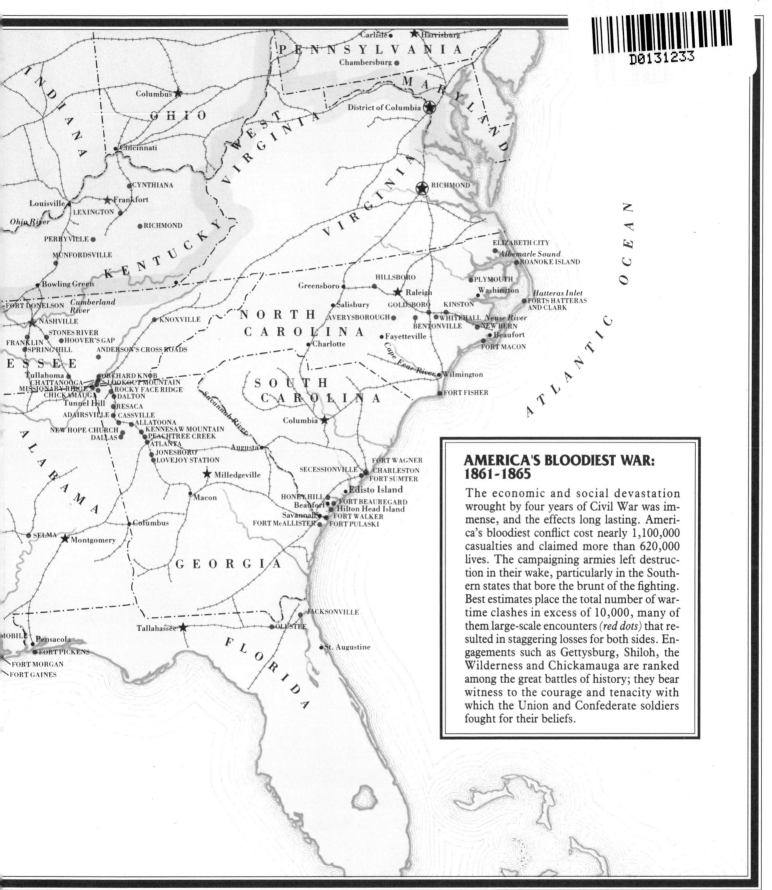

AMERICA'S BLOODIEST WAR: 1861-1865

The economic and social devastation wrought by four years of Civil War was immense, and the effects long lasting. America's bloodiest conflict cost nearly 1,100,000 casualties and claimed more than 620,000 lives. The campaigning armies left destruction in their wake, particularly in the Southern states that bore the brunt of the fighting. Best estimates place the total number of wartime clashes in excess of 10,000, many of them large-scale encounters *(red dots)* that resulted in staggering losses for both sides. Engagements such as Gettysburg, Shiloh, the Wilderness and Chickamauga are ranked among the great battles of history; they bear witness to the courage and tenacity with which the Union and Confederate soldiers fought for their beliefs.

Scale in Miles

0   150   300   450   600

THE TIME-LIFE HISTORY OF THE CIVIL WAR

THE TIME-LIFE
HISTORY OF THE CIVIL WAR

BARNES
&NOBLE
BOOKS
NEW YORK

The Time-Life History of the Civil War,
originally published as *BROTHER AGAINST BROTHER*
Time-Life Books History of the Civil War was produced by
ST. REMY PRESS

MANAGING EDITOR	Kenneth Winchester
MANAGING ART DIRECTOR	Pierre Léveillé
Editor	Dianne Stine Thomas
Art Director	Odette Sévigny
Associate Editor	Pierre Home-Douglas
Contributing Editor	Ian Walker
Editorial Assistant	Megan Durnford
Senior Art Director	Diane Denoncourt
Contributing Art Director	Francine Lemieux
Designer	Shirley Grynspan
Art Assistants	Robert Galarneau, Solange Pelland
Index	Shirley J. Manley
Administrator	Denise Rainville
Production Manager	Michelle Turbide
Production Coordinator	Jean-Luc Roy
Proofreaders	Jane Pavanel, Judy Yelon

Time-Life Books Inc. is a wholly owned subsidiary of
THE TIME INC. BOOK COMPANY

President and Chief Executive Officer	Kelso F. Sutton
President, Time Inc. Books Direct	Christopher T. Linen

TIME-LIFE BOOKS INC.

EDITOR	George Constable
Executive Editor	Ellen Phillips
Director of Design	Louis Klein
Director of Editorial Resources	Phyllis K. Wise
Director of Photography and Research	John Conrad Weiser
PRESIDENT	John M. Fahey Jr.
Senior Vice Presidents	Robert M. DeSena, Paul R. Stewart, Curtis G. Viebranz, Joseph J. Ward
Vice Presidents	Stephen L. Bair, Bonita L. Boezeman, Mary P. Donohoe, Stephen L. Goldstein, Juanita T. James, Andrew P. Kaplan, Trevor Lunn, Susan J. Maruyama, Robert H. Smith
New Product Development	Yuri Okuda, Donia Ann Steele
Editorial Resources	Blaine Marshall
Production Manager	Prudence G. Harris
PUBLISHER	Joseph J. Ward

THE CONSULTANTS

George Daniels, Consulting Editor, is a writer, editor and editorial consultant who has served as senior editor of *Time* Magazine and executive editor of Time-Life Books.

Brian C. Pohanka, Military History Consultant, is an editor, historical advisor and a former senior researcher for Time-Life Books.

THE WRITERS

Ronald H. Bailey, a former *Life* Magazine senior editor, has written 14 non-fiction books and contributed to 40 others, many of them on military history subjects.

Champ Clark, who teaches newsmagazine writing at the University of Virginia, is a freelance writer and a former senior editor of *Time* Magazine.

David Dunbar, a former book editor for Reader's Digest Canada, has authored two books and contributed to six others. He is currently a freelance writer and editor.

William Goolrick, a graduate of the Virginia Military Institute, and a former series director for Time-Life Books, is a freelance writer.

Bryce S. Walker, has served as a correspondent for *Stars and Stripes* in Korea, and as an editor of Time-Life Books. He is presently a freelance writer.

Henry Wiencek, former series editor of the *Smithsonian Guide to Historic America,* is the author of books on the historic architecture of the southern U.S.

This edition published by Barnes & Noble, Inc.
by arrangement with Time-Life Books Inc.

Copyright © 1990 by Time-Life Books Inc.

1995, Barnes & Noble Books

ISBN 1-56619-902-6
(formerly ISBN 0-13-921818-1)

Manufactured in the United States of America

10 9 8 7 6 5 4 3 2 1

CONTENTS

FOREWORD

Twenty years after the Civil War, twice-wounded Union veteran Albion W. Tourgée wrote that Americans should remember "*not* the courage, the suffering, the blood, *but only the causes that underlay the struggle and the results that followed from it.*" Tourgée's comment was prompted by irritation at the flood of books and articles that poured off the presses in the 1880s celebrating the pageantry and heroism of Civil War battles and leaders but saying little about the issues and consequences of that titanic struggle. The flood has rarely ebbed in the century since Tourgée wrote, and it is in full flow again during the 125th-anniversary commemorations of the war.

Many of today's academic historians share Tourgée's view. Far more interesting to them than the campaigns are the Civil War's causes and consequences. Those consequences were enormous. As Mark Twain wrote in 1873, the war "uprooted institutions that were centuries old, changed the politics of a people, transformed the social life of half the country, and wrought so profoundly upon the entire national character that the influence cannot be measured short of two or three generations." Northern victory in 1865 resolved two fundamental, festering questions left unresolved by the American Revolution of 1776: whether this vulnerable experiment in republican self-government could survive in a world of monarchies, empires, czardoms and counterrevolutions; and whether the republic would continue to endure half slave and half free.

Americans were preoccupied by the question of states' rights and national survival during the first three generations of the republic's existence. Some Americans advocated the right of states' secession and periodically threatened to invoke it; in 1860-61 eleven states did invoke it. If allowed to stand, this action would have constituted a precedent that meant the end of the *United* States. The next time a disaffected minority lost a presidential election, there might well be another secession, until the American republic collapsed into numerous petty, squabbling states. "We must settle this question now," said Abraham Lincoln in 1861, "whether in a free government the minority have the right to break up the government whenever they choose." Union triumph in 1865 settled it. No state or region has tried to secede from the United States since.

"The monstrous injustice of slavery," Lincoln had said in 1854, "deprives our republican example of its just influence in the world—enables the enemies of free institutions, with plausibility, to taunt us as hypocrites." With the abolition of slavery by the Civil War, that particular hypocrisy plagued the United States no more. The 13th, 14th and 15th Amendments to the Constitution—the Civil War Amendments—achieved on paper the most sudden and radical social transformation in American history—indeed, in the history of any nation. In a space of five years, four million slaves were emancipated and granted equal citizenship rights with their former masters—at a cost of 620,000 soldiers' lives and the destruction of the social organization and economic infrastructure of half the country. The free-labor capitalism of the North prevailed over the slave-labor plantation agriculture of the South, with tremendous effect on the future of the United States. These were the results and the transformations of which Tourgée and Twain spoke.

James M. McPherson is Edwards Professor of American History at Princeton University. His books include The Struggle for Equality, Marching Toward Freedom, Ordeal by Fire *and the Pulitzer Prize winning* Battle Cry of Freedom.

Yet to deplore a celebration of the campaigns and battles is itself to express a narrow view of the Civil War. For without an understanding of the courage and blood we cannot comprehend the great issues and results. Most of the things we consider important in this era of American history rested on the shoulders of those three million soldiers in blue and gray who fought it out during four years of violence unmatched in the Western world between the Napoleonic Wars and World War I. The campaigns and battles were crucial. They affected everything else. If some of them had come out differently, the future of the United States—indeed, of the world—would have been different.

If General George B. McClellan had been bolder and more aggressive in the spring of 1862, he might have captured Richmond and won the war with only minimal damage to Southern society and slavery. If Robert E. Lee's invasion of Pennsylvania had fulfilled his hopes—if he had won the battle of Gettysburg in the same fashion he had won at Chancellorsville against greater odds two months earlier—the Confederacy could well have triumphed. Even as late as the fall of 1864, if William Tecumseh Sherman had not captured Atlanta, Lincoln probably would not have been reelected and his successor might have been compelled to negotiate peace with an independent Confederacy. Thus an understanding of how and why McClellan was driven back in the Seven Days' battles, the Army of the Potomac triumphed at Gettysburg, and Sherman captured Atlanta is important to understanding how and why American history has developed the way it has during the past 130 years.

For all of these reasons, the story of campaigns and battles told in *Brother Against Brother*—as well as the discussion of the underlying causes and results also to be found herein—is an important one; it is dramatic, gripping, tragic, poignant, sometimes funny and sometimes gruesome. Above all, that story is crucial to a comprehension of America and what it has stood for during the past two centuries.

James M. McPherson

Smoke-belching steamboats dock at the New Orleans levee at the mouth of the Mississippi. The mighty river bound North and South in mutually beneficial trade.

THE TWO AMERICAS

"It is no more possible for this country to pause in its career than for the free and untrammeled eagle to cease to soar," exulted Florida congressman Stephen R. Mallory in 1859. And he had plenty of reason for optimism.

The decade of the 1850s brought the United States exceptional growth and prosperity. The population increased by 35 per cent, to more than 31 million. Railroad trackage more than trebled, reaching 30,000 miles. The production of all kinds of foodstuffs and manufactured goods rose dramatically. And the country had enormous resources to sustain its phenomenal progress: vast unoccupied lands, a network of navigable rivers, incalculable riches in timber, iron, coal, copper, California gold.

It was true that the 1850s also exacerbated the political tensions between North and South. But in the cold light of economics, the sections were interdependent—perhaps inseparable. Southern plantations provided bountiful raw materials for the industrial North, and Northern factories made most of the finished goods consumed by the South. "In brief and in short," concluded Senator Thomas Hart Benton of Missouri, "the two halves of this Union were made for each other as much as Adam and Eve."

Boom Time in the Cotton Kingdom

The famed Southern boast that "Cotton is king!" became increasingly true in the 1850s. Though many plantations thrived on rice, tobacco and other cash crops, more and more land was planted in cotton to meet the demands of British and Yankee textile mills, and more and more slaves were put to work bringing in the harvests. The annual yield soared from two million bales in 1849 to 5.7 million bales in 1859. This amounted to seven eighths of the world's cotton and more than half of all American exports.

Laboring alongside hired whites, a gang of slaves harvests rice under a planter's direction. A planter would consider it a good year if each field slave produced a profit of $250.

A workaday plantation comprises a big house (center) flanked by slave quarters, smokehouses, gardens and stockyards. Large plantations were virtually self-sufficient.

Huntsville, Alabama, has a rural look in this view, painted around 1850. "From the quiet appearance of their towns," said a visiting Yankee, "the stranger would think business was taking a siesta."

A Realm of Sleepy Towns and Scattered Hamlets

"Every step one takes in the South," wrote a British visitor in 1856, "one is struck with the rough look of the whole civilization. Towns and villages are few and far between." Cities were scarcer still, and practically all of them were relatively small; Charleston, Richmond and Savannah each had populations of less than 40,000. Only New Orleans, with about 150,000 inhabitants, was comparable to Northern cities in size and diversity.

The bucolic landscape and the slow, agrarian life were just what most Southerners desired. Said an Alabama politician: "We want no manufactures; we desire no trading, no mechanical or manufacturing classes. As long as we have our rice, our tobacco and our cotton, we can command wealth to purchase all we want."

In Athens, Georgia, the buildings of Franklin College (later the University of Georgia) stand atop a wooded hill (left) across the Oconee River from the terminus of the Georgia Railway. Though Athens was founded in 1801, it had only 3,848 inhabitants by 1860.

Melting Pots
for New Americans

In marked contrast to their Southern counterparts, Northern cities were crowded, bustling, boisterous places, many expanding too fast to digest their growth. The population of New York soared from 515,000 to 814,000 in the 1850s. Chicago, incorporated as a city in 1837 with a population of 4,170, had 112,000 inhabitants in 1860.

Foreign voices were heard on all sides. Between 1850 and 1860, more than 2.8 million immigrants poured into port cities; nearly one half of the New York population was foreignborn. Most of the immigrants drudged long hours for meager pay and lived in squalor. But they adapted readily to their new country, embraced its egalitarian values and made great strides as Americans. By the 1850s, the Irish had become political powers in Boston, Philadelphia and New York, and the Germans were the dominant voting bloc in St. Louis and Milwaukee.

Many Americans resented the foreign influx, but others exalted in it. "We are not a narrow tribe of men whose blood has been debased by maintaining an exclusive succession among ourselves," wrote novelist Herman Melville. "No: our blood is as the flood of the Amazon, made up of a thousand noble currents all pouring into one."

A wild snowball fight among rowdy New Yorkers disrupts traffic in front of P.T. Barnum's curiosity museum in lower Manhattan in 1855. Rivalries between neighborhoods, ethnic groups and political clubs often led to pitched battles in the streets.

The North's "Great, Silent Revolution"

Throughout the 1850s, the North industrialized at almost breakneck speed. By the close of the decade, the Northern states contained four fifths of America's factories, two thirds of the nation's railroad mileage and practically all of its shipyards. The New York *Tribune* described the economic development of the North as "a great, silent revolution." But the revolution was not really noiseless at all. It thrived on clattering, roaring phalanxes of new machines: circular saws, power looms, rotary presses, hydraulic turbines, shoe peggers, sewing machines, steam locomotives, corn planters, wheat drills, reapers, road scrapers, posthole augers. These inventions and countless others made "Yankee ingenuity" an international byword, and when Samuel Colt of Connecticut perfected the use of mass-produced, interchangeable components for his revolver, the British dubbed his method of manufacturing "the American system."

Workers fashion railway forgings at a rolling mill in New Jersey. In the railroad craze of the 1850s, a number of lines went broke by overbuilding or engaging in rate-cutting wars.

Factories in Pittsburgh spew clouds of smoke in this 1838 painting. Pittsburgh owed its success to an enormous vein of bituminous coal that ran beneath the city and to iron-ore deposits nearby.

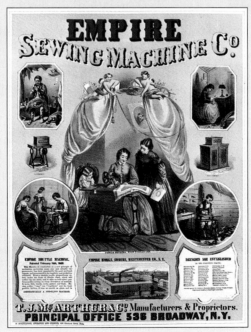

Standing in the bow of a bobbing boat, a Yankee harpooner prepares to deliver the death blow to a foundering whale. In the 1850s, when whaling was at its peak, more than 700 New England-based ships ranged the globe, bringing home catches worth an average of eight million dollars a year.

A sewing-machine advertisement features improved models for the home and workshop. By 1859, Northern factories were turning out 37,000 machines a year.

Pride and Peril in the "Wisest System Ever Devised"

When Andrew Jackson described Americans as "guardians of freedom for the human race," and when James K. Polk spoke of American government as "this most admirable and wisest system ever devised," the Presidents' sentiments were not considered hyperbolic by the vast majority of their countrymen. To Northerners and Southerners alike, such statements represented the truth, pure and simple.

Besides their abiding faith in democratic ideals, Americans everywhere shared an avid interest in the political process that translated those ideals into practice. Patriotic celebrations on the Fourth of July and Washington's Birthday were built around political speeches, and during the rest of the year any candidate appealing for votes could count on drawing a fair-sized crowd. Indeed, electioneering appeared to be a great constant in American life. The visiting English novelist Charles Dickens remarked: "Directly that the acrimony of the last election is over, the acrimony of the next begins."

American politics was a fiercely partisan affair, and for decades, that had been all to the good, spurring the people's interest in national issues, putting new ideas and policies to the test of the ballot box. But as the 1850s drew to a close, thoughtful citizens wondered whether their shared ideals could sustain the nation through its mounting crises—or whether their political passions would split the Union.

Verdict of the People, *painted by noted American artist George Caleb Bingham, shows a street scene in a Missouri town as the results of an election are announced. The facial expressions of the listeners clearly indicate whether their candidate was the winner or the loser.*

THE ROOTS OF CONFLICT

Nothing could keep Edmund Ruffin away from the secession convention. Not grief for his daughter Elizabeth, who had just died in childbirth. Not the heavy storm that had blanketed his plantation in Virginia with nine inches of snow. Now that South Carolina was on the verge of quitting the United States, Ruffin was determined to witness with his own dimming eyes the dawn of the glorious new era.

On December 19, 1860, the old man arrived in Charleston to find the city overflowing with enthusiastic Southern patriots. He was lucky to find a tiny room in the Charleston Hotel. Later that day, Ruffin sat in a jam-packed hall where he met scores of old friends and fellow "fire eaters" who had been leaders in the fight to break up the Union. They watched as David F. Jamison, a gentleman-scholar who lived graciously on the proceeds of a 2,000-acre, 70-slave plantation, called the convention to order using a gavel incised with the word "Secession."

Momentous issues remained to be settled, including a new law code, customs regulations, and negotiations with the government "known as the United States" over transferring Federal property to the new republic of South Carolina. At 1:15 p.m. the following day, all 169 delegates voted to adopt the Ordinance of Secession as read. That evening, the new nation's founding fathers reconvened for the signing ceremony, a two-hour affair that ended with Jamison holding up the completed document. "I proclaim the State of South Carolina an independent commonwealth," he stated. An enormous roar of approval shook the hall.

The convention adjourned, and old Edmund Ruffin—honored with the gift of a pen that had signed the Ordinance of Secession—recorded the jubilant scene: "As I now write, after 10 p.m., I hear the distant sound of rejoicing, with music of a military band, as if there were no thought of ceasing."

The deed had been done. But what actually had happened? According to some Northerners, nothing at all. The United States was a sovereign nation, not a mere confederation of individual states; thus, the republic was indivisible, secession impossible.

Others in the North regarded secession as a constitutional crime so grave that only force of arms would put it right. Most Southerners were willing to fight to defend their action and their way of life. Many on both sides saw secession as the only peaceful way to resolve their quarrels.

In any case, it was the beginning of the end of the early Union—an event that Southerners called the second American Revolution. Looked at another way, it marked the end of the beginning: an abrupt halt to the nation's first phase of helter-skelter growth. It would lead, after four months of increasing hostility, to the deadliest of American wars, a struggle that would drag on for four years and consume the lives of more than 620,000 young Americans, or roughly one out of every 50 citizens.

The war they would engage in traced its roots to the birth of America. With different geographies and climates, North and South had developed radically different economic and social patterns. In the upper Atlantic states, the terrain was hilly and rocky, with the interior heavily forested and difficult of access. These conditions tended to keep farms small and to build up large pools of population along the coast. Many Northern settlers, therefore, became seamen, fishermen, shipbuilders and merchants.

The South, on the other hand, developed a plantation system that relied to a considerable extent on large-scale cultivation of a single cash crop: tobacco, rice, sugarcane or cotton. In a pattern set in Virginia tobacco plantations, intensive one-crop farming quickly exhausted the soil. Rather than sacrifice profits by rotating crops or fertilizing, big planters simply purchased more land—and, more slaves to work the new holdings.

When the Industrial Revolution began in the

Cockades of South Carolina palmetto fronds were worn by Charlestonians to symbolize their defiance of the Union at the secession convention in December of 1860. Later, the cockades were worn throughout the South as emblems of sectional solidarity.

18th century, entrepreneurs in the North moved steadily inland, exploiting the water power rivers provided. With surplus workers from coastal cities, they built the factories and laid the railroads that helped secure the North's position as the industrial heartland of the U.S. Meanwhile, the rift between the two regions was widened by a volatile, boom-and-bust American economy. In the South, small farmers and plantation-owners alike were frequently victimized by Northern factors who paid prices set by the British market. Southerners came to believe that their region had become an exploited agricultural colony of the industrial North. In 1851, an Alabama newspaper published a bitter list of the ways in which the South was serving as a vassal to the North: "We purchase all our luxuries and necessities from the North. Our slaves work with Northern hoes and plow. The slaveholder dresses in Northern goods, rides in a Northern saddle. In Northern vessels his products are carried to market, his cotton is ginned with Northern gins. His son is educated at a Northern college."

Against this backdrop of two divergent Americas arose a series of political crises during the first half of the 19th century. All dealt with the expansion of slavery; all were seemingly resolved, but each deepened sectional hostility.

On February 13, 1819, James Tallmadge, an obscure representative from New York, introduced a resolution that electrified Congress. His measure sought to prohibit slavery in the Missouri Territory, a section of the Louisiana Purchase petitioning to enter the Union as a slave state. The proposed restriction reflected the North's growing antislavery sentiment. It also alarmed Southern planters, who feared that unless cotton cultivation continued to expand, their economy would wither and die as cultivated areas were eventually exhausted.

In addition, the measure threatened to tip the Congressional balance of power in favor of the North. While that region's greater population guaranteed control of the House of Representatives, the Senate still teetered in balance: of 22 states in the nation in 1819, half were free and half were slave.

The volatile issue of the extension of slavery to Missouri touched off an acrimonious debate that spanned two sessions of Congress. Abolitionist Northerners seethed with moral outrage. The Southern planters, trapped in their dependence on slavery, accused Northerners of exaggerating the evils of the institution and challenged the right of the North to meddle in Southern affairs.

Finally, in 1820, Henry Clay of Kentucky hammered out a compromise: Missouri would be admitted as a slave state and Maine would join as a free state, preserving balance in the Senate. In addition, a demarcation line would be drawn at latitude 36°30'. Henceforth, new states north of the line would be free; those to the south, slave.

The Missouri Compromise represented a watershed in American politics. For the first time, an action by Congress had aligned the states against each other on a sectional basis.

Congressman John C. Calhoun of South Carolina reflected this new parochialism in his changing outlook. Once an ardent young nationalist who promoted a national defense, a national bank and a national protective import tariff, Calhoun eventually realized that the import tariffs he had championed protected Northern manufacturers and raised the prices Southerners paid for imported goods.

In 1827, while serving as Vice President under John Quincy Adams, Calhoun made his first break with nationalism. On the Senate floor, he cast the decisive vote against a new tariff bill that threatened to deepen the Southern recession. But the following year, rival politicians rammed an even higher tariff through Congress. Angry Southerners labeled it the Tariff of Abominations, and soon they were blaming it for all their economic ills.

In 1846, the Mexican War provoked another political crisis. David Wilmot, a tobacco-chewing country lawyer from Pennsylvania, introduced a measure that would ban "slavery or involuntary servitude" in any territory acquired as a result of the war. The Wilmot Proviso never became law, but like the Missouri Compromise, it split Congress along sectional lines. "As if by magic," wrote a Boston journalist, "it brought to a head the great question which is about to divide the American people."

In 1848, a defeated Mexico ceded to the United States an immense domain that included all the territory between Texas and the Pacific. Calhoun, his health now failing, argued that the territory was the joint possession of individual states, and that Congress therefore had no authority to intervene on the question of slavery. And since slaves were no more than chattel, Southerners should be free to transport them to new territories as they would mules or oxen or any other material possession. The newly elected president, Zachary Taylor, hero of the Mexican War and a Louisianian, tried to dodge the whole issue. California and New Mexico had not yet been authorized to organize a territorial government, a stage before statehood during which the territory was still a Federal ward. It was then that Congress could meddle in the volatile issue of slavery.

Taylor decided to persuade California, and later New Mexico, to skip the territorial phase and apply directly for statehood, thus removing the Federal government from any slavery decision. By November 1849, California had drawn up a constitution and opted to enter the Union as a free state. New Mexico began a similar procedure.

Proslavery Southerners were outraged by Taylor's maneuverings. They saw a betrayal by one of their own, and threatened secession. Men of moderation on both sides turned to Henry Clay, the aged and ailing "Great Pacificator." In January 1850, Clay proposed that California should enter the Union as a free state. But Congress, he said, should refrain from intervening on the slavery question in other new territories carved from the Mexican cession. Clay also offered resolutions on other seemingly minor issues, including one recommending that Congress enact stiff laws to assist in the capture of runaway slaves.

Clay defended his compromise plan in a series of speeches in the Senate. In his rich voice, the old Kentuckian urged Southerners not to complain if California rejected slavery. And he demanded of Northerners: "What do you want, you who reside in the free states? Have you not your desire in

Kentucky's Henry Clay, whose Compromise of 1850 reconciled North and South for a decade, presented himself as a presidential candidate five times and was five times rebuffed. Out of his disappointments came his famous declaration that he "would rather be right than be President."

Daniel Webster of Massachusetts, whose noncommittal attitude toward slavery often prompted criticism, outraged abolitionists with his speech in favor of the 1850 Compromise condoning slavery. Poet Ralph Waldo Emerson accused him of venality in a bitter couplet: "Why did all manly gifts in Webster fail? / He wrote on Nature's grandest brow, For Sale."

Tall and square-shouldered, with the burning eyes of a visionary, South Carolina's John C. Calhoun was unyielding and passionate in his defense of Southern rights. A visiting Englishman called him "a volcano in full force."

California? And in all human probability you will have it in New Mexico also." He ended by begging Southern extremists "to pause at the edge of the precipice, before the fearful and disastrous leap is taken into the yawning abyss below."

Clay's plea for moderation was countered by John Calhoun, now so weak from tuberculosis that a colleague had to read his speech. In it, Calhoun called on the North to grant slaveholders equal rights in the Western territories, quiet the abolitionist agitation and guarantee the return of fugitive slaves. Barring those concessions, Calhoun proposed that North and South separate and each section govern itself in peace.

Calhoun's challenge was met by the magisterial Daniel Webster, in one of his finest speeches. "I wish to speak today, not as a Massachusetts man, nor as a Northern man, but as an American, and a member of the Senate of the United States. I speak today for the preservation of the Union." Webster implored Northern radicals to soften their position. The Wilmot Proviso, that "taunt or reproach" to the South, was unnecessary because conditions in the West were unsuitable for slavery. "I would not take pains to reaffirm an ordinance of nature," he stated, "nor to reenact the will of God."

Webster's speech infuriated abolitionists but received high praise elsewhere. Even the fiery Charleston *Mercury* lauded his effort: "With such a spirit . . . it no longer seems impossible to bring this sectional contest to a close." By September, Clay's proposals were enacted into law. Clay's Compromise of 1850 was hailed as the Union's salvation. But one of its minor measures would do major damage to the chances of achieving a lasting settlement.

That measure was the Fugitive Slave Law. Runaway slaves were not a serious problem for planters; only about a thousand escaped each year. Even so, the Fugitive Slave Law placed the full power of the Federal government behind efforts to recapture runaways. Professional slave hunters, armed with affidavits from Southern courts, began to scour Northern cities, ferreting out runaways and sometimes kidnapping free blacks, of whom almost 200,000 lived in Northern communities.

The Fugitive Slave Law galvanized the antislavery movement, which had been growing in strength since the 1830s. Of the hundred-odd antislavery groups, abolitionists were the most vociferous. Fiercest of

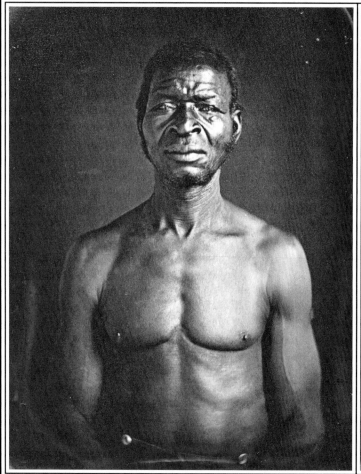

JACK, A SLAVE DRIVER

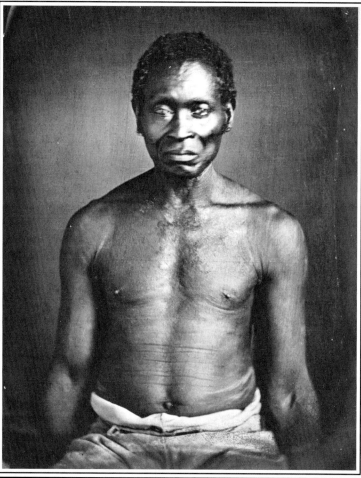

FASSENA, A CARPENTER

Life in Bondage

"I'd rather be dead than be a nigger on one of these big plantations," a white Mississippian told a Northern visitor. For those who were slaves, the plantation life often did lead to an early death.

Born into bondage, very likely sold at least once during the course of his or her lifetime, a slave normally began to work in the fields by the age of 12. From that point on, overwork was his daily portion. One former slave said of his servitude on a Louisiana plantation: "The hands are required to be in the cotton field as soon as it

is light in the morning, and, with the exception of 10 or 15 minutes, which is given to them at noon, they are not permitted to be a moment idle until it is too dark to see, and when the moon is full, they often labor till the middle of the night."

The majority of slaves were fed poorly; many subsisted chiefly on a "hog and hominy" diet, which consisted of a peck of corn and about three pounds of fatty salted meat a week. They were generally clothed in shabby homespun or in cheap fabrics known as "Negro cloth," which were manufactured

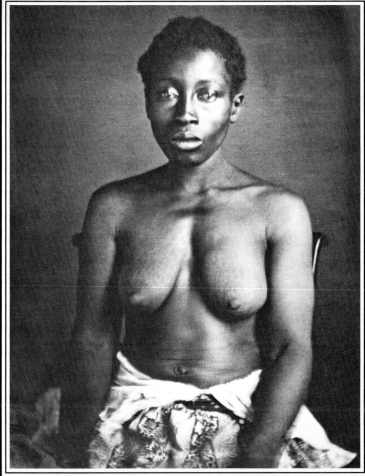

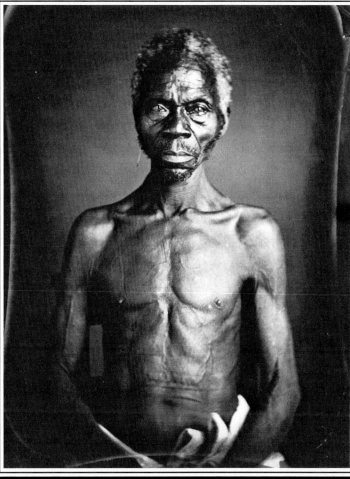

DELIA, OCCUPATION UNKNOWN   RENTY, A FIELD SLAVE

in Northern or English spinning mills. Many children wore only shirts and went shoeless even in winter.

From six to 12 slaves were quartered in each leaky, drafty, dirt-floored, one-room shack. "Their houses," wrote an Alabama physician, "can be but laboratories of disease." What medical care slaves received was primitive at best. Malaria, yellow fever, cholera, tuberculosis, typhoid, typhus, tetanus and pneumonia took terrible tolls. Many slaves were afflicted with worms, dysentery and rotten teeth. Fewer than four out of 100 lived to be 60 years of age. Slaves were kept in a state of fear by punishment and the threat of punishment. They were required to show abject humility when they addressed whites: they had to bow their heads and lower their gaze.

No wonder that slaves—even the ones who received relatively good treatment— yearned for freedom. "O, that I were free!" wrote one slave who finally managed to escape. "O, God, save me! I will run away. Get caught or get clear. I had as well be killed running as die standing."

Four slaves gaze impassively from daguerreotypes taken in 1850. The pictures, among the earliest known photographs of slaves, were part of a study on racial characteristics conducted by scientist Louis Agassiz.

The Breakup
of a Slave Family

Slave families are broken up at a railroad station in Richmond. In most cases, slaves were sold between October and May so they could become accustomed to their new plantations in time for the next growing season.

A slave family sent to auction was seldom sold to a single buyer. And so followed the breakup every slave expected: a child taken from its mother, a couple separated.

The slave family was a tenuous unit to begin with; from the master's viewpoint, couples existed to produce more slaves to be put to work or sold for profit. A man and woman might be matched for breeding purposes against their will. With the master's permission, the couple might have a wedding ceremony, though the slave marriage had no status in law. Since the union might soon end with one partner's sale, a preacher changed the marital vow to say, "Until death or distance do you part."

A dealer's broadsheet announces his willingness to purchase slaves for cash. Many a slave was sold without warning to pay the debts of his owner.

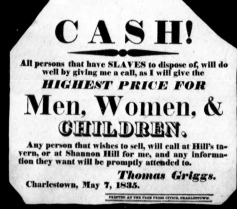

CASH!

All persons that have SLAVES to dispose of, will do well by giving me a call, as I will give the
HIGHEST PRICE FOR
Men, Women, &
CHILDREN.

Any person that wishes to sell, will call at Hill's tavern, or at Shannon Hill for me, and any information they want will be promptly attended to.

Thomas Griggs.
Charlestown, May 7, 1835.

PRINTED AT THE FREE PRESS OFFICE, CHARLESTOWN.

A prosperous planter (below, right) sells a young mulatto—his own illegitimate son.

Tools of Punishment and Intimidation

"He has been gelded, and is not yet well," wrote a Louisiana jailer after he captured a runaway slave. Although such punishment was used to control only the most unruly blacks, nearly all slaves endured some form of brutal coercion. Large plantations were equipped with various instruments of punishment, including a long rawhide whip. Blows from this whip took the skin off the back of an offender. Standard punishment was 15 to 20 lashes, but serious offenders often endured hundreds.

Stripped naked, a slave receives a brutal whipping in front of other slaves. After several blows, the lash usually became wet with blood; as the beating continued, the victim's cries of pain turned into low moans.

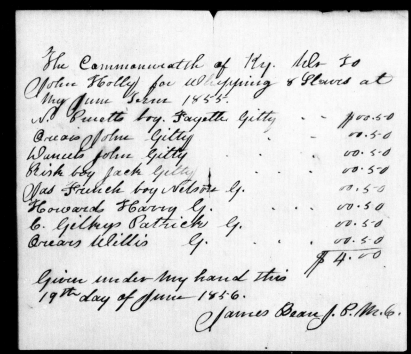

A statement signed by a Kentucky official certifies that a professional slave breaker is owed four dollars for whipping eight slaves.

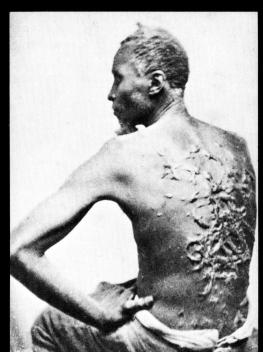

A gruesome network of scars on a slave's back bears witness to a severe whipping—or several. The slave in this photograph escaped during the war and fought as a soldier in the Union Army.

Once the Fugitive Slave Law was on the books, it was no longer enough for a runaway slave, such as Margaret Garner, to reach the North. Cornered in a room in Cincinnati, Garner shows her captors the bodies of two of her children. It was said that she killed the pair rather than see them returned to bondage.

them all was New Englander William Lloyd Garrison, whose zealous conversion to the cause had come in 1830 while serving a seven-week jail term in Baltimore for libeling a merchant who legally ferried slaves up and down the coast. Returning to Boston, Garrison founded the abolitionist newspaper *The Liberator* in 1831.

The North responded to Garrison's call to action. Blacks and whites in Northern cities formed vigilance committees to protect fugitives from slave catchers. In Boston, abolitionist crowds paraded through the streets and clergymen preached civil disobedience to local slave-catching police.

Then came the case of Anthony Burns, a Virginia escapee who had been working at a Boston clothing store. When Burns was arrested by a Federal marshal, an abolitionist crowd stormed the courthouse where he was being held. In the resulting melee, a special deputy was killed; Regular Army troops were called in. With flags flying at half-mast and church bells tolling, Burns was marched through crepe-hung streets to the harbor and put aboard a Virginia-bound ship. "When it was all over," wrote a Boston attorney, "I put my face in my hands and wept."

The tragedy outraged countless Northerners. "We went to bed one night old-fashioned, conservative, compromise Union Whigs," wrote one, "and waked up stark mad abolitionists." Nine states passed personal-liberty statutes, which made it so difficult for slave catchers to get cooperation from Northern authorities that most gave up the chase.

So it was that the nation stood at mid-century in grave peril. The meager chances for a rapprochement between North and South had further dimmed by 1852, as Henry Clay and Daniel Webster followed John Calhoun to the grave, leaving their constituencies in the hands of less seasoned, less patient leaders. At the same time, a new ingredient was added to the North-South quarrels, an ingredient that gave Americans everywhere a preview of their future. It was organized violence, and it erupted in Kansas.

Shortly before midnight on May 24, 1856, James Doyle, a settler well known locally for his proslavery sentiments, heard a knock at the door of his cabin on Pottawatomie Creek in eastern Kansas. When Doyle opened the door, five armed men ordered him and his two oldest sons outside. Beneath a clear prairie sky, they killed the settler with their short, heavy swords and split his sons' skulls like melons, then departed to the wails of Doyle's wife, Mahala. Before the night was over, two other settlers who were known for proslavery views would be slain. John Brown of Osawatomie had come to call.

"Old Man" Brown, as he was known, was a self-styled Angel of the Lord, yearning to smite God's slaveholding enemies. The chain of events that brought this zealot to Kansas had begun in 1854: Congress had voted to allow settlers in the Nebraska Territory, which included Kansas, to decide their own slavery status at the time of admission to the Union as states. Southerners noted a problem, however; the

Missouri Compromise, which prohibited slavery north of 36°30', would effectively ban proslavery settlers from the territories. Thus the vote would be skewed in favor of antislavery settlers.

After a fierce debate, Congress accepted an amendment repealing the part of the Compromise that included the demarcation line. Now, whichever side rushed the most people to the new land would gain control of the territorial legislature—and the authority to write the final word on slavery.

After passage of the Kansas-Nebraska Act, men poured onto the plains. Hundreds of interlopers, called Border Ruffians by the abolitionist press, came over from Missouri to stuff ballot boxes on the March 1855 election day. As it turned out, the trip was unnecessary. Bona fide proslavery settlers far outnumbered their opponents and easily carried the day. The rest of that year saw clashes between Border

Six Kansas Free Staters stand ready to fire their outdated cannon at proslavery troublemakers. Some of the artillery pieces employed in the Kansas conflict were trophies from the Mexican War. Others were even older relics used to fire salutes during Fourth of July celebrations.

Ruffians and Free Staters, who had formed their own provisional government at the town of Lawrence. Among them was John Brown.

In the spring of 1856, the proslavery sheriff of Douglas County went to Lawrence to enforce several arrest warrants, and was shot and wounded in an ambush. Soon after, the Douglas County grand jury returned indictments against several Free Staters, two newspapers and the Free State Hotel—all in Lawrence, and all charged with treason. Arrests were made but the Border Ruffians remained unsatisfied. On May 21 they wrecked the offending presses, bombarded the hotel with cannon and set the Free State Governor's house afire.

The attack produced swift denunciations in Washington. Massachusetts Senator Charles Sumner, for example, delivered an antislavery harangue, singling out Andrew P. Butler, an aging proslavery senator from South Carolina, for having "chosen a mistress who, though ugly to others, is always lovely to him; though polluted in the sight of the world is chaste in his sight—I mean the harlot Slavery." Butler was absent at the time but his cousin, Representative Preston Brooks of South Carolina, came dramatically to his defense. Entering the Senate on May 22, Brooks strode up to Sumner and rained blows on the abolitionist's head with a gutta-percha cane, severely injuring the Senator.

In Kansas, John Brown was already seething over the sack of Lawrence; the news of Sumner's caning pushed him over the edge. The Old Man "went *crazy*," his son reported. He and his "Army of the North" sharpened the swords that they were to use on May 24 to murder James Doyle and his sons.

A warrant was issued for Brown's arrest but he evaded capture. That autumn, backed by U.S. Army troops, newly appointed Governor John Geary at last brought an uneasy quiet to the plains. The whole nation heaved a collective sigh of relief, and talk of disunion subsided—until, in March 1857, the Supreme Court ruled on the legal status of slavery in the territories.

The case involved a slave from Missouri named Dred Scott, whom Army surgeon John Emerson had taken to live first in Illinois and later in the Wisconsin Territory, which the Missouri Compromise had declared slave-free. Emerson eventually brought Scott back to Missouri, where the surgeon died in 1843. Three years later, Scott, with the help of local antislavery lawyers, sued Emerson's heirs for his release, contending that his years in Illinois and Wisconsin had made him free. The case eventually made its way to the Supreme Court, where a decision was delivered by Chief Justice Roger B. Taney, a wealthy Marylander who personally deplored slavery and had freed his own bondsmen.

Taney held that Scott had no right to sue: slaves and freed descendants of slaves were not citizens because at the time the Constitution was written, blacks were "regarded as so far inferior that they had no rights which the white man was bound to respect." Scott's time in Wisconsin had not nullified his slave status, Taney ruled. He was Emerson's property, and slaveholders had an absolute right to take their property into the territories. The Fifth Amendment guaranteed that no person should "be deprived of life, liberty or property without due process of law."

Any law, said Taney, that abridged such a constitutionally protected right was in itself a violation of due process. In other words, the Missouri Compromise violated the Constitution. Dred Scott had lost on all counts. Eventually, a new master would give the elderly slave, his wife and his two daughters what the court would not: freedom.

The South's Pyrrhic victory made old enemies more determined than ever and added new recruits to the ranks of hard-line abolitionists and emancipationists. Now, John Brown was ready to strike again. In July 1859, he rented a farm in Maryland, just across the state line from Harpers Ferry, Virginia (later West Virginia). Brown planned to establish a base in the Alleghenies, invade Virginia and liberate many slaves. He would train the freed blacks and lead them on a larger raid that would foment a general slave insurrection in Virginia. Eventually, he and his army of rebels would found a kind of black state in the South with its own form of government. But first he needed more weapons, so he set his sights on the Federal arsenal in Harpers Ferry.

Late on the cold, rainy night of October 16, John Brown crossed the Potomac and entered Harpers Ferry with a ragtag army of 16 whites (including four of his sons), four free blacks and one escaped slave. The raid began smoothly; Brown's men captured the arsenal and a nearby rifle works without firing a shot

and rounded up several hostages. But the slaves Brown expected to rally by the thousands did not come. The town was thoroughly aroused, and soon telegraph wires flashed a message all over the East: "Negro insurrection at Harpers Ferry!" Several Virginia militia companies arrived the following morning to find townsmen and the raiders in a blistering exchange of gunfire.

While the battle raged all day, townsmen used two bodies for target practice and let a hog chew on a third. By nightfall, six raiders were killed and Brown's sons Oliver and Watson had been wounded, and lay dying in vivid pain. Oliver begged his father to kill him and end his misery. "If you must die, die like a man," Brown replied in cold anger.

The next morning, Brown looked out on 2,000 hostile people, including a company of Washington Marines under the command of Lieutenant Colonel Robert E. Lee of the 2nd United States Cavalry. Lee sent his aide, Lieutenant James Ewell Brown (Jeb) Stuart, forward under a white flag to demand surrender and promise protection from the raiders. Brown met Stuart at the door with impossible counterproposals to the ultimatum. Thereupon Stuart jumped aside and waved his hat as a signal for the Marines to charge. They battered through a door, bayoneted two raiders to death and an officer bludgeoned Brown to the ground. The dreams of "the Lord's avenging angel" had been shattered.

The trial of Brown and six surviving raiders began 10 days later. The injured Old Man was carried into the Virginia court, where he lay on a cot throughout the trial and spoke eloquently in his own behalf. The trial lasted a week; the jury's deliberation 45 minutes. Brown showed not a flicker of emotion as Judge Richard Parker sentenced him to hang for murder and treason. Nor did he utter any last words on the scaffold. But on the way to his execution on December 2, 1859, he handed a guard a final note that predicted national calamity: "I John Brown, am now quite certain that the crimes of this guilty land will never be purged away but with blood."

Months after Brown's execution, on the evening of February 27, 1860, some 1,500 of New York's leading citizens braved a snowstorm to hear a little-known Illinois politician address the cruel problems facing the nation. Abraham Lincoln spoke at Cooper

Union, an institution of free instruction in the arts and applied sciences. The subject of the talk: whether Congress had the Constitutional right to control the extension of slavery to the territories.

Lincoln worried that his affluent audience might snicker at his rural twang and ill-fitting suit, which stretched over his angular frame. But the audience quickly warmed to him; in fact, when he ended his rousing refutation of the Dred Scott decision and his spirited condemnation of slavery itself, his listeners rose and cheered. Later, after his election, Lincoln remarked that this speech more than any other had brought him the Republican presidential nomination.

Perhaps only in an overheated political climate could a man like Lincoln have vaulted to prominence. Two years before, he had startled the nation by nearly unseating Stephen A. Douglas, the powerful Democratic senator from Illinois. Lincoln was already something of a legend in his home state, where widely circulated stories told of his obscure 1809 Kentucky birth, his hardscrabble childhood on the Indiana and Illinois frontiers, his young manhood splitting rails and studying for the bar, and his four terms in the state legislature and one in Congress. He was a masterly politician and a compelling speaker. From his office in Springfield, he had become one of the state's key political forces, first in the service of the Whig Party, and then in the newly formed Republican Party. Now, in the early 1860s, a new America waited to be born and Abraham Lincoln would be its progenitor.

Lincoln's party faced formidable opposition. In the 1856 presidential elections, the Democrats played on secessionist fears, maintaining that Republican ties with abolitionism made the party unacceptable to the South. The tactic worked: Pennsylvanian James Buchanan bested his two opponents, Republican challenger John C. Frémont and former President Millard Fillmore. The Democrats had been granted one final mandate to solve the slavery issue.

Two years later, however, as the Republicans rallied to contest the midterm Congressional elections of 1858, Abraham Lincoln, seeking a national platform, challenged Stephen Douglas for his seat in the Senate. At that time, state legislatures elected United States senators, with the party in control making the selection; public nomination of a candidate was unknown. Nevertheless, Douglas took his opponent

seriously. "I shall have my hands full," he said of Lincoln. "He is the strong man of his party—full of wit, facts, dates. He is as honest as he is shrewd, and if I beat him my victory will be hardly won."

Douglas, in fact, got a taste of exactly how difficult the battle would be when the lanky Westerner challenged him to a debate. The rivals met in seven prominent country towns, drawing crowds—and the press—from far and wide to hear their arguments. As the entire country was caught up in the contest, Douglas played on the prejudices of the voters in speech after speech. Lincoln's views, he claimed, would inevitably lead to full political and social equality for blacks. Stung by the attacks, the challenger associated himself with views that were both antislavery and anti-black—at least when he was speaking in the Democratic strongholds of southern Illinois that were both antislavery and anti-black. Then, before Liberal gatherings, he reverted to more high-minded pronouncements. When Illinois finally went to the polls, the Republicans outvoted the pro-Douglas Democrats by 125,000 to 121,000. However, realigned legislative districts gave Douglas a state house majority and one more senate term.

He may have lost the election but Lincoln had gained national prominence. Winning the Republican nomination for President two years later, he faced a troubled Democratic Party. Nominee Stephen Douglas and the party platform were rejected outright by Southern Democrats in favor of Kentucky Senator John C. Breckinridge. Meanwhile, a faction of Whigs who had established the Constitutional Union Party chose a third opposition candidate, John Bell of Tennessee. The Republicans rallied behind Lincoln.

The campaign was tumultuous. In every town, partisans held parades and bellowed speeches. Liberty and Union were the watchwords of Republican orators in abolitionist New England; Union and economic growth were their themes in mid-Atlantic states, where slavery was a less compelling issue. At the same time, in the Democrats' Southern bastion, the local press sounded the secessionist battle cry. Rather than "submit to such humiliation and degradation as the inauguration of Abraham Lincoln," proclaimed one newspaper, the South would see "Pennsylvania Avenue paved ten fathoms deep with mangled bodies."

Abraham Lincoln was eloquently portrayed by photographers, but his quick-changing facial expressions were beyond the reach of the cameras of the day. When Lincoln spoke, recalled a Chicago Tribune *editor, "the dull, listless features dropped like a mask. The whole countenance was wreathed in animation."*

When the final returns of November 6, 1860 were recorded, the electoral vote reflected with appalling accuracy the nation's sectional split. Lincoln carried every free state except New Jersey; south of the Mason-Dixon line, he won nothing. Bell captured Virginia, Kentucky and Tennessee. The rest of the South went solidly for Breckinridge; Douglas won three of New Jersey's seven votes (Lincoln got the rest) and all of Missouri's nine. Abraham Lincoln, with 180 electoral votes, became President-elect.

Following the election, the momentum toward secession rose to a terrifying pitch. Mary Boykin Chesnut of South Carolina wrote in her diary, "We are divorced, North and South, because we have hated each other so." The South was a tinderbox, needing only one spark to explode into war.

The man who decided where the Civil War would begin arrived in Charleston, South Carolina in late November 1860. He was Major Robert Anderson, the new commander of the three Federal forts in Charleston Harbor: Moultrie, Sumter and Castle Pinckney. Anderson realized that his slightest misstep could touch off warfare—a chilling responsibility.

On the night of December 26, Anderson transferred his men from vulnerable Fort Moultrie to Fort Sumter, on a tiny island 3.3 miles from Charleston. When the evacuation was discovered the following day, secessionists seized Moultrie. Now Sumter swelled in symbolic importance. It was a Federal installation from which the United States could not retreat; it was also a piece of property that the self-declared sovereign state refused to leave in the hands of a so-called foreign power.

At 6 a.m. on January 9, the *Star of the West* relief ship approached Sumter carrying 200 troops from New York. At a South Carolina battery on nearby Morris Island, cadet gunner George E. Haynsworth fired two rounds. His aim was abominable, but arguably, those were the first shots of the Civil War. Fort Moultrie joined in the shelling and within minutes, the *Star of the West* turned and fled. Anderson and South Carolina Governor Francis Pickens exchanged angry notes about the incident, then lapsed into an uneasy truce. Passions elsewhere were inflamed. That very day, Mississippi voted to secede; then in the following weeks, Florida, Alabama, Georgia, Louisiana and Texas.

On February 8, secessionist delegates in Montgomery, Alabama, adopted without dissent the Provisional Constitution of the Confederate States of America. Jefferson Davis, a somber United States senator from Mississippi, was chosen President, and took the oath of office on February 18. In his inaugural address, he told the North that all Southerners wanted was to be left alone, but if attacked, they would defend themselves. Many Northerners agreed with Davis' appeal, and said of the seceded states, "Let the erring sisters go in peace."

Two weeks later, on March 4, 1861, Abraham Lincoln took the oath of office as the 16th President of the United States and addressed the South in conciliatory tones. He had sworn to defend the Union, but he would not initiate aggressive action. "We are not enemies, but friends," he said in a moving coda. Memories of the Revolution still bound them together. These fond sentiments would "swell the chorus of the Union, when again touched by the better angels of our nature." The inaugural did not pacify the South. Emma Holmes of Charleston said the "stupid, ambiguous, vulgar and insolent" speech "is everywhere considered a virtual declaration of war."

Lincoln had been in office just one day when the simmering crisis boiled up again. He received a woe-filled letter from Anderson urgently requesting troops to help him hold position in Charleston Harbor. Still hoping to avert a clash over Sumter, Lincoln ordered former Navy captain Gustavus V. Fox to organize the relief mission and to land only supplies—no reinforcements—unless the Confederates interfered.

For the Confederates' part, they were also making plans for Sumter. On April 10, the Confederate Secretary of War, Leroy Pope Walker, telegraphed the commander of Charleston, a dapper Louisianian named Pierre Gustave Toutant Beauregard, to demand Sumter's immediate evacuation; if he was refused, he was to "proceed in such manner as you may determine, to reduce it." The brigadier general was undoubtedly amused by one of those poignant ironies that often crop up in wartime. While at West Point in the 1830s, Beauregard had studied artillery under an instructor who became his friend and was now his adversary, Major Anderson.

Already, Beauregard had encircled Sumter with artillery. He also controlled 6,000 men of all ages and degrees of training, from fuzz-cheeked boys to gray-

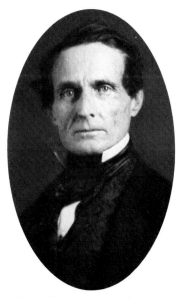

Jefferson Davis was sworn in as President of the Confederate States in Montgomery, Alabama, on February 18, 1861. Four weeks earlier he had left his seat in Washington, saying, "Whatever of offense there has been to me, I leave here. I carry with me no hostile remembrance."

West Pointers at the Crossroads

In the autumn of 1860, the 1,108 officers of the United States Army were scattered across the nation on garrison duty in forts along the coast or in the new Western territories. The news in early November of Abraham Lincoln's election sent a shock wave through the ranks. Secession now loomed, and the officers from the South faced a wrenching decision: to remain loyal to the Union or to resign their commissions and defect to the Southern cause of their home states.

A good index of how the officers chose sides can be found in the West Point class of 1857. Fourteen of the 38 graduates of this class—appear below according to their allegiance. For most of these men and their classmates, the choice was clear: They went the way of their home states. In fact, about 40 per cent of the class "went South," in the vernacular of the day.

The United States Army brass, however, fearing mass defection by Southern officers, tried to bribe the Southerners to remain loyal. E. Porter Alexander *(below),* for example, was offered a tour of duty on the West Coast, far from the likely theaters of war. This, he was told,

Defenders of the Confederacy

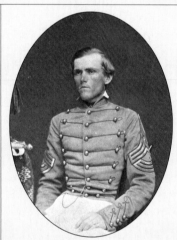

HENRY C. McNEILL, TEXAS
Served on General Sibley's staff;
Colonel of 5th Texas Cavalry.

E. PORTER ALEXANDER, GEORGIA
Chief of Artillery, Longstreet's
Corps; Brigadier General.

RICHARD K. MEADE, VIRGINIA
Engineer, North Carolina;
died of disease, July 1862; Major.

Loyalists for the Union

JOHN C. PALFREY, MASSACHUSETTS
Chief Engineer, 13th Corps; Brevet
Brigadier General.

CHARLES H. MORGAN, NEW YORK
Chief of Artillery and Chief of Staff,
2nd Corps; Brigadier General.

CHARLES J. WALKER, KENTUCKY
Commanded 10th Ky. Cavalry; Chief
of Cavalry, 23rd Corps; Colonel.

would spare him the anguish of raising his sword against his native state of Georgia, his family and his friends.

Alexander refused and became one of four cadets in the class of 1857 to resign upon learning that his home state had seceded from the Union. Eleven other Southerners in the class defected to the Confederate officer corps following the April 12, 1861 hostilities at Fort Sumter. However, three of these men—Richard K. Meade, Manning M. Kimmel and Lafayette Peck—did not join the Confederate Army until they had seen service against the South. Meade, a second lieutenant from the state of Virginia, was in the Fort Sumter garrison during the bombardment and later surrendered to Confederate forces under General P.G.T. Beauregard. One of Meade's West Point classmates, Samuel W. Ferguson, was the Confederate lieutenant who hoisted the Rebel flag over the fort.

During the war, the classmates of '57 served with distinction on both sides. For those shown here, highlights of their service records and their highest career ranks appear below their pictures. Four Confederate and six Union officers rose to the rank of general or its honorary equivalent, brevet general. By the end of the war however, seven of the classmates would be dead.

JOHN S. MARMADUKE, MISSOURI
Commanded cavalry under General Price; captured 1864; Major General.

LAYFAYETTE PECK, TENNESSEE
Instructor; died of disease in Alabama, 1864; Lieutenant.

SAMUEL W. FERGUSON, S. CAROLINA
Commanded a cavalry brigade, W.H. Jackson's Division; Brig. General.

MANNING M. KIMMEL, MISSOURI
Union officer at First Bull Run; joined the Confederacy; Major.

THOMAS G. BAYLOR, VIRGINIA
On staff of General Sherman in Atlanta Campaign; Brevet Colonel.

WILLIAM SINCLAIR, OHIO
Commanded 6th Pennsylvania Reserves; twice wounded; Colonel.

EDWARD R. WARNER, PENNSYLVANIA
Inspector of Artillery, Army of the Potomac; Brevet Brigadier General.

GEORGE RYAN, CONNECTICUT
140th N.Y.; killed at Spotsylvania, Virginia, May 1864; Colonel.

For his defense of Fort Sumter, the taciturn Major Robert Anderson was lionized throughout the North and promoted to brigadier general. "His guides in life," said a relative, were "the Ten Commandments, the Constitution and Army regulations."

Brigadier General P.G.T. Beauregard, commander of the Confederate forces confronting Fort Sumter, was an officer of excellent credentials. An 1838 West Point graduate and a Mexican War hero, he had recently served as a commandant of cadets at West Point.

The fiery trails of projectiles light up the night sky around Charleston as Fort Sumter duels Confederate gun batteries on April 12, 1861. When flame and smoke engulfed the Federal bastion, many women spectators standing near Charleston Harbor wept for the Fort's defenders.

beards like Edmund Ruffin, who had journeyed to Charleston to witness the birth of the new South. The Confederate force was ready for action.

At the fort early on April 12, negotiations for a peaceful surrender at Sumter ended as Beauregard's emissary, Colonel James Chesnut, presented Anderson a formal declaration. By Beauregard's authority it read, "We have the honor to notify you that he will open the fire of his batteries on Fort Sumter in one hour."

At 3:30 a.m., Anderson escorted Chesnut and his party back to their boat. Shaking hands with each one, Anderson said, "If we never meet in this world again, God grant that we may meet in the next."

Back in Charleston, the bells of St. Michael's began pealing; everyone was waiting for the action to begin. It was Lieutenant Henry S. Farley who jerked the lanyard that sent the signal shell arcing high over Fort Sumter. Now no one could stem the tide of events—not Anderson or Beauregard, not Lincoln or Davis. America had spun out of control.

At the sight of the signal shot, Confederate batteries all around Sumter commenced firing. Every Charleston bed emptied. In the darkness before dawn, the citizens raced to rooftops or the waterfront to watch the shells exploding. With 10 officers, 68 soldiers, eight musicians and 43 civilians, Anderson concluded that he could fight only a defensive battle until Captain Fox's relief expedition arrived.

At about 7 a.m., artillery captain Abner Doubleday took it upon himself to fire the first Union shot. His target was a floating battery anchored near Fort Moultrie; he missed. Although cheered by Doubleday's inaccuracy, the Confederates were even more relieved that the enemy had responded. Explained Ruffin, who was firing his own cannon, "I was fearful that Major Anderson did not intend to fire at all. It would have cheapened our conquest."

Noontime found Sumter withstanding the bombardment fairly well. The brick-faced barracks were supposedly fireproof, but some Confederate batteries were lobbing oven-heated cannonballs called "hot shot," which lodged inside the barracks and set the wood aflame. It was not until after 1 p.m. that a lookout sighted the first vessels of the relief expedition beyond the bar at the harbor mouth. Cheers went up as two ships began to head in, but the jubilation was short lived. Aboard the steamer *Baltic*, Fox saw the

fierce bombardment, and put back out to sea; the relief expedition was stymied.

That evening, a rainstorm extinguished the last sparks of Sumter's barracks blaze. Anderson ordered a cease-fire for the night. The Confederates also reduced their barrage, lobbing only four 10-inch mortar shells an hour. On the morning of April 13, the hot shot resumed, and by noon the fort was burning wherever there was wood to set alight. Some soldiers clambered outside the gun embrasures in the face of cannon fire, just to breathe fresh air.

Nearly all the guns of Sumter had been silenced now. The Confederates, sensing triumph was at hand, redoubled their effort. Yet they admired the bravery of their opponents, and when a shot came from Sumter after a prolonged silence, they applauded.

Finally, at 7 p.m., Anderson surrendered. A settlement was reached that was as honorable as a surrender could be. The Confederate troops rejoiced. "A shout of triumph rent the air from the thousands of spectators on the islands and the mainland," wrote Confederate militiaman Augustus Dickert. Beauregard sent a telegram to the Confederate government in Montgomery announcing the news; copies were hurriedly broadcast throughout the South.

Under the terms of the surrender, the Sumter garrison would depart the next day, April 14, 1861. Anderson was in tears that morning, but he was grateful that his old friend Beauregard allowed a 100-gun salute to the tattered Union flag. At about 2 o'clock, the salute began. Thousands watched from boats in the harbor as Old Glory was lowered amid the cannon's roar. A spark prematurely ignited the powder charge in Private Daniel Hough's gun; the explosion tore off the soldier's right arm, killing him instantly. He was the Civil War's first fatality.

Two hours later, with musicians playing "Yankee Doodle," the Federals marched out of the battered fort. The Confederates had fired 3,341 projectiles during 33 hours of bombardment. The barracks were in ruins, the main gate was gone.

Anderson tenderly carried the shot-torn flag, little suspecting that four years hence he would once more raise that very flag over Sumter. The following day, the Federals were homeward bound. The guns had spoken. To the relief of many, the North and the South were finally free to settle their complex differences in the simplest way—by force of arms.

FIRST BLOOD

*"The enemy has assailed my outposts in heavy force.
I have fallen back on the line of Bull Run and will
make a stand at Mitchell's Ford."*

GENERAL P.G.T. BEAUREGARD, JULY 17, 1861

The news of Fort Sumter's surrender raced by telegraph throughout the North and South, igniting an explosion of patriotic fervor on both sides. The South was jubilant. "Flushed faces, wild eyes, screaming mouths hurrahing for 'Jeff Davis' and the Southern Confederacy,' " echoed through Goldsboro, North Carolina, reported a visiting British correspondent. Military bands struck up in Southern capitals from Richmond, Virginia, to Austin, Texas, as volunteers flocked to join the state militias. "So impatient did I become for starting," said one recruit, "that I felt like ten thousand pins were pricking me in every part of my body."

The North reacted to Sumter's fall with hardly less emotion. The 20 million Northerners were stunned, frightened and above all outraged by the attack on the American flag. A mob of angry New Yorkers stormed the offices of the New York *Herald*, forcing its pro-Southern editor, James Gordon Bennett, to display the Stars and Stripes. In Boston, bells tolled all day long. In Milwaukee, a judge and jury walked out of the courtroom to enlist as a group. "Carry terror into the hearts of the Confederates," demanded an editorial writer in *The New York Times*, "conquer them, subjugate them!"

At long last, the waiting was over. After decades of mounting antagonism, of rhetorical bluster in the halls of Congress and of finely wrought compromise over the issues of slavery and states' rights, matters would now be settled in gunsmoke and blood. War had finally come.

Or had it? America's two most powerful men, Abraham Lincoln and Jefferson Davis, both announced their belief that armed conflict might somehow be averted. "Separation is not, of necessity, final," declared the sober-faced Davis, newly installed as the Confederacy's President. Davis was only too aware of the South's limitations. Compared with the North's industrial might, the Confederacy's looked insignificant: The state of New York alone had more factories than all the Southern states combined. Much of the South's armament would have to be captured from Federal stores, or else imported from Europe. Its rail capacity for moving troops and supplies was roughly one third that of the North. And while the Union could recruit from a pool of 3.5 million able-bodied men between the ages of 18 and 45, the South had less than one third that number.

Even so, Davis remained cautiously optimistic. "All we ask is to be left alone," he said. In that spirit he was content to sit back and wait, taking no aggressive military action unless and until the North invaded Southern territory. If that occurred, the South would be prepared.

Back in March, Davis had issued a call for 100,000 Southern volunteers, gallant lads who could be expected to fight with all the extra ardor of men defending their own homes. Under any circumstances, it was an article of Confederate faith that one Southern boy, taught since childhood to ride and shoot, could whip any number of Yankee clerks and shopkeepers. Furthermore, a defensive strategy offered certain military benefits: shorter lines of communication, and a familiarity with local terrain that no invader could possibly possess.

Lincoln, for his part, was equally reluctant to take the offensive. Like Davis, the Union President also clung to a belief that peace might still be salvaged. "I will not say that all hope is yet gone," he asserted. In fact, he was in the uncomfortable position of having virtually no standing army that could force the South to capitulate. More than a decade had passed since the last American war, with Mexico, and whatever Federal troops had not been mustered out were now largely committed to keeping order in the Western Territories.

The Union retained an extensive cadre of senior officers, to be sure—grizzled veterans long in experience. But old age had drained their energies, and their sense of strategy and tactics remained bogged

Two youthful Rhode Island soldiers and a friend, photographed in the first weeks of the war.

Rough-hewn recruits of the 9th Mississippi Infantry gather round a campfire near Pensacola, Florida. Southerners responded as spiritedly as Northerners did to the call for volunteers. In every courthouse town across the Confederacy, soldiers enlisted in companies and chose their officers, often after emotional election campaigns.

in tradition. Many of the most vigorous leaders in the junior grades tended to be Southerners. And they were defecting to the Confederacy in alarming numbers. Too often, Federal regiments were led by parade-ground colonels who had gained their positions through political appointment.

Nonetheless, Lincoln had to act swiftly. On April 15, two days after Fort Sumter's fall, he issued an executive order summoning 75,000 volunteers for three months' service. Then, five days later, he imposed a naval blockade on all Southern ports.

The timing of these decrees was not entirely coincidental. Congress, to which the Constitution assigned the exclusive right to declare war, had just adjourned for its spring recess. Consequently, for the moment, the President was free to act as he saw fit. Furthermore, war was not the issue—or so Lincoln maintained. If the South had no legal grounds for seceding, as many believed, then the President was only using his Constitutional powers to deal with an armed insurrection. With sure political instinct, Lincoln scheduled a special session of Congress for the Fourth of July—by which time the deed would be done, and public opinion in the North would have rallied solidly behind him.

Now it was the South's turn to be outraged. In the eyes of the Confederacy, each state was a sovereign entity, with a perfect right to drop out of the Union whenever it wished. Seven slave states had already done so, and eight others hung in the wings, debating whether or not to march on stage with their Confederate sisters. Virginia, for one, had no trouble deciding. Just two days after Lincoln's call to arms, a state convention in Richmond passed an ordinance of secession.

Virginia's voters still had to ratify the secession order, with the vote scheduled for May 23. The result, however, was a foregone conclusion. With many of her citizens ready for a fight, Virginia saw no need to wait. On April 18, a state militia unit under Captain Turner Ashby launched itself against the U.S. arsenal at Harpers Ferry.

Ashby had picked an easy prize. The arsenal was open to bombardment from surrounding hills, and its small Union garrison judged the place indefensible. So the troops set fire to a stock of 15,000 weapons and then retreated in haste across the Potomac River to Maryland. When the Virginians marched in they found—to their delight—more than 5,000 rifles still usable, and parts for many others.

Two days later, Virginia scored another coup. The Gosport Navy Yard near Norfolk was a major Federal stronghold, and one of the most important naval stations in the country. But Norfolk's commander, the elderly Commodore Charles S. McCauley, on hearing that local militiamen were closing in, decided to retreat. He ordered his men to scuttle or burn every warship that could not put out immediately to sea. Only three vessels, however, got away; the others came to rest on the shallow bottom of the Elizabeth River, among them the burned-out hulk of the U.S.S. *Merrimack*, which the Confederates would later salvage and refit as the ironclad C.S.S. *Virginia*. In addition, the Virginians captured more than 1,000 heavy naval guns, which would bolster Confederate fortifications throughout the South.

In light of these triumphs, a giddy excitement swept the Rebel states. The prospect of a swift and painless victory seemed tantalizingly close. Regiments from Virginia, and soon from all over the South, began pouring into Richmond, ready to move on to anticipated battlefields along the state's northern border. "Every hour there are fresh arrivals of organized companies," an observer wrote. "Martial music is heard everywhere, day and night, and all the trappings and paraphernalia of war's decorations are in great demand."

Inspired by Virginia's zeal, Davis and his cabinet decided to move the Confederate capital to Richmond, shifting it north from small, remote Montgomery, Alabama. The transfer would be completed on May 29. Meanwhile, Tennessee, Arkansas and North Carolina all voted overwhelmingly to join the Confederacy.

The prospect of battle seemed far less appealing to the 61,000 citizens of Washington, D.C. The Union capital spent the war's early weeks teetering on the brink of panic. It had good reason for con-

cern: With only the Potomac River to shield it from Virginia, the city was shut off from the north by Maryland, another slave state. Even if Maryland did not opt for secession—and no one knew which way she would go—the state was rife with pro-Confederacy sentiment. Furthermore, Washington had almost no means of defense. Against an estimated 50,000 men now massing in Richmond, its garrison of Regular Army soldiers numbered a mere 1,000. And although a 1,500-man militia could also be called upon, many of its members were Southern sympathizers, and thus deemed unreliable.

The first reinforcements were several hundred troops from Pennsylvania. Their arrival on April 18, however, was not reassuring. Not only did they come unarmed and poorly trained; they also brought ominous reports of the situation in Maryland. During their march through Baltimore, a mob of secessionists had pelted them with rocks and paving stones.

The next contingent to arrive was the 6th Massachusetts Infantry, one of four volunteer regiments that had been drilling for some months in the Bay State. The regiment traveled south by train, reaching Philadelphia in the early hours of April 19. There its commander—Colonel Edward F. Jones, a businessman from Utica, New York—learned of the trouble in Baltimore. Accordingly, he issued ammunition and ordered his men to load their weapons.

The train reached Baltimore around noon. Here the soldiers had to switch lines, with their railroad cars being hauled individually by horse teams to a southbound terminus on the far side of town. The first seven cars made the transfer without mishap, but the last three were stopped by an angry crowd of 8,000 Rebel sympathizers. The soldiers were forced to quit the cars, and push their way through the mob. Then pistol shots rang out, and a soldier in the front rank fell dead. The officer in charge then ordered his men to open fire. Their fusillade cut a swath through the crowd, and the Bay Staters quick-marched through it. Soon the bulk of the 800-man regiment was heading south over the rails toward Washington. Three soldiers and 12 civilians had been left dead, more than 20 soldiers had been injured, and 130 were unaccounted for.

When the train pulled into the capital at 5 o'clock that evening, Lincoln himself was on the platform to greet it. "Thank God you have come," he

Sentimental Farewells to the Gallant Recruits

The heart-wrenching start of the Civil War came at a time when Americans wore their hearts plainly on their sleeves. It was the springtime of American innocence, when most people believed without question in the ideals and morals they had been taught at school, church and family hearth. And they expressed their beliefs with unabashed emotion, in flowery prose and poetry, and sentimental art.

An endless stream of mawkish domestic scenes, painted for sheet-music covers or lithographs, attests to the fierce patriotism that animated both sides in April 1861. As one work indicated, young men who did not volunteer were scorned: In it, a young woman's father refuses her hand to a suitor in civilian clothes. Poetry in praise of the volunteer bound for battle was hardly less maudlin. The paeans invariably included, as did a Confederate woman's, the information that the beholder's "eyes fill to witness such noble resolution."

Yet the spirit of the time was genuinely heroic, and some contemporaries captured it with true grandeur. Oliver Wendell Holmes Jr., a lieutenant of Massachusetts troops in 1861 (and later a Justice of the United States Supreme Court), wrote of his war-torn generation: "Through our great good fortune, in our youth our hearts were touched with fire. It was given to us to learn at the outset that life is a profound and passionate thing. We have seen with our own eyes the snowy heights of honor, and it is for us to report to those who come after us."

A painting titled The Consecration—1861 *shows the demure sweetheart of a rose-sniffing Union officer "consecrating" his sword. This work, by Philadelphian George Lambdin, was praised in its time for its "genuine sentiment."*

At the war's beginning, the volunteer's departure was a favorite theme for artists. Below, a stalwart Southern youth bids adieu to the old plantation in a work by Nashville painter Gilbert Gaul. The wartime genre of sentimental domestic scenes remained popular for half a century after the war.

declared. Many more troops, however, were still needed to defend Washington.

With the route through Baltimore clearly unsuitable, an alternative course quickly had to be found. The best way seemed to be by ship to Annapolis, on Chesapeake Bay, then by land 40 miles to Washington. Embarkation orders went out to the crack 7th New York, and several Rhode Island units. But soon thereafter, another Massachusetts regiment, commanded by yet another parade-ground amateur, pioneered a faster variation.

Benjamin F. Butler was an ambitious and thoroughly self-approving attorney from Lowell, who had never led so much as a squad of infantry into battle. His lack of such experience, however, did not disturb him one bit. Already he had played an important role in organizing his state's four regiments of volunteers, and he was their overall commander. He had sent the 6th Massachusetts to Washington, and dispatched two others by sea to garrison Fort Monroe, at the mouth of Chesapeake Bay. Now he was in Philadelphia with the 8th Massachusetts, figuring out what to do next. Since secessionists had cut the telegraph line to Washington, he could not wire his superiors for direction.

Butler took his men by train to Perryville on the banks of the Susquehanna River, where he commandeered a large ferryboat and sailed down Chesapeake Bay to Annapolis. Although a branch railroad led on to Washington, there was one problem: Rebel trainmen were in the very process of sabotaging the track. Butler found a broken-down locomotive and a private in his ranks who, miraculously, had worked for the company that had made it. The private jury-rigged the engine into running, several days were spent in hasty track repair. Around noon on April 25, Butler and his regiment chugged into Washington.

The logjam had been broken; henceforth 15,000 men a day could travel the rail line from Annapolis to Washington, and it no longer mattered so much what happened in Baltimore. But a great deal more did happen in Maryland, and once again General Butler played a leading role in the events.

On April 26, Maryland's pro-Union governor called the Maryland legislature into session at Frederick, 50 miles west of Baltimore and 18 miles northeast of Harpers Ferry. There was still a danger that secessionist agitators might panic the legislature

into taking Maryland out of the Union. To neutralize Frederick, Butler was ordered to take a railway junction eight miles from Baltimore on the line to Frederick. At about the same time, Union troops closed in on Baltimore, reinforcing Fort McHenry and garrisoning Fort Morris, and construction crews began restoring the sabotaged railroad bridges.

Butler easily took control of the junction and emplaced artillery batteries. That done, the Massachusetts commander began to grow restless; he wanted a victory that matched his own ambition. Without pausing to seek approval from Washington, he packed his regiment into rail cars and headed for Baltimore. He arrived on the night of May 13, in a thunderstorm, and seized Federal Hill overlooking the city. The next morning the people of Baltimore awoke to find themselves confronted by nearly 1,000 Union troops, with a battery of artillery focused upon the city from the harbor heights.

Butler's coup had been a flagrant breach of military discipline: He had abandoned his post to strike out on a risky venture of his own devising. His superiors in Washington reproved him and withdrew his command, but nearly every Northerner felt an upsurge of gratitude. Butler had faced down the secessionists with a fine show of vigor and daring—at a time when both were in short supply in the Federal military.

Supreme command of the Union forces lay in the hands of the venerable Winfield Scott, America's most senior general and her greatest living military hero. Scott had served the Army with dedication and frequent brilliance for 53 years, and had led it to victory in the Mexican War of 1846-1848. But the handicaps of age, poor health and enormous bulk—he was almost 75, and tipped the scales at nearly 300 pounds—severely limited him. Unable to supervise his troops in the field, Scott exercised command from his desk, where he often toiled for 16 hours a day.

Battles are fought in the front lines, however, and Scott faced a disturbing shortage of experienced field-grade commanders. Pro-Southern officers, many of whom had served with distinction under Scott in earlier days, continued to defect. One of the first to go had been Louisiana's General P.G.T. Beauregard, who conducted the siege of Fort

Men of the 6th Massachusetts fire into a mob of rock-throwing secessionists during the Baltimore riot of April 19, 1861. The regiment's commander, Colonel Edward Jones, wanted to mount an attack on the mob but cooler heads prevailed. The troops eventually boarded a train bound for Washington.

One of the three soldiers killed in the Baltimore melee was 17-year-old Private Luther Ladd.

to stand aside, unsheathing his weapon only in the event that Virginia was attacked.

After this interview, Lee paid a visit to Scott, his friend and mentor, to explain his decision to defect. It was a tearful moment for them both. "You have made the greatest mistake of your life," said the aged general, "but I feared it would be so." Scott was himself a Virginia man, and in the painful irony of a nation at war with itself a delegation of Virginians had already called on him, expecting that he also would defect. The old man cut their spokesman off in mid-sentence. "I have served my country, under the flag of the Union, for more than 50 years," he said, "and so long as God permits me to live, I will defend that flag with my sword, even if my own native state assails it."

Still the problem remained of finding qualified leaders to command the Union troops in the field. Eventually Scott chose two Ohio men. One was the aggressive and self-confident George B. McClellan, a 34-year-old West Pointer who had resigned his commission to go into the railroad business. McClellan commanded the Ohio state militia, and Scott now promoted him to major general in the Regular Army; he would take charge of all Union operations in the Middle West. Then, to assail the Confederate forces in the East, Scott turned to a 42-year-old Mexican War veteran, Major Irvin McDowell. As a recently appointed brigadier general, McDowell would lead the 30,000 soldiers now assembled in the Union capital.

Just before McDowell assumed his new post, the Washington troops made their first armed foray into Southern territory. On May 23, Virginians voted overwhelmingly to ratify the act of secession passed earlier by the Richmond convention. With the Old Dominion now officially a member of the Confederacy, Scott acted with decisive swiftness. Early the next morning, he threw 11 regiments across the Potomac to seize and hold a buffer zone for the capital.

At 2 a.m., under a brilliant moon, the force moved out three columns strong, marching over the Potomac bridges. It easily folded back the thin line of pickets on the Virginia side. The right-hand column pushed west to cut a key rail line. The central column captured Arlington Heights, a vantage point from which the Virginians had been able to monitor

Sumter. He was soon followed by Brigadier General Joseph E. Johnston, the Army's highest-ranking active staff officer. In all, 313 officers—nearly one third of the Army's experienced Regulars—resigned to take up arms against the Union.

The defection that troubled Scott the most, however, was that of Colonel Robert E. Lee. As an officer of engineers, Lee had performed superbly in the Mexican War, and Scott had taken an almost paternal interest in the younger man's career. Now he wanted Lee to lead the Union armies into battle. On April 18, Scott sent an emissary to sound Lee out. "I look upon secession as anarchy," the colonel had said, and allowed that if he owned every slave in the South, he would "sacrifice them all to the Union." But, he sadly concluded, "how can I draw my sword upon Virginia, my native state?" And Lee promised

A Helter-Skelter Rush to Arms

It was, said a Wisconsin politician, "one of those sublime moments of patriotic exaltation when everyone seems willing to sacrifice everything for a common cause." Young men responded with almost manic enthusiasm to Lincoln's call for 75,000 volunteers on April 15, 1861. As a volunteer remarked, joining the army was like small-pox: "It's catching."

Patriotic civilians spared no effort to support the recruits and the recruitment drive. State legislatures put aside political squabbles and passed generous military appropriations. Businessmen set up relief funds to

A crowd of 100,000 New Yorkers jams Union Square on April 20, 1861, for a war rally featuring Major Robert Anderson, the heroic commander of Fort Sumter.

aid the families of soldiers. But the mighty turnout of volunteers created logistical problems that took time to solve. Food distribution was so inadequate that many men got only two meals a day, and they were lucky; in Philadelphia, soldiers had to beg food from civilians. The volunteers were billeted in crude shacks, public buildings and crowded apartments. Transportation to the battle zones was overtaxed, and many recruits found themselves moving south in slow freight cars or the reeking holds of rented steamers.

The discomfort and confusion dampened the ardor of some recruits. Even so, the great majority of volunteers remained in fine spirits, and soon 16 Northern states had exceeded their quotas of volunteers. How many men were headed for Washington? A Massachusetts volunteer answered for his state, "We're *all* a-comin'!"

Six days earlier, Anderson had brought with him from Fort Sumter the flag seen flying from the equestrian statue of George Washington (foreground).

activity in the capital. (That column also seized the spacious Arlington mansion of Robert E. Lee, though it missed finding the owner, who was in Richmond with his family.)

The objective of the left-flank column was the town of Alexandria, a small but vital river port a few miles to the south. Guarded by some 700 locally recruited Virginia militia, it was slated for assault by Colonel Orlando B. Willcox's 1st Michigan Regiment. At the same time, three steamers slid downriver toward the Alexandria waterfront. The vessels carried the colorful 11th New York Fire Zouaves, volunteers from the New York City Fire Department who wore colorful uniforms and were led by the dashing young Colonel Elmer E. Ellsworth. As Willcox marched into Alexandria by land, Ellsworth's Zouaves would attack from the river. Given the advantage of surprise, the two units were then expected to capture the enemy militia.

As it turned out, the plans were thwarted when a Union Naval officer went ashore well before Ellsworth's scheduled dawn landing and—apparently with no authorization—offered the Confederate commander a truce until 9 a.m. if he would withdraw his troops peaceably. His motive, the Navy man said, was to spare Alexandria's women and children any risk from gunfire. The Virginians, thus alerted in advance, decamped in haste just as the Union troops arrived. Only 35 militiamen dawdled long enough to be taken prisoner. And the Union side suffered a stunning loss. As Ellsworth marched into town he spotted a Confederate flag fluttering atop the Marshall House inn. Determined to remove this offensive symbol, the young colonel charged up the inn's staircase with four companions. On his way back down he met the innkeeper, James W. Jackson, who was poised on the third-floor landing with a loaded shotgun. The innkeeper fired, hitting Ellsworth in the chest and killing him instantly. Jackson in turn was immediately slain by one of Ellsworth's men.

Ellsworth had never before led soldiers into combat, but he was already a hero in the North. Glamorously handsome, he was considered an expert on close-order drill. He had transformed his first Zouave unit into the nation's champion drill team. Now he became the first Union officer to die in action, and the North's first martyr.

Despite this setback to Northern pride, the incursion into Virginia had been carried out with smooth efficiency and remarkably little bloodshed. As more Federal troops crossed the Potomac in the weeks that followed, and fortified their position with trenches and redoubts, the stage was set for far deeper thrusts into the Old Dominion.

While the Federal forces on the Potomac made ready for future battle, Union forces to the west were also enjoying some small but gratifying successes. The prime consideration here—as throughout much of Virginia—was control of the railroads. One important link was the Baltimore & Ohio, which ran through northern Virginia from the Ohio River through Harpers Ferry and beyond, and served to bring in troops and supplies from the Western states. Rebel saboteurs had already begun burning the B & O's bridges. And so Major General McClellan, commanding the Union forces in Ohio, moved swiftly to take possession.

McClellan sent his advance columns into northwest Virginia on May 26, and within the week they had seized an important junction at Grafton. The Confederates, badly outnumbered, fell back to the nearby village of Philippi. There, at dawn on June 3, the Ohioans caught them by surprise. "The chivalry couldn't stand," crowed the pro-Union Wheeling *Intelligencer*, referring to the Old Dominion's swashbuckling pretentions. "They scattered like rats from a burning barn."

Over the next month and a half, McClellan's forces poured into northwestern Virginia. They won modest triumphs at Rich Mountain and Carrick's Ford, and secured the region for the Union.

If Virginia's western flank was rolled up with unexpected ease, such was not the case on the state's eastern seaboard. The Union already had a toehold here, at the formidable bastion of Fort Monroe. Located at the mouth of Chesapeake Bay, on a spit of land between the York and James rivers that was called, appropriately, the Peninsula, the fort would be a constant worry to the South. Its powerful guns could play havoc with Confederate shipping; it also provided an opportune base for land probes up the Peninsula toward Richmond, 60 miles to the northwest. It had just one problem: General Scott, bowing to political pressures, had named as its commander

mander none other than Benjamin Butler, the rash and willful Massachusetts officer who had already demonstrated his talent for overstepping orders.

Butler began well enough, occupying the nearby town of Newport News without opposition. Then he began to search for greater glories. Though Scott had forbidden him to take any action without formal approval, Butler decided otherwise. He started laying plans to march up the Peninsula.

The first obstacle in his path was a Confederate defense post at Big Bethel, a village eight miles to the north. Some 1,400 troops of the 1st North Carolina Infantry and supporting units had dug in there, behind earthen embankments, and the Richmond Howitzers had emplaced five cannon. The commander of this force, Colonel Daniel Harvey Hill, knew his business. A distinguished veteran of the Mexican War, he had joined the Rebels from his post as superintendent of the North Carolina Military Institute.

No one in Butler's command could call upon such depth of experience. Of the 7,500 men at Fort Monroe, most were freshly recruited, unseasoned youths led by neophyte officers who knew no more of combat than they had read in army manuals. To compound their problems, Butler had devised an ambitious dawn attack across rugged, unfamiliar terrain. The plan was chessboard perfect—and devilishly tricky to bring off.

The Federals, 4,400 strong, moved out in two separate columns, in the early morning darkness of June 10. There were four regiments of New Yorkers, including a Zouave unit under Colonel Abram Duryée, plus several companies from Vermont and Massachusetts. If all went according to plan, the two columns would converge on Big Bethel at sunrise, catching the defenders by surprise. To lead the attack, Butler chose another Bay State militiaman, Brigadier General Ebenezer Pierce.

The plan began unraveling from the very start. As

the lead units met up in the predawn murk they mistook each other for the enemy, and opened fire. Twenty-one soldiers lay killed or wounded before the firing stopped. By then the Confederates were prepared to give the rest a boisterous welcome.

The main assault began at 9:15, with Pierce's right-flank units. The Federals sprinted forward in parade-ground ranks toward the Rebels' defensive earthworks, only to be met by a punishing volley of well-aimed rifle fire. Then the howitzers opened up. "It seemed as if the balls could never come so thick and fast," a Zouave wrote later. "It was a grand and awful scene," another remembered. The Zouaves fell back in disarray.

Thwarted on the right, Pierce sent in his left-flank troops. Unfortunately for him, a wooded ravine partially obscured the line of advance. When the soldiers crossing it emerged on the far side, they began firing at the troops ahead—only to find that they were shooting their own comrades. Again, the attack collapsed. Another assault on the right proved equally inept. Finally, after barely two hours of fighting, Pierce decided to call a halt. The retreat to Fort Monroe was more a scramble than a march.

Behind him, Pierce left the war's first grim preview of battlefield carnage. Eighteen Yankees lay dead, and more than four dozen others writhed wounded on the ground, shrieking in pain. "One brave boy with his arm torn off cried out to his comrades to avenge him," a Zouave reported. Another youngster showed a hand dangling from a thread of flesh and begged someone to cut it off "as the pain was dreadful."

Confederate casualties were negligible: one dead and 10 wounded. Even so, the defenders were shocked by the scene before them. Cried Lieutenant Benjamin Huske of the 1st North Carolina, "Great God in mercy, avert the awful results of civil war!"

But neither the war nor its consequences could now be avoided, for all the hopeful protestations of both Lincoln and Davis. In the eight weeks since Fort Sumter, the exchanges of gunfire had been few and—as such matters go—relatively bloodless. But the time for sparring was over. As the Union and Confederate armies continued to mass in northern Virginia, a major clash became inevitable. When it occurred, on a hot July day beside a sluggish

Virginia stream with the homely name of Bull Run, the true, sickening dimensions of the conflict ahead became apparent to everyone.

Once again, the prize was a railroad. A few miles south of Bull Run lay the depot of Manassas Junction. Through this key intersection flowed all rail-bound troops and supplies moving north from Richmond to the Confederate front. It was also the terminus of the Manassas Gap Railroad, which cut west through the Blue Ridge Mountains to the lush and fertile croplands of the Shenandoah Valley. Not only was the Shenandoah important for its agricultural bounty, but also for strategic reasons: It was a natural invasion route for Yankees heading south,

Zouaves of the 5th New York make a desperate charge on a Confederate battery at Big Bethel, Virginia. Six Zouaves died in the vain assault, and their garish uniforms, a Confederate said, "contrasted greatly with the pale, fixed faces of their dead owners."

and for Confederate thrusts into Maryland and then east toward Washington. Rail access to the valley was essential.

The Confederates were thus determined to preserve control of Manassas Junction, and the man charged with doing so was the flamboyant General Beauregard, hero of Fort Sumter. Like his counterparts in Washington, Beauregard was plagued with delays and shortages: never enough troops and too little time to train the ones he had. It also greatly pained him that the Yankees now occupied a sliver of Virginia soil around Alexandria. He was constantly shifting strategy, from strengthening his defenses to laying plans for attack.

Confederate troop strength was clearly insuffi-

cient for attack, however, and Beauregard received strict orders forbidding him to take the offensive. While President Davis and General Lee feverishly kept hurrying more regiments forward from throughout the South, Beauregard weighed his own readiness for combat. He wrote that his soldiers "seem to have the most unbounded confidence in me. Oh, that I had the genius of a Napoleon!" Somehow, such modest disclaimers never rang quite true coming from P.G.T. Beauregard.

Rebel spies in Washington were now reporting that the Union command was gearing up for a massive thrust into Virginia, and the general's forward outposts, at Fairfax Court House and Centreville, were too exposed to resist a full enemy assault. Beauregard decided to make his stand at Bull Run.

The stream's brush-covered, five-foot-high banks presented a formidable barrier to any attacker. Only one bridge, a stone span on the Warrenton Turnpike, could support the wagon traffic of an invading army. Soldiers might wade across at a half-dozen or more places—though most such fording sites abutted dense woods where an army would have trouble maneuvering. Beauregard deployed his men to guard the fords, concentrating the bulk of them in the vicinity of Mitchell's and Blackburn's Fords, where open terrain was most likely to attract an invader.

In Washington, 25 miles to the north, Beauregard's former classmate (West Point class of 1838) was busy assembling the Union troops. General Irvin McDowell was in many ways the Confederate general's opposite. Charmless and methodical, he had not the slightest talent for inspiring subordinates. Abstaining from alcohol, tobacco, coffee and tea, he indulged in only one vice: gluttony. "He was such a gargantuan feeder," noted one officer, "and so absorbed in the dishes before him that he had little time for conversation."

McDowell was a capable strategist, however, as his battle plan demonstrated. The Union forces would advance westward along three parallel routes. The two right-flank columns would clear the Rebels from Fairfax Court House and Centreville, a few miles west of Alexandria; then they would stage a diversionary attack on the enemy center at Bull Run. The third column would skirt the enemy's right flank and strike southward, cutting the railroad line to Richmond. This flanking movement, McDowell

Tools of the Soldier's Trade

During the first year of the war, both North and South had to use an array of personal weapons to meet the demands of their expanding armies. Indeed, two years would pass before all the soldiers carried up-to-date firearms. However, a few models of the basic infantryman's weapon soon emerged.

Of brief but vital importance for both armies was the 1842 musket, America's first percussion musket and the first weapon to be truly mass-produced. Manufactured with fully interchangeable parts, it was slowly superseded by the 1855 rifle musket, whose rifled barrel spun the bullet and gave it greater accuracy and longer range than the ball shot from the smoothbore musket. The 1855 rifle musket served as the basis of three improved models, all of which saw extensive use during the war. A similar weapon, the imported Enfield, became the secondary rifle of both armies.

Still more advanced than the Enfield rifle and the 1855 rifle musket was the Sharps, a breech-loading rifle. Conservative ordnance officers distrusted the Sharps' intricate mechanism but, recognizing its greater rate of fire, issued it to selected companies of skirmishers. Eventually the carbine version would be heavily used by Union cavalrymen.

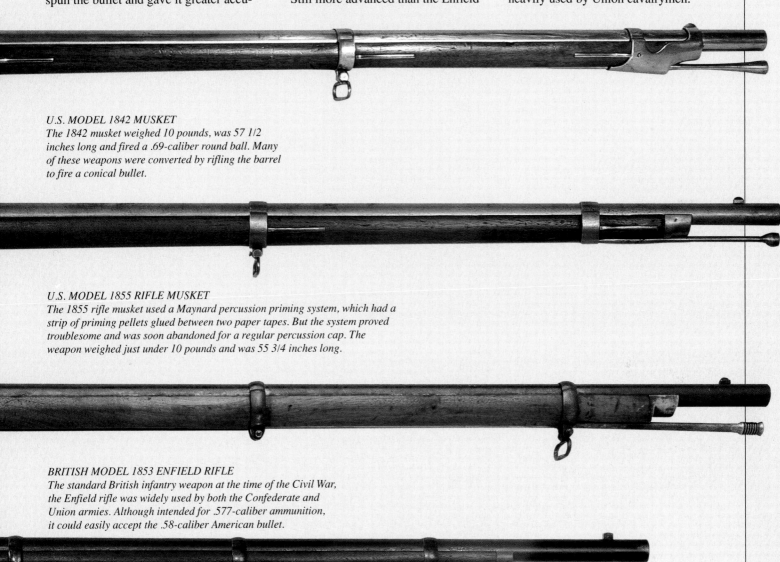

U.S. MODEL 1842 MUSKET
The 1842 musket weighed 10 pounds, was 57 1/2 inches long and fired a .69-caliber round ball. Many of these weapons were converted by rifling the barrel to fire a conical bullet.

U.S. MODEL 1855 RIFLE MUSKET
The 1855 rifle musket used a Maynard percussion priming system, which had a strip of priming pellets glued between two paper tapes. But the system proved troublesome and was soon abandoned for a regular percussion cap. The weapon weighed just under 10 pounds and was 55 3/4 inches long.

BRITISH MODEL 1853 ENFIELD RIFLE
The standard British infantry weapon at the time of the Civil War, the Enfield rifle was widely used by both the Confederate and Union armies. Although intended for .577-caliber ammunition, it could easily accept the .58-caliber American bullet.

SHARPS MODEL 1859 RIFLE
The Sharps rifle had a dropping breechblock, which fell when the trigger-guard lever was pulled down, exposing the bore. A .54-caliber cartridge made of linen was inserted.

Seated among his aides, Union General in Chief Winfield Scott signs the order for General Irvin McDowell's advance at Bull Run. Scott planned to accompany the army in a carriage, to be on hand in case his advice was needed during the battle, but his age and ill-health forced him to relinquish the idea.

hoped, would force the Confederates to abandon Manassas Junction, and fall back to the next defensible line, along the Rappahannock River 15 miles to the south.

Several uncertainties marked this plan, not the least of which was the untried combat ability of McDowell's forces. All too many Union officers were either inactive old veterans or inexperienced youths. Another problem was a lack of tactical intelligence. McDowell could not find any maps that reliably pictured the terrain ahead. But the Union side did have one great advantage: a distinct superiority in numbers.

No fewer than 35,000 Union soldiers would march into battle, the largest force ever mustered in North America. Beauregard, with fewer men, would presumably be compelled to retreat, unless he received massive reinforcements. The closest battle-ready Confederates were four brigades in the Shenandoah Valley, 60 miles to the west—10,000 men in all, under General Joseph E. Johnston. Should Johnston slip past the Federal battalions assigned to cover him, and reach Bull Run in time to join the battle, the results for McDowell could be

catastrophic. The Union general confessed he felt "very tender" about this possibility.

McDowell's three columns moved out at 2 p.m. on a hot, sunny July 16. They trekked along dusty dirt roads through a thinly populated region of low, rolling hills, with dense forests and cultivated fields interspersed with many creeks. Swatches of tangled brush dispelled any possibility of cross-country travel, and at each stream crossing, wagons and cannon tended to bog down in mud. The southernmost column marked time for hours at one such spot as its commander, Brigadier General Samuel P. Heintzelman, ordered his men across single file on a log bridge. Finally, someone thought to start wading. Most troops, however, did not reach their designated bivouacs until 10 o'clock that night, none having hiked more than six miles.

Early next morning the march resumed. The center column under Brigadier General David Hunter reached Fairfax Court House, hoping to catch the Confederate garrison by surprise; the Rebels had already pulled out. Heintzelman's key southern column became hopelessly entangled in rough terrain north of Bull Run.

All day McDowell sat at Fairfax Court House, disappointed at the slow forward movement of his troops. Where, he worried, was Heintzelman's brigade? Hearing no word by evening, the general rode out through the darkness in search of it. He did find Heintzelman—early on July 18. He also discovered what good maps would have told him: that a flanking attack from this direction would be impossible. The battle plan would have to be rethought.

Another problem soon developed elsewhere. Brigadier General Daniel Tyler, in command of the northernmost column, had been ordered to approach the Confederate center and divert its attention with a noisy feint. He had also been told, emphatically, "Do not bring on an engagement."

Tyler reached a crest overlooking Bull Run on the morning of July 18, and surveyed the scene below. Open fields swept down to the stream, and two easy crossings showed themselves: Blackburn's Ford and, a few hundred yards to the west, Mitchell's Ford. An enemy battery could be seen behind them, and a few pickets here and there, but nothing else. He suspected, however, that there might be more. He called up all of Colonel Israel Richardson's brigade and began making preparations to probe across Bull Run.

What happened next was a Union fiasco. The Southerners, well aware how tempting this particular stretch would be for an attacking army, had stationed more than half their troops to defend it. Three full brigades were concealed in brush along the stream's south bank, with another brigade in reserve behind them. In fact, directly in front of Tyler, at Blackburn's Ford, was the brigade of Brigadier General James Longstreet. As Tyler's skirmishers jogged out across the open pasture, Longstreet's sharpshooters opened up.

McDowell's adjutant rode up and advised Tyler to call a halt; the general's demonstration had uncovered the enemy's position and strength, and that was enough. But Tyler had the smell of powder in his nostrils, and a brigade of his own to command; he was more eager than ever to attack. Unit after unit of Federal troops drove in toward Blackburn's Ford, only to be driven back by withering Confederate fire. Finally Tyler saw his folly, and called a retreat. His losses were slight: 19 killed, 64 wounded or missing. But his sacrifice had served no purpose.

When McDowell heard what had happened, he was furious; Tyler received a stern reprimand. Then McDowell sat down to rethink his strategy. Having been forced to discard his original battle plan, he devised another that was nearly its mirror image. This time the Federals would attack from the north, crossing Bull Run upstream at Sudley Ford, and turning the Confederate left flank. At the same time Tyler would make a diversionary gesture at the Stone Bridge on the Warrenton Turnpike.

Beauregard, however, had deployed no troops at Sudley Ford. So tortuous were dirt roads leading to it that he assumed McDowell would not attempt them. Also, he remained convinced that the main Union thrust would be launched against Blackburn's and Mitchell's fords.

The northernmost limit of the Confederate line was a new demi- or half-strength brigade. Its commander, Colonel Nathan Evans, was a gruff, boastful South Carolinian who never went anywhere without an orderly bearing a keg of whiskey strapped to his back. But Evans had one thoroughly redeeming quality: he loved a good fight. He would bear the brunt of the Union attack.

The Confederates also had another hidden ace. After the clash at Blackburn's Ford, a telegraph message had summoned Johnston from the Shenandoah Valley. Over the next two days, the four Shenandoah brigades funneled east via the Manassas Gap Railroad. By the afternoon of July 20, Johnston himself had reached Manassas Junction, ready to plug any gap that opened in Beauregard's line.

The Union brigades, meanwhile, bided their time at Centreville, awaiting wagonloads of fresh supplies. Throngs of civilians arrived from Washington—senators, shopkeepers, ladies with picnic baskets, to watch McDowell thrash the Rebels. Final orders were issued. The army would march on July 21, at 2 a.m., and attack at dawn.

As usual, the army was late. A confusing set of marching orders caused delays on the road south. When that was straightened out, the columns heading for Sudley Ford were encumbered by the confusing network of approach roads. It was 9 a.m. before the lead brigade, under General Hunter, reached the ford.

Even so, Hunter's men had an easy trip across. For some hours the nearest Confederate unit, Nathan Evans' brigade, had been occupied trading shots

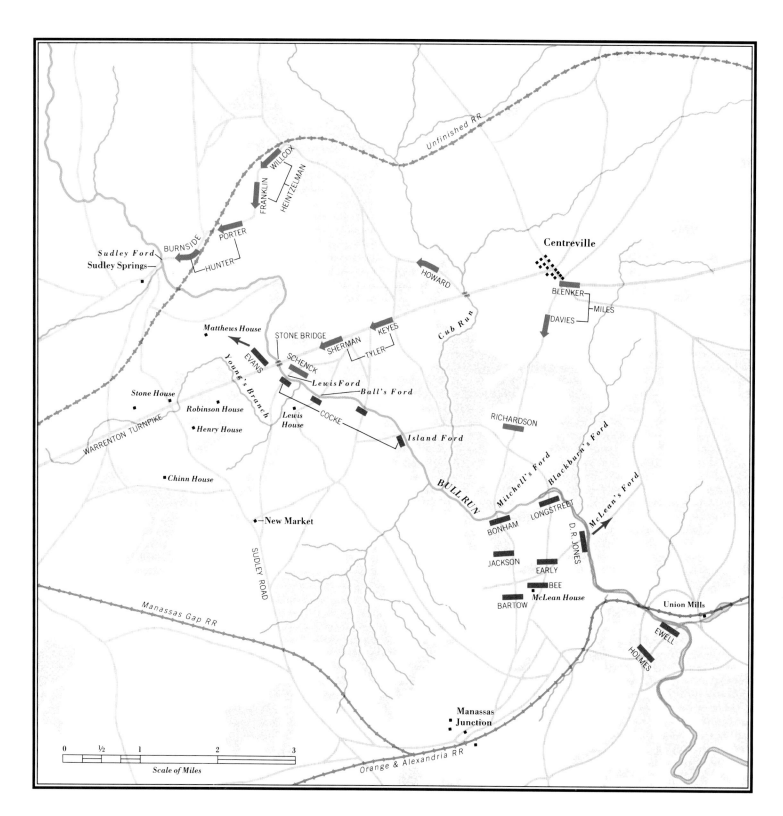

WILLCOX

FRANKLIN

HEINTZELMAN

BURNSIDE

PORTER

Sudley Ford
Sudley Springs

HUNTER

HOWARD

Centreville

BLENKER

MILES

DAVIES

Matthews House

STONE BRIDGE

KEYES

SHERMAN

TYLER

Cub Run

EVANS

SCHENCK

Lewis Ford

Ball's Ford

Stone House

Robinson House

Young's Branch

Lewis House

COCKE

RICHARDSON

Henry House

WARRENTON TURNPIKE

Island Ford

Chinn House

BULL RUN

Mitchell's Ford

Blackburn's Ford

McLean's Ford

LONGSTREET

•—**New Market**

BONHAM

D. R. JONES

SUDLEY ROAD

JACKSON

EARLY

BEE

BARTOW

McLean House

Union Mills

EWELL

Manassas Gap RR

HOLMES

Manassas
Junction

0   ½   1   2   3

Scale of Miles

Orange & Alexandria RR

Unfinished RR

The Battle of Bull Run began as the Union brigades of Colonel Burnside and Colonel Porter (blue arrows, upper left) reached Sudley Ford at 9:30 a.m. on July 21 after a dawn march from Centreville. Three brigades under General Heintzelman followed to bolster the Federal right as other Union troops feinted toward the Stone Bridge and Mitchell's Ford. General Beauregard's Confederate brigades (red boxes) were spread over a six-mile front, with most on the right. Only Colonel Evans' demi-brigade (red arrow) moved to counter the threat to the Rebel left flank.

The punctured pages of a pocket-sized New Testament show where the book stopped a bullet that would otherwise have killed Private A.P. Hubbard of the 4th South Carolina during the Bull Run battle. This was the first of many Bibles that saved the lives of Civil War soldiers.

with a Union column across the Stone Bridge. Tyler, assigned to this diversionary task, this time obeyed orders and held his position. Then, just as Evans realized that no attack was coming, he learned what was really happening. A signalman, perched high above the trees on an observation tower, had spotted Hunter's bayonets glinting in the sun to the north. "Look out on your left," the message came to Evans, "you are turned."

In view of the odds against him, Evans could have withdrawn without apology. Instead, he decided to attack. Leaving four companies to face Tyler at the bridge, he hurried north with the rest. At the crest of Matthews Hill he deployed his men: the 4th South Carolina on the left; and Major Roberdeau Wheat's 1st Louisiana Special Battalion, styled "Wheat's Tigers," on the right. He was just in time: At 9:15 Evans saw the first of Hunter's troops march out of the trees that shaded Sudley Ford.

In the Federal vanguard were two Rhode Island regiments under Colonel Ambrose E. Burnside. Hunter himself was leading them as they started up Matthews Hill. Evans' first volley, however, stopped them in their tracks. Hunter, attempting to steady

them, took a chunk of Rebel lead in his neck and left cheek. As he was assisted from the field he told Burnside, "I leave the matter in your hands."

Burnside brought more troops into line, amid a sprinkling of Rebel bullets. His own horse was shot from under him. Still other Yankee regiments arrived—more than enough to overwhelm the defenders on Matthews Hill. As Burnside adjusted his line, shifting troops and artillery, suddenly he saw the Rebels swarming down the slope toward him.

The Rebels came on screaming, some brandishing bowie knives—500 Louisiana Tigers led by Roberdeau Wheat. The colonel was severely wounded, but the impact of their wild charge threw the vastly more powerful Union force into confusion, and that was all Evans needed. The sally bought time, holding the Federals at bay until reinforcements could be brought in.

The first to arrive were two Shenandoah brigades, one under Colonel Francis S. Bartow, the other commanded by Brigadier General Barnard E. Bee. For the next two hours the Confederates held firm: 5,500 men against a Yankee force roughly three times their number. One company, in fact, lost a third of its men. "The balls just poured on us, struck our muskets and hats and bodies," a Georgia man recalled. "This bold and fearful movement was made through a perfect storm." Another unit sought shelter in a thicket within range of a Federal battery: "Our men fell constantly. The deadly missiles rained like hail among the boughs and trees."

And still the Confederates held on. Yet no store of courage could withstand the Yankee tide forever. Bartow's regiments, on the right, began to fall back. Evans' weary men were also wavering on the left. The Confederates prepared to retire to a new defensive position along the Warrenton Turnpike.

Just then, a gray-clad regiment moved up the road on the right, from the direction of the Stone Bridge. General Bee, in the center, thought the unit had come to reinforce him. He waited to join it to his line. This was a fatal mistake. Once in rifle range, the newcomers unleashed a murderous volley. No friends at all, they were in fact the gray-uniformed 2nd Wisconsin, in the van of Tyler's Yankee regiments now pouring south over the Stone Bridge.

Overwhelmed in front, surprised on the flank, the Confederates fell back in confusion—across the

Warrenton Turnpike, and up the north slope of Henry House Hill. General McDowell galloped up just in time to observe their departure and raised a jubilant shout: "Victory! Victory! The day is ours!" His elation, however, was premature.

All through the morning's fighting, Beauregard had lingered with the bulk of his forces at Mitchell's Ford, where he was convinced the real assault would occur. Johnston, quicker to assess the situation, stood by with growing impatience. Finally he acted. "The battle is there," he declared. "I am going."

Jolted awake from his lethargy, Beauregard began shifting troops to the front. The first to arrive, straight off the Richmond train, were 600 South Carolinians under Colonel Wade Hampton, reputed to be the South's wealthiest planter. Hampton led them forward just as the Confederate line broke—and found himself isolated on the right. He and his men made a fighting retreat. Then came

another Shenandoah brigade: five regiments of Virginians under General Thomas J. Jackson. The general lined up his men just behind the crest of Henry House Hill. There he waited.

Below and on the hill's forward slope, Brigadier General Barnard E. Bee was rallying his men. When he saw Jackson's Virginians holding firm at the end of the plateau, Bee shouted, "There stands Jackson like a stone wall! Rally behind the Virginians!" Bee, who later in the day fell with a mortal wound, had given Jackson his nickname, Stonewall.

By now, at around 2 p.m., some 6,500 Confederates and Colonel William N. Pendleton's 13 cannon had fallen into line behind Henry House Hill. Johnston and Beauregard had ridden up, soon to be followed by the brigades of Colonel Jubal A. Early and Brigadier General Milledge L. Bonham. But the Union force massing before them had risen to more than 11,000 men.

Confederate General Joseph E. Johnston (foreground), arriving at his threatened left flank to reorganize the sagging defense, rallies a Georgia regiment. Colonel Francis S. Bartow, waving a flag at rear, gallops through enemy fire to regroup his shattered forces.

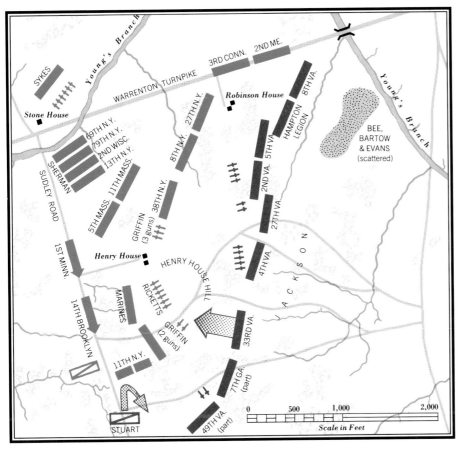

The turning point of the Bull Run battle was reached at about 2:30 p.m. The 33rd Virginia captured the exposed batteries of Captains Ricketts and Griffin near the crest of Henry House Hill, routing the units supporting the batteries: the 11th New York Fire Zouaves and a battalion of U.S. Marines. Federal reinforcements, led by the 14th Brooklyn, reached the scene too late to save the all-important artillery.

moment the Virginians held, then a counterattack drove them back. For the next two hours, all along the line, the two armies surged forward and back, in a tactical confusion of charge and counterassault. At one point Griffin regained his guns, only to be forced back by the 5th Virginia with Beauregard himself in the lead. "Give them the bayonet! Give it to them freely!" the Confederate general cried.

The Union forces began to weaken and hesitate. Beauregard, sensing the decisive moment, led his entire line in attack; the Yankee front simply fell apart. The collapse occurred around 4:30, and McDowell recalled it painfully. "The entire plain was covered with retreating troops," he wrote. "The retreat soon became a riot, and this soon degenerated still further into a panic." The men fell back behind Bull Run, then lurched on homeward along the roads to Washington.

Beauregard sent his forces in pursuit, and they managed to take large numbers of Yankee prisoners. But the Confederates were also worn out, and within a few hours the chase was called off. For the moment it was enough that they retained possession of the field. The first pitched battle of the war had been a resounding Confederate victory.

It had been a surprisingly vicious battle, considering that for most participants it was the awkward first fight of their lives. The Confederates counted 387 killed, 1,582 wounded and 13 missing, and unreported injuries probably swelled the total casualties to 2,000. Fully one fourth of those came from Jackson's brigade. The Union side suffered far worse: at least 470 dead, 1,071 wounded and 1,793—the equivalent of nearly two regiments— either captured or presumed dead.

No one in the Union army appeared to blame McDowell personally. Even Sherman, critical whenever he could be, would credit the general with "one of the best-planned battles of the War." The Federals lost, he went on, because it was also "one of the worst-fought." In fact, the Union army, with rare exceptions, had been atrociously led. A disillusioned New Hampshire soldier put the bitter truth succinctly: "Every order was a blunder and every movement a failure." Yet now there was also a new determination to win, one that moved Federals and Confederates alike to write home the same pledge: "I shall see the thing played out or die in the attempt."

If McDowell had sent his troops forward in a single vigorous assault he would have overwhelmed the Rebels through sheer weight of numbers, gaining the victory he had already claimed. Instead, he began committing his regiments one by one, frittering away his strength in the effort to preserve it. A unit would charge, then fall back under fire, leaving a field of dead and wounded.

The hardest-fought sector was the very summit of Henry House Hill, where in a feat of great daring two Yankee artillery captains, James B. Ricketts and Charles Griffin, had set up two batteries totaling 11 guns. The position was untenable—unless the battery received immediate infantry support. The 11th New York Fire Zouaves came forward to give it, double-quicking up the hill. When they reached the crest, Jackson's Virginians stood up and delivered a crushing volley.

At last Jackson made his move. The 33rd Virginia swept over the hill and captured the guns. For a

59

"SEEING THE ELEPHANT"

The soldiers who fought their first battle at Bull Run on July 21, 1861, were shocked to discover the savagery of combat. To express their reaction to the experience, they adopted a phrase from farm boys who, after attending a traveling circus, spoke with awe of "seeing the elephant." Some of their feelings are captured on these pages in their words and in artists' renderings of critical moments in the daylong battle.

To McHenry Howard of the 1st Maryland Infantry, the baptism of fire at Bull Run came "as if in a dream, the whole thing was so sudden, unexpected and novel." A private in the 8th Georgia wrote, "The whole air sounded as though a large aeolian harp was hung over, around and about us." Another Southerner compared the duel of enemy guns to "two mailed giants hammering each other with huge battle axes."

In this first great clash of the war, officers who were as inexperienced as their men found it next to impossible to maintain discipline. Inexplicably, an entire

Colonel Ambrose Burnside's brigade joins battle with Colonel Nathan Evans' Confederates on Matthews Hill at 9:45 a.m. on July 21. The regiments advancing in

Confederate regiment broke ranks in midcharge and went off to pick blackberries. Captain Charles Griffin of the 5th U.S. Artillery reported that "a great many of our regiments turned right off the field as they delivered their fire. They went right off as a crowd would walking the street—every man for himself, with no organization whatever."

Another Union officer, who had repeatedly shouted orders to his men, said that "they seemed to be paralyzed, standing with their eyes and mouths wide open, and did not seem to hear me."

Troops on both sides were victimized by their lack of physical and mental preparation. Dozens of men, wearing heavy woolen uniforms, burdened with gear and short on water, collapsed of sunstroke in the midsummer heat. Even the soldiers' humane instincts worked against them: scores of men left their units in the lurch to help casualties. "The sufferings of the wounded," wrote an officer of the 11th Massachusetts, "moved the hearts of men who had not by long experience become callous to the sight of human agony."

In the final reckoning, there was not much difference between the Confederates and the Federals in fighting prowess. In such balanced circumstances, resolution alone was bound to count heavily, and the Confederates at Bull Run were unshakably resolved.

Said one Rebel soldier: "The truth is, we were so unused to a fight and determined on victory, that we never dreamed of retiring."

line past the Matthew house (left) *are the 2nd Rhode Island and the 71st New York.*

> *"I leaned down from the saddle, rammed the muzzle of the carbine into the stomach of my man and pulled the trigger. He tried to get his bayonet up to meet me; but he was too slow, for the carbine blew a hole as big as my arm clear through him."*
>
> ADJUTANT WILLIAM W. BLACKFORD, 1ST VIRGINIA CAVALRY

The 11th New York Fire Zouaves, protecting Griffin's and Rickett's batteries on Henry House Hill, stand their ground against a charge by a squadron of Colonel Jeb

Stuart's 1st Virginia Cavalry. Although the Fire Zouaves managed to repulse the attack, they were left shaken and demoralized.

At the turning point of the Bull Run battle, soldiers of the 33rd Virginia Infantry charge the Federal artillery on Henry House Hill. Because the Virginians (visible

through the smoke at right) wore blue uniforms, Captain Charles Griffin of the Federal artillery was mistakenly instructed to hold his fire, and disaster followed.

THE ROAD TO SHILOH

*"No blaze of glory that flashes around the
magnificent triumphs of war can ever atone for the unwritten
and unutterable horrors of the scene of carnage."*

*BRIGADIER GENERAL JAMES A. GARFIELD, 20TH BRIGADE, 6TH DIVISION,
ARMY OF THE OHIO; LATER U.S. PRESIDENT*

One day in May 1861, a demure elderly lady, clad in a black bombazine dress with sunbonnet and veil, drove her carriage into a militia camp on the westerly edge of St. Louis. There was talk that Missouri's secessionist governor, Claiborne Fox Jackson, planned to raid a nearby Federal arsenal using the camp's 700 men, but so far the Union had no proof and was unable to act.

Once inside the camp, the visitor's veil remained in place. She was not, after all, a concerned mother visiting her son, but a wiry little Union captain named Nathaniel Lyon. His red beard well concealed, Lyon scouted the camp, where he saw Confederate flags flying and men carrying weapons plundered from the Federal arsenal at Baton Rouge. It was, as Lyon reported later, a veritable "nest of traitors." A few days after, Captain Lyon returned with 3,000 Home Guardsmen, surrounded the camp and demanded its surrender. The militiamen gave up immediately, and Lyon was a Union hero, though his subsequent actions would prove unwise and have far-reaching consequences.

At any rate, Lyon's excursion into espionage was somehow symbolic of the unconventional war that would be waged in the West, remote from the command centers of Washington and Richmond. Here a general's success could hinge on sheer aggressiveness and innovation.

The stakes in the West were high indeed. In the autumn of 1861, Brigadier General William Tecumseh Sherman was ordered west on a mission to judge the morale of the population in Ohio, Indiana and Illinois, and assess its readiness "to oppose the Southern Confederacy." He was shocked by the lack of preparedness he found, but exhilarated about the strategic opportunities in the vast field of operations between the Allegheny Mountains and the Mississippi. "Whatever nation gets control of the Ohio, Mississippi, and Missouri Rivers," he wrote, "will control the continent."

Western rivers flowed deep into the Confederacy's heartland. In the absence of adequate roads and railroads, their importance as avenues of transportation promised to be crucial. The campaigns that moved up and down those rivers featured several encounters that would change the course of the conflict. The first major battles would be fought for Forts Henry and Donelson, Confederate strongholds on the Tennessee and Cumberland rivers that protected the interior of the middle South. Then, less than a year after war began, a savage struggle would rage for two days along the Tennessee near a Methodist meeting house called Shiloh Church.

While fighting in the West would hinge on controlling the rivers, the key to success lay in the border states of Kentucky and Missouri, where loyalties were so finely balanced that the two states could go either way—with momentous results. Each state had a population of about 1.2 million, greater than that of any Confederate state except Virginia. If both joined the Confederacy, they would increase its size, and presumably its military manpower, by about 25 per cent. A Confederate Missouri would imperil the Union's major routes west, blocking off Kansas and flanking southern Illinois, while giving the South a key stretch of the Mississippi, including its vital junction with the Ohio at Cairo on the southernmost tip of Illinois. If Kentucky joined the Confederacy, it would imperil the blast furnaces, foundries and rolling mills of Ohio.

The battle between secessionists and Unionists in Missouri was bitterly fought. The southeastern counties and the extreme northwestern portions of the state along the Kansas border were solidly for the South. There, guerrilla fighting broke out almost immediately after Lincoln's election in November 1860. Elsewhere in Missouri, neither side was clearly ahead. The state's large German population, however—largely liberal-leaning refugees from the 1848 German revolution—was strongly opposed to slav-

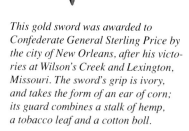

*This gold sword was awarded to
Confederate General Sterling Price by
the city of New Orleans, after his victories at Wilson's Creek and Lexington,
Missouri. The sword's grip is ivory,
and takes the form of an ear of corn;
its guard combines a stalk of hemp,
a tobacco leaf and a cotton boll.*

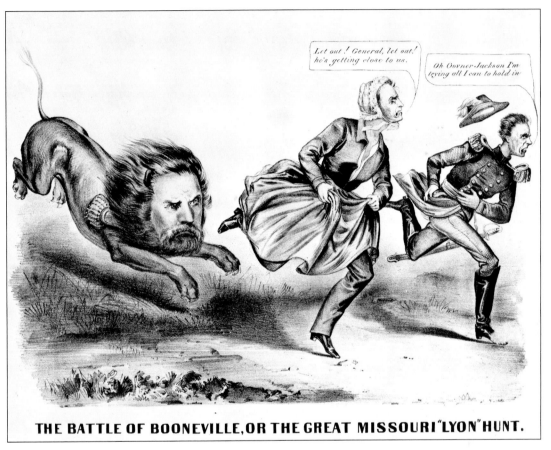

THE BATTLE OF BOONEVILLE, OR THE GREAT MISSOURI "LYON" HUNT.

A Union cartoon satirizes the rout of Confederate forces at Boonville, Missouri, on June 17, 1861. The two Confederate leaders—Governor Claiborne Jackson, dressed as a woman, and General Sterling Price—flee from a charging lion with the face of the Union's Brigadier General Nathaniel Lyon.

ery. Many of them had settled in the thriving river port of St. Louis.

Governor Jackson was openly for secession, but a state-wide convention voted for neutrality. His chief opponent was Frank Preston Blair Jr., a 42-year-old Republican Congressman from St. Louis, and member of a political family that had helped found the Republican Party. It was Blair who acted on rumors of a secessionist plot to seize the St. Louis Arsenal, and had been instrumental in Lyon's foray against the militia camp.

It all might have ended there, with the situation neatly defused had Lyon not paraded the captured Confederate militiamen through St. Louis. Shooting and rioting erupted and, by the end of the day, 28 civilians were dead or dying. The pro-Union Home Guards firmly restored order—so roughly that 3,000 frightened secessionists fled the city. The secessionists dubbed the incident the "St. Louis Massacre," and it roused the countryside against Blair and Lyon.

In the rapid escalation, General Sterling "Pap" Price came to Governor Jackson's aid, taking charge of the secessionist irregulars. Meanwhile, Lyon, who had been promoted to brigadier general, occupied the Confederate capital at Jefferson City, and chased the secessionists across Missouri, routing them in a sharp skirmish at Boonville.

The Confederates retreated southwest toward Arkansas. Jackson kept most of the 3,000 or so troops and gathered new recruits at every step along the way, while Price and a few aides raced on ahead to link up with a 5,400-man column coming north under General Ben McCulloch. The rendezvous took place on July 29, at Wilson's Creek, about 40 miles southeast of Carthage. Counting McCulloch's men, the Confederate ranks had now swollen to 14,000 men, many of them ill-equipped but nonetheless eager and dangerous. By contrast, the pursuing Lyon had seen his own force dwindle to scarcely 6,000 troops as men departed when their 90-day enlistments expired and others deserted as they got farther and farther from home.

Characteristically, Lyon decided to hit the enemy before they attacked him. He planned to strike the Confederate right flank, while a second force of Home Guardsmen under Colonel Franz Sigel swept around from the left.

Lyon had chosen an abysmal place to launch his assault. Wilson's Creek, curving west and south toward the James River, passed between steeply rising bluffs and tall hills cut by ravines. On the west side of the creek, from where Lyon's forces were approaching, there rose a 150-foot spur of land that came to be known as Bloody Hill. The area in which the two armies would clash was cramped: barely 520 yards long by 175 yards wide.

The battle began hopefully for Lyon, with rain keeping the Confederate pickets and foragers under shelter. When shooting erupted on Bloody Hill, a Missourian galloped to inform his commanders that Lyon was upon them. "That's not true!" snapped McCulloch. A moment later, Lyon's shells screamed in from the north, and Sigel's from the south.

For five hours the two sides were locked in a savage struggle amid the brush and scrub oak on Bloody Hill. Sigel's stroke against the Confederate left crumpled against one of the accidents of war. He saw a mass of gray-clad men approaching his column and assumed they were Federals. (At that early stage of the war, the 1st Iowa Infantry also wore gray.) In fact, the gray-backs were McCulloch's men, who charged in a howling frontal assault that sent Sigel's force into a frantic retreat.

The battle finally dwindled, but not before Lyon took a fatal bullet in the chest while leading a charge on horseback. Slowly the two armies disengaged, leaving the Confederates in possession of Bloody Hill, but too tired to pursue. "We watched the retreating enemy through our field glasses," recalled a Confederate general, "and were glad to see him go." The casualties in the struggle were appalling: 1,336 Confederates; 1,317 Federals, or 27 per cent of the entire Union force engaged. Some units on both sides lost more than a third of their number.

The battle was counted a Confederate victory, but it soon became evident that the Union's aggressive little Lyon had accomplished much of his goal; his pursuit had driven the Rebels into the hinterland and had left Missouri's Unionists free to consolidate their position. In the wake of Lyon's capture of Jefferson City, a Unionist convention had declared state offices vacant and had appointed a loyal governor and other officials. The machinery of government and the centers of population and industry remained firmly under Federal control.

The loss of Lyon left a serious gap in Federal leadership. Command of all Federal forces in the West was now in the hands of Major General John Charles Frémont, a volatile, rather romantic man of 48 who had made a glamorous reputation for a series of explorations that mapped the Oregon Trail and the California Trail. Fortunately for the Union, Frémont's opposing commander was regarded as a textbook general who lacked drive and flair. Major General Leonidas Polk had trained at West Point but had left the army to take religious orders in the Episcopal Church, rising to become Bishop of Louisiana.

Shortly after the defeat at Wilson's Creek, Frémont made a major political blunder by placing Missouri under martial law, ordering summary execution for rebels, and proclaiming the slaves in the state to be free. At that time Lincoln was still insisting that the primary purpose of the war was to preserve the Union, not to free the slaves. In fact, he was still hoping to win the loyalty of slaveowners in the border states.

Frémont's declaration of martial law inflamed secessionist forces even further. The political errors were compounded by a military one. After driving off the Federals at Wilson's Creek, Price had plunged north with 10,000 men and had attacked the Federal fort at Lexington, Missouri. The 3,000 Federal troops there had held out valiantly for eight days, but when no help was forthcoming from Frémont, the garrison eventually surrendered to superior numbers.

Stung by this fresh defeat, President Lincoln concluded that Frémont had "absolutely no military capacity," and ordered him relieved of command. But just before Frémont disappeared from the scene, he performed an important service for the army in the West—and the entire nation, for that matter.

The army needed a man to command the troops assembling at Cairo, Illinois, for future offensives to the South. The last officer to be interviewed was a scruffy little brigadier general who had left the Army seven years earlier and had spent recent months try-

Despite his feats as an explorer, John C. Frémont was unsuited to military command both by experience and temperament. "His cardinal mistake," Lincoln wrote, "is that he isolates himself, and allows nobody to see him; and by which he does not know what is going on in the very matters he is dealing with."

ing to find his way into the war. Frémont was impressed with what he called the brigadier's "dogged persistence" and "iron will." And so the command of Cairo went to Ulysses S. Grant.

Grant began the war as a failure, burdened with the reputation of a drunkard who had resigned from the Army under pressure. He had served with distinction in the Mexican War, but subsequent duties at a remote post in California had led him to drink. Whether drinking impaired his military efficiency remained unproved, but in 1854 he resigned—some said to avoid a court-martial. Business failure in civilian life followed.

When war broke out Grant was eager to get back into the Army, but his requests for a commission fell on deaf ears. Eventually, Illinois Governor Richard Yates offered him the command of the 21st Illinois, which was then in a state of mutiny. Grant took over quietly, but, "in a very few days," one of his soldiers wrote, "he reduced matters in camp to perfect order."

The unit's first taste of battle was an important test for Grant. Racked with fear and doubt as he led his men up a hill against a group of Confederate guerrillas, Grant discovered at the top that the foe had fled. The enemy commander, he wrote, "had been as much afraid of me as I had been of him."

From his headquarters at Cairo, Grant demonstrated his newfound confidence by occupying Paducah, Kentucky, at the mouth of the Tennessee River invasion route, thereby countering the movement of General Polk's Confederate troops into Columbus, Kentucky, 40 miles away. Then, ordered to make a feint at the hamlet of Belmont directly across the Mississippi from Columbus, Grant decided not just to annoy the enemy but to make a real attack instead.

On November 6, Grant embarked 3,114 men in transports and next morning launched them against 2,700 Confederates sent by Polk to defend the place. After four hours of bitter fighting, the Confederates scattered and Grant's troops erupted in unruly celebration. Suddenly, Confederate artillery shells rained down among them. Across the river, Polk had watched the battle go against his men and had ordered several fresh regiments to land with heavy

In a Federal officer's sketch of the Battle of Belmont, General Grant's troops set fire to a captured camp, denying its supplies to the Confederates. Although the Union troops eventually retreated and Grant barely escaped with his life, the battle bucked up Federal morale and showed Grant as a general prepared to fight.

supporting fire; the mission was to cut the enemy off from their boats.

Among the Federals, celebration turned to panic. Several officers advised surrender. Not Grant. Said he calmly: "Well, we must cut our way out as we cut our way in"—which was precisely what they did.

As Grant was proving his mettle at Belmont, the Federal command over the region passed to Major General Henry Wager Halleck, a difficult man, much respected and much disliked. His reputation as a theoretician earned him the nickname Old Brains. Halleck's new antagonist, replacing Leonidas Polk as the supreme Confederate commander in the West, was Albert Sidney Johnston, tall, handsome and deeply admired by both sides. "A real general," was Sherman's assessment. Grant had heard that officers who knew Johnston deemed him "the most formidable man that the Confederacy would produce."

Johnston's main problem was quite plain: "He had no army," an aide later said. Unperturbed, Johnston decided to launch an enormous campaign of pure bluff to keep the Federals at bay while he built up his strength. Confederate raiders suddenly ran riot in Kentucky, hitting isolated Federal camps and disrupting recruitment. Gray cavalrymen seemed to be everywhere, but always out of reach; the Federals could never catch them. Sherman, thoroughly befuddled, declared that he would need 200,000 men to deal with Johnston's hordes.

Meanwhile, Johnston went about the urgent business of defending the Cumberland and Tennessee rivers. Halleck also focused his attention on the rivers. The Union high command had been planning for just such a campaign since May 1861, when work began on a river gunboat fleet. By the following winter, a St. Louis riverman and salvage expert, James B. Eads, had produced a fleet of seven ironclad gunboats that would inspire awe wherever they went. Commanded by a tough, no-nonsense salt-water captain, Flag Officer Andrew Hull Foote, the gunboat fleet was expected to be the decisive weapon in the war for the Western rivers.

As the year 1862 began, Grant had seen his army at Cairo alone grow to more than 20,000 men, and he was spoiling to use them in a fight. Fort Henry, defending the Tennessee River, seemed to be a likely target. After repeated requests to a reluctant General

Albert Sidney Johnston, portrayed in 1860 wearing his U.S. Army uniform, became the South's oldest field general at the age of 58. When the highly regarded Texan decided for the Confederacy, Federal officers mourned and Confederates celebrated a victory.

Halleck, Grant at last received permission to launch the attack.

On February 2, Grant loaded 17,000 men onto steamboats and started up the Tennessee escorted by Foote's gunboats. The sight of the great Federal flotilla was daunting enough for the Confederate commander, Brigadier General Lloyd Tilghman, but he was just as worried about the river itself. The waters were rising and would soon flood some of his gun emplacements. He decided to send the bulk of his men 12 miles overland to safety at Fort Donelson on the Cumberland River, while a rearguard of infantry and artillerymen held Grant back.

The Federal gunboats moved in for a quick kill, but they were met by lively fire from the fort. At the

The Federal gunboat flotilla attacks Fort Henry four abreast on February 6, 1862. As the flagship Cincinnati *(left), the* Carondelet *and the* St. Louis *shell the fort, the* Essex *is hit in the boiler and put out of action.*

range of one mile, the Confederates opened up with "as pretty and simultaneous a broadside as I ever saw flash from the sides of a frigate," said one officer. The *Cincinnati* took 31 hits, but the real carnage was on the unfortunate *Essex*. One shot burst a boiler, and many of her officers and crew were scalded to death. Yet in the end, the gunboats and the rising river reduced the fort's active guns to four. After two hours, the Confederates surrendered. That afternoon Grant wired Halleck: FORT HENRY IS OURS. The meaning of the message was clear: Johnston's Tennessee line had been breached. The war in the West was starting to move.

Grant was eager to maintain his army's momentum. The morning after taking Fort Henry, a newspaper correspondent went to see Grant; he had been ordered back to New York and wished to say goodbye. Grant advised him to wait around a day or two. "Why?" asked the reporter. "I am going to attack Fort Donelson tomorrow," was the reply.

General Johnston knew that such an attack had to come and carefully assessed his situation. To defend Tennessee, he had about 45,000 men at his disposal; but the Federals overall had at least twice that number, as well as gunboats that controlled the Tennessee and Cumberland rivers. Johnston assumed that Fort Donelson, defended by 5,000 men, would fall to an attack by gunboats. Though his mind told him that defending Donelson was hopeless, his heart told him to fight. He decided to send 12,000 reinforcements, but made the mistake of dividing the fort's command among three brigadier generals, two of whom,

General Ulysses S. Grant, on horseback (center), watches his troops advance on Fort Donelson, atop the distant ridge. Two black servants carry a wounded Federal

officer (right) to an impromptu field hospital behind an artillery battery (left). The white-bearded horseman is Colonel Joseph D. Webster, Grant's chief of staff.

Gideon J. Pillow and John B. Floyd, were scarcely competent. Only the third, West Pointer Simon Bolivar Buckner, offered any promise.

On February 12, Grant and 15,000 of his troops marched 12 miles from Henry to Donelson. Grant expected the gunboats to destroy the fort's two waterside batteries. Then his troops would move above the fort, threatening the road south over which the Confederates might escape, and bombard their trenches from the rear. On February 13, Grant arranged his ground forces around the fort, intending to capture any Confederates who tried to escape the bombardment.

On the afternoon of February 14, four of Foote's gunboats went into action. Even though his guns had longer range than those in the fort, Foote decided to use the same tactics that had been so successful at Fort Henry: running the boats close to the fort and pounding it point-blank. That, however, turned out to be a mistake.

From the range of 2,000 yards, the boats inflicted some damage on Donelson at little cost to themselves. But as they closed to 400 yards, the Confederate guns shredded the little fleet. The *St. Louis*, its wheel smashed and pilot dead, drifted out of control. The *Pittsburgh* collided with the *Carondelet*, shearing off a rudder. Both boats were taking water through holes in their hulls. The Federal flotilla drifted helplessly away, leaving Fort Donelson still fighting strongly.

However, the resounding Confederate victory over the gunboats did little to lighten the gloom that had settled on Donelson's three brigadiers. They already had decided that the fort was a trap and would cost them their army if they did not get out.

At dawn the next day, Confederates led by General Pillow hit a thin point in the Federal line by the river. All morning a confused battle raged in dense woods, with the Confederates steadily bending back the Federal line commanded by Brigadier General John A. McClernand.

Grant was away at a conference with Foote, having left standing orders that no one should provoke a fight. In his absence, no officer dared issue the necessary orders to counterattack, and the Union troops lost ground. Grant was red with anger when he returned at 1 p.m. and found the command in disarray. But he kept his legendary calm: Surveying the evidence, he realized quickly that the enemy was in

the midst of escape. He told an aide, "the one who attacks first now will be victorious." He ordered McClernand and another division commander, Brigadier General Lew Wallace, to advance and retake the lost ground. And he spread the word himself, galloping down the line with an aide, shouting, "Fill your cartridge boxes, quick, and get into line; the enemy is trying to escape and he must not be permitted to do so." This, Grant said later, "acted like a charm. The men only wanted someone to give them a command."

He then sent a hasty message to Foote asking for a gunboat demonstration against the fort and rode off to urge forward a third commander, Brigadier General Charles F. Smith. "You must take Fort Donelson," he told Smith. "I will do it," said Smith, and Grant noted gratefully that "the general was off in an incredibly short time."

Smith's advance began on Buckner's earthworks. With fixed bayonets, the Federals charged and took the works, from which they could not be dislodged. As the Federal command was reclaiming its ground, the Confederate command was disintegrating. Their position now hopeless, the Confederate generals held a conference at which they formally passed around the command until it landed with Buckner, who used his new authority to surrender. By the time Grant responded, however, Pillow, Floyd and thousands of troops—including a cavalry force under Lieutenant Colonel Nathan Bedford Forrest—had slipped away. The Federals would hear further from Forrest.

The Confederates were now forced to make a broad retreat: Nashville was abandoned amidst panic as a Federal army under Major General Don Carlos Buell approached. The first captured capital of a Confederate state, Nashville was to remain an advanced base and headquarters for the Federal operations in the West.

This bugle was shot from the hand of Frederick Barnhart, a private in Company B of the 15th Indiana, as he was sounding the call at Shiloh. He retrieved and kept the instrument as a memento of one of the War's bloodiest clashes.

Confederate commanders gather for a final council of war on April 5, 1862, the eve of their attack at Shiloh. They are, from left, Generals Beauregard, Polk, Breckinridge, Johnston, Bragg and Hardee.

The defeat at Donelson had shocked the South into giving the Western theater the attention it needed. Leonidas Polk withdrew his men from their stronghold at Columbus, Kentucky. Johnston's new rallying point was Corinth, Mississippi, an important rail junction into which fresh troops now poured from every direction. Major General Braxton Bragg arrived from Florida with 10,000 men; Brigadier General Daniel Ruggles brought 5,000 more. Johnston and his second-in-command, General P.G.T Beauregard, now had 40,000 men under them, with Leonidas Polk, Braxton Bragg, William J. Hardee, and John C. Breckinridge for corps commanders. Things were coming together at last, Johnston felt. Now was the time for the Confederates to make their move in the West.

On the Union side, Grant also had about 40,000 men and urged an immediate attack on Corinth, but Halleck restrained him, ordering Grant to wait until Don Carlos Buell's 55,000-man Army of the Ohio had arrived. Meanwhile, Grant laid plans for the campaign at his headquarters in Savannah, nine miles from a tiny Tennessee River hamlet called Pittsburg Landing. In charge of the camp, Grant placed his old associate who had just rejoined the Army, 42-year-old William Tecumseh Sherman.

On April 2, the Confederate commanders received word that Buell was on his way from Nashville to link up with Grant. "Now is the moment to strike the enemy at Pittsburg Landing," wrote Beauregard that night. Bragg agreed with him, and Johnston consented to an attack on April 4. The army would march the next day, and Beauregard spent the night devising a complicated plan of attack. The plan, suitable only for experienced units, called for three corps to attack in successive waves. He then concocted an equally intricate plan for the march to Pittsburg Landing.

On the morning of the 3rd, Hardee refused to march without written orders, which were not handed him until afternoon; the attack was postponed a day. Then a torrential rain turned the roads to mud, and units became separated, costing another day. Johnston's impatience boiled over: "This is perfectly puerile!" he raged. "This is not war!"

Furthermore, the troops were raising such a clamor that Beauregard was certain that the Federals knew of their presence. He abruptly decided to cancel the attack and return his troops to Corinth. He was, however, mistaken: Although 40,000 Confederates were just two miles from the Federal camps, the Union commanders were convinced of their security, dismissing reports of enemy activity nearby. Sherman,

This photograph of Grant was taken in the early 1850s before he resigned his captain's commission to avoid a court-martial for drinking and neglecting his duty. At the time, he was stationed on the West Coast, apart from his wife and family.

Grant (left) and his friend Alexander Hays, both second lieutenants, stand beside their horses at Camp Salubrity, Louisiana, in 1845. Hays later became a general and was killed fighting under Grant in 1864.

Grant was a 27-year-old quartermaster of the 4th United States Infantry at Sackets Harbor, New York, when this daguerrotype was taken in 1849. Recently married, he lived with his bride, Julia, in cramped quarters at Madison Barracks.

The Union's Homespun Hero

When the 17-year-old named Hiram Ulysses Grant arrived at West Point in 1839, a confusion of West Point records caused him to be listed as Ulysses S. Grant; he left the name so. Years later, Grant became a national figure. Exalted in the eyes of the Northern public, he was in person a shy and reticent man, as plain as homespun. "He was pictured in the popular mind as striding about in the swash-buckler style of melodrama," a Federal officer wrote. "Many of us were not a little surprised to find in him a modesty of mien and gentleness of manner which seemed to fit him more for the court than for the camp."

Approaching the apex of his military career in 1863, Major General Grant poses with his hand on his sword. In fact, he disliked side arms and wore them only rarely.

This portrait of Grant was taken in Vicksburg after his victory there in 1863. "His eyes were dark grey, and were the most expressive of his features," an aide wrote. "His face gave little indication of his thoughts."

Toward the end of the war, Grant and his wife, Julia, sit for a family portrait with their children (from left), Nellie, Jesse, Fred and Ulysses Jr.

like Grant, did not anticipate a Confederate attack. Settled in his camp, near a crossroads and a one-room log church called Shiloh, a Biblical name meaning "place of peace," he had taken only basic precautions; no trenches or earthworks had been dug.

In camp to Sherman's left, brigade commander Colonel Everett Peabody received word of a great sprawl of Confederate campfires beyond the Federal picket lines. He sent out a 300-man reconnaissance force at 3 a.m. on Sunday, April 6. At dawn, just a half mile from camp, the Federals ran into skirmishers from Hardee's corps and exchanged volleys. Hearing the shooting, Peabody sent up reinforcements.

As drum rolls thundered out the alarm, Peabody's division commander, General Benjamin M. Prentiss, galloped up and demanded to know if Peabody had provoked this attack. "Colonel Peabody," he roared, "I will hold you personally responsible for bringing on this engagement." Peabody replied that he was always responsible for his actions. Then he mounted his horse and galloped off to battle.

As the sound of the firing reached Sidney Johnston's temporary headquarters on the Pittsburg-Corinth Road, Beauregard was arguing again for abandoning the battle. Johnston cocked an ear to the guns. "The battle has opened, gentlemen, it is too late to change our dispositions now."

Johnston told Beauregard to stay in the rear, directing men and supplies as needed while he rode to the front to lead the men on the battle line. In doing so, Johnston relinquished control of the battle to Beauregard. It was a confusing move. What made it especially confusing was that the two generals had no unified battle plan. Johnston had telegraphed President Davis that the attack would commence with: POLK THE LEFT, BRAGG THE CENTER, HARDEE THE RIGHT, BRECKINRIDGE IN RESERVE. Beyond this, Johnston envisioned a thrust on his right to prevent the Federal army from reaching the Tennessee River and escaping by water. Then the Confederate line would wheel west, pin the enemy against Owl Creek and force a surrender. Beauregard, for his part, simply wanted to attack in three waves and push the Federal army straight eastward into the Tennessee. And Johnston, it seems, never pressed his subordinate to do otherwise.

Johnston rode forward in high spirits. "Tonight we

will water our horses in the Tennessee River," he said. Around him long lines of silent men were marching through a heavy white mist. Then the rising sun began burning off the mist and the day was revealed—brilliant, but with a touch of softness in the air, a perfect Tennessee Sunday in spring.

As the battle of Shiloh erupted at dawn, Colonel Jesse J. Appler deployed his 53rd Ohio in a field outside their camp and sent word to Sherman. But the General did not want to believe the report. The messenger returned with Sherman's response: "You must be badly scared over there." Then the Federals saw an awesome sight. Hundreds of men, the sun bright on their gun barrels, were moving directly toward the 53rd's right flank. Appler cried, "This is no place for us," and led the retreat from the camp to a brush-covered ridge where the men would await the enemy.

Just then Sherman rode up with his orderly, thinking that the enemy advance was only a reconnaissance in force. In a moment Confederate skirmishers popped up from the brush only 50 yards away. "My God," Sherman cried, "we are attacked!" The Confederates fired. Sherman's orderly was killed instantly and buckshot hit the general's hand. "Appler," Sherman shouted, "hold your position. I will support you." Appler watched goggle-eyed as Sherman galloped off.

As they rushed toward Appler's camp, the Confederates, led by Brigadier General Patrick Ronayne Cleburne, plunged into a sharp ravine that they had not anticipated. In the swampy morass the brigade was dispersed, and Cleburne was left with only about 1,000 men. The Confederates charged out of the ravine and into the camp when the 53rd opened fire, joined by the 1st Illinois Light Artillery. Cleburne reported "an iron storm that threatened certain destruction for every living thing that would dare to cross."

The blast blew the Confederates back down the hill. A second charge was met with another barrage. Flying metal slashed the Confederates, but they grimly charged forward. Colonel Appler's nerve cracked. He bawled, "Retreat and save yourselves!" and ran for the rear, followed by most of the 53rd Ohio.

Still, the hastily organized Federal line refused to collapse completely. Sherman on the right and Prentiss on the left managed to cling desperately to

The uniform coat, worn at Shiloh by Confederate Lieutenant Jeremiah Manasco of the 22nd Alabama Infantry, tells of his terrible wound. A shot shattered his left arm, which was then amputated at the shoulder. Manasco died a month later.

This map shows the disposition of forces at 9:30 a.m. on April 6, 1862 when three Confederate corps (red) attacked Grant's army all across the Shiloh area, pushing toward the Tennessee River. Surprised in camp, the Federal division under General Prentiss and one of Sherman's brigades, under Colonel Jesse Hildebrand, were put to flight. In the Federal rear, Generals McClernand, Hurlbut and Wallace threw units forward to stem the Confederate tide.

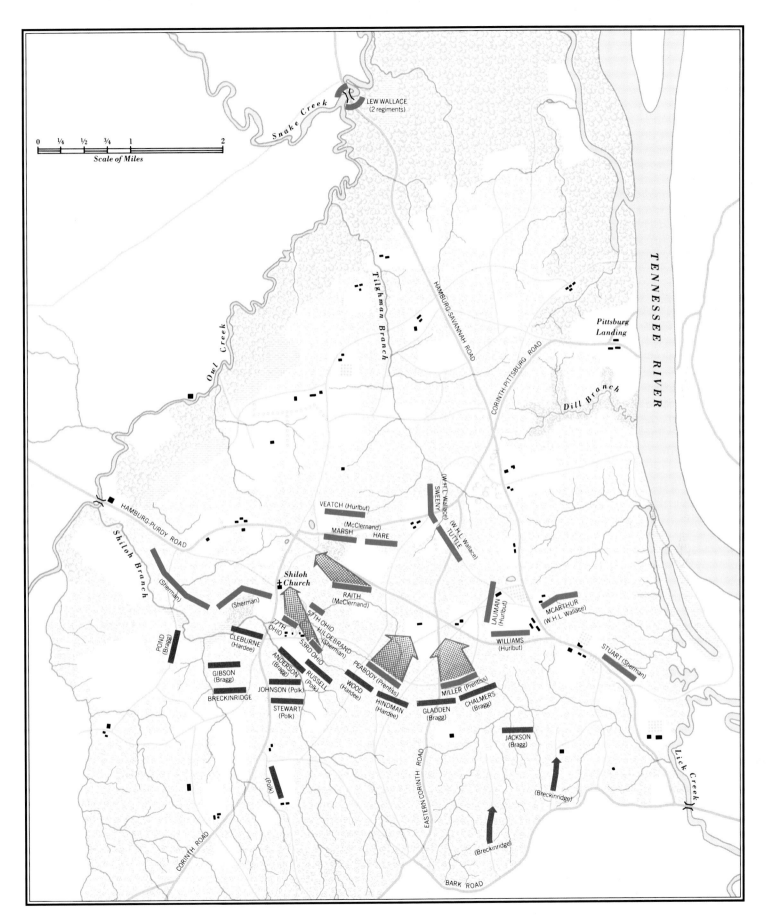

LEW WALLACE
(2 regiments)

0 ¼ ½ ¾ 1   2
Scale of Miles

Snake Creek

TENNESSEE RIVER

Pittsburg
Landing

Owl Creek

Tilghman Branch

HAMBURG-SAVANNAH ROAD

CORINTH-PITTSBURG ROAD

Dill Branch

VEATCH (Hurlbut)

(W.H.L. Wallace)
SWEENY

(McClernand)
MARSH   HARE

(W.H.L. Wallace)
TUTTLE

HAMBURG-PURDY ROAD

Shiloh Branch

(Sherman)

(Sherman)

Shiloh
Church

RAITH
(McClernand)

LAUMAN
(Hurlbut)

MCARTHUR
(W.H.L. Wallace)

POND
(Bragg)

CLEBURNE
(Hardee)

77TH
OHIO

57TH OHIO
HILDEBRAND
(Sherman)

53RD OHIO

WILLIAMS
(Hurlbut)

STUART (Sherman)

GIBSON
(Bragg)

ANDERSON
(Bragg)

RUSSELL
(Polk)

WOOD
(Hardee)

PEABODY (Prentiss)

MILLER (Prentiss)

BRECKINRIDGE

JOHNSON (Polk)

STEWART
(Polk)

HINDMAN
(Hardee)

GLADDEN
(Bragg)

CHALMERS
(Bragg)

JACKSON
(Bragg)

(Polk)

EASTERN CORINTH ROAD

Lick Creek

(Breckinridge)

CORINTH ROAD

(Breckinridge)

BARK ROAD

their ground. Behind them McClernand, the veteran of Donelson, along with Brigadier General Stephen A. Hurlbut and Brigadier General William H.L. Wallace (no kin to Lew Wallace) formed battle lines to stem the Rebel tide. By 8 a.m. it had become clear to the Confederates that Hardee's line was not breaking through as expected, and Bragg began to move up his corps—the second Confederate wave—to press the attack.

Grant was at breakfast at his Savannah headquarters when he first heard the distant cannon. He went onto the porch to listen. He was limping, having sprained his ankle when his horse had fallen in the mud the previous day. "Gentlemen," he said to his staff, "the ball is in motion. Let's be off." He made for his headquarters steamboat, the *Tigress*, from where he dispatched two brief notes calling for reinforcements. One note went to Buell and the other to Brigadier General William Nelson. Buell's army had begun arriving in Savannah, on the east bank of the river, the day before; Nelson's division already was there and the others were near. Johnston had failed in his crucial effort to destroy Grant's army before Buell could link up with it.

On the way to his main camp, Grant paused at Crump's Landing to tell Major General Lew Wallace, another veteran of Donelson, to get his men ready. At about 9 a.m., Grant got his horse ashore and began riding toward the front. As he reached the battle, Prentiss' line was on the verge of collapse. A Confederate bayonet charge swept across 300 yards of open ground and pushed Prentiss' men back to their camp, where they held briefly, then broke and scattered. Fresh Federal units moving up encountered Prentiss' men "rushing back from the front pell mell," as one soldier recalled, "holding up their gory hands, shouting 'you'll catch it!—we are all cut to pieces—the Rebels are coming!' " The panicked troops clogged the road and infuriated the advancing newcomers. Nothing could stop the flight to Pittsburg Landing. The number of Union men hiding at the river's edge grew all day, rising into the thousands.

Meanwhile, Sherman's regiments were giving ground, but still fighting stubbornly. Sherman, his handkerchief wrapped around a wounded hand, seemed to grow calmer as the day progressed, even though four horses were killed under him. He remained boldly upright under fire that made his

Brigadier General William Tecumseh Sherman, portrayed in this rare photograph about the time of Shiloh, was praised as "a gallant and able officer" in Grant's official battle report to General Henry Halleck. Halleck commended Sherman to Washington and got him promoted to major general of volunteers, retroactive to the first day of the battle.

aides flinch. An inspiration to his men, Sherman was watching the action when one of Grant's aides came up. Sherman said to him: "Tell Grant if he has any men to spare I can use them; if not, I will do the best I can. We are holding them pretty well just now—pretty well—but it's as hot as hell." In fact, it was too hot to hold out for very long. At about 10 a.m., Sherman gave the order to fall back. His stand, however, had bought the Federal army a bit more valuable time.

As Prentiss' front dissolved, the Confederates found their own formation in disarray. Some of the soldiers had not eaten in 24 hours and they stopped to wolf down the breakfasts left on the fires in Prentiss' camp and to collect souvenirs. The interlude proved to be a blessing for Prentiss, giving him time to regroup.

Rallying the remnants of his command, perhaps 1,000 men, Prentiss aligned them on an old wagon road about a mile behind their original position. Sunken slightly from use, the road provided some cover. Better still, it was on high ground, fringed with concealing brush and a stout split-rail fence. Much of it commanded a huge open field over which attacking troops would have to move fully exposed. Here, Prentiss and his men decided to stand and fight.

At this point General Hurlbut moved his two brigades to Prentiss' left along the Sunken Road. W.H.L. Wallace placed his three fresh brigades on

Prentiss' flanks, two on Prentiss' right and one far to the left beyond Hurlbut. To the right of Wallace's two brigades stood McClernand's division, then Sherman's. Thus at about 10:30 in the morning, the Federal line was formed again.

Grant rode forward to visit Sherman and found him worried; his division used ammunition of six different calibers and was running out of all six. Grant told him more ammunition was on its way; then he rode off. One of Grant's aides thought things looked "pretty squally," but Grant said, "Well, not so bad. Lew Wallace must be here soon."

On the Confederate side, Johnston was equally confident. When one of Beauregard's aides rode up to ask him for new orders, Johnston said: "Tell Beauregard that we are sweeping the field before us and I think we shall press them to the river." With few instructions, Beauregard was to act as he saw fit.

Johnston seemed to recognize that he had waived control of the battle. Beauregard had moved his headquarters up to Shiloh Church and was using Sherman's tent. Confederate soldiers remembered the fiery little man standing on a stump by the church, wearing his lucky red cap and urging them on. His adjutant, Colonel Thomas Jordan, circulated about the field, sending troops off toward the heaviest firing, a military axiom much favored by Beauregard.

The three Confederate assault lines, which were

At dawn on April 6, Confederates spill out of the thickets around Shiloh Church in a surprise attack on General Prentiss' camp. The startled Federal soldiers retreated beyond their tents. But they soon formed a battle line that slowed down the Confederate onslaught.

now spread across the whole battlefield, were inextricably entwined on the rough and broken ground of Shiloh, and the crushing avalanche that Beauregard had envisioned was deteriorating into raging little fights. Men were often lost; some found themselves in strange units under commanders they did not know. Meeting amid the confusion, Polk and Bragg redivided the command. Bragg would take the right, Polk the center, Hardee the left, with Breckinridge in reserve. The two generals sent messengers to inform Hardee and Breckinridge.

But time was wasting for the Confederates. The Federal line along the Sunken Road was growing stronger by the moment. Both sides brought up artillery and blasted each other's battle line. The Confederates soon got the range of the Sunken Road and laid down a devastating fire.

Scything metal fragments cut down many fresh Federal troops, who were standing erect behind the rail fence. John T. Bell, a 2nd Iowa private, later recalled his experience: "I am lying so close to Captain Bob Littler that I could touch him by putting out my hand when a shell burst directly in our front and a jagged piece of iron tears his arm so nearly off that it hangs by a slender bit of flesh and muscle."

The cannon fire drew the attention of Colonel Jordan, who found a brigade from Major General Benjamin F. Cheatham's division and ordered it to attack. Cheatham's men came on at a trot, closing the distance to 200 yards from the enemy's line. As the Confederates reached 150 yards, the Federal cannon opened up: The long lines rippled like grass in the wind as the shot cut through them. At a range of 30 paces, the Federal riflemen fired, sending Cheatham's men fleeing. On the extreme right of Cheatham's division line, Confederates came crashing through woods and brush toward Hurlbut's position. At a range of 100 yards, the Federal line erupted with gunfire, but still the Confederates came on. Finally, within 10 yards, they were stopped.

The bodies lay in piles, some disemboweled, some headless, some cut in half by cannon fire. Wounded men cried and whimpered. Stumbling out of that hell, a Confederate soldier gasped, "It's a hornet's nest in there." The name stuck.

General Braxton Bragg, now commanding the Confederate right, was determined to crush the Hornet's Nest. He rode up to Colonel Randall Lee

Gibson's fresh brigade and demanded a bayonet charge. Gibson immediately gave the signal, and the men of the 4th, 13th, and 19th Louisiana and the 1st Arkansas started forward. They had not seen the previous attacks, and marched unwittingly across the open field toward the split-rail fence. The 8th Iowa's 800 rifles blazed, and Federal cannon cut swaths with canister and case shot—explosive shells filled with iron balls. Gibson's men went reeling back in confusion under the avalanche of iron. Enraged, Bragg ordered further assaults, which his officers bravely led, but to no avail. Four charges left Gibson's brigade shattered with not an inch gained.

By 2:30 p.m. the Confederate line had been stalled against the Hornet's Nest for more than two hours, stymied all along the line by lack of an overall commander with a coherent strategy. Confederate troops were being wasted in piecemeal attacks, usually without artillery support.

While Gibson's brigade was being chewed up, Johnston's attention was focused on a peach orchard just to the right of the Hornet's Nest. He ordered a charge and personally led some reluctant Tennessee troops into battle. Shortly after reining up, Johnston was seen reeling in his saddle by Governor Isham Harris of Tennessee, serving as volunteer aide on Johnston's staff.

Harris lowered the general to the ground, and discovered that Johnston's boot was full of blood: A Minié ball had nicked an artery in Johnston's right leg. He bled to death before medical help could arrive. In his pocket was a tourniquet that could have saved his life, had anyone thought to use it.

Now the Confederate army would have to make do with Beauregard, a leader who was so far to the rear that he had only a vague idea of what was happening at the front. Beauregard immediately assumed command of the army and ordered that Johnston's body be shrouded for secrecy and the bad news suppressed lest it demoralize the troops. Then he made the mistake of turning his full attention to the troublesome Hornet's Nest. On both sides of the Hornet's Nest, the Federal line was sagging back toward the Tennessee River. Beauregard might have hurled his forces against those crumbling flanks and driven on to Pittsburg Landing. Instead, he seemed obsessed with smashing the Federal center. There had been 11

or perhaps 12 full-scale charges against this position, all of them bloody and unavailing. Clearly a new tactic was indicated. Brigadier General Daniel Ruggles, the white-bearded commander of Bragg's first division, began calling in cannon, and within an hour massed 62 guns in a line facing the Sunken Road.

The guns opened up at 4 p.m. hurling "a mighty hurricane" of shot, in the words of a 2nd Iowa lieutenant. Prentiss' flank began to pull back. On the right, Sherman and McClernand were fighting a desperate withdrawal toward Pittsburg Landing; on their left, there were no troops at all. The Confederates had a clear path to the Tennessee River and the vulner-

In the afternoon of April 6, Generals Sherman and McClernand retreated to Pittsburg Landing, exposing units of W.H.L. Wallace's on the right flank of the Hornet's Nest. The left flank crumbled as General Hurlbut was driven back by furious Confederate attacks. By 5:30 p.m., the defenders of the Hornet's Nest were surrounded and forced to surrender.

able Federal rear. The end was near for the defenders of the Hornet's Nest.

Confederate infantry charges had hammered the flanks backward until the battle line was horseshoe-shaped. A youth with the 15th Michigan remembered the terrible fear of being trapped: "Someone calls out, 'Everybody for himself!' The line breaks, I go with the others with the howling, rushing mass of the enemy pressing in close pursuit."

Confederate troops completely surrounded the Hornet's Nest, where General Prentiss' force had dwindled to 2,200 men. But Prentiss had held his ground through a dozen charges and scourging artillery bombardment, holding back the Confederate advance so Grant and Hurlbut could have the time to put together the new line that was forming at Pittsburg Landing. Prentiss could do no more; he raised a white flag.

Grant's new defensive line ran inland at a right angle from the river above Pittsburg Landing northwestward toward Owl Creek. It was about three miles long and very strong. Lew Wallace was expected to arrive with his fresh division of 6,000 men, for which Grant had waited for hours with mounting impatience and concern. Wallace was in fact delayed by a mix-up over orders and a long march down the wrong road. It was not until 7 p.m. or thereabouts that Wallace's division finally took its position at the far right of the new line. By then the first of General Buell's units had arrived as well.

Crossing the Tennessee River in steamboats, Buell's men could see thousands of Federals on the other side: demoralized fugitives from the battle, some of whom began to swim across the river. One Kentucky general, 300-pound William Nelson, ordered his boat's captain to plow right through the desperate swimmers. When he got ashore, Nelson rode into the mob at the riverbank, swinging his sword and roaring, "Damn your souls, if you won't fight get out of the way of men who will!"

By dusk, it was clear to every man on Grant's new defense line that reinforcements had arrived. Cheer after cheer resounded down the line. The Confederates were not advancing, and the longer they waited, the stronger Grant's new line became.

The Confederates failed to press an attack for several reasons. After the Hornet's Nest collapsed, a number of units spent an hour or so rounding up prisoners. Then, said a Confederate staff officer, "the news of the capture spread; many soldiers and officers believed we had captured the bulk of the Federal army and hundreds left their positions to see the 'captured Yanks.' " Later, thousands of hungry, exhausted Confederates settled down at cook fires or rummaged through Federal tents. Sensing that victory might be slipping out of their grasp, the Confederate commanders finally roused their troops to make a last drive to capture Pittsburg Landing in the hour or so of daylight that remained.

Slowly the exhausted Rebels forced themselves back into battle. On the left, Hardee's and Polk's troops pecked away at Sherman's and McClernand's remnants, with almost no effect. On their right, Bragg's men faced massed Federal cannon across Dill's Branch, a marshy tributary of the Tennessee. "One more charge, my men," shouted Bragg, "and we shall capture them all!" Plunging into Dill's Branch, his troops waded through cold water and clambered up a steep ravine on the other side. There the steady, accurate fire of the Federal artillery cut them to pieces.

Bragg's men were crouching for cover against the sides of the ravine when one of Beauregard's aides galloped up and cried, "The general directs that the pursuit be stopped; the victory is sufficiently complete." Bragg cried, "My God, was a victory ever sufficiently complete? Have you given the order to anyone else?" Then, learning that Polk's regiments were already withdrawing, he said with a sob, "My God, my God, it is too late."

Afterwards it was said that the Confederates had been on the verge of total victory when the withdrawal order ruined their chances. Samuel H. Lockett, Bragg's chief engineer, later wrote, "In a short time the troops were all falling back—and the victory was lost."

The offensive, however, had already ground to a halt before Beauregard ordered the withdrawal. The Confederates, in fact, stood no chance of cracking the compressed Federal line, which was powerfully reinforced by thousands of Buell's fresh troops.

Darkness fell and a terrible night began. The Federal troops had left their wounded behind with their dead on the ground that they had lost. Neither army had any organized system of litter-bearers or medical teams to seek out and treat the wounded men. So most of the wounded just lay there, alone and unable to move, burning with the awful thirst that follows gunshot wounds.

Young Wilbur F. Crummer, of the 45th Illinois, lay exhausted in Grant's battle line. He could hear the shrieks and groans of the wounded. "Some cried for water," he recalled, "others for someone to come and help them. I can hear those poor fellows crying for water." And, he added, "God heard them, for the heavens opened and the rain came." But the deluge that night was no blessing. A cold drizzle began about 10 p.m. By midnight it was a downpour, whipped by a hard, cold wind. Lightning lit up the ghastly field. The wounded suffered on and on; One of Bragg's men said, "This night of horrors will haunt me to me grave." Hogs gorged on the bodies, while many of the wounded crawled to one another for comfort and warmth, and died huddled together.

Scores of wounded dragged themselves to a pond near the Sunken Road, where their blood turned the water red. The next day men saw the rusty color and named the place Bloody Pond. Blood was everywhere on the field. When a Confederate officer's horse balked at dawn, the officer saw that rain had cut a ditch six inches wide down which "ran a band of blood nearly an inch thick, filling the channel." His horse "plunged his foot into the stream of blood and threw the already thickening mass into ropy folds up on the dead leaves on the bank."

All night artillery shells from Federal gunboats on the Tennessee River landed among the wounded with earsplitting roars. And all night the handful of surgeons on both sides were so overworked they could treat only the most seriously wounded. Federal surgeons took over a cabin Grant had used as a headquarters. The bone saws rasped and by morning a pile of limbs lay stacked outside the cabin.

Beauregard withdrew his troops that evening, and sent a wire to President Davis: A COMPLETE VICTORY. He later admitted: "I thought I had General Grant just where I wanted him and could finish him up in the morning." Most Confederates assumed the battle was over; the Federals, they thought, would flee across the river in the dark rather than be driven into the river in the morning.

Beauregard's army was hopelessly scattered; few units made any attempt to regroup. Polk withdrew his division a full three miles. Perhaps because of an encouraging report that Buell's army had marched away, Beauregard ordered no reconnaissance. The report turned out to be entirely false.

The Confederates' prize captive, General Prentiss, discussed the battle freely and made a prediction that no one believed. He boasted, "You gentlemen have had your way today but it will be very different tomorrow. You'll see! Buell will effect a junction with Grant tonight and we'll turn the tables on you tomorrow." Beauregard, however, remained cocky. He spent that night in Sherman's bed.

Tennessee cavalryman Colonel Nathan Bedford Forrest was not so confident. He dressed some of his troops in captured Federal overcoats and sent them scouting behind Federal lines, where they saw unit after unit of Buell's army crossing the river. Forrest raced to pass on their reports, telling General James R. Chalmers, "if this army does not move and attack them between this and daylight, it will be whipped like hell before 10 o'clock tomorrow."

Next, Forrest awakened General Hardee, who told him to take the news to Beauregard. But Forrest could not find Beauregard and returned in frustration to his camp. At 2 a.m. he scouted the river again and saw Buell's soldiers still crossing. Again he awakened Hardee, who told him to keep a bright lookout. This casual dismissal made Forrest furious. Said an aide, "He was so mad he stunk."

Grant, meanwhile, never lost confidence. Sherman found him that night with a cigar clamped in his mouth, his hat turned down against the rain. Sherman thought of discussing the possibility of retreat but changed his mind and said, "Well Grant, we've had the devil's own day, haven't we?" "Yes—lick 'em tomorrow though," Grant replied.

Grant told Sherman that he was going to counterattack at dawn. He said that the time would come, as it had at Fort Donelson, "when either side was ready to give way if the other showed a bold front." To a staff officer he added, "Beauregard will be mighty smart if he attacks before I do."

Though he had a warm and dry command boat at his disposal, Grant spent that night near his men under a tree. His injured ankle kept him painfully awake, so he went back to his cabin—the one that had been taken over for a field hospital. There, the

Working hastily during battle, a Federal surgeon examines a soldier's wounded arm while other casualties await their turn for treatment. The tent facility, set up on the second day of fighting, was the first field hospital established during the Civil War.

A detail of Federal soldiers burns the carcasses of horses killed in action near the peach orchard at Shiloh. In the battle's grisly aftermath, about 500 horses were found dead on the field.

sight of the bloody work going on "was more unendurable than encountering the enemy's fire," he said. He returned to his tree in the rain.

As dawn broke, Federal skirmishers moved forward along the battle line, followed at a distance by the bulk of Buell's and Grant's armies. Neither commander had laid out a firm plan of attack. The troops advanced unevenly over the soggy ground, and soon the Federals crashed into an enemy unit that had spent the night close by their front line. The Confederates fell back steadily, firing as they went.

Elsewhere on the battlefield, Confederate soldiers were jerked awake by the renewed firing. They felt at once an awful sense of dismay: All of them were exhausted, many were hungry, and few had expected to fight again. Yet they climbed to their feet, ready to meet the onslaught. Grant was moving 45,000 troops onto the field, half of them fresh. Beauregard could muster no more than 20,000 men capable of fighting. The battle followed the odds, with Grant's men easily retaking most of the ground they had been forced to cede the day before.

Even so, the Federals encountered savage resistance around Shiloh Church. The Confederates there showed no inclination to give up more ground, and mounted assaults of their own on Grant's huge counterattack. Bragg ordered repeated lunges against the Federal front, resuming the tactics that had already proved so costly. Leading his weary men in a forlorn charge, General Patrick Cleburne, whose brigade had opened the battle, found himself in "a thick undergrowth which prevented my men from seeing any distance, yet offered them no protection from the storm of bullets. My men were dropping all around from the fire of an unseen foe." Cleburne's brigade had numbered 2,750 men on Sunday morning; scarcely 1,700 would survive Shiloh unscathed.

The sheer weight of Federal numbers kept crushing and grinding the enemy formations. Everywhere the situation was hopeless for the Confederates. "The fire and animation had left our troops," one of Beauregard's staff officers wrote later.

About 2:30 p.m. Colonel Jordan presented a painful proposition to Beauregard, carefully expressed in elaborate euphemisms: "General, do you not think our troops are very much in the condition of a lump of sugar, thoroughly soaked with water, but

The beaten Rebels evacuate Corinth, Mississippi. They left behind, said Union General Lew Wallace, "not a sick prisoner, not a rusty bayonet, not a bite of

bacon—nothing but an empty town."

yet preserving its original shape, though ready to dissolve? Would it not be judicious to get away with what we have?"

"I intend to withdraw in a few minutes," Beauregard replied. With orders to form a rear guard, Jordan collected 2,000 soldiers and a dozen artillery pieces and placed them on a ridge just south of Shiloh Church astride the road to Corinth. The Confederate troops began withdrawing at about 3:30 p.m. They moved in orderly fashion, regiment by regiment, until Jordan's men were standing alone. Then they filed off the ridge and down the muddy road in the train of the defeated army.

None of the Confederates retreated far. In sheer exhaustion they began falling out after marching only a mile or two. Soon the entire Confederate army stopped and made camp, where it could easily have fallen prey to a Federal drive. But Grant said, "My force was too much fatigued to pursue. Night closed in cloudy and with heavy rain, making the roads impracticable for artillery by the next morning."

That morning, April 8, the battered Confederates set out for Corinth along a narrow road of deep, churned mud. Forrest was guarding the rear with 350 cavalrymen. In his wake came four of Sherman's Federal infantry brigades along with a cavalry unit. Watching from a rise, Forrest saw Federal skirmishers pick their way through a belt of fallen trees, (which gave the place its name, Fallen Timbers). He ordered an attack.

Forrest drove through the cavalrymen and raced toward Sherman and the infantrymen. "I and the rest of my staff ingloriously fled pell mell through the mud," Sherman said later. "I am sure that if Forrest had not emptied his pistols as he passed the skirmish line, my career would have ended right there."

Instead, it was Forrest's life that almost ended. Leading the charge, he did not see that his men had stopped at the sight of 2,000 leveled Federal rifles; he was galloping right into the enemy line alone. "Kill him! Kill him and his horse!" the soldiers screamed. A Federal jammed his musket into Forrest's side and fired; the heavy ball lifted him in his saddle and lodged against his spine. Despite the wound, Forrest reached down, seized a Federal soldier by the collar, snatched him up onto the horse's rump as a shield and galloped away. As he neared his own men, he flung the Federal to the ground. Forrest

was the last man wounded at the Battle of Shiloh.

Back on the battlefield, scenes of horror lingered. For days, details dug mass graves for the dead. Grant reflected that bodies lay so close together that one could have walked over them for great distances without touching the ground. The casualty totals were shocking and plunged the North and the South into grief and outrage. Each side lost roughly 1,700 men killed and more than 8,000 wounded; but the losses were more severe for the South, which had a much smaller population to draw on for replacements. A Confederate soldier-novelist, George Washington Cable, later said, "The South never smiled again after Shiloh."

The sole reputation to be enhanced at Shiloh was that of the volunteer as a courageous fighting man. Even as the victor, Grant was roundly criticized for allowing his army to be attacked in a dangerously exposed position. President Lincoln was urged to relieve him, but said, "I can't spare this man, he fights."

For all the bloodshed at Shiloh, the battle was just an unexpected interruption in the Federals' campaign to capture the vital rail junction at Corinth. The day after Shiloh, Grant's staff began pulling the army together to get on with the job. Federal troops, commanded by Halleck, arrived on the outskirts of Corinth on May 28; they began bombarding the Confederate defenses the next day.

Beauregard accepted the inevitability of retreat, but mounted a deception that would allow his army to escape intact. Locomotives chugged in and out of town to the accompaniment of loud cheering, as if reinforcements were arriving. The ploy worked: Halleck hesitated until his troops heard the Confederates blowing up supplies that could not be evacuated. On May 30, the Federals took possession of an empty town.

The loss of Corinth shook the Confederate high command. Now, after a year of fighting, the Confederates had lost Missouri, Kentucky, and most of Tennessee; they had also been defeated in Arkansas. New Orleans had fallen, and the Federals were moving up the Mississippi toward the stronghold at Vicksburg. Unless the South could launch a successful counteroffensive, the West would be lost.

THE COASTAL WAR

Neither the Union nor the Confederacy was prepared for war at sea, and in the frantic days following the fall of Fort Sumter, the opposing sides scrambled to acquire vessels of any kind. By the end of 1861, the makeshift naval forces facing each other included revenue cutters, wooden-hulled steam cruisers and a variety of workaday vessels converted to warships.

Simultaneously, each Navy launched operations against the other; the war at sea soon became a battle over commerce vital to the Confederate States. Attempting to cut off Southern exports and European imports, the United States Navy blockaded major Southern ports along the 3,000-mile Confederate coastline.

By 1862, newly commissioned warships were entering the arena—among them, the war's first two ironclads appeared. On March 9, these iron-hulled, armored warships engaged in history's first clash of ironclad against ironclad. At Hampton Roads, Virginia, a strategic waterway vital to both sides, the U.S.S. *Monitor* and C.S.S. *Virginia*—more commonly known as the *Merrimac* (the scuttled frigate from which it was rebuilt)—exchanged powerful blows at ranges varying from a few yards to half a mile. Like boxers, they circled and probed for weak spots, moving in and out. But at whatever range, their armor withstood the test; neither could hurt the other. Tactically, the four-hour duel between the two ended in a draw, but even the Confederates agreed that the *Monitor*, by preventing the destruction of the Union's wooden ships at Hampton Roads, had won a strategic victory.

Thereafter, in the developing coastal war, Federal forces would launch full-scale assaults against New Orleans, Charleston, Mobile Bay and Wilmington, North Carolina. This offensive would reap two benefits: It gained important footholds for incursions into the South, while occupying thousands of Confederate troops that might otherwise have been used for offensive operations.

91

The Siege of Charleston

From the beginning of the war, Charleston, South Carolina was destined to be the scene of a prolonged and bitter struggle in which both sides would expend prodigious amounts of energy. Since Charleston was the site of Fort Sumter, where the first shots of the war tore the Union asunder, Northerners hated the city as they did no other. To Confeder- ates, however, Charleston was a symbol of freedom from Federal tyranny, one they were prepared to defend to the last.

By the spring of 1862, the U.S. Navy's efforts to blockade Charleston Harbor had proved less than a perfect success. Day after day, swift, low-hulled blockade runners took advantage of the harbor's complexities—its three

Inside the desolate ruins of Fort Sumter, Confederate soldiers huddle around campfires on a chill dawn in December 1864 in this painting by Conrad Chapman, a

approach channels, shifting shoals and tricky currents. As the runners defied the Federal patrols, slipping into port with precious supplies for the Confederacy, it became apparent that the only sure way to shut off this supply line from abroad was to capture the city itself.

From August 1863 onward, Charleston was rocked by exploding shells from Union warships and siege guns emplaced on captured islands nearby. "The thunder of artillery," noted an observer, "was as familiar as the noises of passing vehicles in more fortunate cities."

The brunt of the Federal fire was directed at Fort Sumter, the anchor of the harbor defenses. In 280 days of almost incessant bombardment, Federal guns fired about 46,000 rounds at the three-tiered citadel, reducing it to rubble and causing 323 casualties.

Nevertheless, the spiritual capital of the South stood defiant in the face of the Federal siege. It was not until February 17, 1865 that the Confederate troops finally evacuated their positions, and the city of Charleston fell.

22-year-old soldier-artist with the 59th Virginia Volunteers who was commissioned by General P.G.T. Beauregard to document Charleston's heroic resistance.

The Battle of Mobile Bay

The task of wresting Alabama's Mobile Bay from Confederate control was assigned to Rear Admiral David Farragut, who, as a flag officer, had captured New Orleans in 1862. For his assault, Farragut had a flotilla of 14 wooden ships, supported by four ironclad monitors and a force of 2,000 soldiers on the western shore.

The evening of August 4, 1864, the officers and crews wrote to their loved ones with a sense of foreboding: The bay's only navigable entrance was but three miles wide and was guarded by Confederate forts Morgan, Gaines and Powell. To make matters worse, the channel was narrowed by shallow water, impassable obstructions and submerged mines, or torpedoes, which would detonate when struck by a ship's hull.

At dawn on August 5, the fleet launched its attack, braving furious fire from the forts and enemy vessels in the bay. For a time, one Federal ship stalled, blocking the channel. Then the lead monitor struck a mine and went down, taking with her 93 men. Aboard Farragut's flagship, the *Hartford*, an Army signal officer witnessed the battle: "Shot after shot came through the side, mowing down the men, deluging the decks with blood and scattering mangled fragments of humanity so thickly that it was difficult to stand on the deck, so slippery was it."

Despite the fierce opposition, the fleet pushed on into Mobile Bay. All but one of Farragut's vessels had made it through, though some were badly battered. But 145 of his men did not return, and 170 had been wounded. On the Confederate side, casualties numbered 32, yet Federal force was overwhelming. By August 23, all the enemy forts had surrendered; the entire Gulf Coast east of the Mississippi was now closed to Confederate shipping and blockade runners.

At the height of the battle for Wilmington, North Carolina, U.S. Navy sailors and Marines (right), totally untrained for fighting on land, break through the palisades protecting the northeast salient of Fort Fisher—only to be cut down by a fusillade from Confederate infantrymen on the traverse. It appeared that the invaders were repelled, but another, better-prepared division had gained a footing at the other end of the land face, and the Federals eventually carried the day.

Assault on Fort Fisher

The last major port to remain in Confederate control was Wilmington, North Carolina, mightily guarded by Fort Fisher at the entrance of the Cape Fear River. Perched on a bluff, the L-shaped fort remained the final major stronghold to be conquered in order to cut off the last trickle of European supplies bound for General Robert E. Lee's beleaguered army.

Plans were drawn up for a coordinated Federal Army-Navy effort. The first attempt to capture the fort, on Christmas Eve of 1864, resulted in what General in Chief Ulysses S. Grant called, "a gross and culpable failure." Less than three weeks later, however, the Federals were ready to try again. This time every detail of the coming attack was planned in harmony by Major General Alfred H. Terry and his naval counterpart, acting rear admiral David Porter.

As Federal plans unfolded, the future did not bode well for fort commander Colonel William Lamb: His superior, General Braxton Bragg, was refusing to send reinforcements. Thus, when the massive Federal fleet appeared with the Army transports on January 12, 1865, the fort was manned by only 700 to 800 men.

The U.S. Navy's fire, observed Lamb, "was concentrated. Each squadron of the fleet took up its assigned bombardment station, and each ship aimed at a specific target." Meanwhile, 200 small boats hauled by tugs brought ashore 8,000 of Terry's men five miles north of Fort Fisher. Working in tandem, Admiral Porter's gunners, with astonishing precision, cleared the enemy out of each successive gun platform just ahead of the advancing Federal troops. Their fire also turned back 750 of the 1,100 reinforcements finally sent by Bragg.

Once the land face was in Federal hands, the rest of the stronghold was doomed to fall. At 10 p.m. that evening, Major James Reilly, next in command to Colonel Lamb, strode onto the beach in front of the fort, holding a white flag, and surrendered. The coastal war was over.

FROM RICHMOND TO SHENANDOAH

*"At Ball's Bluff, I was hit at 4:30 p.m. I felt as if a horse had
kicked me. First Sergeant Smith grabbed me and lugged me to the
rear and opened my shirt and ecce! two holes in my breast."*

LIEUTENANT OLIVER WENDELL HOLMES JR., 20TH MASSACHUSETTS INFANTRY

Late on the afternoon of July 16, 1861, only five days after Federal troops had been routed at Bull Run, a 34-year-old major general stepped down from a Baltimore & Ohio train that had just pulled into Washington's depot. He was a handsome man, with steady gray eyes, a sandy mustache, and a 45-inch chest that made him look shorter than his height of five feet eight inches. Desperate for a hero, the Northern press awarded him the title of "Young Napoleon." George Brinton McClellan was confident that he could handle the role. "By some strange operation of magic I seem to have become the power of the land," he wrote to his wife. "I see already the main causes of our recent failure; I am sure I can remedy these."

In stark contrast to McClellan's acclaimed arrival was the almost unnoticed departure from Richmond two days later of a gray-bearded, 54-year-old general in the uniform of the Confederacy. Robert E. Lee, undertaking his first field duty of the war, was off to western Virginia on a mission aimed at coordinating the efforts of Confederate commanders who had so far proved themselves adept only at feuding with one another. Upon his return from the mountains, his reputation would be stained by failure, and he would be known by such derisive nicknames as "Evacuating Lee" and "Granny Lee."

Only eleven months hence, troops under McClellan and Lee would collide in a series of conflicts known as the Battles of the Seven Days. When the shooting stopped, one of the generals would be on the road that led eventually to military retirement, while the other would be on the way to renown as perhaps the most revered of American commanders.

In response to an urgent summons from President Lincoln, McClellan had come to assume command of all troops in and about Washington. He found the city in disarray: drunken and demoralized soldiers filled the saloons, and frightened civilians braced for

the worst at the hands of Confederates encamped at Centreville, Virginia, scarcely 25 miles southwest of Washington.

The perfectionist McClellan seemed just the man to straighten things out. The son of a Philadelphia surgeon, he had graduated second in his West Point class and distinguished himself in the Mexican War. In 1857 he had resigned his captain's commission, turned his considerable talents to civilian endeavors and, through rapid promotion, become president of the Ohio and Mississippi Railroad's Eastern Division.

Eleven days after the fall of Fort Sumter, McClellan reentered military service and was soon named to command the Department of Ohio, comprised of volunteer forces from Ohio, Indiana and Illinois. In that capacity, he sent his 20,000 troops into anti-secessionist western Virginia, where they routed the outnumbered enemy in several small clashes that paved the way—despite the subsequent efforts of Robert E. Lee to redeem the Confederate situation—for the region's 1863 admission to the Union as the new state of West Virginia.

As his first task in Washington, McClellan set himself to establishing rudimentary military discipline. More than 1,000 tough Regular Army men, assigned to temporary duty as military police, swarmed through brothels, gambling houses, saloons and hotel lobbies, arresting everyone in Federal blue who lacked written authorization to be away from his post. Within two weeks, practically all the soldiers were either back on duty or in the guardhouse.

Once order among the ranks had been restored, McClellan turned his meticulous attentions to training them. In his diary, Private Alfred Bellard of the 5th New Jersey recalled being "initiated in the misteries of keeping our heels on a line. Toes out at an angle of 45 degrees, chest out and such other positions as tend to make a full fledged veteran out of a raw recruit."

Finally, when the troops were ready, McClellan

A youthful private of the 18th Massachusetts stands with crossed arms in a French chasseur uniform, one of 10,000 bought by the U.S. government in 1861 to help clothe the Army. General George McClellan awarded the jaunty outfits to regiments that displayed special proficiency in drill.

put his newly christened Army of the Potomac on parade in grand divisional reviews. The center of attention was invariably McClellan, who would come galloping down the ranks on his magnificent dark bay war-horse, Dan Webster. As he swept by, the soldiers would cheer, and McClellan would acknowledge their enthusiasm with an endearing gesture. "He went beyond the formal military salute," explained an officer, "and gave his cap a little twirl, which with his bow and smile seemed to carry a little of personal good fellowship to even the humblest private soldier."

Among the few who did not share in the mass adulation of McClellan was his immediate superior, General in Chief Winfield Scott, who scornfully characterized him as "an ambitious junior." For his part, McClellan clearly considered it time for the infirm, 75-year-old Scott to depart. "The old General always comes in the way," McClellan wrote his wife. "He understands nothing, appreciates nothing."

One thing Scott did understand, however, was that McClellan was seriously overestimating the strength of the enemy. Thanks in part to faulty intelligence reports from his secret-service chief, Allan Pinkerton, an energetic Scot who had founded one of America's first private detective agencies, McClellan reckoned that the Confederates facing Washington in early October were "not less than 150,000 strong." In fact, they numbered less than one third of that.

Yet despite his swollen calculations, McClellan sensed an opportunity in the presence of an outlying Confederate position at Leesburg, Virginia, 35 miles up the Potomac from Washington. Hoping to "shake the enemy out of Leesburg" without a fight, he sent a message to Brigadier General Charles P. Stone, commander of a division on the Maryland side of the river about eight miles east of Leesburg, suggesting that, "Perhaps a slight demonstration on your part would have the effect to move them."

McClellan's slight demonstration soon became a major debacle. Late in the evening of October 20, Stone himself supervised a crossing of the Potomac at Edwards Ferry, southeast of Leesburg. At the same time, he sent Colonel Charles Devens, commander of the 15th Massachusetts, to spearhead a second crossing about three miles upstream at Ball's Bluff, where the men could climb up an old cow path as it ascended a steep bank, nearly 100 feet high.

The Edwards Ferry effort was short-lived. Stone got 2,250 men across the river but hesitated when confronted by 500 Confederates, whose number appeared stronger, and withdrew after hearing reports about what was happening at Ball's Bluff.

There, as at Edwards Ferry, the enemy was represented by troops under Colonel Nathan G. Evans, a 37-year-old officer with a reputation as a hard drinker. "When inspiration was slow in coming from Above," wrote one of his artillerymen, "he invoked the aid of his canteen hanging at his side." Yet for all his bibulous habits, Evans was an experienced soldier who had distinguished himself at Bull Run, and upon hearing from sentinels of the Federal threat at Ball's Bluff he began hurrying men in that direction. Once there, they occupied the high ground that commanded an open field where the Union soldiers debouched after climbing the bluff.

Before long, both sides were throwing reinforcements into what turned into a bitter, daylong battle. In command for the Union, with several regiments from his brigade, was Colonel Edward D. Baker, a U.S. Senator from Oregon and a longtime confidant of Abraham Lincoln. The 50-year-old Baker entertained some romantic notions about warfare, and while coming up the cow path he gaily called out lines from Sir Walter Scott's "The Lady of the Lake": "One blast upon your bugle horn is worth a thousand men."

The exuberant Baker had but a short time to live. At about 4:30 p.m., he was out in front of his line, exhorting his men, when a tall, red-haired Confederate soldier jumped out of the nearby woods and emptied his revolver into the politician-soldier. Edward Baker fell with a mortal wound.

As the battle continued, Confederates pressed in from three sides, and by 6 p.m. the Federals stood with their backs to the edge of the bluff. "Charge, Mississippians, charge!" cried Colonel Winfield Scott Featherston of the 17th Mississippi. "Drive them into the Potomac or into eternity!" According to one Confederate, Union troops "seemed suddenly bereft of reason, they leaped over the bluff with mus-

kets still in their clutch, threw themselves into the river without divesting themselves of their heavy accoutrements, hence went to the bottom like lead." At least 100 Federals drowned, while total Federal casualties amounted to more than 50 per cent of the 1,700 who saw action at Ball's Bluff. The Confederates reported only 36 killed, 117 wounded and two missing.

The blundering Battle of Ball's Bluff inevitably aroused a clamor of Federal criticism, especially from senators angered by the loss of their colleague. (Later, they would see to it that Charles Stone was not only relieved of command but clapped into jail.) But George McClellan deftly deflected the wrath of the legislators by shifting part of the blame to General in Chief Scott, whose ineptness, he implied, was an impediment to effective military operations.

Less than a week later the President accepted Scott's offer of retirement, which first had been tendered back in August. As his successor, Scott proposed Major General Henry W. Halleck, a brilliant theoretician who commanded the Federal Department of Missouri. But Lincoln decided instead on the young organizational genius who had created the Army of the Potomac, and on November 1 designated McClellan as general in chief of all Union armies. Two days later, McClellan and an escorting squadron of cavalry were at the railroad depot to salute Winfield Scott as he departed from Washington—and from the army he had served for more than five decades. McClellan watched thoughtfully as the old man was helped aboard the train. Later that day, he wrote to his wife, "I saw there the end of the career of the first soldier of the nation; and it was a feeble old man scarce able to walk; hardly anyone to see him off but his successor. Should I ever become vainglorious and ambitious, remind me of that spectacle."

But even though McClellan had escaped condemnation for Ball's Bluff, he had by no means silenced the rising chorus of those who believed that the time was past due for the Army of the Potomac to stop parading and find employment in a decisive, war-ending campaign. "Forward to Richmond!" trumpeted Horace Greeley's New York *Tribune,* and when some government civilians took up the cry, McClellan began leveling invective at the offenders.

Routed Federal troops scramble down the slope of Ball's Bluff and plunge into the Potomac. "The river was covered with a mass of struggling beings," wrote a Confederate soldier, "and we kept up a steady fire upon them as long as the faintest ripple could be seen."

Politicians, he wrote his wife, were "these inca-pables," and the Cabinet contained "some of the greatest geese I have ever seen."

McClellan's contempt extended even to his spon-sor, President Lincoln, whom he called "the original Gorilla." On the evening of November 13, Lincoln strolled over to the young general's home, only a block from the White House, to discuss strategy. Told that McClellan was out, the President decided to wait for him in the parlor. After about an hour, McClellan arrived, walked past the room without so much as a word, and proceeded upstairs. Lincoln

waited 30 minutes more, then asked a servant to inform McClellan of his presence. The answer came back that McClellan had gone to bed. Five weeks later, the President again went to visit McClellan, who had been stricken by typhoid fever. This time Lincoln was told that the general was too sick to see him, and was turned away at the door.

While McClellan was ill, his critics gathered, most notably in the form of the seven-member Joint Committee on the Conduct of the War, dominated by Congressional Radicals who demanded a swift and ruthless war against the Confederacy. Chaired by Ohio's vindictive Senator Benjamin Franklin Wade, the committee would become a power in the land—and McClellan's bane.

Faced with the Radicals' mounting calls for action, a worried Lincoln summoned two of the ailing McClellan's division commanders, Brigadier Generals Irvin McDowell and William B. Franklin, to the White House on January 10, 1862. "If General McClellan does not want to use the Army, I would like to borrow it," said the President, "provided I could see how it could be made to do something." Lincoln asked the generals for ideas, but they could offer nothing that seemed helpful.

Three days later, Lincoln presided over another White House meeting, this time with several Cabinet officers and four generals—including McClellan, who showed up looking pale and thin. When the Secretary of the Treasury, Salmon Chase, asked him to reveal his military plans, McClellan refused. Some of those present, he said, were "incompetent to form a valuable opinion, and others incapable of keeping a secret," a statement that helped secure Chase's enmity. But by nightfall, McClellan would have an even more dangerous foe in the person of Edwin McMasters Stanton, who was named that day to replace Simon Cameron as Secretary of War.

Stanton, 47, who had served as Attorney General in the last months of the Buchanan Administration, was a gnomelike man with short legs and a massive head. Now, he took the War Department by storm, standing at his high desk, banging his fist on its top and calling out orders in a voice that sometimes rose to a hysterical screech. Before assuming office, he had been careful to cultivate McClellan. Once installed, however, he began declaring that he would "force this man McClellan to fight."

Inspired by such sentiments, the outcry for decisive action eventually reached the point that Ben Wade and his Joint Committee went to the White House to demand that the President fire McClellan. "If I remove McClellan," Lincoln asked somberly, "whom shall I put in command?"

"Well, anybody!" Wade replied.

"Wade, anybody will do for you," said Lincoln, "but not for me. I must have somebody. I must use the tool I have." But Lincoln's doubts about his general in chief continued to deepen. It would have been scant comfort for Lincoln to know that his Confederate counterpart, Jefferson Davis, was also experiencing difficulties with his commanders.

The troubles there had begun soon after Bull Run, when the dashing Louisiana Frenchman, General Pierre Gustave Toutant Beauregard, wrote a letter to friends in the Confederate Congress suggesting that only the government's failure to supply his troops adequately had prevented him from capturing Washington. When the thunderstruck lawmakers asked Davis to reply, the President wrote a mild letter to Beauregard, noting that there was no evidence to support the charge.

Beauregard backed off, but not for long. In submitting his battle report, he seemed to claim full credit for the timely arrival on the Bull Run battlefield of General Joseph E. Johnston's forces. That brought a stiffly worded note in which Davis accused Beauregard of trying "to exalt yourself at my expense." Beauregard thereupon responded with a tasteless, self-justifying open letter that appeared in a Richmond newspaper under the heading, "Within hearing of the Enemy's guns."

To make matters worse, Beauregard kept insisting that his corps was an independent command rather than part of Johnston's army. Indeed, he was so persistent about his claim that an exasperated Davis finally sent him off to the war's Western theater.

That left Johnston in undisputed charge, and his differences with Davis were of long standing, dating back—rumor had it—to a fight over a woman when both were West Point cadets. At any rate, the animosities were exacerbated when the President placed Johnston fourth on the seniority list of five officers he was nominating for full general. Johnston, who had outranked the others in the prewar U.S. Army, reacted with a nine-page letter accusing the President of trying "to tarnish my fair name as a soldier and a man." Davis' brief, scathing reply said that Johnston's complaints were "as unfounded as they are unbecoming."

On February 19, 1862, Johnston was summoned to Richmond for a daylong strategy meeting with Davis and the Cabinet. He brought with him bad news: good spring weather, he said, would soon dry the muddy roads of northern Virginia and make it possible for McClellan to attack with superior force. Johnston recommended a withdrawal to the south

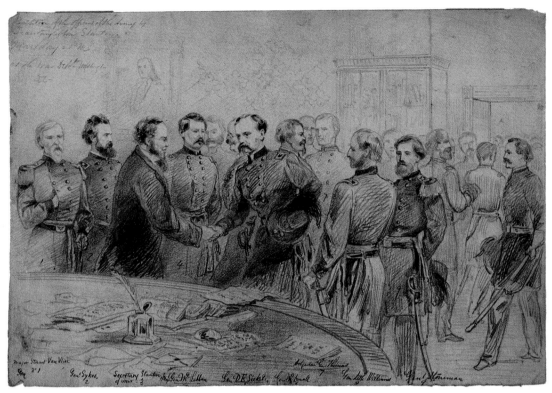

Secretary of War Edwin Stanton, standing beside General McClellan, shakes hands with Brigadier General Daniel E. Sickles at a War Department reception in January 1862. Once a staunch critic of Lincoln, Stanton became a close adviser to the President, who admired Stanton's energy, his willingness to make hard decisions and his single-minded devotion to winning the war.

from Manassas as soon as the roads were solid enough to bear artillery. How far south? Davis asked. Johnston did not seem to know.

On the train back to his Centreville headquarters, Johnston ran into an acquaintance who had already heard talk of the proposed withdrawal—even though, Johnston noted, the man was "too deaf to hear conversation not intended for his ear." Since the government was evidently incapable of keeping a secret, Johnston decided, he would henceforth withhold his plans even from President Davis.

Johnston kept his vow. On March 7, he ordered all his troops east of the Blue Ridge Mountains to head south. By the evening of March 9, most of them were gone, leaving behind a few Quaker guns—logs disguised as heavy field artillery pieces—and smoldering mountains of bacon and salt pork that had been put to the torch to prevent them from falling into the hands of the enemy.

Yet even on March 10, Jefferson Davis was still so ignorant of what was happening that he wired Johnston to promise him reinforcements at Manassas. Not until three days later did Johnston finally get around to telling the President that his army was establishing a new line of defense on the Rappahannock River, nearly halfway to Richmond.

Upon learning of the enemy pullout, McClellan quickly moved his headquarters to Fairfax Court House, about 15 miles west of Washington, which the enemy had vacated. There, he was soon dismayed to learn that Lincoln had removed him as

general in chief of the Federal armies on grounds that he could not devote the necessary attention to other fronts now that he had "personally taken the field" with the Army of the Potomac. Henceforth, commanders of the Federal armies were ordered to report to Secretary of War Stanton.

Adding to McClellan's discomfiture was the fact that the Confederate departure wrecked his pet scheme for the capture of Richmond. For weeks, he had been hoping to transport his troops by ship down Chesapeake Bay to the mouth of the Rappahannock. A few miles up the river, they would land at the hamlet of Urbanna and then march about 60 miles southwest to attack the Confederate capital. Now, however, Johnston's new line south of the Rappahannock put him in a good position to thwart a landing at Urbanna.

After a day of solitary thinking, McClellan came up with another proposal: the army would steam down Chesapeake Bay to Union-held Fort Monroe at the tip of the Virginia Peninsula, a historic tongue of land separating the York and James rivers. Then, using the fort as a secure base, the troops would march up the Peninsula to Richmond.

Lincoln agreed to the design—but only on condition that McClellan leave behind enough troops to give Washington "an entire feeling of security."

And so, on March 17, the first of McClellan's divisions embarked at Alexandria, on the Virginia side of the Potomac. During the next three weeks, nearly 400 vessels shuttled the 200 miles to and from

Fort Monroe. The fleet transported 121,500 men, 14,592 animals, 1,150 wagons, 44 batteries of artillery and 74 ambulances. As a British observer remarked, the logistical accomplishment was truly "the stride of a giant."

McClellan himself arrived on April 2 and took his first look at the ground he had chosen. The Peninsula, nowhere more than 15 miles wide, was heavily wooded and deeply dissected by innumerable small streams. The first major obstacle on the way to Richmond appeared to be at Yorktown, 20 miles up the York River, where the Confederates had built on field fortifications erected by the British during the War of Independence.

The march got under way on April 4, and next afternoon Brigadier General Samuel Heintzelman's III Corps drew up on the marshy ground in front of Yorktown after hard going on roads turned to gumbo by torrential rains. At the same time, Brigadier General Erasmus Keyes' IV Corps was supposed to be swinging around to the left of the Confederate positions. Keyes, however, was bogged down before

"MASTERLY INACTIVITY," OR SIX MONTHS ON THE POTOMAC.

an obstacle he had not anticipated: the Warwick River. According to McClellan's map, the Warwick flowed roughly parallel to the road Keyes had been following. In reality, the river cut directly across the Federals' path.

While McClellan was pondering his problem, he was handed a War Department telegram with bad news: Irvin McDowell's 38,000-man I Corps, which had been expected to leave Alexandria momentarily, was being retained for the defense of Washington. McClellan had claimed that he had left behind more than 73,000 men to protect the capital. As it turned out, however, those troops were widely scattered (nearly half were in the Shenandoah Valley), and only 19,000 second-line troops were available to man the forts around Washington. For a while, McDowell would have to remain where he was.

McClellan fumed. The detention of McDowell's corps, he wrote, was "the most infamous thing that history has recorded." Changing his tactics, McClellan decided to forgo the assault on the Warwick River defenses with infantry, and instead conduct "the more tedious, but sure operations of a siege."

One of the reasons for not pressing ahead was Yorktown's Confederate commander, Major General John Bankhead Magruder, who was using his 11,000 men to stage a theatrical extravaganza. Magruder's artillery fired at everything in sight; his bands played after dark, and on the Warwick River front Confederates marched in and out of a thicket in a seemingly endless column. McClellan, who had no idea that Magruder had set a few hundred men to going around in a circle, grew alarmed. "It seems clear," he wrote to Lincoln, "that I shall have the whole force of the enemy on my hands, probably not less than 100,000 men, and possibly more."

The proposed siege of Yorktown required an enormous amount of labor. For example, McClellan's biggest cannon—seacoast Parrott guns—weighed ten tons each and required teams of up to 100 horses to pull them. Then they had to be maneuvered onto their platforms by elaborate rigs of block and tackle.

All this consumed time, and the longer it took, the more Magruder's charade turned into a reality. After considerable hesitation, Joseph Johnston had begun moving his army from the Rappahannock to the Peninsula on April 10, and during the next few days

the number of Confederates between McClellan and Richmond soared past 50,000.

Finally, by May 3, nearly all the Union siege guns were in place—114 of them, along with more than 300 smaller artillery pieces. That evening, after dark, the Confederates started filing out of their soggy Yorktown fortifications; Johnston, knowing that he could not compete with McClellan's big guns, had decided to retreat toward Richmond. Thus, in the end, McClellan won Yorktown the way he had always wanted to: without a fight.

On May 4, the pursuing Federals caught up with Johnston's rear guard a few miles short of the old colonial capital of Williamsburg, where the Confederates manned a line of fieldworks that consisted of 13 redoubts and extended for about four miles across the narrow neck of the Peninsula. The largest redoubt was Fort Magruder, a bastion 600 yards wide that occupied the center of the line.

At that time, McClellan was still in Yorktown, supervising the embarkation of four divisions; these units he sent 30 miles up the York River to West Point in hopes of cutting off the Confederate retreat. In his absence, nobody seemed to know what to do, and it was not until 7:30 a.m. on the miserable, rainy day of May 5 that Brigadier General Joseph Hooker, who was spoiling for a fight after a month's inaction at Yorktown, took it upon himself to launch his III Corps division in an assault against Fort Magruder.

For two hours or so, Hooker's men made some headway. By then, however, Johnston had sent back reinforcements under Major General James Longstreet, a burly, stolid man who was the most dependable of his division commanders. By about 4 p.m., after a day of seesaw fighting, Longstreet had driven Hooker back into the woods about a mile and a half from Fort Magruder.

Meanwhile, 38-year-old Brigadier General Winfield Scott Hancock, a powerfully built officer with an enormous repertoire of profanity, had led some 2,500 Federals to the right in an attempt to outflank the enemy near the York River. At noon, Hancock's force seized two unoccupied redoubts and took a strong position on a ridge. Longstreet, preoccupied by Hooker's presence on his front, took little notice of Hancock until after 5 p.m., when he sent a reserve division under Major General Daniel Harvey Hill to deal with the problem.

A Northern cartoon mocks Generals George McClellan in Washington and P.G.T. Beauregard in Virginia for their inactivity. When the Confederates withdrew from the Manassas area in March of 1862, another Northern satirist crowed, "It was a contest of inertia and our side outsat the other!"

Shouting "Bull Run!" and "Ball's Bluff!" Hill's men charged hard, forcing back Hancock's skirmishers. But as the Confederates drove to within 30 paces of the ridge's crest, Hancock's whole battle line stood up and opened fire. Then, when the enemy attack buckled and stopped, Hancock galloped to the front and, in a voice hoarse from shouting, gave the decisive command: "Forward! Charge!" The Confederates fled, leaving behind a battle flag, which was proudly displayed by a young Union staff lieutenant named George Armstrong Custer.

The Battle of Williamsburg had cost the Confederates 1,603 men killed, wounded and missing. The Federals had suffered higher casualties: a total of 2,239, including 456 dead. Still, McClellan could now put his men on the road that led directly to Richmond, only 50 miles away, on whose outskirts he anticipated the long-awaited arrival of Irvin McDowell's corps.

McClellan continued to move so slowly that one of his own generals called him the "Virginia creeper." Even so, by May 24 he was so close to Richmond that some of his troops could set their watches by the chimes of the city's churches. Yet any satisfaction McClellan may have felt was dashed by a telegram received that day from President Lincoln: "I have been compelled to suspend General McDowell's movements to join you."

Behind that stunning message lay a Confederate campaign in a theater remote from Virginia's Peninsula, a theater that was conducted by one of the war's most improbable generals—Major General Thomas Jonathan Jackson.

In a sense, this campaign had begun on the morning of November 4, 1861, when the 1,800 men of his Virginia brigade lined up in close column near the Bull Run battlefield. As the soldiers snapped to attention, into the grassy clearing ambled a small, scruffy horse carrying "Stonewall" Jackson, whose disreputable appearance belied his only adornments: the stars and wreath of a general. His coat was a faded relic of the Mexican War era. The visor of his shapeless cap shadowed a grim, bearded face and concealed the blue eyes that took on a feverish glitter in the frenzy of battle. He sat his horse awkwardly, torso bent forward as if leaning into a stiff wind, legs akimbo in flop-top boots, and gigantic feet (estimat-

ed at size 14 although he was only 5 feet 10 inches tall) thrust into shortened stirrups.

Although he disliked speaking to large groups, the general began to address the silent troops. He spoke stiffly at first, but then, caught by a surge of emotion, he rose in his stirrups, stretched out his right hand in the gesture of Joshua, and cried in his high-pitched voice: "In the Army of the Shenandoah you were the First Brigade; in the Army of the Potomac you were the First Brigade; in the Second Corps of this army you are the First Brigade; you are the First Brigade in the affections of your General; and I hope by your future deeds and bearing you will be handed down to posterity as the First Brigade in our second War of Independence. Farewell!"

With that, Major General Thomas Jonathan "Stonewall" Jackson wheeled his horse, Little Sorrel, and rode off. While it was at Bull Run that he had earned his nickname, it would be in the battles ahead in the Shenandoah Valley of Virginia that Jackson would win undying fame.

The Shenandoah was of vital strategic import to the Union and the Confederacy alike, and politicians as well as commanders for both sides were poignantly aware of that fact. "If this Valley is lost," Stonewall Jackson once wrote, "Virginia is lost." By the same token, the Shenandoah Valley in Confederate hands was a salient thrusting into the Union's front; terminating on the Potomac 30 miles northwest of Washington, the Valley menaced the capital's flank. So long as it was controlled by Confederate forces, Federal authorities—and especially Abraham Lincoln—would remain apprehensive.

The man now assigned to hold the Valley for the Confederacy was an unlikely combination of opposites. He was a tender husband but also a pitiless disciplinarian who would, according to one of his soldiers, "have a man shot at the drop of a hat, and drop it himself." He worshiped a gentle God, but like Gideon he would raise a zealot's sword against his impious foe. He was a lifelong hypochondriac, always seeking relief in peculiar diets and quack cures, but as a soldier he imperturbably endured the worst rigors of the field. In battle, the dreary professor who had been known as "Fool Tom" to his bored students at the Virginia Military Institute turned into an inspiring commander.

Now, after establishing headquarters in the Valley town of Winchester, Jackson found himself opposed by a Union army under Major General Nathaniel P. Banks, an amiable, Massachusetts politician who looked splendid in military uniform but knew very little about soldiering.

Despite Banks' ineptitude, Jackson's first efforts to thwart the enemy were spotty at best. For example, on New Year's Day, 1862, Jackson set his tiny army of about 10,000 men on a roundabout march that would eventually take them to the Allegheny mountain town of Romney, where a Federal force threatened the Confederates' western flank. As one man recalled, the day of departure was "springlike in its mildness," and the troops behaved as if they were on a lark. They worked up a bit of a sweat and many of them got rid of their burdensome overcoats and blankets, either depositing them in company wagons or simply strewing them along the road.

Then, suddenly, the fair weather turned foul. A chilling wind whistled out of the northwest, the temperature plunged, snow and sleet fell, and the shivering men began wishing for the gear they had so blithely discarded. But the supply wagons had fallen far behind the marching columns. For hundreds of men there would be no greatcoats or blankets that night.

The march was one that the troops would remember to the end of their days. As they moved during the next two weeks, their path became a treacherous sheet of ice covered by six inches of snow; the temperature kept dropping until it reached about 20 degrees below zero. By the time the expedition got to Romney on January 14, one infantryman recalled, there were "icicles two inches long hanging from the hair and whiskers of every man."

The Federals had already pulled out of Romney, and though Jackson left part of his command to occupy the town, those troops were soon ordered by the Confederacy's War Secretary Judah P. Benjamin to return to Winchester—a piece of interference that almost resulted in Jackson's resigning from the Army and returning in indignation to the Virginia Military Institute.

Early in March, Joseph Johnston's army moved south from the Manassas area, and Jackson was instructed to parallel the withdrawal on the west side of the Blue Ridge Mountains. He left Winchester on March 11, but lurked south of the city, hoping to pounce on Federal soldiers who unwarily pursued.

At about the same time, General Banks was ordered to take most of his army eastward across the mountains to help cover Washington. By March 22, two divisions had gone, leaving only 9,000 men under Brigadier General James Shields in the Valley, where Jackson's cavalry scouts reported their presence at Kernstown, four miles south of Winchester.

Unfortunately for Jackson, the reports mistakenly established the Union force at a mere four regiments. In two days, Jackson marched his men 41 miles, then threw them against Shields' division on March 23 without making further reconnaissance. In a battle marred by confused and even conflicting orders from Jackson, the Confederates were soundly defeated.

Even so, Kernstown had positive results for the Confederates: Federal authorities, now aware that they were confronted west of the Blue Ridge Mountains by an adversary of dangerous belligerency, sent Banks back to the Valley, and, for the first time, denied McClellan the use of McDowell's corps on the Peninsula.

In Richmond, Robert E. Lee doubtless took careful note of the Union response. After his distressing experience in western Virginia, Lee had been shunted into such humdrum jobs as organizing coastal defenses in Georgia. Now, although he had a high-sounding title as Commanding General of Confederate Armies, Lee was in fact no more than the military adviser to a President who had a notorious aversion to taking advice.

In that capacity, Lee could not command; he could only suggest. And that, in an April 21 letter to Jackson, was what he did. In somewhat elliptical language, Lee hinted that an attack by Jackson against Banks in the Shenandoah Valley would have the effect of continuing to pin McDowell to Washington's defenses. That was all the license Jackson would need to launch a campaign of masterful maneuvers.

In his exploits, Jackson would be ably assisted by a soldier every bit as peculiar as himself. The crusty Major General Richard S. Ewell was a chronic dyspeptic, who spoke in a lisp punctuated by frightful oaths. His nervous energies were such, wrote General Richard Taylor—one of Ewell's brigadiers and a man with a gifted pen—that they "prevented

A portrait of Stonewall Jackson painted by a Confederate soldier depicts the general as he appeared during the Shenandoah Valley Campaign. Of Jackson, General Richard Taylor wrote: "Praying and fighting appeared to be his idea of the 'whole duty of a man.' What limit to set on his ability I know not, for he was ever superior to occasion"—except perhaps at the Seven Days' Battles, where Jackson was plagued by an uncharacteristic lethargy.

him from taking regular sleep, and he passed nights curled around a camp-stool in positions to dislocate an ordinary person's joints." He had, wrote Taylor, "a striking resemblance to a woodcock."

Upon heading south, Joseph Johnston had left Ewell's division east of the Blue Ridge Mountains, and now, when placed at Jackson's disposal, it increased the Valley army to 17,000 men.

Thus reinforced, Jackson's army during the seven weeks after Lee's letter marched more than 600 miles, twice traversing the entire length of the Valley. It led Union forces on wild-goose chases and eluded traps set by Federals converging from north, west and east; it fought five pitched battles and numerous smaller actions. Though all the engagements together would not have added up to a single Shiloh, the campaign achieved its strategic objective by again preventing McDowell from joining McClellan. Indeed, even before Jackson had finished befuddling the enemy, the Confederacy's Johnston had taken advantage of McDowell's absence by launching a savage attack against McClellan.

Noting that President Lincoln's order had "simply suspended, not revoked" McDowell's march toward Richmond, McClellan began reaching out to meet the force whose arrival would give him nearly 150,000 troops—a superiority of better than 2 to 1. In so doing, however, he dangerously split his army east of Richmond, with three corps north of the Chickahominy River and two corps south of it.

The Chickahominy was an erratic stream. In dry weather it measured less than 15 yards wide over most of its course. But a slight rise could quickly inundate the adjacent marshes and bottom lands for as much as a mile. In late May 1862, heavy rains had swollen the Chickahominy to its highest level in 20 years, impeding contact between the two wings of McClellan's army.

Keenly aware of McClellan's dilemma, Joseph Johnston determined to attack south of the Chickahominy and overwhelm the Federal left wing—the two corps of Erasmus Keyes and Samuel Heintzelman—before it could be reinforced from across the river. Johnston informed neither President Davis nor General Lee of his intentions. In fact, among Johnston's division commanders, only James Longstreet was entrusted with the overall plan, and even then the word was transmitted orally instead

Footsore and weary, Stonewall Jackson's troops nevertheless raise a cheer as they march past their commander in the Shenandoah Valley.

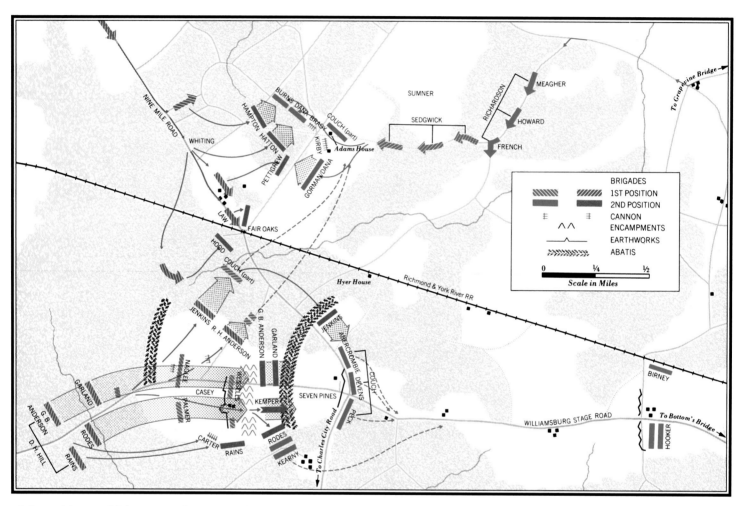

Map labels:
NINE MILE ROAD
WHITING
HAMPTON
HATTON
PETTIGREW
BURNS DANA BRADY
COUCH (part)
KIRBY
Adams House
SUMNER
SEDGWICK
RICHARDSON
MEAGHER
HOWARD
FRENCH
To Grapevine Bridge
GORMAN/DANA
LAW
FAIR OAKS
HOOD
COUCH (part)
Hyer House
Richmond & York River RR
JENKINS R. H. ANDERSON
G. B. ANDERSON
GARLAND
JENKINS
ABERCROMBIE DEVENS
COUCH
BIRNEY
NAGLEE
CASEY
WESSELLS
KEMPER
SEVEN PINES
PECK
GARLAND
G. B. ANDERSON
PALMER
RODES
KEARNY
To Charles City Road
WILLIAMSBURG STAGE ROAD
To Bottom's Bridge
HOOKER
D. H. HILL
RODES
RAINS
CARTER
RAINS

BRIGADES
1ST POSITION
2ND POSITION
CANNON
ENCAMPMENTS
EARTHWORKS
ABATIS
0   ¼   ½
Scale in Miles

of in writing—which was unfortunate, since Longstreet was slightly deaf. Later, Johnston mildly called the result a "misunderstanding."

It certainly was. Johnston's plan called for his 40,000 troops to march along three roads, then strike the outnumbered Federals south of the Chickahominy on their left, on their front and on their right. Longstreet was ordered to take the northern route. This was the Nine Mile Road, which ran roughly parallel to the Williamsburg Road for six miles, then cut southeastward, crossing the railroad at Fair Oaks station and—a mile beyond it—intersecting the Williamsburg Road at Seven Pines.

Instead, on the morning of May 31, Longstreet put his men on the Williamsburg Road, which thrust due east from Richmond through Seven Pines. The mistake not only reduced Johnston's three-pronged

assault to two; Longstreet's men also blocked the path of Major General Benjamin Huger's division as it moved south to the Charles City Road, which angled southeast from Richmond before intersecting with a side road that led northward to Seven Pines.

Throughout the morning, Major General Daniel Harvey Hill, whose division was assigned to smash straight down the Williamsburg Road, waited impatiently for the signal to attack. Finally, at about 1 p.m., upon learning that Huger's lead brigade had come into position on the Charles City Road, Hill sent his men toward Seven Pines. They swarmed forward, straight into a Federal division of green troops under Brigadier General Silas Casey, who tried valiantly and vainly to stem the gray tide. Recalled one Union officer: "Old Casey was as brave as a lion, and remained while his men would

The Battle of Seven Pines, or Fair Oaks, began at 1 p.m. on May 31, 1861, when D.H. Hill's division overran Silas Casey's Federal troops. The second Union line—Darius Couch's division—then held at Seven Pines until flanked by Micah Jenkins' regiments. At 5 p.m. Confederate General W.H.C. Whiting began an unsuccessful series of attacks north of Fair Oaks. The following day, the Confederates pressed the attack by the railroad line north of Seven Pines but were eventually forced back to their original positions.

112

stand; he lost everything but the clothes he stood in."

When Casey's men came streaming down the Williamsburg Road, Keyes sent up reinforcements who managed to re-form the Union lines at Seven Pines by midafternoon. With both sides feeding troops into the fighting, casualties mounted. "Long streams of wounded made their appearance on their way back to the rear in every species of mutilation," wrote a Confederate private.

As the afternoon wore on, the conflict turned into what the Union's Brigadier General Philip Kearny described as "another haphazard battle." Finally, however, Longstreet responded to Hill's urgent calls for help by getting some of his men into action, and two regiments commanded by Colonel Micah Jenkins, a gifted, 26-year-old South Carolinian, sliced through the Union center at Seven Pines. Now, if only General Johnston could send reinforcements down the Nine Mile Road, a decisive victory could be won.

Incredibly, Johnston had not realized until after 4 p.m. that a major battle was being waged. For some reason—"some peculiar condition of the atmosphere," Johnston said later, he had been unable to hear musketry scarcely two miles south.

Once he learned of the true situation, Johnston himself set off down the Nine Mile Road at the head of 10,000 fresh troops commanded by Brigadier General William H.C. Whiting. They were held up at Fair Oaks by fire against their left and rear from fragments of Major General Darius Couch's division, which had been cut off by Jenkins' onslaught against the Union center. Then, just as Couch's outnumbered troops were about to be overwhelmed, help came from an unexpected source.

At about 2:30 p.m., George McClellan had ordered Brigadier General Edwin Sumner, whose division had been posted north of the Chickahominy, to hurry to the relief of the beleaguered Union forces around Seven Pines. An old Army veteran who was known to his troops as Bull because of his bellowing voice, the 65-year-old Sumner was less than imaginative at formulating orders, but he was very good at following them. Now, when informed by one of his engineers that it would be impossible to use the so-called Grapevine Bridge because of the battering it had taken from the rampaging river, Sumner was outraged. "Impossible?" the old soldier roared in defiance. "Sir, I tell you I can cross. I am ordered."

Cross he did, and soon he was bulling his way toward the sound of Couch's gunfire near Fair Oaks. Seeing him come, Darius Couch was overtaken by the feeling that "God was with us and victory ours!"

With Sumner's division in action, the Confederate attack began to sputter, and toward dusk Johnston reluctantly concluded that the battle would have to continue the following day. At about 7 p.m. he rode toward the front to oversee the disposition of his troops. When a staff colonel who was accompanying him ducked at the sound of an enemy shell, Johnston smiled and said, "Colonel, there is no use of dodging; when you hear them they have passed."

Just then a Federal musket ball struck Johnston in the right shoulder. A moment later, a shell fragment slammed into his chest, knocking him to the ground unconscious. When Johnston was carried from the field, command of the Confederate forces fell to Major General Gustavus Smith, a large-framed 41-year-old who had been a rising star in the prewar army until he resigned in 1854 to take up a career as a civil engineer.

Early the next morning, Smith presented a confused plan in which Longstreet would wheel all three divisions of the army's right wing northward and attack toward the railroad east of Fair Oaks. Longstreet protested that the movement would expose his right flank to a Federal counterattack westward along the Williamsburg Road. Smith blithely asserted that the Federals east of Seven Pines had been routed and then tried to mollify Longstreet by offering to call on divisions guarding the Chickahominy if they were needed. Longstreet rode away, apparently compliant, although he in fact had no intention of carrying out his part of the project, convinced that Smith lacked leadership ability.

Longstreet went to General D.H. Hill and told him to dispatch a few brigades to probe the Federal position, a far cry from the massive, three-division attack Smith had envisioned. At 6 a.m. on the morning of June 1, Hill reluctantly sent three brigades against the Federal positions along the railroad. Although the Confederates attacked furiously, they were unable to crack the enemy line. Finally realizing that he would get no help from Longstreet, Hill ordered a withdrawal. At about 2 p.m., the Battle of Fair Oaks (or, as the Confederates called it, Seven

Troops of the 104th Pennsylvania launch a gallant counterattack at Fair Oaks. Holding his own banner aloft, color sergeant Hiram W. Purcell races forward in the

face of advancing Confederates to rescue the flag of a fallen comrade.

A powerful man nearly six feet tall, Robert E. Lee was soft-spoken, polite and even diffident. On the field of battle, his manner changed. "No man who saw his flashing eyes and sternly set lips," said an observer, "is ever likely to forget them."

The Making of a General

When General Robert E. Lee took command of the Confederate forces defending Richmond in June 1862, he was famous yet little known. Steeped in the tradition of *noblesse oblige,* Lee could trace his family's call to the military back eight centuries, to an ancestor who had fought beside William the Conqueror. Lee was brought up to become a gentleman soldier, and he wholeheartedly accepted his obligation. A graduate of West Point in 1829—second in his class, and without a single demerit—his first taste of fighting came during the Mexican War, with a performance that inspired U.S. commander General Winfield Scott to call him, "the very best soldier that I ever saw in the field."

Beneath Lee's aristocratic reserve beat a passionate heart. He was easily moved to tears and wept unabashedly on learning that a close comrade had died. But when anger broke through Lee's façade of studied calm, those who had seen his rage before quickly departed the scene.

Lee was uncanny in judging his opponent's strengths and weaknesses, and in turning both to his advantage. Perhaps his greatest asset, however, was pure audacity—his willingness to run risks, his eagerness to attack, his instinct for taking the initiative at just the right moment.

When it finally came time to serve the Confederate side as its field commander, Lee quickly vaulted to the peak of his profession in just three months—culminating in his victory at the second battle at Bull Run. With that triumph in August 1862, Lee was well on his way to becoming the greatest soldier of the Civil War.

Lee's engraved .28-caliber revolver was given to him by arms manufacturer Samuel Colt in 1855 at the end of Lee's three-year term as Superintendent of West Point. The gun's perfect condition suggests that Lee rarely used it.

Robert E. Lee, 31, radiates confidence in his earliest known portrait, painted in 1838 by William E. West. A doting father to his six children, Lee once complained that soldiering was a profession that "debars all hope of domestic enjoyment."

Pines) ended in deadlock. The Confederates had suffered 6,134 casualties, including 980 killed, while the Federals had incurred 5,031 casualties, of whom 790 were killed.

In the course of the day's battle, the burden of overall command had proved too much for poor Gustavus Smith and he had suffered a temporary nervous breakdown. "I was completely prostrated by an attack of paralysis," he candidly wrote later; but 18 hours after he was relieved of command, "no symptom was manifested." To replace him, on June 2, 1862, President Davis named the army's new field commander: General Robert E. Lee.

Few Southern cheers greeted the appointment. More typically, the Richmond *Examiner* scathingly described Lee as "a general who had never fought a battle and whose extreme tenderness of blood inclined him to depend exclusively on the resources of strategy." But at least one Confederate had a more accurate measure. Shortly after the Battle of Fair Oaks, Colonel Joseph Ives, who had known Lee earlier, was asked by a fellow officer if the new commander had enough audacity for the tasks at hand. Replied Ives: "If there is one man in either army, Confederate or Federal, head and shoulders above every other in audacity, it is General Lee! His name might be Audacity."

An awesome challenge now confronted Lee: although some 50,000 Confederates were arrayed outside Richmond, they faced 100,000 Federal troops. The 2-to-1 mathematics of the situation seemed inescapable: once the Union army launched its assault, Richmond must fall.

Fortunately for Lee, the bloodshed at Fair Oaks had shaken McClellan, who wrote his wife that he was "tired of the battle-field, with its mangled corpses and poor wounded. Victory has no charms for me when purchased at such cost." In that state of mind, McClellan kept his huge force frozen in place astride the Chickahominy, with three corps on the south bank and two on the north, still reaching out to link with the still-promised march of Irvin McDowell's troops from Fredericksburg.

Lee made good use of the time that McClellan granted him. He obtained better rations and uniforms for his troops; he stressed discipline and sobriety (Lee himself took nothing stronger than a little wine); and he tackled the defeatist attitude that afflicted some of his generals. When one of them began drawing diagrams of the inevitable results of a Federal siege, Lee impatiently interrupted him. "Stop! Stop!" he exclaimed. "If we go to ciphering we shall be whipped beforehand."

In fact, what Lee had in mind was nothing less than a full-scale attack against McClellan's isolated right wing north of the Chickahominy. But first he needed to know the exact position of Brigadier General Fitz-John Porter's V Corps, which formed the northern tip of the Union army. To find out, Lee ordered his cavalry chief, Brigadier General James Ewell Brown (Jeb) Stuart to conduct a reconnaissance in force.

Only 29 years old, Stuart was a storybook cavalryman who relished the assignment. On June 12, he set out with 1,200 men on a wild, semicircular ride that during the next three days covered nearly 100 miles and took him all the way around McClellan's army. Upon his return, Stuart reported to Lee that Porter's right flank was "up in the air"—not anchored on any natural obstacle—and vulnerable to attack.

With that news, Lee could proceed with his plan. The key to his offensive was Stonewall Jackson's army, which would march from the Shenandoah Valley and outflank Porter's right. The sound of Jackson's guns to their north would be the signal for three Confederate divisions of about 47,000 men under Major Generals Longstreet, Ambrose Powell Hill and Daniel Harvey Hill to attack from the west and sweep eastward along the Chickahominy's north bank, threatening McClellan's supply line to White House Landing on the Pamunkey River. At a conference with Lee, Jackson agreed to launch his assault early on the morning of June 26 in the first of what came to be known as the Battles of the Seven Days.

At the appointed time, Lee stood on a bluff looking north across the Chickahominy toward the village of Mechanicsville and waited for the shooting to start. But nothing happened until he received a message sent by Jackson at around 9 a.m., indicating that his troops were about six hours behind schedule.

Up at Meadow Bridge, A.P. Hill was chafing at the delay. At 36 and Lee's youngest major general, Hill was a slender, handsome man who liked to wear a

Less than four weeks after the stalemate at Seven Pines, Lee sparked the first battle of the Seven Days by sending most of his forces north against Fitz-John Porter's troops on the Federal right near Mechanicsville. Porter retreated to near Gaines' Mill, and on June 27 the advancing Confederates broke his line behind Boatswain's Creek, forcing him to withdraw south of the Chickahominy. In the next three days Lee's pursuing forces clashed with McClellan's army as it shifted south to the James River. On July 1, both sides girded for a climactic battle at Malvern Hill.

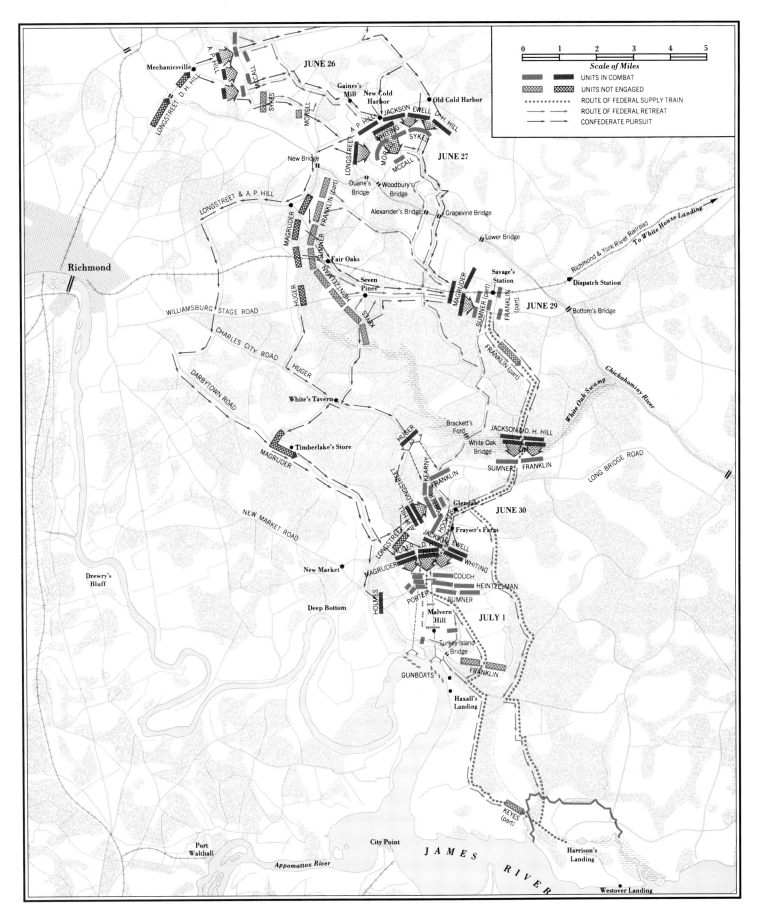

JUNE 26

Mechanicsville
A. P. HILL
McCALL
LONGSTREET D. H. HILL

Gaines's Mill
New Cold Harbor
A. P. HILL
JACKSON EWELL D. H. HILL
SYKES
MORELL
Old Cold Harbor

SYKES
LONGSTREET
MORELL
WHITING
McCALL

JUNE 27

New Bridge

LONGSTREET & A. P. HILL

Duane's Bridge
Woodbury's Bridge
Alexander's Bridge
Grapevine Bridge

MAGRUDER
FRANKLIN (part)

Lower Bridge

Richmond

SUMNER

HUGER

Fair Oaks
HEINTZELMAN

Seven Pines

KEYES

MAGRUDER
SUMNER (part)
FRANKLIN (part)

Savage's Station

Dispatch Station

JUNE 29

Bottom's Bridge

WILLIAMSBURG STAGE ROAD

CHARLES CITY ROAD

HUGER

FRANKLIN (part)

DARBYTOWN ROAD

White's Tavern

Richmond & York River Railroad
To White House Landing

Chickahominy River

White Oak Swamp

Brackett's Ford
JACKSON & D. H. HILL
White Oak Bridge
SUMNER FRANKLIN

Timberlake's Store
MAGRUDER

HUGER
KEARNY
FRANKLIN

LONG BRIDGE ROAD

NEW MARKET ROAD

LONGSTREET
A. P. HILL
HOOKER
HUGER D. HILL
JACKSON EWELL
WHITING

Glendale
Frayser's Farm

JUNE 30

MAGRUDER

New Market

COUCH
HEINTZELMAN

Deep Bottom

HOLMES
PORTER
SUMNER

Malvern Hill

JULY 1

Turkey Island Bridge

GUNBOATS

FRANKLIN

Drewry's Bluff

Haxall's Landing

KEYES (part)

Port Walthall

City Point

JAMES   RIVER

Harrison's Landing

Appomattox River

Westover Landing

Scale of Miles

| 0 | 1 | 2 | 3 | 4 | 5 |

UNITS IN COMBAT
UNITS NOT ENGAGED
ROUTE OF FEDERAL SUPPLY TRAIN
ROUTE OF FEDERAL RETREAT
CONFEDERATE PURSUIT

flaming red battle shirt. He was also extremely high-strung, and by 3 p.m. his patience had run out. Without bothering to notify Lee of his intentions, Hill took his division across the Chickahominy and, toward 5 p.m., launched Brigadier General James J. Archer's brigade in the first of a series of piecemeal attacks against Porter's main defense line, entrenched on high ground behind Beaver Dam Creek.

Not until Hill's assault was well under way did Stonewall Jackson arrive with his vanguard at a place called Hundley's Corner, less than three miles from Hill's northernmost brigade. Jackson could hear the boom of Federal artillery and the rattle of Hill's musketry, and all he had to do was push forward a mile or two to turn the enemy's flank. Instead, inexplicably, he put his men into bivouac and settled down for the night. As one Confederate officer later wrote, Jackson on this day "was not really Jackson. He was under a spell."

Still unaware of Jackson's strange behavior, Lee sent D.H. Hill's lead brigade to aid the embattled troops of A.P. Hill. The result was "as might have been foreseen," D.H. Hill later wrote, "a bloody and disastrous repulse."

At about 9 p.m., darkness ended the Battle of Mechanicsville. Robert E. Lee's first major engagement had been a miserable failure: he had lost 1,484 men killed and wounded. A Federal officer saw wounded and dead Confederates lying along Beaver Dam Creek "like flies in a bowl of sugar." The Federals had suffered only 361 casualties, and

George McClellan ecstatically wired Washington: "I almost begin to think we are invincible."

For all his bravado, McClellan knew that his right flank would be imperiled when Jackson roused himself at dawn. During the night, McClellan ordered Porter to withdraw four miles to the east to an even more formidable position on Boatswain's Creek. There, marsh and fringes of pine trees bordered the steep banks of the sluggish little stream, and the ground on the east bank rose to form a crescent-shaped plateau.

Early on the morning of June 27, when Lee discovered that most of the Federals had vacated their entrenchments behind Beaver Dam Creek, he sent his four commands eastward in three roughly parallel columns with the aim of hitting Porter front and flank. To the north, Jackson and D.H. Hill would head for Old Cold Harbor, hoping to get behind Porter's right flank. In the center, A.P. Hill would pursue Porter's rear guard, supported by Longstreet driving along the north bank of the Chickahominy.

At about noon, A.P. Hill's lead brigade caught up with the Federal rear guard near a gristmill called Gaines' Mill—the name applied to the battle that took place later that day—and sent it scrambling for safety. Then Hill pushed beyond the crossroads at New Cold Harbor and sent his men down a slope to Boatswain's Creek, where the Federals were waiting.

Just as had happened the day before, Lee was unable to get all his forces in line for a coordinated assault. Instead, A.P. Hill attacked first, then D.H.

In the midst of desperate fighting at Boatswain's Creek, south of Gaines' Mill, Colonel Bradley Johnson halts his Confederate 1st Maryland Infantry and drills the ranks under fire after they faltered during a charge. The men quickly recovered, hurled themselves at the Federal line, and drove it back.

Hill, and then Richard Ewell, who had brought his hardened veterans from the Shenandoah Valley along with Jackson's troops. But from his headquarters atop the plateau behind Boatswain's Creek, Fitz-John Porter was, according to his opponent D.H. Hill, conducting the defense "with an ability unsurpassed on any field during the war." One after another Confederate onrush was held at bay.

Not until after 5 p.m. did the principal reason for Lee's problem come riding up in the person of Stonewall Jackson—late again, this time partly because he had taken a wrong road that morning. Yet Lee had only the gentlest of rebukes for the laggardly Jackson. "Ah, General," he said. "I am very glad to see you. I had hoped to be with you before."

About two hours later, Lee launched a general assault, although not all units advanced simultaneously. Among the last to march into action was the so-called Texas Brigade, under Brigadier General John Bell Hood, a 31-year-old Kentucky native with fair hair and beard. When Lee saw Hood ride past, he singled him out for a quick briefing. Pointing to Porter's defenses, Lee asked: "Can you break his line?" Hood said he would try. Lee raised his hat and said, "May God be with you."

And in went the Texas Brigade, surging across the swampy creek, up the slope beyond, and onto the crest of the plateau, just 10 yards from the Federal line. There, for the first time, Hood's men opened fire, and a wall of lead slammed into Brigadier General George W. Taylor's New Jersey brigade. That volley, wrote a Union staff officer, "was the most withering I ever saw delivered. The New Jersey Brigade broke all to pieces."

This was the success Lee so desperately needed. The Federal line began to crumble and Porter's left fell back, stubbornly at first and then in a state approaching panic.

As the beaten Federals retreated across the Chickahominy, an overwrought McClellan expressed his disappointment in an extraordinary telegram to Secretary of War Stanton. "If I save this army now," it concluded, "I tell you plainly that I owe no thanks to you or to any other persons in Washington. You have done your best to sacrifice this army."

Ironically, at any time during the past two days, McClellan and the 60,000 Federals still south of the Chickahominy could easily have taken Richmond.

Instead, McClellan had been mesmerized by the 25,000 Confederates left to defend the city under Magruder, who had put up a spurious show of strength that surpassed even his theatrics near Yorktown, convincing McClellan that he must be facing at least 200,000 troops.

Late on the night of June 27, McClellan astounded his corps commanders by announcing that the Army of the Potomac would abandon its entrenchments before Richmond and move to a new position on the north bank of the James River. The movement began early next morning, with long columns streaming eastward on the Williamsburg Road, then turning south to two bridges over White Oak Swamp.

Although Lee realized by late afternoon that McClellan was on the move, a crucial question remained: was the enemy retreating east down the Peninsula or south to the James? Not until the morning of June 29 was the answer sufficiently clear for Lee to map a hasty plan for pursuit: Jackson would cross the Chickahominy at Grapevine Bridge and link up with the left of Magruder's force, which was to advance eastward against the rear of the retreating Federals. Meanwhile, Longstreet and A.P. Hill would cross the Chickahominy at New Bridge and, in cooperation with Benjamin Huger, knife southeastward to intercept McClellan's troops below White Oak Swamp.

In the event, everything went wrong. The excitable Magruder, almost sleepless for the previous four days, found the Union's three-corps rear guard drawn up in battle lines around their supply depot on the railroad at Savage's Station. Outnumbered nearly 3 to 1, Magruder pulled back to wait for Jackson—who never did show up. Instead, Jackson sent enigmatic word that he had "other important duty to perform"—presumably rebuilding Grapevine Bridge, which took all day. Finally, Magruder launched a half-hearted attack, but the Federal lines stood fast.

By the next morning, the Union army was stretched out like a 10-mile-long snake, its tail at White Oak Swamp and its head on the heights of Malvern Hill overlooking the James. The point of greatest danger was at a crossroads called Glendale. There, near a farm owned by the Frayser family, the two roads from White Oak Swamp converged to form a single route to the James. While McClellan's precious supply wagons waited to get through the bottleneck, they would be vulnerable to assault along a road from the west.

Now, if Jackson swooped down from the north while other Confederates attacked along a road from the west, Lee would have what one of his officers called "the opportunity of his life."

It was not to be. After finally crossing Grapevine Bridge, Jackson tarried to round up about a thousand Federal stragglers. It was nearly noon before he reached White Oak Bridge, which the Federals had just burned. Then, while his men repaired the bridge, Jackson lay down under a tree and went to sleep. He had made no attempt to find an alternative crossing—even though a cavalry officer reported finding a suitable ford about 400 yards upstream.

In the strange lethargy that afflicted him during the Seven Days, Jackson was perhaps affected by the rigors of his Shenandoah Valley campaign and the long march to the Richmond area. According to his chief of staff, the Reverend Major Robert Lewis Dabney, Jackson's fatigue "had sunk the elasticity of his will and the quickness of his invention for the nonce below their wonted tension."

While Jackson dallied, another Confederate general got bogged down. Two miles northwest of Glendale, Huger's lead brigade ran into an obstruction of trees felled by the Federals. Instead of instructing his men to move the logs out of the way, Brigadier General William Mahone ordered them to hack a new pathway through the thick woods that bordered the road. But after a mile-long trail was cleared, Huger rode up and found himself faced by Brigadier General Henry W. Slocum's Union division, which had been drawn up to protect the Federal supply train. Huger, who had already been criticized for his inactivity at Fair Oaks, withdrew into the woods, finished for the day.

Not far to the south, Robert E. Lee was only about a mile away from Glendale, approaching from the southwest with 18,000 men under Longstreet and A.P. Hill. After waiting most of the afternoon in the forlorn hope that Jackson and Huger would start the fighting, Lee ordered an attack at about 5 p.m.

Longstreet went in first, crashing through an understrength brigade in the Union center, and A.P. Hill followed in an attempt to exploit the opportu-

nity. Then, however, a Federal division under General Philip Kearny counterattacked, stopping the enemy rush. For a while it seemed that Kearny would regain all the lost ground, but A.P. Hill rode to the front, seized a flag and tried to lead a wavering regiment forward. When the men hesitated, Hill shouted: "Damn you, if you will not follow me, I'll die alone." Inspired by his courage, the soldiers charged, repulsing Kearny's counterattack.

As darkness fell, the firing flickered out. In the drawn Battle of Glendale, or Frayser's Farm, Lee had lost 3,300 men against 2,853 for the Federals. More significantly, the Union supply wagons were safe at the James River and the infantry would be able to march to Malvern Hill during the night.

For Lee, it had been a day of lost opportunities, and Stonewall Jackson unwittingly pronounced its epitaph. That evening, supping with his staff in front of White Oak Swamp, he dozed while still chewing his food, then jerked awake to announce: "Now, gentlemen, let us at once to bed, and see if tomorrow we cannot do something."

Three miles south of Glendale, Malvern Hill was actually a large plateau that stood more than 100 feet high at its crest. By the morning of July 1, Federal infantry was arrayed in a rough semicircle on the northern rim, and nearly 250 Union guns were emplaced wheel to wheel atop the plateau.

After riding south from Glendale on the Willis Church Road, Lee took up positions on the lower slopes of Malvern Hill. Based on a reconnaissance made by Longstreet, Lee set up his guns both west and east of the Willis Church Road and blasted the enemy artillery with a withering crossfire. For a while, the bombardment made things uncomfortable for the Federals. One Union soldier thought that troops had seldom "lain so long under as hot a fire as my fellows did. It is the most trying position a soldier has to endure, to stand these horrid missiles, crouched low, seeing them strike all about him."

Still, the Confederates were badly outgunned, and at about 3 p.m., Lee finally called off the cannonade. Soon, however, his hopes revived. On the Confederate right, an infantry brigade under Brigadier General Lewis Armistead had moved a short distance forward to dispel some bothersome enemy skirmishers. But Magruder, so wildly excited

A pro-Southern broadsheet printed in England uses a play on names to credit four of Lee's commanders—D.H. Hill, A.P. Hill, Stonewall Jackson and James Longstreet—with halting McClellan's advance on Richmond. In fact, Jackson made little contribution to the Confederate effort.

Greeted by pillars of smoke rising from friendly campfires, the rear guard of the Army of the Potomac completes the eight-mile march from Malvern Hill to Harrison's Landing, capping what one Federal soldier described as either "an inglorious skedaddle or a brilliant retreat." Major General Joseph Hooker was less equivocal. "We retreated," he said, "like a parcel of sheep."

that many thought he was drunk, mistakenly reported to Lee that Armistead had made a significant advance. At that, Lee ordered Magruder to "Press forward your entire command and follow up Armistead's success."

In fact, Magruder's command had mismarched that morning and was not yet in position to attack. Entirely unfazed, Magruder simply commandeered two of Huger's brigades and launched an assault that ended abruptly when it struck a Federal infantry line that was, in the words of one Confederate, "seemingly immovable. It stood as if at dress parade."

Sometime after 5 p.m., D.H. Hill attacked from the center of the Confederate line up a long, open slope that led to the enemy defenses some 800 yards away. Federal cannoneers tore huge gaps in the gray-clad ranks with salvo after salvo of exploding case shot.

Meanwhile, Magruder's men were ready at last, and he sent them into battle piecemeal. When the 15th Virginia Regiment reached a meadow at the base of Malvern Hill, its commander, Colonel Thomas August, was severely wounded by a shell fragment. As stretcher bearers were carrying him

away, August shouted to the troops: "Remember you are fighting for your homes and your firesides. Give them hell, damn 'em!" Moments later, as one witness recalled, "the stretcher-bearers were cut down and the colonel, still bleeding, was tumbled ingloriously into the ditch."

By then, Jackson was moving up his own troops and Ewell's to reinforce D.H. Hill, but it was already too late. Whiting remained idle on the Confederate left, and Lee did not call up Longstreet and A.P. Hill from reserve on the right. There would be no eleventh-hour surge by Lee's army.

Toward 9 p.m., darkness came, the Battle of Malvern Hill was over. That night, the Army of the Potomac gathered up its wounded and followed the path of its supply wagons to Harrison's Landing. The Seven Days had come to an end. During those days, Federal casualties had come to 15,849 against a staggering 20,614 Confederates—nearly one fourth of the men with whom Lee had begun his effort. But the new Confederate commander had accomplished his strategic purpose: Richmond, for now at least, was safe.

123

A Fortress City on the Potomac

"Before the war the city was as drowsy and as grass-grown as any old New England town," journalist Noah Brooks recalled of Washington, D.C. "The war changed all that in a very few weeks."

Indeed, by the spring of 1862, when Stonewall Jackson's Confederate army threatened Washington from the Shenandoah Valley, the Federal capital fairly bristled with defenses. "Long lines of army wagons and artillery were con-

tinually rumbling through the streets," Brooks reported. At the same time construction crews were erecting a cordon of fieldworks that would turn Washington into the most heavily fortified place in the United States.

The architect of this transformation was a 47-year-old engineer, Brigadier General John G. Barnard, whom McClellan had appointed to bolster the city's defenses after the Federal disaster

The 1st Connecticut Heavy Artillery Regiment drills at a fort on the Arlington heights, which command Washington from the Virginia side of the Potomac River.

at Bull Run. Under Barnard's supervision, 3,000 soldiers and civilian laborers constructed dozens of enclosed field forts and batteries occupying every prominent point around the city at intervals of 800 to 1,000 yards.

The forts were relatively simple structures made of wood and earth. Workers dug a ditch around the planned perimeter and piled the dirt inside to form an embankment called a rampart. Heavy guns were positioned on the ramparts on wooden platforms. Then living quarters, powder magazines, guardhouses and bombproofs were erected inside the enclosure.

Between the forts, Barnard's crews built lunettes—crescent-shaped earthen emplacements for fieldpieces—that commanded the approaches to the city. And the whole system was connected by 20 miles of trenches for riflemen.

The massive construction project was carried out with picks and shovels in what a soldier from the 79th New York Regiment called "the hardest kind of manual labor." But when completed and fully garrisoned by 25,000 infantry and 9,000 artillerymen, General Barnard's interlocking network of fortified positions was truly formidable. The once peaceful capital on the Potomac had become a fortress city.

Federal infantrymen guard Chain Bridge, the northernmost of three bridges that spanned the Potomac between Washington and Virginia during the war.

Artillerymen at Battery Martin Scott (inset) stand to their guns on the heights overlooking the Virginia approaches to Chain Bridge. This battery, named for an officer killed during the Mexican War, was one of the first heavy gun emplacements built by the Federals.

Artillerymen at Fort Totten, north of Washington, assemble outside an earthwork bombproof large enough to shelter the entire garrison.

THE BLOODIEST DAY

*"We cannot afford to be idle, and though weaker than our
opponents in men and military equipments, must endeavor
to harass, if we cannot destroy them."*

GENERAL ROBERT E. LEE TO PRESIDENT JEFFERSON DAVIS, SEPTEMBER 3, 1862

As Robert E. Lee rebuilt his battered army in the wake of the Seven Days' Battles, Southerners noted with concern that all the bleeding and dying had not altered the basic situation in Virginia. Pressure began to grow for a radical change in the Confederacy's passive strategy. President Jefferson Davis had been anxious to propitiate the European powers by showing that the Union was the aggressor, but now the critics demanded that he take the offensive instead of merely repulsing Federal attacks. Invade the North, they urged.

Neither side, in fact, had a clear idea of what to do next. In Virginia, a delicate equilibrium existed between the Federals' preponderance of strength and the Confederates' superior leadership. It was difficult to conceive a strategy, to break the stalemate; it was easier to wait for the enemy to make an exploitable mistake.

However, Federal activity—as well as the lack of it—soon set the stage for action, and a dramatic switch in Southern strategy. The conspicuous inactivity, in July 1862, was that of General George B. McClellan, who sat with his Army of the Potomac at Harrison's Landing, 20 miles southeast of Richmond, refusing to renew his attack on the Confederate capital without further reinforcements. McClellan remained adamant despite personal visits by the new Federal general in chief, Major General Henry W. Halleck, and President Lincoln himself.

In sharp contrast to McClellan's quiescence was the storm generated farther north by a newly arrived Federal commander, Major General John Pope, a caustic critic of McClellan's Peninsular Campaign. Tall and burly, with a long beard and quick tongue, Pope was brought from the West where he was credited with zestful leadership in the Federal victory at Island No. 10, a Confederate strongpoint blocking the S bend of the Mississippi River around New Madrid, Missouri—so called because it was the 10th island south of the river's juncture with the Ohio River. Pope's assignment was to create a new force, called the Army of Virginia, from three corps scattered about the northern part of the state.

While Pope was ridiculed by some of his own men for condescension and pomposity (it was said that he signed his orders "Headquarters in the Saddle," which inspired soldiers to joke that he did not know his headquarters from his hindquarters), he was abhorred by his foe. In occupied Virginia he issued decrees holding citizens responsible for guerrilla attacks and called for summary executions of offenders without benefit of trial. Robert E. Lee called Pope "the miscreant" and declared, "He ought to be suppressed."

But it was a minor military move by Pope that prodded Lee into action. On July 12, Pope ordered Major General Nathaniel P. Banks' corps to advance to the Culpeper, Virginia, Court House on the Orange & Alexandria Railroad. Pope's move threatened the vital junction of Gordonsville, 27 miles to the southwest, where the Orange & Alexandria intersected with the Virginia Central line, which linked Richmond to the Shenandoah Valley. By this small step, Pope set in motion a succession of events that would culminate in the war's fiercest single day of combat and exert a profound influence on its future course.

To block the threat to Gordonsville, Lee dispatched three divisions under Stonewall Jackson. This was a daring gamble, for it stripped Richmond of 25,000 troops, more than half its defenders, while McClellan remained within striking distance. By early August, however, it was evident that McClellan intended to withdraw back down the Peninsula rather than renew his campaign against the Confederate capital, and Lee decided to unleash Jackson to deal Pope a preemptive blow.

On August 9, Jackson struck north toward Culpeper with a column of men and wagons that stretched seven miles. That afternoon, in 100-degree heat, the column collided with Banks' blue-clad corps near Cedar Mountain, a low, mile-long ridge.

A worried Lincoln examines a sore-footed McClellan in this cartoon ridiculing the Federal retreat from the Peninsula in 1862. McClellan's failure to capture Richmond did in fact land him in political hot water, but Lincoln defended him at first, saying that his campaign was "the price we pay for the enemy not being in Washington."

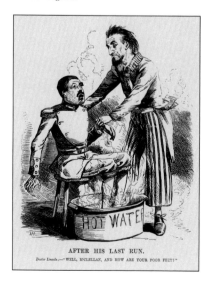

AFTER HIS LAST RUN.

Doctor Lincoln :—" WELL, M'CLELLAN, AND HOW ARE YOUR POOR FEET?*"*

Confederate Major General James Longstreet was characterized by an army comrade before the war as "a hearty, robust man overflowing with good spirits." But in January 1862, three of his children died of scarlet fever. Henceforth, noted one of his staff officers, "he was a changed man, very serious and reserved."

The two sides deployed just north of the mountain and opened up with their cannon. Even though Banks' 9,000 Federals were outnumbered by more than 2 to 1, he elected to attack based upon verbal orders received that morning from General Pope via a courier. (Pope later insisted that he had sent word to remain on the defensive until help arrived.)

At 5 p.m. Banks attacked, ordering Brigadier General Samuel W. Crawford's brigade of 1,700 men to strike Jackson's left flank. Crawford's men emerged from the woods and charged through a newly cut wheat field dotted with neat shocks. They crossed a rail fence, charged into the woods along the road and caved in three Confederate lines. Hand-to-hand fighting raged from tree to tree. In a few minutes, three Confederate brigades were put to rout, including the celebrated Stonewall Brigade, which had been caught up in the assault, outnumbered and outflanked.

Galloping toward the front to stanch the panic in his shattered regiments, Jackson displayed unchar-acteristic emotion. "Rally, brave men, and press forward!" he shouted. "Your general will lead you. Jackson will lead you. Follow me!"

As his beaten units rallied, Jackson raced back to the rear to urge forward Major General A.P. Hill's Light Division, so named for its mobility on the march and in battle. Brigade by brigade, Hill's 12,000 men advanced into battle and broke the Federal spearhead. Nearly 50 per cent of Samuel Crawford's ill-fated brigade was lost. Color Sergeant James Hewison of the 5th Connecticut was so determined to prevent his state flag from being captured that, though twice wounded, he tore the banner from its staff, wrapped it around him and crawled back to Federal lines.

Hill's repeated assaults smashed the center of the Federal line. By 6:30 p.m., the Confederate victory was complete. Urged on by Jackson, Hill's men continued to pursue the retreating enemy to within seven miles of Culpeper before the arrival of a fresh division of Federal troops halted their drive. The Battle of Cedar Mountain had cost Jackson 1,355 men killed and wounded, while Banks suffered 2,377 casualties—nearly 30 per cent of his corps.

Success at Cedar Mountain strengthened Lee's growing streak of opportunism. On August 13 he further exposed Richmond by sending Major General James Longstreet's 30,000-man command north to join Jackson. This shift gave the Confederate expedition a total of 55,000 troops, roughly a man-for-man match with Pope's forces arrayed north of the Rapidan River.

Lee knew it was a gamble to leave Richmond virtually uncovered. McClellan, under orders from Lincoln, had begun moving his troops away from Richmond and down the Peninsula a week previously, but Lee knew his foe's apparent withdrawal might be only a feint. Even so, the Confederate commander realized that there was an equal or greater danger: McClellan's army could leave the Peninsula, steam up the Chesapeake Bay and the Potomac and join Pope to give the Federals overwhelming superiority in northern Virginia. To forestall this, Lee needed to move with both speed and audacity.

On August 25, after learning that the first of McClellan's Federals had arrived at Aquia Landing on the Potomac, and were moving west to join Pope, the Confederate commander decided upon a further

gamble. In the face of the conventional doctrine that called for concentrating forces when faced with an enemy of potentially superior numbers, Lee divided his small army. While Longstreet's 30,000 men demonstrated on the Rappahannock to suggest a frontal attack on Pope's forces, now massed on the opposite shore of the river, Jackson's 25,000 men began a circular flanking march to the north. The aim was to sweep around the Federal right, threaten the rear and force Pope to fall back toward Washington, depriving him of his strong position on the Rappahannock. Longstreet, meanwhile, would follow Jackson north on the same circuitous route, reunite with his forces and strike Pope while the Federals were off balance and before the bulk of McClellan's army could reach the field.

The plan was hazardous in the extreme. If Pope grasped Lee's intentions, he could maneuver his army to keep the two Confederate forces divided and then destroy them separately. "We have record of few enterprises of greater daring," one of Lee's officers wrote later. "To risk cause and country, name and reputation, on a single throw and to abide the issue with unflinching heart is the supreme exhibit of the soldier's fortitude."

Jackson's march into the rear of the Federal army succeeded because of the grit of his soldiers, who largely subsisted on green corn and apples along the route, and Pope's lack of tactical imagination. Stubbornly convinced that Jackson was headed for his old stomping grounds in the Shenandoah Valley, Pope left the route unguarded, including the easily defended mountain passage at Thoroughfare Gap, which led to the plain of Manassas and the railroad junction where Pope's vast supply depot lay. Largely unmolested, the Confederate column covered 60 miles in a little over two days, marching northwest and then turning sharply east at Salem. On August 27, Jackson's vanguard pounced upon the supply depot at Manassas Junction, 25 miles behind Pope's line on the Rappahannock.

The depot covered nearly a square mile, and before they put the torch to it, the ravenous Southerners stuffed their stomachs and their haversacks with food. When the abstemious Jackson ordered the smashing of hundreds of barrels of liquor, some of the men sprawled on the ground and greedily drank from the puddles of alcohol. "I fear that whiskey," Jackson said, "more than I do Pope's army."

Jackson moved his troops the next day to Stony Ridge, a wooded hill seven miles from Manassas, to await the arrival of Lee and Longstreet's command. After deploying there in the late afternoon, a tempting target presented itself below on the Warrenton Turnpike. It was a division of Federal troops, part of the army Pope had been marching to and fro that day—first to the smoking ruins at Manassas, then toward Centreville—in confused response to Jackson's thrust. To Jackson's immediate front was a brigade wearing the black broad-brimmed hats of the Regular Army. But far from being Regulars, these men from Wisconsin and Indiana were mostly untried volunteers. Their commander, Brigadier General John Gibbon, a 35-year-old North Carolinian with three brothers in gray uniform, had attempted to instill confidence by outfitting them with the hats.

Jackson directed artillery fire against the Black Hat Brigade and then attacked with infantry. Gibbon's green Federals, finding themselves suddenly engaged against six enemy brigades outnumbering them by 3 to 1, might well have run, but they held their ground. Two lines, Federal and Confederate, stood 75 yards apart and, for an hour and a half as the light slowly faded, fired as fast as they could load and aim. "They stood as immovable as the painted heroes in a battle-piece," said the commander of one of the Confederate brigades, Brigadier General William Taliaferro. "Out in the sunlight, in the dying daylight, and under the stars they stood, and although they could not advance, they would not retire. There was some discipline in this but there was much more of true valor."

In this brief encounter on a hillside called Brawner's Farm, the Black Hat Brigade lost more than 900 of its 2,100 men; each side counted about 1,300 casualties in all. The next morning, August 29, Longstreet's command arrived on the field. Jackson had remained overnight strongly posted behind an unfinished railroad grade at the base of Stony Ridge. Longstreet's men filed into place on Jackson's right, curving around to straddle the Warrenton Turnpike and completing a 50,000-man Confederate line now nearly four miles long. This ground lay at the western edge of the Bull Run battlefield of the previous year, and within hours it would be bloodied by another major clash of arms, the Second Battle of Bull Run.

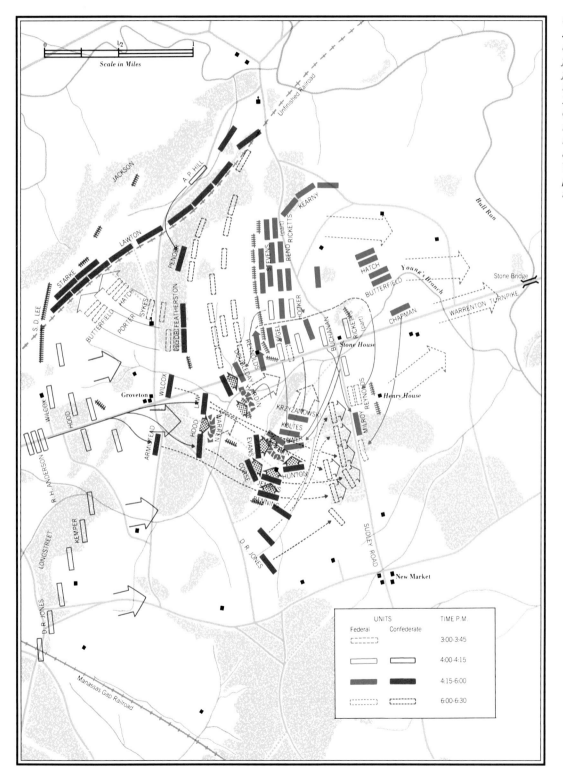

On the afternoon of August 30, 1862, James Longstreet launched a massive attack against the undermanned left flank of John Pope's army. In fierce fighting on Chinn Ridge, the Federal brigades under Brigadier Generals Zealous Tower and Robert Milroy and Colonel Nathaniel McLean were eventually routed, but they gained enough time for Pope to establish a defense on Henry House Hill. North of the Warrenton Turnpike, Jackson began to push eastward toward Bull Run after repulsing determined Federal attacks.

UNITS		TIME P.M.
Federal	Confederate	
		3:00-3:45
		4:00-4:15
		4:15-6:00
		6:00-6:30

The Federals belatedly gathered their forces on the old battlefield that afternoon and began a series of disjointed and largely ineffective assaults. An exception was the charge mounted shortly after 3 p.m. by the brigade of Brigadier General Cuvier Grover, which successfully stormed the railroad embankment in the center of Jackson's front and started up the slope.

As Sergeant Frank Wasley of the 2nd New Hampshire moved forward, he stumbled over a fallen Confederate. Wasley snatched a huge knife from the man's belt and lunged. "Oh, for God's sake," the Confederate cried, "don't!"

Wasley's arm stopped in midstroke. "All right, Johnny!" But the Confederates rallied, forcing back Wasley and the other members of Grover's brigade. The Federals failed to support Grover, who had to fight alone and was eventually driven back at a cost of nearly one third of his 1,500 men.

On Jackson's far left that afternoon, the South Carolina Brigade under Brigadier General Maxcy Gregg beat back the Federals so many times that some of his men had to scavenge cartridges from the wounded and dead of both sides. Gregg, deaf, irascible and indomitable, strode the line waving his old sword from the Revolution. "Let us die here, my men, let us die here," he exclaimed.

Several of the Federal generals were less reluctant to take such a stand. At 6:30 p.m., some five miles to the south, Brigadier General Fitz-John Porter received an order from Pope written two hours earlier: "I desire you to push into action at once." Porter's V Corps was part of the 23,000-man contingent from the Army of the Potomac that had recently arrived from the Peninsula. But because the hour was late and he could see Longstreet's big corps deployed in front of him, Porter refused to obey the orders to attack. Dismissing Porter's report of the Confederate force in front of him as a mere excuse for inaction, Pope was so furious at Porter's failure to advance that he later mounted a successful campaign to have him court-martialed and dismissed from the Army. (For 20 years thereafter, Porter petitioned for a rehearing, and was finally vindicated.)

Despite the setbacks, however, Pope awoke the following morning, August 30, confident of victory. He had reports of Confederate movements to the rear—in truth, units merely readjusting their lines or going back for ammunition. But the worst of his misconceptions was his failure, after nearly 24 hours, to recognize the existence of Longstreet's corps on the Federal left. Bent on pursuing the perceived enemy retreat, Pope shifted Porter's corps to the right, leaving a single division under Brigadier General John Reynolds to face Longstreet's 30,000 men. Pope's refusal to face the truth continued—even after Reynolds' Pennsylvanians ran into a mass of Confederates and recoiled in alarm. That afternoon, Reynolds' corps commander, Major General Irvin McDowell, ordered him north of the turnpike to assist Porter, leaving the Union left virtually undefended.

While Jackson's men repulsed repeated attacks by the Federals now massed north of the turnpike, Longstreet prepared to assault the uncovered sector south of it. At 4 p.m., his 30,000 fresh troops started forward. They found in front of them a battery of guns and two Zouave regiments from New York, the 5th and the 10th, consisting of no more than 1,000 men.

The 5th New York bore the brunt of the assault by the Texas Brigade, one of the best in the Confederate Army. Failing to hear the order to fall back, the Zouaves stood and fought in what Private Andrew Coats called "the very vortex of Hell." No fewer than 124 of the outfit's 490 men were killed outright or died later of wounds—the highest number of fatalities sustained by any infantry regiment in any Civil War battle. Clad in scarlet pantaloons and red fezzes with yellow tassels, the Zouaves' bodies lay so closely together, a Texan recalled, as to give "the appearance of a Texas hillside when carpeted in the spring by wild flowers of many hues."

Pope, concerned now not with victory but mere survival, began shifting troops back to the south to bolster his shattered left. Two crucial pieces of high ground were the keys to extricating his army from possible disaster, and controlling the route of retreat eastward on the Warrenton Turnpike. The first eminence, the treeless plateau called Chinn Ridge, fell about 6 p.m. to the hard-charging Texas Brigade and some Virginia regiments and other units of Longstreet's corps.

Federal survival now hinged upon the second strongpoint, farther east at Henry House Hill, a rise surmounted by the remains of the Henry home that had been destroyed during the First Battle of Bull Run. Jackson had launched an attack on the Federal right at 6 p.m., and Pope's entire line was breaking.

Major General John Pope, the Union commander at Second Bull Run, had a talent for ignoring what he did not wish to hear. At one point in the battle, an officer galloped up to report that the Confederates were turning the Federal left flank—to which Pope replied, "Oh, I guess not."

His fleeing columns jammed the turnpike. But on Henry House Hill, overlooking this endangered artery, two of Pope's most dependable units, Brigadier General George Sykes' brigade of Regulars and Major General Jesse Reno's old brigade, fought like men possessed. In the dying light, they turned back every charge the Confederates could muster. Then, about 8 p.m., it began to rain and the firing subsided. The turnpike turned to mire as the retreating Federals trudged through the mud across Bull Run toward Centreville—hungry, exhausted, dispirited, but alive to fight another day.

The Second Battle of Bull Run, together with the rest of the three-week campaign north of the Rappahannock, had cost the Federals 14,462 men compared to 9,474 for the Confederates. Not the least of the Union's losses were the two generals killed on September 1, two days after Bull Run, in an encounter to the east near Chantilly. The victims were Major Generals Isaac Stevens and Philip Kearny. The one-armed Kearny, in particular, was renowned by both sides for his reckless courage and

aggressive leadership. "There was no place for exultation at the death of so gallant a man," noted Confederate Major Walter H. Taylor.

The Union could ill afford to lose generals of such caliber. The discredited Pope was now finished—"kicked, cuffed, hustled about, knocked down, run over and trodden upon as rarely happens in the history of war," wrote one regimental historian—and presently sent off to a new and inconsequential command in Minnesota. President Lincoln, as he had done in July 1861 after the first Union defeat at Bull Run, turned to George McClellan. The heroic image of the man the troops called Little Mac had been tarnished in the battles around Richmond, but the Army still loved him. "If he can't fight himself," said Lincoln, "he excels in making others ready to fight."

The triumphant Lee now stood on the doorstep of the Union capital, less than 25 miles away. He could not strike directly at Washington—the fortifications ringing the capital were too strong, and the Federal armies regrouping there would soon outnumber his Confederates by more than 2 to 1. But, determined to maintain the momentum he had gained in taking the war to the Federals, he decided to push farther north. "The present," he wrote President Davis, "seems to be the most propitious time since the commencement of the war for the Confederate Army to enter Maryland."

By carrying the war onto enemy soil—albeit a border state—for the first time in the Eastern theater, Lee hoped to achieve at least two military objectives. He wanted to feed his army and horses on Maryland's rich autumn harvest while luring enough Federals away from Washington to prevent another enemy march on Richmond. But he also saw such political possibilities as strengthening antiwar Democrats in the upcoming November elections and inducing the British—and perhaps the French as well—to recognize the Confederacy and even intervene in the war on its behalf.

Lee wrote Davis of his plan on September 3, and without waiting for approval, broke camp and headed north the same day. He intended only a foray into Maryland, not a permanent occupation of enemy territory, which would have been a sharp departure from Davis' stated policy of fighting only to defend the Southern homeland.

It was a ragtag army that began crossing the shallow fords of the Potomac River just above Leesburg, Virginia, on the following afternoon. As one of Lee's brigadiers phrased it, the men had been "marching, fighting and starving" since the Seven Days' Battles in late June. They were gaunt and unshaven, and many were wearing vermin-infested, tattered uniforms. By one estimate, fully a fourth of the army marched barefoot.

Some 20,000 fresh reinforcements from Richmond joined Lee's march, but nearly that many men dropped out. These dropouts were ill and exhausted or simply wanted to sit out the invasion at their homes in northern Virginia. Some stayed behind because they had enlisted to defend their homeland, not to invade the North. The 50,000 men who did march into Maryland were the most determined of the veterans who had driven the Northern invaders from the outskirts of Richmond all the way back to Washington. "None but heroes are left," one of them wrote home.

Reaching the town of Frederick, 20 miles into Maryland, Lee issued his orders for the campaign on September 9. They called for his most audacious scheme yet. Defying the maxims of military science, he divided his army not in two but into four different elements. One wing, under Longstreet, would drive northwest in the first leg of a march that Lee hoped would lead the Confederates on a powerful raid as far north as Pennsylvania. Meanwhile, the other three elements, comprising the bulk of the army, would converge upon the Federal garrison at Harpers Ferry, back in Virginia at the confluence of the Potomac and Shenandoah rivers, to insure Lee's supply route southward into the Shenandoah Valley.

In fragmenting his army, Lee was counting on McClellan to provide a cushion of time. He expected his old foe from the Seven Days to respond to the Confederate foray with his characteristic caution. McClellan did not disappoint him. Marching out from Washington with 84,000 troops to confront the Confederate invasion, McClellan required a week to cover the 50 miles to Frederick. Much of the delay was understandable, however. He had to merge Pope's Army of Virginia with his Army of the Potomac, then work his magic to revitalize defeated and dispirited units. At the same time, he had moved out on a broad front to satisfy the concerns of his

superiors who feared that Lee might circle back into Virginia and attack Washington.

McClellan arrived in Frederick with the main body of troops on September 13, two days after Lee's divided army had left town. In Frederick, another factor that had slowed McClellan—the lack of accurate intelligence about enemy strength and movements—suddenly took a strange turn. On the morning of his arrival, a pair of soldiers from the 27th Indiana, Sergeant John M. Bloss and Corporal Barton W. Mitchell, made an extraordinary discovery in a campground recently vacated by the Confederates: an improvised package of three cigars wrapped in a sheet of paper. Free cigars were a happy discovery, but the wrapper was astounding. The paper, it turned out, contained Lee's complete orders for the four-way split of his army. McClellan read the document with rising excitement. "I have all the plans of the rebels," he telegraphed Lincoln, "and will catch them in their own trap if my men are equal to the emergency. Will send you trophies."

Vowing to "whip Bobbie Lee," McClellan set his big army in motion the following morning. He want-ed to relieve Harpers Ferry and to pounce upon the scattered pieces of the Confederate army where they were pinpointed in Lee's order. To accomplish those goals, he had to get across the formidable ridge known as South Mountain, which was pierced by two principal passes and one smaller pass about a dozen miles west of Frederick. His attempts would provoke two bitter battles during that Sunday.

Most of the Federal army marched up toward the northernmost pass, Turner's Gap, heading for what McClellan mistakenly believed was the bulk of Lee's men at Boonsboro. In fact, Lee and Longstreet had pushed on to Hagerstown with 10,000 men, leaving only a single division under Major General D.H. Hill to guard Boonsboro. The previous night, a Southern sympathizer in Frederick had alerted Lee to the fact that a major piece of intelligence evidently had fallen into Federal hands. To gain time for the capture of Harpers Ferry, he ordered Turner's Gap held "at all hazards." Hill's division hurried back from Boonsboro and put up a gallant fight in the gaps of South Mountain until Longstreet's troops could make the longer march from Hagerstown.

As dusk settles over South Mountain, Federals of Brigadier General John Hatch's division overrun Alabama troops firing from behind stone outcroppings on the wooded crest north of Turner's Gap. Hatch fell severely wounded in the fierce contest and command fell to Brigadier General Abner Doubleday, who launched a sweeping volley that sent the Confederates rushing backward.

By 3 p.m., Hill's exhausted men teetered on the brink of collapse. A half-hour later, Longstreet arrived after a 13-mile march over rough terrain that had taken 19 hours. Major General John Bell Hood led his division toward nearby Fox's Gap. He arrived there in time to plug a big hole in the Confederate line and stave off repeated Federal attempts to crack through on the ridge.

Similar attempts to overcome the main body of the Confederates near the summit of Turner's Gap to the north met with more success. Two divisions from Major General Joseph Hooker's I Corps outflanked Brigadier General Robert Rodes and his 1,200 Alabamians who were covering a spur north of the mountain. On Rodes' right, the Federal division under Brigadier General John Hatch advanced relentlessly from the base of the mountain; on Rodes' left, Brigadier General George Meade pressed the Confederate flank vigorously. By the time darkness had put an end to the struggle, Rodes had lost a third of his brigade; grudgingly, he yielded the high peak and squeezed back into the Gap.

The battle for the third pass that day was waged six miles to the south at Crampton's Gap. In three hours of hard fighting, Major General William Franklin's corps of 12,000 Federals finally overcame the 1,000 defenders at the base of the mountain and then beat back two regiments of reinforcements that attempted to dislodge them from the crest. Franklin probed cautiously at the Confederate defenses beyond Crampton's before deciding to bed down for the night on the mountain despite McClellan's orders to relieve the garrison at Harpers Ferry, now only six miles away.

Although costly to Lee, who had lost 2,700 men compared with McClellan's casualties of 1,800, the defense of the South Mountain gaps had delayed the Federal advance. This allowed the tightening of the Confederate grip on Harpers Ferry, where on Sunday the three other separate wings of Lee's army had completed their encirclement of the 14,000-man garrison. The task of Stonewall Jackson and the other Confederate generals there had been eased by the ineptitude of the Federal commander, Colonel Dixon S. Miles. A gray-bearded veteran with a fondness for hard drink, Miles failed to provide for proper defense of the heights that surrounded the post. Without control of these eminences, wrote a Federal soldier, Harpers Ferry was "no more defensible than a well bottom."

That Sunday night, with the Federals facing almost certain surrender, Colonel Benjamin F. Davis, the Alabama-born commander of the 8th New York Cavalry, sought to salvage something from the debacle. He persuaded Miles to let him make a run for it with the garrison's 1,400 cavalrymen. It was such a risk that one of the officers felt compelled to warn his horsemen that by the next morning they would be "in Pennsylvania, on the way to Richmond or in Hell." Davis not only led his column north to freedom in Pennsylvania; along the way he used his thick Southern drawl to fool the Confederates and hijack a wagon train carrying Longstreet's reserve supply of ammunition. At a time when Davis' old West Point classmate, Major General Jeb Stuart, was riding off with all the laurels for the Confederacy, it was Davis and his men who had pulled off the first great cavalry exploit for the Army of the Potomac.

The breakout could not have been more timely. The next morning, September 15, nearly 50 Confederate guns unleashed their fury on Harpers Ferry. A shell from one of them mortally wounded Colonel Miles, just as the white flags went up. It was the largest capitulation of Federal forces in the entire war—12,500 men, who later would be paroled upon their oath not to take up arms until a comparable number of enemy prisoners were released.

Elated by news of this victory, Robert E. Lee elected to reunite his army and make a stand at Sharpsburg, a little Maryland town 12 miles to the north. While the three other wings were securing Harpers Ferry, Longstreet's troops took up positions on a ridge just east of Sharpsburg in front of a meandering little stream called Antietam Creek. The four-mile-long Confederate line provided woods, fences, outcroppings of limestone and other excellent cover, but it had one troubling feature: Lee's men would have to fight with their backs to the Potomac, which offered only one nearby crossing shallow enough for an escape route. Lee decided to stand in this risky place, a Confederate officer later concluded, only because he did not want "to leave Maryland without a fight."

Lee would have his fight—"a great enormous battle," as a Wisconsin officer would describe it, "a great

tumbling together of all heaven and earth"—but first his foe had to get ready. McClellan took his time pushing across South Mountain and westward to the banks of Antietam Creek six miles beyond. He arrived Monday afternoon and then spent hours reconnoitering the field and attending to every detail of troop deployment. As usual, he was convinced that the enemy had far superior numbers. Lee's army, he had concluded from grossly exaggerated intelligence reports, amounted to "not less than 120,000 men."

Again, McClellan's caution cost him an opportunity—to strike at the enemy when more than half of Lee's army was still at Harpers Ferry. By the time he had his plan of attack prepared on the following afternoon, September 16, most of these Confederate troops were beginning to file into line after an all-night march. Even when all troops were in place, however, McClellan would still have a clear numerical edge of more than 70,000 men to Lee's 40,000. His intention was to commit more than half of his army to the main effort against the Confederate left while a single corps launched a diversionary attack against the enemy right.

The Federal advance finally began at 5:30 a.m. on Wednesday, September 17. It was spearheaded by the I Corps commanded by hard-drinking, tough-talking Joseph Hooker. His three divisions pushed south, guiding their right on the Hagerstown Turnpike and aiming off in the distance for the one-story whitewashed brick church of the German Baptist Brethren—known to the locals as the Dunker Church because the congregation believed in baptism by total immersion. Stonewall Jackson, defending the Confederate left with three divisions, had his main line astraddle the pike about 300 yards north of the church.

Cannon on both sides opened up in a prolonged duel that one Confederate described as "artillery hell." West of the pike, Jeb Stuart had assembled eight cannon from his own horse artillery and a dozen of Jackson's guns. This lethal chorus was joined by four batteries deployed on the high ground across the pike from the Dunker Church. The Federals answered from the north with Hooker's nine batteries and from east of the Antietam with four batteries of 20-pounder Parrott rifles that blazed away at the combined rate of a shot every second.

The cannon proved most fearsome when brought forward to fire shell or canister in support of the

Captain Wilson Colwell of the 2nd Wisconsin was killed on the evening of September 14 as he led two companies of skirmishers against a Confederate brigade at Turner's Gap. Wrote Colwell's commanding officer, "His place can hardly be filled. He was a fine officer and beloved by the whole regiment."

At dawn on September 17, Lee occupied a line between
Sharpsburg and Antietam Creek. Jackson held the
left flank and Longstreet the center. Lee left the right
flank—the area between the town and the lower
bridge—lightly defended in anticipation of A.P. Hill's
arrival. McClellan's plan of attack called for Joseph
Hooker and Joseph Mansfield to hit the Confederate left
while Ambrose Burnside advanced on the enemy's right.

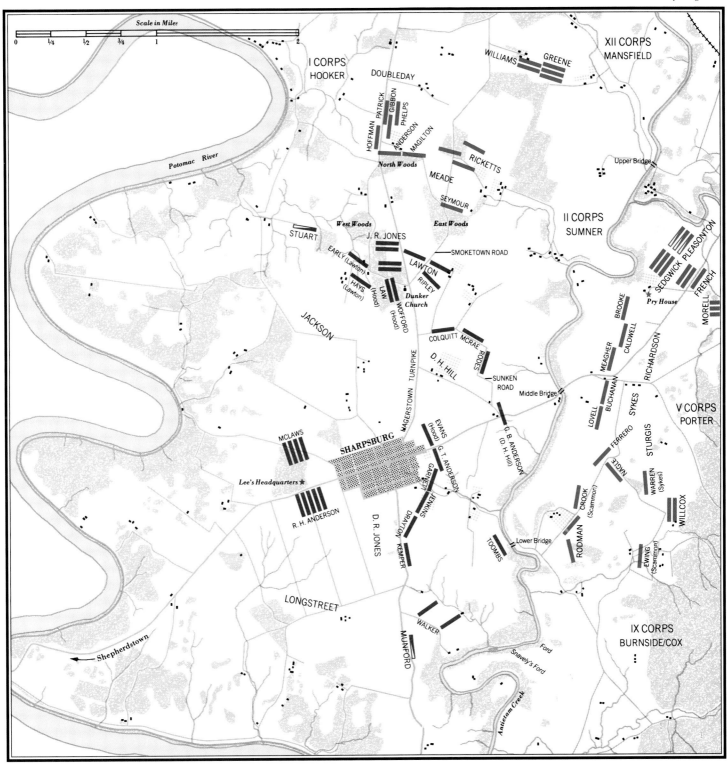

Scale in Miles

0   ¼   ½   ¾   1   2

I CORPS
HOOKER

DOUBLEDAY

XII CORPS
MANSFIELD

WILLIAMS   GREENE

HOFFMAN   PATRICK   GIBBON   PHELPS
ANDERSON   MAGILTON

North Woods

RICKETTS

MEADE

Potomac River

Upper Bridge

SEYMOUR

West Woods   East Woods

II CORPS
SUMNER

STUART

J. R. JONES

EARLY (Lawton)

SMOKETOWN ROAD

LAWTON

RIPLEY

PLEASONTON

HAYS
(Lawton)

LAW
(Hood)

Dunker
Church

SEDGWICK

FRENCH

JACKSON

WOFFORD
(Hood)

COLQUITT   MCRAE

RODES

MORELL

Pry House

BROOKE

CALDWELL

MEAGHER

WAGERSTOWN TURNPIKE

D. H. HILL

SUNKEN
ROAD

Middle Bridge

LOVELL   BUCHANAN

RICHARDSON

SYKES

V CORPS
PORTER

G. B. ANDERSON
(D. H. Hill)

MCLAWS

SHARPSBURG

EVANS
(Hood)

G. T. ANDERSON

FERRERO

STURGIS

Lee's Headquarters ★

GARNETT

JENKINS

NAGLE

WARREN
(Sykes)

R. H. ANDERSON

D. R. JONES

DRAYTON

KEMPER

CROOK
(Scammon)

RODMAN

WILLCOX

EWING
(Scammon)

TOOMBS   Lower Bridge

LONGSTREET

WALKER

Ford

IX CORPS
BURNSIDE/COX

MUNFORD

Snavely's Ford

Shepherdstown

Antietam Creek

141

advancing infantry. When the Federals ran into stiff resistance along the eastern edge of the Hagerstown Turnpike, Hooker ordered up four batteries. These cannon raked a cornfield on David Miller's farm where Confederates had taken cover among stalks that stood higher than their heads. "In the time I am writing," Hooker's official report read, "every stalk of corn in the northern and greater part of the field was cut as closely as could have been done with a knife, and the slain lay in rows precisely as they had stood in their ranks a few moments before."

This 20-acre cornfield rapidly became the

Cornfield, the focus of the fiercest fighting on the Confederate left. Isaac Hall of the 97th New York saw two lines go at it for 30 minutes or so. "They stood and shot one another," he wrote, "till the lines melted away like wax." A brigade of Georgians stayed put despite a 50 per cent casualty rate. The Louisiana Brigade, nicknamed the Tigers, rushed to their aid and drove the Federals back, only to be stopped by the point-blank fire of a battery of 3-inch ordnance rifles that the crews rolled directly into the Cornfield. It was later estimated that the opposing lines surged back and forth through its broken and

Launching the initial assault of the battle of Antietam, Federal troops from I Corps under the command of General Hooker charge with fixed bayonets through the Cornfield, between the East and West Woods. They carry their guns at right shoulder shift to avoid entangling the long weapons in the corn or accidentally stabbing their comrades in the ranks ahead.

under Major Rufus Dawes reached a rail fence separating it from the pasture to the south. Beyond the fence, however, a regiment of Georgians lay waiting in the grass.

All at once, wrote Dawes, "a long line of men in butternut and gray rose up from the ground. Simultaneously, the hostile battle lines opened a tremendous fire upon each other. Men were knocked out of the ranks by dozens. But we jumped over the fence, and pushed on, loading, firing, and shouting as we advanced."

On both sides of the pike, the Confederates were falling back. Dawes' 6th Wisconsin swept forward "loading and firing with demoniacal fury," he recalled, "and shouting and laughing hysterically." It was about 7 a.m., and he was only 200 yards north of the Dunker Church and from the cannon-girded high ground across the pike that was the Federal goal. Jackson's Confederates, with the ranks of the two divisions on either side of the pike dangerously thin, teetered on the edge of collapse. At this critical moment, a long gray line filed through a gap in the fence in front of the church, raising the yip-yip-yip of the Rebel yell. It was Jackson's last reserve, the 2,300-man division of Brigadier General John Bell Hood.

Angry as bears because their first real cooked meal in days—a breakfast of hoecakes—had been interrupted, Hood's hungry troops stormed out of the woods behind the church. They poured into the wide gap opened up by the Iron Brigade and drove the Federals back through the Cornfield. Hood's counterattack—30 savage minutes that he later described as "the most terrific clash of arms, by far, that has occurred during the war"—saved the morning for the Confederates.

But Hood's men paid a price. The vanguard dissolved in a fury of canister shot fired at point-blank range. One of his regiments, the 1st Texas, got caught in a crossfire near the northern edge of the Cornfield. No fewer than nine of the regiment's color-bearers went down in swift succession. In not much more than 20 minutes, the 226-man regiment suffered 186 killed and wounded—a casualty rate of 82.3 per cent, the highest for any regiment in one battle during the war. Finally, as an entire corps of fresh Federals marched onto the field, Hood's division was forced to withdraw back across the pike to the shelter of the West Woods, having lost more than half of its men.

blood-stained stalks no fewer than 15 times in the course of that day.

While the struggle here and at the nearby East Woods was locked in stalemate, the Federal attack had made impressive progress a couple of hundred yards to the west. John Gibbon's Black Hat Brigade led the way down both sides of the pike. These Westerners were proudly bearing a new nickname; Hooker had likened their strength and tenacity the previous day at South Mountain to iron, and now men were referring to the Iron Brigade. They drove past the chaotic Cornfield, and the 6th Wisconsin

Braving a deadly storm of shot and shell, Federal troops from I Corps charge toward the Dunker Church (top right) during the early-morning fighting. The church

marked the southern boundary of the field on which the initial fighting would be waged. The caisson at left marked the approximate apex of I Corps' advance.

"Where is your division?" a brother officer inquired. "Dead on the field," replied Hood.

The Federal reinforcements were the 7,200 troops of Major General Joseph Mansfield's XII Corps. Half of them were raw recruits, and before they could emerge from the East Woods, their 58-year-old commander went down mortally wounded. But his replacement, former Detroit postmaster Brigadier General Alpheus S. Williams, got them moving again toward the Cornfield.

From the Confederate side, Major General D.H. Hill's division shifted north to join the fight but they soon faced a crisis. A brigade of North Carolinians, still shaken by the death of their commander, Brigadier General Samuel Garland Jr. three days before on South Mountain, heard the warning cry of Federals on their right flank and fell to pieces. "In a moment the most unutterable stampede occurred," said their new commander, Colonel Duncan McRae. "The whole line vanished, and a brigade famous for its previous and subsequent conduct, fled in panic from the field."

The Federals belonged to the division of Brigadier General George Greene, a doughty 61-year-old descendant of Revolutionary War hero Nathanael Greene. Sweeping through the gap left by the retreating Southerners, one brigade smashed into the Confederate flank at the northeast edge of the Cornfield, leaving enemy dead "literally piled upon and across each other," according to Colonel Eugene Powell of the 66th Ohio. Greene's other brigade advanced southwest along the Smoketown Road, and drove the Confederate guns from the high ground east of the Dunker Church. Now just 200 yards from the church, they ran into intense rifle fire, halted and sent back for ammunition.

It was only 9 a.m. and already more than 8,000 Americans—Federals and Confederates in almost equal measure—had met death or injury since sunrise.

Lee now took steps to bolster Jackson's beleaguered forces in the West Woods. He committed a reserve division and stripped his right of a division and a brigade. Lee could afford to gamble because he stayed near the battle and was closely attuned to it. He was so absorbed in the fighting, in fact, that he failed to recognize the powder-blackened face of his own son, Robert Jr., an artillery gunner, who had to identify himself to his father.

Lee took notice of stragglers, however. One of them had killed a pig and was hurrying to the rear to cook it. Lee, in a rare burst of fury, ordered the shirker sent to Jackson to be shot. Instead, Jackson thrust the man into the thickest fighting in front of the West Woods, where the culprit redeemed himself—as one Confederate officer remarked, "losing his pig but saving his bacon."

McClellan, meanwhile, remained at his headquarters more than a mile east of the fighting, responding belatedly to events rather than initiating them. His battle plan was already a shambles. The diversionary assault on the Confederate right had been inexplicably delayed, and the main attack on the enemy left had degenerated into a series of disjointed assaults.

Another such assault, belated and ill-coordinated, occurred shortly after 9 a.m. when Major General Edwin Sumner double-quicked a division from his II Corps across the Cornfield and into the West Woods about 300 yards north of the Dunker Church. Sumner, at 65 the oldest general in the Army of the Potomac, charged forward so rapidly that he accidentally left another of his divisions behind in the East Woods. He also made no attempt to learn the tactical situation. He crossed paths with Hooker, who had led the morning's first assault, but the I Corps commander was being carried to the rear with a painful foot wound, and they did not confer. The other Federal corps commander on the scene, General Williams, attempted to brief Sumner, but the old man was fixated on reaching the woods and paid no heed.

Sumner had kept his three brigades stacked one behind the other and did not bother to take the routine precaution of deploying skirmishers to the front or flankers to either side. As he pushed through the West Woods, a torrent of fire erupted on his exposed left with such swiftness and ferocity that it appeared to be a carefully planned ambush. Actually, Sumner unwittingly had been on a collision course with the reinforcements sent by Lee. In a matter of moments, the forest was carpeted with fallen Federals. "Where the line stood the ground was covered in blue," wrote a Georgian.

The Federal lines were crowded so closely together that many men in blue were afraid to fire for fear of hitting their comrades. Others were not so careful, and the 15th Massachusetts found itself taking friendly fire from behind and enemy fire from the front and

The indomitable Clara Barton cut through official red tape and the conventions of society to become an unofficial field nurse with the Army of the Potomac. She served so close to the front lines at Antietam that on one occasion a stray bullet passed through her sleeve, killing a soldier she was caring for. After the war, Barton would found the American Red Cross.

Under fire from Confederate artillery, Federal troops close in upon Rebel positions near the Roulette farm during the advance on the Sunken Road. The ferocity of the fusillade astonished even veteran soldiers. Noticing that "almost every blade of grass is moving," Private Thomas Galwey of the 8th Ohio at first attributed it to "merry crickets. It is not until I have made a remark to that effect to one of our boys and notice him laugh, that I know it is the bullets that are falling thickly around us."

left. It suffered 344 casualties, the greatest number lost by any regiment in either army that day. A company commander in another Massachusetts regiment, Captain Oliver Wendell Holmes Jr., went down with a bullet through his neck. Lying semiconscious, he heard a voice asking, "You're a Christian, aren't you?" Holmes managed to nod. "Well, then," said the voice, "that's all right!" Then the regimental chaplain of the 20th Massachusetts moved on, leaving for dead this future associate justice of the U.S. Supreme Court.

By 9:45 a.m., when Sumner succeeded in getting the last able-bodied Federal out of the West Woods, he had lost nearly half of the division—2,255 men dead, wounded or missing. His disastrous foray also had inadvertently opened a new front in the center of the Confederate defenses, about a half mile southeast of the Dunker Church. The focus of the Battle of Antietam now shifted there from the area north of the church, where Stonewall Jackson—correctly concluding that "The Federals have done their worst"— would continue to hold the line despite attacks by General Greene's division and other enemy units.

The action in the center was triggered when the Federal division that Sumner had left behind in the East Woods veered south and clashed with the thinly held Confederate line. D.H. Hill had only 2,500 defenders there—less than half the attacking Federals—and many of them were worn out from

supporting Jackson on the left earlier that morning. But two of Hill's brigades occupied a superb defensive position at the base of a hill. It was a country lane that jutted eastward from the Hagerstown pike for about a half mile and was so worn down by erosion and the weight of wagons that it dropped several feet below the level of the bordering fields and thus made a perfect rifle trench. The locals called it the Sunken Road, but those who fought there would know it as Bloody Lane.

The Confederates lay in the road and waited patiently while the Federals mounted the crest 100 yards beyond and started down the slope. "Now the front rank was within a few rods of where I stood," recalled Colonel John B. Gordon of the 6th Alabama. "With all my lung power I shouted, 'Fire!' My rifles flamed and roared in the Federals' faces like a blinding blaze of lightning accompanied by the quick and deadly thunderbolt. The effect was appalling. The entire front line, with few exceptions, went down in the consuming blast. Before his rear lines could recover from the terrific shock, my exultant men were on their feet, devouring them with successive volleys."

Line after line of Federals foundered on the long slope in front of Bloody Lane. Then Sumner's third and last division, which had been held in reserve by McClellan, came up and first sent forward one of the

Union's most colorful outfits, the Irish Brigade. Made up largely of Irish immigrants, the unit had been recruited by Brigadier General Thomas Francis Meagher, a flamboyant revolutionary who envisioned this service as training for a war to free his homeland from English rule. As the Irishmen advanced up the slope under their emerald flags, one of the regimental chaplains, Father William Corby, rode back and forth shouting the words of conditional absolution prescribed by the Roman Catholic Church for those who were about to die. Over the crest, hundreds of them fell under the withering fire from the Sunken Road. General Meagher himself went down, he reported later, because his white horse was shot out from under him, but rumors circulated that he was drunk and had fallen off.

Not until noon, after more than two hours of desperate fighting and the loss of a number of key officers, did the Confederate line give way. As the Federals stormed down into the Sunken Road, Confederate generals fought to patch together a new line farther south. D.H. Hill, having lost his third horse of the day, grabbed a musket and rallied the remnants of his infantry. He led about 200 of them forward through an orchard, noting that even "with the immediate prospect of death before them," the men were so hungry they grabbed apples and devoured them on the run.

Trying to skirt the Federal left flank near the Sunken Road, Hill ran headlong into the 5th New Hampshire. A scrappy outfit that would absorb more battle losses during the course of the war than any other Federal regiment, this unit was led by Colonel Edward E. Cross, a crusty adventurer who had spent some years in the West. Cross now demonstrated his battlefield theatrics against Hill's scratch force.

"Put on the war paint!" Cross cried out. Taking their cue, his men tore open cartridges and, like Indians on the warpath, smeared their faces with black powder. "Give 'em the war whoop!" shouted Cross. A bloodcurdling roar went up, and his men sprang forward and broke Hill's attack.

Still, Hill had enabled his superior, Longstreet, to get 20 cannon in place just west of the Hagerstown pike. Wearing a carpet slipper because of a heel blister, Longstreet sat on his mount, calmly directing their fire and—as one artilleryman remembered it—taking an occasional nip from his flask.

His gunners staved off the Federal advance. But his infantry was threadbare—the struggle around the Sunken Road had cost him nearly 2,600 men against Federal casualties of almost 3,000—and dangerously low on ammunition. One of his regiments, the 27th North Carolina, had not a single cartridge remaining and resorted to waving their battle flags to create the illusion of strength.

Another major Federal thrust here in the early afternoon against the center almost certainly would have split Lee's army and probably doomed it. McClellan had the extra men—3,500 cavalry plus Porter's 10,300-man corps, which was waiting only a mile east of the Sunken Road. In addition, Franklin's 12,000-man corps was now available in the northern sector. But shaken by his losses and convinced that Lee might counterattack at any moment, McClellan refused to commit his reserves.

With the Confederate left and center now in stalemate, McClellan's fading hopes for victory rested that afternoon upon the southern sector and his old friend, Major General Ambrose Burnside. As commander of the 11,000-man IX Corps, Burnside was charged with the responsibility of creating a diversion by crossing the Lower Bridge, the southernmost of the three spans across Antietam Creek. But Burnside had shown little initiative while the fighting raged in the north and center. He was offended because McClellan had changed the army's command structure, under which he previously had charge of two corps; now he was in no mood to do more than was asked of him. While waiting for the order to attack, he made no attempt to find fords across the shallow creek. And though Lee had shifted his troops until only 2,000 men occupied the Confederate line for more than a mile from Sharpsburg to below the bridge, Burnside sent no probes across the narrow stone bridge.

Only when he received orders from McClellan a few minutes before 10 a.m. did Burnside attack. Twice he sent troops in brigade strength to take the bridge. And twice they fell back under the fire of Confederate artillery and a brigade of 550 Georgians commanded by Brigadier General Robert Toombs and positioned on the steep wooded bluff rising up on the west bank. Finally, about 1 p.m., Burnside got a brigade across with the help of artillery. These Federals hooked up on the west bank with other units

Major General Ambrose E. Burnside, the affable but incompetent commander of the Federal IX Corps, had no pretensions to military genius. "He was not fitted to command," a fellow general remarked. "No one knew this better than himself."

that had forded the creek north and south of the bridge.

Just when the way appeared open for a full-scale assault on Lee's thin line south of Sharpsburg, there was a new delay of more than an hour. The lead division was out of ammunition and had to be replaced in the assault column through a complicated reshuffling of units. Furious at this further delay, McClellan sent a courier with orders to relieve Burnside of his command if he failed to push ahead at once. But the courier did not have to deliver them. When he arrived, he discovered that Burnside had descended from his hilltop headquarters and was personally directing traffic on the blood-slickened bridge that would thereafter bear his name.

By about 3 p.m.—two hours after the capture of the bridge—the entire IX Corps was across the Antietam. Leaving one division in reserve on the west bank, 8,000 Federals marched westward on a front three quarters of a mile wide. They outnumbered the Confederates south of Sharpsburg by more than four to one. To a Confederate officer watching from the heights up near town, their advance seemed irresistible. "The earth," he wrote, "seemed to tremble beneath their tread." Federal skirmishers soon reached the outskirts of Sharpsburg, which seethed with a sense of impending disaster. A few hundred yards to the south, the Zouaves of the 9th New York, shouting their war cry, "Zou! Zou! Zou!" surged forward to capture the key hill overlooking the town.

The entire Confederate right wing was in shreds, and Lee could not afford to shift reinforcements from the hard-pressed center or left. The fate of his army, perhaps of the Confederacy itself, now focused upon a powerful column of reinforcements still on the march from Harpers Ferry—A.P. Hill's Light Division. The biggest division in Lee's army, and arguably the best, the Light Division reflected the feisty leadership of Major General Ambrose Powell Hill. The men and Hill had shown such lax discipline on the earlier march into Maryland that Stonewall Jackson had felt compelled to suspend him briefly from command. But now Hill was back in the saddle and wearing his flaming red battle shirt.

Lee, waiting anxiously near Sharpsburg, knew that the Light Division was close at hand. As the troops marched north, Hill galloped on ahead to report to Lee, who was so relieved to see him that he dropped his customary reserve and embraced his impetuous

Major General Ambrose Powell Hill, commander of the Light Division, had a gentlemanly exterior that hid a fighting spirit. "At the critical moment," wrote an admiring comrade, "Hill was always at his strongest."

subordinate. It was 2:30 p.m., and Lee now had the reassurance that Hill's men were close at hand. But would they make it in time to stop Burnside?

An hour later, with the Battle of Antietam hanging in the balance, Lee was still peering off to the southeast for some sign of Hill's men. All he could see were the long blue lines of Burnside's advancing Federals. Suddenly in the distance there appeared a gray-clad column flying the Virginia and Confederate flags. It was Hill at last, leading 3,000 men, hundreds more having fallen by the wayside on the march that had brought the division 17 miles in eight hours.

Hill marched his five brigades into the far right of the crumbling Confederate line and prepared to attack. He could not have chosen a better spot: The enemy regiments on the extreme Federal left had failed to keep pace with the units to the north. Hill's troops rushed into the resulting gap. Such was the sense of urgency that Maxcy Gregg did not take the time to shift his brigade of South Carolinians from column of fours into a conventional line of battle but simply shouted, "Commence firing, men, and form the line as you fight."

They charged into a cornfield and hit the 16th Connecticut. These Federals had been in service only three weeks, and many of them had never even loaded their muskets until the previous evening. Within a few minutes, 185 of them went down. As their line disintegrated, the 4th Rhode Island came up on the right. In the high corn it was hard to distinguish between friend and foe, a difficulty compounded by the fact that some of the Confederates were wearing new Federal uniforms appropriated from the Harpers Ferry commissary. The Confederates unleashed volley after volley.

The Connecticut troops broke and ran, then the Rhode Islanders. The rout left the 8th Connecticut far out in advance and isolated, and Hill's men drove it down the hills toward the Antietam Creek. Fresh Federal regiments came up, but these men as well had to fall back under Hill's onslaught. With the Federal far left broken, Brigadier General Jacob Cox feared for the exposed flank of the forward brigades farther north, and he ordered a withdrawal. He and General Burnside then pulled IX Corps all the way back to the west bank of the Antietam despite the fact that, after suffering 20 per cent casualties, they could still field more than 8,500 men—twice the number

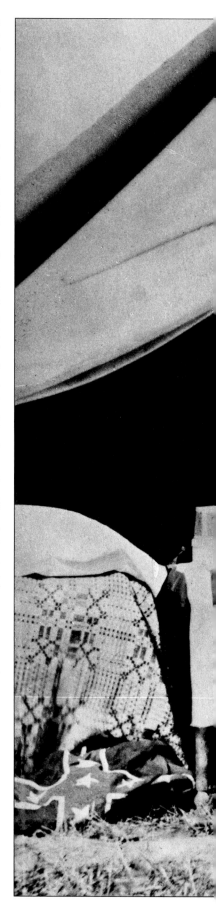

of the enemy troops that were now confronting him.

One of the last Federal regiments to leave the field was the 9th New York Zouaves. At first, the commander, Lieutenant Colonel Edgar A. Kimball, refused to pull out. He had lost more than a third of his men and he was almost out of cartridges, but he wanted reinforcements so he could advance. Kimball yielded only after his division commander personally ordered him to withdraw. As the Zouaves formed to march to the rear, giving up the high ground they had fought so gallantly to gain, Kimball told him, "Look at my regiment! They go off this field under orders. They are not driven off. Do they look like a beaten regiment?" By 5:30 p.m., the hard fighting had ended on the heights overlooking the Burnside Bridge and all along the line. After 12 hours, the Battle of Antietam was over, although random firing continued for another hour or so while men prayed for darkness to put a stop to the slaughter. Never before had so many Americans fallen in combat in a single day.

By the best available counts, casualties numbered 22,726. Federal losses accounted for somewhat more than half: 2,108 killed, 9,549 wounded and 753 missing, for a total of 12,410. The Confederates lost 1,546 killed, 7,752 wounded and 1,018 missing. "No matter in what direction we turned," a Federal officer wrote of the carnage, "it was all the same shocking picture, awakening awe rather than pity, benumbing the senses rather than touching the heart, glazing the eye with horror rather than filling it with tears." One in every four men engaged in the battle had fallen—and for what? Tactically, it was a standoff. The Federals had gained ground, but they had failed to dislodge Lee's army from the ridge in front of Sharpsburg.

A.P. Hill's dramatic arrival on the field had saved the battle for Lee's army, but a day later Lee found it necessary to withdraw back across the Potomac into Virginia, and with that retreat the true import of Antietam began to emerge. The Confederate withdrawal transformed a tactical stalemate into a strategic victory for the North. President Lincoln seized upon this victory as the occasion to issue a document that would lend a new and deeper meaning to the bloodiest day in American history.

On Monday, September 22, five days after Antietam, Lincoln summoned his cabinet members to the White House. He reminded them of the document he had read to them back in July. It had been the first draft of the Emancipation Proclamation, decreeing freedom for the Confederacy's three-and-a-half million slaves. Before the Battle of Antietam, he told the Cabinet, he had made a promise "to myself, and to my Maker" to issue the proclamation if the Confederates were driven out of Maryland. "I think the time has come now."

Though he personally opposed slavery, Lincoln's motives for the proclamation, which was made public on September 24, were more pragmatic than humanitarian. He wanted to sap a source of the Confederacy's economic strength by providing an incentive for slaves to escape. He wanted to mend divisions in the Republican Party, where a majority of congressmen and senators were in favor of abolition. And he wanted to forestall foreign intervention by appealing to world opinion. As it turned out, public opinion in both England and France did, in fact, ensure the countries' neutrality. The Confederacy would have to continue fighting alone, with little hope of foreign help.

There remained one last and ironic consequence of the Union's strategic success at Antietam. On November 5, Lincoln ordered McClellan relieved of command of the Army of the Potomac and replaced by his erstwhile friend Burnside. In addition to demonstrating excess caution at Antietam and then in pursuing Lee at his usual snail's pace, McClellan was a conservative Democrat, whose party stood for limited war and compromise. The Emancipation Proclamation now doomed all possibility of meeting the Confederacy halfway, and the North would continue fighting not only to preserve the Union, but to abolish slavery as well. It could no longer afford a commander who lacked the ardor and ruthlessness required to wage all-out war.

On November 11, following a final review, McClellan boarded his train at Warrenton Junction. The general stepped out onto the rear platform of his car and calmed the distraught men surrounding the train. "Stand by General Burnside as you have stood by me," he urged them, "and all will be well. Goodby lads."

Then the train steamed slowly out of the station, taking McClellan away from the war for the last time. "A shade of sadness crossed his face," noted Colonel Edward Cross of the 5th New Hampshire. "He carried the hearts of the army with him."

A GALLERY OF THE DEAD

In October 1862, Mathew Brady put on display at his New York City gallery a series of photographs that ended once and for all the general public's romantic notions of the war. Taken at Antietam by Brady's colleague Alexander Gardner, the pictures were the first ever of dead Americans on a field of battle; that the corpses were all nameless Confederates made no difference in the impact of Gardner's images. "Let him who wishes to know what war is look at this series of illustrations," Dr. Oliver Wendell Holmes Sr. wrote. Another viewer said: "We recognized the battlefield as a reality, but a remote one, like a funeral next door. Mr. Brady has brought home the terrible earnestness of war. If he has not brought bodies and laid them in our dooryards, he has done something very like it."

THE STRUGGLE FOR TENNESSEE

*"I can never forget, whilst I remember anything, that you gave
us a hard-earned victory, which, if there had been a defeat instead,
the nation could scarcely have lived over."*

ABRAHAM LINCOLN TO MAJOR GENERAL WILLIAM S. ROSECRANS
AFTER THE BATTLE OF STONES RIVER

During the Civil War, railroads emerged for the first time in human history as a crucial factor in the waging of war. By the summer of 1862, the war west of the Appalachians was being fought as much for railroads as for territory. It was clear that whoever possessed the rails held a key to the conflict east of the mountain chain, if only because Robert E. Lee's Army of Northern Virginia was dependent on a constant flow of food, munitions, manufactures and manpower from the South and West.

The region's vital rail junction was Chattanooga, Tennessee. And it was for control of Chattanooga that a vicious struggle began, seesawing through eastern Kentucky and Tennessee, spilling at times into Alabama and Georgia, causing panic as far north as Cincinnati, and framing the great battles of Perryville and Stones River.

After the Federals captured the railroad junction of Corinth, Mississippi, at the end of May, Major General Henry W. Halleck, overall commander in the West, had set his sights on Chattanooga. He dispatched Major General Don Carlos Buell and his Army of the Ohio from Corinth, eastward to Alabama and Tennessee.

Despite a violent temper that repeatedly got him into trouble, General Buell had served with distinction in the Mexican War, receiving three brevet promotions. Thereafter, he had transferred from the 3rd U.S. Infantry to the adjutant general's department, and had worked there creditably for 13 years, rising to the rank of lieutenant colonel. After the Civil War began, Buell was chosen by General George B. McClellan, the Federal General in Chief, to lead the Army of the Ohio, and in that role, he proved to be a cautious, methodical soldier. He was an excellent disciplinarian and a hard worker, but he was also rigid, opinionated and unpopular. Colonel John Beatty of the 3rd Ohio Infantry described him as "cold, smooth-toned, silent."

One of the principal Confederate threats to Buell in East Tennessee was the 56,000-man Army of the Mississippi. That army had been pulling itself together at Tupelo, Mississippi, after its retreat from Corinth, and its former commander, General P.G.T. Beauregard, had been replaced in June by General Braxton Bragg.

Bragg, at 46, shared a remarkable number of traits with his antagonist. Like Buell, he had shown great early promise, graduating fifth in the West Point class of 1837 and later serving with distinction as an artillery officer in the Mexican War, where he also had garnered three brevets. But Bragg was prey to frequent disabling illnesses, from dyspepsia to headaches. Perhaps because of these illnesses, he was exceedingly unpleasant to everyone around him.

Bragg was under general instructions from the War Department in Richmond to strike northward in Tennessee to Nashville, and pierce Buell's now-strung-out Federal army. But decisive action had never been easy for Bragg, and from the beginning his deliberations on how to accomplish his objective had been complicated by his subordinate immediately responsible for Chattanooga, Major General Edmund Kirby Smith. An ambitious, self-centered officer who had no problem making decisions, Smith was nursing invasion plans of his own: Despite the growing threat to Chattanooga, he wanted to strike into Kentucky. He believed that there were thousands of Confederate sympathizers, chafing under the Federal yoke and ready to help him occupy the state.

In early July, Smith unleashed two preliminary raids led by relatively inexperienced cavalry commanders. These raids, with a mandate to disrupt the tenuous Federal supply line extending from Louisville to Buell's army, would have a calamitous effect—both on Buell's advance

The development of new artillery, which proved such a decisive factor in battle after battle in the Civil War, required its own set of equipment and tools. A leather haversack was used to carry rounds from the limber to the rifle.

General Braxton Bragg, an iron-clad disciplinarian, took over the battered Confederate army in Mississippi in June 1862 with orders to strike into Tennessee. Ulysses S. Grant, who had served with Bragg in the Mexican War, remembered him as "a remarkably intelligent and well-informed man."

toward Chattanooga and on Bragg's half-formed plans to strike toward Nashville.

One of Smith's cavalry commanders was Colonel John Hunt Morgan, a wealthy Kentucky businessman, with refined manners and an easygoing style, who savored the glamor of raiding. On July 4, he trotted his cavalry out of Knoxville, Tennessee, bent on harassing the vital Federal supply line between Nashville and Louisville, Kentucky. Plagued by pro-Union bushwhackers who abounded in the East Tennessee mountains, the raiders nevertheless were able to make the 104-mile westward ride across the Cumberland Plateau to Sparta, Tennessee, in three days. There, as Smith and Morgan had expected, the

people were sympathetic to the Confederacy; new recruits flocked to join the raiders.

Morgan left Sparta with his brigade of 1,100 men, to attack a Federal garrison at Tompkinsville, Kentucky, 90 miles to the northeast. Doubtless he relished the idea of taking Tompkinsville. It was defended by a battalion of the 9th Pennsylvania Cavalry, whose troops had occupied Lebanon, Kentucky, in May. They had insulted the women there by using vulgar language and advising them that the only way to preserve their virtue was, as their commander, Major Thomas Jefferson Jordan, put it, "to sew up the bottoms of their petticoats."

On July 9, Morgan's brigade reached Tompkinsville and quickly surrounded the 400 Federal troopers, who were deployed on a thickly wooded hill. After a brief flurry of fire, Jordan surrendered. All the Federal prisoners except Jordan were paroled; presumably for his offense against Southern womanhood, Jordan was sent to prison in Richmond.

Morgan's raiders drove on, and upon reaching the Louisville & Nashville telegraph line, 30 miles north of Tompkinsville, they tapped the wire and began spreading the false information that Morgan intended to strike all the way to the Ohio River and attack Louisville and Cincinnati. The bogus reports were widely believed; alarms were raised throughout the Ohio River valley, and panic spread through Cincinnati and Louisville. To fuel the fear, he rode to the banks of the Ohio northeast of Louisville. Then, sweeping eastward, Morgan launched a three-pronged assault on the town of Cynthiana, south of Cincinnati, taking 300-odd Federal prisoners and a much-needed herd of 300 horses.

In just over three weeks, Morgan's raiders had ridden 1,000 miles, had taken 1,200 prisoners, captured 17 towns and destroyed or turned over to local sympathizers a small fortune in Federal property. More important, as planned, the raid had distracted Federal attention from the advance on Chattanooga.

On July 6, two days after Morgan had left Knoxville, another of Kirby Smith's cavalry commanders, Colonel Nathan Bedford Forrest, had left Chattanooga with 1,000 troopers. Forrest had made himself a reputation, for a daring escape at Fort Donelson and for a slashing rearguard action at Shiloh. Like Morgan, he had been a wealthy businessman before the war and behaved as if born to the saddle and to command. But he had emerged from a background of poverty and little schooling, and he was as rough-hewn as Morgan was polished.

Forrest's chief target was a railroad depot at Murfreesboro, Tennessee, 35 miles southeast of Nashville. There, Forrest and his raiders swooped down on a jail, flushed out its Federal guards and freed a group of Rebel prisoners. According to Confederate Captain William Richardson, one of those rescued, Forrest's eyes were "flashing as if on fire, his face was flushed, and he seemed in a condition of great excitement. To me he was the ideal of a warrior."

Forrest then dashed off to the west of town where his horsemen had run into stiff opposition from Federal forces dispatched from the nearby Union camp on Stones River. With the threat of Federal reinforcements arriving by train from Nashville, some of Forrest's officers proposed a withdrawal, but their commander insisted on staying put. "I didn't come here to make half a job of it," he snapped. "I'm going to have them all."

Forrest devised a ruse. After ordering his men to ride back and forth in order to inflate their numbers in the eyes of the enemy, Forrest sent an intimidating

Major General Don Carlos Buell, who led the Army of the Ohio against Braxton Bragg, was a stickler for discipline and detail, with an ultra cautious approach to combat. Buell had little confidence in his men—and his men had little love for him.

158

John Hunt Morgan posted this broadsheet and others like it as he rode through Kentucky in July 1862, urging the citizens of his native state to rise against "the hireling legions of Lincoln." Morgan's raid attracted some Kentuckians to the Confederate cause, but it frightened many others into enlisting in Union regiments.

note to the Federal commander: "I must demand an unconditional surrender of your force as prisoners of war or I will have every man put to the sword. You are aware of the overpowering force I have at my command, and this demand is made to prevent the effusion of blood." Thoroughly cowed, the Federals surrendered their remaining 450 men and four guns. In Murfreesboro, Forrest had captured 1,200 prisoners, 50 wagons and teams, a battery of artillery and about a quarter of a million dollars' worth of supplies.

When General Buell heard of the wholesale surrender at Murfreesboro, he was outraged. He sent a 3,500-man division to Murfreesboro to stop Forrest, repair the railroad there and keep it open. The division repaired the railroad quickly, but they failed to stop Forrest or to keep the road open. On July 21—the same day he was promoted to brigadier general—Forrest struck again, this time driving north of Murfreesboro, almost into Nashville. He destroyed three railroad bridges and took 97 prisoners. The railroad would be out of commission until July 29.

It had been a fretful summer for the opposing army commanders intent on East Tennessee. With Confederate raiders continually striking at the vulnerable Federal supply lines, General Buell's advance on Chattanooga had stalled in the vicinity of Decatur, Alabama, more than 100 miles west of his objective. On the Confederate side, General Bragg had reorganized and reinvigorated his army, situated in Tupelo roughly 100 miles southwest of Buell. But, characteristically, Bragg seemed incapable of using his forces decisively; he had talked vaguely of striking northward into central Tennessee, but he had not moved.

At the end of July, however, the lull was about to end with a burst of activity that would race like a fast-burning fuse through eastern Tennessee and into the northern reaches of Kentucky. Events would run their course, wildly beyond the control of either Buell or Bragg. Rather, these events would be shaped to a remarkable extent by the cunning Kirby Smith, who had paved the way for an invasion of Kentucky with a single-minded campaign of manipulation waged against his fellow officer, Braxton Bragg.

While Morgan and Forrest were busy striking in the north and the west, Smith had been scheming at his headquarters in Knoxville, 100 miles northeast of Chattanooga. After accolades for his performance in the Shenandoah Valley and at Bull Run, he now resented his assignment to a small western department with little scope for action. But he soon conceived an invasion of Kentucky as a way to relieve his boredom—and to bring himself glory. However, he could not move north while he was chained to the defense of Chattanooga. To free himself for the invasion, Smith would have to persuade others to assume the responsibility of protecting the city; this project he undertook with energy and determination.

Beginning in the last week of June, Smith sent off a spate of alarming messages—to the War Department, to the governor of Georgia and to Generals Robert E. Lee and Bragg. "If the Government wishes Chattanooga secured, a reinforcement of at least 2,000 armed men must be immediately sent there and an officer of ability assigned to the command," one of the messages read. In response to Smith's repeated requests, President Jefferson Davis sent Brigadier General Henry Heth with 6,000 reinforcements, and Bragg reluctantly sent a division of 3,000 men to Chattanooga. But Smith was far from satisfied, and he continued to paint such a grim picture that finally, on July 21, Kirby Smith won his game: Bragg ordered the Army of the Mississippi to Chattanooga.

It was a difficult movement around Buell's interposing army, but Bragg managed the logistics mag-

Panic along the Ohio

"To arms!" the Cincinnati *Gazette* proclaimed in September 1862. "The time for playing war has passed. The enemy is approaching our doors." Indeed, the Confederate armies of Kirby Smith and Braxton Bragg were marching through Kentucky with little but raw Union recruits between them and the Ohio River ports of Louisville and Cincinnati. The citizens of these cities would have to defend themselves.

Major General Lew Wallace, in charge of Cincinnati's defense, declared martial law, threw a pontoon bridge across the river and sent 15,000 civilians to dig fortifications on the Kentucky side. From all over Ohio came a flood of volunteers, known as Squirrel Hunters for the muzzle-loading hunting rifles many of them carried. Wallace soon had 55,000 irregulars manning the earthworks and 16 impressed steamboats armed

with small cannon patrolling the Ohio river.

At Louisville, Kentucky, 130 miles downriver, General William Nelson also mobilized civilians in an attempt to ring the city with earthworks, and he built bridges to the Indiana shore—as much to evacuate the city as to facilitate its defense. Meanwhile, the Union Army of the Ohio, which had driven deep into the South, raced north to intercept the oncoming Confederates.

In frantic flight, the people of Louisville jam the ferry docks on the Ohio River in a rush to evacuate their threatened city. During the crisis, Louisville, a city of

160

Refugees from Louisville, most of them women and children, huddle around campfires in relative safety on the north bank of the Ohio River. As a precaution, they had been ordered to flee their homes after Confederate cavalry raided the outskirts of the city on September 23, 1862.

68,000 people, was described by a reporter as a "howling uproar, filled with troops, teams, dust and the clatterbang of arms."

nificently. He sent his mounted units—the cavalry, artillery and wagon trains, about 5,000 men in all—overland by a circuitous 430-mile route south to Tuscaloosa, Alabama, east to Rome, Georgia, then north to Chattanooga. Because of supply problems and a drought, the 35,000 infantrymen had to be moved by train—a journey of almost 800 miles.

Now freed of his restrictive garrison duties, Smith assembled his men and marched on August 14 to capture Lexington, Kentucky. After sweeping aside some green Federal troops near Richmond, Kentucky, the aggressive 38-year-old Smith moved his headquarters to Lexington and sent a cavalry force to occupy the state capital at Frankfort.

The Confederates now had an open road all the way to the Ohio River, which sent shock waves among the citizens of Cincinnati. President Lincoln, even while preoccupied with disaster much closer to home—Lee's defeat of Pope at Second Bull Run—took time to ask fretfully the whereabouts of General Buell. Kirby Smith, however, had suddenly run out of ideas. Established in Kentucky at last, he went on the defensive and waited to see what Bragg and Buell were going to do.

Buell was sorely tried by the Confederates' drive into Kentucky and by their sharp thrusts at his supply lines. In August, John Hunt Morgan's raiders cut the rail line between Nashville and Louisville by setting fire to a tunnel, causing it to collapse. Unsure of what to do, Buell moved the Army of the Ohio to McMinnville, northwest of Chattanooga, then on September 5 to Murfreesboro. In contrast to Buell's

A Son of Virginia on the Union Side

Brigadier General William Rufus Terrill, who commanded a Federal brigade in Jackson's division at Perryville, saw his family torn asunder by the war. Virginia-born and a relative of both Jeb Stuart and Robert E. Lee, Terrill nevertheless remained faithful to his oath as a U.S. officer, pledged when he graduated from West Point in 1853. The decision to fight for the Union outraged his father, who wrote Terrill a heart-scalding letter in which he threatened, "Do so and your name shall be stricken from the family records."

Despite the pain caused by the family rupture, Terrill proved a brilliant officer, distinguishing himself as an artillerist at the Battle of Shiloh. Promoted to brigadier general, Terrill was commanding infantry in battle for the first time at Perryville when he was killed by a Confederate shell.

Terrill's only brother, James, was also killed in the war while serving as a colonel for the Confederacy in 1864. After the conflict, the Terrill family erected a memorial to the dead brothers on which is carved, "God Alone Knows Which Was Right."

confusion, the three wings of Bragg's army—under Bragg and Major Generals Leonidas Polk and William J. Hardee—drove smartly northward through Tennessee, arriving at Glasgow, Kentucky, on September 14.

Bragg now determined to involve Smith in a joint movement against Louisville, the Federal supply center for Kentucky and Tennessee—the loss of which would cripple Buell's operations. After forcing the surrender of the Munfordville Federal garrison, Bragg and his army moved northeast to Bardstown, where he asked Smith to send supplies and join him. Smith, however, seemed uninterested in any campaign not of his own making and remained in Lexington, leaving Bragg to take Louisville on his own.

Meanwhile, Buell was on the move, marching north with unaccustomed speed from Bowling Green to Louisville, where he arrived on September 25. He then gathered 60,000 of his troops and put them on what he hoped was a collision course with the Confederate forces in Bardstown. There followed almost two weeks of massive, almost comedic confusion as the two armies stumbled through the Kentucky hills groping for one another. The mercu-

rial Bragg first marched northeast to Frankfort believing that the enemy was headed that way, then abandoned Kentucky's capital and hurried back south again to join Polk and Hardee, expecting to find the Federals somewhere east of Bardstown. Meanwhile, Buell had shifted his aim southeast of Bardstown and was moving in that direction.

As they maneuvered through the rugged countryside, troops on both sides suffered from a worsening drought. A Federal of the 50th Ohio wrote: "The boys got some water out of a dark pond one night and used it at supper to make their coffee and to quench their thirst also. What was their disgust next morning to find a dead mule or two in the pond. I imagine that coffee had a rich flavor."

The water situation grew so serious that on the afternoon of October 7, Federal troops commanded by Brigadier General Philip H. Sheridan made a dash for water at Doctor's Creek, a few miles west of the little town of Perryville. Confederate troops of the 7th Arkansas were in the town and put up stiff resistance, but Sheridan's thirsty men would not be stopped. Behind them marched Buell's main army, and there, at Perryville, the combatants came together.

The next day, there were 16,000 Confederates in Perryville, commanded by Polk, preparing to attack 60,000 Federals. Nearby, at Versailles, Bragg was assembling 36,000 troops to face a lone Federal division of 12,000 men. Meanwhile, General Hardee, the author of the U.S. Army's standard text on military tactics, was beginning to sense disaster. After reviewing copies of Bragg's recent orders, he was disturbed enough by what he read to take the risk of lecturing his commanding general. "Don't scatter your forces," he implored. "There is one rule in our profession that should never be forgotten—it is to throw the masses of your troops on the fractions of the enemy." Fight at Versailles or fight at Perryville, he said, but in either case, "strike with your whole strength."

As morning approached, Polk began to realize the strength of the Federal force he was facing; he thought better of attacking. At the same time, Bragg had grown impatient about the situation at Perryville and decided to take personal command there. Arriving at 10 a.m., determined to disperse what he judged to be a small Federal force before concentrating his army farther north, he was distressed to find Polk on the defensive. Immediately, Bragg began shifting troops into assault positions.

Despite the uneven odds, the Confederates were able to drive the Federals from their positions in a series of fierce charges. The Confederates fought gallantly and well, but only survived the precarious situation because of Federal blunders and lack of communication. Remarkably, General Buell did not know until 4 p.m. that his army was engaged in a furious battle: Atmospheric conditions were such that the roar of the guns could not be heard at his headquarters only a few miles from the front. Consequently, he arrived too late to do much more than oversee the existing deployments.

Both sides claimed victory, but in the end, no one gained much at Perryville. According to casualty figures, Bragg was the victor. The Federals had suffered 845 dead, 2,851 wounded and 515 missing. The Confederate casualty toll was 3,396. That night, however, Bragg understood for the first time that he had been fighting the whole Army of the Ohio. He ordered an immediate and hasty retreat to Harrodsburg, where he could concentrate his forces and counter any move by Buell to cut the Confederate line of withdrawal to Tennessee.

To President Lincoln's despair, Buell failed to pursue Bragg's outnumbered and retreating army. He blandly informed Washington that the roads were too rough and the country too barren. Lincoln's reaction was to be expected. On October 23, he replaced Buell with burly, six-foot-tall Major General William S. Rosecrans, who, in contrast to Buell's timidity, appeared to Lincoln to be one of the few real fighters among the Federal generals. Dubbed Old Rosy by his troops, Rosecrans was now 43 years old, with a close-cropped beard and a long, hooked, red nose that some associated with his hard drinking. Quick to anger, the general was just as quick to forgive.

Rosecrans' soldiers expressed enthusiasm at his promotion. But their good will could not change the fact that the problems that had undone Buell remained to be solved. Their commander proceeded to restock his supplies and re-equip his newly dubbed Army of the Cumberland at Nashville. Although Halleck and Lincoln repeatedly prodded their new general for action, Rosecrans refused to budge until his army was ready.

Rosecrans' antagonist was under fire, too; subordinates and fellow generals alike complained that Bragg was hopelessly incompetent. He had, wrote a diarist in Virginia, "a winning way of earning everyone's detestation." Summoned to meet President Davis, an abashed Bragg assuaged his superior with a new plan: He would move his army to Murfreesboro and from there attack Nashville. Around the beginning of November, his troops moved to Chattanooga, then to Tullahoma and finally through the Stones River valley to Murfreesboro.

By Christmas, Bragg's Army of Tennessee was aligned in a long crescent centered on Murfreesboro and facing Nashville. General Hardee commanded the left wing, based in Triune, 14 miles west of Murfreesboro on the McClensville Pike leading south from Nashville. The center, under General Polk, was at Murfreesboro, where Bragg also had his headquarters. The right wing was located at Readyville, 12 miles east of Murfreesboro. There, Major General John P. McCown, once described by Bragg as lacking "capacity and nerve for a separate, responsible command," controlled a division of Hardee's corps.

On Christmas Day, Rosecrans was ready for battle at last. He issued orders for the army to advance on

Murfreesboro the next day. At a council of war that night, he reviewed the plans with his generals. After a while he put an end to the discussion by banging a mug of toddy on a table and springing to his feet. "We move tomorrow, gentlemen! We shall begin to skirmish, probably as soon as we pass the outposts. Press them hard! Drive them out of their nests! Make them fight or run! Fight them! Fight them! Fight, I say!"

Heavy rain, typical of a Tennessee winter, began to fall that night. In the cold, gray dawn, three columns of Federal troops trudged out of Nashville by separate routes. Major General Thomas L. Crittenden, on the left, took three divisions down the Nashville Pike.

Major General Alexander McCook occupied the center with another three divisions and a cavalry brigade, while Major General George H. Thomas held the right with his division plus three brigades. In all, a bit more than half the 82,000 men in the Army of the Cumberland took part in the advance; the rest remained in garrison at Nashville or guarded the railroad to Louisville.

The Federal columns ran into Confederate cavalry units soon after passing the outposts of Nashville. First contact was made by McCook's wing, which at 7 a.m. attacked a Confederate cavalry detachment at Nolensville commanded by Brigadier General John A. Wharton, once a key member of Nathan Forrest's raiders in Tennessee. Withdrawing toward the south, Wharton formed a line on the ridges north of Triune, where his artillery commenced a duel with McCook's guns. General Thomas responded to the firing by stopping his southward march, and turning east to assist McCook.

At about the same time in the northeast, Crittenden ran into Brigadier General Joseph Wheeler's cavalry outposts, deployed north of Lavergne on the Nashville-Murfreesboro road. Later that day, as Crittenden pushed on closer to Lavergne, he encountered stiff resistance from Wheeler's entire brigade, reinforced by a brigade of hand-fighting Tennesseans. A pattern was emerging in which the Federals, instead of making a rapid advance on the main Confederate army, were continually being forced to stop, form a line of battle, and clear their path of stubborn, well-deployed cavalry units.

With the time gained by the cavalry's successful delaying tactics, Bragg began to consolidate his army, calling in McCown and Hardee. Unsure in the face of the three-pronged advance where the main Federal effort would be made, Bragg threw a defensive line across all the approaches to Murfreesboro from the northwest. Polk was placed more than a mile west of the town, where the Stones River curved behind his back, while Hardee was an equal distance out to the northwest, across the river from Polk. Major General John C. Breckinridge's division was positioned directly in front of Murfreesboro, charged with defending the Confederate right.

It was a terrible position for any kind of fighting. Hardee wrote later that "the country on every side was open and accessible to the enemy." It was rough ground, interspersed with limestone shelves, large boulders and deep crevices, and dotted with thick stands of red cedar.

Polk faced his troops to the west in a semicircle across the Franklin road, the Wilkinson Pike and the Nashville Pike. Major General Jones M. Withers' division was placed in the front line, with Major General Benjamin F. Cheatham's division in reserve along the banks of the river. Private Sam Watkins of the 1st Tennessee, wrote later that the line of battle was formed on the wrong side of the Stones River: "on the Yankee side. Bad generalship, I thought."

Federal forces began approaching the river in the late-afternoon gloom on December 29. By the following evening, the Federal line extended from Crittenden's forces, anchored on the west bank of the river in the north, to McCook's troops almost three miles to the south near the Franklin Road. Rosecrans decided to see if he could deceive Bragg about the Federals' intentions. He ordered McCook to extend his right and build many campfires to make Bragg believe that the main threat was on that front.

The ploy was an ancient one, but it apparently fooled Bragg. He ordered the divisions of McCown and Brigadier General Patrick R. Cleburne to cross to the west side of the river and take position on Polk's left, leaving Breckinridge's division virtually alone to defend the Confederate right. As it happened, the two commanders had arrived at identical plans: to attack the other's right flank.

And now the men on both sides settled down at last for a long night of waiting, and popular tunes from both Federal and Confederate regimental bands wafted in the air. Each side took turns yielding to the

General Rosecrans rides into the thick of the fray to direct fire against a Confederate charge at Stones River. The Union left is shown firmly anchored on the river and the railroad running to Nashville, while fresh troops in the foreground move up to secure Rosecrans' right.

music of the other until a Federal band struck up "Home Sweet Home." As a soldier from the 19th Tennessee recalled, "immediately a Confederate band caught up the strain, then one after another until all the bands of both armies were playing 'Home Sweet Home.' And after our bands had ceased playing, we could hear the sweet refrain as it died away on the cool, frosty air."

At about 6 a.m., as the darkness began to turn milky gray, an apparition appeared to the south and southwest of McCook's Federal positions. Blending in with the fog and mist, long gray lines of Confederates—the 11,000 men of the seven brigades of McCown's and Cleburne's divisions—formed like shadows in front of a protective grove of cedars. Quietly, they moved toward the Federal division commanded by Brigadier General Richard W. Johnson, McCown's men on the left and Cleburne's on the right, following 500 yards behind. "We could see the enemy advancing over the open country for about half a mile in front of our lines," the Union's Brigadier General Edward N. Kirk later reported. Slowly at first, then faster, and finally at the double-quick, the Confederates attacked across the cotton and corn fields. They held their silence until they came within close range of Johnson's men. Only then did the Federals hear the wild Rebel yell.

The seven Confederate brigades descended with overwhelming force on brigades commanded by Kirk and Brigadier General August Willich, who had just gone to the rear looking for General Johnson. The fighting was brief but ferocious. Five color-bearers of the 34th Illinois were killed in quick succession before the Confederates seized the colors and pushed the Federal regiment back. Kirk's troops fired point-blank into the massed gray infantry, but the Confederates forged ahead, overrunning Kirk's line, mortally wounding the general and scattering his men.

Within half an hour, the two Federal brigades were destroyed as effective fighting units. Kirk had lost 483 men killed and wounded, and another 376 captured. Willich's brigade suffered 463 casualties, and 700 of his troops surrendered. Most of those retreating did not stop until they reached the Nashville Pike and the railroad cut, three miles to the rear.

The Federal flank had been turned. The flight of Johnson's troops had exposed the right flank of Brigadier General Jefferson C. Davis' division.

167

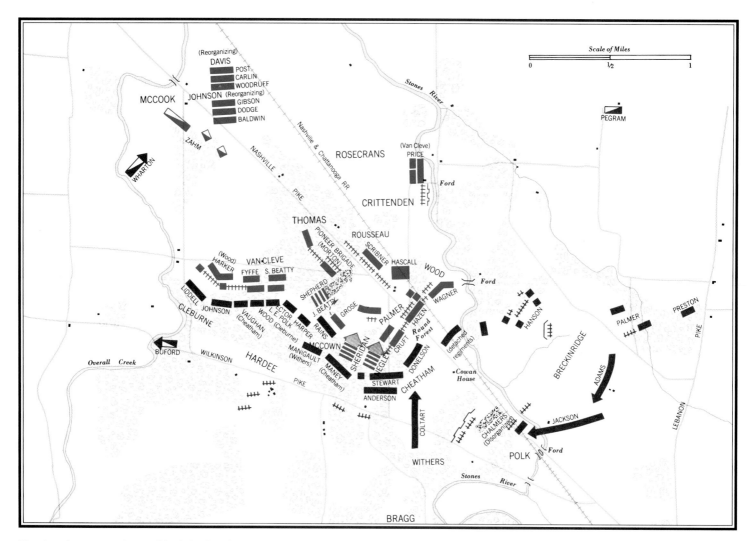

Hearing the commotion on his right, Davis ordered Colonel P. Sidney Post's brigade to bend back part of its line 90 degrees to face the enemy sweep.

Before long, Davis' newly adjusted line—now forming an arc that faced from southeast to southwest—was hit hard by the four brigades of Cleburne's division. But Davis' troops, though greatly outnumbered, stubbornly refused to yield. Their stalwart defense robbed the Confederate drive of its momentum. The Confederates could not push through, and their attack began to falter.

In the Confederate center, meanwhile, part of Polk's corps had joined the assault. But it was a haphazard effort at best; elements of Cheatham's and Withers' divisions were committed piecemeal. And

this failure of command coordination caused the first Confederate setback of the day. General Bragg did what he could to correct his lieutenants' mistakes, but it was too late. For the moment, the opportunity to overwhelm the Union right wing had been lost.

Far to the north, on the Federal left flank, General Rosecrans was initiating his own attack, and had at first appeared unconcerned about the firing from the south. But the sight of retreating soldiers and the mounting cries of attacking Rebels eventually convinced him that something had gone seriously awry.

Major General Lovell H. Rousseau's division was sent to support the sorely pressed Federal flank, where Phil Sheridan's division was now also under fierce attack. Disregarding sheets of Federal fire, the

168

At approximately noon, the Confederate advance on their left has almost run its course and the Federals, their original line folded back on the Nashville Pike like the blade of a jackknife, are stubbornly defending a salient centered on the Round Forest. On the Federal left, Crittenden's brigades have been recalled from east of the river to reinforce the Federal right flank, while Confederate attacks on the Round Forest have been repulsed.

Confederates battered at the line held by three of Davis' and Sheridan's brigades. At one point, the screaming, yelling Rebels surged to within 50 yards of the Union line before being hurled back.

Confederate casualties were so heavy that corps commander Polk threw in fresh brigades of Tennesseans and Texans under Cheatham. Leading the charge of his 9th Texas, Colonel William H. Young proudly recalled that he ordered his regiment "to move forward with a shout, both of which they did." But the assault shattered against the Federal ramparts, and then Sheridan's men rushed forward in a counterattack that drove the Confederates back across the open ground.

The Rebels took a deep breath and came on again. Cheatham and Cleburne reformed their bloodied brigades and fell upon Sheridan and what was left of Davis' division. The men with Davis had fought valiantly, but now they fell back under the terrible pressure, exposing Sheridan's flank. The diminutive "Little Phil" had to act swiftly or all would be lost—and swung his line 90 degrees until it linked up with Rousseau's on the right and two other Federal divisions on the left.

It was now 10 a.m., four hours into the battle, and the Federal line had been hammered into a V-shape. Sheridan's division was at the apex, and the Confederates gave him no respite. On his immediate left were the Illinois regiments of Colonel George W. Roberts' brigade. Roberts was killed and his officers were cut down one by one. Captain Alexander F. Stevenson of the 42nd Illinois, recalled the toll: "Death and blood everywhere. Colonel Harrington, bravely leading the 27th Illinois, was struck by a piece of shell, which tore the jaws from his face; Lieutenant Colonel Francis Swanwick, of the 22nd Illinois, wounded and unable to be moved; nearly 40 per cent of the 42nd and 22nd killed or wounded."

Under such circumstances, Sheridan was forced to conduct a fighting withdrawal northward. He was able to re-form his line just north of the Wilkinson Pike, keeping his right flank in contact with Rousseau. But the Confederate attacks were relentless, despite the awful casualties. One third of Hardee's corps had been killed or wounded, including six brigade and regimental commanders. Polk's corps had suffered 30 per cent losses, most of them in the assaults on Sheridan's lines.

Still, Bragg had reason to be pleased. The enemy's right flank had been shattered, and although Sheridan and Rousseau clung tenaciously to their new positions, their units had been badly mauled. The Confederates were continuing to attack with spirit, and one more great effort might prove decisive.

Rosecrans was galloping from crisis to crisis. At one point, his chief of staff, riding close by his side, was decapitated by a shell, splattering the general with gore. On the left, Rosecrans raced to Colonel Samuel W. Price and ordered him to prevent the Confederate right wing from fording the river. Then he hurried to see how his men were faring on the imperiled right flank. By now, elements of Crittenden's corps were moving along the battlefront, extending the Federal right wing beyond the new lines established by Rousseau and Sheridan.

Around 11 a.m., Rosecrans rode up to Rousseau's position. There he found Sheridan leading his men rearward. Sheridan was furious; he was retreating again not because he had been defeated but because his men were nearly out of ammunition. Sheridan began swearing vividly, but Rosecrans cut him short. "Watch your language," Rosecrans warned. "Remember, the first bullet may send you to eternity."

Sheridan's retreat left a yawning gap in the Federal line. Hardee sent his Rebels plunging into the opening, but they were unable to take advantage of the moment. Then Polk committed his last two brigades in an effort to smash the salient. Under a devastating fire, the attack failed and the brigade counted their dead and wounded. The 8th Tennessee lost 306 of its 472 men; the 16th Tennessee lost 207 men of the 402 who started the advance.

By noon, the Federal line had its apex at a four-acre clump of cedars known as the Round Forest. A deep and easily defended railroad cut ran through the woods about 100 yards west of the river. These features combined to make the Round Forest the field's strongest defensive position. Before the day was over, the soldiers would be calling it "Hell's Half Acre."

Thus far, repeated Confederate attacks against the Round Forest had proved fruitless, largely because of a rocklike stand by a Federal brigade commanded by Colonel William B. Hazen. Hazen's troops, deployed astride the Nashville Pike and the railroad, had held the forest since early morning.

At 1 p.m., Bragg sent an order to Breckinridge,

still off to the right, to provide him with four brigades at once. Until the new units could arrive, a lull descended upon the battlefield. Rosecrans gathered all available artillery on a rise behind Hazen in the Round Forest, while Hazen braced his men for yet another onslaught. Looking to the east, the Federals could see the fresh enemy troops crossing the river. Daylight had begun to fade, but there was time enough for one last desperate Confederate charge.

Polk now committed a foolish error. Instead of waiting for all four brigades to come up, he sent in the first two with no support. In perfect order, the brigades moved forward across a field littered with the mangled, gray-clad bodies from earlier charges.

In the Round Forest, a weary Colonel Hazen watched the Confederate approach with grave concern. "The enemy advanced steadily," he recalled, "and, as it seemed, to certain victory." A number of reinforcements arrived from Rosecrans, and Hazen ordered his men to hold their fire until the Confederates drew nearer. The massed Federal artillery ripped mercilessly into the oncoming lines; and when the enemy at last came into close range, Hazen gave the order to fire. The Round Forest erupted in a flaming volley—and the surviving Rebels fled back across the field, across the grisly carpet of dead and wounded comrades.

Once more the Confederates formed into their battle lines. Once more they charged across the awful field, leaping over the hundreds upon hundreds of bodies lying there. By now the Federals had emplaced 50 cannon on the rise behind the forest, and all of them were firing as fast as their crews could reload. Spencer Tally of the 28th Tennessee would remember, "In the fading light, the sheets of fire from the enemy's cannon looked hideous and dazzling." The Confederates fell back again, leaving behind another layer of bodies. Finally, near sunset, General Hardee gave the order to cease fire.

Despite the frightful losses, the Confederates were generally convinced that victory was theirs. Hardee's report on the day's action did not betray any sense of defeat. "For three miles in our rear, amid the thick cedars and the open fields, where the Federal lines had been originally formed, their dead and their dying, their hospitals and the wreck of that portion of their army marked our victorious advance.

Actually, Rosecrans' brigades were far from dis-

ordered; they simply collapsed in place, exhausted by the day's fight. Rosecrans returned to his cramped log-cabin headquarters along the Nashville Turnpike and called a conference of his corps commanders. He began the meeting by discussing the possibility of retreat, then solicited the opinions of his senior officers. According to one account, General George Thomas fell asleep; but when the word "retreat" was mentioned, he awoke with a start, opened his eyes, looked about with a fierce gaze that had often struck terror into skulkers and muttered, "This army does not retreat." Rosecrans left the meeting and personally scouted a route of withdrawal as far northwest as Overall Creek, one mile behind his lines.

By the time he returned, Rosecrans had decided to remain where he was. He was convinced that his army—depleted though it was—was willing to defend itself for at least another day. He sent a wagon train to Nashville to evacuate some of the wounded, and to return with supplies and ammunition.

Bragg, still in his headquarters, wanted to believe that he had won a major triumph. And he found all the confirmation he needed in reports of the Federal wagons moving north toward Nashville. He sent a telegram to Richmond: "The enemy has yielded his strong position and is falling back. God has granted us a happy New Year." Then he went to bed. The night passed slowly for the men on both sides, kept awake by a cold rain and waiting miserably for the dawn, when the armies would meet once again.

When Bragg awoke on New Year's Day, he was stunned to learn that the Federals were still in their lines. He had been so certain Rosecrans would retreat that he had no plan for continuing the battle. Instead of going to work to devise a strategy, he sank into a curious sort of lethargy.

The Federals had abandoned the Round Forest to consolidate their lines. Polk's corps moved unopposed into the woods, which now harbored pitiful masses of dead and wounded soldiers and animals. Bragg stirred himself enough to order Breckinridge to recross Stones River and take up his original position on the east bank. Despite some minor skirmishes, the rest of the day proved uneventful. Bragg did not order the general attack that his soldiers expected—and dreaded.

The following morning, as an early rain turned to sleet, Bragg ordered his artillery to probe the Federal

The Craft of Field Artillery

During the Civil War, artillery attained a lethal effectiveness that did much to make the conflict one of the deadliest in history. In support of infantry attacks, the guns hurled solid shot and explosive shells into the enemy's formations and fieldworks. On the defense, artillery could be even more destructive, firing shotgun-like canister blasts at close range into oncoming infantry. And rival gunners tried to annihilate each other with counterbattery fire, using shot and shell to wreck guns and blow up caissons full of ammunition.

When the war started, the opposing armies were mainly equipped with antiquated bronze-barreled smoothbore cannons, like this 6-pounder based on an 1840s design. Such guns, firing projectiles only 3.67 inches in diameter, were thought by Federal and Confederate artillerists to lack sufficient power and range. But they continued to be used by both armies, especially in the Western theatre, where newer models were scarce.

Members of General Rosecrans' army turn out in full regalia in a camp near Murfreesboro. Among their weapons were a 3-inch ordnance rifle (left) and a pair of 6-pounder guns.

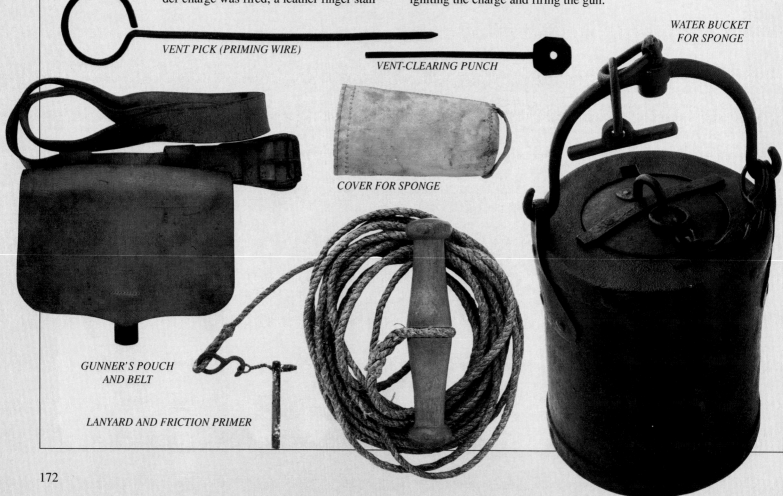

SPONGE-AND-RAMMER

WORM-AND-BRUSH FOR CLEARING BARREL

TRAIL HANDSPIKE

The Tools of a Well-Drilled Team

Experienced gunners working together with precision (*opposite*) could load and fire a fieldpiece twice a minute. The tools of their trade were simple. The largest was a sponge-and-rammer. The sponge swabbed the barrel, removed leftover powder and doused any residual sparks that might prematurely ignite the next charge. The rammer forced the round down the barrrel.

A punch was used to clean out the vent in the top of the barrel through which the powder charge was fired; a leather finger stall closed the vent during loading to extin– guish any sparks still there, and a pick was rammed down the vent to rip open the powder bag after loading. The trail handspike served as a lever to aim the heavy barrel. To fire the piece, a gunner put the friction primer, a two-inch brass tube containing combustibles, including phosphorus, into the vent. He then pulled the lanyard, which yanked a wire through the phosphorus. The matchlike flash traveled down the vent, igniting the charge and firing the gun.

VENT PICK (PRIMING WIRE)

VENT-CLEARING PUNCH

WATER BUCKET FOR SPONGE

COVER FOR SPONGE

GUNNER'S POUCH AND BELT

LANYARD AND FRICTION PRIMER

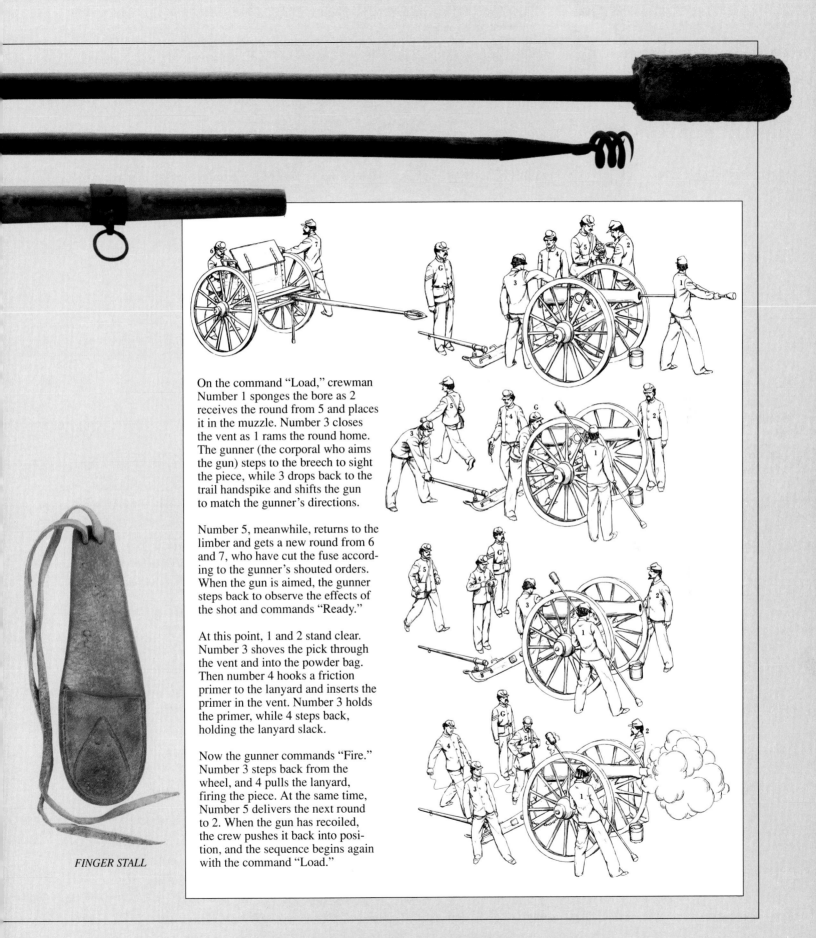

On the command "Load," crewman Number 1 sponges the bore as 2 receives the round from 5 and places it in the muzzle. Number 3 closes the vent as 1 rams the round home. The gunner (the corporal who aims the gun) steps to the breech to sight the piece, while 3 drops back to the trail handspike and shifts the gun to match the gunner's directions.

Number 5, meanwhile, returns to the limber and gets a new round from 6 and 7, who have cut the fuse according to the gunner's shouted orders. When the gun is aimed, the gunner steps back to observe the effects of the shot and commands "Ready."

At this point, 1 and 2 stand clear. Number 3 shoves the pick through the vent and into the powder bag. Then number 4 hooks a friction primer to the lanyard and inserts the primer in the vent. Number 3 holds the primer, while 4 steps back, holding the lanyard slack.

Now the gunner commands "Fire." Number 3 steps back from the wheel, and 4 pulls the lanyard, firing the piece. At the same time, Number 5 delivers the next round to 2. When the gun has recoiled, the crew pushes it back into position, and the sequence begins again with the command "Load."

FINGER STALL

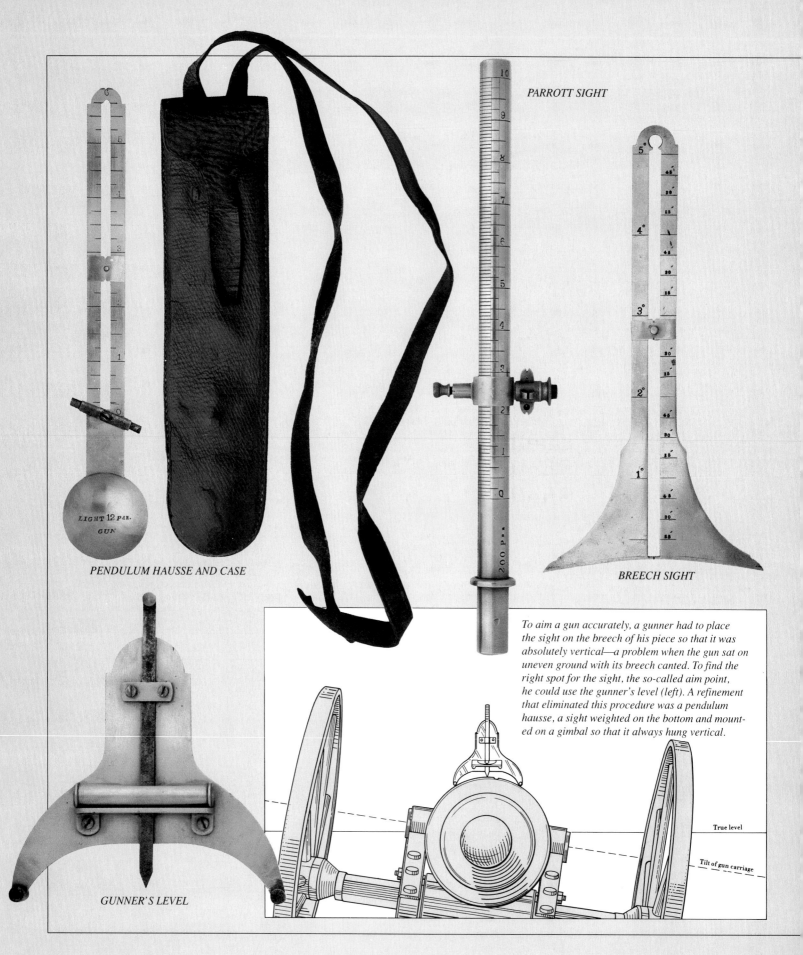

PARROTT SIGHT

PENDULUM HAUSSE AND CASE

LIGHT 12 PdR. GUN

BREECH SIGHT

GUNNER'S LEVEL

To aim a gun accurately, a gunner had to place the sight on the breech of his piece so that it was absolutely vertical—a problem when the gun sat on uneven ground with its breech canted. To find the right spot for the sight, the so-called aim point, he could use the gunner's level (left). A refinement that eliminated this procedure was a pendulum hausse, a sight weighted on the bottom and mounted on a gimbal so that it always hung vertical.

True level

Tilt of gun carriage

174

TABLE OF FIRE ARMS
10-PDR. PARROTT GUN
Charge, 1 lb. of Mortar Powder

ELEVATION In Degrees	PROJECTILE		RANGE In Yards	TIME OF FLIGHT In Seconds
1	Case Shot,	10½ lbs.	600	
2	Case Shot,	10½ lbs.	930	3
2¾	Shell,	9¾ lbs.	1100	3¼
3⅞	Shell,	9¾ lbs.	1460	4¾
4½	Shell,	9¾ lbs.	1680	5¾
5	Shell,	9¾ lbs.	2000	6½
6	Shell,	9¾ lbs.	2250	7¼
7	Shell,	9¾ lbs.	2600	8¼
10	Shell,	9¾ lbs.	3200	10¾
12	Shell,	9¾ lbs.	3600	12⅞
15	Shell,	9¾ lbs.	4200	16⅞
20	Shell,	9¾ lbs.	5000	21⅞

CARE OF AMMUNITION CHEST

1st. Keep everything out that does not belong in them, except a bunch of cord or wire for breakage; beware of loose tacks, nails, bolts, or scraps.
2nd. Keep friction primers in their papers, tied up. The pouch containing those for instant service must be closed, and so placed as to be secure.
Take every precaution that primers do not get loose; a single one may cause an explosion. Use plenty of tow in packing.

(This sheet is to be glued to the inside of Limber Chest Cover.)

The Precise Art of Aiming

To hit his target, a gunner needed to determine three things: the distance to the target, how much to elevate the gun's barrel to throw the projectile that far and how much a crosswind might push the shot off line.

Many Civil War artillerymen became uncannily good at estimating distance and the effects of wind. But aiming the piece for long-range shooting called for some special aids. First, from a table of fire *(above)*, a gunner found the correct elevation in degrees for the distance to his particular target. Next, he placed on the breech of the gun one of the commonly used sights *(opposite, top)*; each was essentially a length of brass notched with an elevation scale in degrees, and each carried a sliding peep hole.

Making sure that the sight was perfectly vertical *(opposite, bottom)*, the gunner slid the peep hole along the rod to the predetermined degree mark. Then he peered through the hole down the barrel and lined up his target. Finally, he elevated the barrel until the muzzle tip was in the line of sight.

Table-of-fire charts, which were pasted on the inside of the ammunition chests carried by limbers and caissons, provided gunners and shell handlers with vital information concerning the performance of various types of guns and ammunition, including the elevations needed for various ranges and the number of seconds the projectile would be in flight.

An Array of Lethal Ammunition

The simplest artillery projectile used in the Civil War was solid shot: deadly iron balls employed mostly at long range. For short-range work there was canister: tin containers that disintegrated when they were fired, scattering a hail of bullets.

Charged projectiles—shells and case shot—exploded after reaching the target. Shells burst into lethal fragments; case shot held a payload of metal balls. These projectiles, used at medium and long ranges, carried either impact fuses or time fuses. The best time fuse, named for a Belgian ordnance expert, was the Bormann fuse, which contained a slow-burning powder. The gunner punched a hole in its thin metal top at one of the marks that indicated the burning time. The flame from the gun's discharge then went into the hole, starting the fuse.

Less reliable but cheaper were paper fuses, which could be cut to size to burn for a specified number of seconds.

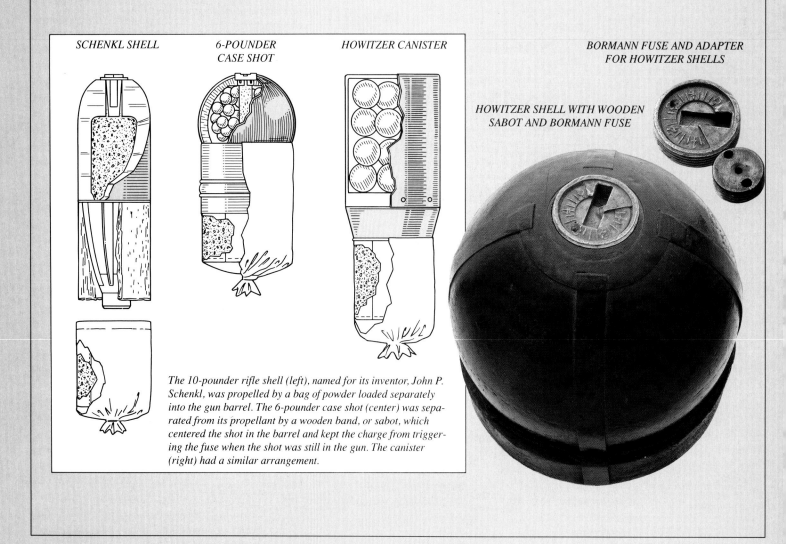

SCHENKL SHELL *6-POUNDER CASE SHOT* *HOWITZER CANISTER*

BORMANN FUSE AND ADAPTER FOR HOWITZER SHELLS

HOWITZER SHELL WITH WOODEN SABOT AND BORMANN FUSE

The 10-pounder rifle shell (left), named for its inventor, John P. Schenkl, was propelled by a bag of powder loaded separately into the gun barrel. The 6-pounder case shot (center) was separated from its propellant by a wooden band, or sabot, which centered the shot in the barrel and kept the charge from triggering the fuse when the shot was still in the gun. The canister (right) had a similar arrangement.

center on the west side of the Round Forest. The 22 Confederate guns spread across the Nashville Pike blazed away for a while, and the Federal batteries responded with vigor, leaving Bragg in no doubt about his enemy's determination to stand fast.

On his own initiative, Breckinridge had spent the morning testing the Federal lines to find out what the Confederates were facing. He found a brigade strongly emplaced with artillery in two lines on a ridge that commanded two fords on the east bank of Stones River. It was part of a division led by Brigadier General Samuel Beatty. The Federals enjoyed the advantages not only of high ground but also of abundant cover and a wide-open field of fire. In addition to Beatty's artillery, six guns of the 3rd Wisconsin Artillery were placed on a hill just west of the river and commanded the open ground in front of the ridge that Beatty occupied.

Thus, when he responded to Bragg's summons to headquarters, Breckinridge was staggered by his general's order to attack the formidable position. Bragg wanted the assault launched at 4 p.m. so that darkness would interfere with any Federal counterattack. Bragg promised the support of Polk's artillery across the river to the southwest and of cavalry brigades on Breckinridge's right flank, but no other reinforcements.

Breckinridge protested vehemently. He sketched the enemy positions in the mud to show Bragg how the Federal artillery was deployed to devastate the planned attack. Bragg's only response was to observe that Breckinridge's Kentuckians had so far suffered less than the others and that it was now their turn to show their mettle. When Breckinridge continued to object, Bragg replied angrily, "Sir, my information is different. I have given an order to attack the enemy in your front and expect it to be obeyed."

Bragg's harsh discipline and uncertain leadership had been fostering resentment among his men ever since he had taken command of the army. And now, in this poisonous atmosphere, Bragg's order very nearly touched off a mutiny. One of the Kentuckians, Brigadier General Roger W. Hanson, was so enraged by the order to mount what he considered to be a suicidal attack that he proposed going to headquarters to kill Bragg. But Breckinridge, a patriot and an obedient soldier, quieted his officers and set to work deploying his 4,500 men.

The Confederate preparations were clearly visible to the men of Beatty's division on the ridge; Rosecrans and his officers began calling reinforcements to the area about 3 p.m. Two divisions and a pair of brigades were moved up to Beatty's left flank on the east bank of the river. Meanwhile, the Federal artillery chiefs began massing more guns on the hill across the river from Beatty's troops; eventually, there would be 58 pieces.

Rain and sleet had been falling all day, and now the infantrymen would have to fight in the miserable wet. Precisely at 4 p.m., Breckinridge shouted, "Up, my men, and charge!" The order was repeated all along the half-mile length of the formation. And as soon as the Confederates stepped off, the guns of Beatty, and those across the river, began to pour down a lethal rain of shells on the attackers.

Breckinridge reported afterward that he was proud of his soldiers' "admirable order" as they advanced westward at a quickstep across the 600 yards of open ground under the barrage. Ignoring their heavy casualties, the Confederates pressed forward toward the ridge, the first rank under orders to fire one volley and then use the bayonet.

The first Confederates to make contact were General Hanson's Kentucky Brigade, called the Orphan Brigade because its native state was in enemy hands. Taking advantage of a protecting fold in the terrain, Hanson's men were able to advance under cover to within 150 yards of the Federal line. The moment they came into view, they drew a volley from Price's men—the 51st Ohio, 8th Kentucky and 35th Indiana—lying behind a rail fence. The Kentuckians let out what an Ohioan called "a most hideous yell," leveled a volley and charged with bayonets flashing. The Federals rose and fired again, but they could not stop the charge.

The Confederates on Breckinridge's right also were relentless. The 20th Tennessee rushed to a fence and leveled volley after volley at the Federals before them. "We had the advantage," recalled Private William J. McMurray, "and the slaughter was terrible."

All along the line, Confederate troops stormed to the top of the crest. The Orphan Brigade and Brigadier General Gideon J. Pillow's Tennesseans crashed into the ranks of Federal defenders, and savage hand-to-hand fighting ensued. The Federals on the ridge faltered and then gave way. As their flight

On the third day of the battle at Stones River, the 2,200 men of Colonel John Miller's Federal brigade ford the shallow river, pursuing General Breckinridge's

Confederates (background) after the failure of their assault. Miller's spirited counterattack, undertaken on his own initiative, was halted only by darkness.

became a rout, they overran Colonel Benjamin Grider's reserve brigade behind them. Grider reported, "I allowed the retreating mass to pass through my lines, the enemy all the time pouring into us a destructive fire."

Grider's Federals fought back fiercely, standing their ground. But Grider's luck did not hold. At about this time, the 6th Kentucky, a regiment of Hanson's that had been pushed out of position in the Confederate charge, arrived unexpectedly on Grider's left flank and slammed into the 19th Ohio. The Ohioans gave way; Grider was flanked, and he gave the order to fall back and rally at the foot of the ridge.

The Confederates raced forward in hot pursuit, sweeping Beatty's entire line before them. In less than 30 minutes, Breckinridge's division had achieved an objective thought impossible. It was time to stop, bring up the artillery and settle in on the ridge for the night. But the sight of the fleeing Federals was too much for the victorious Confederates. They had suffered for six days without hot food or proper shelter; they had slept and fought in the rain and sleet and freezing weather; and now they wanted nothing more than to get the battle over with and comb the Federal camps for supplies. Disregarding their orders and the shouts of their officers, they chased the Federals all the way to the river. The 2nd and 6th Kentucky of Hanson's Orphan Brigade crossed the river, expecting the rest of Breckinridge's men to follow.

But the Confederates were already paying dearly for their zealous charge. The moment they crossed the crest of the ridge, they came into full view of the Federal batteries across the river. At that point, the gunners went to work, and the ferocity of their cannonade, a Federal observer wrote, must have made it seem to the Confederates as though they had "opened the door of Hell, and the devil himself was there to greet them." Shells slammed into the pursuers at the rate of 100 rounds per minute, cutting great swaths from the Confederate ranks.

The pursuit slowed, and the disorganized Rebels began milling about in desperate clusters in the river and on both banks. There, unable to endure the slaughter, they began to retreat back up the slope. At that point, a Federal commander west of the river seized the initiative. Colonel John F. Miller ordered his brigade to attack. While Rosecrans watched approvingly from the crest of a nearby hill, Miller's

brigade charged across the river and slammed into the disorganized remnants of Hanson's and Pillow's brigades. Miller's men were soon followed by other units ordered forward by Rosecrans.

The tide of battle was now reversed. The Confederate officers tried desperately to halt the retreat on the crest of the hill they had just won. General Hanson was slain, and Colonel R.P. Trabue took command of the Orphan Brigade. He managed to stem the general retreat—but only momentarily.

When the Federal counterattackers had driven to within 150 yards of the top of the ridge, Colonel Miller ordered the 78th Pennsylvania to capture a Confederate battery posted on the crest. Miller's men swarmed over the Confederate gunners, killing some and driving away the rest. Jimmy Thorne, a 16-year-old Pennsylvanian, climbed up on the barrel of a Confederate gun, patted it and yelled, "Here it is." By 4:45 p.m., the rout of the Confederates was complete. It was getting dark, and the Federals were willing to quit for the day.

Breckinridge was shattered by the pointless carnage. He watched numbly as his decimated and demoralized troops re-formed their ranks. When he saw how much shorter the lines were, he turned livid with anger at Bragg. A Kentucky officer reported that Breckinridge "was raging like a wounded lion as he passed the different commands from right to left. Tears broke from his eyes when he beheld the little remnants of his own old brigade." Then Breckinridge cried out, "My poor Orphans! My poor Orphans! My poor Orphan Brigade! They have cut it to pieces."

At dawn on January 3, the armies were roughly in the same positions; the weather was still miserable; the wounded continued to suffer and die. During the night, Bragg had learned from cavalry scouts of the arrival of a fresh brigade to reinforce Rosecrans. In addition, captured documents convinced him that Rosecrans now had an overwhelming numerical advantage: 70,000 men to face the 20,000 Confederates still able to fight. At 10 a.m., Bragg conferred with Hardee and Polk; they quickly agreed that retreat was necessary.

The battle at Stones River was finally over. During the afternoon of the 3rd, Bragg began sending his ammunition and supply wagons south toward Shelbyville and Manchester. Polk was ordered to take his troops out during the evening and move to

The 105th Ohio, part of Rosecrans' Army of the Cumberland, marches into Murfreesboro after the battle. Though the fighting left the town unscathed, almost every building had been turned into a hospital for the wounded and dying of both sides. "I have often expressed the desire to witness the terrible strife of a fierce battle," wrote an Illinois soldier in a letter home, "but I can say now that my curiosity is fully satisfied."

Shelbyville. Hardee was to follow in the morning and march to Tullahoma. Behind him, Bragg left 1,700 seriously wounded and sick scattered among the homes of Murfreesboro.

The struggle along Stones River had cost the Confederates severely. Of the 34,732 troops Bragg commanded when the battle began, he lost 9,239 killed or wounded—27 per cent of his strength. Rosecrans lost 9,532 killed and wounded, 23 per cent of the 41,400 Federals engaged. But Bragg's losses were far more serious than the statistics indicated: the Federals could easily replace their casualties, but the thinly populated Confederacy was growing increasingly short of fighting men.

Although Rosecrans was astonished by Bragg's withdrawal, it did not take him long to realize that the outcome represented a major victory for the North. It made Kentucky safe for the Union and secured Nashville as a base for future Federal operations. It boosted the spirits of pro-Union East Tennesseans and dashed the hopes of Confederate sympathizers in central Tennessee and Kentucky. Moreover, for the Lincoln Administration the triumph was a much-needed antidote to the recent Federal defeats at Fredericksburg and at Chickasaw

Bayou, near Vicksburg. The President was elated. "God bless you," he telegraphed Rosecrans.

Bragg, meanwhile, drew censure from newspapers throughout the South. Some even suggested that he had retreated from Stones River against his generals' advice. The allegation was untrue and five of his generals absolved him of the charge. But they also unanimously declared that Bragg did not have their confidence. Confederate Secretary of War James A. Seddon instructed General Joseph E. Johnston to take personal command of the Army of Tennessee and order Bragg to Richmond. But Johnston's failing health rendered him unable to carry out Seddon's order and Bragg remained in command by default.

He continued to reject responsibility for his defeat and placed the blame on his commanders, especially Cheatham, Breckinridge, Polk and Hardee. In Bragg's eyes, the battle just delayed the opportunity to deal the enemy a crippling blow. He knew that Rosecrans would have to take Chattanooga in order to control Tennessee and invade Georgia from the west. And when the Federals moved against Chattanooga, Bragg and the Army of Tennessee would be waiting for them along the banks of the Chickamauga River.

Herman Haupt (far right), field commander of the U.S. Military Railroads, controlled three sections of rail (shown in blue) in Virginia that were vital to the campaigns of 1862 and early 1863. The Orange and Alexandria carried Federal troops and supplies southwest as far as Culpeper. From Manassas Junction, the Manassas Gap line ran west to Front Royal and Strasburg. Farther south, a segment of the Richmond, Fredericksburg & Potomac linked Aquia Creek, on the Potomac, with Falmouth, across the Rappahannock from Fredericksburg.

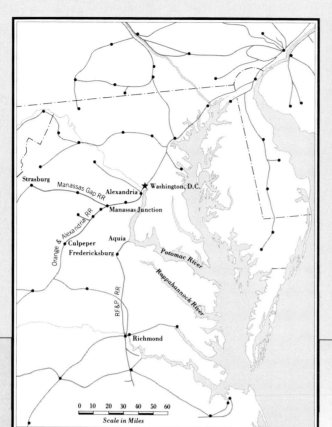

This sprawling yard at Alexandria, Virginia, was the hub of the U.S. Military Railroads. It was linked to nearby Washington by a single bridge over the Potomac.

182

The Nation's Railroads at War

From the start of the Civil War, the Union had a marked advantage in its railway network. There had been a boom in railway construction during the 1850s, most of it in the Northern states. By 1861, the North had 22,000 miles of track, compared with the South's 9,000 miles; the North had a similar edge in rolling stock—and in the capacity to build more of both.

This asset was not immediately exploited. Railroads had never been used on an ambitious scale to transport and supply armies in the field, and some authorities doubted that it could be done—with good reason. Rail systems lacked both uniformity and reliability. Often tracks were built of poor-grade iron rails laid on ties of unseasoned wood; moreover, track gauges varied capriciously from a standard width of 4 feet 8 1/2 inches to widths of 5 and even 6 feet.

Early in 1862 the Union government moved to solve these problems by creating the United States Military Railroads, an agency empowered to coordinate rail service in the North and to control all railroads in occupied territory. To rebuild and run the railroads in northern Virginia, Secretary of War Edwin Stanton recruited 45-year-old Herman Haupt.

A West Point graduate, Haupt was a solemn man of prodigious energy. Among his many accomplishments, he had helped to survey and build a railroad line that crossed Pennsylvania, and he had written a pioneering book on bridge construction.

Haupt rose eagerly to the new challenge and demanded freedom from interference by even the most senior officers, although at first he held only a colonel's commission. He insisted that the army protect the trains from Confederate raiders, and that the trains run on schedule, i.e., incoming supplies had to be unloaded promptly.

In short order he built an efficient transportation network, radiating out of Alexandria, Virginia (*below*), to sustain future offensives, including the Fredericksburg and Chancellorsville Campaigns. By 1862 he was moving 800 tons of supplies a day; and beleaguered Union generals were assured that whatever else might go wrong, at least the railroads would run on time.

A Bustling Hub for Supply Missions

As field boss of the U.S. Military Railroads, Haupt was responsible for supplying and transporting the Federal armies in Virginia while maintaining the rail lines and rolling stock that made those missions possible. Setting up headquarters at the Alexandria rail yard, he purchased additional locomotives, freight cars and rails, and established a Construction Corps to lay track, build bridges and run the repair shops.

The corps was staffed at first by 300 soldiers, but Haupt preferred civilian workers, and he hired them in increasing numbers. He organized the corps into 10-man squads by skills: teamsters, woodcutters, carpenters and mechanics. Haupt had no time for slackers. Anyone unwilling to work 16 continuous hours when necessary was sent packing.

A steam-powered sawmill at Alexandria cuts up timber for use as ties and as fuel for locomotives.

Carpenters of Haupt's Construction Corps plane the edges of wooden planks by hand at the Alexandria lumberyard.

Damaged rails and iron wheels salvaged from wooden cars are collected at Alexandria, where they will be repaired or melted down for recasting.

Men of the Construction Corps excavate a siding in occupied Virginia. A locomotive named for the newly promoted General Haupt stands by to haul away earth.

Building with Speed and Ingenuity

Haupt's pressing assignment in May of 1862 was to rebuild the railroad from the mouth of Aquia Creek, on the Potomac, 13 miles to Falmouth, across from Fredericksburg. Retreating Confederates had wrecked the line, reducing the railhead at Aquia Creek to ruins, tearing up miles of track and burning three bridges. The roadbed itself had been churned by cavalry and turned into a quagmire by constant rain.

Haupt put his newly formed Construction Corps to work around the clock. "I threw out a dragnet and raked in all the lanterns to be found," he wrote. "We unloaded iron by candlelight, put it on cars hauled by soldiers to the end of the track, and kept on laying and spiking all night."

The most daunting obstacle in the path of the Construction Corps was a chasm 80 feet deep at Potomac Creek. Haupt spanned

it with a bridge constructed mostly of fresh-cut logs.

It was perilous work. "We got three men at different times in the river, but fished them out," Haupt reported to the War Department. "A fourth is missing, supposed to be drowned."

After only 21 days of labor, the railroad had been restored and Federal supply trains were chugging along it every hour.

Haupt designed and built the 400-foot-long trestle bridge across Potomac Creek (above) in nine days, using two million feet of green lumber and a crew of inexperienced soldiers. President Lincoln, on a visit, called it "the most remarkable structure that human eyes ever rested on. There is nothing in it but beanpoles and cornstalks." In 1863 Haupt replaced it with a sturdier truss bridge (left); the replacement was accomplished, he wrote, "without delaying a single train for a single minute."

A crude hoist on the wharf in Alexandria (top) raised or lowered a section of track, as the water level dictated, so that rolling stock could be loaded onto barges (bottom) for towing down the Potomac.

The Waterborne Railway

In midautumn of 1862, Haupt received orders to transport unprecedented quantities of food, forage and munitions from depots near Washington to the Federal forces assembling near Fredericksburg.

No rail line connected the two places, but Haupt had set up a supply route down the Potomac River to Aquia Creek and from there by rail to the Fredericksburg area. He also devised a way to avoid the tedious unloading of freight at the transfer points between land and water. His trains ran to the river's edge at Alexandria. There the cars were pushed onto flat-bottomed barges.

Two barges bolted together could hold eight freight cars. Four of them could ferry a typical 16-car train 35 miles to the landing at Aquia Creek in six hours, and put it ashore, ready to roll.

On the rebuilt landing at Aquia Creek, a Federal supply train (left foreground) that has arrived by river is poised to steam toward Fredericksburg.

REBELS RESURGENT

*"Call it what you please, demoralization or discouragement,
we care not to ford rivers, sleep standing and fight running, when
sure defeat always awaits such a doomed army."*

SERGEANT WALTER CARTER, 22ND MASSACHUSETTS, ARMY OF THE POTOMAC

Ambrose E. Burnside was offered command of the Army of the Potomac on three different occasions in 1862, and each time he demurred on grounds that he was not competent to handle so large a force. On November 7, when the third offer was tendered, Major General Burnside at first refused—but then reversed his decision. It was not ambition, nor any surge of self-confidence that caused him to accept what he had once so assiduously rejected; it was the realization that if he continued to balk, the command would go to an officer he detested—Major General Joseph Hooker.

Nothing in Burnside's background had prepared him for the enormity of the task he was about to undertake. He had been plagued by bad luck and self-doubts through most of his life. When he was born in Liberty, Indiana, in 1824, the attending physician could not get him to breathe until he resorted to tickling his nose with a feather. After a mediocre academic career at West Point, Burnside joined the U.S. forces fighting in Mexico, but arrived too late to see action. Burnside languished in frontier assignments for the next six years, resigning from the army in 1853 to manufacture a breech-loading carbine he had invented. The carbine was excellent, but the company proved to be a financial disaster.

When the Civil War broke out, Burnside returned to the army, took command of the 1st Rhode Island Infantry and marched it to Washington. A brigade commander at Bull Run that July, he performed adequately, and was awarded a brigadier's star. His reputation was made early in 1862 when he led an amphibious expedition that conquered Roanoke Island and New Bern, on the coast of North Carolina. That achievement earned Burnside a promotion to major general, command of the army's IX Corps and the confidence of the President. He held the Union left wing at Antietam, but showed little dash or initiative there.

As the new army commander, Burnside was confronted with a situation that had changed dramatically in the two months since Antietam. Robert E. Lee had used the time to reorganize and resupply his badly battered army. For some time, he had been operating with his nine infantry divisions grouped unofficially into two corps under his most reliable generals—James Longstreet and Stonewall Jackson. In October 1862, the Confederate Congress formally approved this organization and created the rank of lieutenant general, to which Longstreet and Jackson were immediately promoted.

Meanwhile, prompted by an increasingly impatient Lincoln, Major General George B. McClellan had been inching his forces south in a weak attempt to intercept Lee before he could return to Richmond. By the time McClellan's men reached Warrenton, Lee had already positioned half his army—the corps led by Longstreet —in Culpeper, 20 miles to the southwest, and directly in McClellan's path. Lee's other corps, under Jackson, had remained in the Shenandoah Valley, posing a threat to the Federals' western flank. At this juncture, a thoroughly disgusted Lincoln had relieved McClellan of command. For McClellan's replacement, the President had few eligible men from whom to choose. Among the candidates, Burnside was brave, loyal and popular—and the one with the fewest apparent liabilities. As so often happened in this war, Lincoln was forced to appoint a less than ideal commander.

Burnside's new responsibilities made him physically ill, but he nonetheless attacked his problems vigorously. On November 9 he forwarded to Washington a bold new strategy for the capture of Richmond. He proposed concentrating his forces along

Whatever his peers thought of his abilities, and opinions were remarkably diverse, almost everyone agreed that General Ambrose E. Burnside had a captivating personality. There was a certain brigandish air about his cheek whiskers that came—by a play upon his name—to be known as sideburns.

Camping in the woods, a refugee family from Fredericksburg bids an emotional farewell to a young man returning to fight with Lee's Confederates. A newspaper reported that about 6,000 residents fled the city for the safety of the countryside, where most had to live on "such scanty and precarious subsistance as is at hand."

the route to the southwest toward Gordonsville, Virginia, to convince Lee that the Federals intended to continue the drive initiated in that direction by McClellan. Then he would shift his army rapidly southeastward from Warrenton to Fredericksburg, cross the Rappahannock River, take Fredericksburg before Lee could block him, then move south and seize Richmond.

President Lincoln was skeptical. He approved the plan, albeit reluctantly, commenting that it "will succeed, if you move rapidly; otherwise not."

Burnside appreciated the need for speed; the attack on Fredericksburg, he stipulated, should be made "as soon as the army arrives in front of the place." To streamline his operations, he proposed reorganizing his command by creating three "grand divisions," as he labeled them, each containing two corps and each with its own staff. To command the grand divisions he would name three major generals: Edwin V. Sumner, William B. Franklin and Joseph Hooker, with well over 100,000 troops at their disposal.

The campaign got off to a propitious start. Sumner's grand division led the way, setting off from the Warrenton area at dawn on November 15. Just after dark two days later, his advance elements marched into Falmouth, a village on the north bank of the Rappahannock a mile upstream from Fredericksburg.

Franklin soon reached Stafford Court House, eight miles north of Falmouth, and Hooker halted at Hartwood, a scant seven miles away.

At that point, Fredericksburg and the heights beyond it were held by just four companies of Confederate infantry, a cavalry regiment and a battery of light artillery. Longstreet's corps was still 30 miles northwest at Culpeper, and Jackson's corps remained in the Shenandoah Valley farther west. Two of Burnside's generals urged him to strike immediately: Sumner, who had learned of a ford not far upstream from Falmouth, asked permission to cross at once and occupy Fredericksburg. Hooker proposed to cross upriver at a place called United States Ford, then strike out for Bowling Green, south of Fredericksburg and only 35 miles from Richmond.

Burnside rejected both proposals, because the weather was threatening and the river already high. Moreover, he was concerned that his overland supply routes from Belle Plain and Aquia Creek, both on the Potomac, were not yet fully in operation. But most important of all, the general was distressed that the pontoons he had requested for bridging the Rappahannock had not yet arrived.

Two shipments of pontoons were to be assembled in the Washington area and sent on different routes to Burnside in the hope that at least one would make it. One load was to be shipped down the Potomac to Belle Plain, then hauled overland. But the steamer was delayed; the pontoons did not reach Belle Plain until November 18, and it took another six days to get them to Burnside, scarcely eight miles away.

The other shipment, sent by wagon train, bogged down in the mud below Washington. By a Herculean effort it was transferred to a steamer in the Potomac. It did not reach Falmouth, however, until the afternoon of November 25.

In the meantime, as Confederate units arrived south of the river, Lee began deploying them for the defense of Fredericksburg. Longstreet's divisions were positioned along a wooded ridge behind the town, which ran southeast for about seven miles from the Rappahannock to a place called Hamilton's Crossing, on the Richmond, Fredericksburg & Potomac Railroad. The Confederate commander had decided against an all-out defense of Fredericksburg itself, because of the presence of Federal artillery along the heights opposite the town. Instead, he posted a brigade under Brigadier General William Barksdale along the riverfront to harass and delay any Federal crossing before withdrawing to the main Confederate lines.

Stonewall Jackson arrived in the midst of a snowstorm on November 29, after a grueling march from the Shenandoah Valley, and his troops were quickly deployed by Lee. Major General Daniel Harvey Hill's division was ordered downriver to Port Royal, and Brigadier General Jubal Early's division was dispatched to Skinker's Neck, 12 miles down river. The division of Major General Ambrose Powell Hill was posted at Yerby's House, six and a half miles southeast of Fredericksburg, and that of Brigadier General William Taliaferro at Guinea Station, four and a half miles south of the town. The four divisions were to guard against any attempt by Burnside to cross downstream and outflank the Confederates. Meanwhile, Major General Jeb Stuart's four brigades of cavalry guarded the army's front and flanks.

Lee's Army of Northern Virginia, 72,564 strong, was at last in place. Facing it, across the Rappahannock, were the 116,683 men of the Army of the Potomac. Never before or after in this war would so many armed men confront each other.

As the Confederate buildup in the Fredericksburg

area continued, Burnside began having second thoughts about an attack directly across the river. Instead of crossing at the town, he decided to make his move downstream at Skinker's Neck, which his engineers had recommended as a crossing site. He called up Federal gunboats from Port Royal to support the attack, but on December 4, Confederate shore batteries succeeded in driving the gunboats back downstream. Then Federal spotters, venturing aloft in balloons, detected Jubal Early's and D.H. Hill's divisions in their camps near Skinker's Neck and Port Royal.

Convinced that Lee had guessed the Federal strategy, Burnside decided to reverse himself and cross his main force at Fredericksburg after all. The attack was set for the morning of December 11. At 2:00 a.m., engineers began building two pontoon bridges at the site of an old rope ferry at the center of Fredericksburg, and another opposite the docks at the lower end of town. Two more bridges were to be built at Franklin's Crossing, downriver from Fredericksburg.

Long before first light, Confederates along the riverbank could hear pontoons splashing into the water and planks thudding into place. At dawn, General Barksdale reported to his superiors that one of the bridges was being rapidly completed and he was about to open fire. A cannon barked twice on Marye's Heights, a thousand yards behind the town, alerting the slumbering Army of Northern Virginia to the long-awaited crossing, and the sound of musketry was immediately heard as sharpshooters along the riverbank commenced a galling fire.

The engineers dropped their implements and fled. Federal artillery opened fire in an effort to drive the sharpshooters from their riverfront positions, but the Confederates were well protected. The guns ceased firing after about an hour to let the engineers go back to work, but the sharpshooters opened up again and sent the bridge-builders racing back to cover.

This frustrating situation continued until about 1 p.m., when the Federals brought all their available artillery—about 100 guns—to bear on the hapless town. During the next two hours, the Federals fired 5,000 shells into Fredericksburg, tearing gaping holes in brick houses, setting wooden buildings ablaze, digging craters in streets and gardens. But the bombardment failed to drive off General Barksdale's men, and when the engineers returned to their work, the

In an improvised amphibious attack, men of the 7th Michigan and the 19th and 20th Massachusetts row pontoons across the Rappahannock River to Fredericksburg while engineers (left) work under fire to complete a bridge. A number of the engineers lie dead or wounded on the bridge planking.

sharpshooters emerged yet again and resumed firing.

Eventually, around 2:30 p.m., Burnside's chief of artillery, Brigadier General Henry J. Hunt, suggested that infantrymen be rowed across in pontoons to clear the opposite shore. As the Federals crossed, they came under heavy fire. But all the pontoons made it to the other side. The men leaped out, formed ranks, and rushed up the nearest street. Within minutes, they had taken 30 prisoners and cleared the area bordering the bridges. Other Federal units then landed, and the attackers pushed further into the town. Barksdale's troops retired street by street, hotly contesting every inch, until at 4:30 p.m., Longstreet ordered them to withdraw to Marye's Heights.

The following day, December 12, passed with Burnside doing nothing more than bringing more troops across the river and pondering his next move. The delay afforded the idle Federals a chance to indulge in one of the war's more discreditable enterprises: the wholesale looting of Fredericksburg. What the troops could not use they demolished; the men smashed mirrors, fine china and alabaster vases; mutilated books, paintings and embroidered draperies; and chopped up antique furniture for firewood. The sacking prompted Private Alfred Davenport of the 5th New York to write, "it made me feel sad to think how comfortable the homes were in time of peace now turned into desolation."

On the southern flank, downriver from Fredericksburg, the Federal advance under General Franklin was also stalled after a promising start on the morning of the 11th. The bridge-builders had been fired on there; six men were wounded and holes were shot in many of the pontoons. But one of the bridges was finished by 9 a.m., and the other two hours later.

The first unit to cross the river at 4 p.m. was a brigade of VI Corps under Brigadier General Charles Devens Jr. One of Devens' regimental commanders decided that the occasion should be marked with proper ceremony, so he ordered a band to lead the way while playing a lively march. The men on the two spans picked up the cadence and fell into step. Both bridges began to sway alarmingly, but before the pontoons were swamped, a staff officer galloped up and ordered the music stopped and the men to break step.

By the time Franklin's dispositions were completed, more than 36 hours had passed since the engi-

neers had begun laying the bridges, and Robert E. Lee had used the time to good advantage. During the night of December 11, he had ordered up two of Stonewall Jackson's divisions, bringing A.P. Hill from Yerby's House to relieve Longstreet's men on the Confederate right, and moving Taliaferro's troops from Guinea Station to provide support. Lee left Jackson's other two divisions, under D.H. Hill and Jubal Early, in place to guard the crossings at Port Royal and Skinker's Neck.

At 5 p.m. on December 12, Burnside rode out to inspect the southern flank. Franklin and his top generals pressed him to approve an all-out attack, but the army commander could not make up his mind. It was only at 7:45 the following morning that Franklin finally received word to move out. Even then, instead of committing Franklin's entire force to the attack, Burnside directed that he send out "a division at least" to "seize, if possible," the heights where Jackson's troops were deployed. At the same time, he ordered General Sumner to send "a division or more" to seize the high ground beyond the town.

Burnside was unaware that D.H. Hill's division had arrived in the Hamilton's Crossing area early on the 13th, after a night's march from Port Royal, and that Jubal Early's division had come up from Skinker's Neck. Jackson now had 30,000 men to defend his 3,000-yard-wide sector.

There was, however, a weak spot in the line. When A.P. Hill had deployed his troops along the forward slope of the ridge on the morning of December 12, he had left a gap of 600 yards between the brigades of Brigadier Generals James H. Lane and James J. Archer. The gap was a wooded area of swampy ground and tangled underbrush in the form of a triangle projecting out beyond the railroad embankment at the base of the ridge for a third of a mile. Hill, assuming that this area was impassable, left it undefended and thus allowed the enemy a covered approach to the heart of the Confederate position.

Above the unmanned area, in the woods along the crest of the ridge, Hill had posted Brigadier General Maxcy Gregg's South Carolina brigade. Gregg, a scholarly lawyer and iron-hearted combat leader, failed to grasp that his was the only line of defense behind the gap.

The Federals moved out under the cover of morning fog at 8:30 a.m., with Major General George

At dawn on December 13, 1862, two Federal grand divisions, having crossed the Rappahannock River, deployed for a frontal assault on the Confederate-held ridge west and south of Fredericksburg, Virginia. In the town itself, Major General Edwin Sumner's Federal II and IX Corps assembled for an attack against Lieutenant General James Longstreet's forces, dug in along Marye's Heights. A mile to the south, Major General William Franklin's I and VI Corps prepared to advance against Lieutenant General Stonewall Jackson's corps. Major General Jeb Stuart's cavalry secured the Confederate right flank, while the divisions of Brigadier General Jubal Early and Major General D.H. Hill hastened from positions downriver to reinforce Jackson's troops.

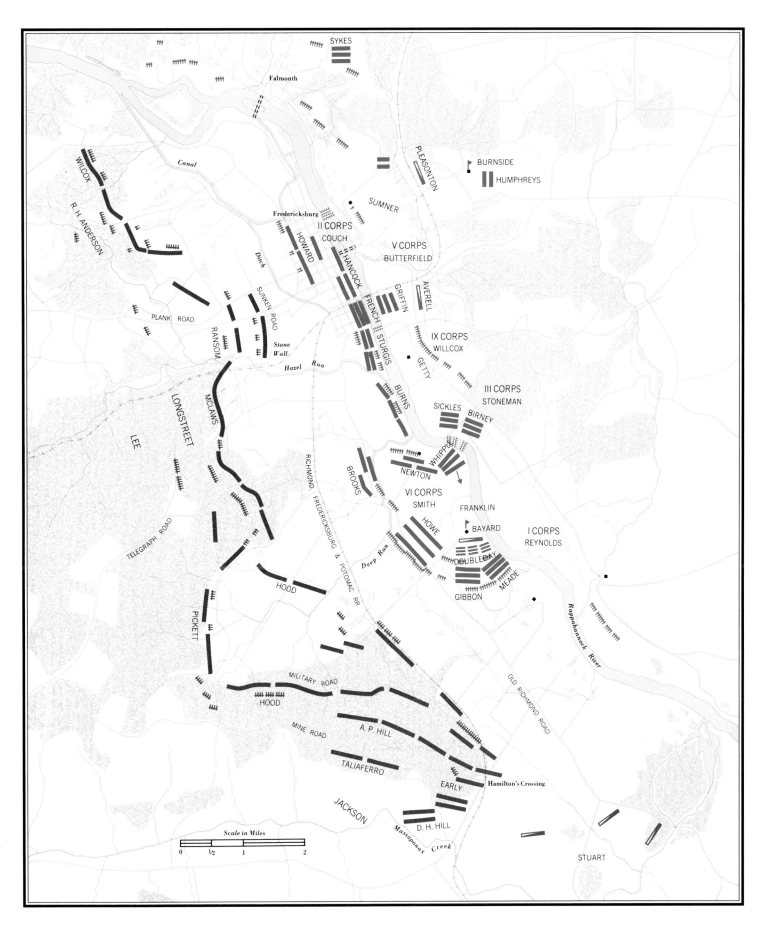

SYKES

Falmouth

Canal

BURNSIDE
HUMPHREYS

WILCOX

R. H. ANDERSON

PLEASONTON

SUMNER

Fredericksburg

II CORPS
COUCH

HOWARD

V CORPS
BUTTERFIELD

HANCOCK

Ditch

PLANK ROAD

SUNKEN ROAD

RANSOM

Stone
Wall

Hazel   Run

GRIFFIN

FRENCH

AVERELL

STURGIS

IX CORPS
WILLCOX

GETTY

LEE

MCLAWS

BURNS

III CORPS
STONEMAN

SICKLES   BIRNEY

LONGSTREET

RICHMOND, FREDERICKSBURG & POTOMAC RR.

BROOKS

WHIPPLE

NEWTON

VI CORPS
SMITH

FRANKLIN

BAYARD

I CORPS
REYNOLDS

TELEGRAPH ROAD

HOOD

Deep Run

HOWE

DOUBLEDAY

MEADE

GIBBON

PICKETT

Rappahannock River

MILITARY ROAD

HOOD

OLD RICHMOND ROAD

MINE ROAD

A. P. HILL

TALIAFERRO

EARLY

Hamilton's Crossing

JACKSON

D. H. HILL

Scale in Miles

Massaponax   Creek

0   ½   1   2

STUART

195

The 114th Pennsylvania Zouaves charge headlong into a Confederate counterattack at Fredericksburg, helping to save the Federal left from disaster after Major General George Meade's men retreated under fire from Jubal Early's division. Colonel Charles Collis, an Irish-born Philadelphian who had raised the Zouave regiment, rides with the colors among his troops, as his brigade commander, General John Robinson (left foreground) lies pinned under his dead horse. Collis, then only 24, received the Medal of Honor for this action.

Traffic Between the Lines

As the armies massed for battle along the Rappahannock River, Confederate and Union soldiers engaged in a lively if illicit trade across the river. The ill-supplied Confederates coveted coffee, sugar, overcoats and shoes—items Federals willingly gave up in exchange for Southern tobacco.

The Rappahannock presented no obstacle to determined and innovative traders.

Rigging a wire across the river near a burned-out bridge, men pulled items of exchange back and forth on a trolley. At a ford above Falmouth, men of the 4th Georgia and 8th Alabama waded through icy water holding haversacks stuffed with tobacco, which they swapped for treasured articles with men of the 4th New York.

A miniature trading fleet of rafts and makeshift boats also plied the waters of the Rappahannock, bearing goods from one side to the other. Invariably, Confederates would christen their vessels *Virginia*, after the ironclad known in the North as the *Merrimac*. And just as often, a craft on its return voyage would be relabeled *Monitor*, which won a strategic victory against the *Merrimac* in March 1862.

In time, the troops established rates of exchange for the most valuable commodities, coffee and tobacco. Enterprising Confederate soldiers would swap 10 pounds of tobacco, which brought $2.50 a pound, for one Federal overcoat. The overcoats were then sent south to Richmond, where each sold for a whopping $100.

On the north bank of the Rappahannock, Union pickets launch a shingle fitted with a paper sail and laden with a cargo of coffee. Confederates across the river wait to return the vessel with tobacco.

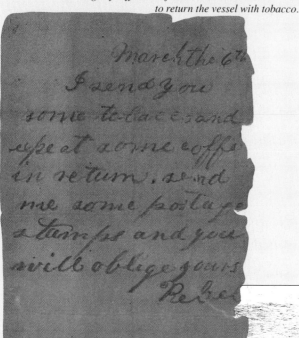

A Confederate's scrawled message, shipped aboard a small boat at Fredericksburg, requests coffee and stamps in trade. Officers on both sides generally overlooked such illegal bartering by the troops.

Federals and Confederates negotiate a trade of coffee for tobacco. Such deals reduced animosity between the two sides. A Confederate who swam the Rappahannock with a load of tobacco reported that the Federals greeted him with "no chaffing or bantering, only roistering welcomes."

Meade's Pennsylvania Division in the lead. Brigadier General John Gibbon's division supported Meade on the right, and the left flank was guarded by Major General Abner Doubleday's division. After marching downriver parallel to the Rappahannock for about 800 yards, the attackers faced right, crossed the Old Richmond Road and formed line of battle.

The fog lifted at about 10:00 a.m. to reveal a spectacular scene. "A slight but dazzling snow beneath, and a brilliant sun above, intensified the leaping reflections from fifty thousand bayonets," Confederate soldier J.H. Moore recalled. "Officers on restless horses rushed from point to point in gay uniforms. Field artillery was whisked into position as so many fragile toys."

As the Federals advanced across the plain, an aggressive young Rebel horse artilleryman, Major John Pelham, galloped down toward the flank of the Union lines with two guns: a Blakely rifle and a 12-pounder Napoleon. Pelham unlimbered his guns and opened fire on the densely massed troops. The lead Federal brigade faltered and came to a halt; Federal artillerymen responded. The Blakely was disabled, but the Napoleon redoubled its fire. Three times Pelham was instructed to withdraw, but only when his ammunition was exhausted did he gallop back down the lane and rejoin Jeb Stuart's division. His bold action had stalled the Union advance for more than half an hour.

Meade's men moved forward again. Confederate artillery opened on them when they were about 800 yards from the heights, tearing huge gaps in their ranks. The line kept advancing, pushing into the triangle of woods that had been left unmanned by the foe. Thousands of men poured through the gap, surged up the hill and stormed into Gregg's position. Many of Gregg's men, thinking there were Confederates to their front, had taken cover from the shellfire, with their arms stacked nearby.

As the South Carolinians leaped for their weapons, the befuddled Gregg dashed along the ranks on horseback and shouted for them not to fire, believing the attackers to be Confederate troops. A wild scramble ensued; many of the unarmed men were slaughtered; the rest fled in disarray. Gregg, a heavyset man in a general's uniform, was an easy target; he soon fell mortally wounded, a Minié ball through his spine.

Then the tide suddenly shifted. Early's and Taliaferro's divisions, held in reserve behind Gregg's position, came rushing through the woods to meet the Federals head-on. Meade's men were driven back down the hill, over the railroad embankment and out onto the plain.

General Gibbon's supporting attack surged up over the railroad embankment and charged into the woods. But the assault was slowed by bitter hand-to-hand fighting with General Lane's brigade, then driven back by a furious Confederate counterattack. For a moment it looked as though the Rebels would drive all the way to the river, but the grayclads ran short of ammunition and, unsupported, they were forced to withdraw.

Less than two hours after the first Federal infantry assault, both sides were back where they started. Franklin's divisions had lost 4,830 men, and Jackson's losses were 3,415. Late in the afternoon, Jackson decided to launch a counterattack and ordered a preliminary movement of artillery. But the movement provoked a furious response from Federal gunners, and seeing that daylight was waning Jackson reluctantly called off the assault.

While Meade and Jackson spent December 13 in a series of attacks and counterattacks that subsided into stalemate, Federal and Confederate forces several miles to the north were pitted in a vicious struggle that ended with one army reeling in defeat and the other celebrating one of its most impressive victories thus far in the war.

After the morning fog had lifted in Fredericksburg, Federal units began their advance on the Confederate positions on Marye's Heights. To reach this objective, they would have to cross a flat and open plain. About 200 yards from the edge of town lay a broad, water-filled ditch, spanned by three narrow bridges; the men would have to form columns and file across the bridges under heavy fire.

On the far side of the ditch, a low bluff offered some cover, and about 350 yards beyond the bluff there was a slight incline where men could get out of the direct line of fire by lying flat and hugging the ground. But elsewhere on the field, there was virtually no protection except for a few scattered houses along the way.

The key to the Confederate position was a lane at the foot of Marye's Heights that would be known lat-

Veteran Fighters of Lee's Legions

The determined-looking men portrayed here were all veterans of Robert E. Lee's Army of Northern Virginia, battle-tested at Fredericksburg and spoiling for further fights. Lee's force, smaller, hungrier and less well equipped than Hooker's Army of the Potomac, was nonetheless formidable: his troops were tightly disciplined, swift on the march, savage in combat, confident and devoted to their commanders. "There never were such men in an army before," Lee himself said. "They will go anywhere and do anything if properly led."

PRIVATE JAMES THOMPSON
Company B, 51st Virginia

PRIVATE GEORGE G. AYOCK
Company B, 30th North Carolina

CAPTAIN CHARLES J. GREEN
Company A, 47th Virginia

PRIVATE THOMAS FONDREN MCKIE
Company A, 11th Mississippi

PRIVATE JOHN D. MILLER
Company H, 3rd South Carolina

CAPTAIN ASHER W. GARBER
Virginia Light Artillery

PRIVATE OTTO KEAN
Virginia Light Artillery

SERGEANT PAGE M. BAKER
1st Louisiana Special Battalion

PRIVATE THOMAS JEFFERSON GOLDMAN
Company D, 44th Georgia

PRIVATE SIMEON CHESTERFIELD PAYTES
Company C, 9th Virginia Cavalry

PRIVATE JOSEPH ABSALOM HIGGINBOTHAM
Company I, 19th Virginia

er as the Sunken Road. The lane was protected on its forward edge by a stone wall four feet high. Troops standing in the Sunken Road could fire comfortably across the shoulder-high wall with minimum exposure to enemy rounds.

The Confederate division commander on Marye's Heights, Major General Lafayette McLaws, had deployed Brigadier General Thomas Cobb's Georgia brigade in the Sunken Road, and had stationed the 24th North Carolina, under Brigadier General Robert Ransom, in trenches that extended the line northward beyond the wall. McLaws had 2,000 men on the line, and 7,000 troops in reserve behind the ridge.

In addition, the Confederate infantrymen were strongly supported by artillery massed on the ridge behind them. The approaches to Marye's Heights were so thoroughly covered that when General Longstreet spotted an idle gun and suggested that it be pressed into service, his artillery chief, Colonel E. Porter Alexander, casually dismissed his superior's concern. "General," he said, "we cover that ground now so well that we will comb it as with a fine-tooth comb. A chicken could not live on that field when we open on it."

Shortly before noon, the Union's II Corps launched its assault. Brigadier General William French's division moved out for the Union attack with Brigadier General Nathan Kimball's brigade in the lead. The men started off in a tightly packed column and came under murderous artillery fire the moment they emerged from the cover of the town. A single shell killed or wounded 18 men in the 88th New York. But the troops closed up and pressed forward, trotting across one of the bridges toward the protective cover of the bluff on the far side.

There the division formed a line of battle, and fixed bayonets before advancing on the heights. Kimball's brigade, already cut up by the artillery fire, slogged grimly up the muddy slope until it was within 125 yards of the Confederate line. Suddenly, a sheet of flame flared from behind the stone wall. Another Confederate volley followed, and then another. Hundreds of Federal soldiers fell dead or wounded under the awful, almost continuous storm of lead. A few men moved to within 40 yards of the wall, firing, reloading and resuming their advance; a few others ran for cover among some houses nearby, but most reeled back from the searing blasts and

fell prone behind the incline, seeking cover from which to fire on the Confederate line. Within 20 minutes, a quarter of Kimball's brigade had been put out of action. Kimball himself was severely wounded in the thigh and had to be carried off the field.

French sent two more brigades forward, and they were blown back, "staggering as though against a mighty wind," said Private Eugene Cory, of the 4th New York Infantry. Now it was the turn of Major General Winfield Scott Hancock's division: Colonel Samuel Zook's brigade charged up the hill with speed and determination and was almost annihilated

Field glasses in hand, General Robert E. Lee, accompanied by General Longstreet (second from right) and several aides, watches the Confederate victory at Fredericksburg unfold from a hilltop near the lines.

by the Confederate fire. The survivors fell back to the incline, and Brigadier General Thomas Meagher's Irish Brigade came on at the double-quick, the men carrying a green flag and wearing green sprigs in their caps to celebrate their heritage. By chance, they faced a sector of the line held by the Irishmen of Colonel Robert McMillan's 24th Georgia Regiment. The Confederates recognized their countrymen by their green emblems, and someone exclaimed, "What a pity. Here come Meagher's fellows." Then the Georgians took aim and mowed down their fellow Irishmen.

In all, seven divisions were hurled against the enemy position at Marye's Heights, at a cost of about 7,000 casualties; but not a single Federal soldier reached the stone wall. In the battle as a whole, the Federal toll came to 12,535, compared with total Confederate losses of about 5,000.

Bitter cold descended on the plain that night. Some of the Federal troops were ordered to hold their positions, and other units remained pinned to the ground for fear of enemy fire. The thousands of wounded still lying on the ground suffered appallingly. They cried for help, for water, for their mothers and for death so piteously that an officer in their midst said "a smothered moan that seemed to come from distances beyond reach of the natural senses" rose up from the battlefield.

Burnside was distraught over the failure of the attack and the cost to his men. He spent the night visiting various units, conferring with their commanders and agonizing over what to do next. He returned to his headquarters and ordered his old command, the IX Corps, to prepare to resume the attack when daylight came, apparently intending to lead the advance in person. But his senior commanders were unanimous in their opposition, and he decided to withdraw the army across the river, leaving behind a force of 12,000 men to hold the town so there would be something to show for the enormous sacrifice. Then he concluded that it would be too dangerous to try to defend the town with such a small force, and on the early morning of December 16th, the last units were withdrawn.

But the army commander remained determined to renew the offensive. He resolved to move a short distance up the Rappahannock, then cross the river and circle to the south to get behind Lee. On January 20, 1863, he issued a proclamation: "The auspicious moment seems to have arrived to strike a great and

Swift Signals via Flag and Telegraph

First Position-or "Ready" First Motion-"One"-"1"

Second Motion-"Two"-"2" "Two-One" - "21"

"One-Two-One-Two"- "1212" "Three"- "3"- or-"Front"

A page from Albert Myer's Manual of Signals *shows part of his flag code. A dip of the flag to the left stood for the numeral 1, a dip to the right meant 2. Combinations of the numbers stood for letters; 21 equaled O, for example, and 1212 indicated P. A forward dip of the flag meant 3. A single 3 marked the end of a word, 22 the end of a sentence, and 333 the end of a message.*

On the eve of the Battle of Fredericksburg, General Ambrose Burnside deployed for the first time in history a military unit—the nascent U.S. Army Signal Corps—equipped with both flags and an electric telegraph for sending messages in the field. Stationed on hills overlooking the battlefield, observers used flags to relay information to Burnside's headquarters to the rear. At the same time, signalmen with Burnside flashed orders from the general over telegraph wires to command posts on his left and right flanks. The swift signaling methods—far faster than the dispatch riders had employed in the past—did not alter the course of this battle, but they would profoundly affect later Civil War campaigns and change the way future wars would be fought.

The founder of the Signal Corps was a sharply intelligent if irascible New York physician named Albert J. Myer. Shortly after graduating from Buffalo Medical College in 1851, Myer enlisted in the Army and served on posts in the Far West. He soon found himself more interested in signals than in surgery, and devised a system of simple flag wigwags.

Summoned to Washington at the outbreak of the Civil War, Myer set up a Signal Corps training school in nearby Georgetown, and began outfitting telegraph units that would accompany, in covered wagons, Federal armies in the field. Before the war's end, Myer's men strung thousands of miles of wire, helping coordinate the movements of huge forces, both on the march and in the heat of battle.

A Signal Corps officer and his men gather on the roof of Army headquarters in Washington, D.C. From here, messages were exchanged with stations in the field. Two of the men hold staffs topped with torches—oil-filled copper cylinders with cotton wicks—that were wigwagged for night messages.

mortal blow to the rebellion, and to gain that decisive victory which is due to the country." Then he formed the army in columns, and as a band played "Yankee Doodle," the men set off. The skies were cloudy that morning, but the air was filled with optimism.

Fog moved in at dusk; by dark, rain had begun to fall. The rain came down harder as the night progressed. By morning, it was falling in torrents, and the roads were dissolving into ribbons of mud. The pontoon and artillery trains became backed up in a two-mile long tangle, delaying the crossing of the Rappahannock all day. Wagons sank up to their wheel hubs, and artillery pieces became mired so deeply that neither 12-horse teams nor gangs of 150 men hauling on ropes could pull them out. Dozens of horses and mules died of exhaustion. The men slipped, foundered and fell sprawling, their shoes sucked off by the mud. As Burnside rode along the column, an irreverent teamster whose mules were hopelessly mired doffed his cap and said, "General, the auspicious moment has arrived."

The rain continued for nearly four days. By the time the storm abated, the army and its animals were worn out, and there was nothing to do but call off the movement and return to camp. Another Union offensive—later labeled the "mud march"—had ended in ignominious failure.

Burnside's officers condemned their commander. But General Hooker outdid them all, telling a newspaper correspondent that Burnside was incompetent and the Administration feeble. The country needed a dictator, Hooker said, and the sooner the better.

The enraged Burnside countered with General Order No. 8, one of the most remarkable and intemperate documents in the annals of the U.S. Army. In it, he condemned Hooker, charging him with "unjust and unnecessary criticisms of his superior officers" and recommending that he be dismissed from the service. Moreover, Burnside wrote that Generals Franklin and Smith, and various other officers critical of his leadership should be relieved or dismissed from the service.

The incensed general hurried to Washington and gave President Lincoln both the order and his resignation. The President must accept one or the other, he said. Lincoln concluded that the situation could not be saved, and regretfully prepared orders relieving Burnside of his command and reassigning his

*Late in January 1863, Federal infantrymen slog knee-deep
across a rain-swollen stream during the infamous "mud
march"—part of a botched offensive that Burnside thought
would give the Union a victory it so desperately needed
after the stunning loss at Fredericksburg. Of the torrential
downpour that lasted four days, a veteran wrote: "The bottom
literally dropped out of the whole immediate country." The men,
he added, were "wallowing, sliding and slipping at every step."*

grand division commanders. But the President insisted that Burnside's services were needed elsewhere and refused to accept his resignation from the Army. Burnside yielded, and later assumed command of the Department of Ohio.

To succeed Burnside, the President selected the obstreperous Joseph Hooker. The choice was a surprising one, but Hooker had one compelling asset—a reputation in the discouraged, defeat-weary Union as a fighting general. A West Point graduate, Hooker had served in the Mexican War, and had been brevetted for gallantry three times. He had earned a reputation as an aggressive commander in the Peninsular Campaign, and at Second Bull Run and Antietam.

He had come to be known as "Fighting Joe"—at least partly through a typographical error. During the Peninsular Campaign, a typesetter for a New York newspaper labeled a story about the action around Williamsburg: "Fighting—Joe Hooker." The tag was only to identify the story at the newspaper and was not for publication; it meant simply that fighting was going on and that Hooker was involved. But when the story was printed, the dash was inadvertently omitted, and the story was headlined, "Fighting Joe Hooker." The sobriquet stuck for the rest of his life.

President Lincoln accompanied the appointment of the new army commander with a letter to Hooker in which he explained that he had placed the general at the head of the Army of the Potomac with some misgivings. Hooker was a "brave and skilful soldier," he said, but had done "a great wrong to the country, and to a most meritorious and honorable brother officer," in his efforts to thwart Burnside.

The President said he had heard, "in such a way as to believe it, of your recently saying that both the army and the government needed a dictator," and he cautioned Hooker that "it was not *for* this, but in spite of it, that I have given you the command. Only those generals who gain successes can set up dictators. What I now ask of you is military success, and I will risk the dictatorship."

The army was in a deplorable condition when Hooker assumed command. The men had not tasted victory since Antietam the previous September; many had not been paid in six months; and they were falling sick by the thousands. Moreover, soldiers were deserting at an alarming rate. Those who remained in camp were either dejected or diseased, or both. Scurvy, dysentery and malnutrition were rife. The shortage of proper food was acute, and poor sanitation was a factor.

The newly appointed army commander set about improving the lot of his troops with energy and determination. By enforcing the regulations involving sanitation—requiring the use of proper latrines, regular bathing and frequent airing of bedding—and by improving rations, he quickly cut the sick call in half. Fresh bread, onions and potatoes were made available several times a week. At the same time, Hooker initiated measures to discourage desertion, granting regular furloughs and filling the empty hours of camp life with drills and instruction periods. The Congress, in the meantime, made arrangements to get the soldiers their back pay.

Hooker also revised his command structure. He dispensed with Burnside's grand division arrangement and ordered his seven infantry corps commanders to report directly to him. He detached the cavalry units from the infantry divisions and organized a separate cavalry corps under Major General George Stoneman. He also set up a Bureau of Military Information to compile and coordinate intelligence reports.

On the other side of the Rappahannock, the winter weather caused terrible suffering in the chronically ill-equipped and ill-fed Army of Northern Virginia. In January, the Confederate command was forced to impose a further drastic reduction in meat and sugar rations. By March, Lee lamented that there did not seem to be enough food to sustain the men, and each regiment was directed to send details to gather sassafras buds, wild onions and poke sprouts.

Another desperate shortage, that of shoes and proper winter clothing, was outlined by a staff officer in a letter to his Representative in the Confederate Congress. Of the 1,500 men available for duty in his brigade, the officer reported, 400 had no shoes. "These men, of course can render no effective service," he said, "as it is impossible for them to keep up with the column in a march over frozen ground."

The Confederates also were handicapped by an acute shortage of manpower. Lee's army, already heavily outnumbered at the Battle of Fredericksburg, was further depleted in February when Longstreet was dispatched with Major Generals George Pickett and John B. Hood to southern Virginia and coastal

Although Major General Joseph Hooker was Lincoln's personal choice to succeed Ambrose Burnside, the President had serious reservations about the impulsive West Point graduate taking over as head of the Army of the Potomac. "I much fear that the spirit which you have aided to infuse into the army, of criticizing their commander, and withholding confidences from him, will now turn upon you," Lincoln wrote in a letter dated January 26, 1863, telling Hooker of his appointment. The President concluded his missive with a final piece of advice, "Beware of rashness, but with energy and sleepless vigilance, go forward, and give us victories."

North Carolina to forage for provisions and defend railroad communications, thereby costing Lee the services of 13,000 troops and three of his most seasoned and reliable commanders.

With Hooker and Lee preoccupied by supply and organizational problems, there was little contact between the two armies during the winter months except for a few cavalry raids and skirmishes. The largest of these occurred near Kelly's Ford, 25 miles northwest of Fredericksburg, upstream from where the Rapidan River merged with the Rappahannock.

The raid was initiated when Federal Brigadier General William Averell, a division commander in General Stoneman's cavalry corps, went to Hooker for permission to take his horsemen up the Rappahannock, cross the river and drive off Confederate cavalry units reported to be in the area. This seemed to Averell to be an opportunity to test the new independent cavalry organization, and perhaps in the process change Hooker's opinion of troopers—scathingly expressed on one recent occasion when Hooker had asked, "Who ever saw a dead cavalryman?"

With Hooker's approval, Averell set out with six full regiments and portions of two others—3,000 cavalrymen in all—and a battery of artillery. The bulk of the horsemen arrived at Kelly's Ford on the Rappahannock on the morning of March 17. Along with dismounted troopers of the 16th Pennsylvania Cavalry, members of the 1st Rhode Island Cavalry splashed across the stream, gained a foothold and took 25 prisoners.

Word of the encounter reached the Confederate Brigadier General Fitzhugh Lee, a West Point classmate and rival of Averell, at Culpeper, 10 miles west of the ford. Lee rode forward and deployed his 800 men in a blocking position on the road between Kelly's Ford and Brandy Station, a small town six miles to the northwest. By chance, he was joined by the redoubtable Jeb Stuart, who was attending a court-martial in Culpeper, and the dashing young Major John Pelham, hero of the Battle of Fredericksburg, who was paying a call on a young lady at nearby Orange Court House.

Averell ordered some of his men to dismount and deploy behind a stone wall a mile and a half from the ford. Fitzhugh Lee directed a squadron of his cavalrymen to dismount and open fire on the Federals behind the wall. Stuart watched over the movement, and Pelham dashed forward in a mounted cavalry charge. The horsemen found a gate and poured through it to try to turn the Federal right. Pelham reined in his horse and shouted "Forward!" to the attacking horsemen. Just then a shell exploded, knocking him from his horse and wounding him with a sliver of metal in the back of his head.

Two cavalrymen placed Pelham across a horse and took him to the rear. His heart was still beating and he survived an ambulance ride to Culpeper. There, surgeons examined the head wound. But before they could do anything to help him, he drew a deep breath and died.

Shortly after Pelham was hit, a Federal counter-attack drove back the Rebels, but Averell ordered a cautious pursuit. When he learned that Jeb Stuart was in the fight, however, he lost any desire he might have had for further action. As he later wrote, he "deemed it proper to withdraw."

The engagement was notable on two accounts. The Federal cavalry corps in its first large-scale fight had demonstrated unprecedented spirit, and the engagement cost the Confederates dearly. They had lost 133 men, compared with 78 Federal casualties, and the death of Pelham deprived them of one of the Confederate army's most promising young officers.

As the spring weather dried the roads, there was mounting pressure on Hooker to resume the offensive. On April 11, the general informed President

Confederate artillerist Major John Pelham, killed at Kelly's Ford at the age of 25, was raised on an Alabama plantation, one of six sons of a physician. Pelham's bravery at Fredericksburg elicited a tribute from General Robert E. Lee: "It is glorious to see such courage in one so young."

At Kelly's Ford on March 17, the 1st Rhode Island and 6th Ohio ride headlong into the 4th Virginia (far left) in one of the war's first large-scale cavalry charges. The battle pitted two former West Point classmates against each other: Brigadier General William Averell and Brigadier General Fitzhugh Lee, a nephew of Robert E. Lee.

Lincoln that General Stoneman would launch the campaign with 10,000 horsemen of his cavalry corps. They were to cross the Rappahannock at least 20 miles upstream, then ride south. After fording the Rapidan they would get behind the Confederate army, severing its lines of communication.

Stoneman set out early on April 13 at a leisurely pace, sending ahead a brigade under Colonel Benjamin Davis. The brigade crossed the Rappahannock at Sulphur Springs, more than 30 miles northwest of Fredericksburg and beat back Confederate detachments guarding the fords. The skies then opened on the hapless horsemen and the Rappahannock rose alarmingly. Stoneman's main body set up camp a dozen miles north of the Rappahannock to await better weather.

The skies finally cleared on April 25, and Hooker decided to adopt a bold new strategy. The cavalry would go ahead with its mission to get behind Lee and cut his supply lines. But instead of waiting for Stoneman's troopers to complete their mission, Hooker would launch his infantry on a strategic envelopment of Lee's army. One third of his army—the V Corps under George Meade, the XI Corps under Oliver Howard and the XII Corps under Henry Slocum—would move up the Rappahannock and cross at Kelly's Ford. These units would then cross the Rapidan River. Meade's corps would double back toward Fredericksburg and clear the way for Major General Darius Couch's II Corps to cross the Rappahannock at Banks' and United States fords.

Couch was then to await further orders at the river, but the other three corps were to reunite 10 miles west of Fredericksburg at a rural crossroads called Chancellorsville—after a large red-brick, white-columned mansion there known as the Chancellor House. While all of this was going on, the VI Corps of Major General John Sedgwick and the I Corps, under Major General John Reynolds, would cross the Rappahannock downriver from Fredericksburg and feign a major attack against the right of Jackson's troops to confuse the Confederate high command.

The Federals began their movement on the morning of April 27. Three days later, the three corps had crossed the Rappahannock and the Rapidan, and were advancing to the southeast through the desolate expanse of scrub pine, oak and dense underbrush known as the Wilderness. By noon, Meade's corps had arrived at Chancellorsville. Slocum's corps reached that point by 2 p.m., with Howard's corps following, and Couch's corps preparing to cross the Rappahannock. Hooker arrived in the evening and issued an order proclaiming that "The operations of the last three days have determined that the enemy must either ingloriously fly or come out from behind his entrenchments and give us battle on our own ground, where certain destruction awaits him."

In the meantime, at Fredericksburg, Robert E. Lee was growing increasingly nervous. The Confederate commander was fully aware of the Federal army's numerical superiority, and to make matters worse, his scouts had been unable to divine where Hooker would strike next. The first sign came during the night of April 28, when Sedgwick's troops started pouring over pontoon bridges across the Rappahannock. Stonewall Jackson, visiting his wife and only child at Yerby House, near Hamilton's Crossing, was alerted to the move and rode to the front. Jubal Early deployed his regiments on the plain, and Jackson ordered A.P. Hill to move his division into position along the crest of the ridge to Early's right. As the day progressed, however, Sedgwick, although poised to attack, made no move. Lee received word that 14,000 men of Howard's XI Corps had crossed the Rappahannock at Kelly's Ford, and other enemy cavalry and infantry units were converging toward Chancellorsville. The threat to the Confederate left was growing and Lee decided to send Major General Richard Anderson's division toward Chancellorsville to cover the roads leading toward Fredericksburg.

When Sedgwick remained inactive on April 30, Lee concluded that the real threat lay to the west and issued orders for a general movement toward Chancellorsville. Jackson was instructed to leave only Early's division in front of Sedgwick's troops, and McLaws was ordered to leave a brigade behind on Marye's Heights.

Jackson's corps marched westward at dawn on May 1 to join Anderson near the Tabernacle Church. On arrival, he found Anderson's men busily digging in and preparing to face an army of superior numbers advancing toward them. That was not Jackson's way. He promptly ordered Anderson's men to pack their tools and prepare to attack. Advancing eastward out of Chancellorsville, Hooker had 70,000 troops marching on a collision course with 40,000 Confederates. God Almighty could not stop him from destroying the Rebel army, he said.

When Hooker's troops reached the far edge of the Wilderness, the vanguard exchanged fire with Confederate skirmishers. Jackson ordered Anderson's men forward, and they assailed the Federals' flanks. Hooker ordered up Hancock's division and they occupied a ridge in open country. Slocum was also holding a strong position, and Meade was advancing unmolested along the River Road.

The Federals so far had suffered little, and they held a strong position on high ground. Yet suddenly, Hooker ordered his astonished corps commanders to break off the advance and pull back to positions they had occupied the night before around Chancellorsville. His subordinates could not believe their ears. Couch was so incensed he went to the army commander's headquarters to protest, but Hooker was adamant. "It's all right, Couch," he said, "I have got Lee just where I want him; he must fight me on my own ground."

The debate over what triggered Hooker's stunning loss of nerve began at once. A few blamed it on alcohol, but most who were around Hooker at the time disagreed. They said he was not drunk, and some expressed the opinion that a drink or two might have improved his performance.

That evening, Generals Lee and Jackson met south of Chancellorsville, near an ironworks called Catherine Furnace. The two generals plotted an attack against Hooker's army. Lee ruled out an assault against the left flank because of the dense trees and underbrush. Two engineers were dispatched to reconnoiter the enemy center, around Chancellorsville.

Then Jeb Stuart rode up to report that Fitzhugh Lee's cavalry had scouted the Federal right flank. It was located about two miles northwest, along the road leading west from Chancellorsville, and was "in the air," meaning that, not anchored on any natural terrain feature, it was vulnerable. The engineers soon returned with a report that the center of the Federal line was invulnerable. The Federal right must be turned, Lee decided—and he left Jackson to figure out a way to do it.

Before dawn, Jackson dispatched his topographical engineer, Major Jedediah Hotchkiss, to gather information about roads from the owner of Catherine Furnace, Colonel Charles Wellford. Hotchkiss returned shortly with a map he had sketched that indicated a circuitous route to the Federal right flank; the route angled southwest and then northwest along the Furnace Road, Brock Road and Orange Plank Road. The two generals listened intently to the major, and Jackson suggested that he take his whole corps around by the concealed route and attack the Federal right flank, leaving only the divisions of Anderson

This map of the opposing forces at Chancellorsville on May 2 traces Stonewall Jackson's daring march parallel to the Federal front. Rear elements of Jackson's column were observed passing the Catherine Furnace ironworks, and two divisions of Major General Daniel Sickles' Federal III Corps attacked the column, taking several hundred prisoners. But the Confederate brigades of Generals James Archer and Edward Thomas turned and threw back Sickles. Jackson, his intention still concealed, reached the Union army's exposed right flank with the bulk of his corps and attacked the unsuspecting Federal XI Corps.

Seated on hardtack boxes in the woods near Chancellorsville, Generals Lee (left) and Jackson make plans to divide their forces and attack Hooker's Federals. Lee holds a map, drawn by Jackson's topographical officer, that charts the concealed route to Hooker's right flank.

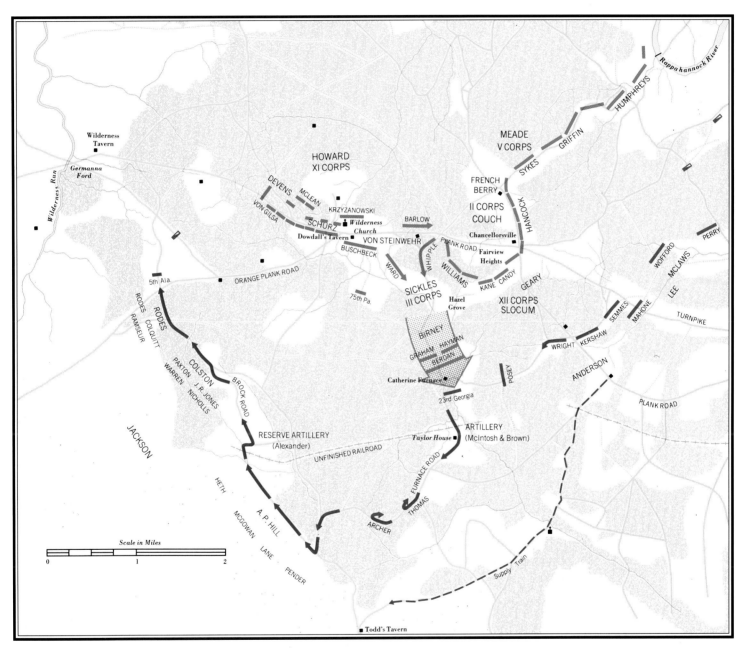

and McLaws behind to hold Hooker firmly in check.

What Jackson proposed was one of the most daring gambles of the war. With the Army of Northern Virginia outnumbered by more than 2 to 1 overall, and already divided between Fredericksburg and Chancellorsville, he was suggesting a further division of forces in the face of the enemy. Leaving only 14,000 men with Lee to face Hooker's 75,000 head-

on, Jackson would take 26,000 men through the woods to Hooker's right. His troops would have to march 12 miles; it would take all day, during which time they would be out of touch with Lee. Despite the danger, Lee's response was unhesitating. "Well," he said, "go on."

Shortly after 8 a.m. on the morning of May 2, Jackson's column came striding through the woods

past the crossroads where Lee was watching. The weather was warm; the men were in high spirits. Jackson rode in the vanguard, urging them on. "Press forward!" he called. "See that the column is kept closed. Press on, press on!"

Brigadier General David Birney, a Federal division commander, spotted the column from a ridge known as Hazel Grove, roughly a mile southwest of Chancellorsville, and sent couriers to Hooker. The army commander dashed off a message to General Howard, whose XI Corps troops were deployed on the right flank to defend against an attack from the south, telling him to be prepared for an attack from the west. The combative Major General Daniel E. Sickles requested permission to attack, and assaulted the rear of the Confederate column with two Federal divisions. The 23rd Georgia Regiment was overwhelmed, suffering 300 casualties, but regiments from Anderson's and A.P. Hill's divisions moved in and held the Federals off, while the rest of Jackson's men marched resolutely on.

At this point, Hooker suddenly changed his mind, jumping to the conclusion from the size of the column and the numbers of ambulances and wagons that the entire Confederate army was retreating. The assumption took hold among Hooker's officers on the right flank, and from that time on they ignored reports of Jackson's approach.

It was around 4 p.m. when the Confederate columns reached the road that led to the Federal flank and began to deploy for the attack in three lines extending a mile on either side of the road. Union General Howard had faced two regiments to the west, but most of the Federals on the flank were relaxing in the sun, laughing, talking and smoking. Some were lying on their knapsacks; others were slaughtering beef cattle. Their arms were stacked, and they were oblivious to their peril.

Jackson gave Brigadier General Robert Rodes the order to attack shortly after 5 p.m. Confederate bugles blared and the bloodcurdling Rebel yell reverberated through the forest, raising a wave of frightened rabbits, deer and foxes. The attackers dashed forward, ignoring the dense underbrush that ripped their clothes and flesh, and overrunning Federal pickets. The astonished men of two regiments that Howard had faced to the west leaped to their arms and fired three volleys, momentarily checking the

Confederate advance before giving ground. Other regiments broke for the rear without firing a shot. Jackson's men rolled inexorably toward Chancellorsville, driving before them brigade after brigade of the hapless XI Corps.

General Hooker was sitting on the porch of the Chancellor House, enjoying the balmy afternoon, when an aide jumped to his feet and shouted "My God! Here they come!" Panic-stricken soldiers along with ambulances and wagons burst into view. Hooker and his aides ran for their horses and galloped directly into the mob, trying in vain to stop the fleeing soldiers. A line was hastily formed, and artillery pieces were hurriedly massed to try to stem the flood of Confederate troops.

As darkness closed in, Jackson's attack began to lose its momentum. In the tangled thickets, officers lost contact with their men, units became scrambled and confused, and the Confederates had no choice but to halt and regroup. Jackson sent orders to A.P. Hill to move up, relieve the exhausted troops and prepare for a night attack. Then, a little before 9 p.m., he rode forward with several of his staff officers to scout the enemy lines. Moving slowly over unfamiliar ground in the moonlight, Jackson and his party worked their way close enough to the Federal positions to hear trees being felled and orders given, and then they started back.

As they approached their own lines, pickets of the 18th North Carolina took them for Federal cavalry and opened fire. Jackson was hit in the right hand and the left arm. One ball severed an artery just below the shoulder. Bleeding profusely and in great pain, he was helped from his horse. At length an ambulance was found, and he was taken to a field hospital at Wilderness Tavern. Chloroform was administered, and his left arm was amputated just below the shoulder. A messenger suddenly appeared. A.P. Hill had been hit; Jeb Stuart was now in command and wanted to know what he should do. "I don't know; I can't tell," Jackson said feebly. "Say to General Stuart he must do what he thinks best."

The Federals, hard hit and off balance, spent the night of May 2 reorganizing, felling trees and forming new defensive positions to stave off another Confederate attack. The new Federal lines formed a loop around Chancellorsville, jutting southwestward to the high ground at Hazel Grove. The arrival of Rey-

Sabers flashing at the Battle of Chancellorsville, the 8th Pennsylvania Cavalry under Major Pennock Huey charges down a narrow road to assist the beleaguered XI Corps, which retreated brigade by brigade under Stonewall Jackson's relentless attack. The gallant Pennsylvanians unwittingly rode straight into Brigadier General Robert Rodes' Confederate division. "We struck it as a wave strikes a stately ship," wrote a cavalryman. "The ship is staggered, but the wave is dashed into spray."

nolds' corps during the night brought the Federal strength at Chancellorsville to 76,000 men. They confronted 43,000 attackers, who were divided into two wings separated by almost a day's march. The situation demanded a strong counterattack, but Hooker was preoccupied with thoughts of defense and the safety of his army.

All through the night, Jeb Stuart, who had suddenly been thrust into command of Stonewall Jackson's corps, reorganized the Confederate lines to prepare for a renewed attack west of Chancellorsville. A.P. Hill's division, now commanded by Brigadier General Henry Heth, moved into the front line, while Brigadier General Raleigh Colston's division formed the second line. The Confederate position was greatly strengthened when the fearful Hooker unexpectedly ordered General Sickles to abandon the high ground at Hazel Grove and pull back closer to the Plank Road and to redeploy his artillery on Fairview Heights. The Confederate artillery commander, Colonel E. Porter Alexander, rushed 30 guns onto the crest of Hazel Grove, and began pouring a devastating fire into the Union lines.

At dawn, Heth's division descended upon the first line of Federal defense across the Plank Road west of Chancellorsville. Brigadier General Samuel McGowan's South Carolina Brigade drove the Federals back south of the road, but was halted by musket fire and forced back when a sea of Union soldiers crashed into the brigade's right flank.

Shortly before the retreat of McGowan's men, two North Carolina brigades, under Brigadier Generals James Lane and William Dorsey Pender, struck the Federal center on either side of the Plank Road. Lane's men brushed aside a green Maryland regiment and overran the log breastwork that constituted the Union second line, but heavy artillery fire and a Federal counterattack broke part of the brigade apart. Pender's brigade linked up with Brigadier General Edward Thomas' brigade to the north and overran two defensive positions before being driven back by a Federal countercharge.

Stuart now ordered Rodes' division to attack. As the men moved forward, some Confederate units were retreating, others were moving laterally to plug gaps in the line, and still others were clinging tightly to their hard-won ground. As a result, Stuart's lines became hopelessly confused. Instead of pushing for-

Confederate cavalry chief James Ewell Brown (Jeb) Stuart, who assumed command of Stonewall Jackson's corps after Jackson was wounded, displayed unexpected proficiency as an infantry commander. Robert E. Lee praised him for his "energy, promptness and intelligence" during the fight at Chancellorsville on May 3.

During the gradual withdrawal of Hooker's forces north from the Chancellorsville crossroads, a Federal battle line braves the onslaught of Jeb Stuart's men. "The crash of the musketry was deafening," recalled Sergeant Rice Bull of the 123rd New York. "We loaded and fired as fast as possible, but still they came on."

Major General Winfield Scott Hancock demonstrated both military skill and great bravery as overall commander of the rear guard that covered the Federal withdrawal on May 3. His corps commander, General Darius Couch, trusted Hancock completely; Couch's only order to Hancock was simply, "Take care of things."

ward, some of Colston's troops flung themselves to the ground and fired over the head of McGowan's brigade. The Stonewall Brigade, Jackson's old command, was ordered into the attack. The brigade went forward, came under a hurricane of fire and was forced to withdraw.

Farther north, Brigadier General Stephen Dodson Ramseur's Rebel brigade came up behind some of Colston's men who were cowering on the ground. Ramseur ordered the soldiers to get up and go forward, but not a man moved. His brigade clambered over them pushing forward and exposing its flank.

Jeb Stuart galloped up to the Stonewall Brigade, which was lying exhausted on the ground, and rode up and down exhorting the men to make yet another effort. The brigade pressed forward, closed the gap on Ramseur's right flank and launched an assault against Federal artillery positioned on the crest at Fairview Heights. But enemy gunners cut them to ribbons, mowing down a third of their number, and the survivors fell back.

Stuart's attack had achieved no breakthrough, but the assaults and the artillery fire from Hazel Grove were wearing the Federals down. At about 9 a.m., the Union right came under attack by two of Rodes' brigades, and the Federal line was driven back on both sides of the Plank Road. General Sickles sent an aide to ask Hooker for reinforcements.

Meanwhile, Hooker was standing on the porch of the Chancellor House with his staff, when a shell from a Confederate battery on Hazel Grove hit a pillar next to him. Part of the pillar struck Hooker on the head, knocking him senseless. Some of the officers thought he was dead, but he regained consciousness and rode off to the rear.

By now, the Confederates were within 500 yards of the Chancellor House, and General Darius Couch was working feverishly to steady the lines of his II Corps. Around 9:30 a.m., he received a summons from Hooker. "Couch, I turn the command of the army over to you," Hooker said, but at the same time, he instructed Couch to order a retreat.

Couch, General Meade and others were bitterly disappointed. They expected the army would attack at last. But it was not to be; with General Hancock's division acting as a rear guard, the Federals withdrew to a new perimeter around Chancellorsville.

Meanwhile, Hooker had sent an order to General

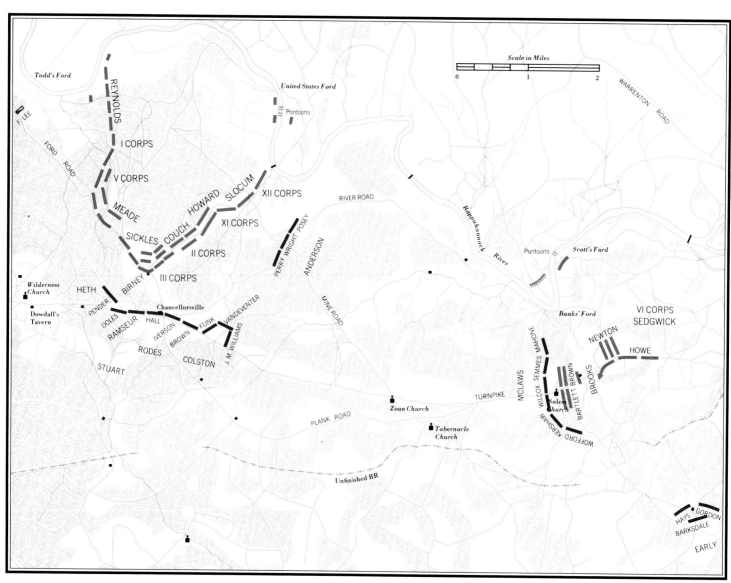

On the afternoon of May 3, the Confederate forces faced the numerically superior Federals on two fronts more than six miles apart. In heavy fighting at Salem Church, 10,000 troops under Major General Lafayette McLaws halted the advance of Major General John Sedgwick's VI Corps from Fredericksburg. Meanwhile, Lee's main force of 25,000 men confronted Hooker's 75,000 men north of Chancellorsville.

Sedgwick telling him to cross the Rappahannock at Fredericksburg late on the night of May 2 and march to Chancellorsville. The directive reflected a complete misunderstanding: Hooker seemed unaware that Sedgwick had long since crossed the river below Fredericksburg, and that the Confederates still had troops in the town. Not surprisingly, therefore, Sedgwick was dumbfounded when he received the orders at about 11 p.m. on May 2.

To follow the orders literally would have been absurd, requiring Sedgwick to recross the river below Fredericksburg that night, move north, throw bridges across at the town under fire, smash through Jubal Early's defenses—and only then march for Chancellorsville. And Hooker expected him to attack the rear of Lee's army at dawn.

Sedgwick decided that the only reasonable course open to him was to take the most direct route to Chancellorsville—the Old Richmond Road north from his bridgehead into Fredericksburg, then the Plank Road west toward Lee. Once again, Federal troops would be forced to advance up Marye's Heights, attacking the same stone wall on which the Army of the Potomac had been smashed in December. But it seemed the only way that Sedgwick could obey his commanding general.

On the morning of May 3, Sedgwick's men pushed out toward the stone wall at the foot of Marye's Heights and were hurled back by a storm of shot and shell. General Gibbon's division crossed the river from Falmouth and joined them. The Federals moved forward, and a column on the left advanced to within 50 yards of the wall before being forced back by a withering fire. Then they charged again and finally overran the position after fierce hand-to-hand fighting.

Sedgwick started his men for Chancellorsville, and Lee dispatched McLaws' division eastward to intercept them. The two forces collided at Salem Church, about four miles west of Fredericksburg. Sedgwick's men charged the Confederates, and came under heavy fire. Although the Confederate line was broken, a counterattack by Alabama regiments shattered the assault and the Federals scampered for the rear.

Two fresh divisions arrived in time for Sedgwick to stabilize his lines, but it was too late in the day to organize a new attack. "We slept in line that night with the dead of the day's battle lying near us," wrote Lieutenant Colonel Martin T. McMahon of Sedgwick's staff. Sedgwick decided to shift his troops northward toward the Rappahannock and form them in the shape of a horseshoe to cover his line of retreat across the river.

On the morning of May 4, Lee arrived at Salem Church to take command of three Confederate divisions converging there. He had intended to destroy Sedgwick's force, but it was late afternoon before everyone was in position for the attack. The assault was badly coordinated and failed to break through the Federal perimeter, but Sedgwick decided to pull his lines closer to the river. At midnight, Hooker summoned his corps commanders for a council of war. He took a vote as to whether they should withdraw or attack. Although a majority voted to attack, Hooker blithely ignored the result and ordered the entire army to pull back across the river. The withdrawal was completed by the morning of May 6, the Army of the Potomac showing much more skill in retreat than it had in battle.

The battle of Chancellorsville would come to be known as Lee's masterpiece. But while inflicting 17,000 casualties on the enemy, the Confederates had suffered 13,000 themselves, and the resources of the South were strained to the point where losses of that magnitude could no longer be sustained. Nor could the South sustain the loss of Stonewall Jackson.

Taken to a field hospital at Guinea Station, about 10 miles south of Fredericksburg, on May 5, Jackson seemed at first to be recovering from the amputation of his arm. But then his surgeon, Dr. Hunter McGuire, diagnosed pneumonia, an illness for which there was no medical help.

General Lee was informed of Jackson's turn for the worse, but he refused to admit that the illness might be fatal. "Tell him to make haste and get well, and come back to me as soon as he can," Lee said. "He has lost his left arm, but I have lost my right."

On Sunday, May 10, Jackson was informed that he probably would not live through the day. In midafternoon, while the room was filled with bright spring sunshine, he said in a firm but quiet voice: "Let us cross over the river and rest under the shade of the trees." And then he died.

Jackson's remains were taken to Richmond and lay in state at the Confederate Capitol. All the city's businesses were closed, and crowds of tearful mourners came to gaze at his coffin. The body was taken to Lexington, where he had taught at the Virginia Military Institute before the war, and he was, in the end, laid to rest in the shade of the trees.

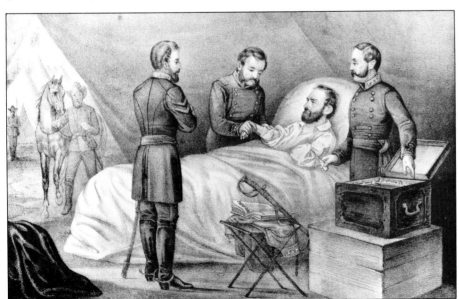

This fanciful engraving of the death of Stonewall Jackson shows him succumbing to his wound in a tent rather than in the small house near Guinea Station where he actually died. When news of Jackson's death was released, wrote Major Henry Kyd Douglas, "a great sob swept over the Army of Northern Virginia. It was the heart-break of the Southern Confederacy."

The Odyssey of the Wounded

Ambulances of the 57th New York Volunteers assemble in front of the regiment for a drill near Fredericksburg, Virginia, in 1864. The vehicles transported the wounded to field hospitals marked by yellow flags (left).

"I was wounded Saturday p.m.," Private Richard Ackerman of the 5th New York wrote his parents after taking a ball through the thigh in the Second Battle of Bull Run. "I laid on the battlefield for 48 hours and then rode in a government wagon for 48 hours more. Last night at one o'clock my wound was dressed for the first time."

Ackerman's ordeal was not unusual. When the war began, neither side had an efficient system for dealing with casualties. The first ambulances were bouncy two-wheeled carts known as "hop, step and jumps." Although these gradually gave way to more stable four-wheeled wagons, the jolting ride over rutted roads could mightily compound the agony of the wounded, and casualties would sometimes suffer contusions from the journey.

Rail and water transport to hospitals in the rear was usually comfortable by comparison. Yet wounded men were sometimes left stranded for days in railroad cars. On other occasions, casualties were packed tight aboard converted riverboats and coastal steamers that lacked even the most rudimentary medical equipment.

In spite of the enormous efforts made to improve hospital facilities during the war, many men who survived the trip to the rear later succumbed to their wounds. Private Ackerman wrote his parents, "Don't think it hard I had to be wounded, for I consider it a merciful dispensation of Providence I wasn't killed." But in late December 1862, four months after he wrote those words, Ackerman died of complications at a Federal hospital in Alexandria, Virginia.

Wounded soldiers recover from surgery on the grounds of a Federal field hospital near Fredericksburg, Virginia, in 1864.

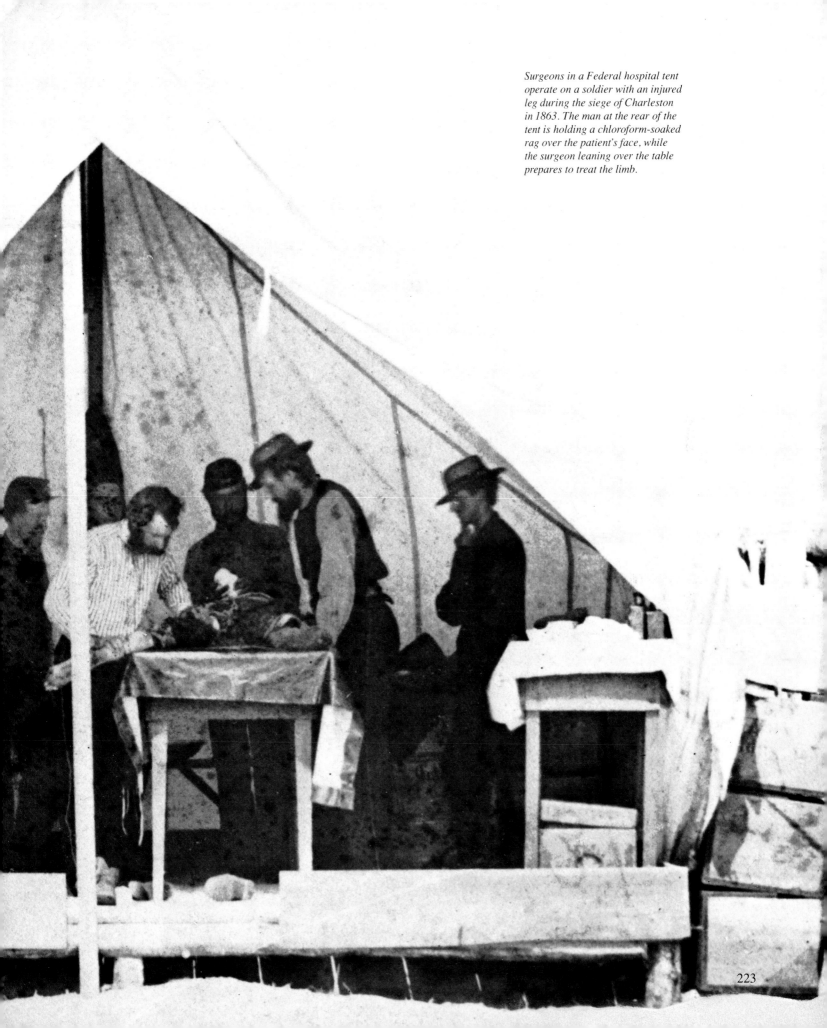

Surgeons in a Federal hospital tent operate on a soldier with an injured leg during the siege of Charleston in 1863. The man at the rear of the tent is holding a chloroform-soaked rag over the patient's face, while the surgeon leaning over the table prepares to treat the limb.

An ambulance convoy pauses in the journey to the large Federal hospital at City Point, Virginia, during the siege of Petersburg in 1864. Four-wheeled ambulances like these had folding bunks for wounded men. At times, the vehicles were so grossly overcrowded that patients were in danger of being smothered en route.

Federal soldiers wounded during the siege of Vicksburg crowd the decks of the Woodford, a former Mississippi riverboat commandeered to serve as a hospital ship. The steamer evacuated thousands of men to hospitals in Baton Rouge and New Orleans before it ran aground and sank in 1864.

Federal casualties of the Battle of Gaines' Mill await transport to the rear aboard flatcars near Richmond in 1862. A locomotive eventually arrived and hauled them to a field hospital at Savage's Station. Many of the men were later captured when the hospital was taken by the enemy.

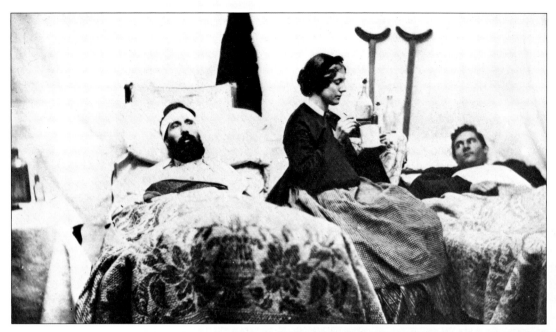

A nurse tends to two recuperating Federals at a hospital in Nashville, Tennessee. Hundreds of female nurses, most of whom were recruited by private relief agencies, served in the permanent hospitals of both sides. Though many lacked formal training, they helped bathe, bandage and comfort the wounded.

Patients lie abed under canopies of mosquito netting in a newly built wing of Harewood Hospital in Washington, D.C. The war spurred a massive construction program to cope with the large numbers of wounded. Such wards were usually one or two stories high and capable of accommodating 40 to 60 patients.

Rows of tents house the overflow of wounded on the grounds of Douglas Hospital in Washington, D.C. By late 1864, the Federal capital and environs had 25 large hospitals, and beds for more than 21,000 patients.

227

WAR ON THE MISSISSIPPI

*"Ships cannot crawl up hills 300 feet high, and it is that part of
Vicksburg which must be taken by the Army."*

REAR ADMIRAL DAVID DIXON PORTER, U.S. NAVY

By early June 1862, the Union governed the Mississippi River at both extremes of the Confederacy, but the center still remained in Rebel hands. Twenty miles north of Baton Rouge, Louisiana, the well-fortified town of Port Hudson controlled all traffic, and another 100 miles upriver, the even more formidable emplacements at Vicksburg, Mississippi, dominated the great waterway. Both strongholds would have to be captured before the Union could open up the river.

That summer the attention of Americans both north and south was drawn to Vicksburg. The bustling little city was one of the jewels of the South, with its own orchestra, a repertory theatre company that specialized in Shakespeare, three daily newspapers and a lecture hall. In the words of local diarist Lucy McRae, the "Queen City of the Bluff" was a place of "culture, education and luxury." Situated on a hairpin bend on the Mississippi River, it was also one of the war's most strategic points.

In addition to commanding the central Mississippi, Vicksburg also served as a critical transfer point for both rail and river traffic bound eastward toward the heart of the Confederacy. Moreover, one of the Confederacy's few rail links to the southwest was the Vicksburg, Shreveport & Texas Railroad. Most of the urgently needed beef and produce from Texas and Arkansas moved along this line. Perhaps as important, European arms, otherwise denied to the South by the Union coastal blockade, found their way into the Confederacy via Mexico, Texas and Vicksburg.

The capture of Vicksburg would not be an easy task, however, for it possessed formidable natural defenses in all directions. The city proper stood on a series of bluffs above the river. Fortifications along these precipices, as high as 300 feet, protected the city from attack by river. The surrounding territory, including the countryside across the river in Louisiana, was a maze of bayous and bogs, much of it impassable to troops on foot. And east of the city,

the line of bluffs abruptly fell away to a plain; the hillsides commanded the eastern approaches.

After the fall of New Orleans on April 26, Flag Officer David Glasgow Farragut had been ordered to steam north immediately. The Federal plan called for him to run the Vicksburg batteries and link up with a squadron of gunboats making its way downriver from Cairo, Illinois, under Flag Officer Charles H. Davis. Along the way, Farragut accepted the surrender of Baton Rouge, Louisiana, and Natchez, Mississippi, without even firing a shot.

But Vicksburg was another matter. When the Federal fleet arrived and demanded capitulation, the city's military governor declared, "Mississippians don't know, and refuse to learn, how to surrender." Taken aback by this response, Farragut was not prepared for an assault on what appeared to be a forbidding fortress. With no immediate solution in sight and suffering from ill-health, he decided to return to New Orleans, leaving only a small force behind to observe the city. Back in New Orleans, however, Farragut received a peremptory order from President Lincoln. The fleet, said the message, must return to Vicksburg immediately. On June 6, Farragut set out once again.

As it happened, Davis was still a long way from Vicksburg. His gunboats had begun their passage downriver from Cairo as planned, but en route, his flotilla had been severely mauled at Fort Pillow by a small fleet of Confederate rams—river steamers equipped with iron prows. Even though the Confederates subsequently evacuated Fort Pillow, the force of rams barred Davis from continuing south until he was joined by a fleet of Federal rams near Fort Pillow on May 25.

On June 6, as Davis' gunboats and the Federal rams approached Memphis, the Confederate flotilla launched a bold attack; but this time the Confederates were outmatched. The Battle of Memphis ensued; of eight Confederate craft that opened the fight, only

This sleeve patch, embroidered with an eagle perched on an anchor, identified U.S. Navy petty officers, including stewards and cooks, masters-at-arms, and boatswain's, gunner's and carpenter's mates.

The Federal ram Monarch *runs down the* General Beauregard *during the battle at Memphis on June 6, 1862. The crowds of pro-Rebel spectators watching the fight from the Memphis riverbank were staggered by the outcome. They had turned out to cheer on their champions, only to see the fleet destroyed.*

one escaped. Now unprotected, Memphis surrendered; finally, Davis' fleet was able to make its way downriver to await Farragut a few miles upstream from Vicksburg.

The second time Farragut arrived at Vicksburg, on June 25, he was better prepared with more troops and transports plus a fleet of mortar schooners that could easily lob their projectiles onto the heights. This time, his vessels blazed past Vicksburg's batteries, with numerous Federal shells accidentally falling amid the homes of Vicksburg. It was the first heavy bombardment the residents had endured, and the first of many to come. The Confederate defenses, however, were scarcely damaged; the powerful enemy batteries still commanded the river.

Three weeks later, on the nearby Yazoo River, the Federals were the victims of a phenomenal exploit. An unknown Confederate lieutenant named Isaac Newton Brown managed to take a partially completed riverboat called the *Arkansas*, and with some scrap iron and disassembled engines and guns, build himself a powerful little armored gunboat. Steaming downriver, Brown first routed a fleet of three Union vessels sent to deal with him, then entered the Mississippi itself and fell upon the huge Federal fleet anchored above Vicksburg. The fierce exchange that

followed was witnessed with indescribable delight by a large audience of townspeople; however, when the battered *Arkansas* finally drew into the Vicksburg docks, she brought with her the realities of war. The ram's decks and deckhouse were a horrendous scene of carnage—blood, hair, brains and bone fragments were everywhere. The *Arkansas* had suffered 12 killed and 18 wounded, and because she was a relatively small boat, the evidence was widespread and chilling. The Federals had fared worse; they counted 17 dead and 42 wounded. The jerry-built *Arkansas* had disabled one vessel and scored hits on many others; every wooden ship in Farragut's fleet had taken at least one hit.

Worst of all for the Federals was the humiliation they had suffered. Farragut reported the episode to Navy Secretary Gideon Welles "with deep mortification." The attack, Welles wrote in his diary, was "the most disreputable naval affair of the war."

The flurry of battles on the Mississippi in the spring and summer of 1862 demonstrated that the North had finally come to terms with a plan proposed in the early days of the war by the aged General in Chief Winfield Scott. In a letter the previous year to the then-rising star of the Union's armed forces, George

The brief career of the Confederate ironclad Arkansas *came to an end on August 6, 1862. After a successful surprise attack on the Federal fleet anchored in the Yazoo River, the* Arkansas *was ordered south to help retake Baton Rouge. En route, the vessel's overworked engines finally gave out; she was set afire by crewmen to prevent her capture by the approaching Federal gunboat* Essex *(left).*

Brinton McClellan, Scott had proposed that a Northern force travel down the Mississippi, clearing out Rebel support from towns like Vicksburg as it moved south. Combined with a sea blockade, the action would strangle the Confederacy into submission.

The scheme, said Scott, would achieve victory "with less bloodshed than any other plan." But the tedious, ungallant nature of the strategy sat badly with Northerners who clamored for a dramatic invasion of Virginia. Horace Greely, the fire-breathing editor of the New York *Tribune*, dubbed Scott's proposal the "Anaconda Plan," after the big South American constrictor snake. Although the plan had failed to find favor it was followed in spirit, and the significance it attached to the key river systems in the Western theater—especially the Mississippi, Tennessee and Ohio—became a key ingredient of the Union's developing military action: in its victories at Forts Henry and Donelson in February of 1862, and in the climactic struggle for Vicksburg the following spring.

While Confederate and Union forces were waging battle on the Mississippi and Yazoo rivers, Major General Ulysses S. Grant, who would play a key role in the effort to capture Vicksburg, was on the Tennessee-Mississippi border wondering about his future. Vicksburg was far from his mind. Since the Battle of Shiloh, everything had started to turn sour for him. His critics, including Major General Henry W. Halleck, commander of all Federal forces in the Department of the West, disparaged his performance on the battlefield. Stories circulated that Grant was a poor officer, and often a drunken one. According to his friend, Major General William Tecumseh Sherman, Grant thought of resigning that summer, but Sherman talked him out of it.

When, in July, Halleck was ordered to Washington to become general in chief of the Federal Army, he summoned Grant to Corinth, Mississippi, and said in parting, "This place will be your headquarters." This seemed to augur increased responsibilities for Grant, but Halleck's first act in his new role was to cut Grant's department, reducing it to about half its former area and half its former troop strength. In the end, Grant had about 100,000 men under him—the Army of the Tennessee and Major General William S. Rosecrans' Army of the Mississippi.

Instead of embarking on an offensive campaign, Grant spent the late summer and early fall of 1862 reacting to Confederate gambits. He had to retake his supply depot at Iuka, Mississippi, after the Confederates seized it on September 14. Then, early in October, Rosecrans won a ferocious defensive struggle at Corinth, which cost the Confederates 4,838 killed, wounded or captured—almost double the number lost by the Federals.

Meanwhile, Halleck had been searching for a commander to replace Grant in the West. No one wanted the job, however, and so on October 25, 1862, Grant was formally named commander of the Department of the Tennessee, which now included everything along the Mississippi River south of Cairo. As the new commander, Grant sent a proposal to Halleck in Washington: He wanted to stop protecting railroads and supply depots and begin to move south toward an objective worthy of some effort—Vicksburg.

Grant was not the only general with his mind set on taking the Mississippi stronghold. Even while he was preparing to march south Grant kept hearing rumors that another Federal commander—Major General John McClernand of Illinois—was raising an army north of the Ohio River to launch an amphibious attack of his own on Vicksburg. An officer whose competence fell far short of his vaulting ambition, McClernand had appealed directly to Lincoln with plans to capture the strategic port. The President, mindful of McClernand's home-state pop-

MAJOR GENERAL WILLIAM T. SHERMAN

ularity and not yet sure of Grant's ability, approved the proposal over Halleck's opposition.

By the time the official orders were issued to McClernand, however, Halleck had managed to whittle down the boastful general's independence. Grant would remain in overall command, and McClernand's operation would be "subject to the designation of the general-in-chief." Still, McClernand's role in the coming offensive against Vicksburg was left unresolved, prompting Grant to launch his attack on Vicksburg before his rival got there first.

Revising his plans for an overland assault on Vicksburg, Grant decided to split his army into two wings. General Sherman would command an expedition of 30,000 men to be transported by a flotilla under David Porter, promoted to Rear Admiral in July 1863, down the Mississippi to the mouth of the Yazoo. There the troops would debark for an assault at a place called Chickasaw Bluffs, just north of Vicksburg. To ease Sherman's task, Grant would continue his southward movement parallel to the Mississippi with the goal of diverting the attention of the Vicksburg defenders.

As often happens to commanders in the field, Grant

was meanwhile distracted from his military objectives by nagging administrative matters, including one that involved a member of his own family. The problem concerned the illicit trade in Southern cotton with Northern industries. Direct cotton trade between the Union and the Confederacy was, of course, banned, but a black market flourished, despite the efforts by Federal field commanders to stamp it out. One day, Grant's father, Jesse, turned up at his son's camp with some friends, the Macks. Grant welcomed them—until he discovered that the friends were cotton speculators hoping to use his father as a way of getting at the supplies in the general's jurisdiction.

Grant was incensed, and sent his father's friends packing. In addition, since the Macks, like many oth-

This fanciful engraving depicts William Tecumseh Sherman's troops storming Chickasaw Bluffs north of Vicksburg. In reality, the Confederate defenders under Brigadier General Stephen D. Lee stopped the Federals at the base of the bluffs.

er traders, were Jewish, the angry Grant issued an order that singled out Jews for expulsion from the area. He was ill-advised and offensive in the extreme. There was a howl of outrage from throughout the North until Lincoln instructed Halleck to cancel the order. Halleck commanded Grant to rescind his order, and the general immediately complied. The fuss abated and a vastly relieved Grant was finally able to turn his full attention to Vicksburg.

At the same time, the Confederates were making extraordinary efforts to improve their defenses in the Vicksburg area. Jefferson Davis had sent Lieutenant General John C. Pemberton, a southern-minded Pennsylvanian, to take charge of Confederate forces in Mississippi, and then had installed over him as commander in the West one of the South's premier officers, General Joseph E. Johnston. Pemberton conceived a double-barreled raid on the Federal rear: First, he ordered Major General Earl Van Dorn to descend with his cavalry on Holly Springs and cut Grant's supply line as the Union general moved south.

While Van Dorn was wrecking Holly Springs, Brigadier General Nathan Bedford Forrest, an unorthodox but highly effective cavalry officer, was leading his Tennessee cavalry brigade against the Federals near Jackson, Tennessee. In a series of engagements, he cut Grant's line of communications at a second point.

The two Confederate raids had a serious effect on Grant's situation. He was now caught in enemy territory without supplies, and he had to hasten back to Memphis the way he had come. He sent word to Sherman shortly before Christmas that his part of their two-pronged attack was no longer possible. But with communications in disarray, Grant's message arrived too late to stop the waterborne assault.

Sherman and Porter were hoping to fall without warning upon the Vicksburg defenses. "The essence of the whole plan," Sherman wrote, was "to reach

Vicksburg as it were by surprise." But the attempt at secrecy was doomed: Neither Grant nor Sherman knew that before the war a planter had installed a private telegraph wire along the west bank of the Mississippi River north of Vicksburg. At about midnight on Christmas Eve, the news flashed along that wire to Vicksburg that a Federal fleet was approaching the city from the north. Thanks to the warning, the Confederate field commander, Brigadier General Stephen D. Lee, had his army ready to meet the advancing Federal troops. On December 26, when Sherman landed on the south bank of the Yazoo four miles northwest of Chickasaw Bluffs, the Confederates numbered about 12,000 on the 10-mile line of bluffs above the Union troops, with another 13,000 on the way.

After marching slowly through swampy ground, the Federals approached the foot of the bluffs on December 28 and spent all day and night probing the Confederate defenses. The following day they began their attack after slogging through bog and bayou, drawing withering fire from the bluff's defenders. Captain William W. Olds of the 42nd Ohio described the scene: "As the storming brigade advanced it found itself in the center of a converging fire, a flaming hell of shot, shell, shrapnel, canister and minie balls. It would be vain to attempt any description of the noise and confusion of that hour."

The attack was a calamitous failure, costing 1,776 Federal casualties to 187 for the Confederates. Another attempt the next day farther upstream to capture Haynes' Bluff also failed; Sherman withdrew to Milliken's Bend on the west bank of the Mississippi. A few days later, in a letter to his wife, the disconsolate general provided a bleak summation of the recent events: "Well, we have been to Vicksburg, and it was too much for us, and we have backed out." To make his draught more bitter, Sherman received a long-delayed message from Grant acting on Washington's order that the command be turned over to McClernand.

Although this wasn't exactly the starring role that McClernand had envisioned, nonetheless he was glad to be back on stage. Taking over command on January 4, 1863, he seized upon a suggestion by Sherman to attack Fort Hindman, on the Arkansas River about 120 miles northwest of Vicksburg. Known to both Federals and Confederates as

Arkansas Post, the fort posed a threat to Federal communications on the Mississippi. It also had only 5,000 men defending it—an easy target for the 30,000-man-strong Federal force.

The Confederates at Arkansas Post fought gamely but on January 11 the entire garrison, along with 17 cannon and 46,000 rounds of ammunition, fell to McClernand's XIII Corps. The minor victory did little to ease Grant's reservations about McClernand, and yet he had no cause to relieve him of command. But one thing was certain: If Grant remained in Memphis, the field command in the Vicksburg assault would fall to McClernand. To Grant, that was unthinkable. On January 29, Grant traveled to

As part of General Grant's strategy to bypass Vicksburg, soldiers dredge a canal across a bend in the Mississippi River. Grant foresaw failure, but, he later wrote, "I let the work go on, believing employment was better than idleness."

Young's Point, Louisiana, just below Milliken's Bend, and took over direct command of the army in the field. The troublesome McClernand was now firmly in hand—at least for the time being.

Farragut had failed at Vicksburg, Sherman had failed, and now it was Grant's turn. During the next two and a half months he would launch no fewer than four amphibious operations aimed at capturing Vicksburg or bypassing it entirely. All were highly unconventional; although he was in a profession that worshiped precedent, Grant was always willing to try something new. He would refer to the attacks as "experiments," yet the general clearly hoped that at least one of the four would, in the end, succeed.

The first of the projects was a canal to cut across the mile-wide peninsula formed by the horseshoe bend of the Mississippi at Vicksburg. If a canal could be completed, the river might rush in and bypass Vicksburg entirely; in that case, Union shipping could do the same. Such a project had been attempted the previous June during Farragut's second Vicksburg expedition; however, an outbreak of malaria and dysentery among the troops had halted the work.

Grant was dubious about the canal, but the resumption of the project was dictated by Abraham Lincoln, a man with as strong a predilection for the unconventional as Grant himself. Grant obediently started work.

Now placed in charge of the renewed attempt, Sherman dismissed the operation as "a pure waste of human labor." The downstream end looked right into the muzzles of Confederate guns across the river; the upstream end was situated on an eddy, which would make it difficult for the river to flow readily into the canal. Still, the army did its best, hampered by the worst rains in memory and was, in fact, on the verge of completing the cut when the river rose, burst through a temporary dam and washed over the canal. When the water had subsided and the Federal crews returned to the canal, the Confederates began shooting at the dredges from across the river. That was enough for Grant, and he called off the project.

Meanwhile, another corps had been given a job that Grant estimated would involve less than a quarter of the effort the canal required. Forty miles northwest of Vicksburg lay Lake Providence, which had once been a bend in the Mississippi but now, because of a change in the river's course, lay a mile inland. However, the lake could be connected to the river again, and once in the lake, Union vessels might be able to pick their way through a chain of waterways to the Red River. That river, in turn, would lead them back to the Mississippi 250 miles below Vicksburg. Troops under Major General James B. McPherson set to work cutting a channel south of Lake Providence but soon floundered in a cypress-filled swampland. Dredging dragged on for two months without much progress, and Grant gave up on this experiment.

By now, Grant's attention was fixed 350 miles north of Vicksburg, where a waterway called the Yazoo Pass branched off to the east from the Mississippi River and led south to the Yazoo River. Once a popular alternate route for ships coming down the Mississippi, the pass had been blocked off at its entrance in the 1850s to provide protection from frequent floods. Grant realized that if Federal forces could descend the Yazoo and land north of Haynes' Bluff, they would be able to bypass the formidable Confederate river defenses there and attack Vicksburg from the east.

The first order of business was to destroy the levee at the pass entrance; which the Federal forces succeeded in doing on February 2. Moving downstream they encountered floating barricades of huge trees felled into the river by the Confederates. But a worse surprise was waiting at Fort Pemberton, where Major General William Loring's 1,500 Confederates commanded a narrow passage in the river. Repeated attempts to steam past the furious gunfire that emanated from the fort proved futile; the Federal force finally conceded defeat and returned back up to the Yazoo Pass.

The fourth of the bayou experiments took place near the southern end of the Yazoo River. Known as the Steele's Bayou Route, the plan was the brainchild of Admiral Porter. Vessels following the incredibly circuitous route would take five waterways and would travel 200 miles to wind up only 20 miles northeast of where they had started on the Yazoo River. Nevertheless, the route outflanked the Chickasaw Bluffs and Haynes' Bluff defenses north of Vicksburg and could carry troops into position for an attack on the city from the rear.

Like the earlier experiments, this one came to grief when the fleet was halted by an impenetrable tangle of willow limbs overhanging the route. To compound the woe, the Confederates got wind of the Union efforts and pounded Porter's ships with heavy fire. Porter sent a frantic message: "Dear Sherman," it read. "Hurry up, for Heaven's sake."

All four experiments had now failed. Confederates who had captured a Federal officer asked him about Grant's intentions: "Hasn't the old fool tried this ditching and flanking five times already?"

"Yes," replied the prisoner, "but he has thirty-seven more plans in his pocket."

The fact was, Grant had only one plan left. With the conclusion of the Steele's Bayou expedition the initial phase of the Vicksburg Campaign was over. It was

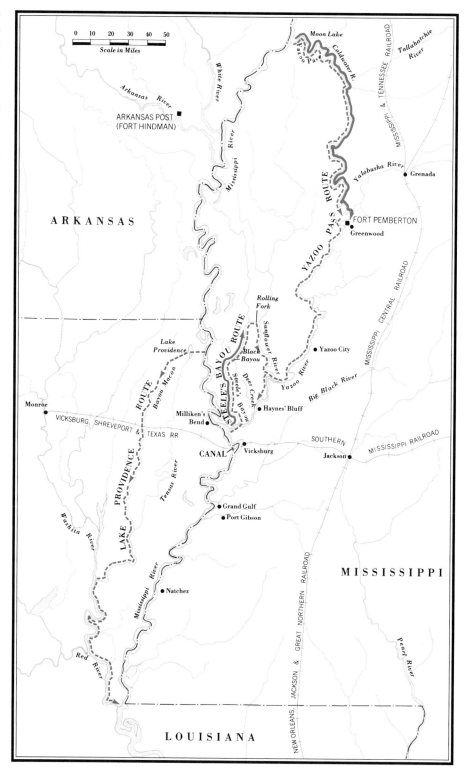

Benjamin H. Grierson, a colonel in the Federal cavalry, was a peacetime music teacher who much preferred playing his jew's-harp to riding a horse. But the 16-day raid he led through enemy territory from La Grange, Tennessee, to Louisiana's capital, Baton Rouge—guided only by a pocket map and a small compass—confounded the defenders of Vicksburg and gave the Union a hero on horseback.

now early April; the weather was growing warmer, and the time for experiments was past. For weeks, while the bayou adventures had been under way, Grant had been spending long hours at his headquarters near Milliken's Bend, puffing his cigar and thinking.

The best approach to Vicksburg, without doubt, had been the one he had begun back in December—down the Mississippi Central Railroad to the town's rear. But to try it again, Grant would first have to move his army from its camps on the Mississippi's west bank back up the river to Memphis, the terminus of the railroad. That movement was manifestly ill-advised for political reasons: Civilian morale in the North had never been lower. In the East there had been no Union success since the costly victory at Antietam the previous September, and there had been one terrible, bloody defeat, at Fredericksburg. All of Grant's experiments had been recognized in Washington as failures, and he was coming under increasing press criticism. The appearance of retreating toward Memphis was now out of the question.

That left only one approach. Grant must take his army still farther down the west bank of the Mississippi, well below Vicksburg. Then he must cross over and attack from the south. This time he would move with three corps, risking everything on a sole throw of the dice. And, finally, he would command the operation himself.

Grant's new plan was bold to the point of rashness. Facing an enemy that outnumbered him almost 2 to 1, he proposed an amphibious landing with no certain way of supplying his army after it was ashore, and with no practical route of retreat open to him if he was defeated. Sherman, his trusted friend, opposed the plan fiercely, as did General McPherson.

General Pemberton's Confederate army, in and around Vicksburg, totaled approximately 60,000 men. Grant had about 33,000 troops available for the landing; of those, fewer than one third could be carried by the Federal transport fleet in the first wave. All of Grant's plans depended on keeping Pemberton confused.

After shifting his men from Milliken's Bend to New Carthage, 20 miles south of Vicksburg on the west bank of the Mississippi, Grant searched for a landing site across the river. He chose a spot 20 miles farther downriver—Grand Gulf—which offered dry ground for the troops. From there Grant's men could

march northwest and flank Vicksburg. But Grant was determined to mask his intentions until it was too late for Pemberton to react effectively.

With masterful guile, Grant sent a division off to distract the Confederates at Greenville, on the east bank of the Mississippi 100 miles north of Vicksburg. He also dispatched a division of McPherson's corps from Lake Providence to join Sherman at Young's Point, northwest of Vicksburg.

By far the most important of his feints, however, was a large cavalry raid south from La Grange, Tennessee, through central Mississippi, an operation that would go down in history simply as Grierson's Raid, and which Grant later described as "one of the most brilliant cavalry exploits of the war." The venture, led by Colonel Benjamin H. Grierson, a cavalryman who—curiously enough—hated horses, magnificently served its purpose. Grierson and his 1,700 raiders rode through eastern Mississippi and Louisiana, capturing the almost total attention of John Pemberton at a time when much more important events were occurring right on his doorstep.

During Grierson's Raid, Grant had come up with yet another distraction for Pemberton: Sherman's corps made a feint against Vicksburg near Chickasaw Bluffs, and the energetic charade had a profound effect on the campaign. Pemberton had dispatched reinforcements in the direction of Grand Gulf to help meet the threat from across the river, but now he received an alarming message from his commander, who was north of Vicksburg: "The demonstration at Grand Gulf must be only a feint. Here is the real attack. The enemy are in front of me in force such as have never been seen before at Vicksburg. Send me reinforcements."

Meanwhile, the naval bombardment of Grand Gulf had begun. Despite the fact that Grant's various diversionary tactics had succeeded admirably, the Union fleet ran into stiff resistance from the 16 artillery pieces emplaced on a 50-foot-high promontory overlooking the river. As Grant watched from a tugboat in the middle of the Mississippi, Admiral Porter's fleet and the Confederate batteries pounded each other for five hours. Grant then went aboard Porter's flagship for a consultation. They had to find a new place to land, with dry ground at the bank and a dry route back to Grand Gulf. That evening soldiers abducted a slave from the east bank and brought him to headquarters. He pointed out a good landing spot: the village of Bruinsburg, eight miles downriver. It was high and dry.

The next day, April 30, troops were put ashore, unopposed, at Bruinsburg. General Grant was jubilant. "I felt a degree of relief," he wrote "scarcely ever equalled since." He was far from victorious, however: "I was now in the enemy's country, with a vast river and the stronghold of Vicksburg between me and my supplies." But Grant was a fighting man, and now at last he could fight. "I was on dry ground on the same side of the river with the enemy. All the campaigns, labors, hardships and exposures that had been made and endured were for the accomplishment of this one object."

The Union troops marched 12 miles inland to the little town of Port Gibson, where Confederate defenders made a brave stand in rough territory with ravines and heavy undergrowth. Grant's army rolled through inexorably, rendering Confederate fortifications at Grand Gulf untenable. The Rebels abandoned Grand Gulf on May 7, and Grant's beachhead was now secure.

Now that Grant was safely across the river he faced the vexing problem of supplies. He planned to send a corps downriver to help General Nathaniel Banks take Port Hudson and then establish a supply line running north from New Orleans. But Banks had suddenly embarked on his own campaign west of the Mississippi. In addition, Grant had another problem: Since the landing he had collected all the vehicles he could find nearby, and the resulting supply train clogged the road from Grand Gulf. This, Grant was convinced, would invite chaos.

His solution to the supply problem revealed a genius for the unconventional and a firm confidence in his men. In order to move with maximum speed, the army would operate independently of supply lines. The men would have to forage, but Pemberton would have no supply trains to hit. In a message to Sherman, Grant outlined his unorthodox strategy: "I do not calculate upon the possibility of supplying the army with full rations from Grand Gulf. I know it will be impossible without constructing additional roads. What I do expect, however, is to get up what rations of hard bread, coffee and salt we can, and make the country furnish the balance."

An ordinary general might have headed straight for Vicksburg. But Grant realized that besieging Vicksburg immediately would expose his rear to attack from Confederates gathering at Jackson. He decided to hit Jackson first, cutting the railroad that supplied Pemberton. Speed was all-important in preventing the Confederates from concentrating their forces. He marched his army north to get between the defenders of Vicksburg and the Confederates at Jackson; two Rebel brigades were already there, and two more had been sent by General Johnston.

General Pemberton could not decide whether to stay in Vicksburg or to venture east and fight. Trying to do both, he moved cautiously out of the town with about 20,000 troops, and left 10,000 men behind. Concentrating his forces near the railroad town of Edwards Depot, 13 miles east of Vicksburg, he waited for Grant's attack. Meanwhile, he sent a brigade of 2,500 men commanded by Brigadier General John Gregg to the town of Raymond, about 15 miles west of Jackson. Pemberton warned Gregg to look for a Federal feint in his direction, but predicted that Grant's main attack would come at the Big Black River, which blocked the way to Vicksburg. Thus Gregg would be in a perfect position to strike Grant's flank and rear.

Pemberton did not suspect that Grant was marching hard not for Big Black and Vicksburg but for Jackson. McPherson's 10,000-man XVII Corps was in the lead—and Gregg's understrength brigade was directly in its path. Early on the morning of May 12 they clashed. With thick woods for cover, Gregg was able to hold off the Federals, and at one point it seemed as if the attack would crumble. Then Major General John A. Logan, commander of McPherson's 3rd Division, appeared on the scene. Nicknamed "Black Jack," and regarded by his troops with awe, Logan spurred his black horse into the midst of his wavering line. With what one soldier called "the shriek of an eagle," Logan rallied the men and launched a counterattack. Decimated by volleys in front and flank, Gregg's Confederates retreated toward Jackson.

The residents of Jackson, meanwhile, were about to welcome a distinguished visitor, General Joseph E. Johnston. Four days earlier in Tennessee, he had received a telegram from Confederate Secretary of War James Seddon ordering him to "take chief command of the forces, giving to those in the field, as far

Sewn by women of Vicksburg for Company 1 of the 28th Mississippi Cavalry, this flag was carried throughout the campaign by Lieutenant Sid Champion, on whose farm the Battle for Champion's Hill was fought.

as practicable, the encouragement and benefit of your personal directon."

Johnston now found himself in the backwash of defeat. Gregg's weary men were straggling into town; Federals were on the outskirts. Pemberton was at Edwards Depot, cut off from Jackson by Union forces so that Johnston had great difficulty communicating with him. After a bloody rear-guard action, the Confederates abandoned Jackson to the Federals on May 14. That night, Grant slept in the same hotel room that Johnston had used the night before. But Grant had no intention of remaining in the Mississippi capital. It was time to strike at his real target.

In this endeavor, he now had a stroke of luck. A Federal spy, hired as a Confederate courier, had been selected by Johnston to carry a message to Pemberton. The spy had brought the message to General McPherson, who now showed it to Grant. The message instructed Pemberton to rendezvous with Johnston's force at the town of Clinton for a cooperative effort to trap General Sherman's force. Pemberton was halfway to his goal when the Federals, forewarned, intercepted his army at a hill on the farm of a man named Sid Champion.

Pemberton had 23,000 men at Champion's Hill to face the 32,000 Federals under Generals McClernand and McPherson. Sherman's corps was en route from Jackson, and Grant had galloped ahead to take command of the battle. At 10:30 a.m, the combative Brigadier General Alvin P. Hovey sent his two Federal brigades in a headlong charge up Champion's Hill, where Pemberton had hastily improvised some defenses. On the Confederate left, the line was stretched so thin that some regiments were separated by as much as 300 yards. Taken by surprise, the Confederates gave way.

Driving the enemy before them, General George F. McGinnis' Federal brigade crested the hill and came face to face with half a dozen Confederate artillery batteries. Just before the guns spewed out their lethal charges of canister, McGinnis ordered his regiments to fall prone. The iron balls whistled harmlessly overhead, and before many of the Confederate gunners could reload or limber up, the blue ranks were upon them. Captain Samuel J. Ridley's Mississippi Battery managed to get off a last round of double-shotted canister that tore scores of Federals to pieces, but the 11th Indiana waded into the Confederates with bayonets and rifle butts, and captured the guns. Ridley fell with six wounds, and later died.

By 1 p.m. the Confederate left was crumbling. Realizing that his army faced disaster, Pemberton issued a frantic call for reinforcements, who launched a fierce counterattack against Hovey's troops on Champion's Hill. Screaming the Rebel yell, they struck with what one Federal called "terrific fierceness," and soon it was Hovey's bluecoats who were falling back.

Grant ordered the nearest troops at hand, two brigades from XVII Corps, to rush to Hovey's aid. As the 5th Iowa moved up, Captain Samuel Byers saw scores of wounded men—"almost whole companies"— streaming down off the hill. The men did not seem demoralized, Byers recalled. "Some of them were laughing, and yelling at us: 'Wade in and give them hell!' "

Approaching the summit with the Federal reinforcements, Byers saw "a solid wall of men in gray, their muskets at their shoulders blazing in our faces and their batteries of artillery roaring as if it were the end of the world. For over an hour we loaded our guns and killed each other as fast as we could."

Sergeant Charles Longley of the 24th Iowa marveled that in the thick of battle a kind of madness gripped the men: "Every human instinct is carried away by a torrent of passion, kill, kill, KILL, seems to fill your heart and be written over the face of all nature." Soldiers on both sides fired the 40 rounds in their cartridge boxes and then scrabbled among the dead for more. On the Federal right flank atop Cham-

Climbing into a hail of Minié balls and grapeshot on May 22, 1863, a sergeant of the 22nd Iowa advances to plant his regiment's colors atop the Confederate breastworks of Fort Beauregard at Vicksburg. The Union attackers were ultimately driven back after suffering their heaviest losses of the campaign.

pion's Hill, the men of the 34th Indiana were in their first big fight. Some of the soldiers, badly shaken, were starting for the rear when General "Black Jack" Logan appeared on the field with what one soldier called "the speed of a cyclone." When the adjutant of the 34th protested that "the Rebels are awful thick up there," Logan roared, "Damn it, that's the place to kill them—where they are thick!" The men of the 34th rallied, and Logan led them forward.

As the afternoon wore on, the defense of Champion's Hill collapsed, and the Confederates, as one officer put it, were "rushing pell-mell from the scene of action." It had been the bloodiest and most decisive engagement thus far in the Vicksburg Campaign. Grant reported 2,441 casualties, Pemberton 3,839. Each side had lost some 400 men killed outright.

To get his troops back to Vicksburg, Pemberton had to cross the Big Black River, 10 miles west of Champion's Hill. As a cover for the retreat, earthworks had been erected on the east bank near the town of Bovina, where the Southern Mississippi Railroad crossed the river. This was Pemberton's last hope of delaying Grant's march on Vicksburg, and he made his position a strong one. But as McClernand's men approached the defenses just after daybreak on May 17, they were full of confidence, while the outnumbered Confederates, many of them still groggy with sleep, were sick of fighting.

The attack was placed in the hands of Brigadier General Michael Lawler, an Irish-born battler of awesome repute: "He is as brave as a lion, and has about as much brains," said a reporter. Galloping back and forth, the 250-pound general deployed his four regiments of Iowa and Wisconsin men at the northern end of the Confederate line and, without waiting for orders, launched a bayonet attack. The exhausted, dispirited Southerners were in no condition to resist. Pemberton, who had ridden up from Bovina just in time to see the end of the battle, ordered his men to fall back to Vicksburg, 12 miles to the west.

With his enemy reeling, Grant ordered four bridges constructed across the Big Black and pushed his men westward. Sherman had now arrived from Jackson, and Grant set out with him to the north of Vicksburg, to establish a base there on the bluffs, which the Confederates had recently abandoned. Both men were so eager, said Grant, that they gal-

loped far ahead of their troops. At last they stood on the bluffs, where, Grant wrote, "Sherman had the pleasure of looking down from the spot coveted so much by him the December before."

Just then, Sherman turned to Grant and made a speech that so impressed Grant that he recalled it distinctly 25 years later. Until that minute, Sherman said, he had doubted the wisdom of Grant's strategy. "This, however," he said, "was the end of one of the greatest campaigns in history," even if Vicksburg should somehow elude capture.

It was a triumphant moment for the Federal forces, and an unspeakably gloomy and bewildering one for the Confederates—not only for the defeated soldiers but also for the stunned citizens of Vicksburg. It was a Sunday no one in that town would ever forget. Rumors of the defeats had spread, and clusters of people gathered on corners after church. No one had any real news, but all suspected the worst. At first, just a few exhausted men drifted through the streets. And then, wrote Mary Loughborough, wife of a Confederate staff officer, "in all the dejected uncertainty, the stir of horsemen and wheels began. Straggler after straggler came by, then groups of soldiers worn and dusty with the long march."

Pemberton still commanded a powerful force of 30,000 men—fewer than Grant's 45,000, but more than enough to defend Vicksburg. And Johnston had about 20,000 troops near Jackson. Furthermore, most of the 10,000 troops Pemberton had left behind in Vicksburg were fresh. These men—the divisions commanded by Major Generals Martin L. Smith and John H. Forney—had been manning the defensive line to the south of town. Now they marched into the city, past the beaten and bedraggled soldiers, to bolster the threatened sections of the line to the north and east. According to Mrs. Loughborough, the men "swung their hats, and promised to die for the ladies—never to run—never to retreat."

When Grant attacked on May 19, he received a rude welcome—in 48 hours an astonishing transformation had occurred among the Confederates. Protected by seven miles of defense works anchored at each end of the river, strengthened by fresh troops, the Rebels had swiftly recovered their spirits and their effectiveness. Grant ordered an assault with all his forces—McClernand on the east, McPherson and

Sherman on the north—but the men had great difficulty advancing through the thick underbrush, felled trees and steep ravines. Soon, they were pinned down by Confederate fire.

Captain J.J. Kellogg, with the 113th Illinois, said he could see "the very sticks and chips, scattered over the ground, jumping under the hot shower of Rebel bullets." His men were pinned down all afternoon in canebrakes. As darkness fell and provided cover, Kellogg's regiment fell back along with the other units that had been similarly pinned down. Grant had lost 942 men, Pemberton 250. It was now clear what the Federals were up against. "This is a death struggle," Sherman wrote his wife after the battle, "and will be terrible."

Grant kept his men busy for the next two days preparing siegeworks. A carefully coordinated assault was set for 10 o'clock on the morning of Friday, May 22. Before the infantry attack, Grant ordered an artillery barrage from every battery in position. At 10 a.m., "as if by magic," recalled Confederate General Stephen D. Lee, "every gun and rifle stopped firing. The silence was almost appalling." Breathless, the Confederates waited. "Suddenly," said Lee, "there seemed to spring almost from the bowels of the earth dense masses of Federal troops, in numerous columns of attack, and with loud cheers and huzzahs, they rushed forward at a run with bayonets fixed, not firing a shot, headed for every salient along the Confederate lines."

Among the charging Federals was the 21st Iowa of General Lawler's brigade. The regiment's objective was the formidable Railroad Redoubt, which guarded the passage of the Southern Mississippi through the town's eastern defenses. Regimental Adjutant George Crooke recalled, "It was a tornado of iron on our left, a hurricane of shot on our right. We passed through the mouth of hell. Every third man fell, either killed or wounded." Eventually survivors from several units gained a foothold on the redoubt, but the Federal success was short-lived—the 30th Alabama mounted a counterattack that cleared the parapet.

Suddenly, out of a pall of smoke, came a lone blueclad figure, Private Thomas H. Higgins of the 99th Illinois, carrying the Stars and Stripes. "At least a hundred men took deliberate aim at him," a Texas private recalled, "but he never faltered. Stumbling over the bodies of his fallen comrades, he continued to advance." Awed by such suicidal courage, some Texans began shouting, "Don't shoot at that man!" while others cried, "Come on, you brave Yank!" Higgins carried his flag right up to the Confederate line, where he was pulled inside the works and captured. Word of his deed spread through the Confederate ranks, and that night he was brought before an admiring General Pemberton. Later, Higgins would be awarded the Medal of Honor, with a citation based in part on the testimony of his Confederate foes.

By now, Grant's attack was floundering all along the line. In some cases soldiers refused to advance, despite the curses and entreaties of their officers. Those regiments that did go forward were pinned down in front of the Confederate works under a scorching sun. For the Federals, the attack on Vicksburg on May 22 had been the bloodiest battle of the campaign. Grant's losses amounted to 3,199 men, 502 of whom had been killed. The Confederates had suffered fewer than 500 casualties.

As the sound of firing died down among the tortured Vicksburg hillsides that Friday, Grant sat on his horse whittling a piece of wood. It had been a savage day and a grueling week, and the Federal troops were still outside the fortifications of the river port. A newspaper reporter heard Grant say quietly: "We'll have to dig our way in."

The Union ring around Vicksburg was 12 miles in length, and Grant's 50,000-man force was stretched thin. In fact, though Pemberton wrote Johnston on May 29 that escape from Vicksburg was impossible, two of the eight roads leading out of town were virtually unguarded by Federal troops. That situation did not last long. General in Chief Halleck, who had treated Grant with icy reserve a few months before, now began eagerly to comply with his requests for reinforcements to help strengthen the Union's hold on the river port. Grant soon had more than 70,000 men in his command. In this iron grip, a Confederate soldier observed grimly, "a cat could not have crept out of Vicksburg without being discovered."

Grant proceeded to lay siege to Vicksburg. As he put it, his strategy was simply to "outcamp the enemy" until their supplies gave out. He also intended to apply constant pressure: Artillery bombarded the Confederates around the clock, and the Union infantry kept pushing their lines closer to the town.

Confederates behind a parapet at Vicksburg hurl lighted artillery shells down on Federal attackers in June 1863. The Federals, who had dug a trench to within 20 yards of the works, fight back with a weapon rarely used before in the war—a hand grenade. Among the primitive grenades employed was the three-pound, dartlike type above, which detonated on impact.

Troops were sent out each night to dig approach trenches, or saps. These were constructed in the traditional zigzag pattern, to prevent the enemy from shooting straight down their length. The Federal forces inexorably pressed forward, until the lead trenches were within a few yards of the Confederate earthworks. At one point, wrote Captain Samuel Byers of the 5th Iowa, "our lines were so close together that our pickets often had a cup of coffee or a chew of tobacco with the Rebel pickets at night. Drummer Bain, of my company, had a brother among the soldiers inside Vicksburg. One night he met him at the picket line, and together they walked all through the beleaguered town."

A favorite meeting place between the lines was an abandoned house that had a good well. There was a severe water shortage in both armies, and thirsty pickets from the two sides would congregate there. Sometimes they became engaged in heated political arguments, but when the discussions grew too vehement the groups would break off—as one man said, "to avoid a fight on the subject."

By mid-June, more than 200 Union cannon were shelling Vicksburg from land while Admiral Porter directed frequent bombardments from the river. The targets of the Federal guns were unquestionably military, but it often seemed to the town's civilian inhabitants that they themselves were the chief targets. The Confederate soldiers in trenches and behind breastworks were well protected; the civilians were more vulnerable, and shells fell all about them. "The general impression is that they fire at the city," wrote Emma Balfour, a doctor's wife, "in that way thinking that they will wear out the women and children and sick; and General Pemberton will be impatient to surrender the place on that account."

The people under bombardment were ill-prepared to endure it, and there was scarcely any relief. Very early in the siege, the Vicksburgers concluded that there was no safety in their houses, and they began burrowing into the hillsides. By the end of the siege, roughly 500 caves had been dug in the yellow clay hills of Vicksburg. Federal soldiers began calling Vicksburg "Prairie Dog Village." Although some people used the caves simply as bombproofs, many lived in them permanently. The temporary shelters, one visitor observed, might be "no larger than a fireplace." But the permanent refuges could be almost

luxurious: many-roomed dwellings equipped with furniture brought from the houses, and with rugs covering the dirt floors.

Even in the best of circumstances, however, cave life was far from pleasant. For some people, the sense of confinement was even worse than the menace of falling shells. "Sometimes," said a man interviewed by Mark Twain after the war, "the caves were desperately crowded, and always hot and close. Sometimes a cave had twenty or twenty-five people packed into it; no turning room for anybody; air so foul, sometimes, you couldn't have made a candle burn in it. A child was born in one of those caves one night. Think of that; why, it was like having it born in a trunk."

Horror stories proliferated about the effects of the bombardment on the residents, and whether true or not, these tales helped undermine morale. Mark Twain was told of a man who was shaking hands with a friend when an exploding shell suddenly left him holding a disembodied hand. The diarist Mary Boykin Chesnut, in faraway Richmond, heard about a three-year-old girl who was struck by a shell: "There was this poor little girl with her touchingly lovely face, and her arm gone."

Despite such accounts, the danger to the inhabitants of the town was more apparent than real. Fewer than a dozen civilians were known to have been killed during the entire siege, and perhaps three times that number were injured. Still, thousands had to endure the torment of living day after day under siege.

The people of Vicksburg expected a rescue attempt at any time. And so did Grant. Joseph E. Johnston, encamped at Jackson, was reportedly raising an army of between 30,000 and 40,000 men, and he worried the Union commander. Johnston, however, faced a cruel dilemma: Although his forces had been strengthened, and were aching to fight, Grant's army still outnumbered Johnston's and Pemberton's together. "Johnston evidently took in the situation," Grant wrote long afterward, "and wisely, I think, abstained from making an assault on us because it would simply have inflicted loss on both sides without accomplishing any result."

In late June, Grant's engineers tried to blast a gap in the Confederate defenses. Soldiers with coal-mining experience were put to work digging a tunnel toward the Confederate entrenchments northeast of

A Confederate soldier and two women in a Vicksburg lane shrink in horror at the sight of a Federal shell with a sputtering fuse. "While comparatively few noncombatants were killed," one resident wrote, "all lived in a state of terror."

town. In only two days, the Federals excavated a gallery 45 feet long; from it, three smaller tunnels radiated out another 15 feet directly under the Confederate redan north of the road to Jackson. On June 25 these tunnels were packed with 2,200 pounds of gunpowder. However, the Confederates above the tunnels had heard the sound of digging and had surmised what was happening. When the charges went off, most of the Confederate troops had already pulled back to a new line.

When Brigadier General Mortimer D. Leggett's Federal brigade charged into the crater made by the blast, they encountered heavy cannon fire. For three days of savage hand-to-hand fighting and grenade attacks, the two sides struggled over the crater, but the Federals had to fall back to their own trenches.

On July 1, the Federals exploded another mine beneath the same redan. It did considerably more damage to the fortifications than the previous attempt; but the Federal officers were now more cautious, and they concluded that the blast had not been devastating enough to justify another assault.

In any case, it was growing increasingly clear—to both the Confederates and the Federals—that the fall of Vicksburg was only a matter of days. Like the people of Vicksburg, the Confederate soldiers were cramped, exhausted and hungry. The troops had been getting inadequate rations since the siege began. The men who retreated to Vicksburg were receiving only one third of the meat and two thirds of the cornmeal that regulations prescribed. And shortages of such staples as salt and coffee had plagued everyone in Vicksburg for months.

A British observer, Lieutenant Colonel James Fremantle, had noted in early May that Mississippians were drinking "a peculiar mixture called Confederate coffee, made of rye, meal, Indian corn or sweet potatoes." Salt was so hard to obtain that Vicksburg residents who owned smokehouses had pulled up the floors to extract the salt left from the meat-curing process over the years. Women went into the fields and gathered tender cane shoots to cook for their children. The one item that was in fairly good supply was peas. Soon after the siege got under way, soldiers began eating a bread made of ground peas, and the civilians followed suit. It was awful—either rub-

Under the command of Major General John A. Logan (right), the 45th Illinois charges into a vast crater blasted out of the Confederate earthworks by a Federal mine on June 25. Confederate Brigadier General Louis Hébert reported that his soldiers had anticipated the explosion and that it created "no dismay or panic among those defending the line."

bery or hard as rock, and in either case foul-tasting.

When all the beef, pork and lamb had disappeared, townspeople and soldiers alike turned, with great hesitation, to other meat. Chaplain William Foster saw some soldiers butchering "what I at first thought was beef." Not until he took a second look at the carcass did he notice "a head with long ears." It was a mule; some people also tried horse flesh. As the siege wore on and hunger spread, several observers noted that dogs—which earlier had run through the streets howling during every bombardment—had all but disappeared, along with cats. A shortage of water was another serious problem, despite the proximity of the great river. The Mississippi was too filthy to drink, and most water supplies were drawn from a limited number of wells and springs, whose capacity was soon strained by the presence of so many soldiers.

As the siege wore on, morale in the town began to droop noticeably. Said Dora Miller, a Unionist trapped in Vicksburg with her husband: "I have never understood before the full force of these questions—what shall we eat? what shall we drink? and wherewithal shall we be clothed?"

The plight of the troops was just as bad. By the end of June, the Confederate soldiers' ration had been reduced to only one biscuit plus a couple of mouthfuls of bacon per day, and Federal soldiers, calling across the trenches, were twitting the hungry Rebels about the arrival of their new general—General Starvation.

The Federals, meanwhile, had accepted a new general of their own. Major General E.O.C. Ord replaced the troublesome General McClernand, who had finally given Grant the justification he needed to relieve him of duty. During the Vicksburg siege, McClernand had continued treating the war as a showcase for his ambitions. He missed no opportunity to claim credit for himself, warranted or not, and his posturing and near-insubordination had earned him powerful enemies throughout Grant's army.

But when he gave a Memphis newspaper a copy of a general order he had distributed to his troops after the May 22 assault—an order full of boasts of his superior tactics and brilliant deeds—Grant could tolerate him no longer. On June 18 he wrote an order relieving McClernand from command and sent him back to Illinois to await further instructions. John A. McClernand would not be seen again in the Army of the Tennessee.

With the Confederates' will to resist visibly weakening, Grant decided to launch another all-out assault on the morning of July 6. By an odd coincidence, General Johnston, at last convinced that he must try something, began during the first week of July to move toward Vicksburg. His intention was to attack Grant on July 7.

But events inside Vicksburg were now moving faster than either general's plans. On July 1, Pemberton sent a message to his division commanders: "Unless the siege of Vicksburg is raised or supplies are thrown in," he wrote, "it will become necessary very shortly to evacuate the place. You are, therefore, requested to inform me with as little delay as possible as to the condition of your troops." The response was unanimous: Not one of the four commanders thought that a successful evacuation was possible. The reason was not lack of food, Pemberton wrote later; it was simply that the men were exhausted.

There was only one course now open to Pemberton. On July 3, a day of scorching heat, he sent a message to Grant under a flag of truce, asking for an armistice so that terms of surrender could be negotiated. Grant's representative replied that only unconditional surrender was acceptable. The next afternoon Pemberton and Grant met for a parley, as hundreds of soldiers watched, lying silently on the earthworks. It was a stiff, uncomfortable encounter. The generals shook hands, but Pemberton was uneasy and bitter, clearly hating every moment of the ordeal. Grant still insisted on unconditional surrender, but he was beginning to consider the difficulties involved in transporting 30,000 prisoners. He decided to offer the Confederates parole—they would be released if they signed an oath promising not to fight again until Federal captives were freed in exchange.

Sometime after midnight, Pemberton sent Grant a message accepting his terms. Grant, sitting in his tent with his son Fred, read the note and spoke quietly to the boy. "Vicksburg has surrendered," he said. It was the 48th day of the siege.

When the Federal soldiers arrived in Vicksburg, their behavior was impeccable. "No word of exultation was uttered to irritate the feelings of the prisoners," wrote the Confederates' Sergeant William Tunnard in some wonder. "On the contrary, every sentinel who came upon post brought haversacks filled with provisions, which he would give to some famished Southerner with the remark, 'Here, Reb, I know you are starved nearly to death.' "

Colonel Samuel Lockett, Pemberton's chief engineer, later remembered that the only Federal cheers he had heard that day came from a Union outfit that raised a shout "for the gallant defenders of Vicksburg."

The fall of Vicksburg was greeted with shock and grief in the South. July 4, 1863 marked the turning point of the Civil War, for on that same day, in the East, Robert E. Lee had retreated after three days of battle at Gettysburg. General Josiah Gorgas, the Confederacy's chief of ordnance, wrote in his diary: "It seems incredible that human power could effect such a change in so brief a space. Yesterday we rode on the pinnacle of success—today absolute ruin seems our portion. The Confederacy totters to its destruction."

On July 9, the Confederate commander at Port Hudson, having learned of Vicksburg's fall, surrendered the garrison. The Mississippi River was at last open to Union shipping along its entire length. On July 16, the unarmed cargo steamer *Imperial* arrived at New Orleans flying the Stars and Stripes, having left St. Louis eight days earlier. The following month, Abraham Lincoln, speaking on the progress of the war, summed up the year's achievement along the Mississippi in a few felicitous words that rang with triumph and satisfaction. "The Father of Waters," he said, "again goes unvexed to the sea."

Confederate guns high above the Mississippi River at Port Hudson, Mississippi, pummel Admiral David Farragut's fleet. At far left, the Federal side-wheeler, Mississippi, *is afire. On July 9, 1863 the town surrendered; the Confederacy's final fortress on the Mississippi was no more.*

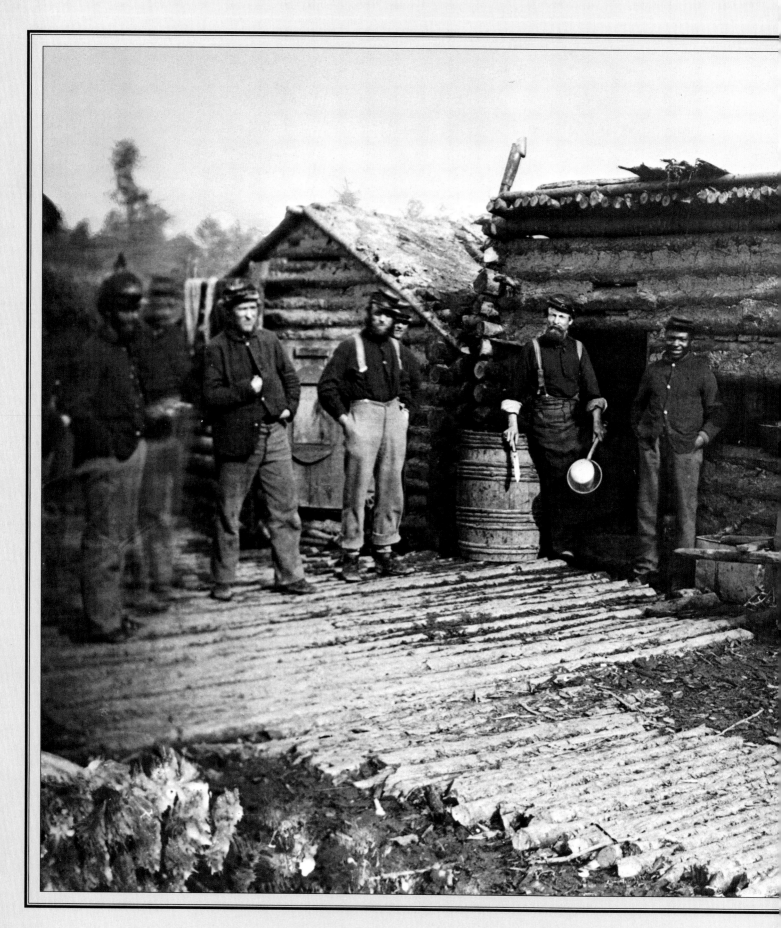

BIDING TIME BETWEEN BATTLES

"I am now very comfortably situated for the winter," a Confederate private wrote his mother in 1863, "having a very nice chimney attached to my tent, and everything that tends to make this unhappy life pleasant and agreeable." Not all were so fortunate, but millions of fighting men North and South made the best of life in camp, finding what comfort they could amid the hardship and tedium of soldiering.

In summer the troops slept in canvas tents, often so cramped that when one man rolled over, the rest had to follow suit. Some Confederates lacked shelter of any kind; they rigged open-air beds by heaping straw or leaves between two logs. In autumn, when the men took up winter quarters, those who could find wood built crude huts, laying split logs on the earth floor and fashioning bunks with mattresses of pine needles. In the absence of canvas or logs, men sought protection from the cold by excavating what they called "gopher holes" in the sides of hills or ravines.

When not drilling or standing guard, the troops read, played cards and wrote letters. In winter they might stage spirited snowball fights, the opposing units arrayed in battle formation with colors flying. Soldiers even made sporting use of a common pest, picking lice and racing them on patches of tent canvas or the flat sides of canteens.

Yet the war was never far away, and the men who had tasted battle grew to cherish their peaceful interludes in camp. Snug in winter quarters near Morristown, Tennessee, in 1863, a Confederate soldier damned his marching orders as "the demon of all our ease and happiness."

As his messmates look on, a Federal soldier takes time out from chopping firewood beside a mud-daubed winter hut near Falls Church, Virginia, in February 1863. The company cook—or "dogrobber," as he was often called—stands beside a former slave, hired as cookhouse servant.

251

Company A of the 5th Georgia Volunteers and their black camp servant lounge before a wall tent in this damaged photograph, taken at Augusta, Georgia, in 1861. The letters CR on the front of the tent stand for Clinch Rifles, the company's informal name.

Seated in the shade in church pews, Federal troops pass the time in camp writing letters, while a fellow soldier mends his clothes. Soldiers carried sewing kits called housewives and took pride in their skill; one boasted of patching his trousers "as good as a heap of women would do."

254

Beneath an arbor, a Federal soldier receives a haircut from an amateur barber. After long campaigns, the men looked forward to such amenities; one Confederate recalled that "the luxury of a shave completed the restoration of a man to decency."

In this rare photograph, Federals attend a Negro minstrel show, one of the most popular forms of entertainment among troops in camp. The band consists, from right to left, of a tambourine player, a banjo player, two guitarists and a minstrel rattling a pair of rib bones in each hand.

Confederate artillerymen play cards beside a tree at their picket post on the Stono River near Charleston in 1861. At left, four slaves prepare a meal in a kettle.

Officers of the 164th New York fish and loll along Pope's Run near Sangster's Station, Virginia, as three Federal sentries guard the railroad bridge above.

GETTYSBURG

*"The struggle was almost hand-to-hand. There was
no wavering or shadow of turning; it seemed as if the last man
would there find his allotted ounce of lead."*

CAPTAIN GEORGE W. VERRILL, 17TH MAINE, IN THE WHEAT FIELD

The leading Confederates appeared as ghostly shapes in the drizzly dawn of July 1, 1863. Lieutenant Marcellus Jones, in charge of pickets for the 8th Illinois Cavalry, spotted the spectral figures as they approached a stone bridge three miles west of Gettysburg, a farm town in southeastern Pennsylvania. Once they reached a range of 700 feet, he fired at a mounted enemy officer, but without visible result. Then, as the eerie gray column shook out into a line of skirmishers a mile and a half wide, Jones prudently withdrew. Without knowing it, he had just discharged the first shot in a military encounter that would swell into a terrible three-day battle, one in which 160,000 Americans would struggle for supremacy within 25 square miles of ground. Years later, long after silence had claimed the blood-soaked countryside, Gettysburg would be remembered. It was the crucial and agonizing turning point in the fortunes of the Confederacy.

The campaign that had brought General Robert E. Lee and his Confederates to Gettysburg was dictated by the same considerations that had prompted his disappointing incursion into Maryland nine months earlier. Now, however, the situation was even more urgent because of worsening supply problems in war-ravaged Virginia. By taking Pennsylvania, Lee would have access to the rich farmlands of that state.

Before marching northward, Lee had exercised the sad imperative of replacing Stonewall Jackson in an effort to carry out a long-needed reorganization. Then, instead of having two cumbersome corps, each comprising about 30,000 men, he divided his army into three smaller and more manageable units.

The I Corps remained under the solid command of James Longstreet, who at that time was in an uneven state of mind. Although he believed that Lee's invasion plan was appallingly risky, he agreed—as he later wrote—on the condition that the campaign be "offensive in strategy but defensive in tactics," forcing the enemy to give battle when the Confederates were in a strong position. Longstreet assumed that Lee had accepted his stipulation; eventually, circumstances would prove him wrong.

Jackson's II Corps was taken over by feisty Lieutenant General Richard Ewell. After losing a leg in the Second Bull Run campaign, Ewell had been absent for nine months. Now, equipped with a wooden limb, he was, presumably, ready to fight again.

To lead the newly formed III Corps, Lee chose a major general he regarded as "the best soldier of his grade." Although Ambrose Powell Hill was indeed a fierce fighter, his impetuous nature had more than once landed him in trouble. How he would respond to higher responsibility remained to be seen.

In addition to this central reorganization, Lee also strengthened the cavalry command of J.E.B. Stuart, who became the preening possessor of five brigades totaling 9,536 men. On the morning of June 8 at Brandy Station, a whistle stop near the Rappahannock River a few miles north of Culpeper, Virginia, Stuart passed this superb force in review before Lee, who afterward wrote to wife: "Stuart was in all his glory." Yet before another day went by, Jeb Stuart would be embarrassed beyond endurance.

Even as Stuart's men returned to their encampments after the grand review, about 11,000 Federal troopers under the Army of the Potomac's cavalry chief, Brigadier General Alfred Pleasonton, moved silently into the woods on the opposite side of the Rappahannock. They had been sent by General Joseph Hooker, commander of that army, with instructions to "disperse and destroy" Stuart's force.

At dawn on June 9, three Union cavalry brigades, and one of infantry, forded the Rappahannock four miles northeast of Brandy Station for a frontal assault

In this depiction of the sort of close combat waged at Brandy Station in Virginia, a Union cavalryman draws blood with his saber, battling over a highly coveted trophy, a regimental flag. A trooper of the 1st New Jersey Cavalry recalled that one guidon changed hands six times during the battle, ending up back with the Federals.

This field glass belonged to Brigadier General Richard B. Garnett, C.S.A., killed at Gettysburg July 3, 1863. Years later his sword was recovered in a pawnshop. No trace of his body was ever found.

against Stuart. A little later, after a delay caused by one of its two divisions becoming lost in the woods, an even larger Federal force splashed across the river five miles downstream and swung around to attack Stuart's right flank and rear.

Stuart was drinking his morning coffee when he heard the rattle of small-arms fire. He was caught completely by surprise. But he rallied quickly, and what ensued was the largest cavalry battle ever waged on American soil, a wild, swirling struggle fought largely for possession of Fleetwood Hill, a commanding north-south ridge that rose about a half mile northeast of Brandy Station.

Typical of the frenzied action was the experience of Adjutant Marcus Kitchen of the 1st New Jersey, who was spurring to the assistance of his fallen regimental commander when two Confederates set upon him. "The first one fired at me and missed," Kitchen recalled. "Before he could again cock his revolver, my saber took him in the neck. The blood gushed out in a black-looking stream; he gave a horrible yell and fell over the side of his horse." Kitchen then rode full-tilt at the second Confederate, but his horse was shot from under him and he hurtled to the ground, where he lay semiconscious while the fight raged around him.

Eventually, Confederate experience and skill prevailed, and by 4:30 p.m., when Pleasonton began pulling back across the Rappahannock, his force had suffered 866 casualties against 523 for the Confederates. But the performance of the Union horsemen against the legendary Stuart had given them new confidence. The Battle of Brandy Station, wrote Adjutant Henry McClellan, one of Stuart's aides, "made the Federal Cavalry."

Stuart himself came under severe criticism for having been caught off-guard. "Vigilance, vigilance, vigilance," intoned the Richmond *Sentinel*, "is the lesson taught us by the Brandy surprise." From Hooker's chief of staff, Major General Daniel Butterfield, came a warning that Stuart would doubtless soon "do something to retrieve his reputation." And so he would—with doleful results for the Rebels.

The day after the cavalry clash, Lee put Ewell's II Corps on the road from Culpeper to the Shenandoah Valley. Ewell briskly captured Winchester, crossed the Potomac, marched through Maryland, and on June 21 entered Chambersburg, 20 miles beyond the Maryland-Pennsylvania border. From there, Ewell would accompany the divisions of Robert Rodes and Edward Johnson as they headed northeast toward Harrisburg, the capital of Pennsylvania. Meanwhile, Jubal Early's division would move eastward to Wrightsville on the Susquehanna River.

As it happened, Early's route took him through Gettysburg, where he easily scattered a regiment of raw Pennsylvania militia. "It was well that the regiment took to its heels so quickly," remarked the sardonic Early, "or some of its members might have been hurt." Before he departed, Early noticed that Gettysburg had a shoe factory, and he sent word back to A.P. Hill that the town might be a good place to get some badly needed footwear.

By June 28, Early was at Wrightsville, where the enemy frustrated his planned crossing of the Susquehanna River by burning a bridge. Rodes had already arrived at Carlisle, and on the night of June 28 a cavalry brigade under Brigadier General Albert Gallatin Jenkins camped on a hill four miles from Harrisburg. It was the northernmost Confederate penetration of the war.

Jenkins reported that Harrisburg looked like easy pickings. But then, on June 29, urgent word came from Lee: Ewell's divisions must immediately withdraw from their advanced positions to join A.P. Hill and Longstreet near Chambersburg, from where they were to march south to Gettysburg. The Army of Northern Virginia was concentrating for battle.

Behind the surprising order lay some startling news. On the night of June 28, Lee had learned from a road-weary spy named Harrison that the Union army had crossed the border into Maryland and was menacing Lee's vital line of communications. Lee immediately ordered his army to assemble. Almost incidentally, Harrison mentioned that Joseph Hooker had been relieved of command, and that the Army of the Potomac was now led by a little-known general, George Gordon Meade.

After Chancellorsville, Abraham Lincoln had been patient with Hooker. But when Hooker did not stir himself to pursue the Confederates until June 25—while Ewell was already starting north from Chambersburg—the President's forbearance reached its limit. Nonetheless, it was Hooker who precipitated his own demise: On June 27, after a minor dispute

On June 10, 1863, Robert E. Lee started his three corps northward toward Pennsylvania (red line). With Lieutenant General Richard Ewell leading, they cut through the Shenandoah Valley and across the Potomac and into the rich farmlands of the Cumberland Valley. Three days later General Joseph Hooker began a parallel march (blue line), moving the Army of the Potomac from the Fredericksburg area to Frederick, Maryland. After screening Lee's bold push for eight days, Major General Jeb Stuart left Salem, Virginia, on June 25 with three-cavalry brigades on a foray (broken red line) that skirted the Federal forces entirely.

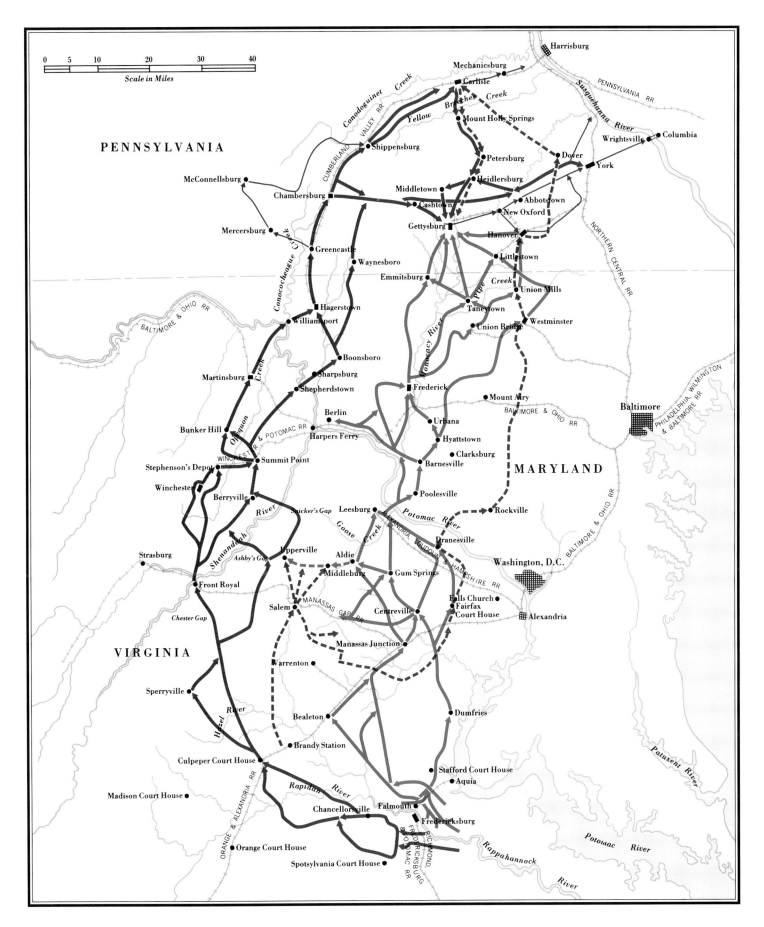

PENNSYLVANIA

Harrisburg

Mechanicsburg

Carlisle

Conodoguinet Creek

VALLEY RR

Yellow Bre_ches Creek

Mount Holly Springs

PENNSYLVANIA RR

Susquehanna River

Columbia

Wrightsville

Shippensburg

Petersburg

Dover

York

CUMBERLAND

McConnellsburg

Chambersburg

Middletown

Heidlersburg

Cashtown

Abbotstown

New Oxford

NORTHERN CENTRAL RR

Mercersburg

Conococheague Creek

Greencastle

Waynesboro

Emmitsburg

Gettysburg

Hanover

Littlestown

BALTIMORE & OHIO RR

Hagerstown

Williamsport

Pipe Creek

Union Mills

Taneytown

Union Bridge

Westminster

Boonsboro

Sharpsburg

Martinsburg

Creek

Frederick

Monocacy River

Shepherdstown

Berlin

Harpers Ferry

Mount Airy

BALTIMORE & OHIO RR

Baltimore

PHILADELPHIA, WILMINGTON & BALTIMORE RR

Bunker Hill

Opequon

WINCHESTER & POTOMAC RR

Urbana

Hyattstown

Clarksburg

Summit Point

WINCHESTER

Stephenson's Depot

Barnesville

MARYLAND

Winchester

Berryville

River

Snicker's Gap

Poolesville

Strasburg

Ashby's Gap

Upperville

Leesburg

Goose Creek

Potomac River

Rockville

Dranesville

ALEXANDRIA, LOUDOUN & HAMPSHIRE RR

Washington, D.C.

BALTIMORE & OHIO RR

Shenandoah River

Middleburg

Aldie

Gum Springs

Front Royal

Chester Gap

Salem

MANASSAS GAP RR

Centreville

Falls Church

Fairfax Court House

Alexandria

VIRGINIA

Manassas Junction

Warrenton

Sperryville

Hazel River

Bealeton

Dumfries

Brandy Station

Culpeper Court House

Stafford Court House

Aquia

Madison Court House

Rapidan River

ORANGE & ALEXANDRIA RR

Chancellorsville

Falmouth

Fredericksburg

RICHMOND, FREDERICKSBURG & POTOMAC RR

Potomac River

Orange Court House

Spotsylvania Court House

Rappahannock River

PENNSYLVANIA

0   5   10   20   30   40
Scale in Miles

261

with Washington authorities, the general fired off a message asking to be relieved, and President Lincoln gratefully acceded.

Thus, at about 3 a.m. on June 28, General Meade, commanding the V Corps, was awakened unceremoniously in his tent near Frederick, Maryland, and was informed that he now commanded the Army of the Potomac. Meade, 47, had earned appointment as a corps commander through his skillful performance at Fredericksburg. Although normally quiet, he was renowned for his hair-trigger temper—as one member of his staff wrote: "I don't know of any thin old gentleman, with a hooked nose and cold blue eyes, who, when he is wrathy, exercises less of Christian charity than my well-beloved chief!"

The sudden promotion obliged Meade to move fast. Although Hooker had bequeathed him no plan, by late afternoon he had devised a strategy. "I must move toward the Susquehanna," he wired General in Chief Henry Halleck, "keeping Washington and Baltimore well covered, and if the enemy is checked in his attempt to cross the Susquehanna, or if he turns to Baltimore, give him battle."

By nightfall on June 29, Meade's army had marched nearly 25 miles and was arrayed along a 20-mile front extending southeast from Emmitsburg, Maryland, near the Pennsylvania border. Next day, ranging north of the foot-soldiers, a Federal cavalry division under a hard-bitten brigadier general named John Buford entered Gettysburg at about 11 a.m. They found the townsfolk wildly excited about the withdrawal, just minutes before, of a Confederate infantry brigade.

That force—commanded by Brigadier General James Johnston Pettigrew of Major General Henry Heth's III Corps division—had acted on Jubal Early's advice: They had come looking for shoes. Pettigrew, however, had pulled out when he spotted Buford's cavalry trotting up the road from Emmitsburg. That afternoon, Pettigrew told Heth what he had seen. When A.P. Hill, who was listening, scoffed at the notion that Federal troops might be in the vicinity, Heth reminded his superior about the shoe factory. "If there is no objection, General," he said, "I will take my division and get those shoes." Hill replied that he had no objections whatsoever.

Early next morning, after his skirmishers had sent Lieutenant Marcellus Jones scurrying for safety, Heth

While commanding at Gettysburg, the usually dour General George G. Meade was, an aide said, "quick, bold, cheerful and hopeful." Though he was normally a bookish type, his performance during the Civil War earned him a reputation for toughness and reliability.

rode onto Herr Ridge, about a mile and a half west of Gettysburg. Nine hundred yards in front of him, on the other side of a swale with a sluggish stream named Willoughby Run threading through it, stood McPherson's Ridge and its 17-acre tract of timber called McPherson's Woods.

Another 500 yards to the east lay Seminary Ridge, crowned by the three-story Lutheran Theological Seminary. North of the turnpike to Chambersburg, Seminary Ridge merged with McPherson's Ridge to form Oak Ridge, which continued northward to an 80-foot-high knob named Oak Hill. A railroad cut ran parallel to the turnpike, some 200 yards to its north and as deep as 20 feet in places.

Heth realized immediately that his Rebels would not make it to McPherson's Ridge without a fight. Deploying his two leading regiments, he ordered them forward toward Willoughby Run. As the soldiers swung down Herr Ridge, they were staggered by salvos from a battery of Federal horse artillery and stopped for a full hour by the furious fire of Buford's dismounted troopers. Then the Confederates came on again. Buford knew that he was badly outnumbered: against Heth's 7,461 men, he had only 2,748, with one in every four a horse-holder. He had already sent an urgent request for reinforcements to Major General John Reynolds, the crisply professional com-

In the initial action at Gettysburg, dismounted troopers of General John Buford's cavalry division hold a defensive line against Confederate infantry at Willoughby Run. "My troops at this place had partial shelter behind a low stone fence, and were in short carbine range," wrote Buford. "Their fire was perfect terrific causing the enemy to break."

mander of I Corps, which was camped twelve miles southwest at Emmitsburg.

Reynolds himself rode onto the battlefield, well ahead of his corps, and asked Buford if he was able to hold out a while longer. "I reckon I can," Buford answered. This was enough for Reynolds. "The enemy is advancing in strong force," he wrote to General Meade at Taneytown. "I will fight him inch by inch, and if driven into the town I will barricade the streets and hold him back as long as possible." Upon receiving the message, Meade was delighted. "Good!" he exclaimed. "That is just like Reynolds, he will hold out to the bitter end."

For Reynolds, who assumed command of the Union force, the bitter end was indeed near. At about 10 a.m., the leading brigade of Brigadier General James A. Wadsworth's 1st Division of I Corps rushed onto the battlefield. Reynolds turned in his saddle to urge some of the men on—and took a skirmisher's Minié ball behind the right ear. Forty-two years old, he fell from his horse, dead.

By then, a Confederate brigade under Brigadier General James J. Archer was recklessly attacking in McPherson's Woods, and only then did its men discover the sort of troops they were up against. Spot-

ting Union defenders wearing the distinctive black felt hats of the I Corps' fearsome Iron Brigade, one Confederate shouted: "There are those damned black-hatted fellows again! Tain't no militia. It's the Army of the Potomac!"

The Iron Brigade soon turned Archer's right flank and caught his men in a killing enfilade. As the Confederates tumbled back, the Iron Brigade came after them, scooping up prisoners—including General Archer, who was taken to Major General Abner Doubleday, the senior officer on the field after Reynolds' death. "Good morning, Archer," said Doubleday, an old Regular Army comrade, "I am glad to see you." Replied Archer: "Well, I am *not* glad to see you—by a damned sight."

All this time, another of Wadsworth's brigades, commanded by Brigadier General Lysander Cutler, had been fighting its own battle north of the Chambersburg Pike on the Union right. There, outflanked by a brigade under Brigadier General Joseph R. Davis (a nephew of Jefferson Davis), two Federal regiments fled toward Seminary Ridge. But as the Confederates pursued, they exposed their own right flank to fire from the south. The Confederates slowed, stopped,

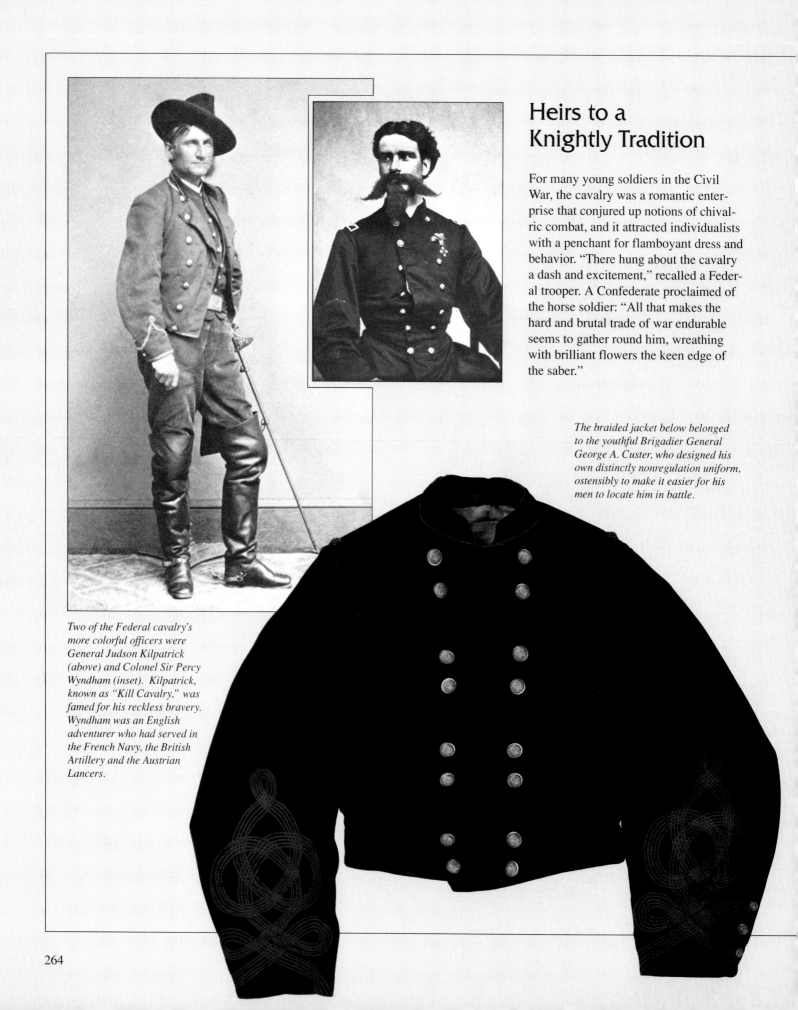

Heirs to a Knightly Tradition

For many young soldiers in the Civil War, the cavalry was a romantic enterprise that conjured up notions of chivalric combat, and it attracted individualists with a penchant for flamboyant dress and behavior. "There hung about the cavalry a dash and excitement," recalled a Federal trooper. A Confederate proclaimed of the horse soldier: "All that makes the hard and brutal trade of war endurable seems to gather round him, wreathing with brilliant flowers the keen edge of the saber."

The braided jacket below belonged to the youthful Brigadier General George A. Custer, who designed his own distinctly nonregulation uniform, ostensibly to make it easier for his men to locate him in battle.

Two of the Federal cavalry's more colorful officers were General Judson Kilpatrick (above) and Colonel Sir Percy Wyndham (inset). Kilpatrick, known as "Kill Cavalry," was famed for his reckless bravery. Wyndham was an English adventurer who had served in the French Navy, the British Artillery and the Austrian Lancers.

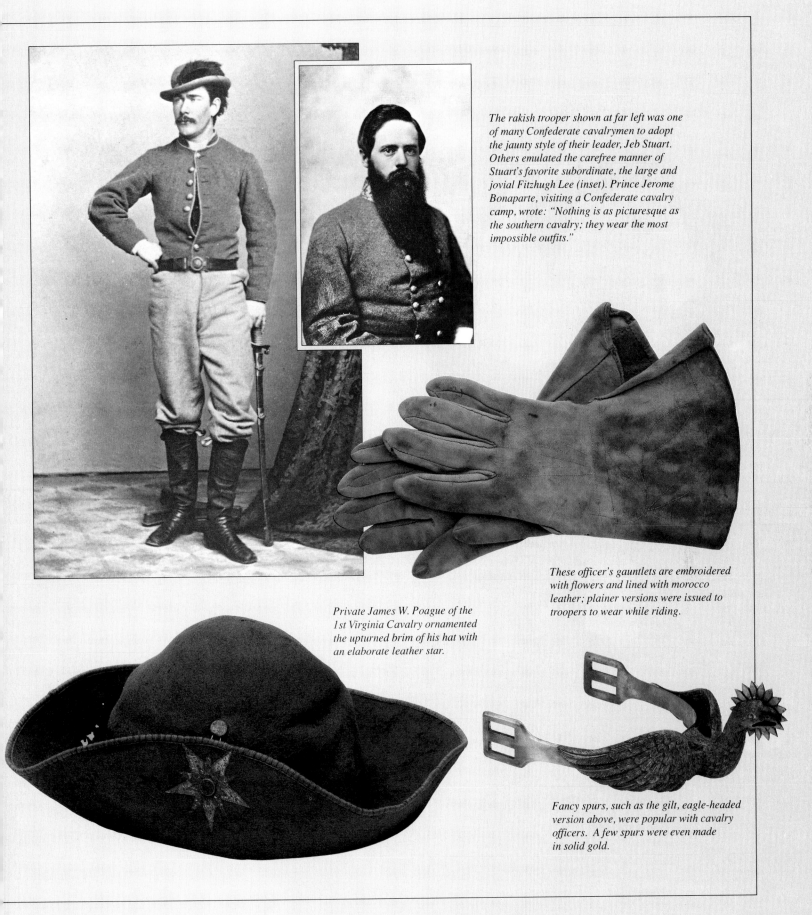

The rakish trooper shown at far left was one of many Confederate cavalrymen to adopt the jaunty style of their leader, Jeb Stuart. Others emulated the carefree manner of Stuart's favorite subordinate, the large and jovial Fitzhugh Lee (inset). Prince Jerome Bonaparte, visiting a Confederate cavalry camp, wrote: "Nothing is as picturesque as the southern cavalry; they wear the most impossible outfits."

These officer's gauntlets are embroidered with flowers and lined with morocco leather; plainer versions were issued to troopers to wear while riding.

Private James W. Poague of the 1st Virginia Cavalry ornamented the upturned brim of his hat with an elaborate leather star.

Fancy spurs, such as the gilt, eagle-headed version above, were popular with cavalry officers. A few spurs were even made in solid gold.

The rugged McClellan saddle, designed by Union General George McClellan, was the best of several types used during the war. The trooper strapped his overcoat across the saddle bow and a poncho and blanket across the cantle. Saddle bags and other items were hung on straps.

Private Elnathan S. Cheney of the 2nd Pennsylvania Cavalry sits proudly astride his mount. Cheney's tack is a mixed bag: He has combined the standard McClellan saddle with a nonregulation bridle.

In bivouac, the 14-inch iron picket pin was driven into the ground and linked by rope to the horse's halter. This arrangement allowed the animal to graze without straying.

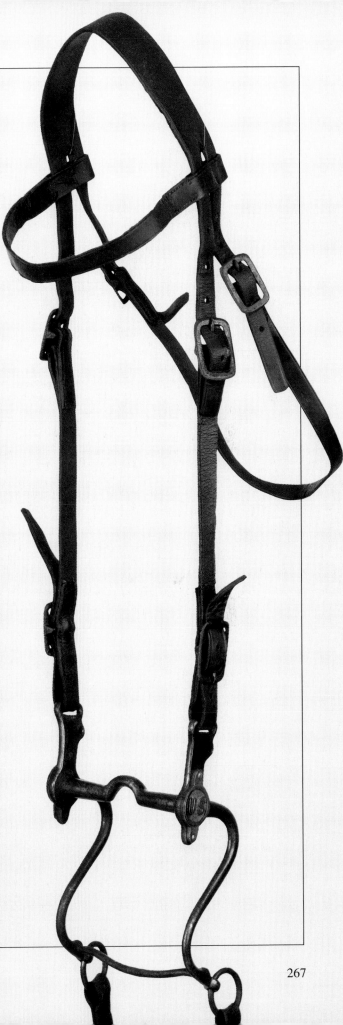

The Importance of Maintaining a Mount

The cavalry trooper was quick to learn that his ability to fight—perhaps even to survive—depended on his horse. Each man acted as his own groom and veterinarian and maintained his own tack. He made certain that saddle and bridle fit properly to keep his mount free of sores, sprains and even internal injuries. And he kept his horse well fed. Indeed, in the Confederate Army, where rations were often scarce, horses ate even when their riders did not.

This single-reined bridle with curb bit was of a pattern introduced in 1863. It replaced a more complicated double-reined model that used two bits, a snaffle and a curb; that rig was discarded after it proved too difficult for novice cavalrymen to control.

267

then broke for the only available cover in sight—the railroad cut.

Milling around in the bottom of the deep cut, hundreds were trapped by Union troops who seized the rim after a brief, brutal exchange of gun butts and bayonets. Davis lost more than half his 2,300 men, most of them as prisoners. As General Heth later reported, the enemy "had now been felt and found to be in heavy force in and around Gettysburg."

At 11 a.m., an uneasy quiet fell over the battlefield. As the Federals readjusted their defenses, yet another battlefield commander took over from Doubleday. He was Major General Oliver O. Howard, who had come in advance of his XI Corps.

Howard had little time to contemplate his new responsibilities. At about 12:30 p.m. the Confederates ran 16 cannon onto Oak Hill in the north and began raking the naked right flank of Cutler's brigade. The guns belonged to Major General Robert Rodes' division of Ewell's corps, which was responding to Lee's summons to return from the northeast. To meet the infantry assault that would surely follow the bombardment, a Union brigade under Brigadier General Henry Baxter raced to deploy at an obtuse angle to Cutler's right, facing generally north from behind a stone wall along the road to Mummasburg.

Just about then the leading elements of Howard's XI Corps came panting into Gettysburg, and Howard hurriedly dispatched two divisions to the north of town. Watching them deploy in a mile-long line, the aggressive Rodes realized that his advantage was rapidly evaporating; shortly after 2 p.m., without even bothering to send out a line of skirmishers, he attacked. Unhappily for the Confederates, the assault was led by brigades under Rodes' two weakest commanders, Colonel Edward A. O'Neal, who had performed clumsily at Chancellorsville, and, on his left, Brigadier General Alfred Iverson Jr., who was widely believed to have achieved his high post through family influence.

The affair was botched from the beginning. Iverson's brigade delayed its advance to give the Confederate artillery more time to clear the way. Pressing on alone down the eastern slope of Oak Ridge, O'Neal's brigade ran full-face into a storm of fire from Baxter's men behind the stone wall. Soon 696 of O'Neal's 1,688 men were casualties and the

brigade reeled back. Having thus disposed of O'Neal's Alabamians, Baxter's troops now changed front, crouching behind another stone wall that ran due south from the Mummasburg road.

Like O'Neal, Iverson had chosen to remain in the rear while his North Carolina brigade went into action. "Unled as a brigade," recalled a sergeant, "we went to our doom. Deep and long must the desolate homes and orphan children of North Carolina rue the rashness of that hour."

From their new position, Baxter's men waited until the enemy troops were only 80 yards away, then delivered a devastating volley that scythed down the Carolinians in a line later described by a Confederate as being "straight as a dress parade." From a spot of relative safety, General Iverson saw a few pitiful survivors waving handkerchiefs in surrender, and he hysterically reported to Rodes that an entire regiment had switched allegiance and gone over to the enemy. The truth was bad enough: Of the 1,384 men Iverson had sent into the 15-minute fight, no more than 400 were present when the brigade was reassembled.

As Iverson's remnants made their way to the rear, Rodes plunged two other brigades into battle. On the far right, Brigadier General Junius Daniel took his 2,162 men southward on McPherson's Ridge, planning to reach the Chambersburg Pike then push down the road to strike Cutler's left flank. It was a promising idea, but Daniel became stalled at the railroad cut, where a savage battle ended in lethal stalemate.

At the same time, 26-year-old Brigadier General Stephen Dodson Ramseur led his small but formidable brigade of 1,027 men into an assault just east of where Iverson had been ambushed. There, Ramseur ran into a Union brigade under Brigadier General Gabriel René Paul, who soon suffered a head wound that left him blind. One after another, Paul's successors went down—until, all told, the brigade had been directed by five different commanders. Finally, as their ammunition ran low, the Federals were forced to give ground foot by foot in the face of overwhelming pressure. As the Confederates closed in from all sides, the rear guard men tore their regimental flag to shreds rather than let it fall into enemy hands.

Meanwhile, on Herr Ridge, a gray-bearded general astride a gray horse was watching the bloody spec-

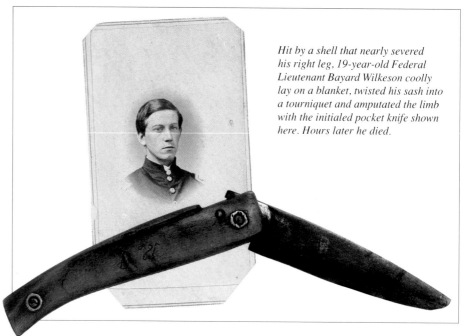

Hit by a shell that nearly severed his right leg, 19-year-old Federal Lieutenant Bayard Wilkeson coolly lay on a blanket, twisted his sash into a tourniquet and amputated the limb with the initialed pocket knife shown here. Hours later he died.

tacle. Robert E. Lee had arrived on the battlefield.

Lee had not desired a major battle, partly because he was still missing the services of his peerless scout, Jeb Stuart. While still in Virginia, Lee had instructed Stuart to screen the right of the army during its northward trek. But Stuart had not yet reported back. Intent on atoning for Brandy Station, he had taken advantage of an ambiguous phrase in Lee's orders to embark on a raid of his own. Consequently, Lee now remained ignorant as to the whereabouts of the rest of Meade's army. From what he could see before him, however, Lee knew that opportunity beckoned.

The long, thin Federal line was bent at a right angle, with XI Corps stretched from east to west and I Corps extending from north to south. Jubal Early, who had brought his division down the Harrisburg road, was ready to assail the Union right, and Rodes was hammering at the angle's apex. If A.P. Hill could renew the assault against the Federal left, the enemy would be caught in a nutcracker's jaws. Realizing that this must be done, Lee ordered Heth's division, supported by that of Major General William Dorsey Pender, to attack.

Heth himself had been knocked senseless by a Minié ball during the morning's fight, but with Pettigrew in command the division pressed toward McPherson's Ridge and outflanked the opposing I

In this depiction of the chaos that swept across Cemetery Hill on July 1, 1863, an exploding shell sends artillery horses crashing to the ground or rearing in wide-eyed terror. During the fighting the remnants of the shattered I and XI Corps were scattered over the hill; had the Confederates continued in their vigorous attack, the Federal forces might have met with disaster.

Corps. During its daylong defense of the ridge, the 1,829-man Iron Brigade had suffered a staggering 1,153 casualties. Now, still fighting, it fell back to Seminary Ridge. Later a Confederate officer riding into McPherson's Woods heard the dreadful howls of the wounded. "I approached some with the purpose of calming them if possible," he recalled. "I found them foaming at the mouth as if mad."

Before the men of the I Corps could catch their breath, Pender's crack division was upon them. A Union battery managed to check the charge for a few minutes, but the Confederates came on again. "Up and down the line," wrote a Union cannoneer with vivid memory, "men reeling and falling; splinters flying from wheels and axles where bullets hit; in rear, horses tearing and plunging, mad with wounds or ter-

ror. Smoke, dust, splinters, blood, wreck and carnage indescribable." Flesh and spirit could stand no more. In a trickle and then a flood, I Corps broke and fled.

Meanwhile, north of Gettysburg, Jubal Early had announced his Confederate presence with crashing artillery fire. In the assault that followed, Brigadier General John B. Gordon's brigade, on Early's right, struck the Union division of Brigadier General Francis C. Barlow head-on. Dreadfully wounded, Barlow fell (Gordon stopped to assist him, and the erstwhile enemies became fast postwar friends) and his division collapsed, sending shock waves along the entire Federal line. One by one, the XI Corps units gave way and went streaming back through Gettysburg. One of Early's officers commented, "It looked as if the end of the war had come."

The end, however, had not yet come. About half a mile south of the Gettysburg town square, the Federal XI Corps division of Brigadier General Adolph von Steinwehr was preparing last-ditch defenses on an 80-foot rise with an ominous name. The rise was called Cemetery Hill, and it was part of a topographic complex that would shape the Battle of Gettysburg. Just to its east, about 100 feet higher, stood boulder-strewn Culp's Hill. Stretching southward for about two miles from Cemetery Hill was Cemetery Ridge, at whose southern end loomed two more hills, Little Round Top and, beyond it, Big Round Top.

Arriving on Cemetery Hill at about 4:30 a.m. was the fifth general of the day to command the Union battlefield force. He was Winfield Scott Hancock, 39, an officer of magnetic presence, whom Meade had hastened from Taneytown to take temporary charge at Gettysburg. As first order of business, Hancock directed Doubleday to take part of I Corps over to Culp's Hill. When Doubleday protested that his men were done in, Hancock rose in his stirrups.

Jeb Stuart's Untimely Ride

Confederates pursue a fleeing wagon while their comrades halt others in the background.

On the morning of June 25, Confederate cavalry leader Jeb Stuart set out from Salem, Virginia, with three brigades of horsemen and rode eastward on a mission to scout and harass the Army of the Potomac. That evening, the troopers discovered to their surprise that a large segment of that army—General Winfield Scott Hancock's entire II Corps—was encamped directly astride Stuart's planned route.

Stuart's 4,800 men could not shoot their way through Hancock's large force. So Stuart faced two options: He could prudently ride back westward and maintain contact with Robert E. Lee's northbound army, or he could ride around Hancock. Characteristically, Stuart decided to follow the more daring course, taking his three brigades on a detour south and east before turning north. In doing so, he put two mountain ranges and the entire Federal army between himself and Lee's right flank.

Committed to his venture, Stuart rushed his troopers past Fairfax Court House and across the Potomac at Rowser's Ford, only a dozen miles from Washington, and then on to Rockville, Maryland.

There, the already weary troopers saw an invigorating sight—a huge Federal wagon train packed with supplies. "The wagons were brand new, the mules fat and sleek and the harness in use for the first time," a Confederate officer later wrote still relishing the memory. "Such a train we had never seen before and did not see again."

The chase was on. Teamsters desperately turned their wagons and fled pell-mell back toward Washington. Stuart's men, howling in delight, rode them down *(left)*. The take was bountiful: 900 mules, 400 prisoners of war, and 125 wagons full of food for the hungry troopers and fodder for their horses.

Ultimately, however, the captured supply train proved more of an encumbrance than a boon to Stuart. The mule-drawn wagons slowed the cavalry's daily pace from 40 to 25 miles—adding, as it turned out, two crucial days to an expedition that had already deprived General Lee of his best mounted scouts for a dangerously long time.

Leaving Rockville on June 28, the Confederate horsemen continued northward into Pennsylvania, cutting telegraph lines, tearing up railroad tracks—and fighting several fierce little battles with bands of Federal cavalry. In one skirmish, near Hanover, Stuart would have been captured or killed by Federal troops had not he and

"Sir!" he roared. "I am in command on this field. Send every man you have!" Doubleday did.

Fortunately for the Federals, Hancock was granted time by a curious mental inertia that gripped the Confederacy's Richard Ewell. During Rodes' piecemeal attacks, Ewell had remained little more than a spectator. Then, as the Federals retreated, both Early and Gordon urged him to push his corps through Gettysburg and onto the hills beyond. In the absence of orders from Lee, Ewell declined. Finally, late in the afternoon, an aide arrived with oral orders from Lee to seize the high ground beyond Gettysburg "if practicable." Given that discretion, Ewell did nothing—and a magnificent opportunity was lost.

Toward the end of the day's fighting, Longstreet arrived on Seminary Ridge well in advance of his corps. Surveying the scene, he calculated that this was the perfect chance to initiate the tactical defense to which he thought Lee had agreed. The army, he told Lee, must swing around the Union left, interpose itself between Meade and Washington, and then take up a strong defensive position. "No," said Lee, ges-

his big mare, Virginia, escaped by leaping a deep, 15-foot-wide ditch; the two sailed over the ravine, a fellow officer recalled, with "Stuart's fine figure sitting erect and firm in the saddle."

Still, there seemed no way to turn westward without encountering large units of the Federal army. Stuart's only chance was to press on to York or even distant Carlisle, hoping to link up with Lee's advance corps under Richard Ewell. The troopers slept in their saddles, many falling off and thudding onto the dusty road. Nearing York on June 30, Stuart found that Jubal Early's division of Ewell's corps had been there but had left hurriedly. Stuart pushed his men mercilessly onward in pursuit.

Arriving near Carlisle at last on July 1, Stuart's advance guard discovered that the town was not in Confederate hands but was held by the Federals under General William F. Smith. The crusty Smith refused to surrender, so Stuart shelled the town (below) and set fire to Carlisle's cavalry barracks. Late that night a courier—one of eight sent out by Lee to scour the Pennsylvania countryside for Stuart—rode up with news of fighting at Gettysburg. At 1 a.m. on July 2, Jeb Stuart began another night ride, galloping south to report to his anxious chief.

A Federal officer rides through Carlisle (center) as shells explode, wounding several New York and Philadelphia militiamen.

turing toward Cemetery Hill, "the enemy is there and I am going to attack him there."

Early next morning, Lee sent out a staff officer, Captain Samuel Johnston, on a scouting expedition in the direction of the Round Tops. Upon his return, Johnston reported that the two hills were unoccupied, while only Federal pickets were posted on the southern portion of Cemetery Ridge. Armed with this information, Lee completed his plans for attack.

Although one I Corps division under Major General George Pickett was still on the road from Chambersburg, Longstreet would march the divisions of General John Bell Hood and Major General Lafayette McLaws southward, then attack along the Emmitsburg road, which slanted northeast toward Cemetery Ridge. After rolling up the Federal left, he would assault Cemetery Hill from the south while the III Corps divisions of Major General Dorsey Pender and Brigadier General Richard H. Anderson assailed it from the west. In the north, Ewell's corps would demonstrate at the sound of Longstreet's guns. If the opportunity arose, Ewell would turn the display into a full-scale attempt to seize Cemetery and Culp's hills.

At about 10 a.m., Lee rode off for a brief visit to Ewell, expecting Longstreet's attack to be under way by the time he returned. But as he started back to his own headquarters, Lee still heard no gunfire. "What can delay Longstreet?" he asked, exasperated. "He ought to be in position by now."

To his dismay, Lee found that Longstreet was still awaiting the arrival of a brigade under Brigadier General Evander M. Law of Hood's division. Law did not show up for another hour, and only then did Longstreet begin to move.

Shortly after Longstreet finally started, the long-missing Jeb Stuart arrived at Gettysburg. According to one of Stuart's aides, Lee reddened at the sight of his cavalry chief and raised his hand as if to strike. "I have not heard a word from you for days," Lee said furiously, "and you the eyes and ears of my army." Lee mastered his anger—but Stuart, who had ridden ahead of his strung-out force, was already too late to help at Gettysburg. Worse, the next day his troops would be fought to a standstill in a massive cavalry battle east of town.

Meanwhile, Longstreet's two divisions had discovered on the way to their jump-off points that when they crossed the rise of Herr Ridge they would be seen by the enemy. To avoid detection, Longstreet ordered a countermarch, then sent his troops down another route along Willoughby Run. All this caused a delay of nearly two hours, and not until about 3:30 p.m. did I Corps begin filing into place west of the Emmitsburg road, with Hood's division on the right, facing the Round Tops, and McLaws' on the left, opposite Cemetery Ridge.

McLaws had been told to expect little or no opposition. Instead, as he wrote later, "the enemy was massed in my front, and extended to my right and left as far as I could see." The large Federal force along the Emmitsburg road was Major General Daniel Sickles' III Corps—and its presence there was almost as unpleasant a surprise to General Meade as it was to McLaws.

During the night and early morning, Union soldiers had thronged the roads to Gettysburg. Meade, who had arrived shortly after midnight, spent the rest of the time arranging his troops. By 9 a.m., Major General Henry W. Slocum's XII Corps held the extreme right on a line running southeast from Culp's Hill, which was itself occupied by Wadsworth's battered I Corps division. Howard's shaky XI Corps, backed by the other two I Corps divisions, was posted on Cemetery Hill.

At Cemetery Hill, Meade's line bent southward, with Hancock's II Corps extending down Cemetery Ridge. Sickles was ordered to position III Corps beyond Hancock on the far Federal left. Later, Sickles was supposed to occupy Little Round Top, a duty he said he would attend to "in due time." He never did, and Little Round Top was left undefended—a fact that Captain Johnston would soon report to Lee.

Sickles, in fact, was completely preoccupied with what he perceived as the weakness of his present position, where Cemetery Ridge lay so low as to be barely perceptible. Adding to his discomfort was the fact that the stretch was commanded by higher ground—on which a peach orchard grew—about half a mile to the west.

Although Sickles asked Meade to ride over to survey his situation, the army's commander instead sent his artillery chief, Brigadier General Henry Hunt, who largely agreed with Sickles' appraisal of the ground. But when Sickles asked if he should move his corps to the Peach Orchard—as it would hence-

Though General James Longstreet disagreed with Robert E. Lee over tactics at Gettysburg, their friendship endured—"affectionate," he later wrote, from "first to last."

forth be called—Hunt temporized. "Not on my authority," he said. "I will report to General Meade for his instructions."

Sickles waited but heard nothing. Finally, after learning from a reconnoitering party that the woods beyond the Emmitsburg road were swarming with Confederates, he determined to act on his own. At 3 p.m., the 10,000 men of the III Corps stepped out, colors flying, bayonets gleaming, drums beating, as if on parade. It was a splendid sight, but at least one watching Union general realized that Sickles was isolating his corps far in front of the rest of the army. "Wait a minute," General Hancock told fellow officers. "You will see them tumbling back."

Unaware of Sickles' move, General Meade summoned his corps commanders to a council of war. But just as Sickles rode up, guns were heard booming to the south. "General, I will not ask you to dismount," Meade said. "The enemy is engaging your front. The council is over." Sickles galloped away and Meade followed soon after.

When Meade arrived at Sickles' sector, he could only have shuddered at what he saw. Aligned along the Emmitsburg road with its right flank completely exposed was the division of Brigadier General Andrew A. Humphreys. To its left, Brigadier General David B. Birney's division occupied the Peach Orchard, then angled sharply off to the southeast. Thus, the two Federal divisions formed a salient that was vulnerable to fire from two sides.

Meade could scarcely restrain his famed temper. When Sickles explained that he had gained the advantage of higher ground, Meade sarcastically interrupted, "If you keep on advancing you will find constantly higher ground all the way to the mountains." Afflicted by second thoughts, Sickles offered to withdraw to his original position. Just then, a shell burst nearby. "I wish to God you could," Meade shouted, "but those people will not permit it!"

Across the way, the Confederate difficulties had continued. Lee's plan was to attack in echelon, starting on the right and moving toward the left, with brigades striking the enemy in a series of trip-hammer blows. As commander of the division on the extreme right, John Bell Hood would open the action by smashing northward along the Emmitsburg road.

But as Hood could plainly see, Sickles' forward movement had knocked the plan askew: if he followed Lee's orders, his troops would suffer ruinous fire from their right. It would be far better, Hood reasoned, to swing his division around the southern edge of the Round Tops—which, his scouts reported, were still unoccupied—and smash the enemy line on Cemetery Ridge from flank and rear.

Three times Hood sent messages proposing this course to Longstreet, and three times the corps commander made identical replies: "General Lee's orders are to attack up the Emmitsburg road." Never before had Hood protested the directives of a superior. Yet now, in clear violation of orders, he launched an assault toward the Round Tops and Devil's Den, a nightmarish jumble of huge boulders that anchored Birney's left, just to the west of Little Round Top.

As the troops advanced, the 15th Alabama of Hood's division on the far Confederate right came under fire from sharpshooters on the wooded west slope of Big Round Top. To clear them out, the regiment, along with most of the 47th Alabama, clawed up the hill. About halfway up, the enemy faded away and the Confederates, sobbing for breath, finally achieved the 305-foot summit.

Colonel William C. Oates, commanding the 15th Alabama, was convinced that he held the key to Gettysburg. If a few artillery pieces could be manhandled up the hill, he reasoned, the guns could blast the enemy line from one end to the other. This exhilarating prospect was soon shattered, however, by the arrival of a staff officer who reported that Hood had

been wounded—his arm smashed by a bursting shell—and that his replacement, Evander Law, wanted Oates to abandon his hard-won perch and seize Little Round Top.

Oates led his small force down into the saddle between the two hills, and was joined on the way by three other regiments. Not a single enemy soldier was in sight. But as the Confederates began to ascend the southern face of Little Round Top, from a natural rampart of rocks less than 50 steps away there suddenly poured what Oates would remember as "the most destructive fire I ever saw."

The Federals behind the barricade had been there a mere ten minutes—and then only as the result of a kaleidoscopic sequence of events. On his way to Sickles' front, Meade had dispatched his chief engineer, Brigadier General Gouverneur Warren, to ensure that troops had been posted on the southern end of Cemetery Ridge. In the process, Warren had climbed Little Round Top and found it peopled only by a few signalmen. Seeing Confederate metal glinting in the woods near the Emmitsburg road, he realized that every moment was now precious.

Aides galloped for help, and one of them came upon Colonel Strong Vincent, a 26-year-old lawyer who commanded a brigade in Meade's old V Corps, which had been posted in reserve. With very little ado, Vincent led his men up the slope of Little Round Top and deployed them among the rocks. The last of Vincent's four regiments to gain the heights was the 20th Maine, composed largely of peacetime fishermen and lumberjacks. As they took their position on a ledge below the summit, Vincent told their commander, Colonel Joshua Chamberlain: "This is the left of the Union line. You are to hold this ground at all costs."

For the 34-year-old Chamberlain, the work of the next hour and a half would earn a Medal of Honor. Hardly had his troops put their backs to the hillside than Oates and his Confederates appeared. From behind their protective rocks, the men of the 20th Maine rose, fired and sent the enemy lurching back. But the Confederates re-formed and came on again—and again and again. The fight, Chamberlain recalled, "swayed to and fro, with wild whirlpools and eddies. At times I saw around me more of the enemy than of my own men; gaps opening, swallow-

ing, closing again with sharp, convulsive energy."

Finally the Federals were down to their last cartridges and the Confederates were rallying for yet another attack. Just then, Lieutenant Holman S. Melcher of the 20th Maine's Company F jumped out in front of the line, yelled "Come on! Come on, boys!" and charged—alone. Moments passed, then a few men followed, and then, with an animal roar, the entire 20th Maine. Stunned, reeling, the Confederates broke and, in Oates' words, "ran like a herd of wild cattle."

The 20th Maine had lost 130 of its 386 men. And though hard fighting was yet to come on other portions of the hill, Little Round Top would remain in Federal hands. Over to their west, the Federals on Little Round Top could see a savage struggle for the Devil's Den. Among the defending Union regiments was the 124th New York, made up of men from Orange County who wore orange ribbons on their coats and called themselves the "Orange Blossoms." Their commander was 37-year-old Colonel Augustus Van Horne Ellis, a harsh, profane soldier more respected than beloved by his men.

As the brawl neared its climax, Major James Cromwell of the Orange Blossoms led a charge that dislodged the attacking Confederates. "The day is ours!" shouted Cromwell—an instant before being struck dead by a bullet. As the Confederates surged back, Colonel Ellis mounted a counptercharge, crying, "My God! My God, men! Your major's down; save him! Save him!" A bullet slammed into Ellis' forehead, and he pitched dead among the rocks.

In the ensuing melee, men in blue and gray sometimes found themselves on opposite sides of the same boulder, reaching around to fire muzzle to muzzle; others used their bayonets to stab blindly around the corners of crevices. The struggle, recalled a Confederate, was "more like Indian fighting than anything I experienced." But when it finally sputtered to an end, the Confederates possessed the Devil's Den. And at that moment, in and around the Peach Orchard to the north, another stage of the chaotic battle was erupting.

Not until about 5:30 p.m.—after Hood's onslaught had passed its fullest fury—did Longstreet finally send McLaws' restless men into action. Under Lee's echelon plan, McLaws' right-flank brigade, com-

With two casualties lying at his feet, Father William Corby stands atop a boulder to give absolution to kneeling troops of the Irish Brigade about to give battle in the Wheat Field. Wrote a Pennsylvania soldier who witnessed the ceremony: "No doubt many a prayer from men of Protestant faith who could conscientiously not bow the knee went up to God in that impressive moment."

manded by Brigadier General Joseph Kershaw, a South Carolina politician who fought as if born to bugles, was the first to strike.

Crossing the Emmitsburg road, three of Kershaw's regiments struck north in a vain attempt to breach Birney's line as it angled back from the Peach Orchard. The remaining two charged eastward to join some of Anderson's Confederates near a patch of ground between the orchard and the Devil's Den that would soon be known simply as the Wheat Field. One of Kershaw's men later recalled the Federal canister fire that raked the regiment as it ran: "Oh the awful, deathly swishing sounds of those little black balls as they flew by us, through us, between our legs and over us."

The Wheat Field changed hands six times on that terrible afternoon. At one moment of Federal crisis, the 532 men of Colonel Patrick Kelly's Irish Brigade were ordered to rush to the field from Cemetery Ridge. Before they left, their chaplain, Father William Corby, mounted a rock and, with the thunder of battle serving as his accompaniment, pronounced upon the kneeling brigade the general absolution—*Dominus noster Jesus Christus vos absolvat*. Father Corby was, however, careful to add that "the Catholic Church refuses Christian burial to the soldier who turns his back upon the foe." With that dubious dogma still ringing loud in their ears, the Irishmen helped restore Birney's line in the Wheat Field.

By then, the Confederates on McLaws' left had crashed into the Peach Orchard, with the Mississippi brigade of Brigadier General William Barksdale, a former U.S. Congressman, leading the assault. At about 6:30 p.m., when the drums began to roll and Barksdale rode to the front of his regiments, an aide saw that his face was "radiant with joy." Barksdale gave a simple command and repeated it time and again while riding toward the enemy: "Forward, men, forward!"

During the attack, the Union's III Corps lost its commander when a cannon shot hit Sickles and left his right leg dangling by a few shreds of flesh. Whatever his faults, Sickles was not short on courage. To counter a rumor that he was dead, he lit up a big Havana cigar and puffed ostentatiously while being carried to the rear.

From the II corps line on Cemetery Ridge, Lieutenant Frank Haskell watched the Confederate tide. "The Third Corps is being overpowered," he wrote later. "Here and there its lines begin to break—the men begin to pour back in confusion—the enemy are upon them and among them. The Third Corps, after a heroic but unfortunate fight, is being literally swept from the field."

After breaking through the Peach Orchard, Barksdale's men headed toward the Trostle farm, not far west of a little stream named Plum Run. There the Confederates were delayed by the gallant stand of a Massachusetts battery of six 12-pounders under Captain John Bigelow. By the time the battery withdrew, it had lost 28 men and four guns, and Bigelow was bleeding profusely from two wounds. But the artillerists had gained precious moments for the arrival of Federal infantry reinforcements.

Among them, called down from the northern end of Cemetery Ridge, was a brigade under Colonel George L. Willard. Led by General Hancock himself, the brigade charged through the elderberry thickets that lined Plum Run. As Barksdale strove to rally his men, he was shot from the saddle. He died that night after gasping to a Federal surgeon, "Tell my wife I am shot, but we fought like hell."

Next came the turn of the Federal XII Corps, temporarily commanded by Major General Alpheus Williams, who had been instructed by Meade to move his men over from Culp's Hill. Since no one had told Williams precisely where to go, he simply headed for the spot where he heard the most noise. After a while, he wrote later, he picked up a trail of "broken gun-carriages, scattered arms, knapsacks, blankets and clothing of all kinds." By the time he joined the battle, however, Barksdale's brigade was on its last legs, and only one of Williams' regiments was required to finish the job. "It met little resistance," Williams recalled, "for the Rebs ran."

Yet even as Barksdale's Confederates broke for the rear, General Hancock saw trouble to the north.

After Barksdale's brigade assailed the Peach Orchard, reponsibility for continuing Lee's echelon sequence passed from Longstreet's corps to A.P. Hill's. Now, Brigadier General Cadmus Wilcox's III Corps brigade was headed straight for a gap on Cemetery Hill that had been left by Federal troops sent to fight in the Wheat Field. Hancock summoned reinforcements, but there was no possibility of them reaching there before Wilcox did. "In some way," Hancock later recalled, "five minutes must be gained or we were lost."

He got his five minutes, and more, from the 1st Minnesota, a small regiment posted behind an artillery battery. Approaching the regiment's commander, Colonel William Colvill, Hancock pointed to the Confederate battle flag and asked: "Colonel, do you see those colors?" Colvill nodded. "Then take them," Hancock ordered. And so it happened, one undersized regiment charging against an entire brigade. Just before the unit reached the Confederates, Colvill shouted, "Charge bayonets." Wrote the regiment's Lieutenant William Lochren: "The men were never made who will stand against leveled bayonets coming with such momentum and evident desperation."

279

A bespectacled General Meade, standing at center, conducts a war council with his general officers in his headquarters at the Leister house on the evening of July 2. After hearing the opinions of his commanders as to what the army should do next, Meade brought the session to a conclusion: the Army of the Potomac would remain in place—and fight Lee when he attacked.

The Confederates crumbled, but not without triumph. Of the 262 Minnesotans who had hurled themselves against Wilcox's brigade, only 47 remained fit for combat. The toll—82 per cent of those engaged—was the highest of any Union regiment in the Civil War.

Wilcox's withdrawal left only the northernmost brigade of Richard Anderson's III Corps division on the field. According to its commander, Brigadier General Ambrose R. Wright, the unit's 1,413 Georgians had worked their way "across that terrible field for more than a mile, under the most furious fire of artillery that I had ever seen."

Nearing the top of Cemetery Ridge, Wright's men drove off some Federal cannoneers behind two stone walls that joined at a right angle. Wright thought he had pierced the Union center. "We were now complete masters of the field," he recorded later, "having gained the key to the enemy's whole line." In fact, Wright was still short of the crest of Cemetery Ridge, and just over it on the opposite slope was the Philadelphia Brigade of Brigadier General John Gibbon's II Corps division.

This veteran outfit was also known as the "Strag-gler Brigade," because of its slack discipline. Only a few days earlier, however, a 28-year-old, spit-and-polish career soldier, Brigadier General Alexander Webb, had taken over and had cracked down hard. The men had grumbled, but they knew that Webb meant business—and when he ordered them to charge at Wright's lodgement, they obeyed.

While so doing, they were joined by Union reinforcements, who began working around the enemy flanks and rear, leaving Wright no choice but to retire. Wright recalled that with "cheers and good order," the Confederates literally cut their way out.

To all intents and purposes, this ended the Confederate assaults against the Union left wing for the day. The entire effort, one of Lee's staff members later admitted, had been woefully disjointed: "There was an utter absence of accord in the movements of the several commands." To make matters worse, General Ewell, confronting the Federal right wing, had frittered away the afternoon hours that might have won the day for the Confederacy. "Greatly did the officers and men marvel," wrote a Confederate of Edward Johnson's division, "as morning, noon and afternoon passed in inaction."

This 12-pounder Napoleon belonging to Battery B, 1st Rhode Island Artillery, was damaged at Gettysburg on the afternoon of July 3, by an exploding shell that took the lives of two of the gunners. After the incident, when the survivors struggled to load the piece, the round—as seen above—became firmly stuck in the dented muzzle and could not be extracted.

By 6:30 p.m., Ewell had already failed in his primary mission of keeping the Federal forces on Culp's and Cemetery hills so busy that they could not go to the aid of their beleaguered comrades along Cemetery Ridge. Yet only at that late hour did Ewell decide to launch a full-scale infantry attack.

Johnson's 5,000-man division moved first, with Culp's Hill as its objective. There it met with 1,310 men under 62-year-old Brigadier General George Sears Greene, whose Federal brigade had been left behind when the rest of the XII Corps went to Cemetery Ridge. A former engineering instructor at West Point, Greene was an expert at building field fortifications, and he had used the time given him by Ewell's dithering to supervise the construction of log-and-earth breastworks that were five feet high.

By the time the Confederates made it to the eastern front of Culp's Hill, darkness was closing in. With the flash of their muskets illuminating the night, the brigades of Brigadier General John M. Jones and Colonel J.M. Williams attacked three times up the steep, boulder-covered hill—and three times they were repulsed. Over to their left, Brigadier General George H. Steuart's brigade fared better, gaining some vacant Federal trenches that Greene's scanty force had been unable to man. There, however, Steuart's men would huddle for the rest of the night, pinned down by fire from the Federals.

On Johnson's right, the Louisiana brigade of

Brigadier General Harry Hays, along with North Carolinians under Colonel Isaac Avery, aimed their assaults at Cemetery Hill and actually burst onto its crest before being driven back down by Union reinforcements who seemed to appear from everywhere.

Then, at about 10:30 p.m., the tumult subsided, although now and then the spiteful crack of a picket's musket could still be heard above the moans of the wounded who lay sprawled on the slopes and meadows of the great battleground.

As Robert E. Lee's thinking evolved that night, the Confederates would attack simultaneously the next morning—Friday, July 3, 1863. Longstreet, reinforced by Pickett's three brigades, would strike at the Federal center, while Ewell assailed the enemy's right. But just as Pickett's men approached the battlefield, a deep growl of gunfire from the direction of Culp's Hill informed Lee that his timetable had been hopelessly upset: Ewell was already engaged.

The Federals had started the fight, opening the day with a heavy bombardment aimed at scattering Edward Johnson's Confederates from the trenches that they had captured the night before. However the Confederates, instead of scrambling back down the hill, attacked. For more than three hours a vicious struggle raged amid what one Union officer called "great rocks that lie there like a herd of sleeping elephants." Finally, a Federal countercharge swept down on Johnson's left and his troops were forced to withdraw. Ewell's infantrymen would do no more fighting at Gettysburg.

On hearing the Federal bombardment, Lee rode to Seminary Ridge to find Longstreet—who again urged that the army maneuver around the enemy and take up a defensive position. But Lee grimly pointed to the Union lines. "The enemy is there," he repeated, "and I am going to strike him." Longstreet asked how many men would participate in the attack. When Lee said about 15,000—an estimate that turned out to be more than 20 per cent high—Longstreet made a final, impassioned plea: "General, I have been a soldier all my life. I have been with soldiers engaged in fights by couples, by squads, companies, regiments, divisions, and armies, and should know, as well as anyone, what soldiers can do. It is my opinion that no 15,000 men ever arrayed for battle can take that position."

281

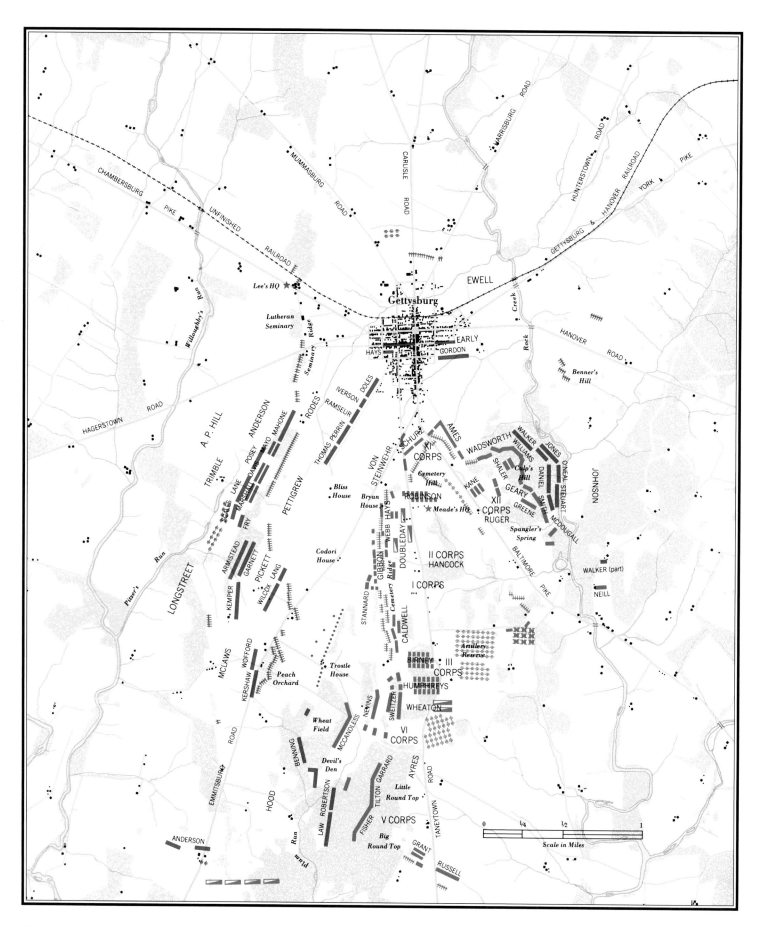

MUMMASBURG ROAD

CARLISLE ROAD

WARRSBURG ROAD

HUNTERSTOWN ROAD

GETTYSBURG & HANOVER RAILROAD

YORK PIKE

CHAMBERSBURG PIKE

UNFINISHED RAILROAD

Willoughby's Run

Lee's HQ ★

EWELL

Gettysburg

Lutheran Seminary

Seminary Ridge

HAYS

EARLY

GORDON

Rock Creek

HANOVER ROAD

Benner's Hill

A. P. HILL

HAGERSTOWN ROAD

ANDERSON

TRIMBLE

LANE

POSEY

MAHONE

MARSHALL DAVIS

PERRIN

IVERSON

DOLES

RODES

RAMSEUR

THOMAS

PETTIGREW

SCALE

FRY

VON STEINWEHR

SCHURZ

AMES

XI CORPS

WADSWORTH

WALKER

WILLIAMS

JONES

ONEAL STEWART

DANIEL

SMITH

JOHNSON

Cemetery Hill

KANE

SHALER

Culp's Hill

GEARY

GREENE

MCDOUGALL

Bliss House

ROBINSON

XII CORPS RUGER

LONGSTREET

Pitzer's Run

ARMISTEAD

GARNETT

KEMPER

PICKETT

WILCOX

LANG

Bryan House

HAYS

WEBB

GIBBON

DOUBLEDAY

Meade's HQ ★

Codori House

Cemetery Ridge

II CORPS HANCOCK

Spangler's Spring

BALTIMORE PIKE

WALKER (part)

NEILL

I CORPS

STANNARD

CALDWELL

Artillery Reserve

MCLAWS

WOFFORD

KERSHAW

Peach Orchard

Trostle House

NEVINS

SWEITZER

BIRNEY

III CORPS

HUMPHREYS

WHEATON

Wheat Field

MCCANDLESS

VI CORPS

EMMITSBURG ROAD

BENNING

Devil's Den

HOOD

LAW

ROBERTSON

FISHER

TILTON

GARRARD

Little Round Top

AYRES

V CORPS

TANEYTOWN ROAD

ANDERSON

Plum Run

Big Round Top

GRANT

RUSSELL

0   ¼   ½   1

Scale in Miles

282

Lee refused to budge. By Longstreet's account, the commanding general "seemed a little impatient, so I said nothing more. Never was I so depressed as upon that day." Longstreet did, however, win on one point: Responding to his plea that the divisions of Hood and McLaws were worn out from the previous day's fighting, Lee agreed to withhold them. With that decision, and with Ewell's corps already depleted, the only Confederate assault of the day would be aimed at the enemy's center.

By 9 a.m., the attacking forces were forming in the woods northeast of the Peach Orchard. On the right was Pickett's division. Its 38-year-old commander, as described by one Confederate officer, was distinguished for the "long ringlets that flowed over his shoulders, trimmed and highly perfumed; his beard likewise was curling and giving out the scent of Araby." Yet despite Pickett's dandyish looks, few ever questioned his courage—and the day's events would give him ample opportunity to achieve the elusive glory he so greatly coveted.

On the Confederate left was Heth's division, still severely shaken from its casualties of the day before; with Heth incapacitated, it was directed again by Pettigrew. To Pettigrew's right rear was the division that had been commanded by Dorsey Pender. But Pender, one of the army's most promising young commanders, had suffered a mortal wound on July 2, and the division was now assigned to 61-year-old Major General Isaac Trimble, a complete stranger to the brigades he was to lead.

At Lee's direction, the attackers would guide on a little, umbrella-shaped clump of trees on the otherwise bare crest of Cemetery Ridge, near the center of the Federal line. But reaching there would be very perilous: there was a gap of nearly a quarter mile between Pickett's left and Pettigrew's right that could not be effectively closed in the woods. To link up, Pickett's division would have to bear to the left while advancing across the open field under fire—a tricky proposition indeed.

To blast a path for Pickett's infantrymen, Colonel E. Porter Alexander placed 75 guns along a front extending 1,300 yards northward from the Peach Orchard. With A.P. Hill's and Ewell's artillery, about 170 Confederate cannon would join in the most colossal bombardment in the nation's history.

Yet just when everything was ready, Alexander received a disturbing note from Longstreet in which the corps commander seemed to place on the 27-year-old artillerist the burden of determining whether the infantry charge should be made. Appalled, Alexander answered that the decision should come before the guns opened fire. Once more, Longstreet instructed Alexander to make the crucial appraisal, and this time Alexander replied: "When our fire is at its best, I will advise General Pickett to advance."

Reluctantly, Longstreet ordered the bombardment to begin. At precisely 1 a.m., Alexander later remembered, the roar of artillery "burst in on the silence, almost as suddenly as the full notes of an organ would fill a church."

Earlier, on Cemetery Ridge, John Gibbon had invited Meade, Hancock and other officers to savor a stew made from "an old and tough rooster" that foragers had scrounged up. After a while, Meade departed, but others were still puffing on cigars when the Confederate batteries opened. Suddenly, Gibbon recalled, "the air was all murderous iron."

With a fine sense of theater, Hancock set out to show every II Corps soldier that "his general was behind him in the storm." Sitting ramrod-straight on

A Panoramic View of the Last Charge

In the Confederate attack that came to be known as Pickett's charge, Robert E. Lee launched 12,000 infantrymen against George Meade's Federals in a do-or-die effort to win the Battle of Gettysburg. Although the Confederates performed valiantly against overwhelming odds, in the end they proved vincible. Less than an hour after they started, 7,500 had fallen, the survivors were retreating in disarray and the Battle of Gettysburg was over.

Twenty years later, in 1883, French artist Paul Philippoteaux re-created Pickett's Charge in a mammoth painting. Originally 400 feet in circumference and 50 feet high, his Gettysburg Cyclorama—so called

Crossing a farm road on a black horse with his staff behind him and the blue II Corps flag flying, General Winfield Scott Hancock urges the 7th Michigan Infantry and the 1st New York Artillery forward to plug gaps in the hard-hit Angle of the Federal line on the gentle slope of Cemetery Ridge. A staff officer later wrote that the sight of the stalwart Hancock, who was badly wounded later that day, gave many soldiers the "courage longer to endure the pelting of the pitiless gale."

because its vast canvas was mounted on the interior walls of a cylindrical building in Gettysburg—depicts the climax of the charge, when the Confederates surged momentarily across a section of the Federal line that was known as the Angle.

Before painting the massive work, Philippoteaux and his assistants spent several months studying the battle site and interviewing Gettysburg survivors. To ensure accuracy of the terrain and scale, they made sketches and took a series of photographs from a platform that was erected just inside the Angle.

The cyclorama was first exhibited in Chicago and advertised as the greatest artistic attraction ever brought to the city. In preparing later versions of the painting for display in Boston, Philadelphia and New York, Philippoteaux conferred with veterans and made additional revisions in an effort to portray with absolute faithfulness one of the horrific events of warfare. Most of the cyclorama scenes are shown on these pages.

With his rearing bay horse reined in tightly, Colonel Norman Hall raises his sword to lead the 19th Massachusetts and 42nd New York forward. Beside him, General Alexander Webb, on a white horse, looks on as the mortally wounded Lieutenant Alonzo Cushing collapses against his cannon with the vow: "I will give them one more shot, Sir." Behind Hall, just left of the clump of trees that served as a guide mark for the Confederate charge, General John Gibbon rides amidst his troops.

Surging over the Federal line at the high point of the charge, Confederates under General Lewis Armistead wave their flags (middle distance) triumphantly around guns they have temporarily captured. In an inaccuracy that was corrected in later versions of the painting, the mortally wounded Armistead—who was in fact on foot that day—is shown here, near his flags, falling backward off his mount. In the foreground, a Federal artillery limber from Cushing's battery heads for the rear.

In the foreground, Federal infantrymen prod Confederate prisoners
rearward at bayonet point while
flaunting the red and white colors
they have seized. In the middle
distance, Confederate General
Richard Garnett—who would soon
be killed—spurs on his gray horse
as he brings his men forward. In the
background, to the right of the Codori
farm buildings on the Emmitsburg
road, Confederate General George
E. Pickett and his staff are seen
as a small cluster of horsemen
observing the battle.

Confusion breaks loose inside the
Angle as a Federal caisson explodes;
beyond it Confederate soldiers, loos-
ing their high-pitched Rebel yell,
swarm thickly over a stone wall to
take on the 71st Pennsylvania in
hand-to-hand fighting. "Every foot
of ground was occupied by men
engaged in mortal combat," wrote
one Federal soldier; an artilleryman
recalled "fighting with handspikes
and rocks and anything we could
get our hands on."

Confederate troops under General
James Johnston Pettigrew charge
across a wheat field and burst through
a rail fence just north of the Angle.
Against them, men of the 71st Pennsylvania stand their ground in a
ragged line as Federal reinforcements
rush up to bolster the endangered
position. In the far distance along

The artist, Philippoteaux, painted
himself into his Gettysburg epic as the
Federal officer who leans against the
tree with a drawn sword, surveying
the scene. In the distance, Pettigrew's
Confederates move across fields that
one man remembered as "covered
with clover as soft as a Turkish
carpet."

North of the Angle, camp servants
and orderlies evacuate Federal
wounded on horses and mules. In the
background, beyond the stone wall,
skirmishers of the 111th New York
pepper the advancing Confederates
with flanking fire. The 12th New
Jersey charges to the New Yorkers'
assistance (top) past Ziegler's Grove
and the Bryan farmhouse. In a letter

The II Corps artillery commander,
Captain John G. Hazard, on horseback and accompanied by a mounted
guidon-bearer, directs Captain
William Arnold in deploying the five
guns of Arnold's Battery A, 1st Rhode
Island Light Artillery. From horse-
drawn limbers, gunners run forward
carrying ammunition for the cannon.

Limbers and caissons of Arnold's battery remain stationary under fire as the wounded lie about a Federal field hospital set up around a haystack. The European-style haystack is one of several minor errors made by the French artist, who was otherwise scrupulously accurate. The tall trees in the background mark the slope of Cemetery Hill, where much of the Federal reserve artillery was massed.

his prancing horse, he rode down the line. More than 20 years after that day, Abner Doubleday would write: "I can almost see Hancock again, followed by a single orderly displaying his corps flag, while the missiles from a hundred pieces of artillery tore up the ground."

Yet despite its awesome volume, the Confederate fire was, in the words of a Federal officer, "by no means as effective as it should have been." With their targets obscured by clouds of gun smoke, many of the Confederate cannon were shooting high. Recalled one Union soldier: "All we had to do was flatten out a little thinner, and our empty stomachs did not prevent that."

Even in the smoke, the Union guns on Cemetery Ridge made easy targets. Among those badly mauled was a Rhode Island battery where a blast ripped away the left arm of Private Alfred Gardner, a devout man who died crying, "Glory to God! I am happy! Hallelujah!"

With all their officers killed or wounded, the surviving Rhode Islanders were forced to retire. The Confederate's Alexander witnessed their departure, and reached a fateful conclusion: the time was ripe for the infantry assault. He scribbled a hasty message to Pickett: "For God's sake, come quick, or we cannot support you. Ammunition nearly out."

On receiving the note at about 3 p.m., Pickett rode to Longstreet and asked if he should advance. Longstreet merely bowed his head, whereupon Pickett declared: "I shall lead my division forward, sir."

Out they went, all three of the attacking Confederate divisions, at a steady pace of about 100 yards per minute, blue flags flapping over Pickett's regiments and red colors over Pettigrew's and Trimble's. Seated on a rail fence, James Longstreet watched them go.

Brigadier General James Kemper, a former Virginia legislator, led Pickett's right-front brigade. To his left rode General Richard B. Garnett, determined to fight despite a severe injury suffered when he had been kicked by his horse. Behind Garnett's brigade was that of gray-bearded General Lewis Armistead, who advanced on foot while waving his black slouch hat from the tip of his sword.

Once clear of the woods, Pickett's division faced 45 degrees left and headed northeast to close with Pettigrew's. The maneuver exposed Pickett's right

to a fearsome raking fire from Union guns on Cemetery Ridge and Little Round Top. With men falling everywhere, the Confederate regiments halted in a swale near the Emmitsburg road and, with parade-ground aplomb, closed the gaps that had been ripped in their ranks.

On Pettigrew's front, disaster soon struck the left-hand brigade of Colonel Robert Mayo. The afternoon before, the 8th Ohio had been sent west of the Emmitsburg road to form a skirmish line. It was still out there, all alone, and its commander, Lieutenant Colonel Franklin Sawyer, was of the decided opinion that battles were for fighting, not fleeing. Facing his men south, Sawyer waited until Mayo's troops were passing about 100 yards away, then ordered a flanking fire against a Confederate brigade that outnumbered his regiment by about 5 to 1. Mayo's men ran to the rear, thereby exposing the left of Joseph Davis' Mississippi brigade, which also began to disintegrate.

Still, Pettigrew's other brigade, led by Colonel James Marshall, continued to advance, and it soon linked up with Pickett's left. Together, the gray lines started up the long slope toward the crest of Cemetery Ridge. Awaiting them on the northern part of the ridge was the II Corps division of General Alexander Hays, which had taken position behind a stone fence that ran southward. About 250 feet north of the clump of oaks that was the target of the Confederate attack, the fence turned to the west for 239 feet. Then it headed back toward the south, forming a salient that would achieve sinister fame as the Angle.

When the enemy neared, an ebullient Hays enjoined his troops: "Now, boys, look out; you will see some fun." Then, with a Confederate brigade about 200 yards to his front, he bellowed "Fire!" and from his line blazed the concentrated fury of 1,700 muskets and 11 cannon. As the Confederates floundered, Hays glimpsed a splendid opportunity. The flight of Mayo's brigade and the shrinkage of Davis' had contracted the Confederate left until it was overlapped by Hays' troops. Hays immediately ordered his northernmost regiment, along with an artillery section, to face south. Within minutes, they directed a fatal flanking fire into Pettigrew's leftover troops.

After watching Hays' maneuver, General Hancock galloped southward to see if a similar move could be executed at the other end of the Federal line. Hancock was severely wounded just as he arrived. As it

Realizing that the battle is lost, Robert E. Lee rides to the rear among Pickett's shattered forces. "He spoke to nearly every man that passed," Colonel E. Porter Alexander recalled, "using expressions such as: 'Don't be discouraged.' 'It was my fault this time.'"

turned out, however, such an envelopment was already in progress.

Edgy about the low ground of their post on the far left of Meade's Cemetery Ridge line, men of a Vermont brigade under Brigadier General George Stannard had moved out and occupied a little knoll about 100 yards to their front. Now, as Pickett's troops slanted past them, the Vermonters wheeled and fired a volley into James Kemper's right flank. Witnessing the attack, Abner Doubleday waved his hat wildly and shouted: "Glory to God, glory to God! See the Vermonters go it!"

The unexpected fire against their right startled Kemper's men, and they began crowding to their left, into Garnett's and Armistead's troops—just as those brigades were also being jostled by Pettigrew's people shrinking from Hays' enfilade on their left. Soon, according to a Confederate officer, the better part of five brigades became "a mingled mass, from fifteen to thirty deep."

As Kemper struggled to restore order, he fell with a bullet in his spine that left him partially paralyzed. Riding up and down exhorting his troops, Richard Garnett disappeared into the inferno. Wrote a Virginia private: "The last I saw of General Garnett he

was astride his big black charger . . . near the stone wall, gallantly waving his hat and cheering the men on." Moments later, Garnett's frenzied, riderless horse came dashing back, horribly wounded and covered with blood. The general was never seen again.

Pickett's mass roiled directly in front of the Angle and the clump of trees, where deadly Union artillery cut wagon-wide swaths in their ranks. One of the batteries was commanded by Lieutenant Alonzo Cushing, who had already suffered a shoulder wound. Now a shell fragment tore into his groin. Yet Cushing remained in action and, as he was shouting orders, a bullet entered his open mouth. He dropped dead and his gunners fled to the rear.

With Gettysburg's moment of decision now close at hand, General Armistead pushed through the Confederate crowd, still brandishing his hat on his sword. "Come on, boys," he cried. "Give them the cold steel! Who will follow me?" While a spine-tingling Rebel yell shrilled across the field, Armistead leaped over the wall and grabbed for one of Cushing's abandoned guns. Then he fell, mortally wounded. His men pressed on, reaching the copse of trees before their triumphant screams were cut short by a Federal volley.

The Terrible Price That Was Paid

The men shown on these pages were among the 50,000 casualties at Gettysburg—30 per cent of all those engaged—making it the bloodiest single battle fought on American soil. Some, like Colonel Paul Revere, were scions of prominent families. Another man, Private Wesley Culp, was remarkable for the irony of his fate: Culp was killed on his father's farm, fighting for the Confederacy. Many soldiers exhibited a grim fatalism, realizing that they were waging a crucial campaign. Lieutenant Colonel Charles Mudge, ordered to launch a suicidal attack, said simply, "It is murder, but it is the order." He died leading the charge.

*Private Denton L. Thompson
148th Pennsylvania, U.S.A.
Killed*

*Major Benjamin W. Leigh
1st Virginia Battalion, C.S.A.
Killed*

*Captain William H. Murray
1st Maryland Battalion, C.S.A.
Killed*

*Colonel George L. Willard
125th New York, U.S.A.
Killed*

*Private James B. Loughbridge
Parker's Virginia Battery, C.S.A.
Killed*

*Lieut. Col. Charles Mudge
2nd Massachusetts, U.S.A.
Killed*

*Private Charles A. Keeler
6th Wisconsin, U.S.A.
Wounded*

*Captain Herbert C. Mason
20th Massachusetts, U.S.A.
Wounded*

*Privates H.J. and L.J. Walker
13th North Carolina, C.S.A.
Wounded*

*Lieutenant J. Kent Ewing
4th Virginia, C.S.A.
Mortally wounded*

*Major Edmund Rice
19th Massachusetts, U.S.A.
Wounded*

*Sergeant Roland Hudson
59th Georgia, C.S.A.
Killed*

*Private Frederick E. Wright
14th Brooklyn, U.S.A.
Killed*

*Lieutenant Daniel Banta
66th New York, U.S.A.
Wounded*

*Sergeant A.H. Compton
8th Virginia, C.S.A.
Wounded and captured*

*Corporal Nelson Gilbert
149th New York, U.S.A.
Wounded*

*Private Wesley Culp
2nd Virginia, C.S.A.
Killed*

*Captain Luther Martin
11th New Jersey, U.S.A.
Killed*

*Sergeant Francis Strickland
154th New York, U.S.A.
Wounded*

*Private John Hayden
1st Maryland Battalion, C.S.A.
Killed*

*Private Samuel Royer
149th Pennsylvania, U.S.A.
Wounded*

*Colonel Paul J. Revere
20th Massachusetts, U.S.A.
Mortally wounded*

The volley came from the 72nd Pennsylvania of the Philadelphia Brigade, just pushed forward by General Alexander Webb, and it stopped the Confederate rush. Then two other Union regiments—the 19th Massachusetts and the 42nd New York—hurled themselves into the fight. Recalled a Massachusetts soldier: "Foot to foot, body to body and man to man they struggled, pushed and strived and killed. The mass of wounded and heaps of dead entangled the feet of the contestants, and, underneath the trampling mass, wounded men who could no longer stand, struggled, fought, shouted and killed. Hatless, coatless, drowned in sweat, black with powder, red with blood, with fiendish yells and strange oaths they blindly plied the work of slaughter."

And then, at last, one by one, by twos and threes, and finally by the hundreds, men in gray began ebbing back down the slope of Cemetery Ridge. They left behind nearly 3,000 combatants—more than half of Pickett's complement.

From a farm just east of the Emmitsburg road, Pickett had viewed their going—and now, watching their return, he wheeled his horse around and rode back toward Seminary Ridge. Later, meeting Lee, he was instructed to prepare his division to repel a possible counterattack. "General Lee," he answered, "I have no division now."

Throughout the next morning, the two armies glowered at each other from ridges scarcely a mile apart. Both were stunned by their losses: the Army of the Potomac had suffered 23,049 casualties, a rate of 25 per cent; official Confederate records would place Lee's losses at 20,448, but the actual figure was probably closer to 28,000, or nearly 40 per cent.

At about 1 p.m. on July 4, lightning cracked, and there began a deluge that, as one man put it, "washed the blood from the grass." Against that apocalyptic background, General Meade composed his congratulations to his army, concluding with an exhortation

The Picture That Moved a Nation

After the battle at Gettysburg, a burial detail came upon a dead Union soldier whose only identification was an ambrotype of three young children found clasped in his hand.

Word of these "children of the battlefield" spread; efforts to identify the father blossomed into a Union-wide campaign. Thousands of copies of the picture *(right)* were circulated. A $50 prize was offered for the best poem about the incident; the winning verse was set to music.

In November 1863 a woman whose husband was listed as missing recognized the picture as one she had sent him before the battle. He was Sergeant Amos Humiston of Company C, 154th New York Infantry.

Proceeds from sales of the photographs and sheet music were used to establish the Soldiers' Orphans' Home in Gettysburg in 1866. Humiston's widow became its first matron, and his children were educated there.

Soldiers of the Federal I Corps cross the Potomac on July 18 in belated pursuit of Lee's retreating forces. The corps had crossed here just the year before, following Lee southward after the Battle of Antietam.

he would later regret: "The commanding general looks to the army for greater efforts to drive from our soil every vestige of the presence of the invader."

Since the beginning of the war, President Lincoln had been trying to convince his commanders that their objective should be the destruction of Lee's army, not the mere possession of real estate. Thus, upon reading Meade's message, Lincoln's face darkened. He slapped his knee in frustration and groaned, "Drive the invader from our soil? My God, is that all?"

It was indeed. At 4 o'clock that afternoon, the Army of Northern Virginia began to pull out, heading for the Potomac—and Virginia. Not until midday on July 5 did Meade start to move his troops from Gettysburg in pursuit. Although the next few days involved some further skirmishes, on July 14 Robert E. Lee watched the last of his troops cross the Potomac at Falling Waters. Then, one Confederate wrote, Lee "uttered a sigh of relief, and a great weight seemed taken from his shoulders."

Despite its anticlimactic aftermath, the Battle of Gettysburg would remain engraved in the national memory. Five years after the war, George Pickett bitterly denounced Lee to former guerrilla leader John Mosby. "That old man," he said, "had my division slaughtered at Gettysburg."

For an instant of memory, men in gray marched beneath fluttering flags up a long, grassy slope. Then Mosby broke the silence. "Well," he said, "it made you immortal."

Four score and seven years ago our fathers brought forth on this continent, a new nation, conceived in Liberty, and dedicated to the proposition that all men are created equal.

Now we are engaged in a great civil war, testing whether that nation, or any nation so conceived and so dedicated, can long endure. We are met on a great battle field of that war. We have come to dedicate a portion of that field, as a final resting place for those who here gave their lives, that that nation might live. It is altogether fitting and proper that we should do this.

But, in a larger sense, we can not dedicate— we can not consecrate— we can not hallow— this ground. The brave men, living and dead, who struggled here, have con-

At the dedication of the Gettysburg National Cemetery, President Lincoln—bareheaded and peering down just to the right of center—prepares to give a brief address.

secrated it, far above our poor power to add or detract. The world will little note, nor long remember what we say here, but it can never forget what they did here. It is for us the living, rather, to be dedicated here to the unfinished work which they who fought here have thus far so nobly advanced. It is rather for us to be here dedicated to the great task remaining before us — that

from these honored dead we take increased devotion to that cause for which they gave the last full measure of devotion — that we here highly resolve that these dead shall not have died in vain — that this nation, under God, shall have a new birth of freedom — and that government of the people, by the people, for the people, shall not perish from the earth.

Abraham Lincoln.

November 19, 1863.

THE FIGHT FOR CHATTANOOGA

"I believe the most fatal errors of this war have begun in an impatient desire of success, that would not take time to get ready, the next fatal mistake being to be afraid to move when all the means were provided."

MAJOR GENERAL WILLIAM S. ROSECRANS, USA

During the first six months of 1863, the armies of General Braxton Bragg and Major General William Starke Rosecrans lay no more than 30 miles apart in central Tennessee, menacing each other's supply lines with cavalry raids but otherwise remaining inactive. Rosecrans, victor in the bloody Battle of Stones River at the turn of the year, had set up his Federal camp around the town of Murfreesboro, scene of the fighting. The cantankerous Bragg, reviled by his Confederates for his harsh discipline and penchant for retreating, withdrew to the southeast. Ordering his men to dig in along the Duck River, Bragg established his headquarters at the small town of Tullahoma.

As a railroad junction Tullahoma claimed a strategic importance, but its overriding value lay in the fact that, fortified by Bragg's army, the town barred Rosecrans and his Army of the Cumberland from their prime objective—Chattanooga. Situated 80 miles southeast of Tullahoma, this modest settlement of 3,500 people on the Tennessee River occupied one of the most crucial crossroads of the war: the intersection of several of the South's vital rail lines. Over these rail routes flowed a great percentage of the Confederacy's arms, munitions, textiles, foodstuffs and manufactures. "If we can hold Chattanooga and Eastern Tennessee," Abraham Lincoln would write, "I think the rebellion must dwindle and die."

Rosecrans had studied the topography around Chattanooga with great care. The easiest approach to Chattanooga from the west was the valley of the Tennessee River, but that valley was easily defended from the high ground on both sides of it. North of the river rose a great mountain, Walden's Ridge; to the south, in Georgia, a series of mountain ranges extended like fingers, pointing toward Chattanooga. These were Raccoon Mountain to the west; Lookout Mountain in the middle—the most imposing, rising more than 2,000 feet above sea level and extending 30 miles; Missionary Ridge; and then Pigeon Mountain on the

east. The ranges were extremely difficult to cross. They were broken by steep passes, with roads so poor that some of them were mere footpaths, and the valleys therein were narrow and equally uninviting.

To get to those mountains surrounding Chattanooga, Rosecrans would first have to take Tullahoma. True to form, the general was in no hurry to begin the attack. He spent weeks in Murfreesboro, strengthening his line of communication and replenishing his supplies. Although Lincoln worried that Rosecrans' inactivity would allow Bragg's Army of Tennessee to slip out of Tullahoma and march 400 miles west to help in the defense of Vicksburg, Rosecrans remained firmly in place; on the contrary, he argued, if forced into the offensive he might well drive Bragg out of Tennessee, encouraging him toward Vicksburg. Thus, in a sort of reverse logic, Rosecrans reasoned that his inaction was actually protecting the Federals who were fighting at Vicksburg.

By June, after weeks of delay that exasperated his superiors in Washington, Rosecrans lost all his reasons for delaying the assault. He had gathered and stored food and forage aplenty; the Confederates' surrender of Vicksburg was just days away; the weather was excellent; and infantry reinforcements had been sent from Kentucky, bolstering Rosecrans' army to 70,000 men. His army now far outnumbered Bragg's forces. On June 24 a wire from Rosecrans arrived in Washington: "The army begins to move at 3 o'clock this morning." Hesitation at an end, the man of many excuses would now act with boldness and confidence, and mount a cam-

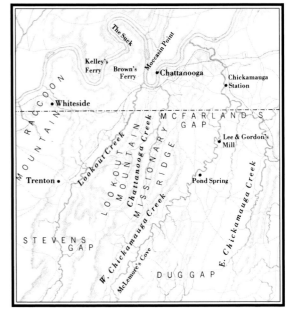

The imposing set of hills that ring Chattanooga, especially to the south of the Tennessee River, made the fight for the town a hellish one for both sides—the most formidable terrain in which major Federal and Confederate forces would clash during the entire Civil War.

The model of a gallant leader, Major General William Starke Rosecrans gallops through shot and shell on a song-sheet cover that was published in his native Ohio at the height of his fame in 1863. Rosecrans impressed his staff and troops with his courage and strategic cunning. "With Rosecrans to lead," wrote one of his junior officers, we think we can go anywhere in the Confederacy."

paign that was a model of planning and execution.

Meanwhile, Bragg prepared for the inevitable onslaught by massing his troops northwest of Tullahoma in a line extending from a ridge west of Shelbyville to Wartrace. Guessing that Rosecrans would attack on the Confederate's left flank, Bragg concentrated most of his forces there.

Rosecrans, however, had devised an elaborate ruse in an effort to outsmart his opponent. While the Federals made a feint to Shelbyville, the bulk of the Union forces headed southeast for McMinnville. Their goal was Manchester, a mere 11 miles from Tullahoma and well in the rear of the Confederate right at Wartrace. By the time Bragg realized the extent of the attack on his right flank it was too late to do anything but pull his troops back to Tullahoma.

The Federals drove on relentlessly, undeterred by a steady rain and long marches. When three Union corps reached Manchester and began closing in on Bragg from the northeast, the fretful Confederate commander decided to abandon Tullahoma and fall back south of the Elk River near Decherd to make a stand. Bragg's troops reached the Elk the next day, July 1, but remained there for only a few hours. Increasingly concerned that Rosecrans would succeed

in flanking him, Bragg resumed his retreat east into the mountains and across the broad Tennessee River to Chattanooga. By July 3, just nine days after he had marched out of Murfreesboro, Rosecrans occupied Bragg's old headquarters at Tullahoma, and was laying plans to pry his foe out of Chattanooga.

Overshadowed by the two great Federal victories the following day at Vicksburg and Gettysburg, the fall of Tullahoma received scant attention in the North. Yet its capture meant that the Confederates had been all but swept from Tennessee at a cost of few Federal casualties. Rosecrans looked for praise from Washington but little was forthcoming. On July 7, Secretary of War Edwin M. Stanton informed Rosecrans that Grant had triumphed at Vicksburg. "You and your noble army now have the chance to give the finishing blow to the rebellion," Stanton added. "Will you neglect the chance?"

Again, Rosecrans refused to move until he was fully prepared. Six weeks passed before he advanced his troops. On August 16 the Federal movement began, with three corps under Major Generals Thomas Crittenden, George H. Thomas, and Alexander McD. McCook, commanding 50,000 troops along a 50-mile front. Bragg expected an attack from the north, across the towering mass of Walden's Ridge, which gave direct access to Chattanooga and led to the vital railroad junction east of the city. But Rosecrans chose a trickier approach from the southwest. Using his favorite ploy of disguising his intentions, Rosecrans sent three infantry brigades under Brigadier General William B. Hazen to feint from the north. Then he moved the bulk of the Federal troops across the river at Stevenson and into the mountains south of Chattanooga. Just as at Tullahoma, Bragg was outmaneuvered, and he had to retreat southward or risk being cut off. Late on September 7 the Confederates gave up Chattanooga, the great prize of the West, without firing a shot, and took to the dusty roads leading south.

Rosecrans was exultant. On the morning of September 9 he telegraphed General in Chief Henry W. Halleck: "Chattanooga is ours without a struggle and East Tennessee is free." He was able to include East Tennessee in his message because on September 2nd and 3rd Major General Ambrose E. Burnside and his 24,000-man Army of the Ohio had occupied Knoxville, to a

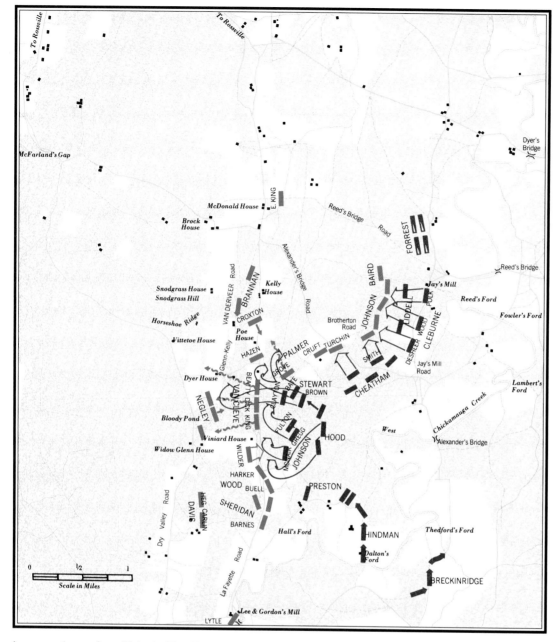

From midafternoon until night on September 19 in the battle of Chickamauga the two armies surged back and forth, roughly along the lines shown here. Having crossed the meandering Chickamauga Creek, the Confederates launched an attack against General Horatio Van Cleve's division, bending back the center of the Federal line. Counterattacks by Union divisions in the center and on the right halted the Confederates' advance. Late in the afternoon General Patrick Cleburne launched an assault that only faltered when twilight gave way to darkness.

joyous welcome from Unionist East Tennesseans. No sooner had Rosecrans announced these two bloodless triumphs than he sent his entire army marching after Bragg in a three-pronged offensive.

Bragg, however, was not in full-scale flight. His withdrawal had been orderly, and he had stopped on September 9 near Chattanooga in the vicinity of La Fayette, Georgia, 30 miles from Chattanooga. Moreover, he was making his own plans to take advantage of the mountainous terrain to trap parts of Rosecrans' army. Civilians were carefully misled by well-briefed Confederate officers to spread stories of panicky flight. Confederates posing as deserters were sent to pour out tales of demoralization in the Confederate ranks.

Bragg kept the Federal forces under almost constant surveillance as they marched through the hills. He tried, unsuccessfully, to trap General Thomas and his 20,000-man Federal corps in McLemore's Cove, a wide, fertile bowl between Missionary Ridge and Pigeon Mountain. A further attempt to snare Brigadier General Thomas J. Wood's division, which had become perilously isolated from Crittenden's corps, foundered because of faulty intelligence reports.

Realizing that his scattered troops were flirting with destruction, Rosecrans consolidated his army; by September 17 the Union forces were closing up near Lee and Gordon's Mill at the mouth of McLemore's Cove, about 12 miles south of Chattanooga. At the same time, Bragg was drawing reinforcements north from Georgia; 12,000 Rebels under Lieutenant General James Longstreet were steaming toward Chattanooga as fast as the battered Confederate railroad system could possibly take them.

Rosecrans wired Washington for extra men. Halleck began shifting troops from Ulysses S. Grant and other commanders, and Lincoln ordered Burnside to hurry southward. But time was running out. The two armies were now lying close together, too close to avoid contact. The opponents were separated now only by a little stream the Cherokees had called Chickamauga, or the River of Blood.

On September 18, Bragg ordered an attack against General Crittenden's XXI Corps on the Federal left at Lee and Gordon's Mill. He hoped to get his troops in motion quickly, turn Crittenden's left and drive the Federals into McLemore's Cove, penning them in and cutting off Rosecrans' line of retreat to Chattanooga. Though Bragg had emphasized the importance of a speedy crossing of Chickamauga Creek, some units were late getting to their crossing points, and Federals slowed the advance at bridges spanning the creek. By the end of the day Bragg had fewer than 9,000 men across the Chickamauga, but the Confederates continued to cross all night. By morning almost three quarters of the army was positioned on the thickly forested west bank, ready to attack.

Rosecrans was ready, too. Unbeknownst to Bragg, his Union foe had extended Crittenden's left on the night of the 17th. Then Rosecrans ordered General Thomas to march XIV Corps around Crittenden to the north. Both leaders labored under misapprehensions: Bragg thought the Federal left was still around Lee and Gordon's Mill; in fact, by the morning of the 19th, it had moved three and a half miles to the north. Rosecrans, just as uninformed, did not know that most of Bragg's army was now on his side of the creek.

Despite all of Bragg's efforts to be the aggressor, it was the Federal side that first took the offensive. After fighting at Reed's Bridge on September 18, Colonel Dan McCook told Union General Thomas that an enemy brigade had crossed the creek. Early on the 19th Thomas ordered Brigadier General John M. Brannan, on the extreme left of the XIV Corps line, to attack the isolated Confederates.

Brannan sent the brigade of Colonel John T. Croxton in the direction of the bridge. On the way, about 8 a.m., Croxton's men encountered Colonel Nathan Bedford Forrest's Confederate cavalry and opened fire. "Our tremendous volley rang along the whole

Discovered at Chickamauga in the 1880s, this brass eagle topped the flagstaff of one of the Federal regiments that fought under Major General George H. Thomas on the second day of the battle. Seven skulls were found scattered near the eagle, testifying to the gallant resistance of the color guard before they were overwhelmed by the onrushing Confederates.

line," wrote a 6th Indiana private. "At first all was smoke, then dust from the struggling steeds. A few riderless horses were running here and there, save which nothing was seen of that cavalry troop. Thus began the Battle of Chickamauga."

Croxton was driving Forrest back toward the creek when a division of Major General William H. Walker's corps, under Brigadier General States Rights Gist—a 32-year-old South Carolinian whose name reflected his father's secessionist ideology—smashed into the astonished Federals with terrific force. Brannan hurried the rest of his division to the assistance of Croxton and was soon heavily engaged. It quickly became apparent that there were more Confederates than a Federal division, let alone a single brigade, could handle. "The enemy bore down upon Brannan like a mountain torrent," wrote the correspondent of the Chicago *Journal*, "sweeping away a brigade as if it had been driftwood."

Thomas rushed up a fresh division, and the Federal lines steadied; Walker countered with another Confederate division. Again the Confederates drove the Federals from their lines, pushing Brannan and his reinforcements all the way back to their starting point. The seesaw battle, stoked steadily by reinforcements, increased in fury, and the din became unearthly. One of Forrest's cavalry officers, Colonel Thomas Berry, wrote that he had been in numerous battles and had never seen one so awful. "The dead were piled upon each other in ricks," he reported, "like cordwood, to make passage for advancing columns." The Chickamauga lived up to its name that day, he said: "It ran red with blood." Despite the carnage, both sides were grimly determined: One Confederate being carried on a litter, his intestines exposed by a terrible wound, waved his hat at fresh troops just coming up and cried, "Boys, when I left we were driving 'em!"

At 2:30 p.m., Major General Alexander P. Stewart's Confederates plunged into the fight. His assault struck the division of Brigadier General Horatio P. Van Cleve and sent it reeling back. The exchange of gunfire was murderous; in just minutes, one of Stewart's brigades lost a total of 604 men—nearly one third of its strength. Nevertheless, Stewart broke the Federal line and seized the La Fayette road, which linked Thomas' corps with that of Crittenden farther to the right, then pushed on to the Glenn-Kelly road. The Confederates now threatened to cut the route between Rosecrans' field headquarters and Chattanooga.

General Bragg, caught off guard by the unexpected beginning of the battle, had not yet ordered a full-scale assault; he was making the mistake of committing his troops piecemeal. Confederate Major General Daniel Harvey Hill later compared Bragg's tactics that day to "the sparring of the amateur boxer" as opposed to "the crushing blows of the trained pugilist."

All day Major General John Bell Hood, who had arrived with the first of Longstreet's divisions, had waited for orders, listening impatiently to the sounds of battle around him. At last, shortly after 4 p.m., he took matters into his own hands. He aligned a division under Brigadier General Evander Law beside that of Brigadier General Bushrod Johnson and launched both divisions in an attack against the Federal right. As his fresh troops marched crisply past Stewart's ragged, exhausted soldiers there was an exchange of banter. A soldier from Hood's Texas Brigade called out a taunt: "Rise up, Tennesseans, and see the Texans go in!"

Hood's attack struck the division of Brigadier General Jefferson C. Davis. As the Confederates descended on his division with blood-curdling yells, the blue regiments gave way from left to right. Last to collapse was the brigade commanded by Norwegian-born Colonel Hans Christian Heg, who was fatally wounded during the fighting. With 696 men killed, wounded or captured, the embattled brigade fell back. For a moment there seemed to be a real possibility of a Federal rout. Hood's and Bushrod Johnson's soldiers approached so close to Rosecrans' headquarters at the home of a young widow named Eliza Glenn that those inside had to shout to make themselves heard over the roar of battle.

General Wood rushed his Federal division into the gap on Davis' right, and now Hood's flank was threatened in its turn. Federal artillery hammered at Bushrod Johnson's left flank. Many Confederates had taken shelter in a ditch along the La Fayette road, and the Federal guns enfiladed the position. Within minutes, recalled a gunner, "the ditch was literally full of dead and wounded." The carnage was so great that one hardened Federal officer quailed: "At this point, it actually seemed a pity to kill men so. They fell in heaps, and I had it in my heart to order the firing to cease, to end the awful sight."

By late afternoon every Federal division but two had been engaged in the battle. One was Brigadier

Colonel Hans Christian Heg's 15th Wisconsin faces withering fire from Georgia troops of General

Henry Benning's brigade at the Battle of Chickamauga on September 19. Heg can be seen falling mortally wounded from his horse at right center.

General James B. Steedman's division, which had been stationed all day far to the north near Rossville, guarding the approaches to Chattanooga. The other, commanded by Major General Philip Sheridan, now made a timely entry, filing into position next to Indiana Colonel John T. Wilder, whose Lightning Brigade was deployed on the right of General Thomas. As Sheridan rode up to Wilder he was preceded by a cluster of pompous staff officers crying out, "Make way for Sheridan! Make way for Sheridan!" Minutes later, after being repelled in sharp fighting, Sheridan's men came running back across the road. Whereupon Wilder's troops, in high amusement, called out: "Make way for Sheridan!"

The day had been a long, arduous, confused and bloody one for both armies. Darkness was beginning to fall and Thomas' troops thought the fighting was through for the day. Little did they realize that a Confederate division under Irish-born Major General Patrick Cleburne was fast approaching the far side of the creek. Cleburne's men had left Lee and Gordon's Mill in midafternoon and toiled northward. As twilight approached, they forded the stream in water armpit-deep, and descended on Thomas.

Screaming the Rebel yell, Cleburne's men rolled irresistibly forward. In hand-to-hand fighting they took three guns, captured nearly 300 prisoners and gained a mile of ground. They did not stop until it became too dark to see what they were doing. Then, as the last firing died away, Cleburne and his soldiers lay down for the night among the dead and wounded.

It was a night that no one there forgot. Litter-bearers worked in the bitter cold, but there were many soldiers who lay between the lines and therefore remained unreachable. "The cries and groans from these poor fellows is perfectly awful," wrote a member of a Federal battery. "They are more dreadful than the storm of bullets that showered on us all day—friend and foe lying side by side, the friends of each unable to assist in the least."

Rosecrans called a council of war that night at the Glenn house. The situation did not augur well. Although the Confederates had not broken the Federal line, they had repeatedly come close—and would be back tomorrow. Reinforced by Longstreet's troops, they now outnumbered the Union side by 67,000 to 57,000 men. By the time the meeting adjourned after midnight, a decision had been reached: The Army of the Cumberland would take a defensive stance on the 20th.

Meanwhile, at a Confederate council, Hood found little enthusiasm among Bragg's officers for the next day's work. As he put it: "Not one spoke in a sanguine tone regarding the result of the battle in which we were then engaged." Bragg restated his strategy: Smash the Federal left and drive Rosecrans into McLemore's Cove, where the enemy could be trapped and annihilated. Lieutenant General Leonidas Polk's right wing would attack at daybreak; Longstreet, who arrived at Bragg's headquarters late that night, would then follow suit with the left wing. The attack was to be in echelon, with the division on the extreme right leading off, and each unit thereafter following the unit on its right into battle.

The Confederate attack, scheduled to begin at dawn, did not get under way until 9:45 a.m. Major General John C. Breckinridge's three brigades led the assault on the Federal left; two of them drove around the end of Thomas' position and smashed into regiments that were just arriving from farther south. The leading Federal brigade, commanded by Brigadier General John Beatty, was forced back until it was behind the Federal left flank. One of Beatty's regiments, the 88th Indiana, had to change front from north to south as the Confederates stormed in behind it. For a brief moment, Breckinridge's division actually seized the road to Chattanooga, but it could not hold on. Beatty was meanwhile calling desperately for help.

Breckinridge's attack was followed by that of the next Confederate division in line, under General Cleburne. As the pugnacious Irishman's troops forged ahead through a pine forest they were suddenly confronted by a line of Federals sheltered behind a formidable log breastwork. The Confederate line was staggered by volleys of musketry and deadly salvos of canister. Unable to break the Federal line, the Confederates took shelter behind the trees and blazed away at the defenders. As Cleburne's assault ground to a stop, General Polk committed two more divisions. Once again the Confederate troops charged toward those forbidding log breastworks. Once again they were thrown back with heavy losses.

Almost continuously, Thomas was sending messages asking for reinforcements, and Rosecrans was deploying units from the right flank of his line and sending them to Thomas as fast as he could free them.

The Union's Major General George Thomas was a firm believer that success on the battlefield was largely "a question of nerve." His performance at Chickamauga followed his philosophy, and earned him the name "The Rock of Chickamauga."

When General Thomas Wood shifted his division to the left at Chickamauga on the morning of September 20, he set in motion a critical sequence of attacks. Longstreet immediately drove into the gap in the Union line with five divisions, led by General Bushrod Johnson. General Thomas Hindman routed Generals Philip Sheridan and Jefferson Davis, and General John B. Hood veered to the right to overrun General John Brannan in the woods. Colonel John Wilder's counterattack slowed but did not halt the onrushing Confederates.

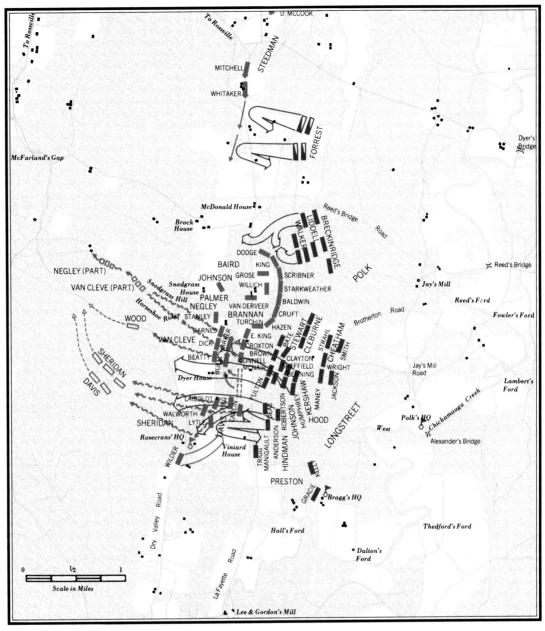

Then, about 10:30 a.m., one of Thomas' staff officers returned from Rosecrans' headquarters with alarming news: Passing along the Federal lines, he had noted a gap near the center, presumably at a point where a division had been pulled out to help Thomas. Whatever the reason, there was a hole, he told Thomas, between the division of General Wood and the division to the north under Major General John H. Reynolds. Informed of the gap, Rosecrans reacted instantly with an urgent message to General Wood, directing him to close up the hole as fast as possible.

Wood was puzzled. He knew that there was no gap: The division of General Brannan was in that position, although drawn back into the forest, where it apparently had escaped notice. Nevertheless, Wood followed his orders and began to move his division.

Around 11:30 a.m. Rosecrans ordered Jefferson Davis forward from his position in reserve to the south to take Wood's place. At the same time two of Sheridan's brigades, in the line to the right of Wood, were sent north to support Thomas. Thus, two Federal divisions and part of a third were in sidelong motion, and now there was a quarter-mile gap in the center of the line where Wood had been. At that moment, entirely by chance, James Longstreet unleashed three divisions—Hood's and Bushrod Johnson's abreast, Brigadier General Joseph B. Kershaw's behind—directly into the Federal gap.

As the juggernaut of 23,000 troops stormed across the La Fayette road and through the fields of the Brotherton farm, stark panic struck the Federal right. Hood was seriously wounded in the attack—his

right leg had to be amputated—but the Confederates swept forward.

On Hood's left, Hindman's division was likewise gaining ground. In minutes the first Federal line, Jefferson Davis' division, was shattered and fleeing in panic. The fugitives plowed into the ranks of the second line, Sheridan's division, throwing those troops into disorder. Soon the better part of Alexander McCook's Federal XX Corps was streaming rearward, toward Rosecrans' headquarters at the Glenn house.

At headquarters, the correspondent and War Department attaché Charles Dana witnessed General Rosecrans, a devout Catholic, crossing himself. "If the general is crossing himself," Dana recalled thinking, "we are in a desperate situation." And indeed they were: "I saw our lines break," Dana said, "and melt away like leaves before the wind." Rosecrans' calm voice rose above the hubbub. "If you care to live any longer," he told his staff, "get away from here." Dana wrote: "Then the headquarters around me disappeared.

The graybacks came through with a rush. The whole right of the army had apparently been routed."

A mile or so to the northeast, Longstreet was jubilant. "They have fought their last man," an artilleryman heard him say, "and *he* is running." The Federals had been fighting with their backs to Missionary Ridge; with heavy fighting continuing across the Rossville road to the north, the only avenue of retreat left to the soldiers fleeing before Longstreet was McFarland's Gap, leading through the ridge to the west. Toward this narrow opening now poured the disorganized units from the army's shattered right wing—the better part of five Federal divisions. As a colonel recalled, "All became confusion. With a wild yell the Confederates swept on far to their left. They seemed everywhere victorious." Late in the afternoon Charles Dana made his way into Chattanooga and sent a grim telegram to Washington. "My report today is of deplorable importance," it began. "Chickamauga is as fatal a day in our history as Bull Run."

With his arm in a sling from his Gettysburg wound, Major General John Bell Hood reels in the saddle as he is struck by a Minié ball while rallying his Texas troops at Chickamauga. Noting that the general was wounded both at Gettysburg and at Chickamauga while riding unfamiliar horses, Hood's omen-conscious Texans concluded that he was safe only when on the back of his favorite roan, Jeff Davis.

The battle was, in fact, far from over. George Thomas, only vaguely aware of what had occurred to the rest of Rosecrans' army, was engaged in the fight of his life. The right of his line, Brannan's division and part of Wood's, faced south from the crest of an elevation that projected from Missionary Ridge. A part of this rise was known as Snodgrass Hill, after a family that lived nearby; the whole of the eminence may not have had a name, but it quickly acquired one—Horseshoe Ridge. The main line faced east from near the La Fayette road. To the rear of the position were the roads leading west to McFarland's Gap, and north to Rossville and Chattanooga.

As a result of Thomas' repeated calls for reinforcements, he now had under him units from three of Rosecrans' corps—perhaps half of the Army of the Cumberland. And he was also collecting a rag-tag-and-bobtail assortment of units from company to brigade strength, plus a number of soldiers of all ranks who had become separated from the rest of the army during the hard fighting on the right. Many officers were behind the breastworks fighting as enlisted men.

The stolid Thomas was not given to dramatics, but as he rode along the lines his very presence bolstered the morale of his battered, powder-stained soldiers. When he came to Colonel Charles Harker's brigade on the left flank he told its commander, "This hill must be held and I trust you to do it." The scrappy Harker replied, "We will hold it or die here."

Thomas ordered a brigade under General Hazen into the line on Snodgrass Hill. The new arrivals were scarcely in position behind some low breastworks, recalled Lieutenant Colonel Robert L. Kimberly of the 41st Ohio, "when the Confederate storm burst." The attacking Confederates, several brigades under the overall direction of Brigadier General Joseph Ker-

The Legendary Johnny Clem

"He was an expert drummer," wrote his sister, "and being a bright, cheery child, soon made his way into the affections of officers and soldiers." He made his way, also, into the hearts of Northerners, who found the "Drummer Boy of Chickamauga" a most appealing war hero.

Ohio-born Johnny Clem ran away to war before he was 10. He was with the 22nd Michigan in its major battles—Shiloh, Perryville, Murfreesboro, Atlanta—but became famous only after the press extolled his exploits at Chickamauga. Armed with a sawed-off musket cut down to fit him, he shot and wounded a Confederate officer who was said to have galloped upon him shouting, "Surrender, you little Yankee devil!" Other stories had him firing furiously after his drum was ripped away by a shell. He was given a sergeant's stripes for valor and awarded a silver medal by the beautiful daughter of Treasury Secretary Salmon Chase.

The war shaped his life: Appointed a second lieutenant in the postwar Army, he served until 1915. When he retired at 65 he was Major General John L. Clem, the last man active in the armed forces who had fought in the Civil War.

Johnny Clem

The Fallen Commanders

The fighting at Chickamauga claimed 35,000 casualties, more than any other battle in the Civil War's Western Theater. "The losses are heavy on both sides," reported Confederate commander Braxton Bragg, "especially so in officers." During the confused fighting in the heavily wooded terrain many senior officers were cut down—including the eight gallant brigade commanders shown here.

General James Deshler, a West Pointer and veteran of the Indian Wars, was killed by a shell while personally inspecting his men's frontline ammunition supply prior to ordering an attack. General Preston Smith and Colonel Philemon Baldwin were hit almost simultaneously at twilight on September 19: Baldwin was riddled with bullets while attempting to rally the men of his old regiment, and Smith was shot when he led his troops into the Federal lines.

Most of the officers who saw death coming faced it with soldierly aplomb. As thousands of Confederates swept toward his beleaguered brigade, General William Lytle, a poet and author, announced calmly to his staff, "If I must die, I will die as a gentleman." Some found strength in their convictions and in the justness of their cause. As he lay dying, Mary Lincoln's brother-in-law, Confederate General Benjamin Hardin Helm, uttered over and over again the single word "victory."

*BRIGADIER GENERAL
JAMES DESHLER, C.S.A.
Killed September 20*

*BRIGADIER GENERAL
PRESTON SMITH, C.S.A.
Mortally wounded
September 19*

*BRIGADIER GENERAL
BENJAMIN HARDIN HELM, C.S.A.
Mortally wounded September 20*

*COLONEL PEYTON H.
COLQUITT, C.S.A. Mortally
wounded September 20*

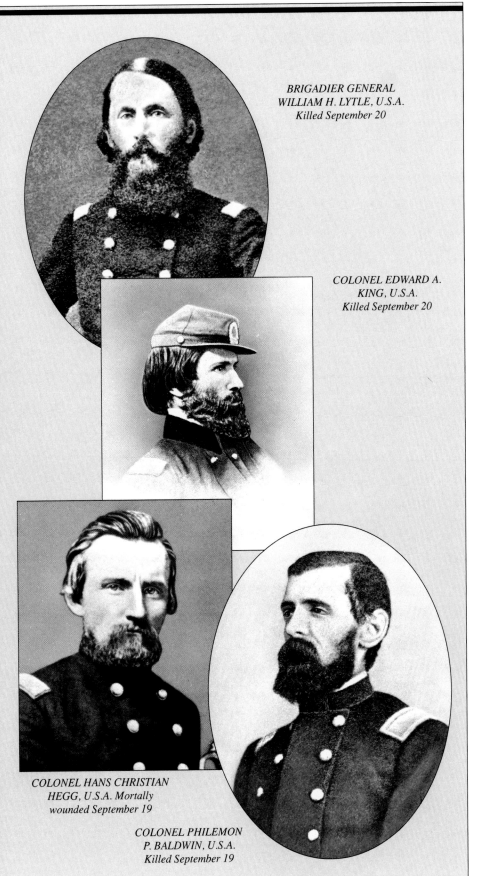

BRIGADIER GENERAL
WILLIAM H. LYTLE, U.S.A.
Killed September 20

COLONEL EDWARD A.
KING, U.S.A.
Killed September 20

COLONEL HANS CHRISTIAN
HEGG, U.S.A. Mortally
wounded September 19

COLONEL PHILEMON
P. BALDWIN, U.S.A.
Killed September 19

shaw, pushed to within 40 paces of the Federal line. There they met such heavy and sustained fire that Kershaw ordered them back. "The slope," said Kimberly, "was strewn with Confederate dead and wounded, but not a man could reach the crest."

Kershaw struck again and again, one ferocious assault after another. Next Bushrod Johnson's and Thomas Hindman's divisions launched another series of charges, aimed like a battering-ram at Thomas' right and rear. It was evident to Thomas that a crisis was at hand; if he could not push Johnson and Hindman back, his escape route would soon be cut off. Worse, his soldiers were running out of ammunition. The men on Horseshoe Ridge were desperately snatching cartridges from the dead and wounded; for a time it looked as if the Federal line would break. "Our troops were driven from the crest, and the enemy's flag waved above it," General Beatty recalled. Beatty rallied his brigade and led it back up the hill, "waving my hat and shouting like a madman." The crest was retaken, but Thomas and his troops were in dire straits and there was no solution in sight. Then, suddenly, help was at hand.

All during the fighting of September 19 and for most of the morning of the 20th, Major General Gordon Granger and his Federal Reserve Corps—consisting in its entirety of three inexperienced brigades—had stood guard with increasing impatience over the Rossville road three miles north of the fighting, as ordered by Rosecrans. As the sounds of battle came rumbling over the fields and more dust and battle smoke rose into the air, Granger fumed. "Why the hell does Rosecrans keep me here?" he cried out. "There is the battle." Climbing up on a haystack, he peered into the distance through his field glasses and exclaimed, "I am going to Thomas, orders or no orders!" He ordered Dan McCook to guard the road with his brigade, and within minutes he was marching off to join the beleaguered Thomas with the remainder of his corps: a single division under General Steedman.

As Granger and Steedman arrived the defenders felt, in Beatty's words, "a throb of exultation." The newcomers had brought not only fresh soldiers but also fresh supplies of ammunition. The burly Steedman galloped into action at the head of his division. When the 115th Illinois wavered in the face of Confederate fire, Steedman snatched up its flag and turned to face the enemy alone. "Go back, boys, go back," he roared, "but the flag can't go with you!" The men rallied and charged once again. Steedman's green soldiers smashed a flanking attack by Hindman's Confederates but at a terrible cost. Of his 3,500 Federals, 20 per cent were killed or wounded in those few minutes; among the casualties were six regimental commanders.

By now all of Thomas' units had taken heavy losses. The total number of men who served under him during the day has been estimated at 25,000; by one account only one quarter of these troops were still in action when Granger showed up. Since that morning, Thomas had fought virtually every brigade in Bragg's army, and toward the end he was fighting them all—Polk's troops as well as Longstreet's.

And still Thomas held. As the shadows deepened, Longstreet redoubled his efforts, hitting the Federal line at every point. By Longstreet's own estimate he sent a total of 25 attacks against the Federals. One of the last, and perhaps the fiercest, came within feet of the Federal breastworks. In places, the opposing soldiers grappled hand to hand before the decimated gray regiments fell back. In the charge, the 1st Alabama Battalion lost nearly 65 per cent of its men; the flag of the 2nd Battalion was pierced by 83 bullets.

Around 4 p.m. Brigadier General James Garfield—Rosecrans' chief of staff and a future U.S. President—arrived after a perilous trip down the Rossville road. From Garfield, Thomas at last learned what had happened to the rest of Rosecrans' army and received instructions from Rosecrans to withdraw from the field immediately. That was manifestly impossible. "It will ruin the army to withdraw it now," Thomas told Garfield. "This position must be held until night." Garfield accordingly dispatched a message informing Rosecrans in Chattanooga that Thomas was fighting off the Confederates and was "standing like a rock." Reprinted in newspapers all over the country, the message made a hero of the doughty XIV Corps commander, who would be known for the rest of his life as the "Rock of Chickamauga."

As twilight descended over the battlefield, Thomas went to work to get his men safely away. The Confederate attacks were continuing with undiminished intensity, and Thomas was once again running low on ammunition as he began his withdrawal. His plan was to pull back his divisions in sequence, starting with the southernmost, under Reynolds. Each division

was to march behind those still in line toward the safety of McFarland's Gap. But at 5:30 p.m., as Reynolds was leaving, the Confederates suddenly launched a savage blow straight toward him, endangering the entire Federal position. General Thomas himself, on the scene, commandeered the brigade led by Brigadier General John Turchin and wheeled the troops around. Gesturing toward the oncoming Confederates, Thomas said, "There they are. Clear them out." Turchin launched a furious attack and sent the Confederates reeling back. In the process his men captured 200 prisoners. Then Turchin rejoined Reynolds' retreating division.

One by one, the hard-pressed units left the field and hurried toward safety. In the end only three regiments—the 21st and 89th Ohio and the 22nd Michi-

Covering the Union withdrawal toward Chattanooga in the late afternoon of September 20, the troops of Brigadier General Absalom Baird—part of General Thomas' main defense—refused to budge. "We held our position, yielding not an inch," wrote Baird. "To fall back was more difficult than to remain."

gan—remained on Snodgrass Hill to hold off the Confederates. General Brannan hurried to Granger and cried: "The enemy are forming for another assault; we have not another round of ammunition—what shall we do?" Granger said, "Fix bayonets and go for them." Brannan immediately led a gallant charge, but without ammunition it was doomed. Within minutes the bloodied defenders were surrounded and overwhelmed. In the three Federal regiments, 322 soldiers were killed or wounded and 563 captured.

The last Federal survivors slipped away after darkness had fallen, when the Confederate fire was diminishing. Without light, Bragg's troops were beginning to fire into one another from the opposite sides of the salient. It had been a brilliant withdrawal under the nose of the enemy. "Like magic," Longstreet wrote lat-

er, "the Union army had melted away in our presence."

Polk got Bragg out of bed to report that the Federal army was in full flight and could be destroyed before Rosecrans had a chance to throw up adequate defenses. But Bragg, said an aide who was present, "could not be induced to look at it in that light, and refused to believe that we had won a victory." Bragg had his reasons for not wanting to continue the fight. His men were exhausted; losses on both sides had been enormous; and although no one yet knew the totals, Confederate casualties had been greater than those suffered by the Federals. The Rebels had lost 18,454 killed, wounded or captured, including nine brigade and two division commanders; Federal losses numbered 16,179, including seven brigade commanders. These had been the bloodiest two days of the war.

The Awesome Repeating Rifles

Most Civil War soldiers on both sides fought from beginning to end with muzzle-loading rifles. But in 1863 several units of the Federal Army of the Cumberland received a supply of revolutionary weapons. The firearms were multishot repeating rifles developed by two ingenious New England gunsmiths, Samuel Colt and Christopher Spencer.

The new weapons immediately proved their value. At the Battle of Chickamauga, two Federal units used their repeaters to devastating effect, helping to prevent a complete Federal rout. In five hours of fighting, the 535 men of the 21st Ohio fired an astonishing 43,550 rounds with their Colt revolving rifles. "My God," said a dazed Confederate prisoner, "we thought you had a division here."

At the same time, Colonel John T. Wilder's mounted infantry brigade broke up a powerful Confederate attack with their Spencer repeaters. "The effect was awful," Wilder reported. "The head of the attacking column seemed to melt away or sink into the earth."

Grouped with one of their officers, five men of the 21st Ohio hold their carefully burnished .56-caliber Colt revolving rifles. To make the new weapon (below), Samuel Colt took the revolving action that he had used in his famous pistols and adapted it to a long-barreled rifle with a full stock.

A foot soldier turned horseman, Private John M. Munson of Wilder's mounted brigade, retains an infantryman's standard outfit—but also carries a Spencer repeater. Most of Wilder's men possessed the full length, 47-inch rifle shown below, but some carried the shorter 39-inch Spencer carbine, which was better suited to use on horseback.

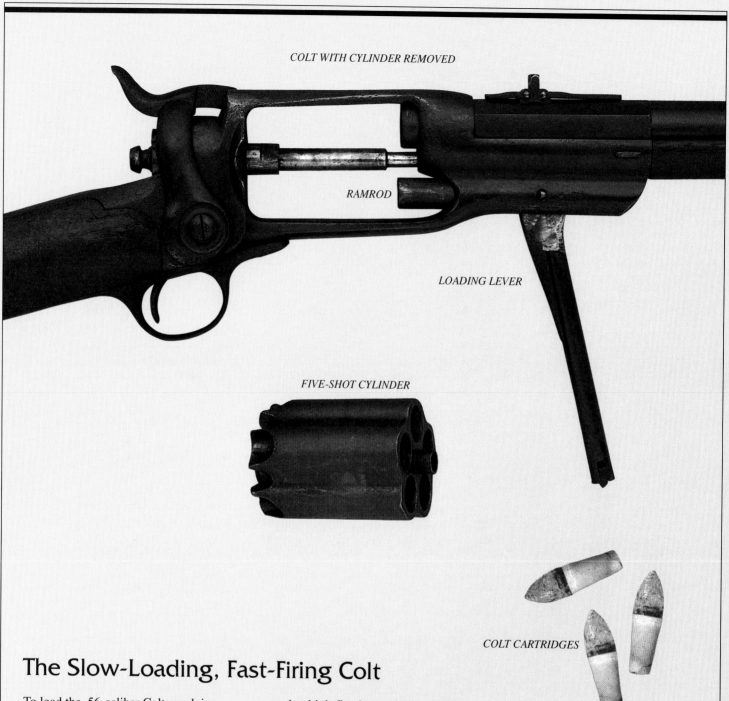

COLT WITH CYLINDER REMOVED

RAMROD

LOADING LEVER

FIVE-SHOT CYLINDER

COLT CARTRIDGES

The Slow-Loading, Fast-Firing Colt

To load the .56-caliber Colt revolving rifle, a soldier first half-cocked the hammer, allowing the cylinder to rotate freely. He then pushed a paper or parchment cartridge, with bullet attached, into one of the cylinder's five chambers. Next he turned the cylinder so that the loaded chamber was in the bottom position, and finally he pulled the lever activating the ramrod, which firmly seated the bullet.

After repeating this process four times more, the soldier placed percussion caps on the nipples that fired each of the chambers. Then, once he had loaded the weapon, a rifleman could fire the five rounds as swiftly as he was able to cock the hammer and pull the trigger—about nine seconds in all.

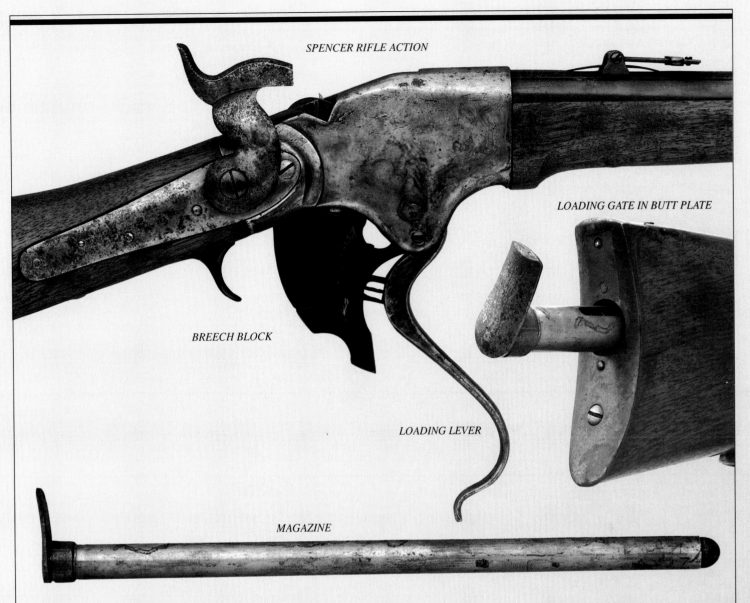

SPENCER RIFLE ACTION

LOADING GATE IN BUTT PLATE

BREECH BLOCK

LOADING LEVER

MAGAZINE

COPPER RIM-FIRE CARTRIDGES

The Rugged, Lever-Action Spencer

Key to the operation of the Spencer rifle was a recently developed copper cartridge that combined primer, powder and bullet in one case. The rifle's hammer detonated mercury fulminate in the cartridge rim. This ignited the powder and discharged the round.

Seven cartridges fitted into a tubelike magazine, which was inserted through the butt. To put a round in the breech for firing, a soldier depressed the loading lever, pulling down the breech block. A spring in the magazine then fed a round into the mechanism. When the soldier raised the lever, the breech block seated the round in the firing chamber. The mechanism also extracted an empty case each time it was loaded.

By September 22, the Federal army was safely within the Chattanooga defenses, and those works were being improved hourly. Moving to the outskirts of the town, Bragg had an idea: If he could occupy Missionary Ridge to the east and Lookout Mountain to the west, he could starve Rosecrans into submission. "We held him at our mercy," he would later say, "and his destruction was only a question of time."

For three days following the Battle of Chickamauga a Federal brigade remained on Lookout Mountain, which commanded the main rail and wagon routes to Chattanooga from the west. Then on September 24, over the strong objections of some of his subordinates, a badly shaken Rosecrans decided that the present position was untenable and withdrew the brigade. Bragg immediately seized the advantage; he occupied Lookout Mountain and posted artillery and sharpshooters along the Tennessee River valley below the ridge, placing Chattanooga under a virtual state of siege.

The Federal army had formerly been getting its supplies by rail from Nashville. After the Confederates occupied Lookout Mountain, supplies could be taken by rail only as far as Bridgeport, 27 miles west of Chattanooga. At this junction the Confederates had burned the railroad bridge across the Tennessee River; the route eastward was dominated by their artillery. From Bridgeport, the Federal wagon trains were forced to take a difficult, 60-mile route that took from eight to 20 days. As the siege wore on, food in Chat-

tanooga grew so scarce that men stole corn from the horses or hunted for it on the ground where the animals had eaten. By mid-October, officers frequently were being assailed by cries of "Crackers!" from men who were now eager to see more of the usually despised hardtack. And the supply route became known as "The Cracker Line."

Amid all this hardship—and with worse trouble threatening— Rosecrans, said correspondent Dana, seemed "dazed and mazy" and "insensible to the impending danger." Although the commanding general ordered that steamboats be built and the railroads supplying Chattanooga be repaired, he had no concrete plan. In Washington, it was becoming increasingly evident to the President that Rosecrans had lost his grip. Lincoln, remarking that Rosecrans was "stunned and confused, like a duck hit on the head," decided that this perilous situation had to be placed in the hands of his most trusted commander.

Ulysses S. Grant was summoned from Vicksburg to a meeting in Louisville, Kentucky, on October 19, with Secretary of War Edwin Stanton. When Stanton asked Grant whether Rosecrans should be relieved of his command, Grant did not hesitate: He urged that Rosecrans be replaced by General Thomas. Grant sent off a flurry of telegrams notifying Rosecrans and Thomas of the changes in command and ordering Thomas to "Hold Chattanooga at all hazards." The reply from the Rock of Chickamauga was immediate: "We will hold the town till we starve." Then Grant set out at all speed for Chattanooga.

On October 23 just as darkness was falling, Grant arrived at Thomas' headquarters "wet, dirty and well," in Dana's words. Early the next morning Grant gave his approval to a plan already set in motion by Thomas for ending the Confederate siege. On the morning of the 27th, two Federal forces—including the key one which glided silently down the meandering Tennessee River on pontoon boats—overwhelmed the Confederates at a landing called Brown's Ferry. They then struck across a peninsula formed by a hairpin bend in the Tennessee, clearing the Confederates from a road that linked Brown's Ferry to Kelley's Ferry—a second landing that could be reached from Bridgeport by steamboat. By taking control of the short stretch between the landings the Federals could get their supplies into Chattanooga with an overland haul of only eight miles. "We've

knocked the cover off the cracker box!" yelled an exultant Federal officer to his men.

An attempt by Confederate Brigadier General Micah Jenkins to recapture Brown's Ferry the following evening failed. Meanwhile, Federal reinforcements were on the way. Major General Joseph Hooker, with 20,000 men dispatched by train from Virginia on September 25, was now advancing toward Bridgeport. And on November 13 Major General William Tecumseh Sherman arrived in Bridgeport from the west with the advance of his four divisions.

Ironically, while the Federal army was strengthening its position, the Confederates were weakening their hold on Chattanooga; Bragg made the dubious decision to send James Longstreet and 15,000 men to attack Burnside at Knoxville. The strategy was questionable, but it did remove from Bragg's sight a general who thought him unfit for command. After Chickamauga, Longstreet and eleven other officers had petitioned President Davis to relieve Bragg, but Davis had stood by his commander. Longstreet's departure, Bragg wrote to Davis on October 31, "will be a great relief to me."

Longstreet was appalled by the order. Without more men he had little hope of prevailing against Burnside's superior forces at Knoxville: 12,000 infantry plus 8,500 cavalry. Worse, Longstreet's departure would leave Bragg with about 40,000 men along an eight-mile line facing a concentrated enemy that, with Sherman's arrival, would number almost 60,000.

In fact, Grant was laying plans to use Sherman's fresh troops to break the Confederate stronghold. Grant was an offensive-minded soldier, and he had found it intolerable to be cooped up in Chattanooga, surrounded by towering hills and trapped by a threatening enemy. "I have never felt such restlessness before," he wrote, "as I have at the fixed and immovable condition of the Army of the Cumberland."

Grant planned his offensive carefully. To defeat the Confederates and retain the town, he would have to attack an enemy entrenched on high ground. Grant had three forces at his disposal. He elected to give what he thought would be the pivotal role in the assault to the Army of the Tennessee, commanded by his old friend, Sherman. Grant viewed the other two forces with less enthusiasm. He suspected that Major General Joseph Hooker and his XI and XII Corps had been sent to him as the castoffs of the Army of the Potomac—Hooker's reputation had been stained at Chancellorsville several months earlier. Grant's third force, Thomas' Army of the Cumberland, had just been through the crushing defeat at Chickamauga, and he was worried about the soldiers' state of mind. Hooker and Thomas were relegated to supporting roles in Grant's plan.

Sherman's target would be the Confederate right—at the junction of Bragg's supply line from the south and his line of communication with Longstreet to the north. Sherman was to march upriver from Bridgeport to Brown's Ferry, cross to the north side of the Tennessee and move into the hills north of Chattanooga. This movement could not be hidden from the watchful Confederates on Lookout Mountain, but Grant hoped to confuse them about where the Federals were going. As Sherman's Army of the Tennessee neared Lookout Mountain, one division was to be detached for a feint against Bragg's left. The rest of Sherman's army would disappear from Confederate view—marching northward, as if to Knoxville. But once safely out of sight on the north side of the river, the men would make camp and lie hidden. Then, in a rapid nighttime move, Sherman was to bridge the river and roll up the Confederate right flank along Missionary Ridge. Bragg would thus be cut off from his supply base at Chickamauga Station and driven away, if not destroyed.

The attack was scheduled for November 21, but heavy rains hampered the progress of Sherman's army from Bridgeport. The roads grew worse and the river began to rise, threatening the pontoon bridge at Brown's Ferry. When all of Sherman's divisions but one had finally crossed the river, the bridge gave way. The soldiers in the division stranded on the far side of the river were quickly reassigned to join General Hooker's forces in Lookout Valley.

Soon after the Army of the Tennessee was safely hidden from the Confederates, a Federal corps crossed the bridge at Chattanooga and moved behind Thomas' defense. This put the finishing touch to Grant's ruse. He hoped that the Confederates, having seen soldiers crossing at Brown's Ferry and, a short time later, seeing soldiers moving across the river into Chattanooga, would conclude that they were the same soldiers.

Much time had been lost—it was now November 22—but Grant was just about ready. Sherman's advance was rescheduled for the 24th of November.

Bragg, thoroughly confused watching all the enemy troop movement, fretted about Sherman's location. Was the Army of the Tennessee preparing for a flanking attack on Lookout Mountain? Was it headed toward Knoxville? Or had Sherman merely reinforced Thomas in Chattanooga? Bragg finally concluded that Sherman was marching on Knoxville, and on November 22 he ordered two divisions to entrain for the north to reinforce Longstreet.

Early on the morning of November 23 Grant set his forces in motion. In Chattanooga Valley, the plain lying between the town and Missionary Ridge to the east, there was a wooded mound called Orchard Knob held by the Confederates. General Thomas was to conduct a reconnaissance in force toward Orchard Knob to see if the Confederate positions in the valley were still occupied. At his discretion, he could seize Orchard Knob. As Thomas was fully aware, the entire operation would be closely watched by friend and foe alike. The Chattanooga Valley and its surrounding hills formed a magnificent amphitheater; Grant wrote later that it was "the first battlefield I have ever seen where a plan could be followed, and from one place the whole field be within one view."

As the troops marched briskly out of the Chattanooga defenses, Grant watched from one of the nearby hills, surrounded by high-ranking officers. "It was an inspiring sight," an observer wrote, "Flags were flying; the quick, earnest steps of thousands beat equal time." Men everywhere stopped to watch. On the hills looming over the plain, clusters of Confederates could be seen staring at the display—like many of the Federals, they believed for a moment that Thomas was staging a grand review. Then, suddenly, the Confederates realized they were under attack and scurried for cover. Those watching in Chattanooga heard a faint cheer from the Knob. And all at once it was over. "The entire movement was carried out in such an incredibly short time," said Charles Dana, "that at half past three I was able to send a telegram to Stanton describing the victory." For a victory it had been—Thomas had seized a mile of ground, as well as Confederate fortifications.

In the game of cat-and-mouse that Grant and Bragg had been playing, Grant had seized the advantage, and he intended to keep it. Sherman's men by now

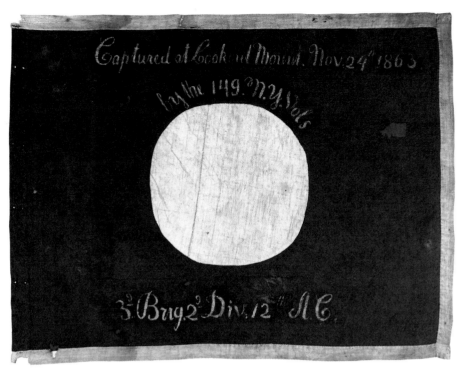

This Confederate flag, carried by a Mississippi regiment in the Battle of Lookout Mountain, was captured during the fighting by Private Peter Kappesser of the 149th New York. The action won fame for Kappesser: He was awarded the Medal of Honor.

were hidden in the woods eight miles northeast of Chattanooga. Just before midnight on November 23, pontoons began ferrying Sherman's men south across the river, and work was started on a bridge. Despite the intense activity, Sherman recalled, "I have never beheld any work done so quietly, so well."

Sherman wasted no time. Once his troops had crossed the Tennessee River, he deployed them in three infantry columns and, about 1 p.m. on the 24th, sent them up the hill just east of the river. Astonishingly, there was virtually no opposition as the attackers ascended. It was not until they reached the summit that Confederate cannon opened up on them. With great difficulty, Sherman's troops dragged their artillery to the top of the slope, and soon a brisk exchange of shells had begun. At last, Sherman, peering about in the rain and mist, had his first opportunity to take stock and now he received a shock. He was on the wrong hill.

Sherman's objective had been the northmost part of Missionary Ridge, known locally as Tunnel Hill because of the railroad tunnel that passed under it. His maps showed Missionary Ridge as a continuous range running almost to the river. In fact, Sherman could now see that there was a sharp break in the ridge, and the hill closest to the river—the one on which he was standing—was a separate eminence. His labors had left him as far from his objective as ever; he had also lost all chance of surprise.

As Sherman stood pondering the deep valley that separated him from his goal on Tunnel Hill, on the other side of the battlefield Joseph Hooker's men were doing their best to redeem their commander's tarnished reputation. In the weeks since Chickamau-

ga, Lookout Mountain—looming, one correspondent said, like "an everlasting thunderstorm"—had taken on a sinister character, symbolizing the frustration of the Federal army. The mountain also provided some Federals with a taunt for Hooker's troops—it had been a wry comment around the Federal campfires for weeks: "On some fine morning General Hooker is going to take Lookout."

Now, in an intermittent fog at dawn on November 24, Hooker's 10,000 men attacked the entrenched Confederates on the north slope of the mountain in a fight that would later be romanticized as the Battle above the Clouds. Some 7,000 Confederates were defending the mountain, but only a fraction of them were in position to contest Hooker's determined assault. Behind a fierce, unrelenting fire, Hooker's men clawed their way up the hill all day, steadily advancing but unable to break the Confederate resistance. As darkness fell they dug in, preparing to renew the fighting in the morning. That night the opposing armies saw the moon in almost total eclipse—regarded on both sides as an ill omen for the Confederates because they were perched on the mountaintop, nearest the moon.

As the sky lightened over the peak on November 25, the Federal troops on the slopes below discovered that the Confederates had departed during the night. Bragg had glumly concluded that his troops had little chance of holding Hooker back. He also feared that his Rebels would be flanked, perhaps cut off, and annihilated the next morning.

At first light, a captain and five men from the 8th Kentucky climbed unopposed to the summit of Lookout Mountain and staged a thrilling pageant. Just before sunrise, carrying a furled U.S. flag, they stepped out onto an overhanging rock. They waited for the sun, and just as its rays hit the peak, the men let loose the flag to the great delight of the thousands watching from below. "Lookout was ours," said one man, "never again to be used as a perch by rebel vultures."

Lookout had not been a major battle; it was more like a "magnificent skirmish," said a reporter, and Federal losses had been remarkably light, about 480 men in all. (A brigade commander, noting that his unit's casualties totaled only 56, felt compelled to apologize for the figure. "It is small," he admitted in his report. "The day was dark, and the men well sheltered with rocks.") Grant later scoffed at the mythol-

ogy that enveloped the fog-shrouded battle: "It is all poetry." Poetry or not, Hooker's troops had achieved one objective and were now available for further fighting. Grant immediately ordered them to set out for Rossville Gap in Missionary Ridge to find—and attack—Bragg's left flank.

As Hooker was setting out from Lookout, Sherman was confidently launching a massive attack on Tunnel Hill. He had an overwhelming superiority of numbers—six divisions totaling 26,000 men against only 10,000 Confederates in two divisions. But the overall commander of those gray divisions on Bragg's right was General Patrick Cleburne. That day Cleburne would add new luster to his reputation as the "Stonewall Jackson of the West." Time after time Sherman's men grimly charged Cleburne's lines, into the teeth of what a soldier in the 6th Iowa called "a terrific storm of musket balls and canister." Each time they were thrown back. At 2 p.m. one of Sherman's generals found his commander sitting on a stone fence, watching the "stinging disappointment" unfold, and reported that Sherman "gave vent to his feelings in language of astonishing vivacity." A short time later Cleburne himself, waving a sword, led a counterattack that took 500 prisoners. Sherman sent word to Grant that his attack had been stopped cold.

Although Grant still had Thomas' Army of the Cumberland poised to strike at the heavily fortified center of Bragg's line, there was no point in sending in Thomas until a Confederate flank had been turned. Sherman's failure to make an impression on the Confederate right lent new urgency to Hooker's advance on Bragg's left. After a pause to rebuild a bridge over Chattanooga Creek, Hooker attacked with alacrity. At around 3 p.m. General John Breckinridge took personal command of the far left Confederate flank, and arrived to find a rapidly developing disaster.

Hooker's forces had driven two regiments from Rossville Gap, and had gained a foothold on the southern slope of Missionary Ridge itself. Breckinridge was heavily outnumbered, and his line to the immediate north had been thinned to reinforce Cleburne. Unable to get additional troops, he could do nothing more than fall back as slowly as possible. Hooker's Federals drove onto the crest of the ridge and routed the defenders, taking hundreds of prisoners. Finally, the destruction of the Confederate flank that Grant had been looking for was under

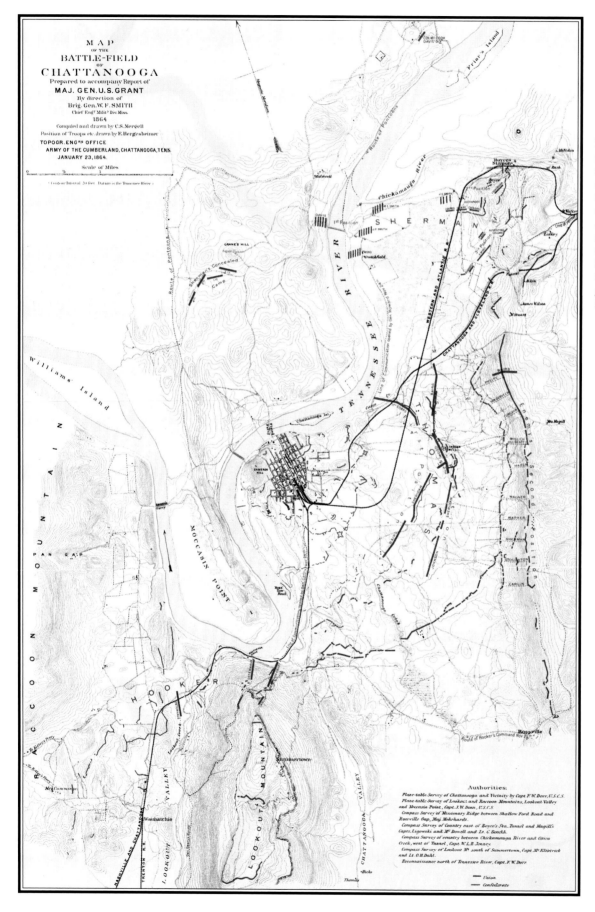

This official U.S. Army map, drawn for General Grant, shows the Confederate entrenchments and the dispositions of Federal troops during the final battles of the Chattanooga Campaign. After Hooker's divisions captured Lookout Mountain and gained control of the Chattanooga Valley beyond, the forces of Thomas and Sheridan began their drive to push the Confederates from Missionary Ridge.

way; but Hooker, not Sherman, was accomplishing it.

Grant and his aides were still attempting to watch the unfolding events from Orchard Knob. The Confederates defending Missionary Ridge had found the range of the little hill by now, and artillery shells were landing uncomfortably close. "When we saw them coming," recalled Charles Dana, one of the observers, "we would duck—that is everybody did except Generals Grant and Thomas and Gordon Granger. It was not according to their dignity to go down on their marrow bones."

The crest of Missionary Ridge was in clear sight. "Bragg's headquarters," said Grant, "were in full view, and officers—presumably staff officers—could be seen coming and going constantly." Grant also thought he could see "column after column" of Confederate reinforcements being rushed to Cleburne. In this he was mistaken, but the prospect worried him. With darkness not far off, he decided to send Thomas forward immediately to relieve the pressure on Sherman. Still lacking confidence in the Army of the Cumberland, Grant gave Thomas only a limited objective: His forces were to take the Confederate rifle pits at the foot of Missionary Ridge and then await further instructions.

Grant had no way of knowing that the obstacle confronting Thomas was far less formidable than it appeared. Bragg had left Breckinridge with only three divisions to defend four miles of line, and he had even further weakened the defenses with faulty command decisions. Unfamiliar with defensive warfare, Bragg had divided his forces along most of his line, sending half of each regiment into the rifle pits located 200 yards in front of the base of the ridge while deploying the rest on the crest. Then Bragg had issued instructions for the men in the rifle pits: If attacked, fire one volley and withdraw up the hill. His order was to have disastrous consequences. Even worse for the Confederates, the still-unfinished breastworks along the top of the ridge had, thanks to an incompetent engineer, been laid out incorrectly. They were sited at the geographic crest—the highest elevation—instead of being placed at the military crest, which was the elevation that commanded the maximum field of fire down the slope.

When the order to attack the Confederate rifle pits was transmitted, Thomas' men, still smarting from Grant's slights, could hardly wait to advance: "We

were crazy to charge," said an Indiana man. An officer reported afterward that in his brigade "all servants, cooks, clerks found guns in some way" and pushed into the ranks.

Once again, the preliminary formation provided a stunning spectacle. As before, Thomas, the consummate drillmaster, formed his ranks with precision, the lines ruler-straight, bands playing, banners fluttering. The troops formed up with Brigadier General Absalom Baird's division on the left, then Generals Thomas Wood's, Philip Sheridan's and Richard Johnson's. When they emerged onto the plain, 20,000 strong, they were a fearsome sight to the Confederates watching from the mountaintop a mile away.

The Confederate guns blasted great holes in the Federal lines, but the attackers continued relentlessly forward. They advanced without firing, skirmishers in front. Soon the main body broke into a spontaneous double-quick run and caught up with the skirmishers. The Confederates held their fire until Thomas' army was within 200 yards. Then they loosed a withering volley. Yet still the Federals pressed on, and most of the Confederates, obeying Bragg's orders, scurried up the ridge.

This movement proved ruinous for the Confederates: It encouraged the Federals, who thought they were watching their enemy taking flight, and dismayed the defenders higher on the ridge who did not know that the friendly forces were retreating under orders. The rifle pits were taken swiftly, and many of the Confederates who had stayed behind were captured. The Federal soldiers lay there, panting but exultant. As the Confederate prisoners were led back toward town, a Union soldier jeered at them, "You've been trying to get there long enough! Now charge on to Chattanooga!"

The triumphant Federals found that they were now exposed to a galling rifle fire from the Confederate entrenchments above them. The colonel of the 8th Kansas declared to his brigade commander, "We can't live here." A sudden restlessness swept the ranks of men milling at the base of the ridge.

A moment later Grant, watching through his binoculars, saw an astonishing sight. A number of blueclad soldiers were starting up the hill. He watched in disbelief as more men followed. Soon long lines of Federal soldiers could be seen laboriously moving up the slope. Grant had never contemplated a major assault

Confederate prisoners crowd a ravine behind Belle Plain, Virginia, waiting for rations from commissary wagons (background). About 7,500 prisoners passed through

A Prisoner's Plight

For most men taken by the enemy, the dismal journey to captivity began in a temporary holding pen near the battlefield. After their names and units had been recorded, they were moved to one of the war's 150 detention centers.

North or South, the inmates were never far from starvation. A South Carolinian noted that his daily prison fare at Point Lookout, Maryland, was a half pint of "slop water" coffee for breakfast and a half pint of "greasy water" soup for dinner, followed by a small piece of meat. The meat available to men on both sides was described in letters and journals as "rusty" and "slimy"—and the other fare was no better. But to near-starving men, any fare would do.

The barracks in many prisons were primitive structures—wet, cold and unsanitary. At Camp Morton in Indianapolis, the barracks had no floors and were so flimsy that snow and rain blew through them; Andersonville prison in Georgia offered no barracks at all. At most installations, filth built up inside and outside the barracks, inviting swarms of pests. The need for clothing was often so acute that the living seized the garments of those who died.

Altogether during the war, about 194,000 Union Troops went into Southern prisons, where 30,000 died. Of the 214,000 Confederates sent north to Union prisons, about 26,000 died. Considering all that the prisoners suffered, however, it was a wonder that anybody at all stayed alive. Survivors of the camps remembered how men would press a thumb into their flesh to see if a discoloration was left in the indentation—a sign of scurvy. Victims of that disease would lose their teeth, along with their hair; then they could not walk, and finally they died.

To escape from this nightmare world was the dream of every prisoner. Eventually, with the coming of peace, prison doors everywhere opened, but the bitterness brought by injury to body and spirit would be felt long afterward.

Belle Plain between May 13 and May 18, 1864, before being shipped to prison at Point Lookout, Maryland.

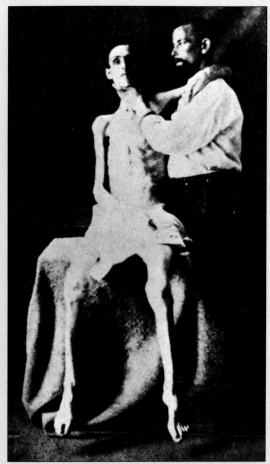

Held upright by a hospital attendant, an emaciated Federal soldier released from Richmond's Belle Isle Prison shows the ghastly effects of starvation and disease. A surgeon who examined former inmates of Belle Isle estimated that 90 per cent weighed less than 100 pounds.

Federal prisoners swelter in the August heat at Andersonville, Georgia, the notorious camp that came to epitomize the evils of Civil War prison camps. More a vast, ill-organized and thoroughly inadequate hospital than a prison, Andersonville needed not guards, but doctors and medicine. The lack of medical care was responsible for a horrendous mortality rate. In the space of less than a year, 13,000 men died at Andersonville.

327

by Thomas' forces. All questions of morale aside, the Army of the Cumberland was probably no stronger—and possibly weaker—than the Confederate force opposing it on the mountain. Moreover, the center of Bragg's line was presumably its strongest point; certainly the terrain there was forbidding. This unplanned attack against a nearly impregnable defensive position was an invitation to disaster. At one point Grant considered calling the men back. Then he decided to wait a few minutes. "It's all right," an officer heard him mutter, "if it turns out all right." And then he said: "If not, someone will suffer."

As Grant deliberated, the Army of the Cumberland was advancing. Under heavy fire from above, the Federals had—in the felicitous phrase used later by a French nobleman who had served on Major General George B. McClellan's staff—"fled forward," toward their tormenters.

The slope was now a scene of swarming activity. The Federals were heavily burdened, carrying nine-pound muskets as well as 40 rounds of ammunition. In addition, most of the troops were wearing overcoats, for the weather had turned bitter cold. Nevertheless, they scarcely hesitated as they crawled and clawed their way up the incline. A member of Bragg's staff, watching the scene with growing incredulity, concluded that the Federals must be drunk.

The ascending soldiers detected the confusion they were causing among their enemy, and were heartened by it. "Those defending the heights became more and more desperate as our men approached the top," said an Illinois soldier. "They lighted the fuses of shells and rolled them down, they seized huge stones and threw them, but nothing could stop the force of the charge."

There was something unearthly about those climbers; nothing seemed to daunt them. The Confederates on Missionary Ridge had demonstrated their courage repeatedly in the months preceding the siege of Chattanooga. But now, as the eerily determined Federals began to reach the crest of the ridge, the resolution of the defenders ebbed. Men threw down their arms and fled, and their panic proved contagious. On the Confederate left, Hooker's troops had driven Breckinridge back two and a half miles from his position, almost as far as Bragg's headquarters on the center of the ridge. Breckinridge now joined the commanding general, who was trying to stop the rout.

Bragg did what he could. A few moments before, when the Union advance had hesitated at the foot of the hill, he thought that the attack had been stopped. He was riding along the crest waving his hat and congratulating his men when the whole position suddenly caved in around him. He said later: "A panic which I never before witnessed seemed to have seized upon officers and men, and each seemed to be struggling for his personal safety, regardless of his duty and his character." Repeatedly, Bragg rode up to groups of his fleeing soldiers, standing in their path and crying: "Here's your commander!" But the soldiers only jeered and brushed past. Breckinridge's response to the chaos around them was more practical, if less soldierly: "Boys," he shouted, "get away the best you can." Indeed, both he and Bragg narrowly escaped capture.

Those watching the scene from Orchard Knob saw the ragged lines of blue reach the crest—in several places at the same time—and, said one observer, "in a few moments the flags of 60 Yankee regiments float along Mission Ridge from one end to the other." A great victory cry swept the ridge as the Federal soldiers realized what they had done. General Granger rode gleefully through the celebrating men, shouting: "I'm going to have you all court-martialed! You were ordered to take the works at the foot of the hill and you have taken those at the top! You have disobeyed orders!"

A soldier of the 8th Kansas never forgot the Confederate panic. "In ten minutes, all that remained of the defiant rebel army that had so long besieged Chattanooga was captured guns, disarmed prisoners, moaning wounded, ghastly dead, and scattered, demoralized fugitives. Mission Ridge was ours."

But not quite all of it. At the north end of the ridge, General Cleburne was for a time unaware of the disaster that had befallen the rest of the Army of Tennessee. "At our end of the line," said one private, "we thought the battle had all gone our way." Cleburne's soldiers were actually cheering their victory over Sherman when word came that the Confederate center had collapsed and Cleburne was in danger of being flanked. Cleburne, the only Confederate general involved in the fighting who had not been routed, was charged with protecting the retreat. Slowly and reluctantly, but in good order, he withdrew from Tunnel Hill and deployed his troops as a rear guard for the broken army.

The fight for Lookout Mountain and Missionary Ridge—soon to be known collectively as the Battle

Generals Granger, Grant and Thomas, on a ledge at left, watch from Orchard Knob as their troops swarm up Missionary Ridge in the background. "What was on the summit they knew not," Granger wrote, "and did not inquire. The enemy was before them; to know that was to know sufficient."

of Chattanooga—had not been especially costly in men compared with the war's major battles—Chickamauga, for example. The Confederate casualty total for the three days—6,700 soldiers killed, wounded or captured—was higher than that of the Union, which lost 5,800 men. Most of the Confederate casualties—4,100 troops—however, were prisoners taken in the attack on Missionary Ridge; only 350 of the 5,800 Federals were captured.

Grant pursued Bragg's forces only briefly; the Federal army was low on rations and he did not think it could live off the barren country below Chattanooga. He also had to send Sherman to the relief of Burnside, besieged at Knoxville by Longstreet. Upon hearing of Sherman's approach, Longstreet decamped.

Confederate forces would return to Tennessee, but the South would never recover from the effects of the fighting around Chattanooga. The gateway to the heart of the Confederacy had been flung open; and by the banks of the Tennessee River, William Tecumseh Sherman was already starting to think about a Federal advance on the city of Atlanta in the spring.

Diarist Sarah Morgan

A CHRONICLE
OF OCCUPATION

"The excitement has reached the point of delirium—we only know we had best be prepared for anything," wrote 20-year-old Sarah Morgan when she heard about the fall of New Orleans in April 1862. The news fed her worst fear—that the Yankees would come up the Mississippi River and conquer her hometown of Baton Rouge, Louisiana's peaceful state capital. Indeed, scarcely a month later, the first Federal gunboats did arrive, and for the next three years, this wellborn young woman set down in a diary her account of life under enemy rule.

The war had divided Sarah's family. A brother living in New Orleans had declared for the Union. Three others were off fighting for the Confederacy. Sarah, her two sisters and widowed mother were left to fend for themselves in Baton Rouge. Pretty and impressionable, Sarah at first found some of the Federal officers as gallant as any Southern gentleman. But as the realities of war came to Baton Rouge, she lost her romantic notions.

In this wartime photograph of Baton Rouge, shops line Laurel Street as it approaches Church Street, where Sarah Morgan lived.

Their vessels anchored in the Mississippi River, Federal sailors in Admiral David G. Farragut's fleet relax on the Baton Rouge riverfront in the summer of 1862.

First Impressions of a Powerful Foe

"About sunset, a graceful young Federal stepped ashore, carrying a Yankee flag, and asked the way to the Mayor's office." Thus did Sarah Morgan describe the capture of Baton Rouge. At first, such polite formalities prevailed. "These people," she confided to her diary, "have disarmed me by their kindness. I admire foes who show so much consideration for our feelings."

Sarah and her sisters received soldiers in their home and took girlish delight in watching the troops drill. "One conceited, red-haired lieutenant smiled at us in the most fascinating way," she gushed. "Perhaps he smiled to think how fine he was, and what an impression he was making." But when a Federal officer offered to place a guard around the Morgan home to protect it against vandals, Sarah advised her mother that acceptance would smack of collaboration. And she worried lest she become too familiar. "Why wasn't I born old and ugly?" she lamented. "Suppose I should unconsciously entrap some magnificent Yankee! What an awful thing it would be!"

Federal soldiers from the troopship Sallie Robinson *form ranks on Main Street. The troops, wrote Sarah, were "stared at unmercifully and pursued by crowds of ragged little boys."*

A family and their slaves comb through the ruins of their burned-out home in August 1862, after the Federals reduced a third of Baton Rouge to rubble.

Before it was gutted by fire, the Louisiana State House was used by the Federals to hold prisoners.

The Ruin of a Town

The honeymoon between Baton Rouge's occupiers and townsfolk ended abruptly in late May of 1862 when Confederate guerrillas wounded three Federal sailors. Federal gunboats retaliated by shelling the city. Then, on August 5, a 2,600-man Confederate force attempted to retake the city and was repulsed only after a bloody fight; each side suffered 84 killed.

Fearing a second attack, the Federals chopped down many magnificent shade trees to furnish wood for abatis. And to provide a clear field of fire around Federal defense lines, houses and other buildings were put to the torch.

Sarah Morgan, who had taken refuge on a relative's plantation, returned to find Baton Rouge "hardly recognizable."

THE KILLING GROUND

*"The assault at Cold Harbor was an attempt, by sheer and furious fighting,
to force the advantage which march and maneuver had missed. It failed at a cost
of life matched by no other fifteen minutes of four years war."*

ADJUTANT JOSEPH MUFFLY, 148TH PENNSYLVANIA, AT COLD HARBOR

General Ulysses S. Grant was at his winter headquarters in Nashville on March 3, 1864, when he received word from the Secretary of War that he was to assume command of all the Union armies. Five days later, Grant reached Washington with his eldest son, Fred, in tow. Through a mixup no one met their train, and when the rumpled officer and the 13-year-old boy presented themselves at the desk of Willard's Hotel, the clerk was thoroughly unimpressed. The conqueror of Vicksburg and Chattanooga signed the register simply "U.S. Grant and Son, Galena, Illinois." The name worked instant magic. The clerk immediately assigned Grant the best suite in the house—the one where Lincoln had stayed before his inauguration.

That evening Grant walked two blocks to the White House, where guests thronged the Blue Room for the weekly reception held by the President and Mrs. Lincoln. Although the two men from Illinois had never met, Lincoln recognized his visitor and stepped forward to pump his hand. "Why, here is General Grant!" exclaimed the President. "Well, this is a great pleasure, I assure you."

When someone in the crowded room cried out, "Stand up, so we can all have a look at you," Grant obliged by standing on a sofa. He remained there, accepting the adulation, for nearly an hour. "For once, at least, the President of the United States was not the chief figure in the picture," recorded a journalist. "The little, scared-looking man who stood on the crimson-colored sofa was the idol of the hour."

Frightened though he may have appeared, Grant now bore upon his shoulders the nation's hopes for bringing to the war in the East the same degree of determination he had displayed in the West. After Gettysburg, Major General George Meade's cautious pursuit of Robert E. Lee had reminded Lincoln of nothing more than "an old woman trying to shoo her geese across a creek." In Virginia during the ensuing eight months, the rival armies had engaged in a dismal campaign of maneuver, marching much and fighting little. Now, Lincoln had selected Grant as the man who could end the impasse.

Grant quickly got down to business. On March 17 he issued General Order No. 1, which began: "I assume command of the Armies of the United States, headquarters in the field, and until notice these will be those of the Army of the Potomac." Meade would continue to lead the fight against Lee, but Grant would map the way—not from Washington or from the West, but from a tent not far from Meade's.

Next, Grant took a train to Cincinnati to confer with Major General William Tecumseh Sherman, whom he had named as his replacement in command of the Union's Western armies. Later, Sherman concisely summarized the grand strategy they had devised during their meeting: "He was to go for Lee and I was to go for Joe Johnston. That was the plan." When Grant returned to the East, his orders to Meade were equally succinct: "Lee's army will be your objective point. Wherever Lee goes, there you will go also."

Grant's design would be put to the test that spring as he led the Army of the Potomac against the forces of Lee in a series of battles whose names would be written in blood: the Wilderness, Spotsylvania and Cold Harbor.

Awaiting the coming of the campaign season, the Army of the Potomac remained in winter quarters north of the Rapidan River, around Brandy Station, Virginia. As one Federal officer wrote, life on the north bank was "miserably lazy. Hardly an order to carry, and the horses eating their heads off."

Grant took advantage of the lull to streamline the army. He disbanded its I and III Corps, which had been decimated at Gettysburg, and distributed the men between II and V Corps. He also

President Lincoln and General Grant (right of center) meet for the first time at a White House reception on March 8, 1864. The artist of this painting was so eager to include portraits of the military heroes of the day that he let his imagination triumph over fact. Generals William Tecumseh Sherman, George G. Meade and George B. McClellan are shown standing in a cluster to the left and Winfield Scott sits among the ladies at right; in reality none of the four were present.

An "ordinary, scrubby looking man with a slightly seedy look," is how distinguished writer Richard Henry Dana Jr. described Ulysses S. Grant, commander of all Union Forces. "He had no gait, no station, no manner." But even Dana conceded that the 41-year-old general had a certain "look of resolution, as if he could not be trifled with."

selected a new leader for the Cavalry Corps: Philip H. Sheridan, a cocky and aggressive 33-year-old major general who had distinguished himself in the West. Sheridan stood but five feet six inches tall, and after he was introduced around the War Department someone remarked to Grant: "That officer you brought on from the West is rather a little fellow to handle your cavalry." Replied Grant: "You will find him big enough for the purpose before we get through with him."

Now, in April, spring was budding, and every veteran knew what it presaged. Wrote Union Private Robert G. Carter in a letter to his parents: "The summer days are almost here, when we shall be wearily plodding over the roads once more in search of *victory* or *death*. Many a poor fellow will find the latter. I dread the approaching campaign. I can see horrors insurmountable through the summer months."

On Wednesday, May 4, Grant began moving his 122,000 troops across the Rapidan, due east of its junction with the Rappahannock, by way of Germanna Ford and Ely's Ford. Beyond the river stood the dark and silent Wilderness, a gray-green expanse, 12 miles wide and six miles deep. A nasty tangle of briers, stunted pines and dense undergrowth, the

Wilderness lay "reaching back in mysterious silence," wrote a Federal soldier.

Somewhere out there, too, in the Virginia countryside, was Robert E. Lee with 61,000 Confederates—all determined to make the Federals pay dearly for every mile they marched.

By 9 o'clock that morning, Confederate scouts had confirmed Lee's prediction of the Federal movement. The general realized the import of the looming battle: The previous night, in his headquarters at Orange Court House, about 20 miles southwest of the Wilderness, Lee had written stoically: "If victorious, we have everything to live for. If defeated, there will be nothing left to live for."

Lee's main force, composed of three corps, was outnumbered 2 to 1 but had the advantage of operating in familiar territory. Closest to the advancing Federals was Lieutenant General Richard Ewell and his II Corps in the vicinity of Mine Run. Upstream on the Rapidan, south of Ewell was Lieutenant General A.P. Hill's III Corps. Ten miles south of Hill was Lieutenant General James Longstreet and his I Corps, newly returned from campaigning in Tennessee. On May 4, Longstreet's position was at Gordonsville, still 30 miles from the Wilderness.

Three roads, roughly parallel, led eastward from Lee's infantry encampments into the Wilderness: the Orange Turnpike, which ran from Orange Court House through Chancellorsville and continued to Fredericksburg; the Orange Plank road, about two miles south of the Turnpike; and the Catharpin road, another two or three miles farther south. On receiving word that his enemy was moving, Lee ordered Ewell forward along the Turnpike. He then instructed A.P. Hill to send two divisions forward on the Orange Plank road, while leaving behind a division to guard against any surprise attack across the upper fords of the Rapidan. Longstreet, farther away than the others, would move up along the Catharpin road. Thus, all three Confederate corps would be aimed at the right flank of Grant's army as it headed south.

The Federals began the march in high spirits, and Major Abner Small of the 16th Maine later recalled "a glorious spring day. Wildflowers were up; I remember them nodding by the roadside. Everything was bright and blowing." But by nightfall, as the men encamped in the sinister Wilderness, a gloomier mood had set in. There were Chancellorsville's skeletons here from the battle the previous year, recently uncovered by the rains of winter. An infantryman kicked at a skull and told his comrades: "This is what you are all coming to, and some of you will start toward it tomorrow."

At that moment, Confederate forces were bivouacking only five miles to the west. Ewell had penetrated two or three miles into the Wilderness, and his lead elements had stopped at a place called Locust Grove. For all his hesitations at Gettysburg, Richard Ewell was now looking forward to a good fight, and he was pleased with the instructions he had received from Lee. "Just the orders I like," Ewell said. "Go straight down the road and strike the enemy wherever I find him."

As anxious as his men to get out of the Wilderness, Grant had the troops on the road by 5 a.m. on May 5. Major General Gouverneur Kemble Warren, a hero of Gettysburg, sent Brigadier General Charles Griffin's division a short distance west on the Orange Turnpike to shield his flank, while Warren himself headed south with the rest of the men from his V Corps. His column was on a country lane about a mile short of the Orange Plank road when he learned that Federal skirmishers had encountered Confed-

erate infantry approaching along the Orange Turnpike.

The Rebels were Ewell's men, and they quickly began forming for action, with Major General Edward Johnson's division deploying on the east edge of a large, bramble-covered clearing, known as Sanders' Field, that straddled the Turnpike.

General Lee, riding with A.P. Hill on the Orange Plank road to the south, knew that his army was not yet ready for a major action: Longstreet's corps was still a day's march away. Lee sent word to Ewell to moderate his advance.

It was too late, however. No sooner had Ewell ordered his commanders to "fall back slowly, if pressed," than Griffin's Federals came swarming out of the thickets. North of the Turnpike, the charge was led by Brigadier General Romeyn Ayres' brigade, which included four regiments of Zouaves. They were pushing across the matted brambles and tangled brush of Sanders' Field when they ran head on into a curtain of Confederate lead—and were struck by

These twisted ramrods, found near the Orange Plank road long after the battle in the Wilderness, bear witness to the chaotic intensity of the fighting there. The muskets of some men grew so hot from repeated firing that ignition occurred even as they rammed a fresh round home, sending the rod flying; in other cases, panic-stricken soldiers simply forgot to withdraw the ramrods before pressing the trigger.

In early May 1864, Ulysses S. Grant launched his army across the Rapidan River in a drive on Richmond. Blocking the way was Robert E. Lee's Army of Northern Virginia. Lee's outnumbered forces intercepted the Federals in the Wilderness, inflicting heavy casualties. The next month, Grant would clash with the Confederates again at two costly battles—at Spotsylvania and Cold Harbor.

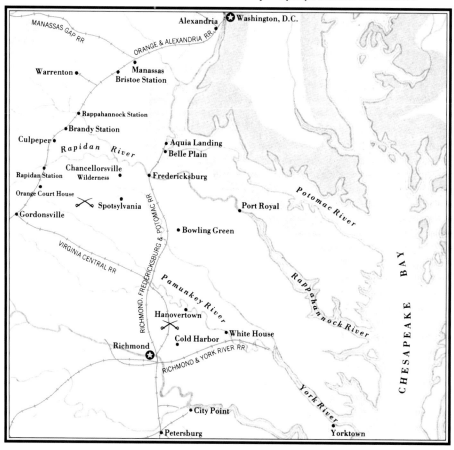

errant Union artillery fire that came from their rear.

Although stunned, the New Yorkers kept pushing forward. "Closing with the enemy, we fought them with bayonet as well as bullet," wrote one officer. "Up through the trees rolled dense clouds of battle smoke, circling about the green of the pines and mingling with the white of the flowering dogwoods." Before they managed to scramble out of the fight, the Zouave brigade had lost 936 of its men.

Meanwhile, across the Turnpike, the Federals were doing better. A division commanded by Brigadier General James Wadsworth, a white-haired 56-year-old patrician who had once studied law under Daniel Webster, had groped through choking thickets to reach Griffin's left flank. Together with some of Griffin's men, the famed Iron Brigade of Wadsworth's division attacked the south part of Sanders' Field and slammed into a Virginia brigade. After a brief, violent struggle, the Iron Brigade surged through a gap in Ewell's line.

At that critical moment, help arrived for the Confederates. Ewell, seeing his center collapsing, had turned his horse and pounded down the Turnpike in search of assistance. He found it in the person of Brigadier General John B. Gordon at the head of a Georgia brigade. The corps commander reined in his horse and shouted to Gordon: "Form at once on the right of the turnpike." Gordon's men went crashing into the Federals, who staggered and gave way.

Griffin's attack was now over. He had been promised help on his open right flank, but the help had never arrived. A bellicose West Pointer and former Indian fighter, Griffin spurred his horse and rode furiously to the army's headquarters near the junction of Germanna Plank road and the Orange Turnpike. Leaping off his horse, he ignored Grant, who was sitting there whittling, and went straight for General Meade, who listened calmly as Griffin cursed at the failure to support his assault.

After Griffin stamped away, Grant got up and approached Meade. "Who is this General Gregg?" he asked, getting the name wrong. "You ought to put him under arrest."

"His name is Griffin, not Gregg," Meade replied. "And that's only his way of talking." Then, in an almost fatherly gesture, Meade reached out and buttoned the coat of his younger superior. The tension broke and Grant went back to his whittling.

While Ewell's and Warren's exhausted corps, separated by about 300 yards, dug in as best they could, the full weight of the battle was developing to the south, along the Orange Plank road. If A.P. Hill's two grayclad divisions could take the junction of the Orange Plank road and the Brock road—the Federals' only accessible north-south route—then Major General Winfield Scott Hancock's II Corps, which had sliced southwest down from Chancellorsville that morning and was now well south of the vital crossroads, would be cut off from the rest of the Army of the Potomac. General Meade ordered Hancock to countermarch northward. Then he dispatched most of a division from Major General John Sedgwick's VI Corps—6,000 veterans under Brigadier General Richard Getty—south on the Brock road to hold the intersection until Hancock could get there.

But Lee also wanted that road junction, and to get it he had a division under Major General Henry Heth, now recovered from the fractured skull he had suffered at Gettysburg. Slowly, Heth's men pushed Getty's back, and when Hancock arrived at the crossroads at 2 p.m. the first officer to reach him reported breathlessly: "Sir! General Getty is hard pressed and nearly out of ammunition."

"Tell him to hold on," Hancock shouted back, and directed his two lead divisions, commanded by Major General David Birney and Brigadier General Gershom Mott, to form up on Getty's left flank. Thus reinforced, Getty attacked, only to be brought up short by a sheet of Confederate fire.

Although the Federal attack had stalled, Lee did not like the look of things. He sent word to Major General Cadmus Wilcox, whose division had been sent earlier to bridge the gap between A.P. Hill and Ewell, to return in support of Heth. That movement reopened the fissure in the Confederate line, and Wadsworth's Federal division, which had been working its way south through dense thickets, soon began moving through the breach.

Earlier in the day, A.P. Hill had been ailing; now, however, in the moment of emergency, his ill health was forgotten. Finding a battalion of the 5th Alabama, which had been left behind to guard prisoners, Hill ordered its men to charge, firing fast and giving the Rebel yell as though regiment after regiment were coming. The screaming attack of the 125 Alabamians stopped Wadsworth's Federals and

Sketching the Common Soldier

An easel stands ready in Forbes' tent-studio.

For Edwin Forbes, an artist for Frank Leslie's *Illustrated Newspaper,* being a spectator at the great battles of the Civil War was, in his words, "nearly as dangerous as being a participant." The 22-year-old Forbes attached himself to the Army of the Potomac at the start of the war and stayed on, armed only with a sketchbook, until the summer of 1864. Energetic and daring, Forbes edged close to the action in battle after battle. Oblivious of the shells and musket fire, he executed quick sketches that he later refined in his make-shift tent-studio to the rear.

When the armies were at rest, the ever-active Forbes drew the common soldier and camp activity. The Wilderness Campaign saw Forbes' talents at their peak. His sketches, a sampling of which are presented on these pages, provide an unglamorized view of the campaign, full of the details that were, as Forbes wrote, "too plain for misunderstanding and far too terrible for any forgetting."

Forbes marveled at the multitude of mule-drawn supply wagons, such as the one shown here, that traveled with the army and "filled the roads on the march."

A teamster known only as Joe leans casually against his wagon. Forbes respected the ability and dedication of the black drivers; he said they seemed to have an "occult understanding" with their mule teams.

Drummer boys, according to Forbes, were "the most picturesque little figures in the Union army." He added that their pranks and high spirits gave "much life to camp or march."

With a pipe in one hand and a newspaper in the other, a weary soldier takes his ease. The men seized such moments whenever they could; Forbes once observed a skirmisher reading while sheltered behind a boulder in the midst of battle.

riveted them firmly in place until darkness ended the fighting.

During that night in the Wilderness, the screams of the wounded rose above the crackle of burning brush. At one point, groping through the darkness, the Union's Major Abner Small "stumbled, fell, and my outflung hands pushed up a smoulder of leaves. The fire sprang into flame, caught in the hair and beard of a dead sergeant, and lighted a ghastly face and wide open eyes. I rushed away in horror." For the men of the struggling armies, the terrors of night would continue with the coming of day.

At 5 a.m. on May 6, Winfield Scott Hancock sent his skirmishers forward to a spattering of musketry that signaled the dawn of a second violent day. Then, with Hancock spurring the men on, 20,000 Federals surged toward Wilcox's and Heth's divisions along a front more than a mile long. Before 7 a.m., the blue host had advanced a mile or more. "We are driving them, sir," a jubilant Hancock shouted to one of Meade's staff officers. "Tell General Meade we are driving them most beautifully!"

In a clearing near the Orange Plank road, Robert E. Lee saw a disaster in the making as Confederates emerged from the woods with Federals bearing down quickly on them. Angrily, he called to Brigadier General Samuel McGowan of Wilcox's division: "Is this splendid brigade of yours running like a flock of geese?"

"General," McGowan replied, "these men are not whipped. They only want a place to form and they will fight as well as they ever did."

By then, the Wilderness itself was taking its toll on the Federals. Disoriented in the thickets, regiments and brigades became hopelessly entangled, and Hancock's assault began to falter—just as James Longstreet's corps came striding up the Orange Plank road, shouldering through the wreckage of Hill's corps and forming to take up the fight. "General, what brigade is this?" Lee asked Brigadier General John Gregg. "The Texas Brigade," replied Gregg. At that, Lee lost all semblance of his famed composure. "Hurrah for Texas," he shouted, waving his hat. "Go and drive out those people."

"Attention, Texas Brigade," Gregg then ordered. "The eyes of General Lee are upon you. Forward . . . march!" As the Texans advanced, Lee began to ride

with them. "Lee to the rear," the men shouted. "General Lee, go back." Yet it was only after several men broke ranks to stop him that the commanding general reluctantly turned toward relative safety.

By midmorning, Longstreet had driven Hancock's troops almost back to their starting point. Then, however, the Federals braced. The battle was settling into stalemate when Lee's chief engineer informed Longstreet of an unfinished railroad bed that led directly into the left of Hancock's line. Under Longstreet's adjutant, Lieutenant Colonel G. Moxley Sorrel, four brigades moved unseen up the cut and burst onto Hancock's exposed flank. Hit before they could change front to face the attackers, the Federal troops began to fall back, and the Union left was close to collapse. When the opposing commanders met years later, Hancock would tell Longstreet, "You rolled me up like a wet blanket."

Yet such was the nature of the tangled Wilderness that neither side could maintain its momentum; by 12:30 p.m. Longstreet's assault had slowed. And next disaster struck the Confederates.

Longstreet, accompanied by other officers, was riding along the Orange Plank road when rifle fire opened up from the woods on his right. Troops of Brigadier General William Mahone's brigade of Virginians were shooting at Confederate troops they mistakenly thought were the enemy—and Longstreet's party was in the line of fire. Brigadier General Micah Jenkins, one of the Confederacy's finest commanders, went down with a bullet in his brain. "At the moment Jenkins fell," Longstreet wrote later, "I received a severe shock from a minié ball passing through my throat and right shoulder."

Longstreet was placed on a litter and carried to the rear with a hat over his face to shield him from the sun. The wounded general could hear men murmuring along the line, "He is dead, and they are telling us he is only wounded." Wanting to reassure them, Longstreet recalled, "I raised my hat with my left hand." As a cheer went up from the ranks, the "burst of voices and the flying of hats in the air eased my pain somewhat."

Almost exactly a year earlier, in the same dismal woods and in similar circumstances, Stonewall Jackson had fallen. But Longstreet's chief medical officer pronounced his wound "not necessarily mortal." In fact, the "Old Warhorse" would indeed eventually

recover. For the present, Lee took over his command.

Late that afternoon, a frustrated Robert E. Lee rode north to where Richard Ewell was still holding his position astride the Orange Turnpike. "Cannot something be done on this flank?" he asked. The answer was yes. John B. Gordon, whose Georgians manned the far Confederate left, had been convinced since morning that his line overlapped that of the Federals to his front, making his opponents vulnerable to a flanking attack.

Upon being told of Gordon's situation, Lee sensed an opportunity to repeat the devastating flanking movement that he and Stonewall Jackson had accomplished at Chancellorsville a year earlier. Accordingly, at about 6 p.m., Gordon's troops attacked with a yell. Almost at once, the Federals broke and fled, and soon wild rumors reached General Meade that all was lost. "Nonsense!" Meade bellowed. "If they have broken our lines, they can do nothing more tonight."

Meade was absolutely right: Darkness put an end to Gordon's attack, and the two-day Battle of the Wilderness finally came to a close. Against about 7,500 Confederate casualties, the Federals had suffered losses of 17,666 men. In the face of much less staggering statistics, previous Union commanders had retreated. Yet before retiring that night, Ulysses S. Grant had a word for a correspondent who was about to depart for Washington. "If you see the President," Grant said, "tell him, from me, that whatever happens, there will be no turning back."

Grant was as good as his word. Despite the heavy losses in the Wilderness, he would continue to press the enemy. On the evening of May 7, after a day of eerie quiet in the Wilderness, the Army of the Potomac set out toward the crossroads hamlet of Spotsylvania Court House, about a dozen miles to the southeast, where Lee's principal supply lines met. Should the Federals seize Spotsylvania, they would be astride the best route to Richmond.

Warren's V Corps led the way, and as the troops marched along the Brock road there came a call of "Give way to the right!" A small cavalcade passed along, headed by Grant on his horse, Cincinnati. Despite orders to be as quiet as possible, the men tossed their hats in the air and gave a great cheer in realization that the agony of the Wilderness was not

to be wasted: Instead of retreating, as they had done so often before, they were moving deeper into enemy territory. "Our spirits rose," one veteran recalled. "That night we were happy."

Less than three hours later, Longstreet's corps, temporarily commanded by Major General Richard H. Anderson, also began moving toward Spotsylvania. Divining Grant's destination, Lee had ordered a rough track cut through the forest; it would give him the shortest route to the crossroads. Clearly a race was on to reach Spotsylvania first.

Marching along the stump-studded path, some of Anderson's men cried out, "Three cheers for General Lee!" and the Rebel yell was echoed from one brigade to another. Three times, according to a South Carolina officer, "this mighty wave of sound rang along the Confederate lines. It seemed to fill every heart with new life, to inspire every nerve with might never known before."

Meanwhile, with a sea of blueclad troops jamming the Brock road, the Federal commanders spent a frustrating night attempting to drive their men forward to Spotsylvania. Despite a peremptory order by Meade to hasten his troops' progress, General Warren watched helplessly as his infantry ground to a halt. It was only at 6 a.m. that he was finally able to get his men moving again. As they started, they heard the popping of carbines in the distance. Fired not by infantry but by cavalry troopers who had ridden ahead, these were the opening shots in the gruesome Battle of Spotsylvania.

In the race for the Spotsylvania crossroads, Confederate horsemen had won, and they were in a blocking position when Union troopers bore down on them. More important, Anderson's weary infantrymen were closer at hand than Warren's Federals, and they were able to reinforce the cavalry. When Warren's soldiers,

This slouch hat, pierced by a bullet at the rear left edge of the crown, bears the clover-leaf emblem of the Federal II Corps. Its owner, Captain Charles Nash of the 19th Maine, was leading a company against General James Longstreet's Confederates in the Wilderness on May 6, 1864, when a bullet sent the hat flying. Nash was not harmed.

On the morning of May 6, Major General Winfield Scott Hancock's Federals seized the initiative, shattering Lieutenant General A.P. Hill's line across the Orange Plank road. Soon, however, General Longstreet's corps arrived from the west and pushed the Federals back, advancing nearly to the Brock road before Longstreet was wounded around noon. Lee launched a second assault against the Union left about 4 p.m., to no avail. A final advance by Brigadier General John B. Gordon's Confederate brigade on the Union right was stymied by darkness and the battle ended in stalemate.

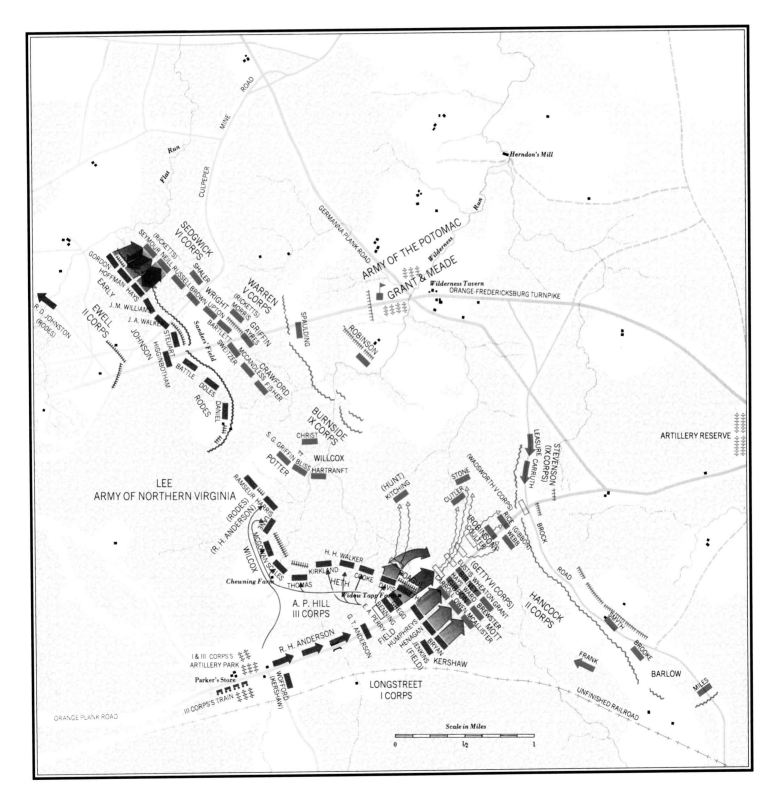

ROAD

Flat Run

CULPEPER

Herndon's Mill

GERMANNA PLANK ROAD

ARMY OF THE POTOMAC

Wilderness Run

GRANT & MEADE

Wilderness Tavern

ORANGE-FREDERICKSBURG TURNPIKE

(RICKETTS)
SEDGWICK
VI CORPS
SEYMOUR NEILL RUSSELL BROWN UPTON

GORDON
HOFFMAN HAYS
EARLY
J. M. WILLIAMS
SHALER

EWELL
II CORPS
J. A. WALKER
JOHNSON
HIGGINBOTHAM
STEUART
BATTLE
DOLES
RODES
DANIEL

WRIGHT
WARREN
V CORPS
(RICKETTS)
MORRIS GRIFFIN
BARTLETT AYRES
SWEITZER
McCANDLESS
CRAWFORD
FISHER

Sanders' Field

SPAULDING

ROBINSON

BURNSIDE
IX CORPS

S. G. GRIFFIN
CHRIST
POTTER
BLISS
WILLCOX
HARTRANFT

(HUNT)
KITCHING

ARTILLERY RESERVE

STEVENSON
(IX CORPS)
LEASURE CARRUTH

LEE
ARMY OF NORTHERN VIRGINIA

RAMSEUR HARRIS
(RODES)
(R. H. ANDERSON)
McGOWAN SCALES
WILCOX

STONE
(WADSWORTH V CORPS)
CUTLER
RICE (GIBBON)
ROBINSON
COULTER
WEBB

BROCK

H. H. WALKER
KIRKLAND
COOKE
THOMAS
HETH
DAVIS
POAGUE
A. P. HILL
III CORPS
Chewning Farm
Widow Tapp Farm

ROAD

(GETTY VI CORPS)
EUSTIS WHEATON GRANT
HAYS WARD BREWSTER
CARROLL OWEN McALLISTER
MOTT

HANCOCK
II CORPS

R. H. ANDERSON
G. T. ANDERSON
BENNING
E. A. PERRY
FIELD
HUMPHREYS
HENAGAN
BRYAN
JENKINS
(FIELD)
KERSHAW

FRANK

SMYTH

BROOKE

BARLOW

I & III CORPS'S
ARTILLERY PARK

Parker's Store
WOFFORD
(KERSHAW)

III CORPS'S TRAIN

LONGSTREET
I CORPS

UNFINISHED RAILROAD

MILES

ORANGE PLANK ROAD

Scale in Miles

0   ½   1

345

Union General John Sedgwick, killed instantly by a sniper's bullet during the Battle of Spotsylvania, lies surrounded by his grief-stricken staff. Major Charles Whittier cradles the general's head while Captain Richard Halstead feels vainly for a pulse and two officers signal for assistance. Crouching next to Whittier is Major Thomas Hyde, who later wrote of Sedgwick as a cherished friend whose "noble heart was stilled at last."

after quick-marching part of the way, came panting onto the scene, they found themselves facing furious volleys from one of Anderson's brigades.

That morning, after establishing his headquarters near Todd's Tavern, Meade at first refused to believe that the Confederates had beaten his army to Spotsylvania. Once convinced, he ordered John Sedgwick's arriving VI Corps to join with Warren in an attack to be made "with vigor and without delay."

Sedgwick, however, could not get in position until 5 p.m., and by then Ewell's 17,000 Confederates were coming in on Anderson's right. The Federal assault, when it came, was halfhearted and poorly coordinated, and the day ended with Spotsylvania still in Confederate hands.

The Confederates spent the hot morning of May 9 strengthening their earthworks. With the arrival of Ewell's corps, Lee had extended Anderson's right on a northeast slant. A.P. Hill's corps, now commanded by Major General Jubal Early because Hill was too ill even to sit up, was posted along Ewell's right rear. By 4 p.m., the Confederate front resembled a ragged V: The flanks bent to meet attacks from either left or right, and a strong salient—which became known to its defenders as the Mule Shoe—protruded northward in the center.

The Mule Shoe bristled with artillery and was shielded by a heavy abatis of felled trees, with branches sharpened and pointed outward. The main trench line, built up with logs and banked earth, was the strongest constructed so far by Lee's men. At right angles to this line ran traverses: mounds of earth that extended rearward and protected the defenders against enfilade fire. And 100 yards to the rear of the principal breastworks, Ewell was building a second set of defenses.

As the opposing sides prepared for battle, the Union was dealt a cruel blow. Trying to reassure some of his men who had been unnerved by fire from enemy sharpshooters, the beloved "Uncle John" Sedgwick said in jest that "they couldn't hit an elephant at this distance." No sooner were the words out of his mouth than a sniper's bullet smashed into his face below the left eye. Later, after twice asking "Is he really dead?" Grant pronounced the loss as costly as that of a division.

Throughout that day and most of the next, Grant probed unsuccessfully for weaknesses in the Confed-

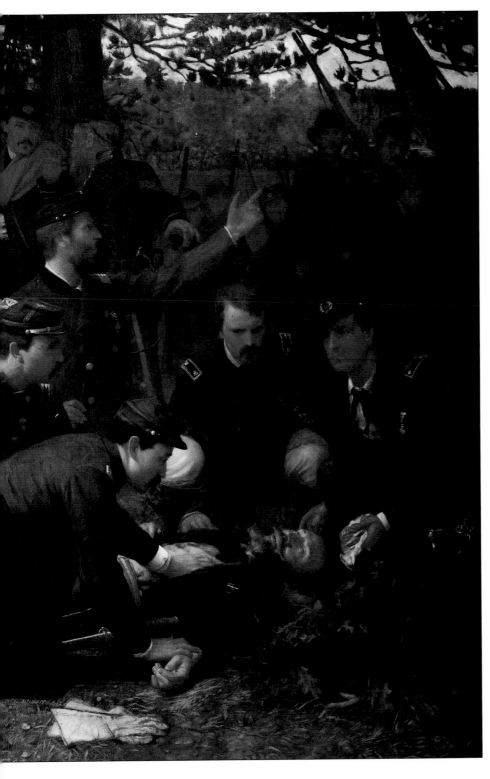

erate defenses. Not until late in the afternoon of May 11 did Brigadier General Horatio G. Wright, who had succeeded Sedgwick in command of the VI Corps, make a reconnaissance and conclude that the Mule Shoe was vulnerable. To assault it, Wright called on Emory Upton, a freckled 24-year-old colonel who commanded one of his brigades.

For some time now, Upton had been preaching a new theory of attack—a hammer blow by a concentrated striking force advancing on a much narrower front than usual. Once this force had shattered a small segment of the enemy's line, a second wave of attackers would pour through the gap and strike the Confederates' flank and rear. To test Upton's idea, Wright gave him 12 veteran regiments totaling about 5,000 men.

At 6:10 p.m., Upton gave the order to charge, bayonets fixed, out of the thick pine woods that stood within 200 yards of the forward Confederate trenches. The Confederates in the Mule Shoe were cooking their meager rations when, according to one of them, someone looked over the works and cried, "Hello! What's this? Why, here come our men on the run from—no, by heavens! It's the Yankees!"

Within five minutes, the leading men in Upton's regiments had made it through the abatis to the parapet of earthworks. "The first of our men who tried to surmount the works fell pierced through the head by musket-balls," Upton recalled. "Others, seeing the fate of their comrades, held their pieces at arms length and fired downward, while others, poising their pieces vertically, hurled them down upon their enemy, pinning them to the ground."

But Upton's spearhead could not sustain itself without reinforcements, and when help failed to arrive the men had no choice but to fight their way rearward. Although they took with them 950 Confederate prisoners, they had suffered about 1,000 casualties of their own.

Grant was disappointed with the results, but he was by no means discouraged. That night an orderly heard him tell Meade, "A brigade today—we'll try a corps tomorrow."

For the job, Grant selected Hancock's II Corps, which would assault the apex of the Mule Shoe at first light on May 12. When Hancock attacked, Major General Ambrose E. Burnside, whose IX Corps had done little fighting in the Wilderness,

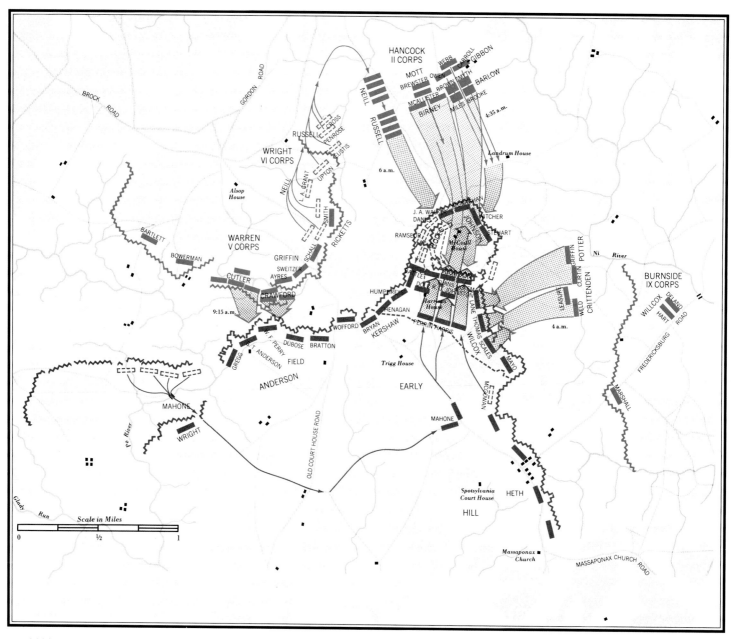

would hit the eastern side of the salient. On the Federal right, Warren and Wright were to stand by to exploit Hancock's advantage.

Unbeknown to the Federal commanders, Robert E. Lee was for once playing into their hands. Anticipating that Grant would move east in search of another route to Richmond instead of butting again at the formidable Confederate works, Lee ordered Ewell to move 22 of his 30 field guns a mile and a half to the rear. From there the guns could be trotted out quickly if Grant attempted to sidle around the Confederate right. But in attempting to prepare for the future, Lee had woefully weakened his present Spotsylvania defenses.

At 4:30 a.m., Hancock's men moved out through thick fog, their way led by a division under Brigadier General Francis Barlow. Greeted by no more than scattered fire as they neared the enemy abatis, Barlow's troops broke into a run. All formation dissolved and the division became a solid mass. Like a great herd of horses, the yelling men stampeded over the Confederate works just east of the Mule Shoe's apex.

On Barlow's right, David Birney's division charged into the trenches held by Edward Johnson's division. The crusty Johnson, stumping around with the aid of a long hickory staff he had used since taking a bullet in the leg two years before, kept hollering "Fire fast! Fire fast!" Soon he was surrounded and, though he swatted at the Yankees with his staff, was taken prisoner along with 3,000 other Rebels. Hancock now possessed a crucial half mile of terrain in the very center of Lee's line.

On May 12 at dawn, 20,000 men of Hancock's II Corps attacked the apex of the Mule Shoe and penetrated into the salient as the battle of Spotsylvania entered its fifth day. The advance was halted by a Confederate counterattack led by General John B. Gordon, with support from Generals Robert Rodes and Jubal Early. Meanwhile, Burnside had hit the eastern face of the salient, and at 6 a.m. Wright joined the attack from the northwest—throwing his men against Rodes' troops in the so-called Bloody Angle.

Lee, meanwhile, had ridden toward the sound of the firing, only to see his own troops streaming past him in full flight. "Shame on you, men, shame on you!" he cried. "Go back to your regiments; go back to your regiments." For once, not even the voice of Robert E. Lee had any effect; the men kept running.

Finally, Lee came upon John B. Gordon, who in command of Jubal Early's old division, was trying to patch together a second defensive line. Lee ordered Gordon to counterattack—and, just as he had done in the Wilderness, gave every sign that he intended to lead the charge himself. "General Lee," Gordon yelled, "you shall not lead my men in a charge. No man can do that, sir. Another is here for that purpose. These men behind you are Georgians, Virginians and Carolinians. They have never failed you on any field. They will not fail you here. Will you, boys?"

"No, no!" the men shouted, and some of them gathered around Lee's horse, Traveller, grabbed the bridle and turned horse and rider back.

At 5:30 a.m., Gordon charged, joined by two brigades of Major General Robert E. Rodes' division on his left. The impact of Gordon's desperate attack pushed the Federals back toward the toe of the Mule Shoe. There, however, the Federal soldiers got into the trenches they had captured earlier, pouring fire into the ranks of the Confederates and stopping Gordon's counterattack.

In the meantime, a savage fight had broken out on the salient's western face, where several brigades of Wright's VI Corps struck hard at the trenches now held by some of Rodes' troops. Once the Federals reached Rodes' works—near a sharp turn in the Confederate line that would win dark renown as the Bloody Angle—a seemingly interminable, hand-to-hand struggle began.

Hour after hour the slaughter continued. Rain fell; wounded men suffocated in the mud and drowned in the flooded trenches. Large oak trees were chopped down by the hail of lead. Some corpses were hit so many times that they simply fell apart. One Confederate remembered a grisly detail from the fighting: soldiers placing the hands of the nearest corpses in such a position that, when the hands stiffened, they formed convenient cartridge holders.

Sometime after midnight, the battlefield at last fell quiet. Far behind the Bloody Angle, a Georgian remembered, a Confederate band began to play "The Dead March" from Handel's *Saul*. And then, unit by unit, Lee's battered defenders quietly moved back to a second line of defense, leaving behind only the corpses of their comrades.

When the morning of May 13 dawned, the Federal troops awoke to find nothing but dead in the salient. In one part of the Bloody Angle measuring no more than 12 by 15 feet they discovered 150 bodies. A Maine lad looking for a friend found a corpse so shot up "there was not four inches of space about this person that had not been struck by bullets." The inconclusive battle for the Mule Shoe had ended.

Two days of fighting at Spotsylvania had cost Lee close to 6,000 men in killed and wounded, and another 4,000 had been captured. Grant's toll was equally devastating—10,920 casualties. On May 20, after a week of stalemate in which casualties mounted without gain in ground for either side, Grant again set his army in motion in an attempt to continue south by sidestepping the Confederates' right flank.

It was a baleful General Lee who set out once more to intercept Grant's army. Only a few days before, while the nightmare struggle in the Bloody Angle was at its hellish worst, he had learned of the death of his cherished cavalry commander, James Ewell Brown (Jeb) Stuart.

On May 11, near a ramshackle former stagecoach inn called Yellow Tavern, directly north of Richmond, Stuart had caught up with two divisions of Philip Sheridan's cavalry, intent on raiding the Confederate capital. Badly outnumbered, the Confederates went on the defensive, with Stuart in the thick of the fighting as usual. By late afternoon, most of the Federals had been cleared out of Stuart's immediate vicinity, and those left behind were mostly troopers who had lost their horses and were trying to get away on foot.

One of them—by some accounts it was a 48-year-old private named John Huff—saw a red beard, a plume, a silk-lined cape, a large figure on a horse 30 feet away. The Federal aimed his pistol, squeezed the trigger and then ran off.

Stuart's chin dropped to his chest, his hat fell off and he clapped a hand over the spot on his right side where the shock had come. "General," shouted a nearby trooper, "are you hit?" "I am afraid I am," Stuart replied in a level voice. Taken in an ambulance to his brother-in-law's home in Richmond, he lingered in excruciating pain before succumbing on the evening of May 12.

Hours after being informed of Stuart's death, the stoic Lee confessed, "I can scarcely think of him without weeping." Lee's work, however, would carry on; at midday on May 21 he put Ewell's corps, to be followed by the rest of the army, on the road to head off the Army of the Potomac. The showdown, he calculated, would come along the steep banks of the North Anna River south of Spotsylvania. If Lee could entrench his troops behind the river, the Confederate force could cover the direct road to the capital as well as protect Hanover Junction, where the Richmond, Fredericksburg & Potomac met the Virginia Central Railroad.

Next morning, Ewell's men filed into place on the south side of the North Anna. After a march of about 25 miles, they were comfortably ahead of Hancock's corps which, leading the way for the Federals, had to cover 34 miles on inferior roads. Anderson came up around noon, and A.P. Hill arrived the next day. All the Confederate forces were in place when the Army of the Potomac approached the river on a wide front after a two-day march; Hancock held the Union left, Burnside and his IX Corps were in the center, and Warren and Wright farther west.

The North Anna, to the eye of General Meade's aide, Colonel Theodore Lyman, was "a pretty stream, running between high banks, so steep that they form almost a ravine, and, for the most part, heavily wooded with oak and tulip trees, very luxuriant." Meade and Grant, however, had little time to notice the stream's natural beauty. Here was Lee, once again strongly entrenched astride the main routes to Richmond, a scant 25 miles away, inviting attack. There was no choice, Grant concluded, but to strike Lee's army head on and hope for a decisive battle that would end the bitter campaign.

Grant wasted no time in ordering Warren's vanguard to ford the North Anna at Jericho Mills and investigate Lee's left. Next to come up was Hancock. Grant sent him and his two lead brigades straight ahead for Chesterfield Bridge, where they encountered opposition from Colonel John Henagan's South Carolina brigade. A fierce artillery duel ensued; after two hours Hancock gained the upper hand, which allowed one of his brigades to charge up a broad,

easy slope and roll over the Confederate position.

Meanwhile, on the Federal right, Warren's men got across the river; but they ran into trouble when A.P. Hill dispatched Cadmus Wilcox's division to strike Warren's right flank. One Federal division—which included the famed Iron Brigade—gave way in panic and stampeded toward the river.

But Wilcox did not have the strength to complete the Federal rout, and Hill, still ailing, did not press his initial advantage. Warren's Union troops dug in that night on the south side of the North Anna. Lee, who was suffering a severe case of diarrhea, later spoke testily to Hill: "Why did you not do as Jackson would have done—thrown your whole force upon those people and driven them back?" Hill accepted the rebuke and made no reply.

On the morning of May 24, the Federal situation appeared promising—at least at first glance. The Confederates had pulled back from the Chesterfield Bridge, and Hancock was able to cross the river virtually unopposed. Wright's Federals, following Warren's, had crossed unimpeded upstream. But overlooked during those hours of seeming success was the key to Lee's defense: Ox Ford.

There, for a half-mile stretch, the south bank of the North Anna was higher than the north bank. On this commanding ground, Lee had placed half of Anderson's corps, along with strong artillery support. Anderson's men could pour down a murderous fire on any Federal troops foolish enough to try to wade the stream around Ox Ford.

With both wings of his army drawn back, Lee's dispositions formed a sort of inverted V, with its impregnable Ox Ford apex pointed at the Federal center. Within that compact, five-mile-long position, the wings could easily reinforce each other, shifting troops to buttress any spot that came under attack.

Grant's position, on the other hand, was decidedly awkward. To reinforce his left with his right, or vice versa, he would have to draw troops back across the North Anna, march them to the proper point, then have them cross the river again. As explained by Confederate General Evander Law, Grant's predicament was that he "had cut his army in two by running it upon the point of a wedge."

Even so, the Federals tried. In the afternoon of May 24, Hancock ordered one of General John Gibbon's brigades to test the Confederate right; although Gib-

bon's entire division was soon involved in a furious fight, the effort ended inconclusively after a heavy rain began to fall. A second attempt, undertaken on the Federal right without authorization by a drunken Union brigadier general named James Ledlie, came to an ignominious conclusion.

Having seen two assaults so strongly opposed, Grant decided that a concentrated push would be folly. He would withdraw before first light on May 27 and sidle yet another time around Lee's right. Despite the setbacks, Grant was in an optimistic mood. "Lee's army is really whipped," he reported to Washington. "I may be mistaken, but I feel that our success over Lee's army is already assured." Events would soon prove him disastrously wrong.

The movements of the two armies followed a familiar pattern. Marching in two columns over narrow, dusty roads, the Army of the Potomac swung wide to the southeast, keeping the North Anna and a confluent river, the Pamunkey, between itself and Lee's forces. Lee, on the other hand, simply marched his men across the cord of the arc that Grant was inscribing to Atlee's Station on the Virginia Central. With only 18 miles to cover—compared with the 40 miles that lay ahead of Grant—Lee's lead units reached Atlee's Station by the afternoon of May 27. As the rest of his three corps arrived, he skillfully deployed them east of the station to block all approaches to Richmond from the Pamunkey.

The following day, preceded by Philip Sheridan's cavalry, the four corps of the Army of the Potomac crossed the muddy Pamunkey on pontoon bridges. Warren and Burnside crossed their corps at Hanovertown, and Hancock four miles upstream. Lee sent two cavalry brigades on a reconnaissance; they collided with Sheridan's forces at a crossroads called Haw's Shop, about three miles west of the Pamunkey, and inflicted heavy casualties in a resulting cavalry battle.

Despite the losses, Grant's corps pushed on, fanning out south and west, and arriving around dusk on May 29 at a sluggish, marsh-fringed watercourse called Totopotomoy Creek. Lee was on the opposite bank with his three corps drawn up in line of battle, and as Lee saw it, the situation was critical. His army had been unable to make up even half the losses it had suffered since May 4. Moreover, Lee's veterans were weak both from sickness and from hunger as severe

as any they had endured. And now there was evidence that Grant was extending his left on a front that Lee could not cover without leaving vulnerable spots in his already weakened line.

Worse news was in the offing: With the arrival of General William F. Smith's 16,000-man Union XVIII Corps on May 30 downstream on the Pamunkey at White House Landing, Grant now had five corps to Lee's three—and the possibility of a clear shot at Richmond. There was no reason why Smith could not move due west from White House Landing to Cold Harbor, three miles southeast of Bethesda Church, where Grant had anchored his left flank. Such a maneuver would extend the Federal left too far south for the Confederate right to check it, and once around Lee's flank, Grant could move on Richmond merely by crossing the Chickahominy River.

Without reinforcements, Lee said he faced "disaster." He wired directly to Jefferson Davis who dispatched Major General Robert Hoke's division of 7,000 men. When word arrived that Hoke was on his way, Lee sent Major General Fitzhugh Lee's cavalry to secure the Cold Harbor crossroads. Fitz Lee's instructions were to hang on by any means until Hoke arrived. Grant recognized the tactical importance of Cold Harbor as well as Lee did, and on May 31 he sent Sheridan and a strong force of cavalry south in the direction of the crossroads to protect the Union army's left flank. The stage was now set for an inevitable collision.

Cold Harbor's name was an anomaly: The cheerless little hamlet possessed no harbor, and the late May temperatures were close to 100 degrees. Located between the Pamunkey and the Chickahominy rivers near the old Seven Days battlegrounds northeast of Richmond, Cold Harbor offered nothing more than a tumbledown tavern in a triangular grove of trees—and a vital intersection where five roads met. One of the roads went eastward to White House Landing and another northwest to Bethesda Church; Grant could use them to maintain his supply lines during his anticipated thrust toward Richmond.

Fitz Lee's cavalry got to Cold Harbor first but was beaten back on the afternoon of May 31 by Federal troopers. Then, as Union and Confederate infantry began to arrive, Richard Anderson sent two divisions to recapture the crossroads. The assault failed miserably, and both sides began digging in.

Barges and other vessels lie moored along the Pamunkey River at White House Landing, where supplies brought by water from Washington and Alexandria, Virginia, were loaded on wagons and hauled to the Federal troops at Cold Harbor. The landing had been General George McClellan's supply depot two years earlier, during the Seven Days' Battles.

On June 1, an assault by the Federal VI and XVIII Corps was repulsed with great slaughter. Still determined to dislodge the Confederates, Grant planned a full-scale attack for the next day, but he was forced to postpone it when Hancock's II Corps was slow in getting into position. The delay gave the Confederates 24 precious hours in which to improve their field fortifications, and they used the time well. "Intricate, zigzagged lines within lines, lines protecting flanks of lines, lines built to enfilade an opposing line, lines within which lies a battery," marveled a newspaper correspondent who later walked over the ground. It was, he concluded, "a maze and labyrinth of works within works." Yet the Confederates folded their trenches into the terrain so ingeniously that, from the Union perspective, the defenses did not look nearly so threatening as those at Spotsylvania or on the North Anna.

But in their bones the Federal infantry knew what they were facing. In the night, as rain turned to drizzle, front-line soldiers began taking off their coats. As Horace Porter, one of Grant's staff officers, walked among them, it seemed that the men were sewing their uniforms—an odd chore at a time like this. Looking closer, Porter found that they "were calmly writing their names and home addresses on slips of paper and pinning them on the backs of their coats, so that their bodies might be recognized and their fate made known to their families at home."

Strangely, Grant had given no specific instructions for the attack he now scheduled for the early morning of June 3. Instead, he left it up to the corps commanders to decide where they would strike the Confederate lines. When General William Smith asked the VI Corps commander, Horatio Wright, about his plans, Wright replied that he was just "going to pitch in." To members of his staff, an appalled Smith denounced the whole attack as "simply an order to slaughter my best troops."

That was exactly what happened. At 4:30 a.m., Union buglers sounded the advance. Along a front of two miles, more than 50,000 infantrymen of the II, VI and XVIII Corps began clambering out of their works and moving on the enemy fortifications, still wreathed in morning mists, several hundred yards away. As they neared their goal, they were met by fire so withering that those who survived were hard pressed to tell what happened. "To give a description

of this terrible charge is simply impossible," a Federal captain wrote later. "That dreadful storm of lead and iron seemed more like a volcanic blast than a battle." Even the Confederate defenders were stunned by the carnage. "It was not war," General Evander Law said later. "It was murder."

The fiercest fighting of all was on the extreme left of the Union line, where Hancock's II Corps was on the attack: Francis Barlow's Federal division on the left, John Gibbon's on the right and David Birney's in support. By chance, Barlow's men hit the only weak spot in the Confederate line, a stretch of low ground on Major General John C. Breckinridge's front that had been turned into a mire by the driving rain. Men of the 7th New York Heavy Artillery, fighting as infantry, led the way over weakly defended parapets, caving in a Confederate brigade and taking more than 200 prisoners, three cannon and a stand of colors. But the Confederates rallied and soon pushed the Federals back to a low swelling of the ground, where they began digging in with bayonets and tin cups.

Almost as badly battered were the veterans of Gibbon's Union division. About 200 yards from their starting point they unexpectedly hit a swamp that cut the division in two. As the swamp widened, so did the gap in the division, which was being peppered hard by skirmishers and pounded by artillery. Two brigades at last sloshed out the other side and, as they struggled toward the enemy trenches, were ripped by fire so intense that, as one Confederate artilleryman recalled, "heads, arms, legs, guns were seen flying high in the air." Unable to continue, Gibbon's men simply dropped to the ground and began digging.

It was the same along the entire line, and by 5:30 a.m., the troops of Hancock's, Wright's and Smith's corps were all hugging the ground. The Union casualties were ghastly: as many as 7,000 men had fallen, the great majority of them in the first 15 minutes. By comparison, the Confederate losses were paltry—fewer than 1,500.

Incredibly, less than two hours later, Meade ordered another attack. But this time he was met by blunt refusals from officers and men alike. "I will not take my regiment in another such charge if Jesus Christ himself should order it!" shouted Captain Thomas Barker of the 12th New Hampshire. Private John Haley of the 17th Maine put it somewhat less

The 7th New York Heavy Artillery of General Francis Barlow's division overruns the first line of Lee's works at Cold Harbor on June 3, 1864, seizing prisoners and turning captured guns on the Confederates. After heavy fighting inside the Confederate works, the New Yorkers were pushed back under murderous fire.

Charge in Cold Harbor
Friday June 3rd 1864.

A. R. Waud

dramatically: "We were tired of charging earthworks."

Faced by such intransigence, Grant eventually abandoned his hopes for a breakthrough at Cold Harbor. Indeed, he even made an apology of sorts to his staff. "I regret this assault," he said, "more than any one I ever ordered."

Still, U.S. Grant was not much of a man for self-recrimination. Although he had lost an astronomical total of 50,000 men while inflicting 30,000 Confederate casualties on the killing ground south of the Rapidan, Grant had no intention of turning away. And on the night of June 12, after nine days of nurs-

ing its wounds, Grant's Army of the Potomac again began heading south—this time toward the Confederate rail hub of Petersburg, Virginia, 22 miles south of Richmond.

Despite his losses at Cold Harbor, Grant still held the advantage. Lee could not move now without exposing Richmond, but Grant could move wherever he pleased, except straight ahead. He had lost the battle but retained his initiative, and although Hancock could truthfully say that his old II Corps lay "buried between the Rapidan and the James," Grant was not looking back at old graves. He was moving on.

BATTLES FOR ATLANTA

"I was unwilling to abandon the ground as long as I saw a shadow of probability of victory; the troops would, I believed, return better satisfied even after defeat if, in grasping at the last straw, they felt that a brave and vigorous effort had been made to save the country from disaster."

MAJOR GENERAL JOHN BELL HOOD AFTER THE BATTLE OF NASHVILLE

On a chilly March day in 1864, two Union officers huddled in a cloud of cigar smoke over campaign maps at the Burnet House, a hotel in Cincinnati, Ohio. Scruffy and rough-hewn, they hardly fit the noble, popular image of high-ranking military leaders. Yet leaders they were, of the most powerful armed force ever assembled on the American continent.

Ulysses S. Grant, dogged and deliberate at age 41, had recently been promoted to lieutenant general, and named supreme commander of all Union armies. His companion was Major General William Tecumseh Sherman, age 44—lanky, volatile, with a weather-beaten face and nervous hands that twitched compulsively at his unkempt sandy hair and wiry red beard. Sherman was Grant's newly appointed successor as commander of Federal forces in the West. On the table before them lay plans for a massive spring offensive: a simultaneous assault on Confederate armies all across the South that, it was hoped, would put an end to the nation's most painful and devastating war.

Ever since the outbreak of hostilities, President Lincoln had been urging his generals to come up with just such a unified strategy. But until now the armies in the East and West had marched to their own separate drummers, with little coordination between them. This situation would soon be rectified: At a signal from Grant, both forces would launch their attack. Grant's Army of the Potomac would cross the Rapidan River and assail the Army of Northern Virginia under Robert E. Lee. At the same time, Sherman would march south from Tennessee into Georgia. He would roll up the Rebel defenses and then, as Grant's order read, "get into the interior of the enemy's country as far as you can, inflicting all the damage you can against their war resources."

With this sweeping directive, Sherman returned to his headquarters in Nashville to prepare his campaign. He would be acting on his own for the first time in years; back in 1861, when he was Union commander in Kentucky, the pressures of leadership had brought him perilously close to nervous collapse. But in the years since he had toughened and matured, sharing with Grant in the triumphs at Vicksburg and Missionary Ridge, and gaining in confidence. A bond had developed between the two Ohio-born generals, so strong that Sherman wrote later, "We were brothers." Or, as he stated more bluntly on another occasion: "He stood by me when I was crazy, and I stood by him when he was drunk; and now we stand by each other always."

Sherman's main objective in Georgia was the city of Atlanta, industrial hub of the Confederate war machine. Here arsenals and factories turned out war matériel of every type, from rifles to cannon, from uniform buttons to wooden coffins. Four rail lines emanated from the city, and along them rode boxcars of armaments and supplies, along with grain and other produce bound for the principal Confederate armies. "Gate City of the South" was how Atlanta's 20,000 citizens styled their home town. Sherman saw it as the entry portal for the swath of destruction he was determined to cut through the Rebel heartland.

One serious obstacle barred Sherman's path: the Army of Tennessee, 45,000 strong, commanded by General Joseph E. Johnston. The Confederates were dug in behind a mountain at Dalton, 30 miles into Georgia and squarely athwart the Western & Atlantic Railroad, the main route south to Atlanta. Dislodging Johnston was vital to Sherman's plans. Unless he secured the railroad, the Union general would be unable to supply his troops with food and ammunition during the coming invasion.

With the launch date planned for the end of April, Sherman had barely a month to get ready. And preparation, he believed, was everything. "The least part of a general's work is to fight a battle," he once declared. So Sherman focused all his intense ener-

Corps badges helped to identify members of the large and complex force—seven infantry corps and one cavalry in three distinct armies—that Major General William Tecumseh Sherman would lead toward Atlanta. The star badge denoted XX Corps of the Army of the Cumberland.

From a low hill, General Sherman watches his troops tramp along a winding Georgia road. In his destructive march to Atlanta and the sea beyond, Sherman waged ruthless, all-out war. Northerners saw him as an avenging angel; to Southerners, he seemed like nothing less than the devil himself.

357

gies on the task, in a tireless frenzy of activity. Sleeping only three or four hours a night, he seemed to be everywhere at once—inspecting troops, barking out orders and dictating telegrams. No stickler for spit and polish, he thought nothing of swimming naked in a brook, or hunkering down at the campfire in his flannel underwear. Well-liked and admired, he was "Uncle Billy" to many men in his command.

The fighting force at Uncle Billy's disposal was impressively strong and experienced. There were three major units: the Army of the Cumberland, nearly 61,000 soldiers under Sherman's old West Point roommate, Major General George H. Thomas; the 24,500-man Army of the Tennessee, once Grant's command, then Sherman's, and now led by their young Ohio protégé, Major General James B. McPherson; and the Army of the Ohio, with 13,500 men under McPherson's 1853 West Point classmate, Major General John M. Schofield. Together they added up to 100,000 troops, most of them hard-bitten veterans hungry for action after a four-month rest in winter quarters.

Moving a force this size posed major problems, however. A single ribbon of track led back from Sherman's jump-off point, Chattanooga, Tennessee, to the main Federal supply depot at Louisville, Kentucky, more than 300 miles to the rear. Along much of its distance the track ran through occupied Southern territory, where it came under frequent assault by Confederate raiders, including Nathan Bedford Forrest, whose elusive Rebel cavalry rampaged at will through the Tennessee mountains.

Unable to stop Forrest, Sherman built a powerful string of blockhouses and signal posts; he also drilled road crews in track repair until damaged rails could be mended as fast as Forrest tore them up. Then, to make sure that nothing would interrupt the flow of supplies to his advancing troops, Sherman stockpiled as much as he could at Chattanooga.

The Union general seized every piece of rolling stock he could lay his hands on; soon a fleet of 100 engines and 1,000 heavily laden boxcars was chugging into Chattanooga. All civilian traffic on the railroad was banned, despite protests from as far east as Washington. Even a shipment of Bibles for the troops was sidetracked. "There is more need of gunpowder and oats than any moral or religious instruction," Sherman snapped.

By the end of April the armies were ready. By Sherman's strict orders, each regiment was limited to one baggage wagon and a single ambulance. Sherman himself made do with a single wagon for his entire field headquarters of clerks and orderlies, and he stuffed all his official papers into his own pocket. He had constructed, he said, "a mobile machine, willing and able to start at a moment's notice." Almost immediately the notice came.

On May 1, a lovely warm Sunday with trees bursting into foliage, Sherman's regiments moved into position. Thomas' massive force took the center, following the railroad south toward Dalton. McPherson trekked overland on the right flank. Schofield's smaller army marched on the left, along a branch line that forked toward Dalton from the northeast. Then on May 5, the same day that Grant launched his offensive against Lee, Sherman crossed into Georgia.

Confederate scouts had quickly spotted the Federal movements, and sped the news to General Johnston at his Dalton headquarters. His position was clearly delicate. The bluecoats outnumbered him by more than 2 to 1. He had pleaded for more troops; but the Confederate government, its attention focused on Grant in Virginia, had been slow to respond. He was promised reinforcements—23,000 men from Southern armies in Alabama and Mississippi. But none had yet arrived.

Johnston had several reasons for optimism, however. In the past five months, since taking command at Dalton, replacing Braxton Bragg, he had performed a seemingly impossible task. The Army of Tennessee, shattered by defeat at Lookout Mountain and Missionary Ridge, had been on the verge of collapse. Morale had reached such depths that soldiers were deserting by the thousands. Patiently, through wise leadership and sheer force of personal example, Johnston had restored the army to fighting trim.

In fact, he was the very model of a commanding general: dashing in appearance, with gold-braided kepi and immaculate gray uniform, while at the same time giving a reassuring air of competence and concern. He would go to heroic lengths to provide for his men, somehow finding them new shoes and extra food, granting brief furloughs all around, and issuing a twice-weekly ration of whiskey and tobacco. In turn, the men idolized him. As a cavalry captain wrote in April, Johnston "infused a new spirit into the whole

mass, and out of chaos brought order and beauty."

Besides his cavalry division, Johnston had seven divisions of infantry, which he divided into two corps. One was led by Lieutenant General William J. Hardee, veteran of Shiloh and Missionary Ridge. The other went to a new arrival—the battered but feisty John Bell Hood, whose left arm was crippled at Gettysburg and whose right leg amputated at Chickamauga. Lionized for his do-or-die aggressiveness, Hood had just been promoted, at age 32, to lieutenant general.

Besides the improved condition of his army, Johnston's second reason for optimism lay in the rugged terrain of northwestern Georgia. Between the Federal forces and his own, and stretching south for almost the 50 miles to Atlanta, lay a series of abrupt hills and towering ridges cut by swift rivers and narrow defiles. The entire region was a natural fortress, laid out by the Almighty as if for its own defense, where a small group of soldiers could be expected to hold off a vastly superior enemy. And defense was Johnston's specialty.

Governments, on the other hand, prefer victories of offense: decisive feats of heroism that rally men's hearts and demonstrate the virtue of their cause. The

Confederate leadership in Richmond bombarded Johnston with numerous suggestions for taking the initiative. But Johnston knew better. He would bide his time, dug into the mountains above Dalton, and wait for the impulsive Sherman to make a blunder. "I can see no other mode of taking the offensive here," he wrote President Davis, "than to beat the enemy when he advances and then move forward."

Sherman refused to oblige him. The Union general had just as little taste for headlong frontal assault. "Its glory is all moonshine," he declared; "even success the most brilliant is over dead and mangled bodies, with the anguish and lamentation of distant families." Furthermore, Sherman had surveyed much of the area 20 years earlier as a young lieutenant; he knew that a direct advance against Confederate lines would be the equivalent of a death sentence for his own troops. Instead, he planned a sequence of lightning-fast flanking maneuvers in hopes of getting at Johnston from the rear.

For the next two months the opposing armies sparred and sidestepped down the road toward Atlanta, Sherman jabbing at the Confederate left flank, and Johnston blocking each thrust just in time to retreat to a new defensive position farther south.

The first clash came on the morning of May 7. A vanguard unit of Thomas' Army of the Cumberland struck a Confederate outpost at Tunnel Hill, where the Western & Atlantic Railroad burrowed through a ridge about a dozen miles northwest of Dalton. The defenders, three cavalry brigades fighting dismounted behind breastworks, delayed the Federal advance for a couple of hours. Then they beat a hasty retreat to the main Confederate line at Rocky Face Ridge.

Johnston could not have picked a stronger position. A 20-mile-long, north-south escarpment that blocked the Federal approach from Tunnel Hill to Dalton, Rocky Face Ridge rose up in a nearly vertical wall to a knife-edge summit. It was virtually unassailable. Several passes interrupted it—at Mill Creek Gap where the Western & Atlantic Railroad cut through, and below this at Dug Gap—but both were heavily fortified. So secure did Johnston believe the ridge to be that he used it to anchor his left flank. He then focused his attention on the more open country north and east of Dalton. Here another rail line, the East Tennessee & Georgia, approached. And here the Confederate general concentrated the bulk of his forces, fully expecting that Sherman would attack from this direction.

Sherman had no intention of invading from the east, nor did he mean to waste his men on futile assaults up Rocky Face Ridge. But he was perfectly content to let Johnston think as much. As Schofield marched down the East Tennessee & Georgia in a display of force with the 13,500-man Army of the Ohio, Thomas' force of 61,000 took up positions confronting Rocky Face, with orders to "occupy the attention of the enemy." The real thrust, however, would be delivered by McPherson's mobile Army of the Tennessee, 24,500 strong—"my whiplash," as Sherman called it. McPherson would skirt the ridge on a wide swing to the right, then cut sharply east through an opening called Snake Creek Gap. Hurrying on, he would hit the railroad depot at Resaca, 15 miles to the Confederate rear, and demolish it, thus severing the enemy's lifeline to Atlanta—all before Johnston knew what was happening.

At first everything moved according to plan. While Schofield feinted at the Confederate right, and Thomas entertained the Rocky Face defenders with noisy forays, McPherson marched undetected into Snake Creek Gap. At dawn on Monday, May 9, he emerged onto the road to Resaca. His soldiers swept aside the single cavalry brigade that Johnston had assigned to defend it. Shortly after noon he sent a note to Sherman: Resaca five miles ahead, no opposition in sight.

Sherman was eating an early supper when the message reached him. He hammered his fist on the table until the dishes rattled. "I've got Joe Johnston dead!" he shouted.

But Johnston remained very much alive. The first of his long-awaited reinforcements, a 4,000-man division from Lieutenant General Leonidas Polk's Army of Alabama, had arrived at Resaca, and Johnston had ordered it to stay there. So when McPherson reached the town's outskirts late Monday afternoon, and surveyed the Confederate position through field glasses, what he saw gave him pause. Greatly overestimating the enemy's strength, he decided to pull back until morning. It was a serious mistake, for that night Johnston, learning that the Federals had swung in behind him, rushed three more divisions to the town's defense. McPherson's sneak attack was a fizzle before it ever began. "Well, Mac," Sherman told him, "you have missed the opportunity of a lifetime."

More Confederate reinforcements poured in over the next several days. A division arrived from Mississippi; then came General Polk with the rest of his army. The portly, 58-year-old Polk, who before the war had been Episcopal bishop of Louisiana, paused for religious offices and baptized General Hood using a horse bucket of consecrated water. Then he took charge of Resaca's defenses. Finally Johnston himself, aware at last of his adversary's battle scheme, moved down from Dalton with his entire force. By Friday the 13th, some 66,000 Confederates were entrenched in an arc around Resaca.

Switching to a new plan, Sherman began probing in strength against the Resaca defenses. For two full days the attacks continued, with negligible result. "We have had a heap of hard fighten," an Alabama soldier wrote his sister, "and have lost a heap of men and kild a heap of Yankes." In fact, some 3,500 Federals were killed, wounded or captured, with Confederate losses amounting to about 2,600.

Not all of Sherman's troops remained at Resaca, however. As the two sides blasted each other, one

A strong-willed widow from Galesburg, Illinois, Mary Ann Bickerdyke had been following the Western armies for almost three years as a nurse before joining Sherman's march to Atlanta. When a surgeon asked her by whose authority she was working in his hospital, Mother Bickerdyke replied, "I have received my authority from the Lord God Almighty. Have you any higher authority?"

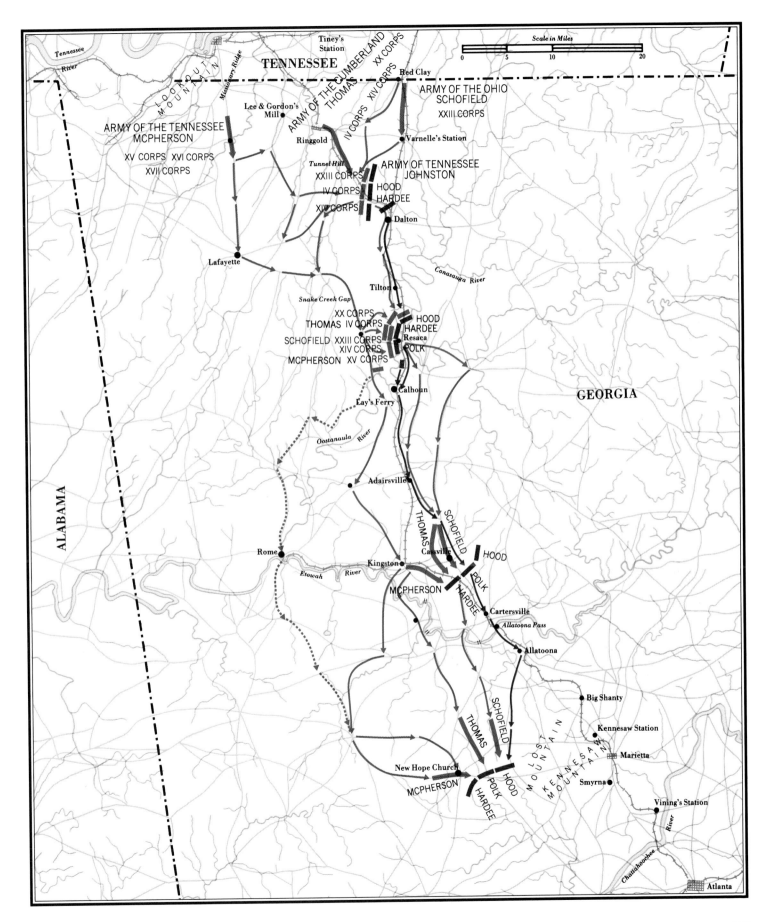

Scale in Miles

0   5   10   20

Tennessee River

TENNESSEE

Tiney's Station

XX CORPS

Red Clay

LOOKOUT MOUNTAIN

Missionary Ridge

Lee & Gordon's Mill

ARMY OF THE CUMBERLAND
THOMAS

IV CORPS XIV CORPS

ARMY OF THE OHIO
SCHOFIELD
XXIII CORPS

ARMY OF THE TENNESSEE
MCPHERSON

XV CORPS XVI CORPS
XVII CORPS

Ringgold

Varnelle's Station

Tunnel Hill

XXIII CORPS
IV CORPS
XIV CORPS

ARMY OF TENNESSEE
JOHNSTON

HOOD
HARDEE

Dalton

Conasauga River

Lafayette

Tilton

Snake Creek Gap

XX CORPS
THOMAS IV CORPS
SCHOFIELD XXIII CORPS
XIV CORPS
MCPHERSON XV CORPS

HOOD
HARDEE
Resaca
POLK

Calhoun

Lay's Ferry

GEORGIA

Oostanaula River

Adairsville

ALABAMA

Rome

Etowah River

Kingston

THOMAS SCHOFIELD
Cassville HOOD
POLK
MCPHERSON
HARDEE

Cartersville
Allatoona Pass

Allatoona

Big Shanty

Kennesaw Station

SCHOFIELD

THOMAS SCHOFIELD

LOST MOUNTAIN

KENNESAW MOUNTAIN

Marietta

New Hope Church

MCPHERSON POLK
HARDEE
HOOD

Smyrna

Vining's Station

Chattahoochee River

Atlanta

361

of McPherson's divisions swung away from the battle and headed south. It reached the Oostanaula River, crossed it "with a bound and a yell and a volley," as one soldier wrote, and established a foothold on the south bank. Once again the Confederate flank had been turned. Forced to disengage, Johnston withdrew down the railroad to a new defense line at Cassville, 25 miles to the southeast.

Sherman followed close behind, his armies advancing along a broad front on either side of the rail line. This gave Johnston the opportunity he had been waiting for. His troops at Cassville, swelled by reinforcements from Mississippi, now numbered nearly 74,000. The Union forces approaching them—Schofield's small Army of the Ohio and a corps from the Army of the Cumberland—amounted to no more than 35,000 men. For the first time Johnston had a numerical advantage, and he resolved to attack. "I lead you into battle," he announced, to the wild cheering of his grayclad regiments. "A sort of halo illuminated every soldier's face," a private recalled. "We were going to whip and rout the Yankees."

It was not to be. As the Confederates marched into position, on the morning of May 19, some Union horsemen were spotted rounding their right wing. It was a mere detachment that by chance had wandered off course, but General Hood, in command on the right, feared much worse. In an uncharacteristic display of cold feet, Hood reported to Johnston that his flank had been turned. The attack was called off. And again the Confederates withdrew.

Their new position was a preselected bastion at Allatoona Pass, where the railroad spanned the Etowah River and then crossed through a narrow cut in the 1,000-foot-high Allatoona Mountains. Sherman remembered the pass from his surveying days, and pronounced it even more unassailable than the "terrible door of death" at Rocky Face Ridge. He would avoid it entirely. Abandoning the railroad, the Union general marched his force cross-country, bridged the Etowah, and closed in on the hamlet of Dallas, 15 miles southwest of Allatoona Pass. Another 15 miles to the south lay the Chattahoochee, the last big river before Atlanta. "We are now all in motion like a vast hive of bees," he reported, "and expect to swarm along the Chattahoochee in five days."

Even in the best of circumstances Sherman's

During the fighting at Resaca on May 14, Federal troops captured the flag of the 38th Alabama, inscribed with the names of some of the regiment's earlier actions in Tennessee and Georgia.

timetable would have been impossible to meet. As it was, another six weeks would pass before the Union armies reached the Chattahoochee, and two weeks more before they stormed the barricades of Atlanta itself. Even then the city would not fall, for the real battles were just beginning.

The first Union soldiers, Thomas' XX Corps under Major General "Fighting Joe" Hooker, reached Dallas on May 25. They walked into a blazing wall of Confederate fire. One division lost 745 men—nearly a tenth of its strength—in the first 20 minutes. As other units arrived and hurled themselves against the Rebel defenses, they too were swiftly repelled. For all the noted agility of Sherman's troops, General Johnston had beaten them to the battlefield.

Exercising his "lynx-eyed watchfulness," as Sherman later called it, Johnston had learned from cavalry scouts of the Federal troop movements. He quickly realized that Sherman was up to his old flanking tricks. In response, he had adroitly shifted his entire army to the Dallas area. It was now entrenched on wooded ridges behind log revetments along a seven-mile arc from Dallas on the left, past the Methodist meeting house at New Hope Church, to Pickett's Mill on the right.

For the next two days the Union regiments struck at the Confederate line, probing for weakness. There was none. In places the opposing armies faced each other across a no-man's-land of blasted tree stumps no more than 20 yards wide. One Union attack, by the 49th Ohio, cost 203 men, more than half the force involved. "We have struck a hornet nest at the business end," a Yankee private declared.

Sherman, with his natural distaste for head-to-head combat, soon disengaged. Movement was not easy, however. Torrential rains had begun to fall, and the marching soldiers churned the red Georgia clay to the consistency of wet cement. But gradually the Federals sidestepped to the east, battling Johnston's skirmishers as they went. By the first week of June both armies had dug into new positions astride the railroad that sustained them.

Sherman inched forward against enemy fire, his soldiers entrenching with each yard gained. It was not a style of warfare Sherman favored. But the mud-clogged roads forestalled any attempt at the kind of swift end run he was famous for. "The skirmish is kept up day and night," wrote a Confederate supply clerk, "and the work of death goes on the while, like the current of the flowing river, slow and even sometimes, and at others as rapid as a cataract."

The work of death was about to accelerate, taking with it one of the Confederate army's leading commanders. On June 14, Leonidas Polk was standing with Generals Hardee and Johnston on the crest of Pine Mountain, when a shell from a Federal gun hit him in the left arm, tearing through his body and emerging from his right side before exploding against a tree. The bishop-general died instantly.

A wave of anguish ran through the Army of Tennessee. Polk had been with it since before Shiloh and while scarcely a military genius, he had served as a spiritual beacon for generals and privates alike. That night, before the Confederates abandoned the mountain stained with his blood, someone chalked a message on the door of a log cabin: "You damned Yankees, you have killed our old General Polk." For his part, Sherman cabled Washington the following day, "We killed Bishop Polk yesterday, and have made good progress today."

The Confederates fell back and relinquished all of their high ground except Kennesaw Mountain, a humpbacked ridge two miles long and 700 feet high, with the Macon and Western Railroad skirting its base. Bristling with cannon and laced with stout revetments, the mountain stood directly in Sherman's path. Knowing that he could not bypass it, his movements curtailed by the glutinous roads, Uncle Billy grit his teeth and resolved on a direct assault.

The bluecoats slogged through the mud toward Kennesaw, bracing against occasional counterattack. At one point Hood, perhaps to make up for his hesitation at Cassville, launched his entire corps against the Federal lines. The Union artillery opened up point blank. Hood's rash attempt—which he had neglected to clear with Johnston—cost him nearly 1,000 men.

By June 24 Sherman's soldiers had reached Kennesaw's base, and three days later they attacked. The assault began with an artillery barrage—200 cannon shattering the morning quiet, and pounding the mountain's defenses. The Confederate guns responded until, said a Federal officer, "Kennesaw smoked and blazed with fire, a volcano as grand as Etna." Then Sherman's divisions started up the slope.

The rains had stopped and the sun beat down through a crystalline sky, raising temperatures toward 100 degrees. The Federals charged uphill against withering fire, faltered and fell back. "The air seemed filled with bullets," an Ohio man wrote, "giving one the sensation experienced when moving swiftly against a heavy wind." So intense was the gunfire that it ignited a large patch of underbrush on the mountain's southern flank.

Scores of Federal wounded lay before the enemy breastworks there, and the flames threatened to engulf them. Defending the trenches were two Arkansas regiments, the 1st and 15th, and their commander, Lieutenant Colonel William H. Martin, saw what was happening. He ordered his men to cease fire. Then waving his handkerchief he leapt onto the parapet. "Come and remove your wounded, they are burning to death," he shouted. "We won't fire a shot until you get them away."

With that the attacking Federals emerged from cover and, assisted by their Rebel adversaries, they carried the wounded men to safety. An Illinois major then approached Martin. Cradled in his hands was a matched pair of Colt revolvers—a token of gratitude for a remarkable act of humanity. Both sides returned to their positions, and the battle resumed.

Meanwhile, a mile and a half to the north, the Federal XV Corps had started up the steep slope of Little Kennesaw on the left and the lesser incline of Pigeon Hill on the right. The main Confederate line stretched out above them 500 yards distant. But the intervening ground was strewn with obstacles like felled timber and boulders; the charge

Patient and friendly with his troops, General Joseph E. Johnston could be curt with his superiors. When Confederate President Jefferson Davis urged him to attack Sherman's force, Johnston listed some obstacles to an offensive with acid brevity: "Chattanooga, now a fortress, the Tennessee River, the rugged desert of the Cumberland Mountains, and an army outnumbering ours by more than two to one."

quickly faltered and the Union troops withdrew.

By noon it was clear to Sherman, watching from a nearby hill, that the attack had failed everywhere. Reports of appalling casualties began filtering in. By final count the Federal losses would run to nearly 3,000 men—Sherman's most expensive morning yet. Confederate casualties were no more than one fourth as high. Reluctantly, Sherman called back his regiments. The Battle of Kennesaw Mountain seemed to have turned into a disaster.

But perhaps it was still too soon to tell. Early that day the Union commander had sent Schofield's troops in a feint to the south, and the reports from that direction were far more encouraging. Schofield had advanced unopposed, and was now turning the enemy's left flank. Sherman came to a startling realization: No longer would he have to batter his armies against the Kennesaw line. With the weather clear and the roads hardening, he could return to his favorite tactics of sly maneuver. A deft sidestep to the south would bring him to the banks of the Chattahoochee, with Atlanta a short way beyond.

As the Federal divisions withdrew from the charred slopes of Kennesaw, Johnston himself hurried south in a vain attempt to block them. He clustered his men in prepared defenses—trenches and revetments dug earlier by black slaves—athwart the railroad on the Chattahoochee's north bank. There he waited; but the enemy never came. Beginning on July 8, and for the next several days, Sherman's armies crossed the rain-swollen river eight miles upstream. Sherman celebrated this achievement by taking a much-needed bath in the river.

On July 11, Uncle Billy wired Washington: "We now commence the real game for Atlanta." News of the Federal crossing threw the citizens of Atlanta into panic. Every southbound train was crammed with fleeing families. Nor did the news sit well with the authorities in Richmond: Why, they wondered, had Johnston not prevented the Union advance?

The Confederate record did not look good. Over the past two months the wily Sherman had fought his way across nearly 100 miles of rugged Georgia hills, slipping past Johnston at every turn, and at a cost of only 12,000 Federal men. Johnston's own losses were somewhat less, to be sure—around 9,000 casualties. But not once had Johnston launched an attack; in fact, he seemed incapable of

doing so. On July 17, as Johnston made ready to meet an expected assault on Atlanta from the east, he received a telegram from the Confederate Secretary of War, James Seddon. Effective immediately, command of the Confederate army would go to General Hood.

Everyone knew Hood's appetite for gunsmoke. As his West Point classmate, John Schofield, warned Sherman, "He'll hit you like hell, now, before you know

Sure enough, no sooner had Hood taken charge than he sent his soldiers in a massed assault against the Federals. Sherman had dispatched McPherson to the east, to rip up the Georgia Railroad and sever Atlanta's supply lines to the Carolinas. Schofield's small army was advancing toward Atlanta in the center. Two miles of marshland separated it from Thomas' greater force, which was moving south on the right toward Peachtree Creek. Hood sensed a flaw in the Federal alignment. He would fling two full corps upon Thomas, catching him in the process of fording Peachtree, before either Schofield or McPherson could come to his aid.

The scheme might have worked had Hood's two corps moved out smartly. But through mistakes in coordinating the attack, the Confederates arrived late at the creek, and found Thomas already established on the south bank. Further errors marred the attack. Instead of advancing in an orderly front, some regiments jumped the gun. The result was a ragged, pell-mell dash in which the assault quickly fell apart.

Hood tried again two days later, on July 22. By now Sherman's armies had closed to within two miles of the city's defenses: Thomas on the north, Schofield beside him in the center, and McPherson on the left wing to the east. Again Hood detected a flaw. While most of McPherson's force was solidly anchored on a prominence called Bald Hill, his extreme left lay open. So Hood decided to try a flanking maneuver of his own. He sent General Hardee's corps on a broad end run to the south, with orders to assail McPherson from behind.

Thus began the Battle of Atlanta, an engagement more savage than any so far in the Georgia campaign. Hardee's men, already battered at Peachtree Creek, marched through the night in order to surprise McPherson at dawn. They arrived weary and late, and it was nearly noon by the time they attacked. As it turned out, McPherson's wing was less exposed than anticipated. A three-hour melee ensued, "a square face-to-face grapple in open field," as an Ohio colonel put it, with charge and counterattack, and much loss of life. Confederate General Walker fell dead; on the Union side so also did McPherson, shot from his horse as he went to inspect his defenses on the flank of Bald Hill.

With Hardee's men stymied, Hood launched a

it." But Schofield also knew Hood's weaknesses, having tutored him in mathematics to prevent his flunking out. Schofield questioned whether Hood had the tactical intelligence—or, indeed, the plain common sense—to command an entire army. Even some of Hood's subordinates had their doubts. Commenting on Hood's promotion, Confederate division commander Major General William H.T. Walker wrote his wife, "Hood has gone up like a rocket. It is to be hoped that he will not come down like a stick."

second assault to the north of Bald Hill. A full corps under Major General Benjamin Franklin Cheatham, waiting in reserve at the Atlanta barricades, flung itself against the Union lines. The startled defenders withdrew helter-skelter, then rallied in a counter-assault, spurred on by the dashing Major General John A. "Black Jack" Logan, who had taken battle-field command of McPherson's army.

The fighting raged until nightfall, and then the guns fell silent. Little ground had changed hands, although many lives were lost. Nonetheless, Hood pronounced the day a success. "It greatly improved the *morale* of the troops," he declared. The cost to his side had been a staggering 8,000 casualties. With 3,000 killed or wounded two days earlier at Peachtree, Hood had now spilled more Confederate blood since assuming command than had the deposed Johnston in all the previous ten weeks. Federal losses, meanwhile, were far fewer: 1,700 at Peachtree, and 3,700 during the Battle of Atlanta. Hood, however, was not about to quit.

A bristling cordon of gun batteries, rifle pits and spiked logs called *chevaux-de-frise* encircled the city of Atlanta, rendering it virtually impervious to direct attack. Sherman, never inclined to waste his army in futile heroics, chose a slower but more effective course. Already he controlled three of the railroad lines into the city. Only the Macon & West-

ern, which ran south and then east toward Savannah, was still in Confederate hands. If he severed this link to the outside world, he might starve Atlanta into submission. So on July 27 he sent McPherson's old Army of the Tennessee—now led by a pious, one-armed New Englander, Major General Oliver O. Howard—to perform the surgery.

Howard swung west behind Atlanta and then down, resting for the night near the rural chapel known as Ezra Church. He prepared to hit the railroad the following day. As a precaution, he ordered his men to pile up breastworks of fence rails and brush, and it was lucky he did. Late the next morning four Confederate divisions, sent down by Hood to block the maneuver, came storming toward him.

When Sherman learned that the fire-breathing Hood was again committing his troops, he was delighted. "They'll only beat their own brains out, beat their own brains out," he said gaily. And as the morning wore on, the Confederates proceeded to do just that. They charged wave upon wave, against nonstop rifle fire, until the grayclad bodies collected, said a Federal soldier, "in windrows, sometimes two or three deep."

The Confederate excursion to Ezra Church cost them another 5,000 casualties, with few Federal losses in exchange. In ten days of command, Hood had lost more than 18,000 soldiers, or nearly one

Part of a mammoth circular painting that went on display in Detroit in 1887, this scene captures with near-photographic detail the Battle of Atlanta, which raged east of the Georgia city on July 22, 1864. Firing from the windows of the Troup Hurt house, Alabamians confront counterattacking Federals at a critical moment in the battle. At left, Union soldiers advance toward a cut on the Georgia Railroad, beyond which can be seen the church spires of the city.

third of the 60,000-man force he had started fighting with. The Confederates were now outnumbered by more than 2 to 1.

That night near the battle site a Yankee picket called out to a Confederate across the way: "Well, Johnny, how many of you are left?"

"Oh," came the weary reply, "about enough for another killing."

For the next several weeks Sherman thrust again at the Macon & Western Railroad—with infantry, with cavalry, and all to no effect. Stymied on every front, Sherman turned his frustration on Atlanta itself. On August 9, Federal gunners poured more than 5,000 shells into the city, killing at least six private citizens, including women and children. Hood sent Sherman a note protesting that the fury of combat was being directed against a civilian population. Sherman replied that Atlanta was an important military arsenal—and the shelling continued.

Messages arrived from Washington as well, on a different topic. The 1864 presidential election was fast approaching, and a war-weary populace appeared ready to vote Lincoln out of office. The next president seemed likely to be none other than ex-general George B. McClellan, who was campaigning on a platform of peace with the South.

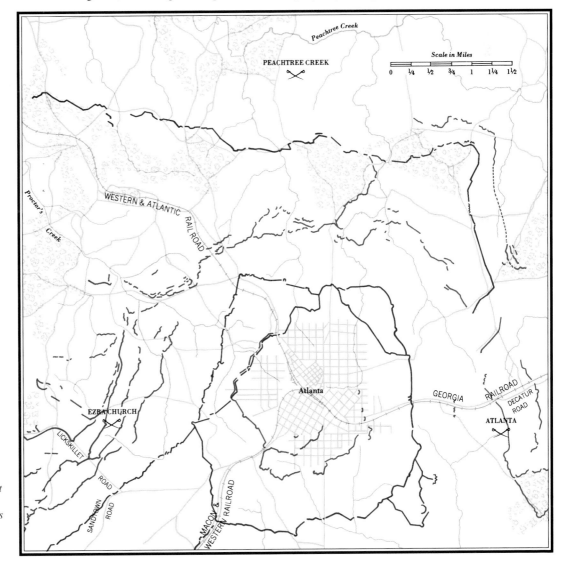

To defend Atlanta against Federal attack, Confederate engineers ringed the city with a network of elaborate fortifications (red). In places the line was little more than a mile from the center of the city—too close to prevent the Federals from shelling Atlanta at will. During the fighting, Union troops built miles of fieldworks (blue), which traced the course of Sherman's shifting operations.

Only a decisive Union victory would preserve the Lincoln government—and, by extension, the Union itself. Sherman was expected to provide that victory.

In the final weeks of August, the Union divisions began disappearing from their trenches around the city. Hood was jubilant. His own cavalry had been raiding the Federal supply lines, and he was fully convinced that Sherman had decided to pack up and go home. Then on August 30 he learned the truth. The Union armies were not retreating, but had marched even deeper into Georgia. They were now fast closing toward the Macon & Western line at Jonesboro, some 20 miles south of Atlanta, and well below Hood's southernmost troop concentrations.

Hood rushed two of his three corps—24,000 men, under Hardee's overall command—to block the Federal advance. Marching all night, the Confederates reached Jonesboro on August 31, and that afternoon they attacked. The Union troops, under Howard, were securely entrenched along a ridge west of town. As on so many occasions over the past weeks, the Confederate attack was an expensive fizzle. Then the following day more Federals arrived—two corps from Thomas' Army of the Cumberland; they swooped down on Hardee's right flank. Already outnumbered, and with more soldiers dropping as the day wore on, Hardee was retreated.

Hardee marched south along the rail line to take refuge at the town of Lovejoy's Station. He was not alone, however. By midafternoon Hood himself had awakened to the extent of the Jonesboro disaster. To avoid being trapped in Atlanta with his lifeline cut, he ordered the city's evacuation. Sad and bewildered, Hood marched south toward Lovejoy's Station with his remaining men, wondering what to do next.

The next day, bands blaring and the Stars and Stripes lifted high, the first Union columns marched into Atlanta. At 6 a.m. on Saturday, September 3, Sherman wired Washington a summary of recent operations and added a trenchant line: "So Atlanta is ours, and fairly won."

The news sent the Union into a frenzy of celebration. Sherman's accomplishment was thereby significant in more ways than one: By capturing the city of Atlanta, his armies had not only deprived the Confederacy of a vital arsenal and rail hub, but they had also strengthened the Union's resolve to continue the war. Lincoln's reelection was virtually

assured. The challenge was now to hold the city.

Hood did not wait long to decide his next move. If the Federals could sever supply lines, so could he. Regrouping his forces—which now numbered some 40,000 men—he headed north to rip up the rail track from Tennessee, which fed Sherman's armies. This forced Sherman to chase after him. For the next two months the Union divisions slogged back through rugged landscape they had already won, past Kennesaw Mountain and Allatoona Pass, fighting as they went to defend the railroad.

Sherman's mood grew more sour. At the start of his campaign he had envisioned a surgical thrust through central Georgia, splitting the Confederacy and destroying its will to fight. Backtracking, he felt, was a loser's game. So Sherman decided on an astonishing gamble: He would simply abandon the railroad. Then, with a fast and self-sufficient force, he would march on through Georgia, living off the land and ravaging the countryside.

Months earlier at Nashville, Sherman had posed

Confederate General John Bell Hood, who succeeded Joseph Johnston as commander of the Army of Tennessee, served in California with the United States Army before the war. In San Francisco in 1855, Hood met William Tecumseh Sherman, then a banker, and was struck by the "piercing eye and nervous impulsive temperament" of the man who was to become his adversary.

Major General George Thomas, shown here with the pocket compass he carried throughout the war, was a stickler for detail, once stating that "the fate of an army may depend on a buckle." But his troops admired him for his methodical ways. Thomas spared no pains, an aide said, to see that his army was "well supplied, well looked after, and always brought to the right place at the right time."

this very idea, and met with sharp criticism. His answer was brief and characteristic: "My soldiers have to subsist even if the whole country must be ruined to maintain them. War is cruelty. There is no use trying to reform it; the crueler it is, the sooner it will be over."

To deal with Hood, who seemed bent on assailing Union strongholds all the way into Tennessee, he sent General Thomas with a large force back to Nashville. With two full corps under Schofield, and extra troops from Missouri, Thomas would have some 70,000 men—ample strength to derail any schemes that Hood might attempt.

Back in Atlanta, Sherman blew up the city's arsenal, and put its industrial area to the torch. Then on November 15, with 62,000 of his toughest campaigners and 2,500 light wagons of essential supplies and munitions, he left the burning city to cut his swath of destruction from Atlanta to the sea.

As Sherman marched south, Hood trudged along in the opposite direction. Most of his troops wore tattered uniforms; some walked barefoot. Nor was Hood himself in much better shape—hobbling on crutches because of his wounds, or riding strapped to the saddle, his mind often clouded by the opiates he took to numb his constant pain. Nonetheless, he was determined to carry the war to the enemy's home ground, into Tennessee, and even to Nashville itself.

The weather had turned bitter; sleet was falling on the morning of November 21, as Hood's army left the Tennessee River heading north. The Confederate objective, some 80 miles distant, was the town of Columbia, Tennessee, on the main turnpike running north to Nashville.

Columbia was the fulcrum of Hood's strategic plan. Some 30 miles south of the city on the turnpike sat Schofield's two Federal corps—about 30,000 men. Nashville itself, with the rest of the Federal army, lay 30 miles to the north. If Hood could reach the town undetected, he would split the enemy in two, and could then confront each half separately on roughly equal terms. The plan might just have worked. But Schofield was well aware of his old classmate's propensity to attack. At the first reports of Confederate movement he rushed two divisions up the turnpike toward Columbia. Then he started up himself with the rest of his force.

When Hood arrived, in falling snow on November 27, he found the enemy entrenched before the town. In best textbook fashion he sent two corps on a flanking movement around the Union left. Anticipating this move as well, Schofield detached an advance corps of men to a new defensive post up the pike at the crossroads hamlet of Spring Hill. There, the Confederates staged a hurried attack, which was cut short by the November dusk. When Hood settled his army down for the night beside the pike opposite Spring Hill, for some reason he neglected to set out pickets.

This was a serious mistake. Under cover of darkness the rest of Schofield's divisions slipped quietly up the turnpike past the bivouacked Confederates. When Hood learned next morning that the enemy had eluded him, he was as "wrathy as a rattlesnake," according to a subordinate. Schofield had escaped, he decided, not through any lapse of his own, but because in the previous day's skirmishing his men had not attacked with sufficient ardor. He would now correct this.

Schofield halted his divisions at Franklin, astride the turnpike 15 miles south of Nashville, where they dug trenches, set up cannon, and awaited Hood's advance. With a broad stretch of open ground in front of him, and a clear field of fire, he was in an ideal position for defense.

Hood arrived on the afternoon of November 30, and prepared an immediate assault. His commanders were dubious. Major General Patrick Cleburne, a hard-hitting Irishman from Arkansas, did not like the look of the enemy emplacements. Nor did Cleburne's friend and fellow Arkansan, Brigadier General Daniel C. Govan.

"Well, general, there will not be many of us that will get back to Arkansas," Govan remarked.

"Well, Govan, if we are to die, let us die like men," Cleburne replied.

The assault began barely an hour before sunset—two full corps of Confederates marching abreast, breaking into a trot, then charging full tilt at the strongest sector of the enemy line. Two Federal brigades, caught out in front, turned and fled toward the barricades. As their companions held fire to let them through, the pursuing Confederates streamed in after them.

So began one of the most savage hand-to-hand struggles of the entire Civil War. The defenders fell back, recovered, and then came on yelling, with their

On November 16, the last of Sherman's troops march east, past ruined buildings as Atlanta burns behind them. A band in the column struck up "John Brown's Body." Sherman said, "The men caught up the strain, and never before or since have I heard the chorus of 'Glory, glory, hallelujah!' done with more spirit, or in better harmony of time and place."

weapons held high. "Some fought with entrenching tools," wrote an Ohio major, "while others clubbed their guns and knocked each other's brains out."

The onslaught drove the Confederates back over the barricades; there they came to earth, pinned down by Federal fire. And so the melee continued, past sunset and far into the night. Occasionally men on both sides of the same parapet climbed to the top, thrust loaded pieces over, and shot blindly. Some soldiers who raised their heads were seized by the hair, pulled over and killed.

And the bodies piled up. "I never saw the dead lay near so thick," wrote a Union colonel. "I saw them upon each other, dead and ghastly in the powder-dimmed starlight." Most of the bodies were Confederate. Six of Hood's generals lost their lives, including Patrick Cleburne; so did 1,750 of Hood's soldiers. According to estimates, the Confederate casualties, including those wounded and taken prisoner, came to a staggering 7,000 men. By contrast, the Federal side lost 1,222 killed or wounded, 1,104 missing and presumed taken prisoner.

A little before midnight Schofield began to withdraw his troops. By 3 a.m. the last Union forces were on their way northward. The Confederate survivors slept where they lay, and Hood was not done yet.

The Confederate commander had marched into Tennessee to attack General Thomas at Nashville; neither common sense nor compassion could dissuade him. By now he could scarcely muster 30,000 men, all of them in tatters, and embittered by defeat. Nevertheless, by the first week in December Hood's Rebels were entrenched in a thin line just south of the city. On December 15, Thomas moved to drive them away, and the outcome was never in doubt.

When Thomas hit Hood's line—with three full corps of battle-ready troops, more than 50,000 men in all—he sent the Confederates reeling backward. The graycoats retreated to new defenses several miles south. The following day Thomas hit them again. They fought with the desperation of men already condemned; against hopeless odds, they held on as long as bone and muscle and heart could endure. But by sundown the Battle of Nashville was over.

In the confusion of retreat, a precise enumeration of Confederate casualties was impossible to make; best estimates put the figure at about 6,400 men. Union losses numbered 3,000 men. But Hood's army now ceased to exist as a fighting force. The general led the survivors back to Georgia, and most of them then made their own way home. On January 13, 1865, Hood asked to be relieved of his command. For all practical purposes, the war in the West had come to an end.

SHERMAN'S MARCH TO THE SEA

As the last fires died out in Atlanta, Major General William Tecumseh Sherman and his troops left the city, passing through 200 acres of ashy desolation. A perilous march through the heart of the Confederacy now awaited the Federals. Approximately 55,000 soldiers traveled on foot, 5,000 on cavalry horses and 2,000 rode caissons or the artillery horses that pulled the army's 65 guns. Each infantryman carried 40 rounds, and the wagon trains held another 200 rounds per man, as well as four portable pontoon bridges. Supplied with only a minimum of food and intending to live off the land, they were embarking on an expedition with an extraordinary purpose. As Sherman had told Grant: "If the North can march an army right through the South, it is proof positive that the North can prevail."

While soldiers pry up track and set fire to rail cars and depot buildings, an officer on horseback scans further scenes of destruction through his telescope.

In all, Sherman commanded four corps, divided into wings of two corps each, which would march to the sea on separate but roughly parallel routes. The northern wing—XIV and XX Corps commanded by Major General Henry Slocum—would head due east from Atlanta toward the town of Augusta. The southern wing, made up of XV and XVII Corps under the leadership of Major General Oliver Howard, would take a southeasterly course toward Macon.

Then, after a week or so of marching, the two wings would veer toward each other, converging on Milledgeville, Georgia's capital. Thereafter, Sherman told Grant, the supply ships should look for him near Hilton Head and Savannah "around Christmastime." This left him only six weeks to march 275 miles.

Sherman's two-pronged advance would enable his army to cut a swath of destruction sometimes 60 miles wide through central Georgia.

373

The Path of Destruction

In the first 10 days the army covered nearly half the distance to Savannah with surprisingly little opposition. Sherman reduced the required day's march from 15 miles to 10, gaining extra time for his foraging parties to gather needed supplies. Meanwhile, the remaining troops could more thoroughly destroy railroad tracks, mills, cotton gins and anything else useful to the Confederacy's war effort. One division, working hard, could wreck 10 miles of road in a day.

When the marchers reached the railroad junction of Millen, there was a notable change in mood. There, as the troops inspected Camp Lawton, a large, recently deserted prisoner-of-war compound, one officer wrote, "Everyone who visited this place came away with a feeling of hardness toward the Southern Confederacy he had never felt before."

The march was now marked with increasing violence and cruelty; unsanctioned gangs of looters went on the rampage as the army moved eastward, and incidents of pillage, robbery and violence increased in frequency. Along the route, slaves of all ages came out to greet their liberators. They came laughing, crying, cheering and praying. But the joyful liberation increasingly became a nightmare, as the streams of refugees grew to unmanageable proportions. This situation led to tragedy—at 100-foot-wide Ebeneezer Creek. As Sherman's troops marched across a portable pontoon bridge, the blacks were held back under guard.

Once the troops were across, the bridge was removed, abandoning the blacks in the path of approaching Confederate troops. As one chaplain reported, there was a "wild rush," during which many of the terrified people plunged into the swift brown water and attempted to swim across; many drowned or were taken by the Confederates.

Leaving Ebeneezer Creek and a devastated South in its path, Sherman's army was nearing its goal. The men were as confident as ever, with little more than 20 miles separating them from Savannah.

Running wild on a Georgia farm, men of a Union foraging party slaughter livestock and cart off hay. Although Sherman's orders expressly forbade trespassing in "the dwellings of inhabitants," many a farm or plantation family would find precious little left to eat once a foraging party had visited.

A column of newly liberated slaves trails behind
Sherman's army—despite Sherman's unwilling-
ness to be burdened with their care. "Thousands
of these poor people left their humble homes,"
wrote one soldier, "and trudged along, with no
idea of where they were going, except that they
were on the highway from slavery to freedom."

Offered free passage to Charleston, families of Confederate officers board a Union steamer at Savannah in January 1865. Sherman had arranged the transport under a flag of truce for those who wanted to join their menfolk in South Carolina.

Savannah in Defeat

During their month-long march, Sherman's men had encountered an opposition more courageous than effective. Preparing to take Savannah, Sherman had stormed and captured nearby Fort McAllister on December 13; the next day he had linked up with a squadron of the Union Navy. Only Savannah itself remained to be taken.

Now, approaching Savannah early on December 21, 1864, the advance guard of Sherman's army received an unexpectedly warm welcome from the port city's mayor. In heavy fog the night before, Savannah's Confederate troops had quietly retreated across a pontoon bridge over the Savannah River. The Federals entered the city of 20,000 without a shot being fired.

The mayor's decision to capitulate was accepted by most of the city's war-weary citizens. Some Savannah residents took detours to avoid walking under the Stars and Stripes, but many families opened their homes to Union officers and charmed them with gracious Southern manners. Sherman, anxious to counter his image as a "Vandal Chief," responded in kind. He kept his troops out of trouble with a succession of drills, inspections and parades.

Savannah's rich and poor mingle as they line up for handouts of flour, salt and bacon, part of a relief shipment donated by the citizens of Boston and New York. With wheat flour selling for $125 a sack before the occupation, and grits going for $16 a bushel, many of the seaport's citizens had taken to eating boiled shrimp for breakfast.

Union soldiers gather outside Savannah townhouses, whose matrons earned needed cash by baking and selling sweet corncakes. "Those Yankees all want something sweet," reasoned one lady, "and we want some greenbacks."

377

DEATH IN THE TRENCHES

Sometime on the evening of June 12, 1864, twelve miles east of Richmond, a Confederate picket at Barker's Mill on the Chickahominy River yelled a question toward the nearby Federal lines: "Where is Grant agoing to elbow us again?"

What the Confederate had no way of knowing was that Ulysses S. Grant was already elbowing again around Robert E. Lee's right flank. In fact, the Union general in chief had just begun a maneuver that would take the Army of the Potomac's 100,000 men a safe distance southeastward along the Chickahominy. Once across that stream, the Federals would march another twelve miles to the broad James River, thence southwest toward their objective: the city of Petersburg, 23 miles south of Richmond.

The gambit signaled a change in Grant's strategy. Instead of striking sledgehammer blows against the Confederates, he would focus his attention on the railroad system that was keeping Lee's army alive. A key to that network was Petersburg, the hub of the Southside Railroad from Lynchburg in the west, the Weldon from North Carolina and the Norfolk & Petersburg from the southeast.

As the Federal effort got under way, even the imperturbable Grant was edgy, lighting one cigar after another, then forgetfully letting them go out. But by June 14, with part of his army safely across the James, Grant was much more relaxed. That day he took a steamer upriver to visit Benjamin Butler, the major general upon whom he was depending for help in his first forays against Petersburg.

Back in early May, Butler had taken his 33,000-man Army of the James on transports up the James River and debarked at Bermuda Hundred, a peninsula formed by a tight bend in the river 15 miles southeast of Richmond. The idea was for Butler to attack either Richmond or Petersburg. Instead, he allowed a Confederate force to block the neck of the peninsula, and had been bottled up there ever since, barely accessible except by waterways.

Now, Major General William F. Smith's XVIII Corps, which had been borrowed from Butler by the Army of the Potomac, was steaming up the James to rejoin its old commander. Grant wanted Butler to augment XVIII Corps to a strength of perhaps 16,000. Then, June 15, Smith would assault the Confederate works at Petersburg. "I believed then, and still believe," Grant would write later, "that Petersburg could have been easily captured at that time."

He had a point. In command for the Confederates at Petersburg, General P.G.T. Beauregard, the hero of Fort Sumter and First Bull Run, had been warning for days about the possibility of a Federal thrust in his direction. But Beauregard's alarms had been largely discounted by Robert E. Lee, who for once could not focus on his enemy's intentions. Lee believed that Richmond was a likelier Federal target than Petersburg; in any event he was convinced that the Union army could not cross the James without being discovered.

Lee was wrong on both counts, and Beauregard was now left to face Smith's approaching troops with a minuscule force of about 2,200 men to defend the city. In his favor, Beauregard had only the imposing strength of the fortifications around Petersburg. A chain of artillery emplacements connected by earthworks and trenches stretched for almost 10 miles, from the Appomattox River east of the city, around to the south and back up the river on the west. The line was studded with redans: triangular projections placed to give the defenders converging fields of fire.

It was called the Dimmock Line, after the engineer who had laid it out, but its strength was largely illusory unless properly manned, and Beauregard simply did not have the numbers to do that.

Despite his overwhelming superiority, Smith was daunted by the defenses. Approaching the main Con-

Few soldiers would have thought, as they sweated out the summer of 1864 at Petersburg, that there would come a time when they would be wearing woolen hoods, which were called balaclavas, to keep warm while they continued assaulting the same city. But the siege of Petersburg, which began in June 1864, ended up lasting right through the winter of 1865 until the dying days of the war.

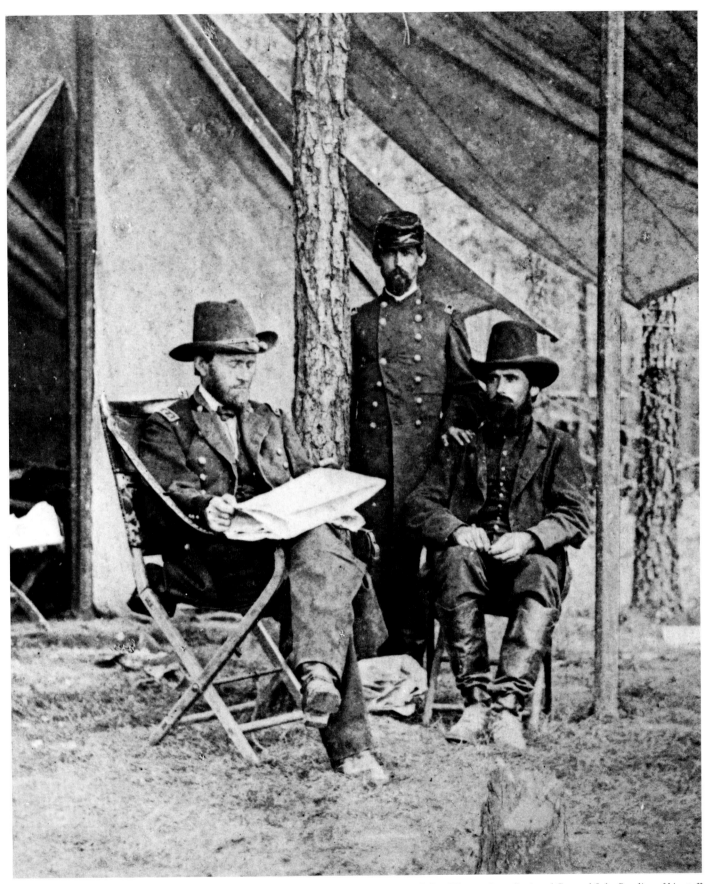

Ulysses S. Grant studies a map at field headquarters in June 1864. With him are Lieutenant Colonel Bowers (standing) and General John Rawlins of his staff.

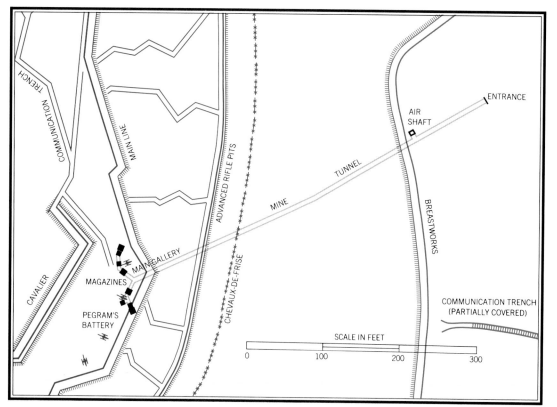

In one of the war's most innovative attempts to break an enemy's defenses, a group of Pennsylvania coal miners dug a tunnel that ended beneath the Confederate works at Petersburg. The miners extended two lateral shafts from the main gallery, which ended directly beneath Captain Richard Pegram's battery. Each shaft housed four magazines that were stocked with black powder and linked to a single fuse that would set off the blast and breach the Confederate line.

federate line at about 1:30 p.m. on June 15, he halted his corps and spent the next five and a half hours making what General Butler later scorned as "interminable reconnaissances." When Smith finally did attack, his infantry rolled over a section of Beauregard's works. As Beauregard later wrote, Petersburg "was clearly at the mercy of the Federal commander, who had all but captured it."

Yet at that moment of brilliant opportunity, Smith decided on a course of action that would later cost him his command. He stopped, explaining the following day that since he "held important points of the enemy's line of works, I thought it prudent to make no farther advance."

Once it had passed, the chance for a swift, decisive blow was gone for good. By the next morning, Beauregard had cobbled together a force of 14,000 men. On June 18, Lee belatedly arrived in Petersburg with the Army of Northern Virginia. For their part, Grant and the Army of the Potomac's commander, Major General George G. Meade, launched a series of disjointed attacks that failed to overcome the Confederate defenses—and cost the Federals 10,000 casualties in the first four days of fighting around Petersburg.

Finally, after another three weeks of sparring, Meade issued an order that the campaign would henceforth progress by "regular approaches." With that began the Siege of Petersburg, which would last until the closing days of the Civil War.

Thus the days of July passed, with the sun burning down and the men hot and sweaty as they dug and dug and dug, with the musketry cracking along the trenches when any soldier was seen by the enemy, and with big guns and mortars thumping away.

The only exception to the general routine was a project undertaken by the 48th Pennsylvania of Major General Ambrose Burnside's IX Corps at the center of the Federal line. In peacetime, these men had been anthracite miners in Schuylkill County, and their commander, Lieutenant Colonel Henry Pleasants, had come up with a novel idea that would grow into one of the war's most dramatic episodes.

As it happened, the early fighting for Petersburg had left the Pennsylvanians only 130 yards from the Confederate line. On a rise to their front was a redan that was occupied by Captain Richard Pegram's Richmond Battery, and entrenchments stretching both north and south. These were occupied by part of a South Carolina brigade commanded by Brigadier General Stephen Elliott Jr. The redan and the trenches that supported it came to be called Elliott's Salient.

Pleasants proposed that his men run a tunnel underneath the redan and blow it up with explosives, thereby opening a breach in the Confederate defenses.

As the scheme was passed upward for approval, Burnside was enthusiastic, but Meade and Grant were decidedly cool. Indeed, the general in chief regarded it merely "as a means of keeping the men

Three sketches detail the toils of Lieutenant Colonel Henry Pleasants' Pennsylvanians. At top right, a lead miner swings his pick while others pack the soil in hardtack crates; at bottom left, kegs of powder hidden in sandbags are hefted to the finished mine, then placed in lateral shafts (bottom right) directly under the target. All this was carried out in sweltering heat, the artist noted, on ground "so slippery as to quickly tire anyone not used to such locomotion."

occupied." Pleasants and his men therefore got little cooperation. They had to scrounge for lumber to shore up the tunnel and, since no one would furnish them with wheelbarrows, they made do with cracker boxes fitted with hickory handles.

Still, the Pennsylvanians pushed on, working in shifts around the clock and burrowing 40 feet a day toward their goal, which lay—according to Pleasants' eventual calculation—precisely 510.8 feet away. Dirt, sand and clay came out of the tunnel in a steady stream until the miners had excavated an estimated 18,000 cubic feet. Because all the material had to be disposed of without drawing enemy attention, the miners spread it carefully over a ravine behind their works.

On July 23 the tunnel was completed, and three days later Burnside submitted a plan for its use. Just before daylight, Pleasants' mine would be detonated and two brigades in columns would surge through the gap left by the explosion. A regiment at the head of one column would peel off to the left and a regiment at the head of the other column would swing to the right, clearing the Rebels from their lines on either side of the flattened fort. Then the remainder of Burnside's corps would pour through the breach.

Next day, in anticipation of the plan's approval, Pleasants began loading the tunnel with four tons of gunpowder. It took the men six hours, until 10 p.m., to place the 320 kegs of black powder, which would be detonated by gunpowder-filled wooden troughs leading from the main gallery, where a 98-foot fuse ran toward the mine entrance. To prevent the force of the explosion from being vented harmlessly out of the tunnel's mouth, earth was tamped into the last 34 feet of the main gallery.

When Meade's order finally came down, it enraged Burnside by making a major change in his tactical dispositions. To spearhead the advance, Burnside had selected his freshest division, commanded by Brigadier General Edward Ferrero. But Ferrero's men were black (they comprised the only division of U.S. Colored Troops in the Army of the Potomac) and Meade fretted lest it be said "that we were shoving these people ahead to get killed because we did not care anything about them." The black soldiers would join the assault after it was well under way.

Burnside protested vehemently, but Grant agreed

with Meade. Forced to pick another unit, Burnside ducked the responsibility by having his other three division commanders draw straws. The winner—or loser—was Brigadier General James Ledlie, a known weakling, drinker and coward.

Now the great moment was at hand. At 3:15 a.m. on Saturday, July 30, Colonel Pleasants entered the tunnel, lit the fuse and came running out. Fifteen minutes passed. Nothing happened. Another 15 minutes. Still nothing. At 4:15, Pleasants allowed two volunteers to go into the tunnel to investigate. The fuse had gone out at a splice. The men relit it and raced for safety.

At 4:40 a.m., someone on the Federal line shouted, "There she goes!" Then, according to a Union staff officer, "a vast cloud of earth is borne upward, one hundred feet in the air, presenting the appearance of an outspread umbrella, descending in the twinkling of an eye with a heavy thud!"

Where the Confederate redan had been, there yawned an enormous hole—the Crater—200 feet long, 50 feet wide and 25 to 30 feet deep in the center. It was filled, a Union lieutenant wrote, "with dust, great blocks of clay, guns, broken carriages, projecting timbers, and men buried in various ways—some up to their necks, others to their waists, some with only their feet and legs protruding from the earth." At least 22 gunners of Pegram's Battery and 256 men of the 18th and 22nd South Carolina died in the blast.

The way into Petersburg lay open to Burnside's men. But the blast had disconcerted them almost as much as it had the Confederates. The cloud thrown up by the explosion, explained one of Ledlie's aides, "appeared as if it would descend immediately upon the troops waiting to make the charge." Some of Ledlie's men scurried to the rear; others were too stunned to move. It took at least ten minutes before they were able to re-form and advance. And when they did they crowded to the edge of the Crater, then descended into it and began milling about, extricating wounded Confederates and hunting souvenirs. Meanwhile, the Rebels on either side of the Crater had recovered and had thrown up a barricade of sandbags across the main trench south of the breach. To the north, the 17th South Carolina spread out into the connecting trenches and traverses, hoping to confine the attackers to the Crater.

Clearly, the Federals were in sore need of leader-

The eruption of the mine under the Confederate defenses at Petersburg on July 30, 1864 raises a plume of debris on the horizon as Union officers look on in the foreground. The explosion signaled a heavy barrage by Federal batteries, including the 10-inch mortars at center, emplaced between traverses built of wicker gabions.

ship, but it was not to come from General Ledlie. He was huddled in a bombproof to the rear, comforting himself with a bottle of rum. He was soon joined there by General Ferrero, who had remained behind after sending his inexperienced men into battle—and disaster. As one Union officer recalled the scene, Ferrero's black troops "literally came falling over into this crater on their hands and knees; they were so thick in there that a man could not walk."

Three hours had passed since the detonation of the mine, and the Federals had only succeeded in cramming an estimated 10,000 troops into the area of the Crater. At that chaotic moment, the black troops in the Crater received new orders from Ferrero in his hideout to advance.

Their suicidal charge soon collided with a countercharge by a brigade that Lee had rushed north to help plug the gap in the Confederate line. The Federals were heavily outnumbered outside the Crater, and they received little help from within. Isolated and hit hard, the Union regiments broke and ran, closely pursued by Confederates who had been enraged to discover that they were fighting black troops. Recalled a Virginia private: "I saw Confederates beating and shooting at the negro soldiers as the latter, terror-stricken, rushed away from them."

Around the Crater, other Federals were making a desperate stand. "The men were dropping thick and fast," recalled a Union officer, "most of them shot through the head. Every man that was shot rolled down the steep sides to the bottom, and in places they were piled up three and four deep."

At about 1 p.m., Major General William Mahone ordered what would be the decisive Confederate charge. As the grayclad troops poured over the rim of the Crater, some Federals fought hand to hand, others tried to surrender, and several hundred simply ran for their lives. "The slaughter was fearful," recalled one of Mahone's officers, especially among blacks.

By about two o'clock the battle was over. The Federal forces had suffered 3,500 casualties against Confederate losses of about 1,500. Within hours, the Confederates were entrenching a new line—in front of the Crater. As for General Grant, he now recognized the chance he had missed to take Petersburg, and perhaps end the war. "Such opportunity for carrying fortifications I have never seen before," he said, "and do not expect to see again."

But the commander of the Union armies would have little time for rueful retrospection: On the same day that the Battle of the Crater was fought, Confederate cavalry burned Chambersburg, Pennsylvania, sending shivers throughout the North. The raid had been launched from Stonewall Jackson's old stomping ground, the Shenandoah Valley, which had been in turmoil for weeks.

Throughout the war, the Confederates had held tenaciously to the fertile Shenandoah Valley despite repeated enemy incursions. With Grant's elevation to general in chief, however, the Federals had strengthened their campaign to control the strategic corridor. Their efforts resulted in a dramatic sequence of events.

In late April 1864, a Union army of 9,000 men

Major General John C. Breckinridge, commander of the Confederate Department of Western Virginia in 1864, was vilified in the North for turning against the Union he had served as Vice President before the war. In December 1863 The New York Times greeted with open delight a rumor that Breckinridge had been killed in action: "If it be true that a loyal bullet has sent this traitor to eternity, every loyal heart feels satisfaction and will not scruple to express it."

under Major General Franz Sigel began moving sluggishly southwestward through the Valley. Not until mid-May did it near the town of New Market, just west of Massanutten Mountain, a 45-mile-long ridge. There, Sigel's force ran up against a much smaller Confederate force commanded by Major General John C. Breckinridge. Included in Breckinridge's contingent was a group of more than 200 cadets, ranging in age from 15 to 25, who had been summoned from their studies at the Virginia Military Institute in the Valley town of Lexington.

The leaders of the competing forces could scarcely have been more dissimilar. The tall, congenial Breckinridge had served as Vice President of the United States and in the U.S. Senate; in 1860, he had run a respectable race for President as the candidate of the Southern wing of the fractured Democratic Party. Sigel, on the other hand, was a martinet with a confusing habit of shouting commands in his native German. A superintendent of schools in St. Louis, Missouri, when the war began, he had been given swift military preferment—primarily to encourage enlistment among the North's 1.25 million German-American people.

Shortly after 11 a.m. on May 14, a Union gunner atop Manor's Hill on New Market's northern outskirts was astonished to see Breckinridge's entire army coming at the Federals "like a swarm of bees." Easily driven from the eminence, Sigel's troops withdrew a short distance northward and re-formed on Bushong's Hill.

After taking a few minutes to restore his formations, Breckinridge ordered another charge. So far, he had held the boy-soldiers of VMI in reserve, but soon there was need for them. When Federal artillery destroyed a section of the advancing Confederate line, a staff officer galloped up to Breckinridge and shouted that the day would be lost if the enemy spotted the gap and counterattacked.

"Put in the cadets," urged the officer.

"They are only children," protested the general. But then, after a few moments' thought, he gave the command: "Put the boys in, and may God forgive me for the order."

With a cheer, the cadets surged forward into the Federal shot and shell, one after another of them going down under the enemy's fire. One youngster clawed at the grass in his death agony. Another

ripped the shirt from his chest to display his mortal wound as he toppled backward. Reaching their objective, a rail fence north of an orchard, the boys knelt, raised their muskets and fired a volley. As a Federal officer recalled, "A streak of fire and smoke flashed across the field." The gap in the Confederate line was closed.

There was still more fighting to be done that day, and the cadets were in the thick of it, further ensuring their place in legend by capturing a field piece. By the time the Federals finally fled from the field, ten of the boys from VMI—the school where Stonewall Jackson had taught before the war—lay dead and another 47 were wounded, almost one fourth of their number. For those who survived, reward came immediately after the battle, when General Breckinridge rode over to the exhausted group.

"Well done, Virginians," Breckinridge said proudly. "Well done, men."

Once Sigel had taken to his heels, Robert E. Lee could no longer afford to keep Breckinridge in the Valley. On May 19—just as Grant was moving around the Confederate right at Spotsylvania and heading for Cold Harbor—Breckinridge departed to join Lee's Army of Northern Virginia. That same day, the hapless Franz Sigel was replaced by 62-year-old Major General David Hunter, a disputatious career officer and ardent abolitionist.

Confronted only by the skeleton Confederate forces that Breckinridge had left behind, Hunter quickly headed south through the Valley in an orgy of burning that climaxed on June 12, when he achieved a measure of revenge for New Market by putting the torch to the Virginia Military Institute. "A vast volume of black smoke rolled above the flames and covered half the horizon," recalled a Federal staff officer. "The Institute burnt out about 2 p.m. and the arsenal blew up with a smart explosion. The General seemed to enjoy this scene."

Hunter's pleasure, however, would be short-lived: Even as VMI was still aflame, Lee dispatched Lieutenant General Jubal A. Early to the Shenandoah Valley at the head of the II Corps he had recently taken over from an ailing Lieutenant General Richard Ewell. Early's orders were twofold: to rid the Valley of Hunter and, if he thought it possible, to drive toward Washington, D.C., and force the Federal gov-

Young Eliza Clinedinst—known to grateful Virginia Military Institute veterans after her marriage as Mother Crim—opened her doors to the wounded and hungry alike in the wake of the fighting at New Market. Among those she comforted was a 15-year-old cadet who, though unscathed, seemed helpless after the ordeal of battle. "He wanted his bread spread with preserves," she recalled. "He sat down just like a little child to eat from Mother's hand."

Amid bursting shells and flashes of lightning, the cadets of VMI charge through the smoke toward a Federal battery. "I think it would have been impossible to eject from six guns more missiles than these boys faced in their wild charge," marveled a Union officer.

Lieutenant General Jubal A. Early was "arbitrary, cynical, with strong prejudices; he was personally disagreeable; he made few admirers or friends either by his manners or his habits," said Early's adjutant general. "He acted as though he would be ashamed to be detected in doing a kindness; yet many will recall little acts of General Early which prove that his heart was naturally full of loyalty and tenderness."

ernment to protect its capital by drawing troops from Grant as he tried to tighten his grip on Petersburg and Richmond.

Early seemed just the man for the job. Among the grimmest of Confederate commanders, he was a cynical former lawyer from southwest Virginia, a misogynist bachelor with a coarse and unbridled tongue. Around an ever-present wad of chewing tobacco, Early expressed himself with a profanity and a sarcasm so biting that he could move men to laughter or outrage with equal facility. But Early could fight, and he swiftly set about proving it.

After his depredations at Lexington, Hunter had crossed the Blue Ridge Mountains and was preparing to attack Lynchburg, where an important Confederate rail center was located. Early arrived there on June 17 and, scarcely pausing for breath, ordered two brigades to push west toward the advancing enemy. On June 18, as a Federal officer recalled,

"the Confederates attacked us with great violence." Realizing that he was doing battle with Jubal Early's veteran II Corps, Hunter hastily withdrew to the sanctuary of the Kanawha Valley of West Virginia.

The way to the North was now open to Early, who quickly put his 10,000 men on the road. Marching northeastward down the Valley, they crossed the Potomac at Shepherdstown on July 5. A few days later, Confederate cavalry arrived at the little city of Frederick, Maryland, whence a major road led south to Washington. To get to the capital, however, Early would have to cross the Monocacy River about three miles southeast of Frederick. He soon found that his route was blocked by Federals deployed on high ground just beyond the river.

The Union force was commanded by Major General Lew Wallace, who had been consigned to the war's backwaters after incurring Ulysses S. Grant's displeasure at Shiloh. Now, although massively outnumbered, Wallace put up a sturdy fight, forcing Early to delay his march on Washington for a precious 24 hours. Eventually, Wallace's old critic, General Grant, would conclude that Wallace had contributed more to the Federal cause by losing the Battle of Monocacy "than often falls to the lot of a commander to render by means of a victory."

The value of Wallace's action lay in the fact that Grant, alarmed by Early's incursion, had sent 15,000 men of the VI and XIX Corps north to defend the Federal capital; they would begin filing into the city's defensive line on the afternoon of July 11.

Around noon that day, Early arrived at a point where he could see Fort Stevens, the northernmost of Washington's fortifications, and beyond it the dome of the U.S. Capitol. "The works were but feebly manned," he wrote later. But before he could get his weary men in position to attack, the Federal reinforcements had started to arrive, and the opportunity was gone.

Although Jubal Early could take dour satisfaction in having accomplished his mission of forcing Grant to send troops who would otherwise have been used in the siege of Petersburg, he concluded that night that he would have to withdraw. Still, he remained for another day—and thereby gave the President of the United States a rare opportunity to see what the shooting war was like.

Visiting Fort Stevens, Abraham Lincoln took a

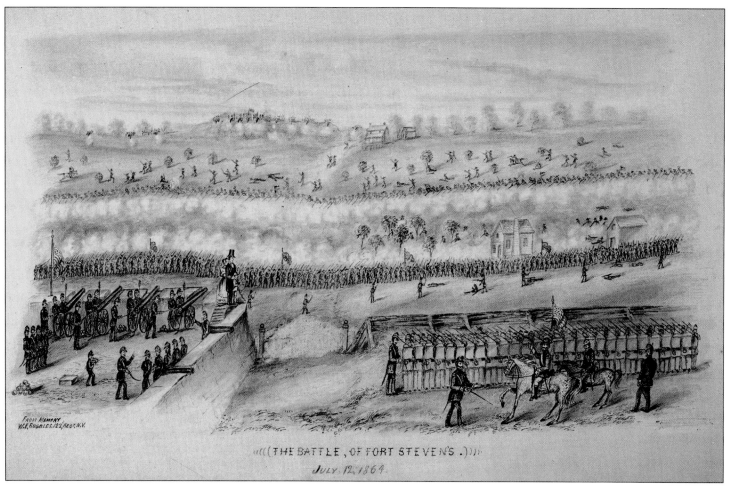

(((THE BATTLE, OF FORT STEVEN'S .)))
JULY. 12, 1864.

position on the parapet. There, despite protests, he remained until a busy young lieutenant colonel named Oliver Wendell Holmes Jr. saw this unprepossessing civilian exposed from the waist up to Confederate fire. "Get down, you damn fool, before you get shot," Holmes snapped—and only when the civilian sat down did the future Supreme Court justice realize whom he was addressing. Lincoln compromised, sitting behind the parapet instead of standing on it. Still, he continually leaped up to see what was happening.

On July 12, Early started marching his men westward; two days later they re-crossed the Potomac at White's Ford, 30 miles northwest of Washington. En route, he continued to harry the North, and on August 1—two days after Chambersburg, Pennsylvania, was put to the torch by Confederate horsemen—Grant announced that he was sending Major General Philip Sheridan to take command in the Valley with instructions "to put himself south of the enemy and follow him to the death."

President Lincoln, who took many barbs about his own appearance, once described Phil Sheridan as "a brown, chunky little chap, not enough neck to hang

him, and such long arms that if his ankles itch he can scratch them without stooping." Yet despite his peculiar looks, Sheridan radiated energy to the point that a newspaper artist called him a "little mountain of combative force."

Instead of putting all his dynamism to work at once, however, Sheridan bided his time, maneuvering in a manner that brought on some minor engagements and meanwhile building up his force to 30,000 men—more than twice Early's numbers. Only then, on September 19 as the armies faced each other across Opequon Creek just northeast of Winchester, Virginia, did Sheridan attack.

For eight hours, the struggle that would be known to the defenders as Third Winchester (battles had been fought there also in 1862 and 1863) and to the Federals as the Battle of Opequon Creek swayed back and forth until the Confederates were forced into an L-shaped perimeter. At about 4:30 p.m., Brigadier General George Crook's VIII Corps assailed Early's left wing, which was facing north, while Major General Horatio Wright's VI Corps attacked the Confederate right from the east.

Sensing victory, Sheridan rode up and down his lines, pausing only to shout, "We've got 'em bagged,

President and Mrs. Lincoln observe the repulse of Jubal Early's Confederates from the walls of Fort Stevens, north of Washington, in this somewhat fanciful postwar drawing. The President did stand for a time atop the wall but he was accompanied by Federal officers; Mary Todd Lincoln remained prudently under cover.

by God!" That night, having inflicted about 4,000 casualties (including Brigadier General Robert Rodes, who was mortally wounded), Sheridan reported, "We have just sent them awhirling through Winchester, and we are after them tomorrow."

In fact, it was September 22 before the Federals caught up with Early, who by then was ensconced on Fisher's Hill, a steep, densely wooded ridge south of Strasburg, Virginia, with his right anchored against the nose of Massanutten Mountain. Although Fisher's Hill was known from previous fighting as the Gibraltar of the Valley, Sheridan was undismayed. Crook outflanked the Confederate left and rolled up Early's thin line. That night, hounding the Confederates southward, Sheridan kept bellowing at his men, "Run, boys, run! Don't wait to form! Don't let 'em stop!" When some soldiers protested that they were too tired to continue, Sheridan shot back: "If you can't run, then holler!"

By the time the Federals finally stopped at Harrisonburg, Virginia, 50 miles southwest in the Valley, Early's troops had marched through Port Republic and on up into the Blue Ridge Mountains.

With Early licking his wounds—and receiving reinforcements that would soon bring his battered army to 21,000 men—there ensued what generations of Valley residents between Staunton and Strasburg would recall as the time of "the Burning." Across a 20-mile-wide swath, Sheridan's soldiers moved northeastward in the autumn of 1864, setting aflame every conceivable source of food and comfort to the enemy. Sheridan himself later reported the razing of 2,000 barns, 120 mills and half a million bushels of grain, along with the confiscation of 50,000 head of livestock. However, by the time the Federals neared the end of their destructive trek, Early was on their trail, doggedly following the pillars of smoke as they plumed skyward.

By October 17, the 31,000 men of three Federal corps were camped north of Strasburg along the eastern bank of Cedar Creek, which for the final five miles of its course flows southeastward to its confluence with the North Fork of the Shenandoah. The Valley Turnpike, running southwestward for five miles from Middletown to Strasburg, crossed Cedar Creek at the midway point, the two features describing a gigantic *X* across the terrain.

From a nearby mountain, one of Early's division commanders, General John B. Gordon, saw that the enemy's left flank was not anchored to any defensive position. If Gordon's troops could ford the Shenandoah downstream from its confluence with Cedar Creek, they could roll up the exposed flank while Early, with the other two divisions, could strike up the Valley Turnpike against the Union center.

At nightfall on October 18, the flanking movement began. As Gordon later recalled, "The long gray line like a great serpent glided noiselessly along the dim pathway." Long before dawn, Gordon's 7,000 men reached a ford across the Shenandoah, less than a mile from the left of Crook's VIII Corps. At about 5 a.m., howling the Rebel yell, three divisions under Gordon struck—just as Early threw his force against the VIII Corps front.

Taken completely by surprise, the bewildered troops of Crook's corps came undone; a Federal staff officer remembered seeing "wagons, ambulances, artillery, soldiers without commanders, commanders without soldiers, every fellow for himself, moving backwards in sullen discouragement in the faces of the yelling victors."

Although they were by no means as shaken as VIII Corps, the Federals' XIX and VI Corps were also forced to retreat until they reached a ridge west of Middletown. There, the relatively intact VI Corps, under the temporary command of Brigadier General George Washington Getty, braced itself; for nearly two hours it fought off repeated Confederate charges while XIX Corps re-formed behind its right flank and Crook tried to rally VIII Corps on its left. Then, deciding his men could not withstand another attack, Getty withdrew to a new defensive line a mile north of Middletown.

The Confederates followed, and at midday the battle reached a fateful juncture. Although Gordon argued hotly that one more charge would win the day, Jubal Early blinked. "It was now apparent," he said in his official report, "that it would not do to push my troops further. They had been up all night and were much jaded." Thus, as Gordon disgustedly wrote, "We waited, waited for weary hours" until the Federals "had time to recover their normal composure and courage."

More specifically, Early had given Phil Sheridan the time he needed to seize control of the battle.

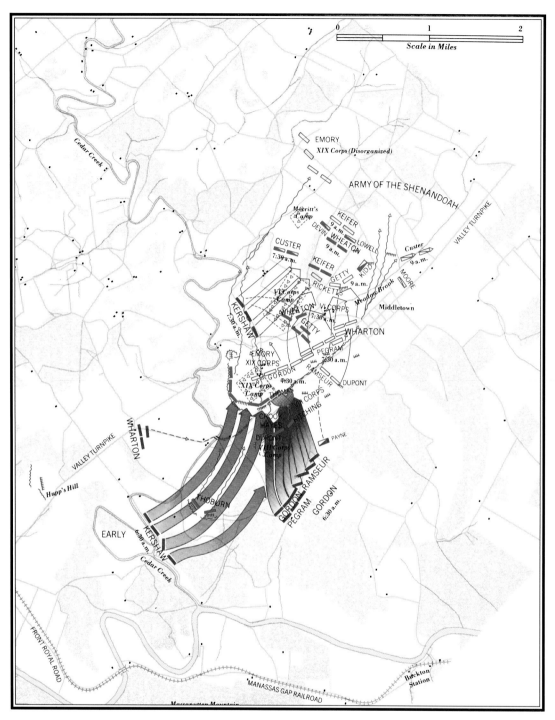

Scale in Miles

At 5 a.m. on October 19, Jubal Early launched a surprise attack on the Federal army camped between Cedar Creek and Middletown. Three Confederate divisions under General John Gordon swept through the camps of Brigadier General George Crook's VIII Corps, while Major General Joseph Kershaw's division on the left routed Colonel Joseph Thoburn's two Federal brigades. The Confederates pressed their advantage, driving XIX Corps from an entrenched position near Belle Grove plantation; but between 7 a.m. and 9 a.m. they were slowed by the dogged resistance of the Federal VI Corps. Major General Philip Sheridan, absent when the battle began, arrived on the field at 10:30 a.m. and rallied his troops on a line north of Middletown.

Thus far the Federals had fought the battle at Cedar Creek without Sheridan's guidance; Little Phil had spent the night of the 18th at Winchester, after returning from a trip to Washington to discuss Union strategy with chief of staff Henry Halleck. Arising at 6 a.m. on the 19th, he had taken his breakfast and mounted for the ride south to rejoin his army. By the time he met his cavalry escort at a creek south of Winchester, the sound of distant firing had risen to "an unceasing roar." Worried, Sheridan moved faster. "Just as we reached the crest of the rise beyond the stream," he recalled, "there burst upon our view the appalling sight of a panic-stricken army."

Barking orders as he went, the fiery little general on a big black gelding named Rienzi began one of the most famous rides in military history.

"As he galloped on," a staff officer remembered, "his features gradually grew set, as though carved in stone, and the same dull red glint I had seen in his piercing black eyes when, on other occasions, the battle was going against us, was there now." Encountering some fleeing men, Sheridan brought them up short: "Come on back, boys! Give 'em hell, God damn 'em! We'll make coffee out of Cedar Creek tonight!" And when Brigadier General William Emory reported that a division of his XIX corps was now ready to cover a retreat, Sheridan flared: "Retreat, hell! We'll be back in our camps tonight."

Incredibly, Sheridan managed to establish a solid, two-mile-long line within two hours. Then he rode along the entire front, showing himself to every soldier. "I'll get a twist on these people yet," he yelled. "We'll raise them out of their boots before the day is over!" At that, a Federal officer recalled, "Cheers seemed to come from throats of brass, and caps were thrown to the tops of the scattering oaks."

Around 4 p.m. an ominous silence fell over the field. At last, wrote a member of Sheridan's staff, the order came: " 'Attention!' rings down the line. 'Shoulder arms! Forward! *March!*' And with martial tread and floating flags the line of battle is away."

Among those attempting to stem the Federal rush was one of the rising stars of the Confederacy, Major General Stephen Dodson Ramseur, who had been given the command of Early's old division shortly after his 27th birthday. Now, wearing a flower on his lapel to honor his newborn daughter, Ramseur rode up and down his line, keeping his men firmly in hand. As the enemy pressed in from three sides, Ramseur's horse went down; he mounted another, which was also shot; then he found a third and was preparing to mount when a rifle ball pierced both his lungs. Ramseur, mortally wounded, was carried to the rear.

Then, across the seething battlefield, Federal cavalry bugles blared. Adding their weight to the charge, Brigadier General Wesley Merritt's horsemen on the left and Brigadier General George Custer's on the right thundered toward the Confederate flanks. As a Union officer put it, "Flesh that is born of woman could not stand such work as this." Early's soldiers turned in flight, and from some woods to the west, a Vermont captain watched them go. Later, he would remember "a great, rushing, turbulent, retreating army, without line or apparent organization, hurrying and crowding. Back across the sea of half-upturned faces of the enemy we could see the Union flags advancing amid the belt of smoke and flame that half encircled the doomed Confederates."

By the time Jubal Early's Army of the Valley finally halted at New Market, it was finished as a fighting force. By Early's begrudging estimate, his army had suffered almost 3,000 casualties—1,860 killed or wounded, 1,050 taken prisoner. The Confederates had inflicted 5,665 casualties, of whom 644 were killed and 3,430 wounded. But the Federals still had a numerical advantage of close to 2 to 1.

The Valley Campaign was over at last. Never again would fighting beyond the Blue Ridge Mountains provide distractions from the ugly war in the trenches that by now extended from south of Petersburg to Richmond.

Since the Federal failure at the Crater, the fighting around Petersburg had settled into a deadly pattern, with Grant hammering first with his right fist and then, when Lee shifted troops to fend off the blow, with his left. On August 14, Major General Winfield Scott Hancock launched an offensive north of the James River against the extreme Confederate left, fighting to within seven miles of Richmond before the Confederates, reinforced from the south, beat off the attack. Four days later the Union met with more success, when Major General Gouverneur Warren's V Corps attacked the weakened enemy line south of Petersburg and seized a stretch of the Weldon Railroad, one of Lee's supply lines.

By such measures, Grant was able to tighten his grip on the beleaguered district. Yet not until late September was he offered a chance for a real breakthrough—and when it came, Grant himself was among the Federals responsible for muffing it.

At the first bend in the James south of Richmond, Lee's defensive line straddled the river, anchored on the north at Chaffin's Bluff, Virginia, where the Confederates occupied a fortified camp. Located at the camp's southeast corner was a formidable obstacle named Fort Harrison, consisting largely of a parapet with enclosed gun positions, fronted by a row of sharpened stakes to entangle charging infantry.

Early on the morning of September 29, some 8,000 Federal men of Major General Edward O.C. Ord's XVIII Corps assailed Fort Harrison and quickly overwhelmed its garrison of 800 inexperienced artillerists. Here was a priceless opportunity: If he could quickly capture the rest of the fortified camp, Ord could then advance on Richmond, only eight miles away.

Yet in their rush at the fort the Federals had become disorganized, and once inside, the exhilaration of their victory delayed the restoration of order. An hour or so passed before Ord was able to patch together a small force, which he led himself. In the futile process, Ord suffered a leg wound, and his command passed to his senior subordinate, an inept brigadier general named Charles Heckman.

For two hours, Heckman threw his individual brigades piecemeal into a series of clumsy attacks that exposed them to brutal enfilading fire. And then, just as a lull was settling over the field at about 10 a.m., General Grant rode into Fort Harrison.

Although the signs of impending failure must have been evident to Grant's practiced eye, the general in chief unaccountably did nothing to remedy the worsening situation. Instead, he simply scribbled a message to Major General William Birney, commander of the X Corps, which had just seized a nearby fort on the James, saying that Ord's XVIII Corps was ready to advance on Richmond. Then Grant departed—and, as Confederate reinforcements poured into the Chaffin's Bluff defenses, the Federal opportunity to take Richmond quickly faded away.

Nonetheless, the fight at Fort Harrison had scared the Confederates; a few days later a depressed Robert E. Lee informed Secretary of War James Seddon that things could not long continue this way. While Grant extended his lines and added to his numbers, the Army of Northern Virginia could "only meet his corps, increased by recent recruits, with a division, reduced by long and arduous service."

For the first time, Lee began to speak openly of the possibility of losing Richmond. He needed time to find more men, more food, more ammunition and more horses. His hope now was to hang on until cold, wet weather put a temporary end to Grant's incessant attacks. "We may be able, with the blessing of God, to keep the enemy in check until the beginning of winter," he wrote. "If we fail to do this the result may be calamitous."

And so the Confederates held on, their condition steadily deteriorating. On the last Thursday of November, proclaimed Thanksgiving Day by President Lincoln (who was doubtless thankful for having won reelection earlier in the month), the Federal armies outside Richmond enjoyed a feast of turkey or chicken, pies and fruit. There was no such cele-

bration for Lee's troops. Instead, wrote a South Carolina captain, "We lay in grim repose."

As much as Lee may have looked toward its coming, the winter of 1864-65 was a death watch. Poisoned by inflation, the Confederate economic system was collapsing. In 1861, one gold dollar had been equivalent to $1.03 in Confederate money. As 1865 began, a dollar in gold equaled almost $60 Confederate. In Richmond, hungry, threadbare citizens were paying $45 Confederate for a pound of coffee, $100 for a

As a shell bursts overhead, General Grant calmly writes a dispatch from Fort Harrison, captured a few hours earlier by Federal troops. "Those standing about instinctively ducked their heads," wrote Horace Porter, Grant's aide, "but he paid no attention to the occurrence, and did not pause in his writing, or even look up."

pound of tea and $25 for a pound of butter—when those items were available at all.

To Lee, the most worrisome problem was a shortage of troops. Since 1861 the Confederacy had put about 750,000 soldiers in the field; in all theaters there were now fewer than 160,000 on duty. The rest, one officer said, had been "worn out and killed out and starved out." To remedy the situation, teenagers and men in their sixties were being enrolled in reserve units; a lieutenant assigned to one such ragtag outfit said it "presented every stage of manhood from immature boyhood to decrepit old age."

As always, the suffering was worst for the soldiers. "Starvation, literal starvation," reported General Gordon. After a spasm of fighting south of Petersburg, Lee bitterly complained that, "Some of the men have been without meat for three days, and all are suffering from reduced rations and scant clothing, exposed to battle, cold, hail and sleet." Yet the commanding general did not have it much better. An Irish politician who visited Lee was invited to dinner. "He had two biscuits," said the guest, "and he gave me one."

Yet Robert E. Lee was never content simply to defend, and with the first harbingers of spring he moved to attack by calling in General Gordon—who had, at 32, become the youngest of his corps commanders—and asked him to find a likely place to batter through the enemy works.

It was three weeks before Gordon came back with a proposal. Near the center of the Federal line east of Petersburg stood a bristling strong point named Fort Stedman. It was located at a place where the opposing entrenchments lay only 150 yards apart—so close, Gordon thought, that the Confederates could take it with a rush. "The tremendous possibility," Gordon wrote later, "was the disintegration of the whole left wing of the Federal Army, or at least the dealing of such a staggering blow upon it as would disable it temporarily."

Launched at 4 a.m. on March 25, the assault appeared at first to be a smashing success. Advancing in three columns, the Confederates swarmed over surprised Federal pickets, punched into Fort Stedman and overwhelmed its defenders. But there, as the Federal army came to life, they stalled.

Responsible for the threatened sector of the front was the Federal IX Corps under Major General John G. Parke, who had been startled that morning to discover that, while General Meade was away at Grant's City Point headquarters, he was the acting commander of the Army of the Potomac. Yet Parke reacted decisively. With two divisions already on the line, he immediately called on Brigadier General John Hartranft's reserve division to move toward the breach. Soon, the Confederacy's Gordon recalled, the surrounding hills were "black with troops."

By 8 a.m., four hectic hours after Gordon's attack had begun, the Confederate situation seemed hopeless, and Lee ordered a withdrawal. In his army's last offensive gasp, he had lost 3,500 men while inflicting about 1,000 casualties. As for the Federals, the only change caused by the assault was that a divisional review, scheduled for that morning, was put off until the afternoon.

On Sunday, March 26, the day after the failed endeavor at Fort Stedman, General Lee informed President Davis that Richmond and Petersburg were doomed. Now, Lee felt, his job was to get his troops away to the southwest, where they could join forces in North Carolina with General Joseph E. Johnston, whose own army had recently been helpless in opposing the Federal legions of Major General William Tecumseh Sherman.

Late on the following afternoon, Sherman himself arrived by steamer at City Point, where Grant and a few staff members were on hand to meet him as he stepped ashore. After his devastating march through Georgia, the red-haired Ohioan had persuaded Grant to let him deal out the same treatment to the Carolinas: Columbia, the capital of South Carolina, had been turned into a sea of flames on February 17; Charleston, the cradle of the Confederacy, had been abandoned by the Confederacy that same day; Sherman's men had surged into North Carolina during the first week in March. On March 23, General Johnston sent Lee a harshly realistic message: "Sherman's course cannot be hindered by the small force I have. I can do no more than annoy him."

At City Point, Sherman and Grant greeted each other, as one officer recalled the scene, like "two schoolboys coming together after a vacation." That night and the next day they conferred with Admiral David D. Porter and another distinguished City Point visitor—President Lincoln, who was staying aboard the steamer *River Queen*.

General Sherman (left) argues a point with General Grant, President Lincoln and Admiral Porter during their meeting to discuss strategy and peace terms aboard the steamer River Queen *in late March 1865. Porter later wrote of Lincoln's attitude toward the South: "His heart was all tenderness."*

With the end of the war obviously in sight, Sherman naturally wanted to know what the President's policy toward the defeated Confederacy would be. Lincoln's answer was clear: As soon as the fighting stopped, the people of the South "would at once be guaranteed all their rights" as citizens of a common country. "I want no one punished," Porter remembered Lincoln as saying. "Treat them liberally all around. We want those people to return to their allegiance to the Union and submit to the laws."

With that in mind (and it would later haunt him), Sherman returned to North Carolina. On the following day, Grant launched the campaign that would at last break the back of the Confederacy.

Grant had anticipated that Lee would attempt a juncture with Johnston, and he had made plans to prevent it. As Grant saw it, the crucial area of operations would be a rectangle southwest of Petersburg that was 10 miles across, east to west, and eight miles deep. It was bounded on the north by the Southside Railroad; on the east by the Weldon Railroad; on the south by the Vaughan road to the village of Dinwiddie Court House; and on the west by a road leading north from Dinwiddie to the Southside Railroad—by way of a crossroads called Five Forks.

Grant ordered General Warren's V Corps, followed by Major General Andrew Humphreys' II Corps, to march five miles south along the Vaughan road until the troops were beyond the Confederate right flank. From there the infantry was to press north toward the enemy line, forcing the Confederates to come out of their trenches to protect their rear and the Southside Railroad.

It was raining on March 29, and the going was hard for Warren's troops. "We went slipping and plunging through the black slimy mud in which pointed rocks were bedded," a Federal officer recalled, "now stumbling over a rotten tree, now over the stiffening corpse of some poor comrade by whose side we might soon lie."

Although the heavy rain continued on the 30th, Warren and Humphreys edged closer to the Confederate trenches. Meanwhile, Philip Sheridan—back from the Shenandoah Valley and once again in command of the Federal cavalry—sent a division of horsemen northward from Dinwiddie toward Five Forks. Upon approaching the vital intersection, however, the troopers found 5,000 infantrymen of Major General George Pickett's division entrenched and in a fighting mood. After a brief exchange of fire, the Federals fell back and reported that the enemy intended to hold Five Forks.

Not until April 1, after a day of maneuvering and sporadic fighting, were the Federals ready to assail Five Forks. According to Sheridan's plan, his dismounted cavalry under Brevet Major General Wesley Merritt would feint toward Pickett's right and pin down his center while Warren's infantry assaulted the

Confederate left, which was bent back at a 90-degree angle to the north. But as the day passed and Warren still was not in position, Sheridan suffered agonies of frustration. "He made every possible appeal for promptness," a staff officer wrote, "dismounted from his horse, paced up and down, and struck the clenched fist of one hand against the palm of the other, and fretted like a caged tiger."

Yet in one way the delays may actually have helped Sheridan. Lulled into a false sense of security by the failure of the Federals to attack, George Pickett and the cavalry's Major General Fitzhugh Lee had gone off north shortly after 2 p.m. to feast at a shadbake hosted by a fellow general on the north bank of Hatcher's Run. The two officers told no one where they were going. The repast was a leisurely one, liquor may have been served, and Pickett was still enjoying the afterglow when, shortly after 4:15 p.m., the Federals struck at Five Forks.

Aimed at the angle of Pickett's bent line, the assault almost missed its mark; instead of being crushed by the combined weight of two divisions on the Federal right, the vital spot was hit only by the division of Major General Romeyn Ayres—with Phil Sheridan nearby and yelling encouragement. "We'll get the twist on 'em, boys!" Sheridan cried. "There won't be a grease spot of 'em left!"

As Ayres' men pushed forward, they were staggered by a Confederate volley and started to fall back. To rally them, Sheridan seized his personal flag and held it high. "Bullets were now humming like a swarm of bees around our head," wrote a staff officer, "and shells were crashing through the ranks. All this time Sheridan was dashing from one point of the line to another, waving his flag, shaking his fist, encouraging, entreating, threatening, praying, swearing, the very incarnation of battle."

Under Sheridan's inspired leadership, the Confederate left was broken, and by the time Pickett finally got back to the field his men were already being driven to the west. "It has been an evil day for us," a Confederate captain wrote in his diary. "My heart sickens as I contemplate this day's disasters."

The day was a disaster for General Warren as well. Since morning, Sheridan had been fretting over Warren's tardiness, and criticized his dispositions. Now, as the gunfire died away, Sheridan ordered Brigadier General Charles Griffin to assume command of V Corps. When the word reached Warren he went to Sheridan and asked him to reconsider. "Reconsider, hell!" said Sheridan. "I don't reconsider my decisions. Obey the order!"

Thus Gouverneur Warren, a hero of Gettysburg, ended the war in disgrace. (Fourteen years later, a court of inquiry exonerated Warren—three months after he had died.)

Word of the victory at Five Forks was carried to Grant by one of his staff officers, Lieutenant Colonel Horace Porter, who leaped from his horse and found himself "rushing up to the general-in-chief and clapping him on the back with my hand, to his no little astonishment." Grant endured Porter's enthusiasm without comment, then turned to General Meade and said quietly: "Very well, then, I want Wright and Parke to assault tomorrow morning at four."

At that appointed hour on the Sunday morning of April 2, Union artillery on the Petersburg front opened with the greatest bombardment of the 10-month siege. "From hundreds of cannons, field guns and mortars came a stream of living fire," recalled a Federal sergeant; "the shells screamed through the air in a semi-circle of flame."

On the Union right, Horatio Wright's VI Corps brushed enemy pickets aside and, despite heavy losses, managed to breach the Confederate trenches at several points. All along VI Corps' front, an officer reported, the Confederates were soon "swept away and scattered like chaff before a tornado."

Unaware of the break in his line, Lieutenant General Ambrose Powell Hill had ridden to Lee's headquarters near Petersburg for a conference. Soon Lieutenant General James Longstreet, still recovering from the wound he had sustained in the Wilderness, arrived in advance of the reinforcements he was bringing from north of the James River. The three generals were discussing the bleak situation when an officer burst in to report that Hill's lines had been struck and broken and that Federal skirmishers were approaching. Hill mounted his horse and raced away to try to stem the Federal flood.

Heading southwest with a courier on the Boydton Plank Road, Hill spotted two Federals in the trees ahead. "We must take them," snapped Hill, drawing his revolver. The bluecoats—Corporal John Mauk and Private Daniel Wolford of the 138th Pennsylvania—took cover and leveled their rifles. "If you fire,

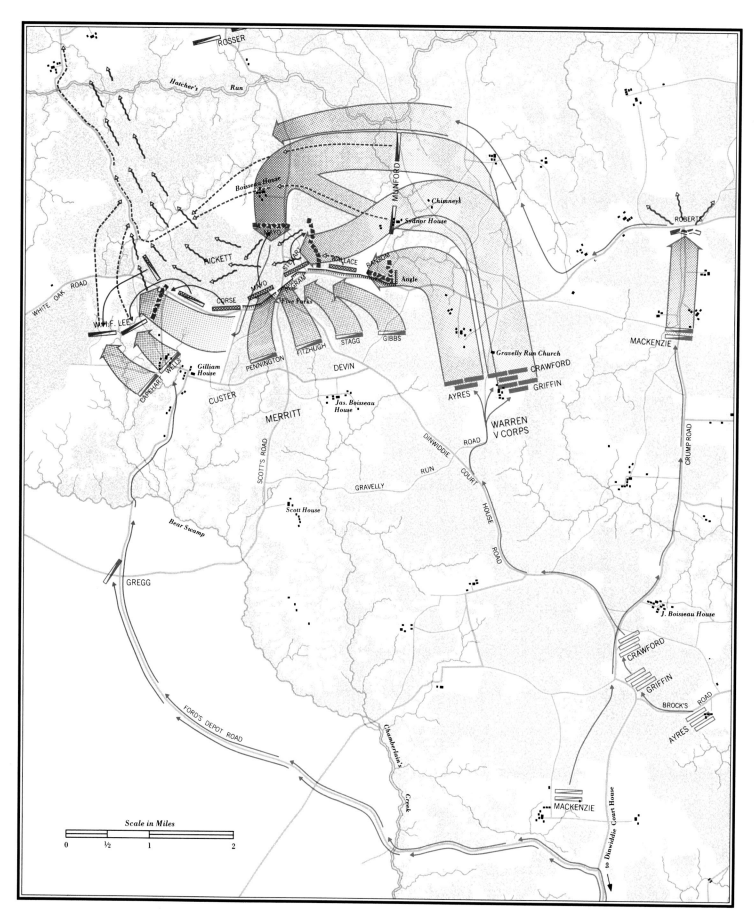

ROSSER

Hatcher's   Run

Boisseau House

MUNFORD

Chimneys

Sydnor House

PICKETT

WALLACE

Angle

MAYO

STUART

WH.F.LEE

MAYO

PEGRAM

PICKETT

ROBERTS

CORSE

Five Forks

CAPEHART

WELLS

Gilliam
House

PENNINGTON

FITZHUGH

STAGG

GIBBS

MACKENZIE

WHITE OAK ROAD

DEVIN

Gravelly Run Church

CRAWFORD

AYRES

GRIFFIN

SCOTT'S ROAD

CUSTER

Jas. Boisseau
House

WARREN
V CORPS

MERRITT

DINWIDDIE

ROAD

COURT

GRAVELLY   RUN

Scott House

HOUSE

CRUMP ROAD

Bear Swamp

ROAD

GREGG

J. Boisseau House

CRAWFORD

GRIFFIN

FORD'S DEPOT ROAD

BROCK'S   ROAD

AYRES

Chamberlain's

MACKENZIE

Creek

to Dinwiddie Court House

Scale in Miles

0   ½   1   2

396

you'll be swept to hell," shouted Hill's courier, G.W. Tucker. And then, bluffing: "Our men are here—Surrender!" Hill echoed the cry: "Surrender!"

The answer came as spitting lead, and a bullet from Mauk's rifle pierced Hill's heart. He was dead before he hit the ground. Tucker rode back to headquarters and reported to Lee, whose eyes filled with tears. "He is at rest now," Lee murmured, "and we who are left are the ones to suffer."

Later that morning, Lee sent a telegram to General John C. Breckinridge, the Confederacy's recently appointed Secretary of War: "I advise that all preparation be made for leaving Richmond tonight." A messenger took a copy of the wire to President Davis while he was attending services at St. Paul's Episcopal Church. "Mr. Davis arose," a parishioner wrote later, "and was noticed to walk rather unsteadily out of the church."

By nightfall, Jefferson Davis and members of the Cabinet, the Archives and the Treasury of the Confederacy were on their way to Danville, Virginia. Then, over the objections of Richmond's city fathers, the Confederates set fire to the city's warehouses to keep the valuable contents out of the hands of the Federals. The flames quickly spread.

With the departure of civil authorities, the streets of Richmond were taken over by a menacing mob: thieves, prostitutes, Army deserters and convicts who had broken out of the penitentiary. "It was an extraordinary sight," recalled newspaper editor Edward Pollard; "disorder, pillage, shouts, mad revelry of confusion." As the hours passed, "the sidewalks were encumbered with broken glass; stores were entered at pleasure and stripped from top to bottom; yells of drunken men, shouts of roving pillagers, wild cries of distress filled the air and made the night hideous."

All the while, Robert E. Lee's widely dispersed army was streaming over five separate routes toward the pretty, red-brick town of Amelia Court House, which lay about 35 miles west of Petersburg on the Richmond & Danville Railroad.

Lee arrived there on April 3, only to make an appalling discovery. During the last days of the siege, he had asked the Confederate Commissary Department to collect a store of food in Richmond. It had been done: 35,000 rations were gathered in the capital, and Lee wanted them sent ahead to Amelia. But

that order had somehow gone astray during the confusion of Richmond's final hours, and Lee now found an abundant cache of artillery caissons, ammunition and harness—but not a single ration.

For a moment, according to one officer, Lee seemed "completely paralyzed." But he quickly mastered himself and sent foraging parties out into the countryside that had already been scoured repeatedly for food. The delay was critical. To the south, Grant's Federals were already racing along a course roughly parallel to Lee's, hoping to get ahead of the Army of Northern Virginia and cut off its escape route.

When the foragers returned during the morning of April 5, their wagons were virtually empty. Yet Lee had no choice but to put his troops on the road without having eaten. His route of march would pass through Rice's Station on the Southside Railroad, seven miles northwest of Burkeville. Once there he could receive food by rail from Lynchburg, then march west to that city or, preferably, head south to the Danville route and follow it to Johnston's army. But with the Federal forces closing in fast he would have to hurry.

Leading the strung-out army was Longstreet's corps. Later came Lieutenant General Richard Anderson's small corps and the Richmond garrison, commanded by the veteran General Richard Ewell. Bringing up the rear was Gordon's corps.

By the time Longstreet reached Rice's Station on the morning of April 6, a gap had opened between his rear and Anderson's vanguard. At 11 o'clock, Anderson was still five miles away; ahead of him were the two branches of Sayler's Creek, a tributary of the Appomattox. When a Confederate wagon train moved unprotected into the widening gap, Federal riders attacked, killing drivers, cutting horses loose and setting wagons on fire. To protect the rest of the wagons, Ewell ordered those still behind him to take a road forking off to the north. General Gordon, however, was not informed of the change; when he reached the fork, he followed the wagons—as he had been doing all day—and thereby veered away from the rest of the army. Thus, Lee's outnumbered army had been split into three diverging parts. Of these, the one made up of Ewell's and Anderson's command was facing the most immediate danger.

Anderson's brigades crossed one of the branches of Sayler's Creek and pushed three quarters of a mile

The Grim Testing
of Black Troops

SIC SEMPER TYRANNIS

22 TH REGT U.S. COLORED TROOPS.

The banner carried by the 22nd Regiment U.S. Colored Troops pictures a bayonet-wielding black soldier overpowering a Confederate. The Latin motto at top, meaning "Thus Always to Tyrants," had an ironic thrust; it was also the state motto of slaveholding Virginia.

Charging at the run, men of the 22nd U.S. Colored Troops capture a Confederate entrenchment on the Dimmock Line outside Petersburg on June 16, 1864. One of the unit's officers wrote afterward, "I never saw troops fight better, more bravely, and with more determination and enthusiasm."

More black soldiers, totaling 38 regiments, served with the Union armies during the lengthy sieges of Petersburg and Richmond than in any other campaign during the Civil War. In that grim crucible they erased the doubts about their fighting ability that had been harbored by Ulysses S. Grant and other Federal generals—and by white troops on both sides. Blacks fought desperately in the chaos of the Battle of the Crater, one brigade suffering 1,324 casualties, and later they took the lead in assaults on New Market Heights and other Confederate strongholds. For individual gallantry in these attacks, 23 black soldiers earned the Congressional Medal of Honor.

One winner, Sergeant Major Christian Fleetwood, wrote that the reason his fellow blacks fought so intensely was to prove their bravery to the world. They "stood in the full glare of the greatest searchlight, part and parcel of the grandest armies ever mustered on this continent," Fleetwood said, competing "with the bravest and the best" and "losing nothing by comparison."

down the road, where they found three of Sheridan's cavalry divisions blocking the way. Horatio Wright's VI Corps had been following Sheridan, and now it swung to the north to come up behind Ewell. Confederate Private W.L. Timberlake watched as VI Corps deployed. "The corps was massing into the fields at a double quick," he wrote, "the battle lines, blooming with colors, growing longer and deeper at every moment, the batteries at a gallop coming into action front. We knew what it all meant."

What it all meant was a battle in which the Confederate situation was hopeless: The Rebels were badly outnumbered and woefully weary. While Wright launched the infantry assault against Ewell, the Federal cavalry slammed into Anderson from the opposite direction. The Confederates "lost all formation and went across country," wrote a New York sergeant, "our boys chasing up and gathering them in." By the end of the one-sided Battle of Sayler's Creek, 6,000 Confederates had been taken prisoner,

A cavalry escort leads the carriages of Confederate officials fleeing Richmond across the James River on the night of April 2. "The waters sparkled and rushed on by the burning city," recalled a soldier who had guarded the bridge. "Every now and then, as a magazine exploded, a column of white smoke rose up, instantaneously followed by a deafening sound."

including Richard Ewell and seven other generals.

To the north of Anderson and Ewell, Gordon found himself in similarly desperate straits when a bridge across Sayler's Creek collapsed, slowing his march while General Humphreys' II Corps came up on his rear. The Confederates fought savagely until Gordon saw that further resistance was hopeless. Then, one Confederate wrote, Gordon "gave us orders to save ourselves, showing us the way by galloping his horse down the hill and fording the creek." On the opposite side, Gordon pulled together what remained of his command and marched toward Farmville, a few miles west on the south bank of the Appomattox River.

At Rice's Station, Lee and Longstreet also determined to head for Farmville, where they could join Gordon's remnants, cross the Appomattox River, burn the bridges behind them and get a little breathing space before marching west for Lynchburg. In the event, however, General William Mahone's rearguard division delayed in burning a key bridge the following day, April 7, destroying only four of its 21 spans and allowing Humphreys' corps to get across. After that, as if in atonement, Mahone's men dug in near Cumberland Church, three miles north of Farmville, and stubbornly held off the advancing enemy until darkness finally ended one of the worst two-day periods in Confederate history.

That night at Farmville's Prince Edward Hotel—where Lee had slept the night before—General Grant received word from Sheridan that provisions for Lee's army had arrived by rail at Appomattox Station, 26 miles to the west. Sheridan intended to start for the junction the following day; if he could beat Lee to those rations, the chase might be over.

Having digested that news, Grant wrote a short message to Lee: "The results of the last week must convince you of the hopelessness of further resistance. I feel that is so, and regard it as my duty to shift from myself the responsibility of any further effusion of blood, by asking of you the surrender of that portion of the Confederate States army known as the Army of Northern Virginia."

North of the Appomattox River, Lee and Longstreet were together when Grant's demand for surrender arrived at 9:30 p.m. After reading the message, Lee passed it without comment to Longstreet, who glanced at it and responded: "Not yet." In reply to Grant, Lee wrote, "Though not entertaining the opinion you express of the hopelessness of further resistance on the part of the Army of Northern Virginia, I reciprocate your desire to avoid useless effusion of blood, and therefore, before considering your proposition, ask what terms you will offer on condition of its surrender." Then Lee started his army for the village of Appomattox Court House, two miles northeast of Appomattox Station, where the Confederates' precious provisions were now stored.

On the fine spring morning of April 8, Lee was still on the road when a courier brought Grant's answer to his inquiry. There would be only one condition, said Grant. It was "that the men and officers surrendered shall be disqualified from taking up arms again against the government of the United States until properly exchanged."

Although this was a far more generous offer than Lee had expected from "Unconditional Surrender" Grant, the Confederate commander was not yet ready to lay down his arms. Instead, he asked Grant to meet him between their lines at 10 o'clock the next morning—not to negotiate a surrender but, as Lee put it, merely to see how "your proposal may affect the Confederate States forces under my command and tend to the restoration of peace."

Grant received Lee's reply that night—and it only added to his miseries. During the day, he had been afflicted by what a staff officer described as "one of his sick headaches, which are rare but cause him fearful pain, such as almost to overcome his iron stoicism." Stopping for the night at a farmhouse near Curdsville, he sought relief by bathing his feet and applying mustard plasters to his wrists and the back of his neck. Now, upon reading Lee's message, he shook his throbbing head and said in dismay: "It looks as if Lee still means to fight."

That same evening, Lee summoned his top commanders to his headquarters northeast of Appomattox Court House. The situation could hardly have been bleaker. That afternoon, Union cavalry had seized Appomattox Station—and, with it, four freight trains loaded with food for Lee's army. Now, as the darkness deepened, the Federal II and VI Corps were only 10 miles to the east; the red glow of enemy campfires burnished the sky to the south; and, to the west, Sheridan's cavalry was "hovering around," as a Virginian recalled, "like ill-omened birds of prey, awaiting their opportunity."

Yet for all their awful dilemma, the Confederate generals determined to try again to escape. At first light, Gordon's corps would lead an attempted breakout to the west.

And so, on the early morning of April 9, the old II Corps of the Army of Northern Virginia—which had fought at Chancellorsville under Stonewall Jackson, at Gettysburg under Richard Ewell, in the Shenandoah Valley under Jubal Early and at Petersburg under John Gordon—went into its last battle. For three hours, while Federal infantry added its massive weight to the cavalry that had originally blocked Gordon's way, the uneven struggle continued. But then, when Lee sent a staff officer seeking an assessment of the situation, Gordon could only reply: "I have fought my corps to a frazzle, and I fear that I can do nothing unless I am heavily supported by Longstreet's corps."

There was no chance of that: Longstreet was already facing imminent attack from the east by the Federal II Corps. Reading Gordon's message, Lee murmured as if to himself: "There is nothing left me but to go see General Grant, and I had rather die a thousand deaths."

Although Lee had not yet received a reply to his request for a 10 a.m. meeting with Grant to discuss the general subject of peace, he assumed that the session would take place; at 8:30, he started east on Traveller, his beloved mount through most of the war. On the way, however, he was given a message stating, in effect, that Grant had no intention of meeting with him for any reason other than accepting the surrender of the Army of Northern Virginia.

Lee's options had now run out, and he could only ask that Grant agree to "a suspension of hostilities pending the adjustment of the terms of the surrender of this army." While couriers raced to find Grant, Lee wearily threw himself down under an apple tree—and waited.

Shortly after 11 a.m., a horseman with Lee's letter rode up to Grant, who had paused to rest in a clearing. Grant read it impassively, then told his chief of staff, Brigadier General John Rawlins, to read it aloud. When Rawlins finished, there was silence. Someone called for three cheers, but the response was feeble. Then Grant smiled. He suddenly felt

wonderful. "When the officer arrived," he said, "I was still suffering with the sick headache; but the moment I saw the note I was cured."

Grant immediately dictated a crisp reply to Lee, explaining his whereabouts and saying he would "push forward to the front for the purpose of meeting you." When Lee read Grant's note, he rode toward Appomattox Court House. Nearing the hamlet, he asked Colonel Charles Marshall of his staff to ride ahead and arrange for a meeting place. In the village,

After evacuating Richmond and Petersburg on April 2, Lee gathered his forces at Amelia Court House. Grant hurled his armies in pursuit, sending Sheridan's cavalry to block Lee's line of march. Amid constant fighting, the Confederates were forced farther west. After clashes at Sayler's Creek and around Farmville, Lee turned toward Lynchburg only to find his way blocked at Appomattox.

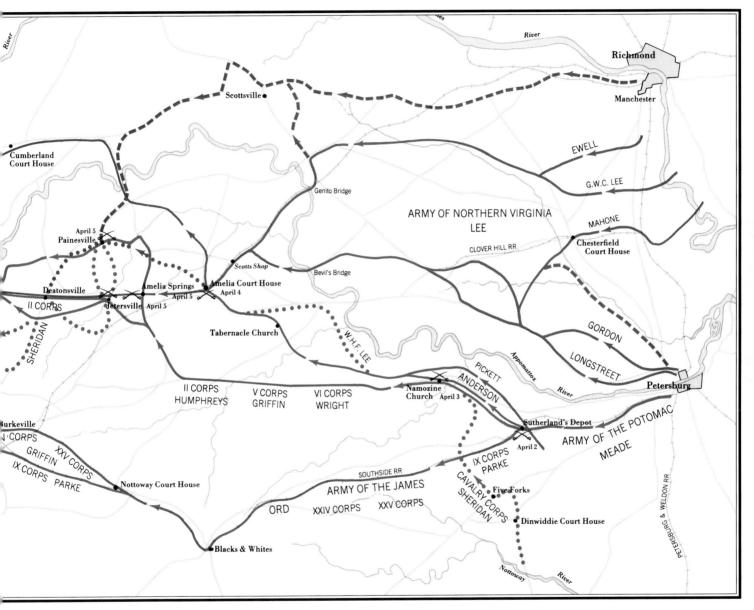

Marshall noted, only a few brave inhabitants were outside, and he asked "the first citizen I met to direct me to a house suitable for the purpose."

By remarkable coincidence, the house selected—a pleasant, tree-shaded, two-story brick structure with a colonnaded porch—belonged to a merchant named Wilmer McLean. He had once owned a farm near Manassas Junction in northern Virginia, and it had been used as General Beauregard's headquarters during the First Battle of Bull Run. McLean was a patri-

otic Southerner, but by March of 1862 he had had quite enough of soldiers, and he moved to the sleepy little community of Appomattox Court House. "Here" he told his family, "the sound of battle will never reach you." But the war in its waning moments had found them again.

Lee arrived at the McLean house at 1 p.m. Grant, accompanied by a number of his officers, entered the parlor about half an hour later. Lee rose to his feet and the two commanders shook hands. They were a study in contrasts. Tall, white-bearded and dignified, Lee had put on his best uniform and wore his finest sword; Grant, slouched and red-whiskered, wore a mud-spattered sack coat and carried no sword. At Grant's behest, several more Federal officers were beckoned into the parlor. Those who could find chairs sat down; others stood against the walls.

As Grant prepared to discuss the surrender, he suddenly became "sad and depressed. I felt like anything rather than rejoicing at the downfall of a foe who had fought so long and so valiantly." To put off the moment, Grant began chatting about the old days in the Regular Army. Lee brought him back to the main topic. "I suppose, General Grant," he said, "that the object of our present meeting is fully understood. I asked to see you to ascertain upon what terms you would receive the surrender of my army."

Getting down to business, Grant confirmed his original, generous offer. "That is," he explained, "the officers and men surrendered to be paroled and disqualified from taking up arms again until properly exchanged, and all arms, ammunition and supplies to be delivered up as captured property."

Grant's words must have lifted a great burden from Lee. Yet after Grant had put the terms on paper, the Confederate commander hesitated. Finally he said, "There is one thing I would like to mention. The cavalrymen and artillerymen own their own horses in our army. I would like to understand whether these men will be permitted to retain their horses."

"You will find the terms as written do not allow this," Grant said slowly. "Only the officers are allowed to take their private property."

"No, I see the terms do not allow it," said Lee. "That is clear." He was evidently loath to ask for the favor, but it was obviously important to him.

Then Grant relented. He would, he said, instruct his parole officers "to let all the men who claim to own a horse or mule to take their animals home with them to work their little farms."

"This will have the best possible effect on the men," Lee said with relief. "It will be very gratifying and will do much toward conciliating our people."

The two generals signed the surrender document at about 3 o'clock. After they shook hands again, Lee led the way out to the porch. Federal soldiers in the McLean yard came to attention and saluted the defeated enemy leader. Lee returned the salute and

mounted Traveller. Just then, Grant was coming down the steps from the porch. He stopped and, without a word, removed his hat. Lee raised his hat in return and slowly rode away.

Soon the Federal camps were erupting in joy. Crusty George Meade, who had been so sick that he scarcely left his ambulance all week, jumped on a horse and took off at a gallop, waving his hat and shouting at the top of his lungs: "It's all over, boys! Lee's surrendered! It's all over!"

"The scene in our brigade after General Meade passed was absolutely indescribable," recalled an officer. "Men shouted until they could shout no longer; the air above us was for half an hour filled with caps, coats, blankets and knapsacks." Another soldier told of "huge, lumbering, bearded men" who "embrace and kiss like schoolgirls, then dance and sing and shout, stand on their heads and play at leapfrog with each other."

One somber thing remained to be done. The Confederates had hoped there would be no formal laying down of arms—that instead they would be permitted to leave their muskets and colors stacked in their encampments for Federal authorities to gather up. But this was one concession Grant would not make. He wanted an official ceremony, something that none of the participants would ever forget.

April 12, 1865, the day selected for the last rites of the Army of Northern Virginia, was cold and gray. Honored with command of the ceremony was Brigadier General Joshua Chamberlain, who once long ago had made his stand with the 20th Maine at Little Round Top. Chamberlain aligned his Federal troops on both sides of the road leading through Appomattox, then watched intently as the Confederate column crossed the valley and marched up the avenue, silent but for the familiar sound of tramping feet.

"On they come," Chamberlain wrote, "with the old swinging route step and swaying battle flags." General John Gordon led the column; behind him, the first unit in the line of march was the Stonewall Brigade, now reduced to barely 200 men.

Gordon sat erect in his saddle, but his head was down and his expression dark. The men behind him were equally grim. As the column neared the double line of Union soldiers, Gordon heard a spoken order, a bugle call and an electrifying sound: the clatter of

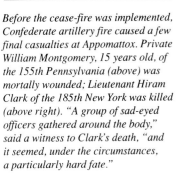

Before the cease-fire was implemented, Confederate artillery fire caused a few final casualties at Appomattox. Private William Montgomery, 15 years old, of the 155th Pennsylvania (above) was mortally wounded; Lieutenant Hiram Clark of the 185th New York was killed (above right). "A group of sad-eyed officers gathered around the body," said a witness to Clark's death, "and it seemed, under the circumstances, a particularly hard fate."

hundreds of Federal muskets being raised to the shoulder in salute. Gordon's head snapped up. Comprehending in an instant, he wheeled his mount toward Chamberlain. As the animal reared, then dipped its head toward the ground, Gordon raised his sword aloft and brought its tip down to his toes in a sweeping response to the Union tribute. He shouted a command, and the advancing Confederates came from a right shoulder shift to shoulder arms—returning the salute.

It was, said Chamberlain, "honor answering honor," and it was hard to say who was the more moved. "Many of the grizzled veterans wept like women," said Confederate Major Henry Kyd Douglas, "and my own eyes were as blind as my voice was dumb." "On our part," Chamberlain wrote, "not a sound of trumpet more, nor roll of drums; not a cheer, nor word, nor whisper of vain-glorying, nor motion of man standing again at the order, but an awed stillness

rather, and breath-holding, as if it were the passing of the dead."

After the exchange of salutes, the ragged veterans in gray turned to face Chamberlain, dressed their lines, fixed their bayonets and stacked their muskets. Then, Chamberlain wrote, "lastly—and reluctantly, with agony of expression—they fold their flags, battle-worn and torn, blood-stained, heart-holding colors, and lay them down." This was the most painful part of the ordeal; said one North Carolinian: "We did not even look into each other's faces."

The next day, Chamberlain recalled, "over all the hillsides in the peaceful sunshine, are clouds of men on foot or horse, singly or in groups, making their earnest way as if by the instinct of an ant, each with his own little burden, each for his own little house."

By the evening of April 13, most of them were gone. The Army of Northern Virginia, mighty in battle, was no more.

405

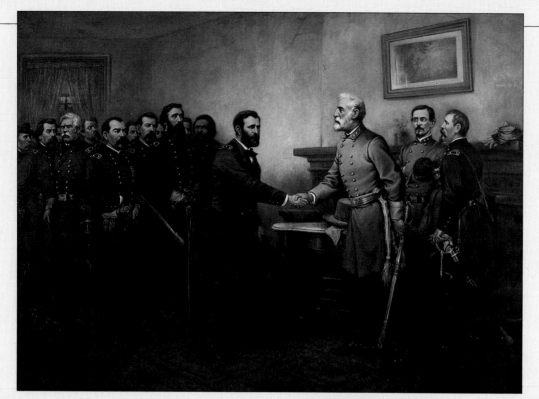

Varied Views of the Surrender

No event in the Civil War inspired more works of art than the historic capitulation of Robert E. Lee to Ulysses S. Grant at Appomattox Court House. Yet the artists were hampered by a dearth of accurate details about the interior of Wilmer McLean's house and what transpired there. No photographer was present, nor were any sketches made during the proceedings. In later years an impossible number of officers claimed that they had been in McLean's 16-by-20-foot parlor at the time the surrender was signed—and even the recollections of the men who were actually there were frequently contradictory.

Within minutes after Lee left the McLean house, Federal officers began a feverish hunt for souvenirs of the occasion. By the time the first artists visited the site, the parlor had been refurnished, further complicating their task. But they persisted; three of the best of their efforts are shown here.

One of the earliest versions of the surrender was painted in 1867 by French-born Louis Guillaume, a prominent Richmond artist. Although he utilized sketches of the McLean parlor, his work contains a number of errors. The size of the room is exaggerated, and the tables and chairs painted by Guillaume were replacements for the original furniture, which had been carried off as souvenirs. But the most obvious error was placing Grant and Lee at the same table; in fact, Grant and Lee sat at separate tables, about five feet apart.

The most accurate version of the surrender was painted by Thomas Lovell during the centennial of the Civil War. The proportions of the room are correct, as is the placement of the participants. General Lee and Colonel Marshall are at far left; the officers behind Grant are, from left, Philip Sheridan, Orville Babcock, Horace Porter, Edward O.C. Ord, Seth Williams, Theodore Bowers, Ely Parker and George Custer. Including Custer was one of the artist's few mistakes; by most accounts, he did not enter the McLean parlor.

THE NATION REUNITED

"The war feeling here is like a burning bush with a wet blanket wrapped around it. Looked at from the outside, the fire seems quenched. But just peep under the blanket and there it is, all alive, and eating, eating in."

JOHN TROWBRIDGE, NORTHERN CORRESPONDENT TOURING THE SOUTH IN 1866

During the Civil War, the men of the North and South fought 10,455 major and minor engagements, and 360,222 Union soldiers were joined in death by an estimated 258,000 Confederates. Yet at the time of Lee's surrender to Grant, the war had yet to claim its most powerful and perhaps its most poignant victim.

On March 4, 1865, Abraham Lincoln, looking gaunt and worn beyond his 56 years, had delivered his second inaugural address in Washington from a wooden platform built out from the Capitol's East Front. His eloquent words, delivered in less than five minutes from a single sheet of paper, were imbued with the spirit of reconciliation.

"With malice toward none," Lincoln concluded, "with charity for all; with firmness in the right, as God gives us to see the right, let us strive on to finish the work we are in; to bind up the nation's wounds; to care for him who shall have borne the battle, and for his widow, and his orphan—to do all which may achieve and cherish a just and lasting peace, among ourselves, and with all nations."

As Lincoln spoke of his hopes for peace, there sat amid the audience a handsome young actor with dark, glittering eyes. His name was John Wilkes Booth; he was an ardent Southern sympathizer; and within a few weeks he would murder the 16th President of the United States.

Booth's plot, conceived as early as August 1864, had originally entailed abducting Lincoln, carrying him to Richmond and holding him as hostage for the release of Confederate prisoners of war, who could then return to the fighting fronts. To that end, Booth had recruited a small gang of ne'er-do-well accomplices. For various reasons, however, Booth's kidnapping schemes were frustrated one after another. Discouraged by failure, Booth's band of conspirators all but broke up.

Then, on the morning of Good Friday, April 14, 1865, Booth learned that President and Mrs. Lincoln, along with Ulysses S. Grant, would attend that night's performance of *Our American Cousin*, a farcical comedy then on the boards at Ford's Theatre, six blocks from the White House. In feverish haste, the actor rounded up all the other conspirators he could find. But now all thoughts of abduction were gone: Instead, Booth set into motion a plan to assassinate President Lincoln, General Grant and Vice President Andrew Johnson.

When he discovered later that day that Grant would not attend the play that evening, Booth instructed one of his accomplices to kill instead Secretary of State William Seward. All three assassinations should take place at 10:15 p.m., Booth decided. Then the killers would gallop south, cross the Potomac and reach safe haven in the South.

Shortly before 8:30 p.m., Abraham and Mary Todd Lincoln entered Ford's Theatre and slowly made their way to the presidential box, accompanied by Major Henry Rathbone and his fiancée, Clara Harris. A little after 10 p.m., John Wilkes Booth, a small derringer pistol concealed on his person, walked through the theater lobby and up the stairs to the dress circle. There he paused, looking around as if counting the house; then, moving swiftly, he slipped into the corridor behind the presidential box.

As roars of laughter arose at one of the play's more comedic lines, Booth slipped into the presidential box and approached Lincoln's rocking chair from the right side. The President was leaning forward with his hand on the railing, looking down at someone

Abraham Lincoln, seated at the left of the small lectern, waits to deliver his second inaugural address to an audience that included John Wilkes Booth. Some scholars of photography place Booth behind the white railing at top, just in front of the marble statue.

A hand-colored lithograph celebrates the 1864 reelection of Lincoln, shown with his new Vice President, Andrew Johnson. The poster heralds an era of patriotism, peace and plenty: The scales of Justice are in perfect balance, commerce thrives on land and sea, and twin cornucopias pour forth an abundance of food, manufactured goods and arms.

ABRAHAM LINCOLN.   ANDREW JOHNSON.

PRESIDENT AND VICE-PRESIDENT.

in the orchestra. Booth's derringer flashed and its single bullet struck behind Lincoln's left ear, tearing into his brain. The President reflexively threw up his right hand; then he slumped in his rocker.

The assassin shouted a word that sounded like "Freedom!" and Major Rathbone lunged toward him. Dropping his empty pistol, Booth drew a knife, slashed the officer's left arm to the bone and then leaped the 12 feet toward the stage below. Yet though John Wilkes Booth was famous for his onstage acrobatics, his right spur caught in one of the decorative flags, causing him to land off-balance and breaking a bone in his lower left leg.

Still, Booth was able to get to his feet, brandishing his knife and snarling, "*Sic semper tyrannis!*" ("Thus always to tyrants"). Escaping across the stage in what one witness described as a kind of bullfrog hop, he made his way to the theater's rear exit, mounted a waiting horse—and vanished into the night.

While Booth was making his getaway, the unconscious form of President Lincoln was carried across 10th Street to a lodging house kept by one William Peterson. Lincoln was laid on a bed too short for his lanky frame; even after he was arranged in a diagonal position, his feet protruded over the bedside.

In the nightmarish vigil that followed, as many as 90 persons, including Cabinet members and 16 physicians, moved in and out of the tiny room in which the President was dying. But there was no question about who was in charge: Almost from the beginning, War Secretary Edwin Stanton assumed command, issuing a flood of instructions for the pursuit of the assassin and any possible accomplices, and even going so far as to order that a hysterical Mary Lincoln be barred from her husband's sickroom.

At 6:40 a.m., Dr. Albert King, one of the attending physicians, jotted in a notebook that Lincoln's breaths were "prolonged and groaning—a deep, softly sonorous cooing sign at the end of each expiration." Five minutes later, King wrote: "Respiration uneasy and grunting, lower jaw relaxed." At 7 o'clock, Lincoln was "still breathing at long pauses."

Then, about nine hours after Booth's bullet had entered his brain, the President's chest rose, fell, and did not rise again. At 7:22 on the morning of April 15, 1865, Abraham Lincoln was dead.

At 11 o'clock that morning, Chief Justice Salmon P.

One of John Wilkes Booth's favorite photographs was this signed print, a brooding portrait that hints at a hidden side of his nature. As fellow thespian Clara Morris observed, "He was so young, so bright, so gay—so kind. I could not have known him well."

Chase administered the oath of office to the new President of the United States. He was Andrew Johnson, born of common clay in North Carolina, who had remained largely illiterate until, at the age of 18, he had moved to Tennessee, set himself up as a tailor and married a shoemaker's daughter who taught him to write. Thanks to native intelligence and a devotion to hard work, he had prospered.

Although Johnson had entered local politics as a Democrat, he was selected as Lincoln's running mate to present a united front in the 1864 elections. He seemed eminently suited to the purposes of Radical Republicans in Congress. As the War Governor of Tennessee, he had displayed a virulent hatred of the South's slave-holding aristocracy. Thus, on the evening after Lincoln died, Senator Benjamin Wade of Ohio, a leading Radical, strode into Johnson's suite at Washington's Kirkwood House, grasped the new

The fateful moment: John Wilkes Booth squeezes the trigger of his .44-caliber, single-shot derringer, mortally wounding President Lincoln on the night of April 14, 1865. When the audience that evening at Ford's Theatre realized what had happened the building was filled with "the shouts, groans, curses, smashing of seats, screams of women, cries of terror," an eyewitness later recalled.

President by the hand, and declared: "Mr. Johnson, I thank God that you are here. Lincoln had too much of the milk of human kindness to deal with these damned rebels. Now they will be dealt with according to their deserts."

At first, Johnson seemed to justify the Radicals' faith. On April 17, for example, Major General William Tecumseh Sherman met with the Confederacy's General Joseph Johnston near Raleigh, North Carolina, to arrange for the surrender of Johnston's army. Doubtless recalling the policy of conciliation that Lincoln had explained to him in a meeting only

a few weeks before, Sherman offered astoundingly lenient terms. They provided not only for the surrender of all remaining Confederate forces, with the men permitted to keep their weapons, but for the readmission of the Confederate states to the Union, with full rights of citizenship and no prosecution.

When the news reached Washington, authorities were aghast, and Stanton even suggested treasonous motives on Sherman's part. In his first major test, the new President held firm. Sherman was forced to renege on his terms, and on April 26, General Johnston was required to sign a surrender document based on the one given Robert E. Lee at Appomattox.

Early that same day, John Wilkes Booth had been tracked down and shot to death in a burning barn near Bowling Green, Virginia. Eight persons, accused as accomplices, were haled before a military commission of retributive mind. Jefferson Davis, whom Stanton suspected of having masterminded the assassination, was also charged as a co-conspirator, as were several other Confederate authorities.

Davis was captured near Irwinsville, Georgia, at dawn on May 10, while trying to reach Confederate forces west of the Mississippi. His first thought was to escape, but his wife restrained him. "God's will be done," he muttered, and surrendered with dignity.

Weary and unwell, Davis half expected to be executed. Instead he was taken to Fort Monroe, Virginia, and placed in heavily guarded solitary confinement to await his destiny. It turned out to be a long wait. Profoundly depressed, the former President languished until May 1867, when, in the absence of persuasive evidence against him, he was simply released on bond, never to be tried.

However, of the eight wretches who did appear in the dock of the military commission, all were convicted. Four were sent to serve sentences in the Dry Tortugas, a chain of islands off the Florida coast. And, on July 7, 1865, the hangman's noose ended the lives of Lewis Paine, a sullen giant who had very nearly slashed Seward to death; George Atzerodt, a besotted loafer who had lost his nerve to execute his assigned task of murdering Andrew Johnson; David Herold, a dimwitted youth who had accompanied Booth on his flight, and Mrs. Mary Surratt, keeper of a Washington boarding house where her son John (who escaped) had met with other conspirators.

By then, to the vast consternation of the Radicals, Andrew Johnson had begun to veer away from their ruthlessly punitive policies, favoring instead the gentler course that Abraham Lincoln would have steered. On May 29 Johnson issued a proclamation granting pardons and returning property to virtually all citizens of the former Confederate states who would take an oath of allegiance to the Union. Worse yet, at least from the Radical point of view, the President began issuing a series of decrees that in effect offered Southerners rapid control of their state governments. Albeit requiring Southern delegates to ratify the 13th Amendment to the Constitution, end-ing slavery, Johnson's plan nonetheless assured a South ruled by whites.

The Radicals fumed. Congressman Thaddeus Stevens asked his colleagues if there were "no way to arrest the insane course of the President." To Senator Charles Sumner, it seemed that Johnson was giving away the victory won by the North. "This Republic cannot be lost," he ranted, "but the President has done much to lose it."

A showdown came in April 1866, when the Radical-led Congress overrode the President's veto of legislation extending the life of the Freedmen's Bureau, which gave the North an economic and political stranglehold on the South. After that display of strength, the future of reuniting the nation would be determined by a despotic Congress.

So began the doleful period of U.S. history that would be known as Reconstruction. Like the Civil War itself, Reconstruction would take far longer, cause more agony and claim more lives than anyone could imagine when it began. During the dozen stormy years to come, Andrew Johnson would escape conviction on impeachment charges by the margin of a single Senate vote; with the torch and the noose as their weapons, such quasi-military Southern societies as the Ku Klux Klan and the Knights of the White Camelia would arise against infestations of Republican carpetbaggers and scalawags; during his two terms as a Reconstruction President, the good name of Ulysses S. Grant would be stained by the corruption he permitted to exist around him.

Remarkably—or perhaps not so remarkably—it was the men who had fought the war in blue and gray who eventually took the first steps toward healing its hatreds. Beginning in the mid-1870s, Union and Confederate veterans held joint reunions, shared wartime memories and returned captured battle flags to the states whose regiments had lost them.

And so it came to pass that in 1875, Brigadier General William Francis Bartlett, a much-wounded Union hero, could arise and declare at ceremonies in Massachusetts that he was "as proud of the men who charged so bravely with Pickett's division on our lines at Gettysburg, as I am of the men who so bravely met and repulsed them there."

Surely, even as Bartlett spoke, there could be heard somewhere in the distance the fading roll of drums and the receding tramp of marching feet.

Taken in February 1865, this portrait of Lincoln captures the serenity and compassion of a man buffeted by four years of agonizing decisions and worries brought on by the Civil War. Only one print was made from the glass negative, which broke during developing.

413

APPENDIX

Statistics kept for the Federal forces during the Civil War recorded only the total number of enlistments. Since many men enlisted more than once during the course of the war, it is difficult to arrive at the total number of men who served. The total number of enlistments in the Union forces between 1861 and 1865 was *2,778,304*.

The number of enlistments in the U.S. Army was *2,672,341* (including *2,489,836* whites; *178,975* blacks; *3,530* Indians).

The number of enlistments in the U.S. Navy and Marines was *105,963*. Taking the multiple enlistments into account, it is probable that about two million individuals served in the Federal ranks.

Owing to missing and destroyed records, Confederate statistics are difficult to compile. Estimates of total Confederate enlistments range from *750,000* to *1,227,890*.

STRENGTH OF THE ARMIES
Comparison of Federal and Confederate forces. (These numbers reflect men present for duty on the day given.)

	USA	CSA
January 1, 1861	14,663 (REG.)	--------
July 1, 1861	186,751	112,040
January 1, 1862	527,204	258,680
March 31, 1862	533,984	--------
June 30, 1862	--------	224,146
January 1, 1863	698,802	304,015
January 1, 1864	611,250	277,970
June 30, 1864	--------	194,764
January 1, 1865	620,924	196,764
March 31, 1865	657,747	--------
May 1, 1865	1,000,516	--------

Federal Army and Navy

Average age at time of enlistment: 25.8 years.
Average height at time of enlistment: 5'8"
Average weight at time of enlistment: 143 1/2 lbs.
Civilian occupations:

FARMERS----------------------- 48%

MECHANICS------------------- 24%

LABORERS--------------------- 16%

COMMERCIAL---------------- 5%

PROFESSIONAL-------------- 3%

MISCELLANEOUS------------ 4%

Nationality:

NATIVE AMERICANS-------------- 75%

FOREIGN BORN---------------------- 25%

The half million foreign-born troops came from:
Germany, 175,000; Ireland, 150,000
England, 50,000; Canada, 50,000; Others, 75,000.

Confederate Army and Navy

No complete statistics exist for Confederate volunteers. In one study of 11,000 men enlisting in 1861-62 from eleven states, the age range was 18-35 years.

A second study of 9,000 men listed in 107 muster rolls from seven states (including the city of New Orleans) shows the following civilian occupations:

FARMERS------------------------ 69%

LABORERS---------------------- 5.3%

TRADE & MECHANICS------- 9%

COMMERCIAL---------------- 5%

STUDENTS--------------------- 8%

PROFESSIONAL-------------- 2.1%

OTHER------------------------- 1.6%

The Regiment as called for by Confederate and Federal regulations.

Field and Staff

1 Colonel
1 Lieutenant Colonel
1 Major
1 Adjutant
1 Quartermaster
1 Surgeon
2 Assistant Surgeons
1 Chaplain (none in
    Confederate regulations)
1 Sergeant Major
1 Quartermaster Sergeant
1 Commissary Sergeant
1 Hospital Steward
2 Principal Musicians

Company

1 Captain
1 First Lieutenant
1 Second Lieutenant
1 First Sergeant
4 Sergeants
8 Corporals
2 Musicians

1 Wagoner
82 Privates

10 Companies---------845 to 1,010 officers and men.
Field and staff---15 officers and noncommissioned officers.

Heavy Artillery Regiments (U.S.) 12 Companies----1,800 officers and men.

Organization of an Army

2 Battalions = 1 Regiment
3-4 Regiments = 1 Brigade
3 Brigades = 1 Division
3 Divisions = 1 Corps

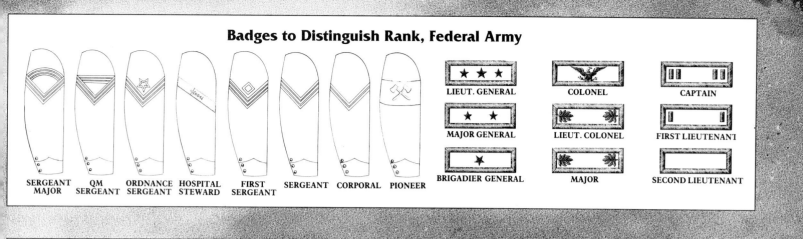

Badges to Distinguish Rank, Federal Army

SERGEANT MAJOR	QM SERGEANT	ORDNANCE SERGEANT	HOSPITAL STEWARD	FIRST SERGEANT	SERGEANT	CORPORAL	PIONEER

LIEUT. GENERAL	COLONEL	CAPTAIN
MAJOR GENERAL	LIEUT. COLONEL	FIRST LIEUTENANT
BRIGADIER GENERAL	MAJOR	SECOND LIEUTENANT

Badges to Distinguish Rank, Confederate Army

SERGEANT MAJOR	QM SERGEANT	ORDNANCE SERGEANT	FIRST SERGEANT	SERGEANT	CORPORAL

	GENERAL	
COLONEL		CAPTAIN
LIEUTENANT COLONEL		FIRST LIEUTENANT
MAJOR		SECOND LIEUTENANT

Federal Casualties

Federal Army

Killed in action or mortally wounded----------------------------- 110,100   67,088 KIA
                                                                                        43,012 MW

Died of disease----------------------- 224,580
Died as prisoners of war------------- 30,192
Nonbattle deaths--------------------- 4,114 accident
                                                       4,944 drowned
                                                       520 murdered
                                                       104 killed after capture
                                                       391 suicide
                                                       267 executed by
                                                          Federal authorities
                                                       64 executed by the enemy
                                                       313 sunstroke
                                                       2,043 other causes
                                                       12,121 cause not stated
Total nonbattle deaths---------------- 24,881
Wounded in action-------------------- 275,175

Federal Navy

Killed in action or mortally wounded----1,804
Died of disease or accident--------------- 3,000
Wounded in action------------------------ 2,226

Total casualties, 1861 to 1865------------ 642,427

Confederate Casualties
(statistics incomplete)

Confederate Army

Killed in action or mortally wounded---94,000
Died of disease--------------------------- 164,000
Died as prisoners of war------------------ 31,000
Wounded in action------------------------ 194,026
Total casualties, 1861 to 1865----------- 483,026

Confederate Navy No statistics available

Federal General Officers killed or mortally wounded in battle

Army Commanders
Maj. Gen. James B. McPherson--------Atlanta

Corps Commanders
Maj. Gen. Joseph K. Mansfield-------- Antietam
Maj. Gen. John F. Reynolds------------ Gettysburg
Maj. Gen. John Sedgwick--------------Spotsylvania

Division Commanders
Maj. Gen. Isaac I. Stevens------------- Chantilly
Maj. Gen. Philip Kearny--------------- Chantilly
Maj. Gen. Jesse L. Reno---------------- South Mountain
Maj. Gen. Israel B. Richardson-------- Antietam
Maj. Gen. Amiel W. Whipple---------- Chancellorsville
Maj. Gen. Hiram G. Berry-------------- Chancellorsville
Maj. Gen. James S. Wadsworth-------- Wilderness
Maj. Gen. David A. Russell------------ Opequon (1864)
Brig. Gen. William H. Wallace-------- Shiloh
Brig. Gen. Thomas Williams----------- Baton Rouge
Brig. Gen. James S. Jackson----------- Chaplin Hills
Brig. Gen. Isaac P. Rodman------------ Antietam
Brig. Gen. Thomas G. Stevenson------ Spotsylvania
Brig. Gen. (Brevet) James A.
    Mulligan---------------------------- Winchester (1863)

Brigade Commanders
32 Brigadier Generals, 35 Colonels serving as brigade commanders. Total: 67

Confederate Generals killed or mortally wounded in battle

Army Commanders
Gen. Albert Sidney Johnston-------- Shiloh

Corps Commanders
Lieut. Gen. Thomas J. Jackson------ Chancellorsville
Lieut. Gen. Leonidas Polk----------- Pine Mountain
Lieut. Gen. Ambrose P. Hill-------- Petersburg

Division Commanders
Maj. Gen. William D. Pender------- Gettysburg
Maj. Gen. J.E.B. Stuart------------- Yellow Tavern
Maj. Gen. William H. Walker------- Atlanta
Maj. Gen. Robert E. Rodes---------- Opequon (1864)
Maj. Gen. Stephen D. Ramseur----- Cedar Creek
Maj. Gen. Patrick R. Cleburne------ Franklin
Brig. Gen. John Pegram------------- Hatcher's Run

62 Brigade Commanders

Prisoners of War

All prisoner statistics are based on partial or unverifiable statistics.

Federal Prisoners:

211, 411 prisoners of war-------------------------- 16,668 paroled on the field
30,218 died in prison
mortality rate: 15.5%

Confederate Prisoners:

462,634 prisoners of war-------------------------- 247,769 paroled on the field
(including surrenders)
25,976 died in prison
mortality rate: 12%

The Bloodiest Battles
Total casualties

Gettysburg
Federal 23,053---Confederate 28,063

Seven Days' Battles
Federal 15,849---Confederate 20,614

Chickamauga
Federal 16,170---Confederate 18,454

**Chancellorsville/
Second Fredericksburg**
Federal 16,845---Confederate 12,764

Antietam
Federal 12,410---Confederate 10,316

Second Manassas/Chantilly
Federal 16,054---Confederate 9,286

Shiloh
Federal 13,047---Confederate 10,694

Fredericksburg
Federal 12,653---Confederate 5,309

Regimental Losses

Federal
Most men killed or died of wounds during term of service.

1st Maine Heavy Artillery★-------------- 23 officers, 400 men
5th New Hampshire Infantry------------ 18 officers, 277 men

Most men killed or died of wounds in a single battle.
1st Maine Heavy Artillery---------------- ★Petersburg, June 18, 1864
210 killed
5th New York Infantry-------------------- 2nd Bull Run, August 30, 1862
117 killed

★Heavy Artillery regiments had greater numerical
strength than infantry and took greater casualties.

Confederate
Most casualties suffered during a single battle.

26th North Carolina------------- Gettysburg---------86 killed 588 wounded
6th Alabama--------------------- Seven Pines--------91 killed 277 wounded
4th North Carolina-------------- Seven Pines--------77 killed 286 wounded
44th Georgia--------------------- Mechanicsville----71 killed 264 wounded
1st South Carolina Rifles------- Gaines' Mill-------81 killed 140 wounded

Due to incomplete or missing records, no accurate losses
can be determined after July 1863.

INDEX

*Federal officer's "Burnside Hat,"
named after the general of that name.*

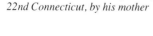

*Shirt made for Private Edgar Yergason,
22nd Connecticut, by his mother*

*Mathew Brady, the most famous photog-
rapher of the Civil War*

Uniform and personal effects of Lieutenant Robert S. Ellis Jr. of Virginia, killed at Gettysburg

Superintendent's residence, Virginia Military Institute, burned by General Hunter's Federals in 1864

A view of Confederate batteries at Drewry's Bluff, Virginia, on the James River, painted by engineer officer John Ross Key

Songsheet cover to one of numerous funeral marches composed after the assassination of Abraham Lincoln

A Federal drummer boy, photographed in the field

Major General George Meade and Admiral David Porter, two of the Union's highest ranking officers

Sword carried by an officer of the U.S. Army's Medical Staff

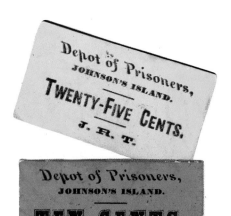

Two types of scrip used as currency by Confederate prisoners of war at Johnson's Island, Ohio

A recruiting poster for the 12th Massachusetts Battery, promising service under General Nathaniel Banks.

The Union Army Refreshment Saloon in Philadelphia, which served meals to troops bound for the front

Chevaux-de-frise, sharpened wooden stakes used as portable obstructions in siege warfare, such as that waged at Yorktown, Virginia

A Northern child clad in a miniature version of the popular Zouave uniform

PICTURE CREDITS

Credits are read from left to right, separated by semicolons from top to bottom.

8-9 Tulane University Art Collection. 10 In private collection. 11 Courtesy Jay P. Altmayer/photo Larry Cantrell; courtesy George E. Jordan/photo John Miller. 12 Courtesy Harry M. Rhett Jr., Huntsville, Alabama/photo George Flemming. 14-15 University of Georgia Libraries/photo Michael W. Thomas. 14-15 Library of Congress. 16-17 Courtesy Virginia E. Lewis/photo Harold Corsini. 17 Library of Congress; Old Darmouth Historical Society; courtesy of the New York Historical Society. 18-19 Collection of The Boatmen's National Bank of St-Louis. 20 Museum of the Confederacy. 21 Library of Congress. 22 Darmouth College Library; New York Historical Society. 23 Beinecke Rare Book & Manuscript Library, Yale University. 24-25 © President & Fellows of Harvard College, 1982, all rights reserved, courtesy Peabody Museum, Harvard University, daguerreotype by J.T. Zealy/copy Hillel Burger. 26-27 Chicago Historical Society. 27 Library of Congress; courtesy Grand Central Art Galleries, Inc. 28 State Historical Society of Wisconsin; the John Judkyn Memorial, Bath, England; Western Reserve Historical Society. 29 Courtesy Grand Central Art Galleries, Inc. 30 Kansas State Historical Society, Topeka. 32-33 Western Reserve Historical Society. 34 Chicago Historical Society/photo Alexander Hesler. 35 Museum of the Confederacy. 36-37 Courtesy United States Military Academy Library, West Point, N.Y./copy Al Freni. 38-39 Library of Congress/Photri; 38 Courtesy the Art Commission of the City of New York/photo Al Freni; courtesy of the City Council of the City of Charleston, South Carolina. 40 Courtesy Kean E. Wilcox. 41 Library of Congress. 43 Indianapolis Museum of Art, James E. Roberts Fund; from the collection of the Birmingham Museum of Art, gift of John E. Meyer/photo George Flemming. 44 Courtesy Gil Barrett. 44-45 Courtesy of the New York Historical Society. 46-47 Courtesy of The New York Historical Society. 49 The Meserve Collection of Mathew Brady Negatives, National Portrait Gallery, Smithsonian Institution, Washington, D.C. 50-51 Courtesy of The New York Historical Society. 52-53 National Rifle Association/photo Leon Dishman; Fort Ward Museum, City of Alexandria, VA/photo Henry Beville; courtesy Harris Andrews/photo Fil Hunter; Fort Ward Museum, City of Alexandria, VA/photo Henry Beville. 54 Library of Congress. 56 Map by Walter W. Roberts. 57 The Museum of the Confederacy/photo Henry Beville. 58 From *Battles and Leaders of the Civil War*, Vol. 1, published by The Century Co., 1884-1887. 59 Map by Walter W. Roberts. 60 McLellan Lincoln Collection, John Hay Library, Brown University. 62-63 From *Deeds of Valor*, Vol. 1, published by the Perrien Keydel Company, Detroit, Michigan, 1906. 64-65 Courtesy Sidney King. 66 Museum of the Confederacy/photo Larry Sherer. 67 Library of Congress. 68 State Historical Society of Missouri. 69 From *The American Soldier in the Civil War*, published by Stanley-Bradley Publishing Co., New York. © 1895, courtesy Library of Congress. 70 National Archives No. 111-BH-1172. 71 U.S. Naval Academy/Beverley R. Robinson Collection. 72-73 Chicago Historical Society #1920-1645. 74 City of Niles, Michigan Fort St. Joseph Museum. 75 From *Life of General Albert Sidney Johnston* by William Preston Johnson, published by D. Appleton & Co., N.Y. 1878. 76 Library of Congress; courtesy Samuel Charles Webster, from *The General's Wife. The Life of Mrs. Ulysses S. Grant*, by Isobel Ross © Isobel Ross, published Dodd, Mead & Company, N.Y.; Ohio Historical Society. 77 Chicago Historical Society Neg. No. ICHi-10503, Library of Congress (2). 78 Collection of Philip Baron Envis, courtesy Moss Publications. 79 Map by Walter W. Roberts. 80 Christopher Nelson. 81 American Heritage Picture Collection. 82-83 Courtesy the Cincinnati Historical Society. 84 Map by Walter W. Roberts. 87 From *Battles and Leaders of the Civil War*, published by The Century Co., New York, 1884; Library of Congress. 88-89 From *Le monde illustré*, Photo Musée de la Marine, Paris. 90-91 Courtesy Jay P. Altmayer/photo Larry Cantrell. 92-93 Painting by Conrad Wise Chapman, courtesy Museum of the Confederacy, Richmond, VA/photo Larry Sherer. 94-95 Painting by William Heysham Overend, courtesy The Wadsworth Atheneum, Hartford, Gift of the Citizens of Hartford by subscription, May 24, 1886/photo Al Freni. 96-97 Courtesy Beverley R. Robinson Collection, U.S. Naval Academy Museum, Annapolis, Maryland. 98 U.S. Army Military History Institute/copy Robert Walch. 99 Painting by Alexander Lawrie, West Point Museum Collections, U.S. Military Academy/photo Henry Groskinsky. 100-101 Library of Congress. 103 Library of Congress. 104 Library of Congress. 107 Library of Congress. 109 John Adams Elder: General Thomas Jonathan Jackson, in the Collection of The Corcoran Gallery of Art, Gift of William Wilson Corcoran. 110-111 Painting by Charles Hoffbauer, courtesy Virginia Historical Society/photo Henry Groskinsky. 112 Map by Walter W. Roberts. 114-115 Painting by William T. Trego, courtesy Bucks County Historical Society/photo Al Freni. 116 National Park Service/photo Larry Sherer; painting by William Edward West, Washington Custis/Lee Collections, Washington & Lee University, Lexington, VA/photo Thomas C. Bradshaw. 117 Painting by James A. Elder, on loan to Lee Chapel Museum, Washington & Lee University, Lexington, VA/photo Larry Sherer. 119 Map by Walter W. Roberts. 120 Maryland Historical Society, Baltimore. 122 Providence Public Library. 123 Library of Congress. 124-125 Library of Congress. 126-127 Western Reserve Historical Society, inset, Library of Congress. 128-129 National Archives, Neg. No. 111-B-383. 130 Library of Congress. 131 Courtesy Lee-Fendall House. 133 Library of Congress. 134 Map by Walter W. Roberts. 135 Library of Congress. 136 Sketch by Alfred R. Waud, Library of Congress. 138-139 Courtesy Frank & Marie-T. Wood Print Collections, Alexandria, VA. 140 State Historical Society of Wisconsin Neg. No. WHi(x3) 40390. 141 Map by Walter W. Roberts. 142 American Heritage Picture Collection. 144-145 Painting by Thure de Thulstrup, courtesy Seventh Regiment Fund, Inc./photo Al Freni; 146 National Archives, 111-B-1887. 147 From *Battles and Leaders of the Civil War*, Vol. 2, published by The Century Co., New York, 1887. 148 Meserve Collection National Portrait Gallery, Smithsonian Institution, Washington, D.C. 149 Old Court House Museum, Vicksburg, Mississippi, 150-151 Library of Congress, courtesy James R. Mellon. 152 Library of Congress. 154 John L. McGuire Collection, courtesy William A. Frassanito. 155 MOLLUS-MASS/USAMHI, courtesy William A. Frassanito. 156 City of Alexandria, Fort Ward Museum/photo Larry Sherer. 157 Confederate Memorial Hall/photo Bill van Calsem. 158 National Archives Neg. No. 111-B-4326. 159 Kentucky Military History Museum/photo Mary S. Rezny. 160-161 Courtesy Frank & Marie-T. Wood Print Collection, Alexandria, VA. 162 Courtesy Brian Pohanka. 163 Painting by William Travis, Smithsonian Institution, Washington, D.C. 166-167 From *Battles of the Civil War 1861-1865:The Complete Kurz & Allison Prints*, published by Oxmoor House, Inc., Birmingham, Alabama, 1976. 168-169 Map by William L. Hezlep. 171 Manassas National Battlefield Park/photo Larry Sherer; The Western Reserve Historical Society, Cleveland, Ohio. 172 City of Alexandria, Fort Ward Museum/photo Larry Sherer (2); Richard Catter Collection/photo Larry Sherer (4); City of Alexandria, Fort Ward Museum/photo Larry Sherer; Richard Catter Collection/photo Larry Sherer; City of Alexandria, Fort Ward Museum/photo Larry Sherer; Richard Catter Collection/photo Larry Sherer. 173 Artwork by Donna J. Neary 174 City of Alexandria, Fort Ward Museum/photo Larry Sherer; artwork by William J. Hennessey, Jr. 176 Manassas National Battlefield Park/photo Larry Sherer; artwork by William J. Hennessy Jr.; Richard Catter Collection. 178-179 Library of Congress. 181 Drawing by Horace Rowdow, West Point Museum Collections, United States Military Academy/photo Henry Groskinsky. 182 Map by William L. Hezlep; National Archives Neg. No. 111-B-6161. 182-183 William Gladstone Collection, U.S. Army Military History Institute (USAMHI)/copy A. Pierce Bounds. 184 The Western Reserve Historical Society, Cleveland, Ohio; National Archives Neg. No. 111-BA-1729. 185 National Archives Neg. No. 77-F-194-6-42. 186 Library of Congress. 187 Library of Congress; Western Reserve Historical Society, Cleveland, Ohio. 188 National Archives Neg. No. 111-BA-1734; National Archives Neg. No. 77-F-194-6-1. 188-189 Library of Congress. 190 Painting by Emanuel Leutze, State of Rhode Island and Providence Plantations/photo Henry Groskinsky. 191 Painting by D.E. Henderson, Gettysburg National Military Park Museum/photo Larry Sherer. 192 Painting by Thure de Thulstrup, courtesy Seventh Regiment Fund, Inc./photo Al Freni. 195 Map by Walter W. Roberts. 196-197 Painting by C. Rochling, courtesy John Henry Kurtz. 198 Fredericksburg National Military Park/photo Larry Sherer; from *Army Sketch Book: Thirty Years After, an Artist's Story of the Great War*, by Edwin Forbes, published by Fords, Howard & Hulbert, New York, 1890 (2). 200-201 Courtesy Bill Turner; courtesy George Batts; courtesy Bill Turner (2); Museum of the Confederacy/photo Larry Sherer; courtesy Bill Turner; from *The University Greys: Company A, Eleventh Mississippi Regiment, Army of Northern Virginia, 1861-1865*, © 1940 by Maud Morrow Brown, published by Garrett and Massie, Inc., Richmond, VA; courtesy T. Sherman Harding; courtesy John Goldman; courtesy Harris Andrews; courtesy Samuel P. Higginbotham II/copy Larry Sherer. 202 Color lithograph after a painting by Henry A. Ogden, Library of Congress. 203 Courtesy Frank & Marie-T. Wood Print Collections, Alexandria, VA. 204 From *A Manual of Signals*, by Albert J. Myer, published by D. Van Nostrand, New York, 1868. 205 Library of Congress. 206 West Point Museum, U.S. Military Academy/photo Henry Groskinsky. 209 National Archives Neg. No. 111-B-3320. 210 Courtesy Frank & Marie-T. Wood Print Collections, Alexandria, VA. 211 Museum of the Confederacy, Richmond, VA/photo Larry Sherer. 212 From *Battles and Leaders of the Civil War*, Vol. 3, published by The Century Co., New York, 1887. 213 Map by Walter W. Roberts. 214 Painting by A. Tholey, Fredericksburg National Military Park/photo Larry Sherer. 216 Courtesy Valentine Museum, Richmond, VA. 216-217 Courtesy Frank & Marie-T. Wood Print Collections, Alexandria, VA. 217 National Archives Neg. No. 111-B-4165 219 Museum of the Confederacy, Richmond, VA/photo Larry Sherer. 220 Courtesy Terence P. O'Leary/photo Peter Ralston; National Archives, Neg. No. B-50. 222 Library of Congress. 222-223 MOLLUS-MASS/USAMHI/ copy Robert Walsh. 224 The Western Reserve Historical Society, Cleveland, Ohio. 224-225 National Archives, Neg. No. CN-11090. 225 Courtesy Roger Hunt/copy Robert Walch. 226 MOLLUS-MASS/USAMHI/copy Robert Walch. 226-227 Library of Congress. 227 Library of Congress. 228 Courtesy Paul DeHaan. 229 Painting by Alexander Simplot, Chicago Historical Society, No. 1932-31. 230 Courtesy Missouri Historical Society, St-Louis. 231 Library of Congress. 232 Courtesy Mark Katz, Americana Image Gallery. 232-233 Courtesy Frank & Marie-T. Wood Print Collections, Alexandria, VA. 233 Library of Congress. 234 Map by William L. Hezlep. 234-235 Courtesy Frank & Marie-T. Wood Print Collections, Alexandria, VA. 237 Courtesy Lloyd Ostendorf Collection. 239 Old Court House Museum, Vicksburg, Mississippi/photo Bill van Calsem. 240 Painting by Thure de Thulstrup, courtesy Seventh Regiment Fund Inc./photo Al Freni. 242 Milwaukee Public Museum/photo David A. Bush. 243 Courtesy Frank & Marie-T. Wood Collections, Alexandria, VA. 244 Library of Congress. 245 Painting by Howard Pyle, private collection, courtesy the Brandywine River Museum, Chadds Ford, Pennsylvania. 246-247 Photograph courtesy The Kennedy Galleries, New York City. 247 U.S. Army Military History Institute/copy Robert Walch. 248 Photograph courtesy The Kennedy Galleries, New York City. 250 National Archives, Neg. No. 111-B-252. 252 Courtesy John Canole. 253 Collection of the Rochester Museum & Science Center, Rochester, New York. 254-255 The Lightfoot Collection. 256 Library of Congress. 257 The Western Reserve Historical Society, Cleveland, Ohio. 258 Museum of the Confederacy, Richmond, VA. 259 Wadsworth Atheneum, Hartford, The Ella Gallup Sumner and Mary Catlin Sumner Collection/photo Joseph Szaszfai. 261 Map by Walter W. Roberts. 262 Painting by Thomas Hicks, War Library and Museum of the Military Order of the Loyal Legion of the United States (MOLLUS)/photo Larry Sherer. 263 From *Recollections of a Private: A Story of the Army of the Potomac*, by Warren Lee Goss, published by Thomas Y. Crowell, New York, 1890. 264 Courtesy Chris Nelson, National Archives Neg. No. 111-B-2750, Custer Battlefield National Monument, Crow Agency, Montana/photo Dennis Sanders. 265 Bill Turner; Valentine Museum, Richmond, VA; Museum of the Confederacy, Richmond, VA/photo Larry Sherer (2); War Library and Museum, MOLLUS/photo Larry Sherer. 266 Courtesy J. Craig Nannos/photo Larry Sherer. 267 Courtesy James C. Frasca Collection/copy Andy Cifranic; courtesy J. Craig Nannos/photo Larry Sherer. 268-269 Painting by James Walker, The J. Howard Wert Gettysburg Collection and Civil War Antiquities/photo Larry Sherer. 270 The J. Howard Wert Gettysburg Collection and Civil War Antiquities/photo Larry Sherer. 271 Painting by W.H. Shelton, courtesy Gettysburg National Military Park/photo Larry Sherer. 272 From *Battles and Leaders of the Civil War*, Vol. 2, published by The Century Co., New York, 1884. 273 Painting by Charles B. Cox, First Regiment Infantry Museum, Philadelphia/photo Larry Sherer. 275 Courtesy Mark Katz, Americana Image Gallery. 276 Painting by Peter F. Rothermel, Collections of the State Museum of Pennsylvania/photo Henry Groskinsky. 278 Painting by Paul Wood, The Snite Museum of Art, Notre Dame, Indiana/photo Steve Moriarty. 279 Kean Archives, Philadelphia, Pennsylvania; The Armed Forces Museum, Armed Forces Institute of Pathology, Washington, D.C./photo Dan Cunningham. 280 MASS/MOLLUS/USAMHI/copy A. Pierce Bounds. 281 Rhode Island State House/photo Mark Sexton. 282 Map by Walter W. Roberts. 282 Library of Congress. 284-289 Circular painting by Paul Philippoteaux, Gettysburg National Military Park/photo Henry Groskinsky. 291 Kean Archives, Philadelphia, Pennsylvania. 294 Gettysburg National Military Park Museum of Confederacy, Richmond, Virginia; courtesy Dave Mark Collection/copied Herb Peck Jr.; War Library and Museum, MOLLUS/copy Larry Sherer; courtesy Bill Turner; MASS/MOLLUS/USAMHI/copy A. Pierce Bounds; courtesy Alan T. Nolan; USAMHI/copy Pierce Bounds; From *Histories of the Several Regiments and Battalions from North Carolina in the Great War 1861-65*, Vol. IV, edited by Walter Clark published by the State, Nash Brothers, Book and Job Printers, Golboro, N.C. 1901; courtesy Herb Peck. 293 Courtesy William Gladstone Collection; Gettysburg National Military Park; State of New York, Division of Military & Naval Affairs/copy Robert Ricardo; courtesy Michael J. McAfee; from *8th Virginia Infantry*, by John E. Divine © 1983 by H.E. Howard, Inc. Lynchburg, VA; courtesy Michael J. McAfee; Gettysburg National Military Park; courtesy Chris Nelson; Pennsylvania Historical & Museum Commission, Division of Archives & Manuscripts, (MG 218 General Photograph Collection); Eric Davis Collection, Baltimore/copy Jeremy N.P. Ross; courtesy Terence P. O'Leary; The J. Howard Wert Gettysburg Collection and Civil War Antiquities/copy Larry Sherer. 295 Painting by David Blythe, National Baseball Hall of Fame and Museum Inc., Cooperstown, New York/photo Frank Rollins. 296-297 Courtesy James Mellon Collection, handwritten text from *The Face of Lincoln*, compiled and edited by James Mellon © 1979 Penguin Inc., published by Viking, New York. 298 William L. Clements Library, University of Michigan. 299 Map by Walter W. Roberts. 300 Map by Walter W. Roberts. 301 Tennessee State Museum/photo Bill LaFevor. 302-303 Painting by Alfred Thorsen, State Historical Society Wisconsin. 305 Map by Walter W. Roberts. 306 Sketch by Frank Vizetelly by permission Houghton Library. 307 Library of Congress. 308 Library of Congress; Mass. Commander, Military Order of Loyal Legion of US & the US Army Military History Institute/copy A. Pierce Bounds (MASS/MOLLUS/USAMHI); Erik Davis Collection; courtesy Mark Katz, Americana Image Gallery. 309 National Archives # 165; Allan Cebula Collection at US Army Military History Institute/copy Pierce Bounds; *War Letters of Colonel Hans Christian Heg*, edited by Theodore C. Blegen, published by Norwegian-American Historical Association, Northfield, Minnesota, 1936; from *History of the Sixth Regiment Indiana Volunteer Infantry*, by Charles C. Briant, published by Wm. B. Burford, Indianapolis, 1891. 310-311 Painting by Harry J. Kellogg, Minnesota Historical Society; 312 War Library & Museum, MOLLUS/photo Larry Sherer. 313 Courtesy Cincinnati Historical Society; courtesy C. Paul Sloane/copy Arthur Soll. 314 War Library and Museum, MOLLUS/photo Larry Sherer. 316-317 Tennessee State Museum/photo Bill LaFevor. 318-319 Museum of the Confederacy, Richmond, VA/photo Larry Sherer. 320 Courtesy The New York Historical Society, New York City. 322-323 Courtesy Frank & Marie-T. Wood Print Collections, Alexandria, VA. 324 Library of Congress. 326 National Archives, Neg. No. 165-A-441. 327 Library of Congress. 329 Painting by Thure de Thulstrup, courtesy Seventh Regiment Fund, Inc./photo Al Freni. 330 From *A Confederate Girl's Diary*, by Sarah Morgan Dawson, published by Houghton Mifflin Company, Boston and New York, 1919; Albert Shaw Collection, *Review of Reviews Photographic History of the Civil War*/copy Larry Sherer. 332 U.S. Army Military History Institute/copy Robert Walch, inset, Department of Archives and Manuscripts, Louisiana State University, Baton Rouge, Louisiana. 334-335 Department of Archives and Manuscripts, Louisiana State University, Baton Rouge, Louisiana. 336 Painting by Paul Louvrier, West Point Museum Collections, U.S. Military Academy/photo Henry Groskinsky. 337 Painting attributed to Francis B. Carpenter © by White House Historical Association/photo National Geographic Society. 338 Drawing by Alfred Waud, Library of Congress. 339 Homer Babcock Collection/photo Larry Sherer. 342 Drawings by Edwin Forbes, Library of Congress. 342 Painting by Julian Scott, courtesy Robert A. McNeil/photo Sharon Deveaux. 344 James C. Frasca/photo Andy Cifranic. 345 Map by William L. Hezlep. 346 Painting by Julian Scott, Drake House Museum/Plainfield Historical Society/photo Henry Groskinsky. 348 Map by Walter W. Roberts. 351 Library of Congress. 352-353 Library of Congress. 355 Drawing by Alfred W. Waud, Library of Congress. 356 L. M. Strayer Collection/photo Brian Blauser. 357 Special Collections (Orlando Poe Collection) West Point Library, U.S. Military Academy/photo Henry Groskinsky. 361 Map by Peter McGinn. 360 Kean Archives, Philadelphia. 361 From *The Photographic History of the Civil War*, Vol. 2, edited by Francis Trevelyan Miller, published by The Review of Reviews Co., New York, 1912. 362 Alabama Department of Archives & History. 363 Drawing by Alfred R. Waud, Library of Congress. 364 Painting by Thure de Thulstrup, courtesy Seventh Regiment Fund, Inc./photo Al Freni. 366 The Atlanta Cyclorama, City of Atlanta/photo Henry Groskinsky. 367 Map by William L. Hezlep. 368 Library of Congress. 369 West Point Museum Collections, U.S. Military Academy/photo Henry Groskinsky; painting by Alexander Lawrie, West Point Museum Collection, U.S. Military Academy/photo Henry Groskinsky. 370-371 Courtesy Frank & Marie-T. Wood Print Collections, Alexandria, VA. 372-373 Library of Congress. 374 From *Battles and Leaders of the Civil War*, Vol. 4, published by The Century Co., New York, 1887; New York Historical Society. 375 National Archives Neg. No. 111-BA-2086. 376-377 Courtesy Frank & Marie-T. Wood Print Collections, Alexandria, VA. 378 Confederate Museum, Charleston, S.C./photo Thomas P. Grimball III. 379 Library of Congress. 380 Courtesy Frank & Marie-T. Wood Print Collections, Alexandria, VA. 381 Map by Walter W. Roberts. 382 Drawing by Alfred R. Waud, Private Collection. 383 National Archives #111-B-4591. 384 Painting by E.I. Andrews, Kentucky Museum, Western University, Bowling Green/photo Bill LaFevor. 385 MVI Archives, Lexington/copy Michael Latil. 386 Painting by Benjamin West Clinedinst, Jackson Memorial Hall, VMI, Lexington/photo Michael Latil. 387 Valentine Museum, Richmond, VA. 388 Drawing by W.E. Ruggles, The Ruggles Collection, University Library, Dundee, Scotland. 390 Map by Walter W. Roberts and William L. Hezlep. 392 Painting by Benjamin West Clinedinst from *Campaigning with Grant* by Horace Porter, published by The Century Co., New York, 1897. 394 Painting by George Peter Alexander Healy, The White House Collection. 396 Map by Walter W. Roberts. 398 The Edward L. Bafford Photography Collection, Albin O. Kuhn Library and Gallery, University of Maryland Baltimore County/copy Alan M. Scherr; painting by Andre Castaigne, West Point Museum Collection, U.S. Military Academy/photo Henry Groskinsky. 400 Library of Congress. 402 Map by William L. Hezlep. 405 Courtesy Chris Calkins/copy Larry Sherer; from the original by R.F. Zogbaum, from *Harper's New Monthly* Magazine, April 1898. 406 Painting by Thomas Nast, Galena-Jo Davies County History Museum/photo James Quick; painting by Tom Lovell, © 1969 407 National Geographic Society; Painting by Louis D. Guillaume, Appomattox Court House/photo Ronald H. Jennings. 408 Louis A. Warren Lincoln Library and Museum, Fort Wayne, Indiana/photo Scott Simpson. 409 The Western Reserve Historical Society, Cleveland, Ohio. 410 Richard J.S. and Kellie O. Gutman Collection, from *John Wilkes Booth Himself*, Hired Hand Press, Dover Massachusetts, 1972. 411 Courtesy Frank & Marie-T. Wood Print Collections, Alexandria, VA. 412 National Portrait Gallery, Smithsonian Institute, Washington, D.C. (NPG.M-81.1). 414 Photograph of the 2nd Michigan Infantry at Fort Wayne, Indiana, courtesy of the Burton Historical Collection of the Detroit Public Library/copy Nemo Warr. 416 Insignia from Civil War Atlas, Plate 172, courtesy Frank & Marie-T. Wood Print Collections, Alexandria, VA. 417 Photograph of unidentified Union Artillery Battery at Morris Island, South Carolina, courtesy Library of Congress. 418 Photograph of the United States National Military Cemetary, Alexandria, VA, courtesy The Western Reserve Historical Society, Cleveland, Ohio. 420 Photograph of Confederate prisoners at Camp Morton, Indiana, courtesy the Western Reserve Historical Society, Cleveland, Ohio. 422 Courtesy Don Troiani/photo Al Freni; courtesy Don Troiani/photo Henry Groskinsky. 423 Library of Congress. 424 Courtesy Samuel P. Higginbotham II/photo Larry Sherer; Virginia Military Institute Museum, Lexington, Virginia/photo Michael Latil. 425 Painting by John Ross Key, Museum of the Confederacy, Richmond, VA/photo Katherine Wetzel; Library of Congress. 426 Courtesy Kean E. Wilcox; (Orlando Poe Collection) Special Collections, U.S. Military Academy Library/copy Jeremy Ross. 427 City of Alexandria, Fort Ward Museum/photo Henry Beville; Follett House Museum, Sandusky, Ohio/photo Andy Cifranic. 428 Courtesy Norman Flayderman/photo Henry Groskinsky. 429 Kean Archives, Philadelphia, Pennsylvania; Library of Congress; courtesy Chris Nelson/copy Larry Sherer.

ACKNOWLEDGMENTS

For help given in the preparation of this book, the editors wish to thank the following: Graphor Consultation, Dominique Gagné, Maurice Gagnon, Daniel German, Elizabeth W. Lewis, Daniel McBain, Jennifer Meltzer, Rosalind Stubenberg, Diane Ullius, Jocelyn Wakefield, Nathalie Watanabe.

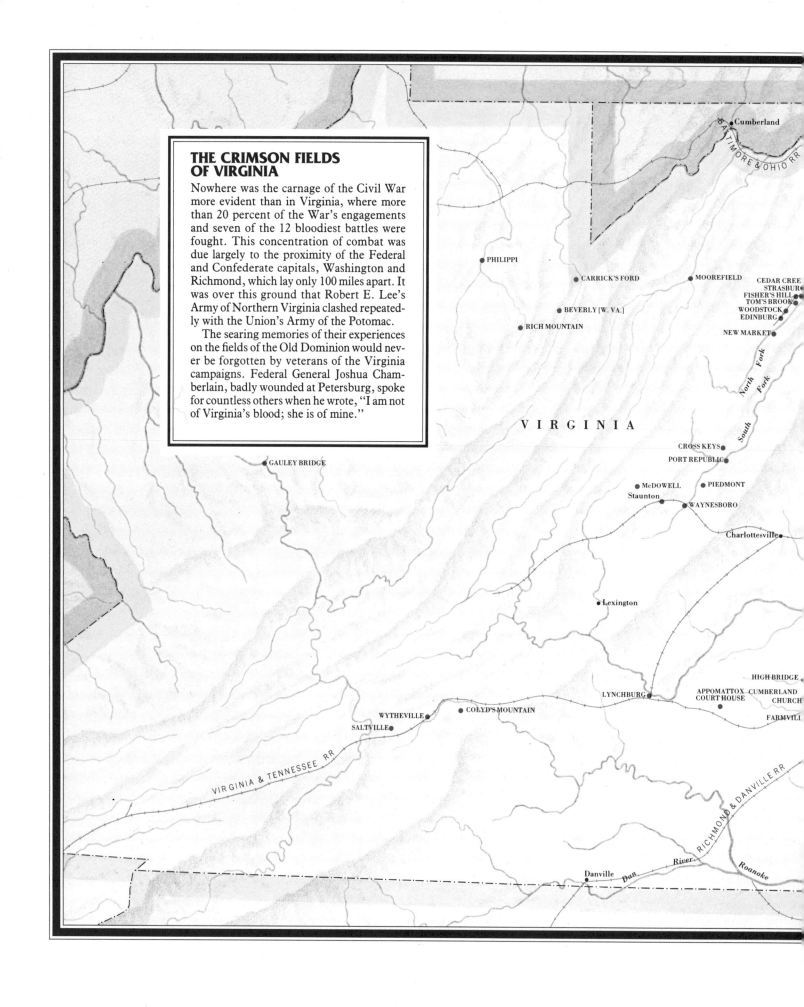

THE CRIMSON FIELDS OF VIRGINIA

Nowhere was the carnage of the Civil War more evident than in Virginia, where more than 20 percent of the War's engagements and seven of the 12 bloodiest battles were fought. This concentration of combat was due largely to the proximity of the Federal and Confederate capitals, Washington and Richmond, which lay only 100 miles apart. It was over this ground that Robert E. Lee's Army of Northern Virginia clashed repeatedly with the Union's Army of the Potomac.

The searing memories of their experiences on the fields of the Old Dominion would never be forgotten by veterans of the Virginia campaigns. Federal General Joshua Chamberlain, badly wounded at Petersburg, spoke for countless others when he wrote, "I am not of Virginia's blood; she is of mine."

BALTIMORE & OHIO RR

Cumberland

PHILIPPI

CARRICK'S FORD

MOOREFIELD

CEDAR CREE
STRASBUR
FISHER'S HILL
TOM'S BROOK
WOODSTOCK
EDINBURG

BEVERLY [W. VA.]

RICH MOUNTAIN

NEW MARKET

North Fork

South Fork

V I R G I N I A

CROSS KEYS
PORT REPUBLIC

McDOWELL

PIEDMONT

Staunton

WAYNESBORO

GAULEY BRIDGE

Charlottesville

Lexington

HIGH BRIDGE

LYNCHBURG

APPOMATTOX
COURT HOUSE

CUMBERLAND
CHURCH

FARMVILL

WYTHEVILLE

COLYD'S MOUNTAIN

SALTVILLE

VIRGINIA & TENNESSEE RR

RICHMOND & DANVILLE RR

Danville

Dan River

Roanoke